Federal Tax Research

NINTH EDITION

William A. Raabe, Ph.D., CPA
The Ohio State University

Gerald E. Whittenburg, Ph.D., CPA
San Diego State University

Debra L. Sanders, Ph.D., CPA
Washington State University, Vancouver

Roby B. Sawyers, Ph.D., CPA, CMA
North Carolina State University

Contributing Author

Steven L. Gill, Ph.D.
San Diego State University

SOUTH-WESTERN
CENGAGE Learning

Australia • Brazil • Japan • Korea • Mexico • Singapore • Spain • United Kingdom • United States

SOUTH-WESTERN
CENGAGE Learning·

Federal Tax Research, Ninth Edition, International Edition
William A. Raabe, Gerald E. Whittenburg, Debra L. Sanders, Roby B. Sawyers

VP/Editorial Director: Jack W. Calhoun

Publisher: Rob Dewey

Senior Acquisitions Editor: Mike Schenk

Associate Developmental Editor: Julie Warwick

Editorial Assistant: Ann Mazzaro

Marketing Manager: Natalie Livingston

Marketing Coordinator: Nicole Parsons

Manufacturing Buyer: Doug Wilke

Permissions Acquisitions Manager: Mardell Glinski Schultz

Senior Art Director: Michelle Kunkler

Production Manager: Jean Buttrom

Content Project Management: PreMediaGlobal

Production House/Compositor: PreMediaGlobal

Black & White Cover Image: © Comstock Images

Color Cover Image: © Shutterstock Images/kentoh

Library of Congress Control Number: 2010939159

International Edition:

ISBN-13: 978-1-111-22166-9

ISBN-10: 1-111-22166-9

Cengage Learning International Offices

Asia
www.cengageasia.com
tel: (65) 6410 1200

Australia/New Zealand
www.cengage.com.au
tel: (61) 3 9685 4111

Brazil
www.cengage.com.br
tel: (55) 11 3665 9900

India
www.cengage.co.in
tel: (91) 11 4364 1111

Latin America
www.cengage.com.mx
tel: (52) 55 1500 6000

UK/Europe/Middle East/Africa
www.cengage.co.uk
tel: (44) 0 1264 332 424

Represented in Canada by Nelson Education, Ltd.
tel: (416) 752 9100/(800) 668 0671
www.nelson.com

Cengage Learning is a leading provider of customized learning solutions with office locations around the globe, including Singapore, the United Kingdom, Australia, Mexico, Brazil, and Japan. Locate your local office at: **www.cengage.com/global**

For product information: **www.cengage.com/international**

Visit your local office: **www.cengage.com/global**

Visit our corporate website: **www.cengage.com**

AVAILABILITY OF RESOURCES MAY DIFFER BY REGION. Check with your local Cengage Learning representative for details.

Printed in the United States of America
1 2 3 4 5 6 7 15 14 13 12 11

Dedications

This book is dedicated to our academic mentors.

William A. Raabe
Norton M. Bedford
Gerald D. Brighton
Christine M. Purdie
Joseph J. Schultz, Jr.
Eugene Willis

Gerald E. Whittenburg
William H. Hoffman
James W. Pratt
John J. Willingham
Allan R. Bailey

Debra L. Sanders
William Raabe
Philip M. J. Reckers
Theodore Saldin
Robert Wyndelts

Roby B. Sawyers
David E. Hoffman
Charles W. Christian
J. Hal Reneau
Philip M. J. Reckers
Joseph J. Schultz Jr.

Steven L. Gill
Susan Porter
Susan Gill
Lynne Krapf

William A. Raabe, Ph.D., CPA, teaches graduate tax courses at the Fisher College of Business of The Ohio State University, and at the Capital University (OH) Law School. He is a leader among business school tax faculty in incorporating technology developments into curricula for the educational development of tax professionals.

Dr. Raabe's teaching and research interests focus on multi-jurisdictional taxation and financial planning, and he is recognized as the leader among business school academics in the fields of state and local income, sales, and property taxation. Dr. Raabe is the author and editor of approximately 20 books, *including South-Western Federal Taxation, Schedule M-3 Compliance*, and the *Multistate Corporate Tax Guide*. He has coached student teams to the national finals of the Deloitte Tax Case Competition (from three different universities) and of the PricewaterhouseCoopers Tax Policy Competition ("xTax").

Dr. Raabe is an editorial board member for the AICPA *Tax Adviser* and the ATA *Journal of Legal Tax Research*. He has received university-wide recognition as the winner of the AMOCO Foundation Award for Teaching Excellence, and the Wisconsin Institute of CPAs named him the Educator of the Year.

Gerald E. Whittenburg, Ph.D., CPA, EA, is a professor in The Charles W. Lamden School of Accountancy at San Diego State University. A graduate of the University of Houston, Dr. Whittenburg is interested in individual and corporate taxation, tax pedagogy, and tax research methodology.

Dr. Whittenburg is also an author of the textbook *Income Tax Fundamentals*. In addition, he has published articles in journals such as *Accounting Education: An International Journal, Accounting Review, Advances in Taxation, Practical Tax Strategies, Taxes—The Tax Magazine, Group Decision and Negotiation, Journal of Business and Accounting, Journal of Legal Tax Research, Journal of Taxation of Investments, Journal of Taxation of Employee Benefits, Journal of Taxation of Financial Institutions, Valuation Strategies, Journal of Small Business Strategy, The Tax Adviser,* and *Journal of Accounting Education*. He has received numerous awards for teaching, including the Trustee's Outstanding Faculty Award for the entire California State University System. Dr. Whittenburg was awarded a Fulbright Fellowship (2003) to the Ukraine. In addition, he has been a visiting scholar at the University of Adelaide (1999 and 2005) and the University of South Australia (2009 and 2010).

Debra L. Sanders, Ph.D., CPA, is a professor in the Department of Accounting and Associate Director of the Masters of Accounting Program at the Vancouver campus of Washington State University. Dr. Sanders received her undergraduate degree (anthropology), Masters (taxation) and Ph.D. (accounting) from Arizona State University.

Dr. Sanders publishes in both academic and professional journals. Her work has appeared in the academic journals *Behavioral Research in Accounting, National Tax Journal, The Journal of the American Taxation Association, Advances in Taxation,* and *The International Journal of Accounting*. Professional journals that have published her articles include *State Tax Notes, Taxation for Accountants, Taxation for Lawyers, The Review of Taxation of Individuals, Taxes—The Tax Magazine, The Tax Adviser,* and *Journal of Financial Planning*. She is also an author on the South-Western Federal Taxation series of textbooks.

Roby B. Sawyers, Ph.D., CPA, CMA, is a professor in the Poole College of Management at North Carolina State University. He earned his undergraduate accounting degree from the University of North Carolina at Chapel Hill, his masters from the University of South Florida, and his Ph.D. from Arizona State University. He has taught a variety of undergraduate and graduate tax courses at both North Carolina State and University of North Carolina-Chapel Hill and has been a visiting professor in the International Management Program at the Catholic University in Lille, France, and the Vienna School of Economics and Business (Wirtschaftsuniversitat Wien). He has also taught continuing education courses for the AICPA, NCACPA, BDO Seidman, McGladrey and Pullen, and PricewaterhouseCoopers.

In addition to being on the author team of *Federal Tax Research*, Dr. Sawyers is an author of *Managerial Accounting: A Focus on Ethical Decision Making* (Fifth Edition), *Managerial ACCT* and writes frequently for leading academic, policy, and professional tax journals.

Dr. Sawyers has been an active member of the AICPA's Tax Division, having served on the Tax Executive Committee, Tax Legislation and Policy Committee, chair of the Trust, Estate and Gift Tax Technical Resource Panel, and chair of the AICPA's task force on estate tax reform.

Steven L. Gill, Ph.D. is an assistant professor in The Charles W. Lamden School of Accountancy at San Diego State University. He received an undergraduate degree in accounting from the University of Florida, a Masters in taxation from Northeastern University, and a Ph.D. in accounting from the University of Massachusetts. Prior to entering academia, Dr. Gill worked in the field of accounting for 12 years, including roles in public accounting, internal audit, corporate accounting, and, ultimately, as a vice president of finance.

Dr. Gill's research interests include a concentration in taxation including mutual funds and college savings (529) plans, and wider interests in corporate internal control structure and weaknesses, management overconfidence, and earnings quality. Dr. Gill has taught at both the undergraduate and graduate levels, and his teaching interests include taxation and financial accounting.

Brief Contents

Contents

The Ninth Edition of *Federal Tax Research* reflects the global nature of tax research and the changing nature of the tax profession. Now more than ever, our text is *the* essential learning tool for tax research, and *Federal Tax Research 9/e* remains justifiably the market leader among tax research texts.

This popular book has been prepared as a comprehensive, stand-alone reference tool for the user who wishes to become proficient in Federal tax research. It is written for readers who are familiar with the fundamentals of the Federal income and transfer tax law, at a level that typically is achieved on the completion of two comprehensive introductory courses in taxation in either the accounting program in a business school or second- or third-year courses in a law school.

Nearly every accounting, tax, and tax law student can benefit from the algorithms and strategies found in this book. The text is most appropriate for:

- Upper-level accounting students in a business school (i.e., seniors in a four-year program or those in the fifth year of a 150-hour program) who desire additional information concerning the practice of taxation.

- Those who are enrolled in a non-tax graduate program in business administration (e.g., an MBA or MS—management program) and would like further practical training in the functions of taxation in today's business environment.

- Second- or third-year law school students, especially those who desire a more detailed and pragmatic introduction to a specialized tax practice.

- Those who are commencing a graduate degree program in taxation, in either a business school or a law school, and require a varied and sophisticated introduction to the procedures of tax research and to the routine functions and implications of a tax practice.

- Practicing accountants and attorneys who need an introduction, an update, or a refresher relative to tax practice and research as an element of their career paths.

Structure and Pedagogy

Too often, existing textbooks ignore the detailed, pragmatic approach that students require in developing effective and efficient tax research skills.

That is why we have included an unprecedented degree of hands-on tax research analysis throughout the text. This book does not simply discuss tax research procedures or the sources of the Federal tax law, nor does it provide a mere sample of the pertinent tax reference material. Rather, the Ninth Edition reflects our conviction that readers learn best by active learning and real-world experience with the most important elements of the Federal tax law. We have applied this conviction to the many important features of the Ninth Edition, including the following:

- NEW: An entire chapter on Financial Accounting Research (Chapter 10) has been added. Increasingly, tax professionals are finding that an understanding of financial accounting for income taxes is a required competency. This chapter provides an overview of accounting for income taxes as well as a detailed description of the content, structure, and use of the FASB Accounting Standards Codification Research

System (CRS). Students will benefit by knowing how to perform both tax and accounting research to bring more value to their prospective employers.

- NEW: Exercises, problems, and research cases have been added and updated to provide the most relevant applications possible.

- NEW: Coverage of tax services (previous Chapter 6) and legal services (previous Chapter 7) is combined into one chapter (Chapter 6), putting all tax research services together to make comparisons easier.

- Spotlight on Taxation boxes appear in every chapter to provide additional research tips, tax information, news, background, and factors to consider in developing a tax research solution.

- The new internal design with colored text is visually appealing for students and instructors.

- An introduction to the tax profession provides details on such valuable topics as preparer penalties, statutes of limitation, interest conventions, and return selection for IRS audits.

- The book's focus on tax planning fits perfectly with this growing trend in tax practice.

- The text has been thoroughly updated with developments that affect those who conduct tax research, including revisions to Circular 230, IRS organizational structure and enforcement functions, and other principles that control tax practice.

- Hundreds of exercises and discussion questions allow the reader to learn by exploring the reference materials in a well-developed tax library in their research strategies.

- Assignments allow students to construct case briefs, file memos, client letters, and other elements of a comprehensive client file—vital skills they will need in practice.

- Hundreds of reproductions, illustrations, and new screen captures have been excerpted from the most important tax reference materials and expose students to the real world of tax research. The screen captures are included to keep the text visually stimulating to students of all learning styles.

- Summary charts, diagrams, and other study aids are integrated throughout the text that summarize the elements of primary and secondary sources of Federal tax law and encourage students to develop their own research routines and techniques.

Focus on Online and Computerized Research

The use of online databases and computerized research has become indispensable in tax practice. Accordingly, the text includes the deepest analysis of the computer research tools available to assist with researching tax in an online and computerized environment. Other important features include the following:

- NEW: The new CCH IntelliConnect interface and WestlawNext interface are included to provide students with cutting-edge tax research tools.

- The review of tax ethics has been expanded, including tax and non-tax sources of guidance for the conduct of today's tax practice.

- More material than ever has been provided on the role of tax research on the CPA exam.

- The Quiz Yourself feature at the end of each chapter directs students to the online quizzes located on the book's Web site through **www.cengagebrain.com**. Here, students will have access to online quizzes, complete with immediate answers and feedback for questions answered incorrectly. The feedback will direct students to the section of the chapter that contains the correct answer.

Students can also access chapter by chapter key words, flashcards and crossword puzzles to enhance the studying experience. At the **CengageBrain.com** home page, search by author name (Raabe), by title (*Federal Tax Research*) or by ISBN (1111221642) using the search box at the top of the page. This will bring you to a link for the 9th edition of *Federal Tax Research*. After clicking the link, you can access all resources by clicking "Access Now".

- The instructor's portion of the Web site for the text, located at **www.cengagebrain.com**, includes the solutions for the end-of-chapter material, a generous test bank with a 25 percent increase in questions, instructor PowerPoint slides, and lecture notes to help guide instructors through the course. The Web site also offers online and computerized exercises and a sample tax research memo. Instructors can access the instructor resources at either **CengageBrain.com** or at **http://login.cengage.com**. If you are new to Cengage Learning books, you will need to register with Cengage Learning by creating a new instructor account. Instructors will be directed to the Cengage Learning dashboard after logging in. Here, you may add any Cengage Learning book to your 'bookshelf', including the 9th edition of *Federal Tax Research* simply by searching by the author, title or ISBN (1111221642). After adding the book to your 'bookshelf' you will be able to access the links to the Instructor Companion Site and accompanying resources.

As a result, we believe that the Ninth Edition is indispensable to learning and performing real-world online and computerized tax research.

Using the Text

The main tax services are reviewed in a hands-on manner. Learning how to use the services is explained through example projects that guide the reader with step-by-step explanations and screen shots to illustrate what is actually seen on the screens. The text's exercises, cases, and advanced cases offer enough variety in both difficulty and subject matter that they may be assigned to individual readers, or to student groups of two or three, for their optimal use. The instructor also should consider giving each student in the course a different research case to complete, thereby discouraging joint work.

Given both the nature of the tax research process and the limited tax research databases available to most firms and universities, the instructor must take care to assign discussion materials for which the necessary resources are available and also to work through the assignment himself or herself, to ascertain that one's target solution to the assignment reflects the very latest in the development of the Federal tax law.

The instructor may want to defer the assigning of certain research cases until a specific research service is discussed, which will provide additional illustrations. Alternatively, the reader could be encouraged to rework a previous assignment as specific research services are introduced.

Acknowledgments

We are grateful to the following reviewers of the Eighth Edition who provided valuable comments and insights, which guided us in the development of the Ninth Edition.

Steven J. Arsenault, College of Charleston

Rose L. Bailey, LL.M, CPA, Esq., East Carolina University

Janie Blankenship, Del Mar College

Rafi Efrat, California State University, Northridge

Stephen Gara, Drake University

Tracie Nobles, Austin Community College

Lucia Smeal, Georgia State University

Mark R. Solomon, Walsh College

Jonathon Tingley, University at Albany

Dr. Scott A. Yetmar, Cleveland State University

We wish to thank all of the book's student and faculty readers who have provided their detailed feedback and suggestions. Without your responses our efforts would have been greatly diminished in scope. Any errors, of course, are the sole responsibility of the authors.

We welcome your comments and suggestions for further improvements to this text. Please feel free to use the following addresses to convey these remarks:

William A. Raabe
Fisher College of Business AMIS
The Ohio State University
Columbus, OH 43210
raabe@fisher.osu.edu

Gerald E. Whittenburg
The Charles W. Lamden School of Accountancy
San Diego State University
San Diego, CA 92182-8221
g.e.whittenburg@sdsu.edu

Debra L. Sanders
Department of Accounting, College of Business
Washington State University, Vancouver
Vancouver, WA 98686-9600
dsanders@vancouver.wsu.edu

Roby B. Sawyers
Department of Accounting, College of Management
NC State University
Raleigh, NC 27695-8113
roby_sawyers@ncsu.edu

Steven L. Gill
The Charles W. Lamden School of Accountancy
San Diego State University
San Diego, CA 92182-8221
sgill@mail.sdsu.edu

William A. Raabe
Gerald E. Whittenburg
Debra L. Sanders
Roby B. Sawyers
Steven L. Gill

October 2010

CHAPTER 1

Introduction to Tax Practice and Ethics

LEARNING OBJECTIVES

- Describe the elements of modern tax practice in the United States.
- Distinguish between open and closed transactions.
- Identify sources of legal and ethical standards that guide those who engage in tax practice.
- Examine in detail the major collections of ethical standards that bear upon tax practitioners today.
- Place tax issues in a broader context of ethics and morality.
- Understand the limitations on tax research by CPAs and other nonattorneys.

CHAPTER OUTLINE

$\mathbf{A}$T THE START OF the second decade of the twenty-first century, tax practice and tax research are continuing to evolve into an electronic and paperless reporting system. For example, in 2010 over 80 percent of individual taxpayers e-filed their tax returns. In keeping with this continuing transition to an all-electronic tax system, tax research is almost 100 percent computer based. The Uniform CPA Exam recognizes this transition and includes a set of "simulation" questions that require that the candidate demonstrate accounting and tax research skills by completing short computer research cases online. However, before the tax practitioner can complete a tax research project, he or she must understand the tax research process and all its elements, and how each element relates to solving a specific tax problem. The primary purpose of this book is to inform the user on how effectively to obtain tax research results in a timely and efficient manner.

The practice of taxation is the process of applying the tax law, rules, regulations, and judicial rulings to specific transactions to determine the tax consequences to the taxpayer involved. There are many ways to practice tax. One can practice tax directly through jobs such as a CPA, tax attorney, **Enrolled Agent (EA)**, or commercial income tax return preparer. In addition, tax can be practiced indirectly by such individuals as controllers, accountants, CFOs, and others who do tax work as part of their other duties. An understanding of taxation and the tax practice environment is essential to the individual who wants to have a position in the tax area.

Taxation is the process of collecting revenue from citizens to finance government activities. In a modern technological society such as that of the United States, however, taxation comprises an interaction among several disciplines that is far from simple. The tax system is derived from law, accounting, economics, political science, and sociology (Exhibit 1-1). Principles of economics, sociology, and political science provide the environment, while law and accounting precepts are applied in a typical tax practice.

EXHIBIT 1-1:   Elements of Taxation

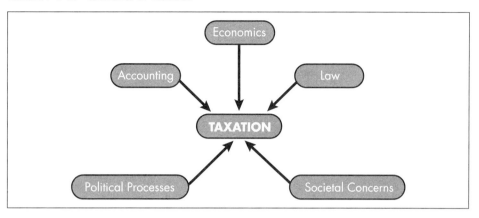

Tax policy questions concerning the effects that a specified tax law change will have on economic growth, the effects of projected inflation on the implementation of the tax law and vice versa, and the effects of the tax law on the United States' balance of payments are addressed by economists. Political scientists, economists, and sociologists, alternatively, examine an issue such as who bears the ultimate burden of a tax, how a tax bill becomes law (including practical effects of the legislative process), the social equity of a tax, and whether a tax is discriminatory. Attorneys interpret (and often create) taxation statutes, and accountants apply the tax laws to current or prospective economic transactions.

Elements of Tax Practice

The tax laws of a democratic country such as the United States are created by a political process. In recent years, the result of this political process has been a law that levies taxes on income, sales, estates, gifts, and other items that usually are reflected by the accounting process. Thus, tax practice can be described as the application of tax legislation to specific accounting situations. The elements of modern tax practice can be separated into three categories: compliance, planning, and litigation, which are all supported by tax research. How these elements of tax practice fit together is illustrated in Exhibit 1-2.

Tax Compliance

In general, **tax compliance** consists of the gathering of pertinent information, evaluation and classification of such information, and the filing of necessary tax returns. Tax compliance also includes other functions necessary to satisfy government requirements, such as representation at a client's Internal Revenue Service (IRS) audit. Commercial tax preparers, EAs, attorneys, and CPAs all perform tax compliance to some extent. Non-complex individual, partnership, and corporate tax returns often are completed by commercial tax preparers. EAs, attorneys, and CPAs usually are involved in the preparation of more complex tax returns; in addition, they provide tax-planning services and represent their clients before the IRS. The elements of tax compliance and administration are examined in more detail in later chapters.

Tax Planning

Tax planning is the process of arranging one's financial affairs to optimize tax liabilities. While that usually means minimizing current tax payments, that is not always the case.

EXHIBIT 1-2: Elements of Tax Practice

```
                        Tax Practice

                        Tax Research

  Tax Compliance        Tax Planning        Tax Litigation
```

However, whereas **tax avoidance** is the legitimate object of much of modern tax practice, **tax evasion** constitutes the illegal nonpayment of a tax and cannot be condoned. Fraudulent acts of this sort are unrelated to the professional practice of tax planning.

Tax planning can be divided into two major categories: **open transactions** and **closed transactions**. In an open transaction, the tax practitioner maintains some degree of control over the attendant tax liability because the transaction is not yet completed; for example, the title to an asset has not yet passed. If desired, some modifications to an incomplete transaction can be made to receive more favorable tax treatment. In a closed transaction, however, all of the pertinent actions have been completed; therefore, tax planning may be limited to the presentation of the facts to the government in the most favorable, legally acceptable manner possible.

SPOTLIGHT ON TAXATION

Case Quotation

There is nothing inherently illegal or immoral in the avoidance of taxation (i.e., tax planning) according to the tax system's rules. The eminent judge Learned Hand best expressed this doctrine in the dissenting opinion of *Commissioner v. Newman*, 159 F.2d 848 (CA-2, 1947):

"Over and over again, courts have said that there is nothing sinister in so arranging one's affairs as to keep taxes as low as possible. Everybody does so, rich or poor, and all do right, for nobody owes any public duty to pay more than the law demands: taxes are enforced extractions, not voluntary contributions."

Tax Litigation

A specialized area within the practice of taxation is the concentration on **tax litigation**. Litigation is the process of settling a dispute with another party (here, usually the IRS or a state revenue department) in a court of law. Typically, a tax attorney handles tax litigation that progresses beyond the initial appeal of an IRS or state revenue department audit result. Accountants and other financial advisers can also serve in a support capacity. Later chapters of this book contain additional discussions of the various opportunities and strategies available in tax litigation.

Tax Research

Tax research is undertaken to answer taxation questions. The tax research process includes the (1) identification of pertinent issues, (2) determination of proper authorities, (3) evaluation of the appropriateness of these authorities, and (4) application of these authorities to specific facts. Tax research methodology, sources of Federal tax law, and tax research tools are examined in Chapters 2 through 10 of this book.

Rules and Ethics in Tax Practice

A person who prepares tax returns for monetary or other compensation, or who is licensed to practice in the tax-related professions, is subject to various statutes, rules, and codes of professional conduct. All tax practitioners are regulated by **Circular 230**, Regulations Governing the Practice of Attorneys, CPAs, EAs, Enrolled Actuaries, and Appraisers before the IRS. The ethical conduct of an attorney is also governed by the laws of the state(s) in which he or she is licensed to practice. Most states have adopted, often with some modification, guidelines that are based on the **American Bar Association (ABA)** Model Code of Professional Responsibility or the newer ABA Model Rules of Professional Conduct.

CPAs who are members of the **American Institute of Certified Public Accountants (AICPA)** must follow its Code of Professional Conduct and any other rules generated by the state board(s) of accountancy. The AICPA has also produced a series of Statements on Standards for Tax Services (SSTS), which contain advisory guidelines for CPAs who prepare tax returns.

Although CPAs who are not members of the AICPA are not bound by the Code of Professional Conduct and the SSTS, those rules and standards are a useful source of guidance for all members of the profession. Statutory tax law also specifies certain penalties and other rules of conduct that apply to everyone (e.g., attorneys, CPAs, and EAs) in addition to their respective professional standards, and also to commercial tax preparers who are not attorneys, CPAs, or EAs. Chapter 13 addresses these rules. The basic overlapping sources of rules and ethics for tax practitioners are illustrated in Exhibit 1-3.

CIRCULAR 230 (For complete text, search "Circular 230" at www.irs.gov.)

Circular 230, which constitutes Part 31 of the Treasury Department Regulations, is designed to provide protection to taxpayers and the IRS by requiring tax preparers to be technically competent and to adhere to **ethical standards**. Circular 230 contains the following definition of **practice before the IRS** in Section 10.2 of Subpart A:

> ... *matters connected with presentation to the Internal Revenue Service or any of its officers or employees relating to a client's rights, privileges, or liabilities under laws or regulations administered by the Internal Revenue Service. Such presentations include the preparation and filing of necessary documents, correspondence with and communications to the Internal Revenue Service, and the representation of a client at conferences, hearings and meetings.*

Under this definition, practice before the IRS consists primarily of the representation of clients during audit procedures, such as a meeting with a revenue agent on behalf of a client to establish the correctness of a taxpayer's return. The preparation of tax returns or the furnishing of information to the IRS in response to a request for such information is not considered practice before the IRS. (Tax return preparation rules are addressed by

EXHIBIT 1-3:   Sources of Rules and Ethics for Tax Practitioners

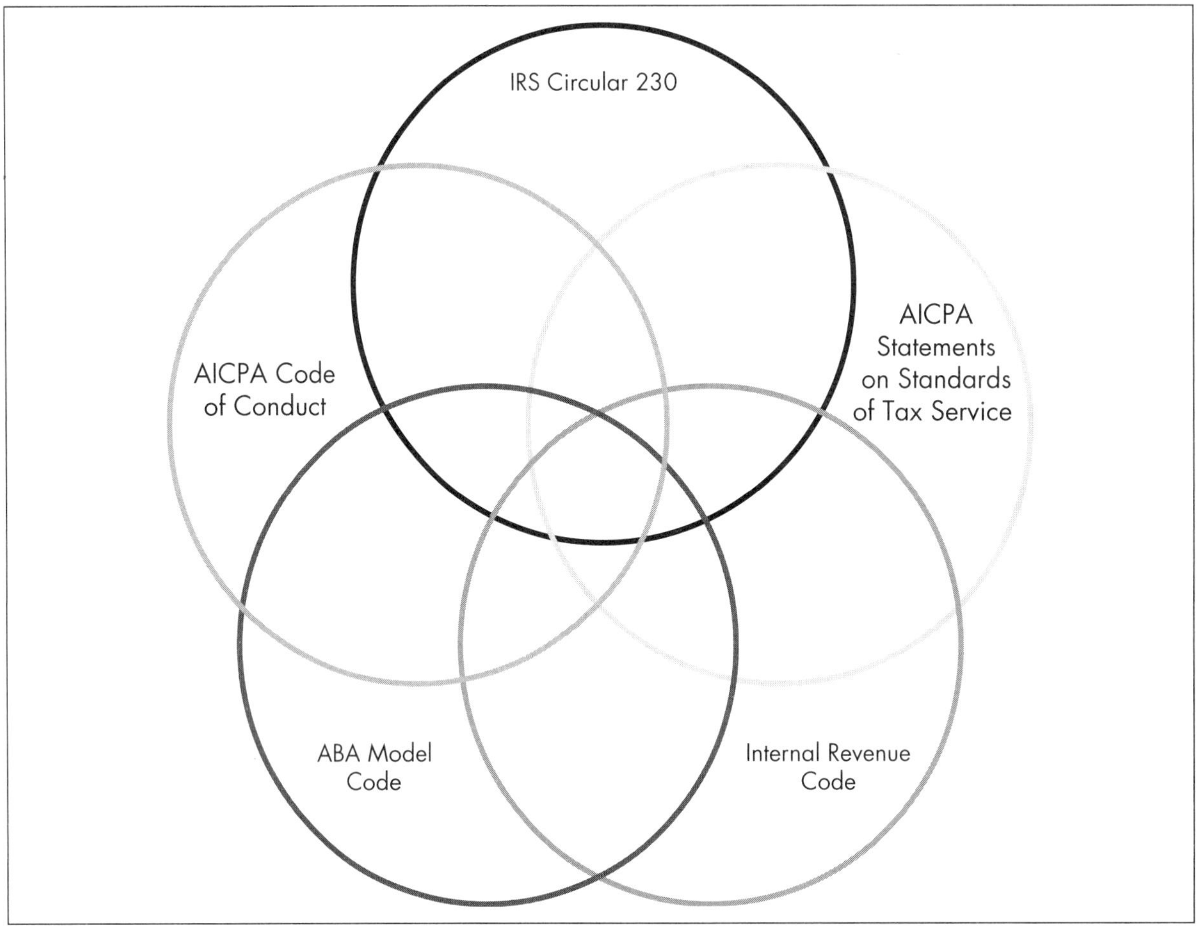

various statutes discussed in Chapter 13.) Circular 230 also states who may conduct such a practice and sets forth the disciplinary procedures that apply. In addition, CPAs, lawyers, and tax return preparers are (or may be) regulated by the states. As a result, there can be additional statutes, regulations, and requirements that must be met by individuals who practice in certain states.

Who May Practice [Circular 230 §10.3]   Under Section 10.3, Subpart A, of Circular 230, the following individuals may practice before the IRS:

1. Attorneys

2. CPAs

3. Enrolled agents

4. Enrolled actuaries

To qualify under this rule, an attorney must be a member in good standing of the bar of the highest court in any state, possession, territory, commonwealth, or the District of Columbia. Likewise, CPAs and enrolled actuaries must be qualified to practice in any state, possession, territory, commonwealth, or the District of Columbia. No further substantive examination is required.

Enrolled Agents (EAs) [Circular 230 §§10.4, 10.5, and 10.6] Individuals who are not attorneys or CPAs can qualify to practice before the IRS by becoming an EA. An EA is someone who has either passed a special IRS examination or worked for the IRS for five years. The procedures for becoming an EA are detailed in Circular 230, Subpart A, §§10.4, 10.5, and 10.6. EAs have the same rights as attorneys and CPAs to represent clients before the IRS. Under Circular 230, an EA must renew his or her enrollment card on a three-year cycle.

The Enrolled Agent Special Enrollment Examination (SEE) is an online exam given throughout the year that consists of three parts. The length of each part is 3.5 hours (not including the pre-examination tutorial and post-examination survey). The parts of the examination are:

- SEE1 Part 1 – Individuals

- SEE2 Part 2 – Businesses

- SEE3 Part 3 – Representation, Practices, and Procedures

A multiple-choice format is used on the SEE. Following are example questions from the SEE:

1. Which of the following entities are required to file Form 709, United States Gift Tax Return?

   a. An individual

   b. An estate or trust

   c. A corporation

   d. All of the above

2. Supplemental wages are compensation paid in addition to an employee's regular wages. They do not include payments for:

   a. Accumulated sick leave

   b. Nondeductible moving expenses

   c. Vacation pay

   d. Travel reimbursements paid at the Federal Government per diem rate

3. There are five tests which must be met for you to claim an exemption for a dependent. Which of the following is not a requirement?

   a. Citizen or Resident Test

   b. Member of Household or Relationship Test

   c. Disability Test

   d. Joint Return Test

For additional information on the SEE, see the Prometric Testing Web site: **www. prometric.com/irs.**

For each enrollment cycle, EAs, like attorneys and CPAs, must meet certain continuing education requirements as defined in Subpart A, §10.6. For an EA's enrollment card to be renewed, he or she must complete 72 hours (i.e., an average of 24 hours per year) of qualifying continuing education for each three-year enrollment period. In addition, a minimum of 16 hours of continuing education credit must be completed during each year of an enrollment cycle. Subpart A, §10.6(f) defines what qualifies as continuing education for EAs.

Circular 230 allows an individual to be an attorney or CPA and an EA simultaneously. Being both an EA and an attorney or CPA might be useful to certain tax practitioners who practice across state lines. The EA's card is effectively a national license to practice before the IRS anywhere in the United States (including territories). In addition, most state taxing agencies grant an EA the right to practice before that state agency.

For more information on EAs, see the following two Web sites. The first site is EA information on the IRS's Web page at **www.irs.gov/taxpros/agents,** and the second is the Web site of the National Association of Enrolled Agents (NAEA) at **www.naea.org**.

Limited Practice without Enrollment [Circular 230 §10.7]   In Circular 230, the IRS has authorized certain individuals to practice without being an attorney, CPA, or EA. Individuals (with proper identification) can represent themselves under §10.7(a) and participate in IRS rule making as provided for under §10.7(b). In addition, under §10.7(c), individuals (with proper identification and authorization, IRS Form 2848) are allowed to represent taxpayers in the following special situations:

1. An individual may represent a member of his or her immediate family.

2. A regular full-time employee of an individual employer may represent the employer.

3. A general partner or regular full-time employee of a partnership may represent the partnership.

4. A bona fide officer or regular full-time employee of a corporation (including a parent, subsidiary, or other affiliated corporation), an association, or organized group may represent the corporation, association, or organized group.

5. A trustee, receiver, guardian, personal representative, administrator, executor, or regular full-time employee of a trust, receivership, guardianship, or estate may represent the trust, receivership, guardianship, or estate.

6. An officer or regular employee of a governmental unit, agency, or authority may represent the governmental unit, agency, or authority in the course of his or her official duties.

7. An individual may represent any individual or entity before personnel of the IRS who are outside the United States.

Tax Return Preparers [Circular 230 §10.7]   Any unenrolled person who signs a tax return as having prepared it for a taxpayer is authorized to conduct "limited practice" before the IRS (with proper taxpayer authorization) under §10.7(c)(viii). Circular 230 requires that such person must not be disbarred or suspended from practice before the IRS or his or her profession. A tax return preparer can make an appearance as the taxpayer's representative only before the Examination Division of the IRS. A tax return preparer may not represent a taxpayer before any other IRS division, including the

Appeals and Collection Divisions [IRS Publication 947]. In addition, the following actions are outside the authority of an unenrolled preparer [Rev. Proc. 81-38, 1981-1 C.B. 386]:

1. Executing a claim for refund for the taxpayer.

2. Receiving checks in payment of any refund of taxes, penalties, or interest for the taxpayer.

3. Agreeing to later assessment or collection of taxes than is provided for by the applicable statute of limitations.

4. Executing closing agreements with respect to tax liability or other specific matters for the taxpayer.

5. Executing waivers of restriction on assessment or collection of a tax deficiency.

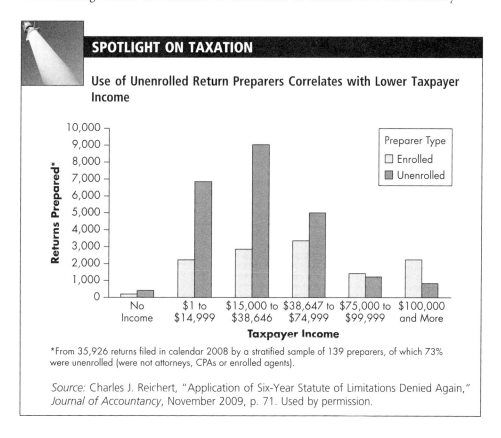

SPOTLIGHT ON TAXATION

Use of Unenrolled Return Preparers Correlates with Lower Taxpayer Income

*From 35,926 returns filed in calendar 2008 by a stratified sample of 139 preparers, of which 73% were unenrolled (were not attorneys, CPAs or enrolled agents).

Source: Charles J. Reichert, "Application of Six-Year Statute of Limitations Denied Again," *Journal of Accountancy,* November 2009, p. 71. Used by permission.

Proposed Requirements for Tax Return Preparers The IRS has proposed that beginning in 2011, tax return preparers who prepare all, or substantially all, of a Federal tax return (for compensation) will be subject to new requirements, including:

1. Requiring all paid tax return preparers to register with the IRS, pay a fee, and obtain a preparer tax identification number (PTIN). If you already have a PTIN, you must still register under the new process.

2. Requiring competency tests for all paid tax return preparers except attorneys, CPAs, and enrolled agents who are active and in good standing with their respective licensing agencies.

3. Requiring continuing professional education of 15 hours per year for all paid tax return preparers except attorneys, CPAs, and enrolled agents.

4. Conducting tax compliance checks on all tax return preparers.

5. Extending Circular 230 ethics standards to all preparers.

For additional information on the proposed tax return preparer requirements, see the IRS Web site. The frequently asked questions (FAQ) section on the proposed requirements is currently located at **www.irs.gov/taxpros/article/0,,id=218611,00.html**.

Practice Before the IRS [Circular 230 Subpart B] Subpart B of Circular 230 provides a set of rules of conduct for those individuals authorized to practice before the IRS. Attorneys, CPAs, and EAs must observe the following rules of conduct (among others) when practicing before the IRS:

1. A tax practitioner must furnish information, on request, to any authorized agent of the IRS, unless the practitioner has reason to believe that the request is of doubtful legality or the information is privileged [§10.20(a)].

2. A tax practitioner must provide the Director of Practice of the IRS, on request, any information concerning the violation of any regulation pertaining to practice before the IRS. The tax practitioner must testify in a disbarment or suspension proceeding, unless there is reason to doubt the legality of the request or the information is privileged [§10.20(b)].

3. A tax practitioner who knows of client noncompliance, error, or omission with regard to the tax laws must advise the client of that noncompliance, error, or omission [§10.21].

4. Practitioners must not unreasonably delay matters before the IRS [§10.23].

5. Practitioners must not accept assistance from or employ a disbarred or suspended person or a former IRS employee who is disqualified from practice under another rule or U.S. law [§10.24].

6. Partners of government employees cannot represent anyone for which the government employee-partner has (or has had) official responsibility [§10.25]. For example, a CPA firm with an IRS agent as a partner cannot represent any taxpayer that is (or was in the past) assigned to the IRS agent/partner.

7. No former government employee shall, subsequent to his or her government employment, represent anyone in any matter administered by the IRS if such representation would violate other U.S. laws [§10.25].

8. No tax practitioner may act as a notary public for his or her clients [§10.26].

9. Fees for tax work must not be contingent or unconscionable [§10.27], and a practitioner must not negotiate a taxpayer's refund check [§10.31].

10. No tax practitioner can represent conflicting interests before the IRS unless he or she has the express consent of the directly interested parties [§10.29].

11. In general, a practitioner must, at the request of a client, promptly return any and all records of the client that are necessary for the client to comply with his or her Federal tax obligations. The practitioner may retain copies of the records returned to a client [§10.28].

Due Diligence [Circular 230 §10.22] Section 10.22 of Circular 230 requires tax practitioners to use **due diligence** in preparing tax returns and in their practice before the IRS. Due diligence is not defined in Circular 230. However, the Second Circuit in *Harary v. Blumenthal*, 555 F.2d 1113 (CA-2, 1977) has held that due diligence requires that the tax practitioner be honest with his or her client in connection with all IRS-related matters. In the view of the IRS, the failure to exercise due diligence involves conduct that is more than a simple error, but less than willful and reckless misconduct (Coursebook Training 994-102, IRS, December 1992). In determining if a practitioner has exercised due diligence, the IRS uses several factors, including the nature of the error, the explanation of the error, and other standards that apply (e.g., the AICPA SSTS that are discussed later in this chapter). In essence, due diligence means a tax practitioner should use reasonable effort to comply with the tax laws.

EXAMPLE 1-1

Judy is a CPA who fails to include rental income on a tax return she completed for a client. The omitted rental income was from a new rental property purchased by the client this year and therefore had not been reported on prior years' tax returns. The taxpayer did not mention the new rental property to Judy in any communications with her. Under these circumstances, Judy has exercised due diligence in preparing the tax return. However, if Judy also kept the rental income records for the new rental property and still omitted the income from the tax return, then she would not be exercising due diligence.

Contingent and Unconscionable Fees [Circular 230 §10.27] Section 10.27 regulates fees charged by tax practitioners and restricts the use of unconscionable and contingent fees. A practitioner may not charge an **unconscionable fee** in connection with any matter before the IRS. This term is not defined in Circular 230. If a tax practitioner charges a fee that is out of line with some measure of the value of the service provided to a client, then the fee would be unconscionable. For example, a CPA could not charge a fee of $10,000 to an unsophisticated taxpayer (such as an elderly person) for simple tax work that most CPAs would complete for less than $500.

Except for a few exceptions as discussed below, a practitioner may not charge a contingent fee for services rendered in connection with matters before the IRS. Practitioners may charge **contingent fees** for services rendered in connection with the Service's examination of, or challenge to, (1) an original tax return; or (2) an amended return or claim for refund or credit where the amended return or claim for refund or credit was filed within 120 days of the taxpayer receiving a written notice of the examination of, or a written challenge to, the original tax return. The intent of this exception is to discourage the tactical preparation of a refund claim or amended return filed late in the examination process.

A practitioner may also charge a contingent fee for services rendered in connection with a claim for credit or refund filed solely in connection with the determination of statutory interest or penalties assessed by the IRS, and for services rendered in connection with any judicial proceeding arising under the Internal Revenue Code.

A contingent fee is any fee that is based, in whole or in part, on whether or not a position taken on a tax return or other filing avoids challenge by the Internal Revenue Service or is sustained either by the Internal Revenue Service or in litigation and includes a fee that is based on a percentage of the refund reported on a return, that is based on a percentage of the taxes saved, or that otherwise depends on the specific result attained.[1]

EXAMPLE 1-2

Oak Corporation has been audited by the IRS for its tax return filed two years ago. The controller of the company completed the original return. The IRS is asserting that Oak underpaid its taxes by $100,000. Oak contacted Joe, a CPA, and engaged him to handle the appeals process with the IRS. In this situation, Joe can use a contingent fee arrangement. (For instance, Joe's fee could be 30 percent of any amount by which he could get the IRS to reduce the assessment.)

Solicitation and Advertising [Circular 230 §10.30]   An attorney, CPA, or EA may use public communication to obtain clients under §10.30 of Subpart B. Types of public communication allowed by this provision include billboards, telephone books, and advertisements in newspapers, on radio, and on television. However, such public communications must not contain false, fraudulent, unduly influencing, coercive, or unfair statements or claims. If done in a dignified manner, examples of items that a practitioner may communicate to the public include (1) his or her name, address, and telephone number, (2) names of individuals associated with the practitioner, (3) a factual description of services offered, (4) credit cards accepted, (5) foreign language ability, (6) membership in professional organizations, (7) professional licenses held, and (8) a statement of practice limitations. Attorneys, CPAs, and EAs also must observe any applicable standards of ethical conduct adopted by the ABA, the AICPA, and the NAEA.

Best Practices [Circular 230 §10.33]   Section 10.33 of Circular 230 states that tax advisors should provide clients with the highest quality representation concerning Federal tax issues by adhering to best practices in providing advice. According to Circular 230, the best practices rules are aspirational. Thus, a practitioner who fails to comply with best practices will not be subject to discipline by the IRS. Still, tax professionals are expected to observe them to preserve public confidence in the tax system.

Best practices to be observed by all tax advisors include the following:

1. Communicating clearly with the client regarding the terms of the engagement. For example, the advisor should determine the client's expected purpose for and use of the advice and should have a clear understanding with the client regarding the form and scope of the advice or assistance to be rendered.

2. Establishing the facts, determining which facts are relevant, evaluating the reasonableness of any assumptions or representations, relating the applicable law (including potentially applicable judicial doctrines) to the relevant facts, and arriving at a conclusion supported by the law and the facts.

3. Advising the client regarding the importance of the conclusions reached, including, for example, whether a taxpayer may avoid accuracy-related penalties under the Internal Revenue Code if a taxpayer acts in reliance on the advice.

4. Acting fairly and with integrity in practice before the IRS.

---

[1]In July 2009, Treasury proposed amendments to Section 10.27 clarifying the definition of contingent fee. The modified sentence would state that "A contingent fee includes a fee that is based on a percentage of the refund reported on a return, that is based on a percentage of the taxes saved, or that otherwise depends on the specific **tax** (emphasis added) result attained."

According to Circular 230, these procedures help to ensure best practices for tax advisors. In addition, tax practitioners with responsibility for overseeing a firm's practice of providing tax advice or of preparing tax returns should take reasonable steps to ensure that the firm's procedures for all members, associates, and employees follow "best practices procedures."

Tax Return Positions [Circular 230 §10.34]   Section 10.34 of Circular 230 provides return preparer practice standards for practitioners who practice before the IRS. At the time this book went to print, the status of Circular 230 section 10.34 was uncertain. On September 26, 2007, Treasury published proposed amendments to section 10.34. These proposed amendments were intended to conform the professional standards under Circular 230 section 10.34 with the new "more likely than not" civil penalty standards for return preparers found in IRC Section 6694 at that time.[2] However, in October 2008, Congress revisited IRC Section 6694 and lowered the standard for undisclosed positions to "substantial authority." Consequently, the proposed standard for Circular 230 section 10.34 is higher than the general standard in IRC Section 6694.

As of December 2010, we are expecting changes to the proposed amendments to Circular 230 section 10.34 which will once again align Circular 230 with IRC Section 6694's substantial authority standard.

Covered Opinions [Circular 230 §10.35]   Circular 230 imposes strict standards on **covered opinions**. This term includes written advice (including electronic communications such as e-mail) concerning one or more Federal tax issue(s) arising from the following:

1. A transaction that is the same as or substantially similar to a transaction that, at the time the advice is rendered, the IRS has determined to be a tax avoidance transaction and identified by published guidance as a listed transaction under 26 CFR 1.6011-4(b)(2).

2. Any partnership or other entity, any investment plan or arrangement, or any other plan or arrangement, the principal purpose of which is the avoidance or evasion of any tax imposed by the Internal Revenue Code.

3. Any partnership or other entity, any investment plan or arrangement, or any other plan or arrangement, a significant purpose of which is the avoidance or evasion of any tax imposed by the Internal Revenuc Code, if the written advice:

    a. Is a reliance opinion, which is written advice that concludes at a confidence level of a greater than 50 percent likelihood that one or more significant Federal tax issues would be resolved in the taxpayer's favor.

    b. Is a marketed opinion, which is written advice that the practitioner knows or has reason to know will be used or referred to by a person other than the practitioner (or a person who is a member of, associated with, or employed by the practitioner's firm) in promoting, marketing, or recommending a partnership or other entity, investment plan, or arrangement to one or more taxpayers.

    c. Is subject to conditions of confidentiality.

    d. Is subject to contractual protection.

---

[2]On May 25, 2007, IRC Section 6694 was amended by Congress to revise the "realistic possibility" standard to a more stringent "more likely than not" standard. The civil penalty standards in Section 6694 are discussed in more detail in Chapter 14.

Procedures to Ensure Compliance [Circular 230 §10.36]   Section 10.36 requires a practitioner who has principal authority and responsibility for overseeing a firm's practice of providing advice concerning Federal tax issues must take reasonable steps to ensure that the firm has adequate procedures in effect to ensure compliance with §10.35. Any such practitioner can be subject to discipline for failing to comply with the requirements of §10.36.

SPOTLIGHT ON TAXATION

E-mail Disclaimer

Because of Circular 230 covered opinions rules, most CPAs and other tax advisors include some form of blanket disclaimer in the tag line of all their e-mail and other written correspondence sent to clients. An example of such a disclaimer would be:

> I am required by IRS Circular 230 to inform you that, unless otherwise expressly indicated, any Federal tax advice contained in this communication, including attachments and enclosures, is not intended or written to be used, and may not be used, for the purpose of (1) avoiding tax-related penalties under the Internal Revenue Code or (2) promoting, marketing, or recommending to another party any tax-related matters addressed herein.

Other Written Advice [Circular 230 §10.37]   A practitioner must not give written advice (including electronic communications) concerning one or more Federal tax issues if the practitioner:

1. Bases the written advice on unreasonable factual or legal assumptions (including assumptions as to future events).

2. Unreasonably relies upon representations, statements, findings, or agreements of the taxpayer or any other person.

3. Does not consider all relevant facts that the practitioner knows or should know.

4. In evaluating a Federal tax issue, takes into account the possibility that a tax return will not be audited, that an issue will not be raised on audit, or that an issue will be resolved through settlement if raised.

When applying the provision, all facts and circumstances, including the scope of the engagement and the type and specificity of the advice sought by the client, will be considered in determining whether a practitioner has failed to comply with this section.

Circular 230 can be found on the IRS's Web site at **www.irs.gov/pub/irs-pdf/pcir230.pdf**.

AICPA Code of Professional Conduct

Members of the AICPA are subject to the Institute's Code of Professional Conduct. The Code is relevant to all of the professional services performed by CPAs, including those services provided in the practice of public accounting, private industry, government, or education. Changes adopted in 1988 were believed necessary to reflect the significant changes in the profession and the environment in which CPAs practice, although the basic tenets of ethical and professional conduct remained the same. One of the most significant changes was the expansion of the rules to apply to all members in all fields of practice, except where the wording of the rule limits the application to a specified field of practice. Under the prior Code of Ethics, only members engaged in the practice of public accounting were required to observe all of the rules. Other members, such as those in the fields of education, government, and industry, were subject only to the rules requiring integrity and objectivity and the rule prohibiting members from performing acts discreditable to the profession.

In addition, the rule prohibiting a CPA in public practice from engaging in a business or an occupation concurrently with the practice of public accounting, which would create a conflict of interest in rendering professional services, was deleted from the Code of Professional Conduct. The members of the Institute felt that such conflicts of interest are effectively prohibited under new Rule 102, Integrity, and Objectivity.

The Code of Professional Conduct was designed to provide its members with the following:

1. A comprehensive code of ethical and professional conduct.

2. A guide for all members in answering complex questions.

3. Assurance to the public concerning the obligations and responsibilities of the accounting profession.

The AICPA Code of Professional Conduct consists of two integral sections: the principles and the rules. The principles provide a foundation on which the rules are based. The principles suggest that a CPA should strive for behavior above the minimal level of acceptable conduct required by law and regulations. In addition to expressing the basic tenets of ethical and professional conduct, the principles are intended to provide a framework for the CPA's responsibilities to the public, clients, and colleagues. Included are guidelines concerning the member's responsibility to perform professional services with integrity, objectivity, and **independence**.

The rules consist of a set of enforceable ethical standards that have been approved by a majority of the members of the AICPA. These rules are broad in nature and apply to all of the professional services that a CPA performs, whether in the practice of public accounting or in the fields of education, industry, or government. The only exceptions to the rules occur when their wording indicates that their application is limited to a specified field of practice only, or with respect to certain activities of those who are practicing in another country. In the latter case, however, the CPA must adhere to the ethical standards of the foreign country.

Any failure to follow the rules under the Code of Professional Conduct may result in the offender receiving admonishment, suspension, or expulsion from membership in the AICPA. The rules apply not only to the CPA, but also to those employees who are under his or her supervision, partners or shareholders in the practice of the CPA, and any others who act on the CPA's behalf (even if they are not compensated for their activities). As previously discussed, the Code of Professional Conduct is applicable to all of the professional services performed by a CPA, including services rendered in the fields of public accounting, such as tax and management advisory services, education, industry, and government.

In addition to the principles and rules, the Code of Professional Conduct provides for three additional promulgations: interpretations of rules, ethics rulings, and "ethics features." Interpretations of Rules are issued by the Division of Professional Ethics of the AICPA and provide additional detailed guidelines for the scope and application of the rules. These guidelines are enforceable, and the CPA must be prepared to justify any departure from them.

The Division of Professional Ethics of the AICPA also issues ethics rulings to further explain the application and interpretation of the rules of conduct and to provide interpretations of the rules in specific circumstances. A member who, in similar circumstances, departs from the findings of these ethics rulings must be prepared to justify such departure. In addition, the Division of Professional Ethics publishes a column in the *Journal of Accountancy* dealing with issues of professional ethics. These informal articles are intended to address issues raised in questions submitted by members of the AICPA. The questions and answers contained in the articles are not considered formal rulings by the AICPA.

Rule 101: Independence   Under Rule 101, a CPA (or CPA firm) in public practice must be independent of the enterprise for which professional services are being provided. Independence is required not only for opinions on financial statements, but also for certain other reports and services where a body of the AICPA has promulgated standards requiring independence. A CPA is not independent if one or more financial relationships exist with a client during the period of professional engagement or at the issuing of the opinion. Thus, independence is impaired if a CPA:

1. Had or was committed to acquire any direct or material indirect financial interest in the client.

2. Was a trustee of any trust or executor or administrator of any estate if such trust or estate had or was committed to acquire any direct or material indirect financial interest in the client and (i) The covered member (individually or with others) had the authority to make investment decisions for the trust or estate; or (ii) The trust or estate owned or was committed to acquire more than 10 percent of the client's outstanding equity securities or other ownership interests; or (iii) The value of the trust's or estate's holdings in the client exceeded 10 percent of the total assets of the trust or estate.

3. Had a joint, closely held investment that was material to the covered member.

4. Except as specifically permitted in interpretation 101-5, had any loan to or from the client, any officer or director of the client, or any individual owning 10 percent or more of the client's outstanding equity securities or other ownership interests.

5. During the period of the professional engagement, a partner or professional employee of the firm, his or her immediate family, or any group of such persons acting together owned more than 5 percent of a client's outstanding equity securities or other ownership interests.

6. During the period covered by the financial statements or during the period of the professional engagement, a firm, or partner or professional employee of the firm was simultaneously associated with the client as a(n):

    a. Director, officer, or employee, or in any capacity equivalent to that of a member of management.

    b. Promoter, underwriter, or voting trustee.

    c. Trustee for any pension or profit-sharing trust of the client.

These independence standards also apply to a CPA who is restricted to doing tax work in a partnership with other CPAs who are examining related financial statements.

For instance, a tax partner in a CPA firm should not own stock in a client whose financial statements are audited by her partners in the firm, even though she may have nothing to do with the audit of that client's statements.

Rule 102: Integrity and Objectivity   All professional services by a CPA should be rendered with objectivity and integrity, avoiding any conflict of interest. A CPA should not knowingly misrepresent facts or subordinate his or her judgment to that of others in rendering any professional services. For example, in a tax practice the CPA may be requested to follow blindly the guidelines of a government agency or the demands of an audit client. Rule 102 prohibits such blind obedience. Prior to the most recent revision of Rule 102, a CPA in tax practice could resolve doubt in favor of the client. This phrase was omitted in the revised language because resolving doubt in favor of a client in an advocacy engagement is not considered an impairment to integrity or objectivity and thus need not be specifically "allowed."

Rule 201: General Standards   The CPA must comply with the following general standards, as well as any interpretations of such standards, of the AICPA Code of Professional Conduct:

1. The CPA must be able to complete all professional services with professional competence.

2. The CPA must exercise due professional care in the performance of all professional services.

3. The CPA shall adequately plan and supervise the performance of all professional services.

4. The CPA must obtain sufficient relevant data to afford a reasonable basis for any conclusion or recommendation in connection with the performance of any professional services.

The standard requiring "professional competence" recognizes the need for members of the profession to commit to a program of professional development, learning, and improvement. Such a program of professional continuing education is also recognized in the standard of "due professional care."

Rule 202: Compliance with Standards   A CPA, whether providing tax, management advisory, audit, review, compilation, or other professional services, must comply with all standards promulgated by bodies designated by the AICPA Council.

Rule 203: Accounting Principles   A CPA is prohibited from expressing an opinion that financial data of an entity conform with Generally Accepted Accounting Principles if those statements or other financial data contain any material departure from the profession's technical standards. In some cases where a departure is present but the financial statement or other financial data would have been misleading without that departure, a member may be able to comply with this rule by describing the departure, the effect of the departure, and the justification for it.

Rule 301: Confidential Client Information   A CPA in the practice of public accounting must not disclose confidential client data without the specific consent of the client. However, Rule 301 does not apply in the following situations:

1. If there is a conflict with Rules 202 (Compliance with Standards) and 203 (Accounting Principles) as set forth by the AICPA Code of Professional Conduct.

2. If the CPA is served with an enforceable subpoena or summons, or must comply with applicable laws and government regulations.

3. If there is a review of a CPA's practice under AICPA or state society authorization.

4. If the CPA is responding to an inquiry of an investigative or disciplinary body of a recognized society, or where the CPA is initiating a complaint with a disciplinary body.

In connection with this rule, members of the investigative bodies who may be exposed to confidential client information are precluded from disclosing such information.

SPOTLIGHT ON TAXATION

Confidentiality

A Texas District Court held that the identities of taxpayers who hired the accounting firm of KPMG to participate in a tax shelter later identified as potentially abusive by the IRS were not protected from disclosure under the §7525 confidentiality privilege for communications between taxpayers and federally authorized tax practitioners. Disclosing taxpayers' identities to the IRS would only reveal their participation in these shelters, and it would not reveal any confidential communications made regarding these tax shelters. *John Doe 1 and John Doe 2 v. KPMG,* 93 AFTR 2d 2004-1759 (DC N. Tex.).

Rule 302: Contingent Fees   A CPA in public practice cannot charge or receive a contingent fee for any professional services from a client for whom the CPA or the CPA's firm performs audit, review, certain compilations, or an examination of prospective financial information. For example, a fee schedule of $5,000 for a qualified audit opinion and $35,000 for an unqualified opinion would not be allowed. Rule 302 also prohibits a CPA from preparing an original or amended tax return, or claim for a tax refund for a contingent fee.

A contingent fee is defined here as a fee established for the performance of any service pursuant to an arrangement in which no fee will be charged unless a specified finding or result is attained, or in which the amount of the fee is otherwise dependent on the finding or result of such service. Solely for purposes of this rule, fees are not regarded as being contingent if fixed by courts or other public authorities or, in tax matters, if determined based on the results of judicial proceedings or the findings of governmental agencies.

Rule 501: Acts Discreditable   A CPA must not commit an act that is discreditable to the profession. This rule is not specific as to what constitutes a discreditable act; however, violations have been found when the CPA committed a felony, failed to return client records after a client requested them, signed a false tax return, or issued a misleading audit opinion.

Rule 502: Advertising and Other Forms of Solicitation   A CPA in public practice cannot seek clients through false, misleading, or deceptive advertising or other forms of solicitation. In addition, solicitation by the use of coercion, overreaching, or harassing conduct is not allowed. The Institute has placed no restrictions as to the type, media, or frequency of a CPA's advertisements or on the artwork that is associated with them. Under Rule 502, an activity would be prohibited:

1. If it created false or unjustified expectations of favorable results.

2. If it implied the ability to influence any court, tribunal, regulatory agency, or similar body or official.

3. If it contains a representation that specific professional services in current or future periods will be performed for a stated fee, estimated fee, or fee range when it was likely, at the time of the representation, that such fees would be substantially increased and the prospective client was not advised of that likelihood.

4. If it contains any other representations that would be likely to cause a reasonable person to misunderstand or be deceived.

For example, a radio spot that states a CPA firm "can beat the IRS every time" would be in violation of Rule 502.

Rule 503: Commissions and Referral Fees　A CPA in public practice cannot charge or receive a commission or referral fee from a client for whom the CPA or the CPA's firm performs audit, review, certain compilation work, or an examination of prospective financial information. Thus, under Rule 503, a CPA who does only tax or other nonaudit work for a client may accept or pay a commission. However, the CPA must disclose the commission to the client or other party in the transaction. In addition, a member who accepts or pays a referral fee for recommending or referring any service of a CPA must disclose that fact.

Rule 505: Form of Organization and Name　CPAs may practice public accounting only in the form of organization permitted by state law or regulation whose characteristics conform to resolutions of the AICPA Council. Under Rule 505, a CPA cannot practice under a firm name that is misleading. The names of one or more past owners may be included in the firm name of a successor organization. In addition, all partners or members of a firm must be members of the AICPA if a firm is to designate itself as "Members of the AICPA."

Statements on Standards for Tax Services

To assist CPAs, the AICPA has issued a series of statements as to what constitutes appropriate standards for tax practice. These SSTS delineate a CPA's responsibilities to his or her clients, the public, the government, and the profession. The SSTS is a set of enforceable standards. They are intended to specifically address the problems inherent in the tax practitioner's dual role in serving the client and the public. The statements are intended to supplement, rather than replace, the AICPA Code of Professional Conduct and Circular 230. They are designed to address the development of tax practice as an integral part of a CPA's practice and the changing environment in which tax practitioners must operate, including the rapidly changing tax laws.

SSTS No. 1: Tax Return Positions　Under SSTS No. 1, a member should determine and comply with the standards, if any, that are imposed by the applicable taxing authority with respect to recommending a tax return position, or preparing or signing a tax return. If the applicable taxing authority has no written standards with respect to recommending a tax return position or preparing or signing a tax return, or if its standards are lower than the standards set forth in the SSTS, then the standards in SSTS No. 1 apply.

This Standard provides that, in providing professional services that involve tax return positions, a member should have a good-faith belief that the position has at least a **realistic possibility** of being sustained administratively or judicially on its merits if challenged. In addition, a member may recommend a tax return position if the member concludes that there is a reasonable basis for the position and advises the taxpayer to appropriately disclose that position. Thus, a member may prepare or sign a tax return that reflects a position if a member has a reasonable basis for the position and that position is *appropriately disclosed.*

A member may reach a conclusion that a position is warranted based on a well reasoned construction of the applicable statute, well-reasoned articles or treatises, or pronouncements issued by the applicable taxing authority, regardless of whether such sources would be treated as authority under Internal Revenue Code Section 6662 (Accuracy-related penalty on underpayments). A position would not fail to meet these standards merely because it is later abandoned for practical or procedural considerations during an administrative hearing or in the litigation process.

In cases where the member believes that the taxpayer may have some exposure to a penalty, the statement suggests that the member advise the taxpayer of such risk. Where disclosure of a position on the tax return may mitigate the possibility of a taxpayer penalty under the Internal Revenue Code, the member should consider recommending that the taxpayer disclose the position on the return. Additionally, a member should not recommend a tax return position or prepare or sign a tax return reflecting a position that the member knows could exploit the audit selection process of a taxing authority, or serves as a mere arguing position advanced solely to obtain leverage in a negotiation with a taxing authority.

SSTS No. 2: Answers to Questions on Returns   Before signing a return as the preparer, a member should make a reasonable effort to obtain from the taxpayer appropriate answers to all questions on the taxpayer's tax return. Where the taxpayer leaves a question on the return unanswered and reasonable grounds exist for not answering the question, the member need not provide an explanation for the omission. The possibility that an answer to a question may prove disadvantageous to the taxpayer, however, does not justify omitting the answer.

Reasonable grounds may exist for omitting an answer to a question on a return. For example, such an omission is acceptable in the following situations:

1. The pertinent data are not readily available and are not significant to the determination of taxable income (or loss) or the tax liability.

2. The taxpayer and member are genuinely uncertain as to the meaning of the question on the return.

3. An answer to a question is voluminous. (However, assurance should be given on the return that the data can be supplied upon examination.) In this regard, a notation on Form 1120 and related schedules that information will be provided on request is not considered acceptable (IRS Brooklyn District Newsletter No. 47, 10/89).

SSTS No. 3: Certain Procedural Aspects of Preparing Returns   In preparing or signing a return, the member ordinarily may rely without verification on information that the taxpayer or a third party has provided, unless such information appears to be incorrect, incomplete, or inconsistent. A more formal audit-like review of documents or supporting evidence is generally not required for a member to sign the tax return. Where material provided by the taxpayer appears to be incorrect or incomplete, however, the member should obtain additional information from the taxpayer. In situations where the statutes require that specific conditions be met, the member should determine, by inquiry, whether the conditions have been met. For example, the Code and Regulations impose substantiation requirements for the deduction of certain expenditures. In such a case, the member has an obligation to make appropriate inquiries.

Although members are not required to examine supporting documents, they should encourage the taxpayer to provide such documents when deemed appropriate. For example, in the case of deductions or income from a pass-through entity, such as a partnership, the entity's documents might be useful in preparing the owner's tax returns.

The member should make proper use of the prior year's tax return when feasible to gather information about the taxpayer and to help avoid omissions and errors with respect to income, deductions, and credit computations.

SSTS No. 4: Use of Estimates   A member may prepare tax returns that involve the use of the taxpayer's estimates if it is impractical to obtain exact data and if the estimated amounts appear reasonable to the member. In all cases, the estimated information must be supplied by the taxpayer. However, the member may provide advice in connection with the estimate. When the taxpayer's estimates are used, they should be presented in such a manner as to avoid the implication of greater accuracy than exists. Situations where the use of estimates may be appropriate include cases where the keeping of precise records for numerous items of small amounts is difficult to achieve, where data are not available at the time of filing the tax return, or when certain records are missing.

The use of estimates in making pertinent accounting judgments where such use is not in conflict with the Internal Revenue Code is not prohibited under this statement;

SPOTLIGHT ON TAXATION

The Cohan Rule

SSTS No. 4 is similar to (and somewhat based on) the estimation rule in the 1930 *Cohan* case [8 AFTR 10552; 39 F2d 540; 2 USTC ¶ 489]. George M. Cohan was a producer of Broadway shows (Yankee Doodle Dandy, for example) in the early part of the twentieth century. As such, his work involved a substantial amount of travel and entertaining in connection with his production of Broadway shows. George did not keeps records of these travel and entertaining (T&E) expenses; he just estimated them for tax purposes (over $55,000 for his 1921 through 1923 fiscal years) and deducted them on his income tax returns. The Board of Tax Appeals (the predecessor to the Tax Court) upheld the IRS's disallowance of all (100 percent) of the estimated T&E deduction due to lack of proper substantiation. However, the Second Circuit of Appeals disagreed and said that Cohan obviously incurred such expenses and that a reasonable estimate would be acceptable in calculating taxable income.

This is sometimes referred to as the **"Cohan Rule"** and is still in effect today. However, Congress has modified the Cohan Rule by changing the Code for certain transactions. For example, the Cohan rule may no longer be used to allow the deduction of estimated amounts of certain kinds of business expenses—namely, travel and entertainment expenses (including away from home travel expenses), and listed property expenditures (including local travel expenses). The current rules (see §274) required detailed substantiation of such expenditures.

such judgments are acceptable and expected. For example, the income tax regulations permit the use of a reasonable estimate for accruals if exact amounts are not known.

Although in most cases the use of estimates does not necessitate that the item be specifically disclosed on the taxpayer's return, disclosure should be made where failure to do so would result in misleading the IRS about the accuracy of the return. For example, disclosure may be necessary where the taxpayer's records have been destroyed in a fire or where the taxpayer has not received a Schedule K-1 from a pass-through entity at the time the return is filed. Tax practitioners should make their taxpayers aware that the tax law does not allow estimates of certain income and expenditure items, and that more restrictive substantiation requirements apply in cases of certain expenditures, such as travel and entertainment expenses.

SSTS No. 5: Departure from a Position Previously Concluded in an Administrative Proceeding or Court Decision The recommendation by a member as to the treatment of an item on a tax return should be based on the facts and the law as they are evaluated at the time during which the return is prepared or signed by the member. Unless the taxpayer is bound by the IRS to the treatment of an item in later years, such as by a closing agreement, the disposition of an item in a prior year's audit, or as part of a prior year's court decision, the member is not prevented from recommending a different treatment of a similar item in a later year's return. Thus, a member may sign a return that contains a departure from a treatment required by the IRS in a prior year, provided that the member adheres to the standards in SSTS No. 1.

In most cases, a member's recommendation as to the treatment of an item on a tax return will be consistent with the treatment of a similar item consented to in a prior year's administrative proceeding or as a result of the prior year's court decision. In deciding whether a recommendation contrary to the prior treatment is warranted, the member should consider the following:

1. Neither the IRS nor the taxpayer is bound to act consistently with respect to the treatment of an item in a prior proceeding. However, the IRS tends to act consistently in similar situations.

2. The standards under SSTS No. 1, Tax Return Positions, must be followed. In determining whether such standards can be met, the member must consider the existence of an unfavorable court decision and the taxpayer's consent in an earlier administrative proceeding.

3. In some cases, the taxpayer's consent to the treatment of an item in a prior administrative or judicial proceeding may have been due to a desire to settle the issue or a lack of supporting data, whereas in the current year these factors no longer exist.

4. The tax climate may have changed for a given issue since the prior court decision was reached or the prior administrative hearing concluded.

SSTS No. 6: Knowledge of Error: Return Preparation and Administrative Proceedings The member must advise the taxpayer promptly, regardless of whether the member prepared or signed the return in question, when he or she learns of an error in a previously filed tax return, an error in a return that is the subject of an administrative proceeding, or a taxpayer's failure to file a required return. Such advice should include a recommendation for appropriate measures the taxpayer should take. However, the member is neither obligated to inform the IRS of the situation, nor may he or she do so without the taxpayer's permission, except as provided by law.

The term error includes any position, omission, or method of accounting that, at the time the return is filed, fails to meet the standards set out in SSTS No. 1. An error also includes a position taken on a prior year's return that no longer meets these standards due to legislation, judicial decisions, or administrative pronouncements having retroactive effect. However, an error does not include an item that has an insignificant effect on the taxpayer's tax liability. The term administrative proceeding does not include a criminal proceeding.

If the member is requested to prepare the current year's return, and the taxpayer has not taken action to correct an error in a prior year's return, the member should consider whether to proceed with the preparation of the current year's return. If the current year's return is prepared, the member should take reasonable steps to ensure that the error is not repeated.

A member should advise a taxpayer, either orally or in writing, as to the correction of errors in the prior year's return. In a case where there is a possibility that the taxpayer may be charged with fraud, the taxpayer should be referred to an attorney.

SSTS No. 7: Form and Content of Advice to Taxpayers In providing tax advice to taxpayers, the member must use judgment that reflects professional competence and serves the taxpayer's needs. The member must assume that any advice given will be used to determine the manner of reporting items on the taxpayer's tax return; therefore, the member should ensure that the standards under SSTS No. 1 are satisfied. When providing advice that will be relied on by third parties, the member's responsibilities may differ. Neither a standard format nor guidelines have been issued or established that would cover all situations and circumstances involving written or oral advice from a member. When giving such advice to taxpayers, in addition to exercising professional judgment, the member should consider each of the following:

1. The importance of the transaction and amounts involved.

2. The specific or general nature of the taxpayer's inquiry.

3. The time available for development and submission of the advice.

4. The technical complexity involved.

5. The existence of authorities and precedents.

6. The tax sophistication of the taxpayer.

7. The need to seek other professional advice.

8. The type of transaction and whether it is subject to heightened reporting or disclosure requirements.

9. The potential penalty consequences of the tax return position for which the advice is rendered.

10. Whether any potential applicable penalties can be avoided through disclosure.

11. Whether the member intends for the taxpayer to rely upon the advice to avoid potential penalties.

EXHIBIT 1-4: Summary of AICPA Statements on Standards for Tax Services

SSTS	Summary of Contents
No. 1	Specifies the standards for professional services that involve tax positions
No. 2	Explains how a member should handle answering questions on a tax return
No. 3	Describes the procedural aspects of preparing a tax return
No. 4	Defines when a member can use an estimate in preparing a tax return
No. 5	Explains what a member should do about items on a current return when similar items were audited on a prior year's return or were the subject of a judicial hearing
No. 6	States what a member should do upon learning about an error in a prior year's tax return
No. 7	Establishes standards for the giving of tax advice to taxpayers

Written communication is recommended in important, unusual, or complicated transactions, while oral advice is acceptable in more typical situations. In the communication, the member should advise the taxpayer that the advice reflects his or her professional judgment based on the current situation and that subsequent developments may affect previous advice, such as stating that the position of authorities is subject to change.

When subsequent developments affect the advice that a member has previously communicated to a taxpayer, the member is under no obligation to initiate further communication of such developments to the taxpayer unless a specific agreement has been reached with the taxpayer, or the member is assisting in the application of a procedure or plan relative to such advice.

Exhibit 1-4 summarizes the main topic of each of the AICPA SSTS. The complete text of the SSTS can be found on the AICPA Web site at **www.aicpa.org/Research/Standards/Tax/Pages/default.aspx**.

Sarbanes-Oxley and Taxation

In 2002, Congress passed the Sarbanes-Oxley Act, which addressed the corporate management abuses that took place during the 1990s and early 2000s in publicly traded American corporations. These corporate governance breakdowns culminated in spectacular business failures such as with Enron, WorldCom, Global Crossing, Waste-Management, Sunbeam, and others, and led to the eventual failure of the Big Five CPA firm of Arthur Andersen.

The Sarbanes-Oxley Act made it "unlawful" for an auditor to provide any of the nonaudit services listed in the Act. In addition, the Act provided that a registered public accounting firm "may engage in any nonaudit service, including tax services, that is not described [in the list of nine specifically prohibited services] for an audit client only if the activity is approved in advance by the audit committee of the issuer" in accordance with the Act. The prohibited services are as follows:

1. Bookkeeping or other services related to the accounting records or financial statements of the audit client.

2. Financial information systems design and implementation.

3. Appraisal or valuation services, fairness opinions, or contribution-in-kind reports.

4. Actuarial services.

5. Internal audit outsourcing services.

6. Management functions or human resources.

7. Broker or dealer, investment adviser, or investment banking services.

8. Legal services and expert services unrelated to the audit.

9. Any other service that the Public Company Accounting Oversight Board determines, by regulation, is impermissible.

It should be noted that tax compliance work is not one of the prohibited services. However, tax work is subject to the pre-approval process. The audit committee needs to know about the proposed tax-related services in order to pre-approve them. Many corporations now take work to CPA firms other than the auditor, rather than seek approval of the audit committee. As a result, many companies divide their audit and tax work between different firms. This appears to be an unintended result of the Sarbanes-Oxley Act.

Investors, on the other hand, would probably prefer that the audit committee be aware of everything that is going on within a company and actually pre-approve the work instead of having the work go elsewhere. Currently, the audit committee may not even be aware if someone other than the auditor is being used for non-audit work. Such decision making remains hidden from audit committee review. Tax practitioners will have to wait to see how this contradiction plays out. Perhaps audit committees will grow more comfortable with their Sarbanes-Oxley responsibilities and this division of traditional audit and tax work may decline in future years.

In addition to being a response to corporate governance and accounting transparency failures, the Sarbanes-Oxley Act is a response to the general failure of business ethics. For example, the proliferation of abusive tax shelters and super-aggressive tax avoidance strategies (which are discussed shortly) are examples of other problems involving business ethics.

ABA Model Code of Professional Responsibility

The ABA Model Code of Professional Responsibility includes nine canons, which may be thought of as statements of principles. Canon 6, for instance, requires an attorney to represent a taxpayer competently. Each canon is followed by a series of ethical considerations (ECs), which in turn are supported by disciplinary rules (DRs). The ECs are aspirational in character, setting forth objectives toward which all attorneys are to strive. The DRs set forth minimum standards of conduct. Any failure to abide by the DRs may subject the attorney to disciplinary procedures and punishment.

In nearly all jurisdictions, the ABA Model Code was adopted by the appropriate policy agency, although sometimes modifications were made. In August 1983, the ABA adopted the Model Rules of Professional Conduct, which, in a majority of the states, have substantially replaced the Model Code as the guide for attorney professional conduct.

The ABA has a Standing Committee on Ethics and Professional Responsibility that answers questions concerning ethics and professional conduct. Requests for opinions from the committee should be directed to the American Bar Association Center for Professional Responsibility in Chicago.

Neither the ABA Model Code nor the Model Rules have the force of law. Each was designed to be adopted by the appropriate agencies that govern the practice of law in the states. In many jurisdictions, the state's supreme court is charged with policing the practice of law; in other states, the legislature bears this responsibility. Attorneys should consult their own jurisdiction's ethical guidelines to determine whether the provisions of the ABA Model Code or the Model Rules, or some modification of these doctrines, have been adopted.

The current status of the ABA Model Rules can be found on the ABA Web site at **www.abanet.org/cpr/mrpc/mrpc_toc.html**.

Nonregulatory Ethical Behavior Models

Since the turn of the twenty-first century, nonregulatory ethical models have become more relevant and applicable to professions such as accountancy and law. Tax practitioners need to be aware that there is substantially more to ethical behavior than just following the rules of ethics or conduct of professional organizations such as the AICPA or the ABA. The regulatory rules are generally straightforward and usually list a defined set of acts that are prohibited by members of the profession. For example, under SSTS No. 6, a CPA cannot disclose an error in a client's tax return to the IRS without the client's permission. On the other hand, nonregulatory ethics involve making choices that are not always clearly spelled out, such as disclosure of client tax information.

Ethical Dilemmas

An ethical dilemma occurs when someone is faced with a situation to which there are no clearly defined answers, such as by regulation or law. In other words, there are multiple "right" answers (or put another way, no obviously wrong answers).

EXAMPLE 1-3

Bill, a CPA, has been requested by his CPA firm employer to join "The Macho Men," a private club. Most of the movers and shakers (i.e., clients and potential clients) in town are members of this club. However, the club does not allow female members. If you were Bill, what would you do? How do you think Bill's female co-workers would feel about him joining a club that discriminates against women? There is no "right" answer to these questions because they are ethical dilemmas to which there are several right answers.

As illustrated in this example, making the choice in an ethical dilemma can be complicated. How, then, is a person supposed to deal with a situation such as this? The answer can be assessed through several generally recognized forms of ethical reasoning.

SPOTLIGHT ON TAXATION

Quotation

"Ethics is knowing the difference between what you have the right to do and what is the right thing to do."

—Supreme Court Justice Potter Stewart

Ethical Reasoning

There are several approaches to resolving an ethical dilemma. Len Marrella notes that three common lines of reasoning are used to solve an ethical dilemma.[3] These are called end-based reasoning, rule-based reasoning, and care-based reasoning. Each of these approaches attempts to provide a framework in which to resolve an ethical dilemma.

End-Based Ethical Reasoning   End-based ethical reasoning was popular in the 1800s. Its main tenet was that an action was right if it produced at least as much net good as any alternative action could have produced. Hence, an ethical decision was the one that did the most good for the largest number of people. In summary, competing ethical solutions are resolved in terms of the "end-result."

John Stuart Mill was a proponent of this philosophy. He encouraged individuals to examine the consequences of various alternatives and to rely heavily on facts when making ethical choices.[4] The steps used to apply end-based reasoning can be summarized as follows:

1. Identify the courses of action available.

2. Identify stakeholders who will be impacted by the various choices of action and what benefit or harm may come to them as the result of a given choice.

3. Choose the action with the greatest benefits and the least amount of harm.[5]

To a CPA this type of decision making is similar to cost–benefit analysis. However, applying cost–benefit analysis to an ethical decision is not as easy as applying it to a financial decision. The real problem is that end-based reasoning does not consider justice, fairness, integrity, and similar concepts in arriving at a choice. Ethicists consider this to be one of end-based reasoning's major failings.

Rule-Based Ethical Reasoning   Rule-based reasoning is based on what is referred to as "Kantian ethics," which were derived from the writing of the German philosopher Immanuel Kant. He held that individual actions should be such that we would accept similar behavior from everyone else. Kant believed rules are made to apply to everyone and there were no exceptions—period. According to Kant, lying and stealing were always unethical, and therefore there is no such thing as a "white lie" to protect someone's feelings or reputation. This thinking today is usually referred to as "Zero Tolerance" and many times leads to unjust results. For example, what if a six-year-old first grader is expelled from school for bringing a plastic picnic knife to school to eat his lunch, in violation of the no-weapons policy at his school. Is this fair or just?

Care-Based Ethical Reasoning   Care-based reasoning is found in the moral teachings of almost every culture and religion. In Western culture it is called the "Golden Rule," which states, "Do unto others as you would have them do unto you." From an ethical reasoning point of view, it advises one to make decisions that would result in the treatment you yourself would like to receive. Care-based reasoning can be described as doing what is "fair and just."

---

[3]*In Search of Ethics: Conversations with Men and Women of Character* (DC Press, 2001).

[4]Manuel Velasquez et al., "Thinking Ethically: A Framework for Moral Decision Making," *Issues in Ethics*, Vol. 7, No. 1, (Winter 1996).

[5]Ibid.

EXHIBIT 1-5: Sources of Ethical Behavior and Impacts

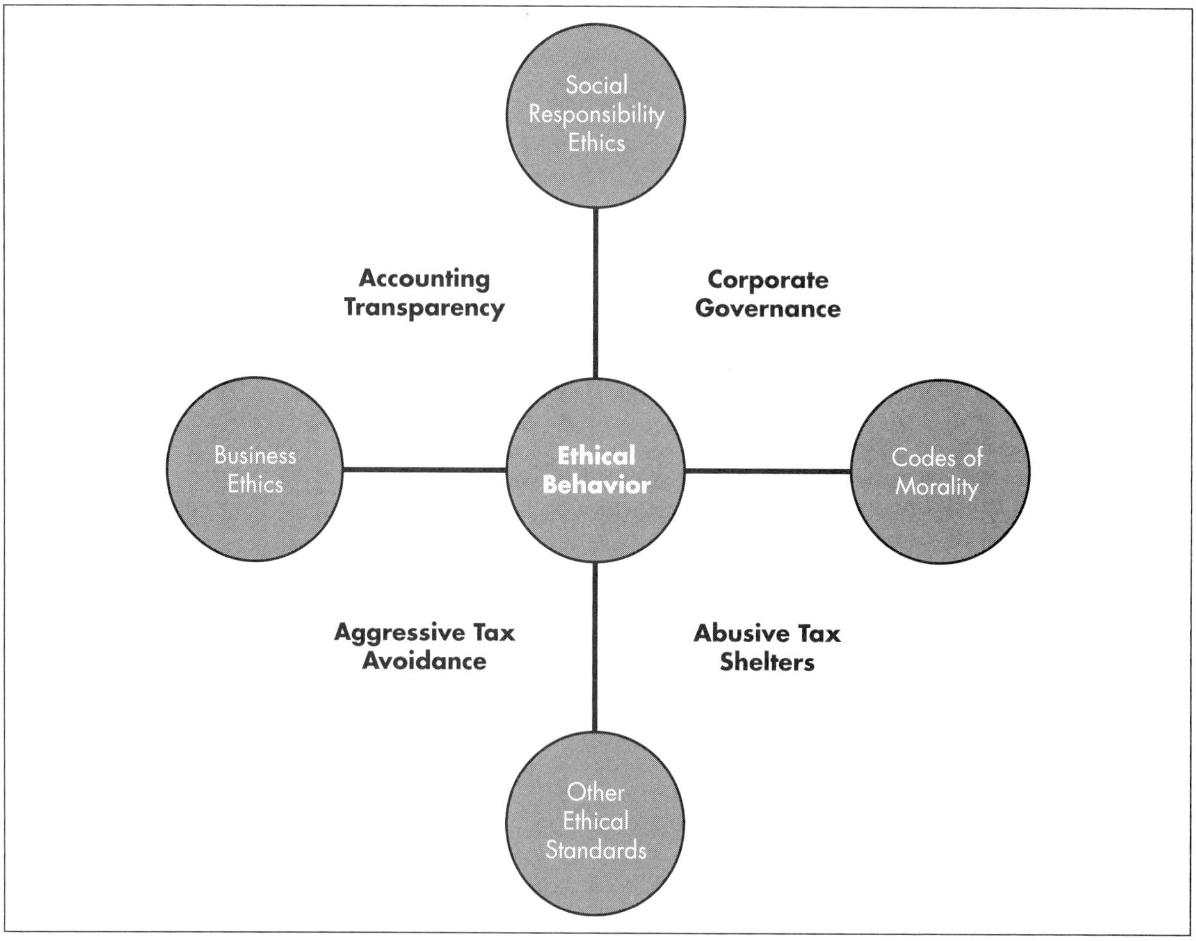

Ethical Professional Behavior

Professional ethical behavior is the result of the interaction of personal morality, social responsibility, business ethics, and other general ethical standards. Exhibit 1-5 illustrates these ethical standards and shows possible business and accounting areas that could be affected by ethical failures.

Morality

The subject of morality fills tens of thousands of books. Publications as diverse as the Bible and popular novels examine morality in one way or another. When something is judged to be morally right or wrong (or good or bad), the underlying standards on which such judgments are based are called moral standards.

According to some people's moral standards, cheating "just a little" in computing a tax liability is morally acceptable. Most people in the United States believe that everyone cheats a little on their taxes. Cheating significantly may be viewed differently, but where is the dividing line between morally acceptable tax cheating and morally wrong tax evasion? Under the self-assessed tax system in the United States, different moral standards provide different answers—from complete honesty to various degrees of dishonesty. The tax practitioner must be ready to work with clients holding various systems of morality and to accept the consequences of the moral choices made, including the possibility of losing a client, paying fines and penalties to the IRS, or even going to jail.

Social Responsibility

The tax practitioner must be aware of social responsibility in areas such as environmental protection, equal opportunity, and occupational safety. Since World War II, society has held the business world increasingly responsible for meeting certain non-economic standards. In 1970, Milton Friedman, the Nobel Prize-winning economist, said that the "social responsibility" of business is merely to increase profits. Nevertheless, the prevailing sentiment today is that business and the professions should return something to society to make it better, not just make a profit. For the tax practitioner, this could mean going beyond the minimum legal responsibility to provide equal opportunity in the hiring of employees by making special recruitment efforts, or it could mean volunteering time to help charitable organizations with their tax problems.

Business Ethics

In recent years, one of the major topics in the business world has been the question of business ethics. Many people believe that ethics has application only in one's personal life, not in the business or professional arena. Like Milton Friedman, they think that the only business of business is to make a profit. This view is popular because people who work in business or professions must concern themselves with producing goods and services to earn a profit, and it is easier to measure profit than it is to make value judgments. People are more comfortable discussing problems in terms of profits rather than in terms of the ethical impact of the entity and its actions. Few business and professional people are trained in ethical analysis, and, therefore they usually are not familiar with how to evaluate a problem in terms of ethics.

SPOTLIGHT ON TAXATION

Quotation

"The income tax has made more liars out of the American people than golf has".
—Will Rodgers

EXAMPLE 1-4

Bruce owns a successful small business. The business is operated as a corporation. During the year, Bruce makes numerous personal long-distance phone calls from the office, uses the company credit card to purchase gas for his family's personal automobiles, sends personal items using the company's FedEx account, and is reimbursed by the company for meals and entertainment expenditures that are primarily personal in nature. These items are deducted by the corporation on its tax return. Would you sign this company's Form 1120 as the tax return preparer? If you also audited this company, what would you do about these transactions?

That business and professional organizations have ethical responsibilities is readily apparent to anyone who reads the popular press. The recent Wall Street scandals involving Goldman Sachs and Lehman Brothers are prime examples of society holding business to a standard of ethical conduct. Most of the big CPA firms have settled lawsuits (both in and out of court) against them for millions of dollars for what was, in part, a business ethics failure.

Tax Planning Ethics

In addition to the previously discussed corporate governance issues addressed in the Sarbanes-Oxley Act, there are many examples of suspect ethics practices in the area of taxation. Following are some "classic" examples of the aggressive tax planning arrangements that have been promoted over the years by CPAs, lawyers, and others.[6]

EXAMPLE 1-5

Cerveza Corporation is primarily in the beverage supply business. The taxpayer classifies itself as a security dealer and then marks down (and claims a tax deduction for) its accounts receivable based on the contention that it is not marketable and some of the accounts will not be paid. This practice was prohibited by Congress in 1998.

EXAMPLE 1-6

Sneaky Inc., a corporation based in the United States, pays $600,000 to buy an expiring foreign copyright that has one royalty payment left. The last payment is for $800,000, less $240,000 of foreign tax credit (30 percent of $800,000). On this deal the buyer has lost $40,000 ($600,000 payment less $560,000 net final royalty), but has purchased a $240,000 foreign tax credit that can be used to offset $240,000 of tax on Sneaky's other foreign income.

EXAMPLE 1-7

Cheater Corporation borrowed $300,000 and used the proceeds to purchase a $2,000,000 single premium life insurance policy. The policy is a universal life insurance policy. Like many life insurance policies, this policy pays interest that is tax-free on the cash value of the policy. As a result of this transaction, the corporation receives an interest deduction for the loan and earns tax-free interest on the policy. This type of transaction was stopped by Congress in 1996.

SPOTLIGHT ON TAXATION

Ethics

The taxing authorities of several U.S. states post the names of delinquent taxpayers on their Web site. The stated purpose of the postings is to "shame" the taxpayers who have not paid their state taxes into paying them. Although this posting clearly is legal, is it ethical? For example, suppose a family has a child with leukemia and has horrendous medical bills and cannot afford to pay their taxes. Should they be held up to ridicule because they are doing the right thing and taking care of their child, even if it prevents them from paying their taxes?

---

[6]For an expanded discussion of tax planning abuse during the 1980s and 1990s, see "Tax Shelter Hustlers," *Forbes*, December 14, 1998, 198.

Other Ethical Standards

The study of non-regulatory ethics could be expanded to cover such other issues as public policy, religious beliefs, and cultural values, issues that are beyond the scope of this text. Most of such topics would be addressed in a university course on ethics or business ethics. A tax practitioner can expand his or her understanding of the application of ethics to accounting and business situations by referring to the books and articles on the following reading list:

- Mary Beth Armstrong, *Ethics and Professionalism for CPAs* (Cincinnati: South-Western Publishing Co., 1993).

- Leonard J. Brooks, *Business and Professional Ethics for Directors, Executives, and Accountants* (Mason: South Western Business & Professional Publishing, 2004).

- Rogene Buchholz, *Fundamental Concepts and Problems in Business Ethics* (Englewood Cliffs, NJ: Prentice Hall, 1989).

- Denis Collins and Thomas O'Rourke, *Ethical Dilemmas in Accounting* (Cincinnati: South-Western Publishing Co., 1994).

- Thomas Donaldson, *Corporations and Morality* (Englewood Cliffs, NJ: Prentice Hall, 1983).

- Len Marrella, *In Search of Ethics: Conversations with Men and Women of Character* (Sanford, FL: DC Press, 2001).

- Manuel Velasquez, *Business Ethics: Concepts and Cases*, Sixth Edition (Englewood Cliffs, NJ: Prentice Hall, 2006).

- Manuel Velasquez et al., "Thinking Ethically: A Framework for Moral Decision Making," *Issues in Ethics*, Vol. 7, No. 1 (Winter 1996).

The following are examples of non-regulatory ethics dilemmas that could arise in a business, accounting, or tax setting. As shown in these examples, the application of ethics to tax and business situations is not clear-cut. Many times, doing what is "right" may not be possible. The tax practitioner is faced with challenges on how to apply proper business ethics on a daily basis.

EXAMPLE 1-8

Hilary is a CPA who is a sole practitioner. This year, one of her clients, Gold Corporation, opened a new division in Europe. Gold is a longtime client of Hilary's, and she is anxious to keep it. However, Hilary has no experience in international tax and would not be able to give Gold the kind of tax advice needed for the new division. The ethical question is whether Hilary should inform the client of her lack of knowledge in this area and risk losing the client, or whether she should remain silent and "wing it" on the international tax issues. What should Hilary do in this situation?

EXAMPLE 1-9

Patrick is a CPA who is a partner in a successful local CPA practice. The state in which Patrick lives has a 40-hour annual continuing professional education (CPE) requirement. If the CPE requirement is not met, a CPA will have his or her license suspended and will not be able to practice. Patrick is approached by the Flight-by-Night CPE Company about signing up for some of its CPE courses.

The representative tells Patrick that the company will report that Patrick attended the courses so that he gets the CPE credit, even if he does not attend. Because Patrick is overloaded with work, he considers this a "low hassle" way to get his CPA license renewed. Would it be ethical for Patrick to obtain his CPE credit this way?

EXAMPLE 1-10

Devona is an auditor in the Boston office of a large international CPA firm. She is sent on an inventory observation for a new client of the Houston office of the firm. The Houston office gives her a six-hour budget for the job. When she arrives at the client's office, Devona discovers that the Houston office has substantially underestimated the size of inventory to be counted. The client has a $20,000,000 inventory comprising more than 6,000 different items. The client plans to use 20 hours to complete the count. Devona is up for promotion, and she does not want to risk a negative personnel review because she overran the budget on this job. Therefore, she considers spending the budgeted six hours on the observation and then signing off in the audit work papers that she completely observed the inventory. Devona thinks this would be acceptable since she perceives there is only a small risk of a material misstatement of the inventory. Would it be ethical for Devona to do this?

EXAMPLE 1-11

Last year, one of Andy's clients, Trout Corporation, had a significant tax problem. Andy needed 35 hours of research time to arrive at an answer to Trout's problem. This year, another of Andy's clients, Bass Corporation, had the same problem. Because of his experience with Trout, Andy could solve Bass's tax problem in three hours. The ethical question is whether Andy should bill Bass for three hours or 35 hours of professional consulting time. There are two ways to look at this situation. Andy only spent three hours on the job, so he should only bill for three hours of time. Yet, there is "value" in Andy already knowing the approach to take on the Bass matter, so perhaps he should bill for that knowledge and not just for the actual time spent working on the problem. What should Andy do in this situation?

EXAMPLE 1-12

Betty is negotiating a transaction on behalf of one of her clients, John Carp. During the process, Betty becomes aware that the other party to the transaction does not adequately understand the tax consequences of the proposed transaction, which are highly favorable to Carp. In fact, if the transaction were completed as proposed, the other side would suffer significant negative tax consequences. Ethically, should Betty inform the other party of the potential negative tax consequences of the proposed transaction?

SPOTLIGHT ON TAXATION

Quotation

"When morality comes up against profit, it is seldom that profit loses."

—Shirley Chisholm

Ethics Training and Education

State Boards of Accountancy are the organizations with the responsibility to license and regulate the practice of public accountancy in each state. Recently, the state boards as a group have increased the ethics training for initial licensing and license renewals in response to highly publicized ethical lapses. All states have some form of ethics training to become a CPA, and most states have some form of ethics training requirement to maintain a CPA license. These ethics requirements vary from state to state. If one has a question about a state's requirements, it is best to refer to the Internet for the most current information on a specific state. Links to state-specific Web sites can be found at the *National Association of State Boards of Accountancy* Web site at **www.nasbatools.com**.

Legal Research by Certified Public Accountants

Over the years, the tax community has addressed the issue of whether the practice of tax law by a CPA or other nonattorney constitutes the **unauthorized practice of law**. The problem stems from the tax law itself, passed in 1913. The provisions of early tax law called for an income tax, but the statute was not specific about the accounting methods to be used in implementing it. In fact, not until 1954 was a formal statutory effort made to address accounting issues in the computation of taxable income. For this reason, many attorneys avoided tax work, allowing CPAs to fill the void.

When a CPA resolves an issue in most non-routine tax situations, he or she is, to some extent, solving a legal problem. The issue is not whether the CPA is rendering legal service, but rather how much legal service is provided. When does the CPA cross the mythical boundary and begin an unauthorized practice of law? Neither these professions nor the courts have promulgated binding guidelines on this issue. Instead, the Federal agencies seem to have taken the lead in attempting to solve this problem.

Historical Developments

Lowell Bar Association v. Loeb, 315 Mass. 176, S2 N.E.2d 27 (1943), addressed the issue of the unauthorized practice of law by nonattorneys engaged in tax practice. The Lowell Massachusetts Bar Association sued Birdie Loeb, a commercial tax preparer, for her preparation of simple wage-earner tax returns. On appeal, the court held that the preparation of "simple" tax returns did not constitute the unauthorized practice of Massachusetts law because tax return preparation could not be identified as strictly within the legal discipline. Tax practice includes interaction among various disciplines, including law, accounting, economics, political science, and others.

Subsequent courts attempted to adopt the Lowell "wholly within the field of law" test in other jurisdictions, but they found that defining the boundaries of the legal profession was so difficult and the 1943 opinion was so general and vague that the Lowell precedent was of little value in other situations.

Probably the best-known case concerning a tax accountant's unauthorized practice of law is *Bercu*, 299 N.Y. 728, 87 N.E.2d 451 (1949). Bercu was an accountant who consulted with a client concerning whether sales taxes that were accrued, but not yet paid, could be deducted on a tax return. The taxpayer who requested this advice was not one of Bercu's regular clients. Bercu advised the client that the sales tax could be deducted when it was paid. Bercu presented a bill to the client and, when it was not paid, sued the client to collect the fees.

Ultimately, the State Court of New York held that it was not proper for Bercu to render services in such a situation. The court indicated that Bercu could have provided this type of service and answered the sales tax question had it been incidental to the tax return work he regularly performed for his clients.

This "incidental to accounting practice" test became the chief issue in several subsequent cases concerning the unauthorized practice of law. In a Minnesota case, *Gardner v. Conway*, 234 Minn. 468, 48 N.W.2d 788 (1951), a person who was neither an attorney nor a CPA attempted to answer difficult and substantial questions of law. The court held that the practitioner improperly gave advice to the client and rejected the "incidental to practice" test as an approach to providing guidelines for the definition of tax practice.

In a California case, *Agran v. Shapiro*, 127 Cal. App.2d Supp. 807, 273 P.2d 619 (1954), CPA Agran prepared returns, performed research, and represented his clients before the IRS. Agran's preparation of Shapiro's return involved extensive research—including more than 100 court cases, Code sections, and Regulations—concerning a question involving the proper treatment of a net operating loss. Upon completion of the work, the CPA presented his bill and, when he was not paid, sued Shapiro to collect. Agran was found by the court to have engaged in the unauthorized practice of law and, therefore, was unable to collect his fees. In its decision, the California Superior Court relied on *Gardner v. Conway* and rejected the "incidental to practice" test that Agran used in his defense. The court did not decide, however, whether the authorization to practice before the IRS preempted the right of the state to regulate tax practice.

In *Sperry v. Florida*, 373 U.S. 379, 83 S.Ct. 1322 (1963), the U.S. Supreme Court held that a Federal statute that admitted nonattorneys to practice before Federal agencies (in this case, the Patent Office) took precedence over state regulation. In late 1965, Congress enacted Public Law 89-332, amending prior law and allowing CPAs to practice before the IRS. Although this law added to the force of the Sperry decision as it applied to CPAs, Sperry still provides for the preemption of Federal regulations and statutes in matters of practice before other Federal agencies.

In 1981, the AICPA and the ABA held a conference for attorneys and CPAs to address some of these definitional questions relative to tax practice and the unauthorized practice of law. The stated purpose of this session was to "promote understanding between the professions in the interests of the client [taxpayers] and the general public." This National Conference of Lawyers and CPAs issued a statement in November 1981, reaffirming that clients [taxpayers] are best served when attorneys and CPAs work together in tax practice. The text of the statement identifies eight areas related to income taxation and three areas related to estate and gift planning in which such professional cooperation should be encouraged. The statement lacks any form of exclusionary language. Indeed, it asserts the following:[7]

> *Frequently, the legal and accounting phases (of tax practice) are so intertwined that they are difficult to distinguish. This is particularly true in the field of income taxation where questions of law and accounting are often inextricably intertwined.*

CPAs and Other Nonattorneys

Currently, CPAs and other nonattorneys who practice tax law before the IRS are in little danger of entering into the unauthorized practice of law provided they avoid providing general legal services. This can be accomplished if CPAs and other nonattorneys do not themselves engage in the following kinds of general law activities:

- Expressing a legal opinion on any non-tax matter.
- Drafting wills or trust instruments.

[7]For a complete discussion of this conference statement, see the *Journal of Accountancy* (August 1982).

- Drafting contracts.

- Drafting incorporation papers.

- Drafting partnership agreements.

Taxpayers can draft any of these documents themselves without the services of an attorney. If a CPA's client wishes to handle personal legal affairs in this manner, the CPA (exercising caution) can render professional advice without running afoul of the case law concerning the unauthorized practice of law.

As long as CPAs and other nonattorneys stay within the practice of tax, and do not cross over into the practice of general law, the control exercised by Circular 230 and the AICPA Code should ensure that virtually all tax compliance, planning, and research activities that are provided by adequately trained nonattorney CPAs constitute the "authorized practice of law."

SUMMARY

In addition to the tax return preparation statutes that are discussed in Chapter 13, CPAs, attorneys, EAs, and others who practice before the IRS are faced with various sets of overlapping rules of conduct. Circular 230 applies to anyone who practices before the IRS. Members of the legal and public accounting professions are subject to additional codes of ethics and conduct.

Similarly, cultural codes of morality and social responsibility form general boundaries relative to acceptable behavior by a taxpayer or tax professional. When engaged in tax practice, one must always be aware of the appropriate rules of conduct and conduct oneself in accordance with those rules.

QUIZ YOURSELF

Reinforce the tax research information covered in this chapter by completing the online quizzes located at the Federal Tax Research Web site at **www.cengagebrain.com.** At the CengageBrain.com

home page, search for the *Federal Tax Research*, 9e ISBN (1111221642) using the search box at the top of the page. This will take you to the product page where you can access the quizzes.

KEY WORDS

By the time you complete this chapter, you should be comfortable discussing each of the following terms. If you need additional review of any of these items, return to the appropriate material in the chapter or consult the glossary to this text.

American Bar Association (ABA), p. 7
American Institute of Certified Public Accountants (AICPA), p. 7
Circular 230, p. 7
closed transactions, p. 6
Cohan Rule, p. 23
contingent fees, p. 13

covered opinions, p. 15
due diligence, p. 13
Enrolled Agent (EA), p. 4
ethical standards, p. 7
independence, p. 17
open transactions, p. 6
practice before the IRS, p. 7
realistic possibility, p. 22
tax avoidance, p. 6

tax compliance, p. 5
tax evasion, p. 6
tax litigation, p. 6
tax planning, p. 5
tax research, p. 7
unauthorized practice of law, p. 35
unconscionable fee, p. 13

DISCUSSION QUESTIONS

Note: A copy of Circular 230 is needed to answer many of these discussion questions. Obtain a complete copy of Circular 230 from www.irs.gov.

1. In a modern, industrial society, the tax system is derived from several disciplines. Identify the disciplines that play this role in the United States. Explain how each of them affects the U.S. tax system.

2. The elements of tax practice fall into what major categories in addition to tax research?

3. What is tax compliance as practiced in the United States? Give several examples of activities that can be classified as tax compliance.

4. Several groups of individuals do most of the tax compliance work in the United States. Identify these groups and describe briefly the kind of work that each group does. In this regard, be sure to define the term Enrolled Agent.

5. What is tax planning? Explain the difference between tax evasion and tax avoidance and the role of each in professional tax planning.

6. Tax planning falls into two major categories, the "open" transaction and the "closed" transaction. Discuss each type of transaction and describe how each affects tax planning.

7. What is tax litigation? What type of tax practitioner typically handles tax litigation on a taxpayer's behalf?

8. In tax litigation, what is usually the role of a Certified Public Accountant?

9. Define tax research. Briefly describe the tax research process.

10. Who issues Circular 230? Which tax practitioners are regulated by it?

11. CPAs must follow the rules of Circular 230. In addition, CPAs in tax practice are subject to two other sets of ethical rules. Give the name and the issuer of both of these sets of rules.

12. Beginning in 2011, tax return preparers who prepare all, or substantially all, of a Federal tax return (for compensation) will be subject to new requirements. Discuss these requirements. Why do you think the IRS made these changes?

13. The term "practice before the IRS" includes the representation of clients in the United States Tax Court for cases being handled under the "small tax case procedure." True or false? Explain your answer. (IRS adapted)

14. The rules that govern practice before the IRS are found in Circular 230. Discuss what entails practice before the IRS and state which section of Circular 230 contains the definition.

15. There are two ways to become an EA. Briefly explain what they are and give the subpart and section references in Circular 230 where the details of becoming an EA are found.

16. The Enrolled Agent Special Enrollment Examination (SEE) is an exam that consists of three parts. What topics are covered in each part?

17. When is the Enrolled Agent Special Enrollment Examination (SEE) given, and how long is each part?

18. EAs are subject to Continuing Education (CE) requirements. Briefly describe the CE requirements and give the reference to where the details can be found in Circular 230.

19. Leigh, who is not an EA, attorney, or CPA, is employed by Rose, a CPA. One of Rose's clients has been notified that his 2007 income tax return has been selected for audit by the IRS. Rose had prepared the

return and signed it as preparer. Rose has been called out of town on a family emergency and would like for Leigh to represent the client. Leigh cannot represent the client even if she has Rose's written authority to do so and has the client's power of attorney. True or false? Explain your answer. (IRS adapted)

20. Regular full-time employees are allowed to represent certain organizations before the IRS without being an attorney, CPA, or EA. Name the organizations that can be represented by full-time employees, and cite where you found that authority in Circular 230.

21. Jane's mother is in a nursing home and cannot travel. There is a problem with her mother's tax return from the previous year, and the IRS needs to discuss the matter with her at the local IRS office. Is it possible for Jane to handle this matter without having to hire professional tax representation? Reference your answer to the appropriate part of Circular 230.

22. A practitioner could be suspended from practice before the IRS if the practitioner employs, accepts assistance from, or shares fees with any person who is under disbarment or suspension from practice before the IRS. True or false? Explain your answer. (IRS adapted)

23. A tax practitioner may not advise a client under Circular 230 to take a position on a document, affidavit, or other paper submitted to the IRS unless the position meets what standard under Circular 230 §10.34?

24. Under Circular 230, may an attorney, CPA, or EA advertise on television? On the Internet? If so, what standards are applied to the advertisements?

25. Can a tax practitioner who is a CPA form a CPA partnership with an IRS agent who is also a CPA? What limits (if any) would be placed on such a partnership?

26. If a tax practitioner finds an error in a prior year's tax return, what action must he or she take (if any) under Circular 230? What subpart and section addresses this situation?

27. Is a tax practitioner required to adhere to the Best Practices standard under Circular 230 §10.33? Explain.

28. What are the four Best Practices under Circular 230 §10.33?

29. Explain the difference between a "reliance opinion" and a "marketed opinion" under Circular 230 §10.35. How does Circular 230 §10.36 apply the Covered Opinion requirement of §10.35?

30. A practitioner cannot give written advice under Circular 230 §10.37 in what situations?

31. Practicing CPAs generally are subject to the AICPA Code of Professional Conduct. What is its stated purpose?

32. The rules under the AICPA Code of Professional Conduct are enforceable ethical standards. Broad in nature, they generally apply to all of the services that are performed by a CPA who is an AICPA member. Identify the two situations in which the application of the rules may be limited.

33. In what situation may a CPA under the AICPA Code of Professional Conduct accept a commission?

34. Under Rule 101 (Independence), a CPA (or CPA firm) is not independent if one or more financial relationships exist with a client during the period of professional engagement or at the issuing of the opinion. Discuss situations in which the CPA's independence may be impaired.

35. Under Rule 102 (Integrity and Objectivity), a CPA who is engaged in tax practice may resolve a doubtful area in favor of his or her client. Explain.

36. A CPA must meet certain qualitative standards under Rule 201 (General Standards). Discuss the four general standards of this rule.

37. In each of the following independent situations, state which AICPA Code of Professional Conduct (if any) is violated by a CPA in public practice.

    a. The CPA opens a tax practice and names the new firm "Jill's Super Tax."

    b. In return for recommending a certain investment to an audit client, a CPA receives a 5 percent commission from the broker who sells the investments.

    c. A taxpayer is being assessed by the IRS for an additional $100,000 of tax. The CPA offers to represent the taxpayer for a fee that is equal to 25 percent of any amount by which he can get the IRS to reduce its assessment.

    d. A CPA places an advertisement in the local newspaper that states that she is the "Best CPA in the Western World." The advertisement further states that, because of her great skill, the CPA has considerable influence with the IRS and the United States Tax Court.

    e. A CPA partnership has eight partners, six of whom are members of the AICPA. On its letterhead, the firm designates itself as "Members of the AICPA."

    f. A CPA who is not in public practice is convicted of helping to run a large illegal drug operation.

38. Under Rule 301 of the AICPA Code of Professional Conduct, a CPA must not disclose confidential client data without the specific consent of the client. Under what conditions might a disclosure of confidential information without the client's consent be appropriate?

39. What are the SSTS? Who issues them? Discuss their principal objectives.

40. When must a member tax practitioner follow SSTS when preparing or signing a return?

41. What threshold does SSTS No. 1 provide for a tax practitioner regarding tax return positions? Could disclosure of the position influence that threshold?

42. According to SSTS No. 2, a tax return should be signed by a member only after reasonable effort has been made to answer all of the questions on the return that apply to the taxpayer. What are some of the reasonable grounds under which a member may sign a return as the preparer even though some of the pertinent questions remain unanswered?

43. What guidelines are provided by SSTS No. 3 as to the reliance by a member on information supplied by the taxpayer for use in preparing the taxpayer's return?

44. A member may use estimates in completing a tax return according to SSTS No. 4. When might the use of estimates be considered appropriate?

45. Last year a taxpayer was audited by the IRS and an item of deduction on the tax return was disallowed. On this year's tax return, the taxpayer would like to deduct a similar item. Discuss the circumstances under which a member may allow the taxpayer to take the deduction on the current year's return and still comply with SSTS No. 5. Under what conditions must special disclosure be made by the member?

46. When a member learns of an error in a previously filed tax return or learns of an error during an audit, how is he or she to respond and still be in compliance with SSTS No. 6?

47. What situations are addressed by No. 7?

48. The Sarbanes-Oxley Act prohibits CPA firms from providing certain services to publicly traded corporate audit clients. Is doing tax compliance work for an audit client one of the prohibited transactions? If such tax work is allowed, who must approve it?

49. Differentiate between the ABA Model Code of Professional Responsibility and that organization's Model Rules of Professional Conduct.

50. Who sets ethical rules for attorneys in the various states?

51. What is an Ethical Dilemma?

52. The text discusses three types of ethical reasoning. Identify them and give a short description of each.

53. Ethical professional behavior is the interaction of several standards. Identify these standards and briefly describe each.

54. How does the term "the unauthorized practice of law" apply to CPAs?

55. List several services or products that a CPA or EA purposely should not make a part of a tax practice in order to minimize exposure to a charge of the unauthorized practice of law.

EXERCISES

Note: A copy of Circular 230 is needed to answer many of these Exercises. Obtain a complete copy of Circular 230 from www.irs.gov.

56. Obtain a complete copy of Circular 230 from www.irs.gov. Summarize what is discussed in each of the following sections of Circular 230:
    a. Subpart A, §10.4(b)
    b. Subpart B, §10.21
    c. Subpart B, §10.26
    d. Subpart B, §10.29

57. Obtain a complete copy of Circular 230 from www.irs.gov. Summarize what is discussed in each of the following sections of Circular 230:
    a. Subpart C, §10.51(b)
    b. Subpart A, §10.6(e)
    c. Subpart A, §10.2(e)
    d. Subpart B, §10.27

58. Obtain a complete copy of Circular 230 from www.irs.gov. Summarize what is discussed in each of the following sections of Circular 230:
    a. Subpart A, §10.2(e)
    b. Subpart A, §10.7(c)(viii)
    c. Subpart B, §10.24
    d. Subpart B, §10.34

59. Obtain a complete copy of Circular 230 from www.irs.gov. Summarize what is discussed in each of the following sections of Circular 230:
    a. Subpart B, §10.33
    b. Subpart B, §10.35
    c. Subpart B, §10.36
    d. Subpart B, §10.37

60. Obtain a complete copy of Circular 230 from www.irs.gov. Which subpart and section of Circular 230 discusses each the following topics:
    a. Solicitation
    b. Negotiation of a taxpayer's refund checks
    c. Depositions
    d. Authority to disbar or suspend from practice before the IRS

61. Obtain a complete copy of Circular 230 from www.irs.gov. Which subpart and section of Circular 230 discusses each the following topics:

    a. Conflicting interests

    b. Tax shelter opinions

    c. Disreputable conduct

    d. Assistance from disbarred or suspended persons

62. Obtain a complete copy of Circular 230 from www.irs.gov. Which subpart and section of Circular 230 discusses each of the following topics:

    a. Practice of law

    b. Information to be furnished

    c. Fees

    d. Who may practice before the IRS?

63. Obtain a complete copy of Circular 230 from www.irs.gov. Which subpart and section of Circular 230 discusses each of the following topics:

    a. Best Practices

    b. Covered Opinions

    c. Tax Return Positions

    d. Due Diligence

64. Obtain a complete copy of the AICPA Code of Professional Conduct from www.aicpa.org. Summarize what is discussed in each of the following rules of the AICPA Code of Professional Conduct. Give a simple example of a transaction or an action relevant to each rule.

    a. Article VI, ¶ para 1

    b. Rule 201, ¶ .02 201-1

    c. Rule 502, ¶ .03 502-2

    d. Rule 504, ¶ .01

65. Summarize what is discussed in each of the following SSTS:

    a. SSTS No. 1

    b. SSTS No. 4

    c. SSTS No. 6

66. What is the precedent-setting value of each of the following cases:

    a. *Lowell Bar Association v. Loeb*

    b. *Bercu*

    c. *Sperry v. Florida*

67. Obtain a complete copy of Circular 230 from www.irs.gov. Ms. E is an EA who prepared the tax returns for Mr. A and Mr. B (buyer and seller, respectively). Ms. E may not, under any circumstances, represent A and B before the IRS with regard to this buy and sell transaction. True or false? Explain your answer. (IRS adapted)

68. Obtain a complete copy of Circular 230 from www.irs.gov. A full-time employee of a sole proprietorship may represent his or her employer in an examination by the IRS without being an EA, attorney, or CPA. True or false? Explain your answer. (IRS adapted)

69. Obtain a complete copy of Circular 230 from www.irs.gov. An unenrolled tax preparer who has not prepared the tax return of John Gomez may represent John before an IRS revenue agent in the conduct of an examination, provided that the unenrolled tax preparer has obtained written authorization from John. True or false? Explain your answer. (IRS adapted)

70. Obtain a complete copy of Circular 230 from www.irs.gov. EAs, attorneys, and CPAs shall exercise due diligence in preparing or assisting in the preparation of documents and other papers relating to IRS matters. True or false? Explain your answer. (IRS adapted)

71. Obtain a complete copy of Circular 230 from www.irs.gov. Which of the following statements may not be used when an EA advertises? Explain your answer. (IRS adapted)

    a. Name, address, and office hours
    b. Names of associates of the firm
    c. Claims of quality of service that cannot be verified
    d. Membership in professional organizations

72. Obtain a complete copy of Circular 230 from www.irs.gov. The IRS Director of Practice may take into consideration a petition for reinstatement from any person disbarred from practice before the IRS after a period of how many years? Explain your answer. (IRS adapted)

    a. Never
    b. Two years
    c. Three years
    d. Five years

73. Inclusion of which of the following statements in a CPA's advertisement is unacceptable under the AICPA Code of Professional Conduct? Explain your answer.

    a. Julie Adams, CPA, Fluency in Chinese
    b. Julie Adams, CPA, MBA, Big State University, 2010
    c. Julie Adams, CPA, Free Initial Consultation
    d. Julie Adams, CPA, I Always Win IRS Audits

74. Which of the following situations would most likely result in a violation of the practitioner's ethical standards? Explain your answer.

    a. A CPA is controller of a bank and grants permission to the bank to use his "CPA" title in the listing of the bank officers in the bank's publications.
    b. A CPA who is also a member of the bar represents on her letterhead that she is both an attorney and a CPA.
    c. A CPA, the sole shareholder in a professional accountancy corporation, uses the term "and company" in his firm's title.
    d. A CPA who writes a newsletter on financial management topics grants permission to the publisher to solicit subscriptions.

75. Which of the following situations would provide an acceptable case for using a taxpayer's estimated figure in the preparation of a Federal income tax return? Explain your answer.

    a. The taxpayer has the necessary data available, but is busy with a pressing public offering and has not had the time to look through her records for the information.
    b. The data are not available at the time of filing the return, and the estimated amounts appear reasonable to the CPA.

 c. The taxpayer has the data available at the time of filing the return but feels that the data do not fairly represent the results of her business operation and therefore desires to use an "estimate."

 d. The taxpayer, relying on the income tax regulations that allow the use of reasonable estimates under certain circumstances, desires to use an estimate to determine the amount of his deduction for entertainment expenses.

76. According to the AICPA Code of Professional Conduct, CPAs in tax practice who are representing a taxpayer in a formal controversy with the government are permitted to receive contingent fees because:

 a. This practice establishes fees that are commensurate with the value of the services rendered.

 b. Attorneys who are in tax practice customarily set contingent fees.

 c. Determinations by tax authorities are a matter of judicial proceedings that do not involve third parties.

 d. The consequences are based on the findings of judicial proceedings or the findings of a government agency.
  Explain your answer.

77. The AICPA Code of Professional Conduct states that a CPA shall not disclose any confidential information in the course of a professional engagement, except with the consent of the client. This rule should be understood to preclude a CPA from responding to an inquiry that is received from:

 a. An investigative body of a state CPA society.

 b. The Trial Board of the AICPA.

 c. A CPA-shareholder of the taxpayer corporation.

 d. An AICPA voluntary quality review body.
  Explain your answer.

78. A taxpayer's records are destroyed by fire. A CPA prepares the tax return based on estimates and other indirect information she has obtained. Under the SSTS, she should:

 a. Disclose the use of estimates to the IRS.

 b. Not disclose the use of estimates to the IRS.

 c. Charge the taxpayer a double fee.

 d. Not prepare a return based on estimates.

 e. Have an attorney prepare the return.
  Explain your answer.

79. Obtain a complete copy of Circular 230 from www.irs.gov. With regard to the categories of individuals who may practice before the IRS under Circular 230, which of the following statements is correct? Explain your answer. (IRS adapted)

 a. Only EAs, attorneys, or CPAs may represent trusts and estates before any officer or employee of the IRS.

 b. An individual who is not an EA, attorney, or CPA and who signs a return as having prepared it for the taxpayer may, with proper authorization from the taxpayer, appear as the taxpayer's representative, with or without the taxpayer, at an IRS Appeals Office conference with respect to the tax liability of the taxpayer for the taxable year or period covered by the return.

 c. Under the limited practice provision in Circular 230, only general partners may represent a partnership.

 d. Under the limited practice provision in Circular 230, an individual who is under suspension or disbarment from practice before the IRS may not engage in limited practice before the IRS.

80. Obtain a complete copy of Circular 230 from www.irs.gov. If an EA, attorney, or CPA knows that a client has not complied with the revenue laws of the United States with respect to a matter administered by the IRS, then the EA, attorney, or CPA is required under Circular 230 to:

 a. Do nothing until advised by the client to take corrective action.

 b. Advise the client of the noncompliance.

    c. Immediately notify the IRS.

    d. Advise the client and notify the IRS.
       Explain your answer. (IRS adapted)

81. Obtain a complete copy of Circular 230 from www.irs.gov. Answer each of the following questions:

    a. What is found in Subpart A, §10.7(a) of Circular 230?

    b. In Circular 230, where are the rules on tax shelter opinions found?

    c. Describe the requirements of Rule 301 of the AICPA Code of Conduct.

    d. Which SSTS discusses the use of estimates in preparing a tax return?

    e. Under SSTS No. 1, a member must have a good-faith belief that a recommended position has a _____ possibility of being sustained if challenged.

82. Obtain a complete copy of Circular 230 from www.irs.gov. Answer each of the following questions:

    a. What is found in Subpart C, §10.51 of Circular 230?

    b. In Circular 230, where are the rules on knowledge of client omissions found?

    c. Describe the requirements of Rule 503 of the AICPA Code of Conduct.

    d. Which SSTS discusses the requirements for verifying a tax client's information?

    e. Under SSTS _____, a member must use judgment that reflects and serves the taxpayer's needs.

83. The exam to become an EA has three parts. Go to the IRS Web site at www.irs.gov and determine what is tested on each part of the exam. Describe the content of each part.

84. Go to the NAEA Web site at www.naea.org. Who is the current president of the NAEA and in what city is the headquarters located?

85. Go the AICPA Web site at www.aicpa.org. Find SSTS No. 2 and print out the complete statement.

86. Go to the IRS web site at www.irs.gov. What is the form number of the Application for Enrollment to Practice before the IRS? Print out a copy of the form to hand in.

87. Go to the IRS web site at www.irs.gov. Do a publication search and find the most recent Circular 230. Print out the title page of the Circular 230 you found to hand in.

88. Many states have an ethics education requirement to become a CPA. Determine each of the following state's ethical education requirements to become a CPA:

    a. California

    b. Texas

    c. Ohio

    d. Your home state

RESEARCH CASES

Note: A copy of Circular 230 is needed to answer many of these Research Cases. Obtain a complete copy of Circular 230 from www.irs.gov.

89. Professor Andy Accrual works for a big state university. The state has negotiated a set of special airfares with various airlines for state employees to use when traveling on state business. These fares are lower, and they do not have restrictions on changing, cancellation, and so forth. Andy is aware that the airlines never check to see if he is on state business when he books such a fare. He has decided that he would like to go to Hawaii on short notice for a well-earned mini-vacation. When he checks the Internet for airfares, he

discovers that the cheapest fare he can find is $700 per person. However, the fare for state employees traveling on business to Hawaii is only $400. Although he is traveling for personal reasons, in your opinion is it ethical to use the special state employee airfare for his vacation? Would this qualify as an ethical dilemma?

90. Donna Deduction is a staff accountant for Dewey, Cheatham, and Howe, LLP. She and other staff raid the office supply cabinet for office supplies to take home to use. In addition to the standard paper, pens, paper clips, and so forth, the staff takes home inkjet cartridges and other high-cost supplies. During the year, Donna takes home supplies worth over $500. In your opinion, is this ethical behavior? If Donna does a significant amount of work for the firm at home, would your opinion change?

91. You are a CPA in practice who has just obtained a new client. Another CPA completed the tax returns for the prior three years. The client has operated his business as an S corporation during the three-year period. After starting work on this year's tax return, you notice that the S corporation has an October 31 fiscal year-end. After examining the file, you discover that three years ago, when the S corporation adopted the fiscal tax year, a §444 election was not made. In addition, the S corporation has not maintained the proper required "minimum deposit account" with the IRS.

    The client wants your advice on what to do now. You determine that there are three options: (1) you can do nothing and hope the IRS does not find out, (2) you can notify the IRS of the mistake and pay any interest and penalties, or (3) you can elect a calendar year and hope the IRS does not notice the current invalid fiscal year. What potential nonregulatory ethical issues do you see in this situation that could influence your decision on any recommendation?

92. You are a CPA in practice and have a long-term client who is involved in a nasty divorce proceeding with her husband. The client has assets she deposited in a bank account in the Grand Cayman Islands. There is U.S. taxable interest on the deposits. Because she does not want her husband to know about the deposits, she asks you to report the interest on her tax return in such a way that it will not "tip off" her husband to the existence of the account. You can handle this request by reporting the interest through Schedule C (instead of Schedule B) on her tax return and thus avoid making the source of the income known. What potential nonregulatory ethics issues do you see in this situation?

93. Ahi Corporation is one of your clients in Hawaii. The company had a good year last year and owes the IRS $100,000,000, due on March 15. There are no penalties or interest due to the IRS. One of Ahi's employees approaches you with the following plan to benefit from the so-called "float" on the large payment due to the government. First, Ahi Corp. will courier its tax return and payment to the U.S. Virgin Islands. There, the tax return will be mailed to the IRS Service Center in Fresno by certified mail on the return's due date, March 15. By doing this, the employee thinks it will take at least six days for the tax return to reach the IRS and for them to cash the $100,000,000 check. Ahi can earn 7 percent after tax on its money, so the interest earned during these six days because of the float is $19,178 per day [($100,000,000 × .07/365 days]. Thus, the total interest earned on the float for six days would be $115,068 ($19,178 × 6 days).

    a. Would you recommend Ahi complete this transaction?

    b. What potential ethics issues do you see in this situation?

94. John Haddock owns 75 percent of Haddock Corporation. The other 25 percent of the stock is held by John's wife, Marsha. You are a tax manager assigned to prepare the corporate tax return for Haddock. While working on the return, you note that Haddock Corp. pays rent to John for a building he owns with his son, John, Jr. The rent being paid is at least three times the normal rate for rentals of similar property in that area of town. You report this observation to the partner on the engagement. She tells you that it is all right to deduct the payments because Haddock Corp. has been doing it for several years, and the IRS never has objected. Under your firm's policy, managers sign the tax return for clients.

    a. Would you sign this tax return?

    b. What potential ethics issues do you see in this situation?

95. You are negotiating a transaction for your client, Shark Corporation. Parties on the other side of the deal ask you for information about the structural stability of a building, which is a significant part of the transaction. Coleman, Shark's tax director, tells you to say that everything is all right when, in reality, the building has substantial hidden damage. Coleman tells you to say this because it would be more favorable to Shark's position in the transaction.

    a. How would you respond to Coleman's request?

    b. What if you have already told the other side that the building is fine when you learn about the problems?

    c. What other potential ethics issues do you see in this situation?

96. Big CPA Firm has many partners in one of its local offices. Two of these partners are Tom, a tax partner, and Alice, an audit partner. Because of the size of the office, Tom and Alice do not know each other very well.

    Tom has a tax client, Anchovy Corporation that is in severe financial trouble and may have to file for bankruptcy. Anchovy is a customer of Sardine Corporation, one of Alice's audit clients. Accounts receivable on Sardine's books from Anchovy are significant. If Anchovy goes bankrupt, it could cause serious problems for Sardine. Alice is unaware of the bad financial condition of Anchovy.

    a. Can Tom disclose to Alice the problems at Anchovy?

    b. What if Anchovy goes under and takes Sardine with it?

    c. What potential ethics issues do you see in this situation?

97. You are the tax manager in a CPA office. One of your clients, Snapper Corporation, is also an audit client of the firm. The CFO of Snapper invites you and the audit manager for a one-week deep-sea fishing trip to Mexico, all expenses to be paid by Snapper. The audit manager says that you both should go and just not tell your supervisor at the CPA firm any details (like who paid the expenses) about the trip.

    a. Would you go on the trip?

    b. Would you tell your supervisors at the CPA firm if the audit manager went on the trip without you?

    c. What other potential ethics issues do you see in this situation?

98. Clara comes to an attorney's office in need of assistance with her husband's estate. Her husband, Phil, a factory worker, had been a saver all his life and owned approximately $1,500,000 in stocks and bonds. Clara is relatively unsophisticated in financial matters, so the attorney agrees to handle the estate for 17 percent of the value of the estate. The normal charge for such work is 3 to 5 percent of the estate. The widow agrees to the 17 percent arrangement. The attorney then hires CPA Charles for $10,000 to compute Phil's estate tax on Form 706 and to prepare other appropriate documents.

    a. Under Circular 230, does Charles have any responsibility to inform the widow that she is being significantly overcharged by the attorney?

    b. What potential ethics issues do you see in this situation?

99. Darlene works for Big CPA Firm. When she was being interviewed, Darlene was told by a partner in the firm that she was not to underreport her time spent on various engagements. However, after working for a few months, she discovers that everyone in her office "eats time." Because she is not eating time like everyone else, Darlene is always over budget. She is beginning to get a reputation as a "budget buster." As a result, none of the senior tax staff wants her on their engagements. She is getting the worst clients and bad reviews from the people for whom she works. It appears that unless she starts eating time, Darlene's future with the firm is limited.

    a. What would you recommend Darlene do?

    b. What potential ethics issues do you see in this situation?

100. Freya is an accountant working on the tax return of a high-tech client. After reviewing the work papers, she discovers that there is a pattern of double billing the U.S. Navy for various projects done by the tax client. She brings this to the attention of her manager on the job, and he tells her that it is not the CPA firm's business what the client does since this is not an audit engagement.

    a. What would you recommend Freya do at this point?

    b. What potential ethics issues do you see in this situation?

101. Jenny is an accountant for an international energy corporation. She oversees the accounting for certain associated offshore entities. The amount of funds involved in the entities is substantial. At the end of the year, she notices that the accounting information from the offshore entities is not included in the consolidated financial statements of the corporation, but is reported on the consolidated tax return. She inquires about this and she is told that the corporation does not report the financial information from the offshore entities since it would lower the earnings of the main corporation. Jenny is sure that this is not the proper accounting and tax treatment for the entities.

    a. What would you recommend Jenny do at this point?

    b. What potential ethics issues do you see in this situation?

102. Eric is a tax manager for a national CPA firm that audits Penny-Pinching Bank (PPB). Eric and his staff prepare and review the tax return for PPB. One day, at an alumni football tailgate party, he meets another alumnus who Eric discovers is on the Audit Committee of PPB. The Audit Committee member/alumni was unaware that Eric's CPA firm is doing PPC's tax return.

    a. What would you recommend Eric do at this point?

    b. What potential ethical and practice issues do you see in this situation?

103. Dodger Corporation has been in the manufacturing business in the United States for over 100 years. A tax consultant has proposed that Dodger use a "corporate inversion" to nominally move its headquarters to an island in the Atlantic Ocean. The operating headquarters will remain in the United States, along with all of its employees, its plant and equipment, and most of its customers. By undertaking this corporate inversion and technically moving its headquarters offshore, Dodger can defer or avoid paying U.S. corporate income tax. For all practical purposes, however, it remains a U.S.-based company.

    a. What would you recommend Dodger do about the proposed corporate inversion?

    b. What potential ethics issues do you see in this situation?

104. For the last 10 years, Ricky, 40, and Lucy, 35, were married and you prepared their joint tax returns for those years. Last year they divorced, and both remained as your tax client. Under the dissolution decree, Ricky has to pay Lucy $4,000 per month alimony, which he does for the current year. You as an Enrolled Agent have completed Ricky's tax return for the current year and you deducted the required alimony payments to Lucy on his Form 1040. Lucy comes to you to prepare her tax return and refuses to report her alimony received as income. She states, "I am not going to pay tax on the $48,000 from Ricky." She views the payments as gift for putting up with him for all those years of marriage." Lucy will not budge on reporting this alimony as income.

    a. Under Circular 230 could you sign the Paid Preparer's declaration on this return?

    b. Give a specific Circular 230 section as to why or why not?

Tax Research Methodology

TAX RESEARCH IS THE process undertaken to answer taxation questions relevant to the researcher's needs. The tax research process is a multistep process that includes an algorithm discussed in this chapter. The tax researcher should become efficient at tax research since these professional services can be very expensive for the client, or the time spent on research can take away valuable time that could be used for other activities of the tax practitioner. Unnecessary time spent doing tax research could be used by the tax practitioner to produce additional tax revenue or to give him or her additional personal time for other activities.

SPOTLIGHT ON TAXATION

The Complexity of Taxation

The complexity of the tax system (and thus tax research) can be shown in a quote by Pam Olson, the former Treasury Assistant Secretary for Tax Policy. When speaking to a group of tax specialists, she quoted an e-mail sent to her by a tax attorney, who said:

"It is difficult to predict the future of an economy in which it takes more brains to figure out the tax on our income than it does to earn it."

The tax research process is similar to that of traditional legal research. The researcher must find authority, evaluate the usefulness of that authority, and apply the results of the research to a specific situation. One can identify two essential tax research skills. The first is the ability to use certain mechanical techniques to identify and locate the tax authorities that relate to solving a problem. The second entails a combination of reasoning and creativity and is more difficult to learn. A tax researcher must begin with native intelligence and imagination and add training and experience properly to apply the information found.

Creativity is necessary to explore the relevant relationships among the circumstances and problems at hand to find a satisfying (and defensible) solution. In many cases, no legal authority will exist that is directly on point for the problem. If such a situation exists, the researcher must combine seemingly unrelated facts, ideas (including those that he or she has derived from previous research work), and legal authority to arrive at a truly novel conclusion. This creative ability of the researcher often spells the difference between success and failure in the research process.

Outline of the Tax Research Process

As the tax problems of the client become more significant, the related tax research can become time consuming and thus expensive to the client. A moderate tax research problem often takes up to eight or 10 hours of research time, and the bill for these services may approach or even exceed $5,000. Because of the costs that are involved, the tax researcher must work as efficiently as possible to obtain the solution to the client's problem. The researcher needs a framework for the research process so that he or she does not waste time and effort in arriving at a solution to the problem.

The tax research process can be broken down into six major steps (Exhibit 2-1). Tax researchers, especially those without a substantial amount of experience at the task, must approach the resolution of a tax problem in a structured manner so that the analysis of the problem will be thorough and the solution complete.

EXHIBIT 2-1: Steps in the Tax Research Process

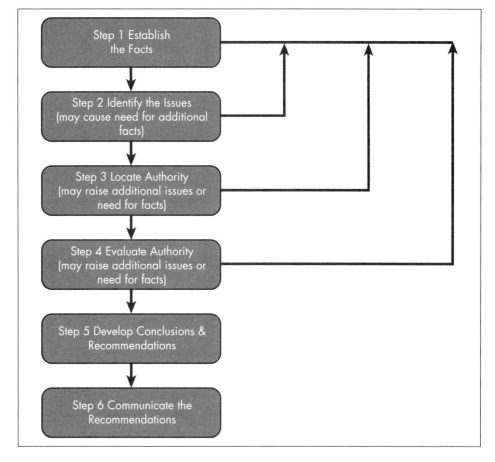

Step 1: Establish the Facts

All tax research begins with an evaluation of the client's factual situation. To find the solution to a problem, the researcher must understand fully all of the facts that could affect the related tax outcome. Many beginning tax researchers make the mistake of attempting to research a problem before they completely understand all of the relevant facts and circumstances.

Moreover, a tax researcher may approach the tax research process so rigidly that he or she ignores new factual questions that arise during the other steps of the research task. The tax researcher may engage in several rounds of fact gathering, including those necessitated by additional tax questions that arise as he or she is searching for or evaluating the pertinent tax authority. These research "feedback loops" are not endless, although they might seem to be. The best tax researcher is one who can balance the need for efficiency against the need for thoroughness.

Significant tax facts that often influence the client's situation include the following:

- The client's tax entity, for example, individual, corporation, trust.

- The client's family status and stability.

- The client's past, present, and projected marginal tax rates.

- The client's place of legal domicile and citizenship.

- The client's motivation for the transaction.

- The relationships among the client and other parties who are involved in the transaction.

- Whether special tax rules apply to the taxpayer due to the type of business in which the taxpayer is engaged (i.e., he or she is a farmer, fisherman, or long-term contractor).

- Whether the transaction is proposed or completed.

Fact gathering can present many practical problems for the researcher. Often, the client will (wittingly or not) omit information that is vital to a solution. He or she may not believe that the information is important or may have personal reasons for not conveying the information to the practitioner. In such cases, the researcher must persist until all of the available information is known. In some cases, facts that initially appear to be irrelevant may prove to be important as the research project progresses. The researcher, therefore, should pay attention to and record all details that the client discloses. Efficient tax research cannot be completed until the factual situation is clear; without all of the facts at hand, the researcher could make costly false starts that, when additional pertinent facts become known, must be discarded or redone, often at the client's (or, worse, at the researcher's) expense.

In gathering facts relative to a research problem, the researcher also must be aware of the non-tax considerations that are pertinent to the client's situation. For example, the client may have economic constraints (such as cash flow problems) that could preclude the implementation of certain solutions. In addition, the client may have personal preferences that will not accommodate the best tax solution to the problem. For instance, assume that the client could reduce his own income and estate tax liability by making a series of gifts to his grandchildren. However, because the client does not trust the financial judgment of the grandchildren, he does not want to make any such gifts to them during his lifetime. Accordingly, the researcher must look for alternative methods by which to reduce the client's total family tax burden.

Step 2: Identify the Issues

A combination of education, training, and experience is necessary to enable the researcher to identify successfully all of the issues with respect to a tax problem. In some situations, this step can be the most difficult element of a tax research problem.

Issues in a closed-fact tax research problem often arise from a conflict with the IRS. In such a case, one can easily ascertain the issue(s). Research of this nature usually consists of finding support for an action that the client has already taken.

In most research projects, however, the researcher must develop the list of issues. Research issues can be divided into two major categories, namely, fact issues and law issues. **Fact issues** are concerned with information having an objective reality, such as the dates of transactions, the amounts involved in an exchange, reasonableness, intent, and purpose. **Law issues** arise when the facts are well established, but it is not clear which portion of the tax law applies to the issue. The application of the law might not be clear because of an apparent conflict among code sections, because a genuine uncertainty may exist as to the meaning of a term as used in the **Internal Revenue Code**, or because there are no provisions in the law that deal directly with the transaction at hand.

When undertaking a research project where the issue may end up being challenged in court, the researcher must be sure to address all of the issues in the tax return. The legal concept of ***collateral estoppel*** bars relitigation on the same facts or the same issues. Therefore, the practitioner must make sure that his or her case is researched fully and that no issues that could be resolved in the client's favor have been overlooked. If such an issue is not addressed in the original case, it may be lost forever.

In many situations, a research project may encompass several tax years. The researcher must be aware of any fact or law changes that occur during the period that might affect the results of the research project. The pertinent facts or law may be subject to changes that will cause the researcher to arrive at different conclusions and recommendations, depending on the tax year involved. Seemingly, simple situations can often generate many tax research issues. In the process of identifying tax issues, the researcher might discover that additional facts are necessary to provide sufficient answers for the new questions. The taxpayer in the following example is used to illustrate the potential for complexities in merely identifying tax research issues.

EXAMPLE 2-1

The KML Medical Group of Houston would like to hire a new physician from Atlanta. However, the new physician owns a home in Georgia on which she will sustain a loss if it is sold in the current housing market. KML approached the Happy Care Hospital, the institution at which the group practices, and asked whether it would reimburse the new physician for the loss to facilitate her move to Texas. The hospital agreed to reimburse the physician this year for her $120,000 realized loss.

A tax researcher might address or clarify at least the following issues in making recommendations concerning tax treatment of the reimbursement:

- Why did the hospital reimburse the physician?

- Is there any parent-subsidiary relationship between the hospital and the KML Medical Group?

- Do any members of the KML Medical Group have an equity or debt interest in the hospital?

- Does the reimbursement constitute gross income to the physician?

- If the reimbursement does constitute gross income to the physician, is it treated as active, passive, or investment income?

- Is the new physician classified as an employee of the hospital?

- Should the hospital report the payment to the physician on a Form 1099 or W-2?

- Should the hospital withhold any income or FICA tax on the reimbursement?

- Can the hospital deduct the reimbursement as a trade or business expense?

- Should the physician consider the reimbursement and/or the loss on the sale of her residence in computing her moving expense deduction?

- If the reimbursement is considered gross income to the physician, when should the amount be included in the physician's income?

- Is the reimbursement subject to any restrictions such as the physician's continued employment? For how long?

- Is the reimbursement to the physician considered an additional amount realized on the sale of her residence?

- Can the reimbursement be considered a gift from the hospital to the physician?

Imagine how the question concerning whether the physician's gross income (if any) was ordinary income might lead to further questions concerning her potential employee status, income tax and FICA withholding, and reporting issues.

Tax Research as an Iterative Process   The process of tax research is iterative in the sense that, once an answer is found, it often causes a new issue to appear and thus requires the gathering of more information. In other words, the tax research process is not strictly linear. This relationship between facts, issues, and answers is illustrated in Exhibit 2-2. The tax research process requires *mechanical skills* and *critical thinking*. Mechanical techniques are gained and sharpened through both knowledge and experience. *Knowledge* is usually gained through education in universities and other formal class work. *Experience* is obtained through working in the field and dealing with real tax problems on a recurring basis.

Critical thinking is the hardest skill for the researcher to develop. To some extent, it depends on native ability, but a person can be taught the elements of logical analysis and can learn to watch for common pitfalls in evaluating information. Being able to analyze and solve a problem is something the tax researcher must master if he or she is to earn a living in this field. Knowledge is useless when it cannot be applied to solve the problem at hand. The following example illustrates how both mechanical skills and critical thinking are used to solve a tax research problem.

EXHIBIT 2-2:   Interaction among Research Facts, Issues, and Solutions

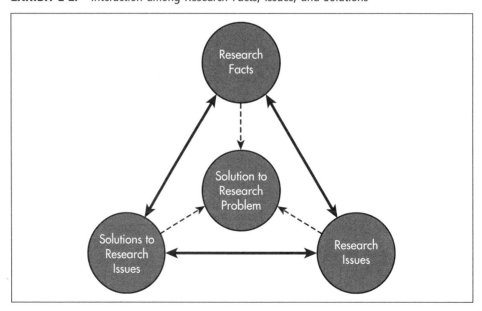

EXAMPLE 2-2

This year, Chris Lee, a client of your CPA firm, sold stock in Slippery Bank (a publicly traded company with a limited market) to Kolpin Corporation for $100,000. Chris has records that show the stock was acquired 10 years ago and has a basis of $135,000. He personally owns 30 percent of Kolpin Corporation. At first glance, the tax researcher would conclude that Chris would have a capital loss of $35,000, which would be deductible against his current-year long-term capital gains of $50,000. This situation appears to be straightforward. The problem could become complex, though, if someone at the CPA firm asked questions about the other owners of Kolpin. What if Chris's wife, Judy Lee, owns Kolpin stock? The researcher must back up in the research process and gather more facts to determine how many shares she owns.

Suppose Judy Lee owns 25 percent of the Kolpin stock. Now the tax practitioner (you) is faced with new facts and issues; §267 of the Internal Revenue Code suggests that the loss might be disallowed. By looking at §267(b)(2), you would find that losses between an individual and a corporation are disallowed if "more than 50 percent in value of the outstanding stock of which is owned directly or indirectly, by or for such individual." You then need to know what "indirect ownership" is. Looking further in the Code, you would find in §267(c), "An individual shall be considered as owning the stock owned, directly or indirectly, by or for his family." Finally, in §267(c)(4), you would discover, "The family of an individual shall include only his brother and sisters (whether by whole or half blood), spouse, ancestors, and lineal descendants."

Armed with this new information, it becomes clear that Chris is a related party to Kolpin Corporation within the meaning of §267. He owns more than 50 percent of the stock, 30 percent directly and 25 percent indirectly through his wife. As a result, the $35,000 capital loss is not allowed to Chris, and he cannot use it to offset his other capital gains.

SPOTLIGHT ON TAXATION

Quotation

"All the Congress, all the accountants and tax lawyers, all the judges, and a convention of wizards all cannot tell for sure what the income tax law says."

—Walter B. Wriston

Step 3: Locate Authority

Once facts have been gathered and the issues defined, the tax researcher must locate legal authority that relates to the issue(s). Authority comes from many sources, including Congress, the courts, and the IRS. Since the inception of the 1913 tax law, several hundred thousand pages of such authority have been produced. To solve a given problem, the researcher must find the appropriate authority in this massive amount of information.

In general, tax authority can be classified as either primary or secondary authority. **Primary authority** is an original pronouncement that comes from statutory, administrative, and judicial sources. **Statutory sources** include the U.S. Constitution, tax treaties, and tax laws passed by Congress. Statutory authority is the basis for all tax provisions. The Constitution grants Congress the power to impose and collect taxes and authorizes the creation of treaties with other countries. The power of Congress to implement and collect taxes is summarized in the Internal Revenue Code, the official title of U.S. tax law. The Internal Revenue Code constitutes the basis for all tax law, and therefore it serves as the basis for arriving at solutions to all tax questions.

The other primary sources of the tax law, administrative and judicial authority, function primarily to interpret and explain the application of the provisions of the Internal Revenue Code and the intent of Congress. **Administrative sources** include the various rulings of the Treasury Department and the IRS, which are issued in the form of Regulations, Revenue Rulings, and other pronouncements. **Judicial sources** consist of the collected rulings of the various courts on Federal tax matters. The primary sources of the tax law will be discussed in detail in Chapters 3, 4, and 5. **Secondary authority** consists of interpretations of primary authority and is an unofficial source of tax information. Examples of secondary authority include tax services, journals, textbooks, treatises, and newsletters.

The distinction between primary and secondary sources of authority has become more important since the enactment of §6662, which imposes a penalty on substantial understatements of tax, except where the taxpayer has "substantial authority" for the position taken on the return. The regulations under §6662 specify the sources of "substantial authority" to include the provisions of the Internal Revenue Code, temporary and final Regulations, court cases, administrative pronouncements, tax treaties, and congressional intent as reflected in committee reports. This list also includes Proposed Regulations, Private Letter Rulings, Technical Advice Memoranda, Actions on Decisions, General Counsel Memoranda, Information or Press Releases, Notices, and any other similar documents published by the IRS in the Internal Revenue Bulletin. Treatises and articles in legal periodicals, however, are not considered substantial authority under this statute.

Secondary authority is useful when conflicting primary authority exists, when there appears to be no extant primary authority, or when the researcher needs an explanation or clarification of the primary authority. During the past 15 years, as the support staffs of government agencies and (especially) federal courts have decreased in number or otherwise become inadequate, more dependence has been placed on the secondary authorities of the tax law, even by the IRS, the Treasury Department, and the court system. The beginning researcher must be careful, though, not to rely too heavily on secondary authority and to always read any pertinent primary authority that is referred to in the secondary sources.

Because of the vast amount of tax authority that is available, the tax researcher would have a tremendous problem in undertaking a tax research problem for a client if it were not for commercial **tax services** and treatises. Several publishers have produced coordinated sets of reference materials that organize the tax authority into a usable format, making the Internal Revenue Code much more accessible. These commercial tax services are useful in that they often provide simplified explanations with footnote citations as well as examples illustrating the application of the law. These tax services may lead the tax researcher, via the footnote references, to the primary source that is pertinent to the question at hand.

Traditionally, tax services have been classified as either annotated or topical. The annotated services are organized in Internal Revenue Code section order, while the topical services are arranged by topic, as defined by the publisher's editorial staff. However, the use of computers has significantly blurred the differences between the organization of commercial tax services. With hypertext linking, any of the tax services can be used from a Code or topical orientation. Exhibit 2-3 includes a listing of some of the current major commercial tax services. The tax services are discussed in detail in later chapters.

Court decisions are published in sets of bound volumes called court reporters. Examples of publishers and court reporters would include those produced by the Government Printing Office (GPO): Tax Court of the U.S. Reports, West Publishing Company: *Federal Reporter*, Research Institute of America (RIA): *American Federal Tax Reports*, and Commerce Clearing House (CCH): *United States Tax Cases*. Chapter 5 discusses in detail the means by which to find court cases in these (and other) reporters.

Both CCH and RIA provide "citators" as part of their tax services. A citator is a reference source that enables the researcher to follow the judicial history of court cases. The citators are discussed in detail in Chapter 7. The GPO prints many of the pronouncements of the IRS. The primary publication for IRS authority is in a set of bound volumes, titled Cumulative Bulletin. Chapter 4 includes a detailed discussion concerning the use of this authority.

Tax journals are another source of information that can be useful to the tax researcher. By reading tax journals, a tax practitioner can become aware of many current problem areas in taxation. She can also increase her awareness of recent developments in the tax law, tax compliance matters, and tax planning techniques and opportunities. Numerous journals, ranging from law reviews to *Cosmopolitan*, publish articles on current tax matters. The tax researcher typically is interested in publications devoted to scholarly and professional discussions of tax matters. Among these publications, each tax journal usually is written for a specific group of readers. Exhibit 2-4 lists several useful tax journals, their publishers, and the target readership of each.

EXHIBIT 2-3: Major Tax Services

Publisher	Title of Tax Service	Orientation
Research Institute of America (RIA)	*Tax Coordinator 2d*	Topic
Research Institute of America (RIA)	*United States Tax Reporter*	Code
Commerce Clearing House (CCH)	*Standard Federal Income Tax Reporter*	Code
Commerce Clearing House (CCH)	*Tax Research Consultant*	Topic
Bureau of National Affairs (BNA)	*Tax Management Portfolios*	Topic
LexisNexis	*Tax Advisor – Federal Topical*	Topic
LexisNexis	*Tax Advisor – Federal Code Reporter*	Code

EXHIBIT 2-4: Selected Tax Journals

Journal	Publisher	Target Readership
Journal of Taxation	Warren, Gorham & Lamont—Thomson Reuters	Sophisticated tax practitioners
Practical Tax Strategies	Warren, Gorham & Lamont—Thomson Reuters	Tax practitioners in general practice
The Tax Adviser	American Institute of CPAs	Members of AICPA and other tax practitioners
TAXES	Commerce Clearing House	General tax practitioners

Step 4: Evaluate Authority

After the researcher has located authority that deals with the client's problem, he or she must evaluate the usefulness of that authority. Not all tax authority carries the same precedential value. For example, the Tax Court could hold that an item should be excluded from gross income at the same time that an outstanding IRS Revenue Ruling asserts the item is taxable. The tax researcher must evaluate the two authorities and decide whether to recommend that his or her client report the disputed item.

In the process of evaluating the authority for the issue(s) under research, new issues not previously considered by the researcher may become known. If this is the case, the researcher may be required to gather additional facts, find additional pertinent authority, and evaluate the new issues. This interaction is illustrated in Exhibit 2-1.

Step 5: Develop Conclusions and Recommendations

After several iterations of the first four steps of the tax research process, the researcher must arrive at his or her conclusions for the tax issues raised. Often, the research will not have resulted in a clear solution to the client's tax problems, perhaps because of unresolved issues of law or incomplete descriptions of the facts. In addition, the personal preferences of the client must also be considered. The "ideal" solution for tax purposes may be entirely impractical because of other factors that are integral to the tax question. In any of these cases, the tax practitioner must use professional judgment in making recommendations based on the conclusions drawn from the tax research process.

SPOTLIGHT ON TAXATION

Changing a Research Conclusion

The changing nature of a tax research conclusion can be illustrated as follows. When Congress created Roth IRAs, a procedure was set up for taxpayers to convert a regular IRA into a Roth IRA by paying the tax on the conversion over a four-year period. After making the conversion, however, many taxpayers reexamined their tax situation and found that the Roth conversion was not as good a deal as originally thought. In this case, however, there was a way out. The tax law gave taxpayers a "second chance" by allowing them to "recharacterize" the Roth IRA conversion back to a regular IRA (within a certain period). Many taxpayers opted to change their converted Roth IRA back into a regular IRA.

Where unresolved issues exist, the researcher might inform the client about alternative possible outcomes of each disputed transaction and give the best recommendation for each. If the research involved an open-fact situation, the recommendation might detail several alternative courses of future action (e.g., whether to complete the deal, or how to document the intended effects of the transaction).

In many cases, the researcher may find it appropriate to present his or her recommendation of the "best" solution from a tax perspective as well as one or more alternative recommendations that may represent much more workable solutions. In any case, the researcher will want to discuss with the client the pros and cons of all reasonable recommendations and the risks associated with each course of action.

Step 6: Communicate the Recommendations

The final step in the research process is to communicate the results and recommendations of the research. The results of the research effort usually are summarized in a memorandum to the client file and in a letter to the client. Both of these items usually contain a restatement of the pertinent facts as the researcher understands them, any assumptions the researcher made, the issues addressed, the applicable authority, and the practitioner's recommendations. An example of the structure of a simple tax research memo is shown in Exhibit 2-5. The memorandum to the file usually contains more detail than does the letter to the client.

EXHIBIT 2-5: Tax Research Memo

Raabe, Whittenburg, Sanders & Sawyers
Certified Public Accountants
San Francisco, CA

Relevant Facts:

Specific Issues:

Conclusions:

Support:

Actions to Be Taken:

_____ Discuss with client. Date discussed: _____

_____ Prepare a memo or letter to the client.

_____ Explore other fact situations.

_____ Other action. Describe:

Preparer: _____

Reviewer: _____

In any event, the researcher must temper his or her communication of the research results so that it is understandable by the intended reader. For instance, the researcher should use vastly different jargon and citation techniques in preparing an article for the *Journal of Taxation* than in preparing a client memo for a businessperson or layperson who is not sophisticated in tax matters. Chapter 11 provides additional guidelines and formats for client memoranda and other means of delivering the results of one's research. In addition, an excellent Web site to help the tax researcher improve his or her written tax communication is **www2.gsu.edu/~accerl/home.html**.

Overview of Computerized Tax Research

The body of knowledge that encompasses the field of taxation grows at a phenomenal pace. Since 1975, Congress has enacted more than two dozen major tax and revenue bills that have had a significant effect on U.S. taxpayers. In addition, each year hundreds of new Treasury Regulations, court decisions, Revenue and Private Letter Rulings, Revenue Procedures, and Technical Advice Memoranda are issued.

The avalanche of tax-related information is not expected to decrease during the foreseeable future. The abundance of available information as well as the complexity of the tax laws that have been enacted since 1975 have made it even more difficult and time consuming to conduct thorough and effective research concerning a tax-related issue.

Whenever a diligent tax professional is providing advice or other services to a client, he or she must be cognizant of the latest legislative changes and judicial decisions. Furthermore, he or she must be able to draw upon, and sort through, the vast body of established tax knowledge and to apply statutes and administrative and judicial rulings to the current tax issue.

Most tax professionals conduct a significant portion of their tax research using computer resources. The vast amount of storage available on a computer, coupled with the computer's fast retrieval of information, has made electronic tax research invaluable for the tax profession. The tax practitioner has two chief ways to find computer information for tax research purposes: (1) online subscription systems and (2) online free (non-subscription) Internet sites.

Computerized tax online services can be accessed via compatible handheld devices and computers that the user already owns. Some popular computer subscription systems are shown in Exhibit 2-6, and examples of online free Internet sites are shown in Exhibit 2-7.

Electronic online tax research systems are relatively simple to operate. Normally, the user will have no trouble utilizing the system after he or she has devised an effective search command or query. After the documents are received, the user must evaluate them and decide whether further research is required. As in using the tax research methodology itself, electronic searching requires a combination of technical knowledge, experience, and creativity in approach.

Benefits of Using a Computerized Tax Service

Historically, tax research usually began with the consultation of topical and annotated tax services or tax-related text. In most instances, the user first had to consult a topical index to locate the appropriate page or pages on which to begin his or her research. Any time that a tax service is accessed by way of its topical index, however, the user is relying on someone else's judgment (i.e., the service's editors) or performance (e.g., the staff of

EXHIBIT 2-6: Examples of Online Tax Resources

Name	Description
RIA Checkpoint	A Web-based tax research service that contains all the RIA material on Federal, state, local, and international taxation. Checkpoint contains all RIA analytical material such as the *Tax Coordinator 2d* and the *United States Tax Reporter*. All public domain information such as the Internal Revenue Code and Regulations, U.S. tax treaties, IRS publications and pronouncements, and court cases are available on this system.
CCH IntelliConnect	A Web-based tax research service that contains CCH's tax services (*Tax Research Consultant* and *Federal Income Tax Reporter*) and other Federal, state, local and international legal and tax information. All public domain information such as the Internal Revenue Code and Regulations, U.S. tax treaties, IRS publications and pronouncements, and court cases are available on this system.
Kleinrock	Owned by CCH, Kleinrock's ATX service uses the same IntelliConnect platform as the CCH services. However, ATX is designed for small firm tax practitioners conducting tax research and includes primary source material, including the Internal Revenue Code, Regulations, Rulings and Other Documents, Letter Rulings and IRS positions, IRS publications, Circular 230 and Tax Court and federal tax cases. It also includes practitioner-oriented state and local tax products, access to CCH journals, and federal and state forms.
Tax Analysts	A Web-based tax research service called the Federal Research Library that includes the Internal Revenue Code, Regulations, Treasury Decisions, IRS taxpayer publications, Revenue Rulings, Revenue Procedures, Notices and Announcements, and over 100,000 court opinions.
LexisNexis Tax Center	Besides containing all Federal and state tax research material, LexisNexis gives you access to expert analytical materials from CCH, Tax Analysts, BNA, and Kleinrock. In addition, LexisNexis has extensive libraries of newspapers, magazines, journals, patent records, and medical, economic, and accounting databases.
Westlaw	Westlaw and WestlawNext contain all Federal, state, local, and international legal sources, including court cases, administrative releases, and statutory information. All government documents (e.g., IRS publications, court cases) are also available on this system. It also offers BNA and some CCH products.
BNA Tax & Accounting	BNA Tax & Accounting focuses on providing a practitioner-to-practitioner approach to analysis and commentary through its Tax Management Portfolios, Daily Tax Report, and online content.

EXHIBIT 2-7: Examples of Online Free Tax-Related Internet Sites

Site Name	Internet Address	Description
Tax Sites	**www.taxsites.com**	This site includes indexes to other tax, accounting, and legal Web sites. Links to commercial, Federal government, state, local, and international Web sites.
Internal Revenue Service	**www.irs.gov**	Taxpayers can find tax forms, instructions, publications, and other IRS information.
Ernst & Young	**www.ey.com**	This Web site contains a large amount of tax and accounting information from the staff of E&Y.
Deloitte Tax LLP	**www.deloitte.com**	The Deloitte Tax LLP Web site contains a large amount of tax and accounting information from the staff of Deloitte Tax LLP.
Thomas	**thomas.loc.gov**	This site provides legislative information from the Library of Congress.
Will Yancey's Home Page	**www.willyancey.com**	This site offers indexes to other tax, accounting, and legal Web sites as well as links to commercial, Federal government, state, local, and international Web sites.

the database or library for proper treatment of update material) as to what is important with respect to the specific topic.

Moreover, the desired information may not be located, even if it exists in the proper place in the database, because the keyword for which the user is looking is not the same word that was used by the editor in the index to discuss the issue that is the subject of the search. It is also possible that, when the index was prepared, the topic of the search was ignored because it was not as important a topic as it is today.

The primary benefit of using a computerized tax service is that such a resource makes it possible for the user to index any significant term, that is, by using it as a search term in a query. By creating his or her own indexes, the researcher is not bound by the limitations that are imposed by a third-party editor or data processor. Once the central computer is accessed with a proper search request, the service's software will electronically scan the designated files and retrieve all of the documents that contain the word or words included in the query. Thus, the user is able to bypass the predefined list of topics that constitute the subject's index and perform his or her search directly on the documents themselves.

Another benefit of using a computerized tax research system is that the user can tailor his or her query to fit the requirements of a specific tax problem. Because the user defines the precise specifications of the query, computerized research is exceptionally flexible. Each search request can be made as specific or as broad as desired, depending on the issue to be researched. If they are properly structured, computerized search queries can result in the research process being conducted with greater speed and thoroughness, and they can reduce the amount of time spent on that phase of the research task.

Such speed and flexibility are best realized as the researcher moves among pertinent tax documents. Most of the electronic services allow this capability through hypertext linking. Generally, when a hypertext link is indicated, typically through a different color for the text, the user can move to the related document so indicated with a click of the mouse or keyboard. For instance, the researcher could be reading a court case that refers to §2032A. By clicking on the hypertext link character, he or she is taken directly to the text of the Code section for direct perusal of the statutory language. Similarly, links can be made to pertinent Regulations or to similar court documents in a manner that the researcher could not accomplish by hand. As the number of available tax documents becomes more voluminous, the importance of moving among the documents quickly is met only with an electronic tax research tool.

Online services are updated many times a day. A researcher generally is able to retrieve recent court decisions and administrative rulings from a computerized service almost immediately upon release by the source of the document. In addition, the computerized services include one or more of the daily tax news summaries, such as BNA's *Daily Tax Report* or Tax Analysts' *Tax Notes Today*. In this regard, a computerized tax service allows a tax researcher to stay on top of the latest news and developments without incurring additional subscription costs for the standalone services.

Computerized services are particularly useful in researching case law. Every word that is contained in a case is included in the database of the computerized service. Thus, the user can save time by directly accessing only those cases that contain the key terms of his or her search. For example, all of the cases that deal with unreasonable compensation can be accessed within seconds, simply by using *unreasonable compensation* as a search request.

An additional benefit of using a computerized tax service is that certain documents no longer are available in print. For example, full printed transcripts of Actions on

Decision and slip opinions normally are not published. However, these documents often may be obtained from the databases of an electronic tax service.

A computerized research service also can be used to obtain regularly published documents to which the researcher does not have access. For example, the full text of Private Letter Rulings is available on most computerized tax research databases. By using a target or filter feature in a computerized service, a tax practitioner can thus obtain only the ruling needed, without subscribing to an expensive loose-leaf service for the entire year.

Because of its inherent advantages, the Web-based tax service has become the standard source for current and archival tax research material.

Factors in Choosing a Computerized Tax Service

In *Computer-Assisted Legal and Tax Research* (Prentice-Hall), Thomas and Weinstein propose that a potential subscriber consider the following factors when choosing a computerized tax database.

- *Database contents.* Does the service provide specialty libraries that will be important in the researcher's work and that are unavailable elsewhere?

- *Search capabilities.* While the search commands and requirements are similar among the commercial tax services, some of the electronic services allow direct reviews of editorial information, and others encompass the Shepard's citations service.

- *Training.* Each of the services offers some level of educational training, either at the user's office or at a regional training center. The proximity, depth, and quality of such seminars may differ among services and across the country.

- *Customer support.* Other forms of contact with the user, such as to develop more sophisticated search techniques or to provide necessary repair services, should be available to the subscriber.

- *Price.* One must consider the cost of the time required to perform the research itself as well as that of necessary equipment or special software.

Using a Computer in Tax Research

In the first part of this chapter, we presented a model of the tax research process. In this model, steps 1 and 2 of the tax research model are (1) to establish the facts and (2) to identify the issues related to the research question(s). The next step in the research model is to locate tax authority with which to solve the research question. In most situations, the tax researcher uses a computer in step 3 of the model in order to find the required authority (or to conclude that there is no authority on the subject). The process of finding tax authority using a computer can be broken down into several steps, as shown in Exhibit 2-8.

Step 1: State the Issue as a Question

After the tax researcher has established the facts and identified the issues that he or she needs to resolve, the issues should be stated as a question to be answered. For example, suppose the researcher has a client who is a self-employed attorney. As part of her trade or business, the attorney incurs substantial travel expenses during the year. She has learned that if she buys airline tickets in advance and extends her visit over a Saturday

EXHIBIT 2-8: Steps in the Computer Research Process

Step 1	State the Issue as a Question	The step comes after establishing the fact and identifying the issues.
Step 2	Identify the Keywords	One needs to use words that are on point to get best results.
Step 3	Construct a Computer Research Query	One needs to use wildcards and connectors to get the best results.
Step 4	Select a Database and Execute the Search	One needs to use a database that finds what is needed without returning too much information.
Step 5	Interpret and Refine the Search	Results may require the researcher to return to a previous step.

night, she will receive a large savings on airfare. Usually, an extra day of meals and lodging can save many hundreds of dollars in her airfare travel expenses. In the current year, she has spent $4,000 in extra Saturday night expenses to save $12,000 in airfare. The research question in this situation could be stated as:

Are the additional travel costs (primarily meals and lodging) of staying over a Saturday night in order to save substantial amounts on the business airfare deductible?

Step 2: Identify the Keywords

Once the research question has been stated, the researcher must next identify the keywords to construct a proper query in the next step. In the preceding research question, the keywords could be as follows:

- Meals and lodging
- Travel
- Saturday
- Deductible
- Airfare

The researcher is looking for words that, when entered into a computer, will find tax authority that is "on point." If the correct keywords are not identified, tax researchers cannot find the authority needed or could be led down blind alleys.

Step 3: Construct a Computer Research Query

Computer tax research systems use a query in order to begin the search for the authority needed by the researcher. The construction of the query varies for each commercial computer tax research system, but many similarities exist between the systems. All tax computer research systems recognize various types of connectors to construct a research query. Generally, computer tax services, such as *RIA Checkpoint*, have 10 to 15 search connectors available, but most tax research searches can be accomplished by using several basic connectors. The syntax of the four most useful connectors in RIA Checkpoint is shown in Exhibit 2-9.

In addition, the tax services allow the use of wildcard (universal) character(s). For example, in *RIA Checkpoint*, an "*" (asterisk) at the end of a root word finds all variations

EXHIBIT 2-9: Selected RIA Checkpoint Search Connectors

Connector	Example	Description
And	stock and securities	Finds documents with both the term stock and the term securities in them.
Or	stock or securities	Finds documents with either the term stock or the term securities in them.
/n	stock/15 securities	Finds documents where the term stock is within 15 words of the term securities.
Not	stock not securities	Finds documents with the term stock, but not the term securities.

of that word. Thus, the word "deduct*" will find deduct, deducted, deduction, deductible, and so on. Other computer tax services use similar methods to construct tax research queries.

Computer tax services are continually being updated. Users should check the appropriate help menu of whichever computer tax service is being used to determine how to construct a query and to find other new features.

Step 4: Select a Database and Execute the Search

Once the query is constructed, the researcher must log on to and choose a database to search. Each computer tax research system contains numerous databases. As an example, RIA Checkpoint contains the following databases (among many others):

- All Federal Databases
- Federal Editorial Material
- *Federal Tax Coordinator 2d* (a tax service)
- Source Material: Cases
- Source Material: Code, Committee Reports, Regulations, Tax Treaties
- Source Material: IRS Rulings and Releases
- Source Material: Tax Court and Federal Procedural Rules
- WG&L Journals

Continuing our example of the deductibility of Saturday night expenses, we could choose to search "All Federal" using a query such as travel/25 Saturday. See Exhibit 2-10. If we executed this search on *RIA Checkpoint*, we would find several references to the fact that the IRS has issued Private Letter Ruling 9237014 that states that the extra expenses incurred for staying over a Saturday to get a lower airfare are deductible as part of the expenses of the business trip.

Step 5: Interpret and Refine the Search

After executing a computer tax search, often the query produces too little or too much information. If there is too little information, the search query must be broadened. For example, other keywords may be used or proximity connectors may be relaxed. On the

EXHIBIT 2-10: RIA Checkpoint Query and Database Selection Screen

other hand, if the query generates too much information, then the search should be tightened. For example, fewer libraries or more unique keywords may be used or proximity connectors may be used or narrowed.

Each computer tax service (e.g., LexisNexis, Westlaw, RIA Checkpoint, CCH Intelli-Connect) uses its own format for conducting tax searches. However, all services (including those conducted on Google or Yahoo!) use the same basic steps in executing such searches. In all computer tax systems, the researcher must state the issue, select the keywords, construct a query, choose a database, execute a search, and interpret and refine the search.

IRS Web Site Research

The IRS maintains an excellent Web site (**www.irs.gov**) where someone interested in tax information can conduct limited tax research. While the IRS Web site is not a full-service tax research resource, it does contain searchable and downloadable tax information such as tax forms, instructions, publications (e.g., Publication 17), and other IRS information. The IRS Web site also has a limited search engine that uses several of the basic connectors and recognizes wildcard characters, as shown in Exhibit 2-11.

The wildcards "*" and "?" are also allowed by the IRS search engine. Using these wildcards, you can find documents that contain words that have similar spellings but are not stemmed variants. For example, air* finds documents that contain air, airline, and airhead. Entering "?at" finds documents that contain cat and hat, while "??at" finds documents that contain that and chat. For complete information on how to conduct IRS Web site searches, go to **www.irs.gov/help/search_help.html**.

EXAMPLE 2-3

Last year, Doris's daughter and her husband moved into her home. This year, Doris has supported both of them for the entire year. Doris would like to know if she can claim a dependency exemption for her son-in-law. Doris could go to the IRS Web site and click the search button. She could then search terms such as "son-in-law" and "dependent." See Exhibit 2-12. The IRS search engine should return several IRS publications (e.g., Pub. 501) that will inform Doris she can claim a deduction for her son-in-law.

Tax Research Practical Considerations When a tax researcher undertakes an engagement, there are several practical factors to consider. These factors can influence the research project on several levels. The primary goal of a researcher should be to produce results in the most accurate and efficient manner possible. The following factors should be considered when conducting tax research engagements:

- *Engagement Time Cost.* A tax researcher has to be efficient in using his or her time. Research time is very expensive, sometimes amounting to several hundred dollars per hour of cost to the client. The researcher has to make sure that the time spent on the project is used efficiently and effectively in order to provide value to the client.

- *Potential Tax Liability Involved.* Not every tax research engagement has the same relative value to a client. A tax transaction involving millions of dollars in tax liability is different from one that affects several thousand dollars in tax liability. The researcher has an obligation to a client not to waste the client's money on a low cost/benefit issue.

EXHIBIT 2-11: IRS Web Site Connectors

Boolean Connectors	
OR	Space
AND	+
NOT	−
ADJ	"enclose in quotes"

EXHIBIT 2-12:   IRS Web site Search Page

© Comstock/Jupiter Images.

What is the point of incurring $5,000 in research time to save $3,000 in taxes? The new staff researcher should always be aware of their research budget and check with their supervisor if they are concerned about the time spent on a specific research project.

- *Accuracy Threshold.* One of the issues facing a tax researcher is how definitive a research result must be. Is the additional time spent to increase the certainty of a conclusion from 70 percent to 95 percent worth the additional cost? Related to the issue is the amount of tax liability involved along with the client's tolerance for risk.

- *Ethics.* Chapter 1 covered many of the ethical requirements for tax professionals. These requirements should always be kept in mind when undertaking a research project and reaching a conclusion. The final question to the tax researcher should be: "Have I met the appropriate ethical standards in reaching my conclusion?"

Tax Research on the CPA Exam

The CPA exam is the examination that all individuals must pass if they wish to obtain a CPA license in one of the 50 states and other jurisdictions (e.g., Puerto Rico) of the United States. The exam is prepared by the American Institute of CPAs and is administered through the National Association of State Boards of Accountancy (NASBA). NASBA information can be found at the following Web site: **www.nasba.org/**.

NASBA contracts with testing centers around the United States, which actually give the exam. The CPA exam is a computer-based exam that tests accounting knowledge (e.g., financial accounting, taxation, auditing) and a set of supporting "soft" skills deemed to be important to the practice of public accountancy. The skills required for the CPA Exam include the abilities to communicate, perform research, and analyze information, as well as other higher-order skills such as judgment and understanding [The CPA Exam Alert, AICPA (January/February 2003) p. 3]. The necessary skills as defined by the Board of Examiners are as follows:

- Communication is the ability to effectively elicit and/or express information through written or oral means.

- Research is the ability to locate and extract relevant information from available resource material.

- Analysis is the ability to organize, process, and interpret data to provide options for decision-making.

- Judgment is the ability to evaluate options for decision-making and provide an appropriate conclusion.

- Understanding is the ability to recognize and comprehend the meaning and application of a particular matter.

CPA exam candidates are required to demonstrate their ability to apply these skills in each section of the Uniform CPA Examination in the context of the content knowledge.

The CPA exam, which is 14 hours in total, is given in four parts. These parts can be taken separately as long as all four parts are passed within certain time limitations. The CPA Exam parts are as follows:

1. *Auditing and Attestation (AUD).* [four hours] This section covers knowledge of auditing procedures, generally accepted auditing standards and other standards related to attest engagements, and the skills needed to apply that knowledge.

2. *Business Environment and Concepts (BEC).* [three hours] This section covers knowledge of general business environments and business concepts that candidates need to know in order to understand the underlying business reasons for and accounting implications of business transactions, and the skills needed to apply that knowledge.

3. *Financial Accounting and Reporting (FAR).* [four hours] This section covers knowledge of generally accepted accounting principles for business enterprises, not-for-profit organizations, and governmental entities, and the skills needed to apply that knowledge.

4. *Regulation (REG).* [three hours] In addition to business law, this section includes significant coverage of Federal taxation (income, gift, and estate). Areas of testing include federal tax processes, procedures, accounting, and planning as well as federal taxation of property transactions, individuals, and entities. Ethics and professional and legal responsibilities are key components of the section, requiring candidates to be familiar with Treasury Department Circular 230, the AICPA Statements on Standards for Tax Services, and relevant Internal Revenue Code sections and related

Regulations. Topics covered under Federal tax procedures include due dates and related extensions of time, the IRS audit and appeals process, the judicial process, the required disclosure of tax return positions, substantiation requirements, penalties, and the statute of limitations.

To demonstrate knowledge and skills in this section, candidates are expected to conduct research of issues and alternative tax treatments using relevant professional literature, formulate conclusions, and prepare documentation to support conclusions and tax positions. Much of the material tested in the REG section of the exam involving ethics, professional and legal responsibilities, Federal tax procedures, and, of course, tax research is included in this book.

The AUD, REG, and FAR sections of the exam contain two types of questions: (1) multiple choice (standard objective questions) and (2) task-based simulations. With simulations, the candidates demonstrate their ability to research professional and legal databases, identify relevant authority, and draw conclusions to solve a problem. The BEC section of the exam includes multiple choice questions and written communication tasks.

SUMMARY

Tax research is a complex process. The researcher must complete all of the steps in the research process to arrive at a solution to or recommendation for the client's tax problem. Moreover, the steps delineated in Exhibit 2-1 (or iterations of them) must be completed in their proper order to minimize the possibility of errors in evaluating the authority, arriving at conclusions, or making recommendations. If the process is abbreviated, the researcher risks failure to properly serve the client, which could result in the payment of unnecessary taxes by the client or in the payment of damages by the tax practitioner to the client.

QUIZ YOURSELF

Reinforce the tax research information covered in this chapter by completing the online quizzes located at the Federal Tax Research Web site at **www.cengagebrain.com.** At the CengageBrain.com home page, search for the *Federal Tax Research*, 9e ISBN (1111221642) using the search box at the top of the page. This will take you to the product page where you can access the quizzes.

KEY WORDS

By the time you complete this chapter, you should be comfortable discussing each of the following terms. If you need additional review of any of these items, return to the appropriate material in the chapter or consult the glossary to this text.

administrative sources, p. 56
collateral estoppel, p. 53
fact issues, p. 52
Internal Revenue Code, p. 52

judicial sources, p. 56
law issues, p. 52
primary authority, p. 55
secondary authority, p. 56

statutory sources, p. 55
tax journals, p. 57
tax services, p. 56

DISCUSSION QUESTIONS

1. What is the purpose of tax research?

2. What are the basic steps in conducting tax research? Briefly discuss each step in the tax research process.

3. What are the two chief tax research skills, as identified in this text? Explain the importance of each basic skill.

4. The tax researcher must find the facts as the first step in tax research. Give examples of the kind of information that a tax practitioner might want to obtain.

5. What are some of the potential pitfalls in the first step of the tax research process?

6. In each of the following independent situations, indicate whether the item generally would be a tax (T) or a nontax (NT) consideration in solving a tax research or tax planning problem.

   a. The taxpayer would like to set up a private foundation to reduce her annual income tax liability.

   b. The taxpayer has a very poor cash flow because of prior investments; therefore, he has a limited ability to make "tax-advantaged" investments.

   c. The taxpayer wants to transfer as much of her property to her grandchildren as possible. However, she does not want any of the property to fall into the hands of the grandchildren's mother (her daughter-in-law).

   d. The taxpayer lived through the Great Depression of the 1930s and does not like investments with any risk, such as owning stocks or bonds.

   e. The taxpayer likes to maintain liquid investments, such as money market funds and certificates of deposit in insured banks and savings and loan institutions.

7. In each of the following independent situations, indicate whether the item generally would be a tax (T) or a nontax (NT) consideration in solving a tax research or tax planning problem.

   a. The taxpayer hates to pay Federal taxes. He will take any legal action to avoid paying any Federal income, estate, or gift taxes.

   b. The taxpayer does not trust the United States banking system and moves all her money to a bank in Switzerland.

   c. The taxpayer is married and his spouse is financially naïve. Since he is in bad health, the taxpayer wants to make sure his wife will be taken care of financially if he were to suddenly die.

   d. The taxpayer wants to purchase rental real estate. He wants to make sure that he will not be subject to a high state tax where he buys.

   e. The taxpayer owns city of San Diego bonds instead of putting his money in a commercial bank.

8. Identify and briefly describe the two major types of tax research issues.

9. What is collateral estoppel? How does it affect tax research and planning?

10. Tax law provisions tend to change over time. Explain how this might affect tax research and planning.

11. In the tax research process, the researcher has an obligation to the client to evaluate authority. Do the precedents in all tax authority carry the same value? Explain.

12. Primary tax authority can be classified as statutory, administrative, or judicial. Briefly describe each.

13. Classify each of the following items as a primary (P) or secondary (S) tax research authority:

    a. The Internal Revenue Code

    b. A Tax Court case

    c. A textbook on corporate taxation

    d. Treasury Regulations

    e. An IRS Revenue Ruling

14. Classify each of the following items as a primary (P) or secondary (S) tax research authority:
    a. A U.S. District Court Case
    b. An IRS Revenue Procedure
    c. Code §162
    d. The Daily Tax Report newsletter
    e. An article on recent tax rulings on inventory valuation in Practical Tax Strategies

15. Classify each of the following items as a primary (P) or secondary (S) tax research authority:
    a. An article in the *Journal of Taxation*
    b. Taxes on Parade (a newsletter)
    c. A Supreme Court decision on a tax matter
    d. The U.S./Australia Income Tax Treaty
    e. A discussion on earnings and profits in the RIA Tax Coordinator 2d Tax Service

16. Briefly characterize and distinguish between annotated tax services and topical tax services.

17. What is a court reporter? Name three organizations that produce court reporters.

18. Who publishes each of the following court reporters?
    a. United States Tax Cases
    b. Federal Reporter
    c. American Federal Tax reports
    d. Tax Court of the U.S. Reports

19. What kind of information can be found in a citator?

20. Name the primary bound publication where IRS pronouncements can be found.

21. Tax practitioners use the term "tax service" all the time. What is a tax service?

22. What is the target readership of each of the following tax journals?
    a. *TAXES*
    b. *Journal of Taxation*
    c. *Practical Tax Strategies*
    d. *The Tax Adviser*

23. Specific items of tax authority have different "values" in helping the tax researcher to solve his or her problem. Explain this statement and describe how it applies to the tax research process.

24. Step 5 in the tax research process is concerned with reaching a conclusion or making a recommendation. If one has not found a clear answer to a tax research problem, how is a conclusion or recommendation to be reached?

25. The final step in the research process typically involves a memorandum to the client file and/or a letter to the client communicating the results of the research. List the items that should be found in the body of both of these documents.

26. It has been said that the tax research process is more circular than linear. Do you agree with this statement? Explain your answer.

27. What is deemed to be substantial authority under the Internal Revenue Code §6662 Regulations? Why is this important?

28. Describe an online tax research system. What are the two advantages of such a system over a standard printed tax service?

29. Give the Web address of three free online Internet sites where someone could find information on various aspects of taxation.

30. What is computerized tax research, and why is it necessary for the tax professional to be able to use computerized techniques to conduct tax research?

31. Briefly describe what is contained in each of the following tax services:
    a. RIA CheckPoint
    b. CCH IntelliConnect
    c. LexisNexis
    d. Westlaw and WestlawNext

32. What are the disadvantages of using a computerized tax service?

33. List four benefits of using a computerized service to conduct your tax research.

34. What are the major steps in developing an effective computerized tax research query?

35. If you were researching an issue and the computer informed you that it had located 1,000 pertinent documents, what would you do to reduce the number of retrieved documents to a more reasonable number?

36. What are the search connectors discussed in the text used by RIA Checkpoint? Describe how each operates.

37. For the following RIA Checkpoint databases state if they generally contain primary or secondary authority: (1) *Federal Tax Coordinator 2d*, (2) Source Material Cases, (3) Source Material IRS Rulings and Releases, and (4) WG&L Journals.

38. What is the Internet address of the Internal Revenue Service's server?

39. What are the connectors used by the IRS Web site search engine?

40. What are the two "wildcards" used by the IRS Web site search engine? Explain how each operates.

41. Where can someone find additional information on searching techniques available for use on the IRS Web site?

42. One of the practical factors that could influence a tax research project is "engagement time cost." Discuss how this might influence your completion of a tax engagement.

43. One of the practical factors that could impact a tax research project is "potential tax liability involved." Discuss how this might influence your completion of a tax engagement.

44. One of the practical factors that could affect a tax research project is "accuracy threshold." Discuss how this might influence your completion of a tax engagement.

45. How might ethics considerations impact a tax research engagement?

46. The computerized Uniform CPA exam has four parts. Identify them and briefly state what is covered in each part.

47. The Uniform CPA exam has a stated set of "supporting skills" that it tests. What are these skills? Do you think they should be tested on the Uniform CPA exam?

48. The online CPA exam is given throughout the year in certain "testing periods." Use a Web search (e.g., Google or Yahoo!) to determine the dates of such testing periods.

49. Go online and find the nearest CPA exam testing site to your location.

EXERCISES

50. Use your university's tax library (or other library assigned by your instructor) to discover the breadth of tax journal offerings. List any five tax journals and the publisher of each.

51. The purpose of this exercise is for you to locate publications that frequently are used in tax research. Give the call number and location (i.e., floor, room, stack) in your library, and the major color of the binding of the publication, for each of the following references. If a publication is not available, state that it is not.

    a. RIA's *United States Tax Reporter*

    b. CCH's *Standard Federal Income Tax Reporter*

    c. BNA's *Tax Management Portfolios*

    d. RIA's *Tax Coordinator 2d*

52. Find out whether each of the following court reporters is available in your library. Give the call number and location (i.e., floor, room, stack) for each reference. If a reporter is not available, state that it is not.

    a. *American Federal Tax Reports*

    b. *United States Tax Cases*

    c. *Tax Court of the U.S. Reports*

    d. *Federal Reporter*

53. Determine if each of the following tax journals is available in your library. What is the most current issue in your library? List the author(s) and title of any two articles from the most recent issue.

    a. *Journal of Taxation*

    b. *Practical Tax Strategies*

    c. *Journal of International Taxation*

    d. *The Tax Adviser*

    e. *TAXES*

54. Is the Internal Revenue Code found in separate volumes in each of the following tax services? If so, in how many volumes?

    a. CCH's *Standard Federal Income Tax Reporter*

    b. BNA's *Tax Management Portfolios*

    c. RIA's *Tax Coordinator 2d*

55. Find a copy of the Cumulative Bulletin in your university's library. By looking in a volume, list three different tax research sources published in a Cumulative Bulletin.

56. Locate a copy of the *American Federal Tax Reports* in your library. List two courts that have decisions published in this court reporter.

57. Locate a copy of CCH's *United States Tax Cases* in your library. List two courts that have decisions published in this court reporter.

58. In your university's library, locate the CCH and RIA citators. How many volumes does each contain?

59. Determine if your campus has any of the following online tax research services available for student use. If a service is available on your campus, describe how you would gain access to that system for research projects in your tax classes. If a service is not available on your campus, state where you might be able to find it.

    a. LexisNexis

    b. RIA Checkpoint

    c. Westlaw and WestlawNext

    d. CCH IntelliConnect

60. Go to the IRS Web page (www.irs.gov) and print out a copy of the most recent Instructions for Form 3903 of Form 1040.

61. Go to the IRS Web page (www.irs.gov) and print out a copy of the most recent Instructions for Form 4952 of Form 1040. You may first need to download the Adobe Acrobat Reader software to be able to view or print the form. The software is provided free of charge by Adobe through a link on the IRS page.

62. Go to the IRS Web page (www.irs.gov). What IRS publication number addresses tax rules that apply to personnel in the armed forces? Print the first page of the IRS publication to hand in.

63. Go to the IRS Web page (www.irs.gov). What IRS publication number addresses tax rules for pension and annuity income? Print the first page of the IRS publication to hand in.

64. Go to the IRS Web page (www.irs.gov). Find information on abusive tax shelters. Give an example of an abusive tax shelter listed by the IRS.

65. Go to the IRS Web page (www.irs.gov). Find a copy of Form 1040-PR, the Puerto Rico individual tax return. Print out and turn in page 1 of the 1040-PR Form.

66. Go to the IRS Web page (www.irs.gov). Find a copy of Form 1040-C (PDF) U.S. Departing Alien Income Tax Return. Print out and turn in page 1 of the 1040-C Form.

67. Go to www.taxsites.com and give the complete Web address for each of the following sites:
    a. The California Franchise Tax Board
    b. The New York Department of Taxation and Finance
    c. The American Institute of CPAs (AICPA)

68. Go to www.willyancey.com and give the complete Web address for each of the following sites:
    a. The Hawaii Department of Taxation
    b. The Vermont Department of Taxes
    c. The American Taxation Association

69. Go to www.willyancey.com and give the complete Web address for each of the following sites:
    a. The Alabama Department of Revenue
    b. The Colorado Department of Revenue
    c. National Tax Association

70. Go to the Practitioners Publishing Co. Web site (ppc.thomson.com) and locate the most recent Practitioners Tax Action Bulletin. Print out a copy of the bulletin.

71. Go to the IRS Web page (www.irs.gov) and find the most recent IRS Publication 1542, Per Diem Rates. What is the maximum per diem rate for lodging and meals and incidental expenses (M&IE) for each of the following towns?
    a. Miami, Florida
    b. Palm Springs, California
    c. San Antonio, Texas

72. Go to the IRS Web page (www.irs.gov) and find the most recent IRS Publication 1542, Per Diem Rates. What is the maximum per diem rate for lodging and meals and incidental expenses (M&IE) for each of the following towns?
    a. Buffalo, New York
    b. Honolulu, Hawaii
    c. Spokane, Washington

73. Go to the IRS Web page (www.irs.gov) and find the most recent IRS Publication 1542, Per Diem Rates. What is the maximum per diem rate for lodging and meals and incidental expenses (M&IE) for each of the following towns?

   a. Denver, Colorado

   b. Kansas City, Missouri

   c. Orlando, Florida

74. Locate and print out the Web site home page of each of the following CPA firms.

   a. Ernst and Young LLP

   b. Deloitte Tax LLP

   c. BDO Seidman LLP

   d. PricewaterhouseCoopers LLP

75. Locate the Web site home page of each of the following CPA firms. Give the city location of the firm's main (home) office.

   a. KPMG LLP

   b. Grant Thornton LLP

   c. Dixon Hughes PLLC

   d. Moss Adams LLP

76. Jennifer owns 200 acres of land on which she grows flowers for sale to local nurseries. Her adjusted basis in the land is $30,000. She receives condemnation proceeds of $20,000 from the state for 10 acres of her land on which a new freeway will be built. The state also pays her $30,000 for the harmful effects that the increased auto exhaust might have on her flowers. List as many tax research issues as you can to determine the tax consequences of these transactions. Do not attempt to answer any of the questions you raise. Simply identify the research issues.

77. Joey parked his car on the top of a hill when he went to watch the X games in San Diego. He did not properly set his brakes or curb the wheels when he parked the car. When he returned from the games, he found his car had rolled down the hill, smashed into Nick's house, and injured Nick, who was watching TV in his den. Joey does not have car insurance. List as many tax research issues as you can to determine the tax consequences of this accident. Do not attempt to answer any of the questions you raise. Simply identify the research issues.

78. John and Marsha are married and filed a joint return for the past year. During that year, Marsha was employed as an assistant cashier at a local bank and, as such, was able to embezzle $75,000, none of which was reported on their joint return. Before the defalcation was discovered, Marsha disappeared and has not been seen or heard from since. List as many tax research issues as you can to determine the tax consequences of this crime. Do not attempt to answer any of the questions you raise. Simply identify the research issues.

79. In the current year, Dave receives stock worth $125,000 from his employer. The stock is restricted and cannot be sold by Dave for seven years. Dave estimates the stock will be worth $300,000 after the seven years. List as many tax research issues as you can to determine the tax consequences of this transaction. Do not attempt to answer any of the questions you raise. Simply identify the research issues.

80. On December 1, 20X1, Ericka receives $18,000 for three months' rent (December, January, and February) of an office building. List as many tax research issues as you can to determine the tax consequences of this transaction. Do not attempt to answer any of the questions you raise. Simply identify the research issues.

81. Formulate a search query to determine whether your client is required to include in gross income the proceeds from redemption of a tax-exempt bond, purchased in 1988 and called by the school district this year. Redemption proceeds were $90,000, and the 1988 purchase price on the secondary market was $76,000. Give an example of a computer search query using only the following RIA Checkpoint connectors: "and," "or," "/n," and "not."

82. Formulate a search query to determine the provisions of the treaty between the United States and Germany relative to fellowship income received by a business student during a summer internship with the German Department of Price Controls. Give an example of a computer search query using only the following RIA Checkpoint connectors: "and," "or," "/n," and "not."

83. Formulate a search query to determine whether your client is required to capitalize fringe benefits and general overhead that is attributable to employees who are building an addition to your client's factory during a "slack time" at work. Give an example of a computer search query using only the following RIA Checkpoint connectors: "and," "or," "/n," and "not."

84. Formulate a search query to determine whether your client can retroactively elect to change its accounting method. Give an example of a computer search query using only the following RIA Checkpoint connectors: "and," "or," "/n," and "not."

85. Formulate a search query to find all of the cases in which the word constructive occurs within 10 words of the word dividend. Give an example of a computer query using only the following RIA Checkpoint connectors: "and," "or," "/n," and "not."

RESEARCH CASES

86. Sam Manuel has been employed on a full-time basis as an electrical engineer for the past three years. Prior to obtaining full-time employment, he was self-employed as an inventor of complex electronic components. During this period of self-employment, most of his projects produced little income, although several produced a significant amount of revenue.

    Due to the large expenditures necessary and the failure of the majority of the products to produce a profit, Sam was forced to seek full-time employment. After obtaining full-time employment, he continued to work long hours to perfect several of his inventions. He continued to enjoy relatively little success with most of his products, but certain projects were successfully marketed and generated a profit. For the past two years, Sam's invention activity has generated a net loss.

    a. List as many possible tax research issues as you can to determine whether the losses may be deducted.

    b. After completing your list of tax research issues, list the keywords you might use to construct a computer tax research query.

87. Matthew Broadway was a partner in the law firm of Johnson and Smith, a partnership of 20 partners, for the past 10 years. Without the knowledge or consent of the other partners, Matthew worked on a highly complicated acquisition and merger project for six months, at all times using the resources of the law firm. Several months later, the firm for which Matthew provided the professional services made out a check for $300,000 to the firm of Johnson and Smith. Matthew insisted that the fee should rightly be his, while the firm disputed his claim. Because of the dispute, the fee was held in escrow until the following year when the dispute was settled.

    The dispute was settled with Matthew agreeing to withdraw from the partnership. Included as part of the withdrawal agreement was a clause that specified he would receive $45,000 of the $300,000 fee, with the law firm retaining the remainder. Six months later, Matthew received a total payment of $125,000, which included the $45,000 fee, from Johnson and Smith.

    a. List as many possible tax research issues as you can to determine the tax treatment of the $125,000 payment received by Matthew.

    b. After completing your list of tax research issues, list the keywords you might use to construct a computer tax research query.

88. Juanita Sharp purchased a large parcel of property for $120,000. A short time after purchasing the property, Sharp submitted plans for the division of the parcel into six lots and the construction of three single-family residences on three of the lots. The city permits required that the property be divided into six lots and that street improvements and water and sewer access be provided. Sharp spent $22,000 for the street, water, and sewer improvements. As a result of the improvements, the value of each of the three vacant lots increased by $1,000, based on an appraisal completed subsequent to the completion of the improvements. The costs of constructing the three single-family residences totaled $200,000.

    a. List as many possible tax research issues as you can to determine how the original purchase price of $120,000, the $22,000 cost of the improvements, and the $200,000 cost of the construction of the homes should be allocated to the basis of each of the lots for purposes of determining gain or loss on the sale of the lots.

    b. After completing your list of tax research issues, list the keywords you might use to construct a computer tax research query.

89. Tom and Donna were divorced three years ago. At the time of their divorce, they owned a highly appreciated residence. Tom remained half-owner of the house, but he moved out and allowed Donna to continue living in the house. In the current year, Tom and Donna sold the house for $300,000. Last year, Tom purchased a new house for $190,000.

    a. List as many possible tax research issues as you can to determine tax treatment(s) available to Tom on the sale and purchase of the residence.

    b. After completing your list of tax research issues, list the keywords you might use to construct a computer tax research query.

90. Vincent Vineyard, MD, is a very successful physician in Temecula, California. He earns approximately $800,000 per year from his medical practice. His two children have graduated from college and he and his wife are now "empty-nesters." Vincent, Jr., is an officer in the Navy and his daughter Valerie is an engineer in Texas. Vinny has had an interest in wine and grape growing for many years. Now, with more time to devote to other activities, Vinny recently started a winery with an initial investment of $1,000,000. Since the winery is new, he expects it to be eight to 10 years before the winery makes a profit. Vinny would like your advice as to any potential tax problems he might have with his new winery investment.

    a. What additional information might you want in this situation?

    b. Where might that information come from?

    c. Are all the given facts pertinent? Which (if any) are irrelevant?

    d. What is the primary research question you would try to answer?

    e. Are there any additional research question(s) you want to address?

91. Ned Naive operated several franchised stores, and at the home office's suggestion he consolidated its payroll and accounting functions with Andy the Accountant. Andy is not a CPA. Last year, Andy began embezzling taxpayer's escrowed tax withholdings and failed to remit required amounts for the four quarters. The IRS assessed Ned penalties for failing to make the proper withholding deposits during the year.

    a. What additional information might you want in this situation?

    b. Where might that information come from?

    c. Are all the given facts pertinent? Which (if any) are irrelevant?

    d. Where might that information come from?

    e. What is the primary research question you would try to answer?

    f. Are there any additional research question(s) you want to address?

92. Dr. Diego Dissolution is recently divorced and has some questions regarding payments he is making to his ex-wife (Mrs. D.). Diego is 45 years old and has a successful dental practice. Mrs. D. was divorced from her first husband six years ago. Diego is paying $12,000 per month to Mrs. D. He wants to know if the tax payments on the $12,000 per month are deductible.

    a. What additional information might you want in this situation?

    b. Where might that information come from?

    c. Are all the given facts pertinent? Which (if any) are irrelevant?

    d. What is the primary research question you would try to answer?

    e. Are there any additional research question(s) you want to address?

93. Phred Phortunate won his state lotto two years ago. His lotto ticket was worth $10 million, which was payable in 20 annual installments of $500,000 each. Phred paid $1 for the winning ticket. The lotto in Phred's state does not allow winners to receive their payout in a lump sum. Phred wanted all of his money now, so he assigned his future lotto winnings to a Happy Finance Company for a discounted price of $4.5 million. Assignment of lotto winnings is permitted by Phred's state lotto. Phred filed his tax return and reported the assignment of the lotto winnings as a capital gain ($4.5 million–$1) taxable at a 15 percent rate.

    a. List as many possible tax research issues as you can to determine whether Phred correctly reported his lotto winnings.

    b. After completing your list of tax research issues, list the keywords you might use to construct a computer tax research query.

94. The Mucho Oro Indian Tribe operates a casino on its reservation in Arizona. The casino is very profitable, and therefore the tribe has excess money to invest. The tribe is approached by an entrepreneur who wants to build an outlet mall next to the casino. The entrepreneur would like to operate the outlet mall as an S corporation. Both he and the tribe would be shareholders in the new S corporation.

    a. List as many possible tax research issues as you can to determine whether this plan of organization would be allowed under the current tax law.

    b. After completing your list of tax research issues, list the keywords you might use to construct a computer tax research query.

95. Your client, Barney Green, and his wife, Edith, attended a three-day program in Honolulu, entitled "Financial, Tax, and Investment Planning for Investors." The Greens went to Hawaii several days early so that they could adjust to the jet lag and be ready for the seminar. The $3,000 cost of the trip included the following expenses.

First-class airfare	$1,200
Hotel (seven days)	800
Program fee	300
Meals and other expenses	700

The Greens have records to substantiate all of the above expenditures in a manner that is acceptable under §274.

    a. List as many possible tax research issues as you can to determine whether the Greens can deduct any or all of the $3,000 of expenditures on their current-year tax return.

    b. After completing your list of tax research issues, list the keywords you might use to construct a computer tax research query.

    c. Execute a computer search using your query. For simplicity, select the IRS Publications database from whichever computer tax service you use. Summarize your findings.

96. Ban Vallew has a son, Katt, by a previous marriage, who is in the custody of his ex-wife. Katt Vallew has a history of emotional disturbance, and he has been sent to a psychiatrist for several years for this problem. This year he has become so disturbed, manifesting violence at home and school, that he had to be sent to a special school in Arizona for problem children. This school is very expensive ($2,000 per month), the cost of which Ban pays for. Ban would like to determine whether he is entitled to the medical expenses deduction (over 7.5 percent of adjusted gross income) for the cost of sending his son to this special school.

    a. List as many possible tax research issues as you can to determine tax treatment(s) available to Ban on the payments to the special school.

    b. After completing your list of tax research issues, list the keywords you might use to construct a computer tax research query.

    c. Execute a computer search using your query. For simplicity, select the IRS Publications database from whichever computer tax service you use. Summarize your findings.

97. Linda Larue suffered from arthritis. Her chiropractor advised her that she needed to swim daily to alleviate her pain and other symptoms. Consequently, Linda and her husband, Philo, purchased for $100,000 a new home that had a swimming pool, after selling their old home for $85,000. If the Larues had constructed a pool at their former residence, it would have cost $15,000 to build, and it would have increased the value of their home by $8,000.

    a. List as many possible tax research issues as you can to determine whether the Larues can deduct any of their current-year expenditures for Linda's arthritis.

    b. After completing your list of tax research issues, list the keywords you might use to construct a computer tax research query.

    c. Execute a computer search using your query. For simplicity, select the IRS Revenue Rulings database from whichever computer tax service you use. Summarize your findings.

98. Gwen Gullible was married to Darrell Devious. They were divorced two years ago. Three years ago (the year before their divorce), Darrell received a $250,000 retirement plan distribution, of which $50,000 was rolled over into an IRA. At the time, Gwen was aware of the retirement funds and the rollover. The distribution was used to pay off the couple's mortgage, to purchase a car, and to cover living expenses. Darrell prepared the couple's joint return, and Gwen asked him about the tax ramifications of the retirement distributions. He told her he had consulted a CPA and was advised that the retirement plan proceeds used to pay off a mortgage were not taxable income. Gwen accepted that explanation and signed the return. In fact, Darrell had not consulted a CPA.

    One year ago (after the divorce), Gwen received a letter from the IRS saying they had not received the tax return for the last full year of marriage. On advice from a CPA, Gwen immediately filed the return (she had a copy of the unfiled return). The Internal Revenue Service notified Gwen that no estimated payments on the retirement distribution had been paid by Darrell, and that she owed $60,000 in tax, plus penalties and interest.

    a. List as many possible tax research issues as you can to determine whether Gwen is liable for the tax, interest, and penalties.

    b. After completing your list of tax research issues, list the keywords you might use to construct a computer tax research query.

    c. Execute a computer search using your query. For simplicity, select the IRS Revenue Rulings database from the computer tax service you use. Summarize your findings.

99. Several years ago, Maurice and Maureen (both Mo, for short) Morris, a married couple from Ohio, purchased a used piano at an auction sale for $150, and the piano was used by their daughter for piano lessons. In the current year, while cleaning the piano, Mo and Mo discovered $14,467 in cash tucked inside the piano. Being unable to ascertain who put the money there, after consulting with local authorities, the Morrises kept the $14,467 (which, in accordance with Ohio law, is legal).

    a. List as many possible tax research issues as you can to determine whether the Morrises are liable for any tax on the money they found. *Is it taxable? When? what kind of income?*

    b. After completing your list of tax research issues, list the keywords you might use to construct a computer tax research query. *"found money", "found income", "gross income", "property" "recognized year"*

    c. Execute a computer search using your query. For simplicity, select the IRS Publications database from whichever computer tax service you use. Summarize your findings. *if they keep the $, they recog income.*

100. Trevor just recently purchased a beautiful house on a hillside in sunny California at a cost of $1 million. One evening while enjoying a barbeque on his patio and after a particularly heavy rain, Trevor is surprised to see his neighbor's house disappear in a mudslide. Visibly shaken, Trevor makes immediate efforts to sell his home. Although the view from his lot has improved considerably, he meets severe buyer resistance when forced to explain why he lacks one set of neighbors. Trevor's best offer, made by a family just arrived in town, is $500,000. Trevor reevaluates his life insurance portfolio, places his personal affairs in order, and decides not to sell. Presuming the landslide caused no physical damage to his property; does Trevor have a casualty loss?

    a. List as many possible tax research issues as you can to determine Trevor's potential casualty loss deduction from the decrease in value of his house.

    b. After completing your list of tax research issues, list the keywords you might use to construct a computer tax research query.

    c. Execute a computer search using your query. For simplicity, select the IRS Publications database from whichever computer tax service you use. Summarize your findings.

97.

a) 1. Can a pool be considered a medical expense
*   -yes*
*   6. Does arthritus qualify*
*   2. what is their agi*
*   3 Basis of home sold*
*   4. How much can be deducted?*
*   5. when can they deduct?*
*   6. Are maintenance exp included?*
*   7. Is the basis of diagnosis important*

b) "medical expenditure", "swimming pool", "arthritus",

c) do on own

Primary Sources of Federal Tax Law

CHAPTER 3

Constitutional and Legislative Sources

LEARNING OBJECTIVES

- Outline the primary and secondary sources of the Federal tax law.
- Describe in detail the nature and structure of the statutory sources of the tax law, including the Constitution, tax treaties, and the Internal Revenue Code.
- Delineate how statutory tax law is created and how tax research resources are generated in this process.
- Determine how to locate the statutory sources of the tax law.
- Discuss how the tax researcher can carefully interpret the Internal Revenue Code.

CHAPTER OUTLINE

Questions about income taxation, unlike many other areas of law, are based primarily in the underlying statute. As a result, the first step in locating potential authority in a tax matter usually consists of identifying the pertinent Code section(s). The current statutory source is in the Internal Revenue Code (IRC) of 1986. In addition, a tax researcher may need to examine the legislative history of a tax provision. Furthermore, it may be necessary to understand the constitutional foundation and associated tax treaties that may affect the Code section(s) in question.

In this chapter, we take a closer look at the tax research process and how the primary tax law sources are used to help the tax researcher arrive at a solution to his or her client's tax problems.

Tax professionals utilize three primary sources of the tax law, mirroring the constitutional division of the function of the Federal government. The three sources are as follows:

- Statutory sources, or the legislative branch.

- Administrative sources, or the executive branch.

- Judicial sources, or the judicial branch.

Thus, the constitutional and legislative tax sources often are referred to as the "**statutory sources**."

Sources of Federal Tax Law

As mentioned in the previous chapter, the sources of the Federal tax law can be classified as **primary authorities** or **secondary authorities**. Chapters 3 through 5 of this text include detailed examination of the primary authorities and their use in the tax research process. The sources of the Federal tax law to be examined here and in the next two chapters are presented in outline form in Exhibit 3-1. In Chapter 3 we examine the statutory sources of the U.S. Constitution, tax treaties, and the Internal Revenue Code. The reader should refer to this outline while reading this text to maintain perspective as to the relationships between each of the sources discussed.

History of U.S. Taxation

Although the Massachusetts Bay Colony enacted an income tax law in 1643, the first U.S. income tax was not created until the Civil War. An income tax law was passed at that time to help the North pay for the cost of fighting the war. This Federal income tax law was passed on August 5, 1861. The tax was not generally enforced, but some limited collections were made under the law.

This first Federal income tax was levied at the rate of a modest 3 percent on income between $600 and $10,000, and 5 percent on marginal incomes in excess of $10,000. Later, in 1867, the rate was a flat 5 percent of income in excess of $1,000. The Civil War income taxes were allowed to expire in 1872. In 1894 another income tax act was passed by Congress. By this time, however, the income tax had become an important political issue. The southern and western states generally favored the tax, and the eastern states generally opposed it. The tax had developed into an important element of the Populist political movement. In *Pollock v. Farmers' Loan and Trust Co.*, 157 U.S. 429,

EXHIBIT 3-1: Framework of Primary Sources of Federal Tax Law

Statutory Sources (Chapter 3)	Judicial Sources (Chapter 5)
• U.S. Constitution	• Supreme Court
• Tax Treaties	• Courts of Appeals
• Internal Revenue Code	• District Courts
Administrative Sources (Chapter 4)	• U.S. Court of Federal Claims
• Treasury Regulations	• Tax Court
• Revenue Rulings	• Tax Court, Small Cases Division
• Revenue Procedures	
• Other written determinations	
• Miscellaneous IRS publications	

15 S.Ct. 673 (1895), the Supreme Court held that the income tax was unconstitutional because it was a constitutionally prohibited "direct tax."

The supporters of the income tax decided to amend the Constitution so that there would be no question as to the constitutionality of a Federal income tax, applying progressive rates to diverse sources of income. The proposed amendment was sent to the states on July 12, 1909, by the Sixty-First Congress; it was ratified on February 3, 1913. The new Sixteenth Amendment to the Constitution stated:

The Congress shall have the power to lay and collect taxes on incomes, from whatever source derived, without apportionment among the several States, and without regard to any census or enumeration.

A copy of a 1913 individual tax return (Form 1040) is shown in Exhibit 3-2. It should be noted that individual taxpayers were allowed a $3,000 ($4,000 for married taxpayers) "specific exemption" before they had to start paying income tax at a 1 percent rate. The 1 percent bracket went up to $20,000 of taxable income before a surtax of an additional 1 percent was added. The surtax eventually reached 6 percent at a taxable income of $500,000. Thus, the maximum marginal tax rate in 1913 was 7 percent (1 percent regular tax plus 6 percent surtax).

The 1913 specific exemption is similar to the current standard deduction. If $3,000 in 1913 were price-level adjusted into today's dollars, it would be more than $63,000. Thus, an individual taxpayer would not pay any Federal income tax until he or she showed taxable income of over $63,000 if an equivalent exemption were in place today.

Before the Sixteenth Amendment was ratified, Congress passed a corporate income tax in 1909. This tax also was challenged at the Supreme Court level, in *Flint v. Stone Tracy Co*, 220 U.S. 107, 31 S.Ct. 342 (1911). The Court held that this tax was constitutional because it was a special form of excise tax on the privilege of operating in the corporate form, using income as its base, rather than a (prohibited) direct income tax.

EXHIBIT 3-2: 1913 Individual Form 1040

TO BE FILLED IN BY COLLECTOR.	Form 1040.	TO BE FILLED IN BY INTERNAL REVENUE BUREAU.
List. No.	**INCOME TAX.**	*File No.* ....
.... *District of*	**THE PENALTY** FOR FAILURE TO HAVE THIS RETURN IN THE HANDS OF THE COLLECTOR OF INTERNAL REVENUE ON OR BEFORE MARCH 1 IS $20 TO $1,000.	*Assessment List* ....
Date received	(SEE INSTRUCTIONS ON PAGE 4.)	*Page* .... *Line* ....

UNITED STATES INTERNAL REVENUE.

RETURN OF ANNUAL NET INCOME OF INDIVIDUALS.

(As provided by Act of Congress, approved October 3, 1913.)

RETURN OF NET INCOME RECEIVED OR ACCRUED DURING THE YEAR ENDED DECEMBER 31, 191 ....

(FOR THE YEAR 1913, FROM MARCH 1, TO DECEMBER 31.)

Filed by (or for) .... (Full name of individual.) *of* .... (Street and No.)

in the City, Town, or Post Office of .... *State of* ....

(Fill in pages 2 and 3 before making entries below.)

1. GROSS INCOME (see page 2, line 12) . . . . $
2. GENERAL DEDUCTIONS (see page 3, line 7) . . . . $
3. NET INCOME . . . . $

Deductions and exemptions allowed in computing income subject to the normal tax of 1 per cent.

4. Dividends and net earnings received or accrued, of corporations, etc., subject to like tax. (See page 2, line 11) $
5. Amount of income on which the normal tax has been deducted and withheld at the source. (See page 2, line 9, column A)
6. Specific exemption of $3,000 or $4,000, as the case may be. (See Instructions 3 and 19) . . . .

Total deductions and exemptions. (Items 4, 5, and 6) . . . . $

7. TAXABLE INCOME on which the normal tax of 1 per cent is to be calculated. (See Instruction 3) . $
8. When the net income shown above on line 3 exceeds $20,000, the additional tax thereon must be calculated as per schedule below:

		INCOME.	TAX.
1	per cent on amount over $20,000 and not exceeding $50,000 .	$	$
2	" " 50,000 " " 75,000 .		
3	" " 75,000 " " 100,000 .		
4	" " 100,000 " " 250,000 .		
5	" " 250,000 " " 500,000 .		
6	" " 500,000		

Total additional or super tax . . . . $
Total normal tax (1 per cent of amount entered on line 7) . . $
Total tax liability . . . . $

Who Pays the Income Tax?

Historically, the 1913 income tax was strictly a tax on wealthy and high-income taxpayers (i.e., a "select tax"). The original post-Sixteenth Amendment income tax applied to less than 1 percent of the population (i.e., 1 in every 271 adults). It was not until the end of World War II that the income tax became a broad-based tax that applied to the majority of the population (i.e., a "mass tax"). However, the percentage of taxpayers who do not pay federal income tax is on the rise.

As of 2009, roughly 47 percent of households did not pay any Federal income tax.[1] Some in that group received additional money from the government because they qualified for refundable tax breaks. The vast majority of households making up to $30,000 do not pay Federal income taxes, as do nearly half of all households making between $30,000 and $40,000. The percentages drop as you move up the income scale. Twenty-two percent of those making between $50,000 and $75,000 end up with no Federal income tax liability, as do 9 percent of households with incomes between $75,000 and $100,000.

SPOTLIGHT ON TAXATION

Quotation

"Taxes are the dues that we pay for the privileges of membership in an organized society."

—Franklin D. Roosevelt

Tax Protesters

In recent years, the income tax has been attacked in the courts on the basis that it is unconstitutional. For instance, some protesters have asserted that since the U.S. currency is no longer based on the gold standard, the Sixteenth Amendment's measure of income, and therefore the tax itself, is invalid. Others have asserted that the Federal income tax law forces the taxpayer to surrender his or her Fifth Amendment rights against self-incrimination. Federal courts, however, have denied virtually all of the protesters' challenges.

Congress has passed several laws to discourage tax protesters. For instance, a taxpayer is subject to a $5,000 fine if he or she files a "frivolous" tax return as a form of protest against the IRS or the U.S. budgetary process. This fine would be levied, for example, when the taxpayer files a blank tax return accompanied by a note suggesting that the Federal income tax is unconstitutional or that the taxpayer wishes to protest against tax revenues going to the creation of nuclear weapons. A number of lower courts have upheld the constitutionality of this fine [e.g., *Schull*, 842 USTC ¶ 9529 (D.C., Va.)].

The Tax Court can impose a penalty, not to exceed $25,000, if the taxpayer brings a "frivolous" matter before the Court. Under §§6673 and 6702, a frivolous matter is where the intent is to delay the revenue collection process and where the proceedings are found to be groundless, or where the taxpayer unreasonably failed to pursue available administrative remedies. Sanctions can also be imposed against tax practitioners who participate in the litigation of frivolous tax return positions.

U.S. Constitution

The Constitution of the United States is the source of all Federal laws of the country, including both tax and non-tax provisions. In addition to the Sixteenth Amendment, however, the Constitution contains other provisions that bear upon the taxation process. For example, the Constitution provides that Congress may impose import taxes but not export taxes. Moreover, the constitutional rights of due process and of the privacy of the citizen apply in tax, as well as non-tax, environments.

---

[1]http://money.cnn.com/2009/09/30/pf/taxes/who_pays_taxes/index.htm

The Constitution also requires that taxes imposed by Congress apply uniformly throughout the United States. For instance, it would be unconstitutional for Congress to impose one Federal income tax rate in California and another rate in Vermont. Moreover, except as provided by the Sixteenth Amendment, the Constitution still bars per capita and other direct taxes, unless the revenues that are generated from these taxes are apportioned to the population of the states from which they were collected.

The Federal courts have upheld the constitutionality of the estate and gift taxes because they are in the form of excise taxes on (the transfer of) property rather than direct taxes on individuals. Thus, one can conclude that, for better or worse, most future judicial challenges to the constitutionality of the elements of the Federal tax structure probably will be fruitless.

One can find copies of the U.S. Constitution in many textbooks, encyclopedias, dictionaries, and in publications such as *The World Almanac* and *Wikipedia*. The Constitution is also reproduced in Volume One of the United States Code, as published by the Government Printing Office.

An excerpt from the U.S. Constitution can be found in Exhibit 3-3. The Constitution can also be found at various Internet sites. An example of such a site is **www. archives.gov**.

Tax Treaties

Tax treaties are agreements negotiated between countries concerning the treatment of entities subject to tax in both countries. The United States has entered into treaties with most of the major Western countries of the world. The overriding purpose of such treaties (also known as tax conventions) is to eliminate the "double taxation" that the taxpayer would face if his or her income were subject to tax in both countries. In such a case, a U.S. citizen who has generated income from an investment in the United Kingdom usually would be allowed a credit on her U.S. income tax return to the extent of any related U.K. taxes that she paid.

Any tax matter can be covered in a tax treaty with another country. Many times, there are multiple tax treaties with a given country. For example, one treaty will address income tax issues, while another treaty covers estate tax, and a third treaty addresses excise taxes. An example of a portion of a tax treaty is shown as Exhibit 3-4.

In addition to the tax treaties, the U.S. government enters into non-tax international agreements that are not formal tax treaties; however, in many respects they function like one. Along with other provisions, these agreements address tax issues involving the parties associated with the agreement. Examples of such international agreements include the North American Free Trade Agreement (NAFTA) and the General Agreement on Tariffs and Trade (GATT). Other agreements might address the exchange of tax, banking, and securities information among citizens of one or more countries.

Treaties are an important source of Federal law. Most treaties do not address tax issues, but the ones that do have a far-reaching effect. When dealing with a research problem that has international connotations, the researcher must locate, read, and evaluate any tax treaty that applies to the client's problem. The researcher cannot rely on the more typical sources of tax research information because these references usually address only domestic tax precedents. Tax treaties often address issues such as the following:

- How to treat the business and investment income of the visiting taxpayer.

- When the visitor is subject to the host country's tax laws.

- How to offset the possibility of taxing the same income or assets more than once.

- How to compute the taxable amount in the host country.

- To what extent host-country withholding taxes are applied to the visitor's transactions.

- How taxes levied by a state/province/canton are treated by the taxpayer.

- What tax disclosures must be made by the visitor.

EXHIBIT 3-3: United States Constitution Excerpt (with original spelling)

WE THE PEOPLE of the United States, in Order to form a more perfect Union, establish Justice, insure domestic Tranquility, provide for the common defence (sic), promote the general Welfare, and secure the Blessings of Liberty to ourselves and our Posterity, do ordain and establish this Constitution for the United States of America.

Article I

Section. 1. All legislative Powers herein granted shall be vested in a Congress of the United States, which shall consist of a Senate and House of Representatives.

Section. 2. The House of Representatives shall be composed of Members chosen every second Year by the People of the several States, and the Electors in each State shall have the Qualifications requisite for Electors of the most numerous Branch of the State Legislature.

No Person shall be a Representative who shall not have attained to the Age of twenty five Years, and been seven Years a Citizen of the United States, and who shall not, when elected, be an Inhabitant of that State in which he shall be chosen.

Representatives and direct Taxes shall be apportioned among the several States which may be included within this Union, according to their respective Numbers, which shall be determined by adding to the whole Number of free Persons, including those bound to Service for a Term of Years, and excluding Indians not taxed, three fifths of all other Persons. The actual Enumeration shall be made within three Years after the first Meeting of the Congress of the United States, and within every subsequent Term of ten Years, in such Manner as they shall by Law direct. The Number of Representatives shall not exceed one for every thirty Thousand, but each State shall have at Least one Representative; and until such enumeration shall be made, the State of New Hampshire shall be entitled to chuse (sic) three, Massachusetts eight, Rhode Island and Providence Plantations one, Connecticut five, New York six, New Jersey four, Pennsylvania eight, Delaware one, Maryland six, Virginia ten, North Carolina five, South Carolina five, and Georgia three.

When vacancies happen in the Representation from any State, the Executive Authority thereof shall issue Writs of Election to fill such Vacancies.

The House of Representatives shall chuse (sic) their Speaker and other Officers; and shall have the sole Power of Impeachment.

Section. 3. The Senate of the United States shall be composed of two Senators from each State, chosen by the Legislature thereof, for six Years; and each Senator shall have one Vote.

Immediately after they shall be assembled in Consequence of the first Election, they shall be divided as equally as may be into three Classes. The Seats of the Senators of the first Class shall be vacated at the Expiration of the second Year, of the second Class at the Expiration of the fourth Year, and of the third Class at the Expiration of the sixth Year, so that one third may be chosen every second Year; and if Vacancies happen by Resignation, or otherwise, during the Recess of the Legislature of any State, the Executive thereof may make temporary Appointments until the next Meeting of the Legislature, which shall then fill such Vacancies.

No Person shall be a Senator who shall not have attained to the Age of thirty Years, and been nine Years a Citizen of the United States, and who shall not, when elected, be an Inhabitant of that State for which he shall be chosen.

The Vice President of the United States shall be President of the Senate, but shall have no Vote, unless they be equally divided.

EXHIBIT 3-4: A Portion of a Tax Treaty

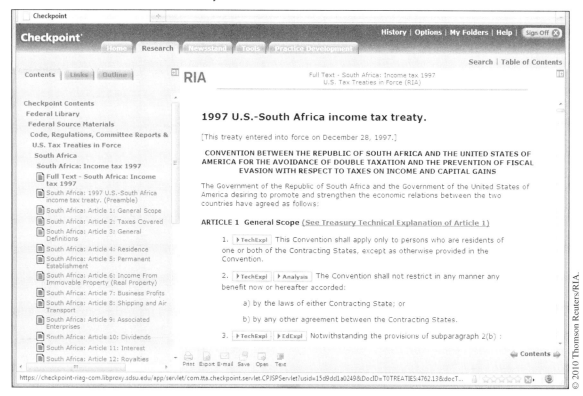

The Constitution provides that "Laws of the United States which shall be made in pursuance thereof; and all Treaties made, or which shall be made, under the Authority of the United States, shall be the supreme Law of the Land." An Internal Revenue Code provision and a provision under a treaty will sometimes conflict. In such a case, both of the provisions cannot represent the law; the one adopted later in time generally controls.

EXAMPLE **3-1**

Prior to 1980, the United States negotiated treaties with several countries that allowed foreign taxpayers to sell U.S. real estate and not pay tax on gains. Under these treaties, nonresident aliens and foreign corporations could avoid U.S. taxes on real estate if the gains were treated as capital gains and were not effectively connected with the conduct of a U.S. business. Because of this favorable treatment for foreign investors, many U.S. farmers felt foreign investors were bidding up the price of farmland in the United States.

This and other concerns led Congress to pass the Foreign Investment in Real Property Tax Act (FIRPTA) of 1980. Under §897, FIRPTA makes gains and losses by nonresident aliens and foreign corporations taxable by treating such transactions as effectively connected with a U.S. trade or business. This provision overrides any treaties in effect at that time by making foreign capital gains on real property taxable for transactions after 1984. If an existing treaty was renegotiated prior to 1985, the new treaty could designate a different effective date for §897; however, the designated effective date could not be more than two years after the signing of the renegotiated treaty.

This later-in-time rule appears to be a simplistic approach to the complex interaction of the Code and treaty provisions. The courts have presented interpretive guidelines to be used in resolving inter-statutory conflicts. One such guideline is that, where possible, equal effect should be given to both statutes; congressional intent to repeal a statute should not be assumed. A significant judicial history also exists for the interaction of treaties and the Code. In fact, as with conflicts between statutes, courts usually attempt to reconcile the apparent conflict in a way that gives consideration to both the treaty and the Code provisions.

The equality of the two types of provisions is indicated in §7852(d) of the Code, which provides that neither a treaty nor a law shall be given preferential status by reason of its being a treaty or a law. The language of both the Code and the Constitution make this clear. The only codified exception to this rule is that treaty provisions in effect in 1954 and which conflicted with the 1954 Code as originally enacted are given precedence over the existing provisions of the 1954 Code, but not over later amendments to the Code. Section 894 states that due regard shall be given to any treaty obligation of the United States that applies to the taxpayer when applying the provisions of the Internal Revenue Code.

Treaties are authorized by the U.S. Constitution. Under Article II, Section 2, of the Constitution, the President of the United States is allowed to enter into treaties with other countries after receiving the advice and consent of the Senate. The President may also enter into other international agreements that have effects on the Federal tax structure. Such agreements need not be ratified by the Senate; however, they are implemented by Congress in accordance with existing Federal laws. However, tax treaties usually are initiated by the State Department, not the Treasury. Generally, tax treaties do not address the U.S. state and local tax effects of the citizens and transactions covered by them.

Treaties may be terminated in several ways. They may expire because of a specific congressional time limitation, be superseded by a newer treaty, or be terminated by the countries' mutual actions.

Tax researchers often find it necessary to examine the provisions of tax treaties. Tax treaties can be found in both the online and printed versions of most tax services, at the government Web sites of many countries, and in many legal publications such as West's *United States Code Annotated*.

The Legislative Process

To understand how to research tax issues, the tax researcher must have a grasp of the Federal legislative process. The tax law of the United States, like automobiles and hot dogs, is created in a multi-step process. At each stage in the creation of a tax law, Congress generates additional items of information, each of which may be useful in addressing a client's tax problem.

Most tax legislation begins in the House of Representatives. In the House, tax law changes are considered by the **Ways and Means Committee**. Upon approval by this committee, the bill is sent to the full House of Representatives for its approval. The bill then is sent to the Senate, where it is referred to the **Finance Committee**. When the Finance Committee approves the bill, the proposal is considered by the entire Senate.

If any differences between the House and Senate versions of the tax bill exist (which is almost always the case), the bill is referred to a **Joint Conference Committee**, where these differences are resolved. The compromise bill must be approved by both houses of

EXHIBIT 3-5:   Legislative Process to Amend the Tax Law

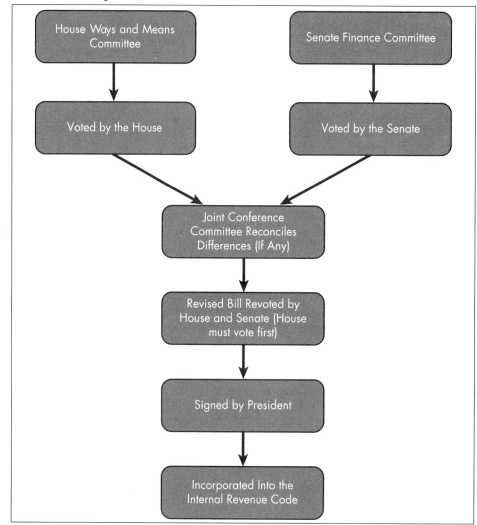

Congress before it is forwarded to the President. If the President signs the bill, the new provisions are incorporated into the Internal Revenue Code. If the bill is vetoed by the President, however, it is not enacted unless Congress overrides the veto with a sufficient revote. Exhibit 3-5 summarizes the usual steps of the legislative process as it is encountered relative to tax legislation.

At each step in the legislative process, the appropriate committee of Congress produces a **Committee Report**, which explains the elements of the proposed changes and the reasons for each of the proposals. These Committee Reports are an important tool for tax researchers. In many situations where the tax law is unclear, or when recent legislation has been passed, they can provide insight concerning the meaning of a specific phrase of the statute or of the intention of Congress concerning a certain provision of the law. Committee Reports typically result from the deliberations of the Ways and Means Committee, the Finance Committee, and the Joint Conference Committee. A "General Explanation" of tax legislation occasionally is prepared by the Joint Committee on Taxation (the "Blue Book"). Exhibit 3-6 reproduces a portion of such a Committee Report.

EXHIBIT 3-6: Committee Report

Conference Report 107-84: ECONOMIC GROWTH AND TAX RELIEF RECONCILIATION ACT OF 2001, PL 107-16

Present Law
Under the Code, gross income means, "Income from whatever source derived" except for certain items specifically exempt or excluded by statute (sec. 61). There is no explicit statutory exception from gross income provided for amounts received by Holocaust victims or their heirs.

House Bill
No provision.

Senate Amendment
The Senate amendment provides that excludible restitution payments made to an eligible individual (or the individual's heirs or estate) are: (1) excluded from gross income; and (2) not taken into account for any provision of the Code which takes into account excludable gross income in computing adjusted gross income (e.g., taxation of Social Security benefits).

The basis of any property received by an eligible individual (or the individual's heirs or estate) that is excluded under this provision is the fair market value of such property at the time of receipt by the eligible individual (or the individual's heirs or estate).

The Senate amendment provides that any excludible restitution payment is disregarded in determining eligibility for, and the amount of benefits and services to be provided under, any Federal or federally assisted program which provides benefit or service based, in whole or in part, on need. Under the Senate amendment, no officer, agency, or instrumentality of any government may attempt to recover the value of excessive benefits or services provided under such a program before January 1, 2000, by reason of failure to take account of excludible restitution payments received before that date. Similarly, the Senate amendment requires a good faith effort to notify any eligible individual who may have been denied such benefits or services of their potential eligibility for such benefits or services. The Senate amendment also provides coordination between this bill and Public Law 103-286, which also disregarded certain restitution payments in determining eligibility for, and the amount of certain needs-based benefits and services.

Eligible restitution payments are any payment or distribution made to an eligible individual (or the individual's heirs or estate) which: (1) is payable by reason of the individual's status as an eligible individual (including any amount payable by any foreign country, the United States, or any foreign or domestic entity or fund established by any such country or entity, any amount payable as a result of a final resolution of legal action, and any amount payable under a law providing for payments or restitution of property); (2) constitutes the direct or indirect return of, or compensation or reparation for, assets stolen or hidden, or otherwise lost to, the individual before, during, or immediately after World War II by reason of the individual's status as an eligible individual (including any proceeds of insurance under policies issued on eligible individuals by European insurance companies immediately before and during World War II); or (3) interest payable as part of any payment or distribution described in (1) or (2), above. An eligible individual is a person who was persecuted for racial or religious reasons by Nazi Germany, or any other Axis regime, or any other Nazi-controlled or Nazi-allied country.

Effective Date
The provision is effective for any amounts received on or after January 1, 2000. No inference is intended with respect to the income tax treatment of any amount received before January 1, 2000.

Conference Agreement
The conference agreement follows the Senate amendment, with three changes. First, the definition of eligible individuals is expanded to also include individuals persecuted on the basis of physical or mental disability or sexual orientation. Second, interest earned by enumerated escrow or settlement funds are also excluded from tax. Third, the provision disregarding excludible restitution in determining eligibility for and the benefit calculation of certain Federal or Federally assisted programs is deleted.

To convert a session number into the second year of the applicable congressional session, multiply the session number by 2 and subtract 212 (the number of years from 1788 to 2000). For example, the second year of the one-hundred-ninth Congress is 2006 [(109 × 2) 212 = 06].

Committee Reports generally are referred to by Public Law number. Every bill that Congress passes is assigned such a number. For example, the Tax Reform Act of 1986 was designated as P.L. 99-514. Public Law is abbreviated as "P.L." in this context. The prefix of the numerical designation (here, 99) refers to the session of Congress that passed the law. The suffix of the Public Law number (here, 514) indicates that this was the five-hundred-fourteenth bill that this session of Congress adopted.

Congressional sessions last for two years; therefore, the researcher may find it useful to construct a method by which to identify the two-year period in which a tax law was passed. Recent and forthcoming sessions of Congress are identified as follows:

Congressional Sessions	Years
One-hundred-ninth	2005–06
One-hundred-tenth	2007–08
One-hundred-eleventh	2009–10
One-hundred-twelfth	2011–12
One-hundred-thirteenth	2013-14

Where to Find Committee Reports

When a new tax law is passed, the pertinent Committee Reports are released in the Internal Revenue Service's weekly Internal Revenue Bulletin. The texts of the 1954 Committee Reports relative to the Internal Revenue Code are found not in the Cumulative Bulletin, but in the United States Code Congressional and Administrative News. All of the pre-1939 Revenue Act Committee Reports are reprinted in the 1939 Cumulative Bulletin.

The Committee Reports and other legislative items can also be found in most subscription online tax services (e.g., RIA Checkpoint) and on various non-subscription Internet sites such as the following:

- **http://thomas.loc.gov**

- **http://waysandmeans.house.gov**

- **http://finance.senate.gov/**

CCH and RIA both publish a collection of Committee Reports (or excerpts thereof) whenever a major new tax law is passed. If a tax researcher wants to find the Committee Reports that underlie a statutory provision, he or she also can use reference materials that are included in the bodies of most of the commercial tax services or in the index to the Cumulative Bulletin.

The Committee Reports Findings List in CCH's Citator, Volume M–Z, is a good place for the tax researcher to locate Committee Reports by P.L. number. See Chapter 7 of this text for a detailed review of the use of citators.

In addition to the Committee Reports, the Floor Debate Report may be of value to the tax researcher. The Floor Debate Report includes a summary of what was said from the floor of the House or Senate concerning the proposed bill. It may include some detailed or technical information that is excluded from the Committee Report. The Floor Debate Report is included in the Congressional Record for the day of the debate.

Internal Revenue Code

After the Sixteenth Amendment was ratified in 1913, Congress passed a series of self-contained revenue acts, each of which formed the entire income tax law of the United States. For about two decades, Congress passed such a free-standing revenue act every year or two. By the 1930s, however, this series of revenue acts, and the task of rewriting the entire tax statute so often, had become unmanageable. Thus, in 1939, Congress replaced the revenue acts with the Internal Revenue Code of 1939, the first fully organized Federal tax law.

Although the concept of a freestanding tax Code, as part of the entire United States Code, was a good idea, the organization of the Internal Revenue Code of 1939 left little room to accommodate subsequent changes to the law. Accordingly, the 1939 Code was replaced with a reorganized, more flexible codification in 1954. Due to extensive revisions to the Code that were made as part of the Tax Reform Act of 1986, the statute was renamed the Internal Revenue Code of 1986. Thus, although the statute still follows the 1954 numbering system and organization, the official title of the extant U.S. tax law is the Internal Revenue Code of 1986, as Amended.

The principal sources of tax laws of the United States since 1913, then, have been identified as follows:

Period	Principal U.S. Tax Law
1913–39	Periodic Revenue Acts
1939–54	Internal Revenue Code of 1939
1954–86	Internal Revenue Code of 1954
1986–Present	Internal Revenue Code of 1986

Many provisions of the 1939 Code were carried over to the Internal Revenue Code of 1954 without substantive change; some of these sections were adopted into the Code verbatim, although all of the sections were renumbered as part of the 1954 reorganization.

SPOTLIGHT ON TAXATION

Growth of the Code

If you think the tax law is getting more complex, you are correct. According to the Tax Foundation, in 1955 the Internal Revenue Code contained 106 Code sections and 409,000 words. Today there are about 1,000 Code sections containing more than 2,139,000 words.

The **Internal Revenue Code** is part of the United States Code, which is a codification of all of the Federal laws of the United States. The elements of the United States Code are organized alphabetically and assigned title numbers. Accordingly, the Internal Revenue Code constitutes Title 26 of the United States Code; its neighbors in the U.S. Code at one time included "Insane Asylums" and "Intoxicating Liquors."

Organization of the Internal Revenue Code

The Internal Revenue Code is organized into an outline form with multiple levels or subdivisions. The primary levels found in the Code are as follows.

    Subtitles
      Chapters
        Subchapters
          Parts
            Sections
              Subsections

Subtitles of the Code are assigned a capital letter to identify them (currently A through K are used). Generally, each subtitle contains all of the tax provisions that relate to a well-defined area of the tax law. Exhibit 3-7 identifies the subtitles of the current Code. The tax researcher spends most of his or her time working with Subtitles A, Income Taxes; B, Estate and Gift Taxes; and F, Procedure and Administration. The other subtitles typically are used only from time to time for special research problems.

Each subtitle contains a number of chapters, numbered, although not continuously, from 1 through 100. These chapter numbers do not start over at each subtitle; rather, they are used in ascending order throughout the Code. Thus, for example, there is only one Chapter 11 in the Internal Revenue Code, not 11 of them. Each chapter contains the tax provisions that relate to a more narrowly defined area of the tax law than is addressed by the subtitles. Most of the subtitles include several chapters. Exhibit 3-8 examines the numbering system of the chapters of the Internal Revenue Code, concentrating on selected important chapters.

The chapters of the Internal Revenue Code are further divided into subchapters. Typically a subchapter contains a group of provisions that relate to a fairly specific area of the tax law. Subchapters sometimes are divided into parts, which may be divided into subparts. Letters are used to denote subchapters, and the lettering scheme starts over with each chapter. Thus, there may be a Subchapter A in each chapter.

EXHIBIT 3-7:   Subtitles of the Internal Revenue Code, as Amended

Subtitle	Tax Law Included
A	Income Taxes
B	Estate and Gift Taxes
C	Employment Taxes
D	Miscellaneous Excise Taxes
E	Alcohol; Tobacco; Miscellaneous Excise Taxes
F	Procedure and Administration
G	Joint Committee on Taxation
H	Presidential Election Campaign Financing
I	Trust Funds

EXHIBIT 3-8:   Key Chapters of the Internal Revenue Code

Chapter	Subjects Included
1	Normal Taxes and Surtaxes
2	Self-Employment Tax
6	Consolidated Returns
11	Estate Taxes
12	Gift Taxes
61	Administration/Information
79	Definitions

Many times, tax practitioners use the subchapter designation as a shorthand reference to identify a certain area of taxation. For example, Subchapter C of Chapter 1 of Subtitle A of the Internal Revenue Code includes many of the basic corporate income tax provisions. Thus, when a tax practitioner wants to refer to a corporate tax matter, he or she often simply identifies it as a "Subchapter C" issue.

EXHIBIT 3-9: Subtitle A: Table of Contents Excerpt

Subtitle A Income Taxes §§1-1564
  Chapter 1 Normal Taxes and Surtaxes §§1-1400t
    Subchapter A Determination of Tax Liability §§1-59b
      Part I Tax on Individuals §§1-5
      Part II Tax on Corporations §§11-12
      Part III Changes in Rates During a Taxable Year §§15-15
      Part IV Credits Against Tax §§21-54
      Part VI Alternative Minimum Tax §§55-59
      Part VII Environmental Tax §§59a-59a
      Part VIII Supplemental Medicare Premium [Repealed] §§59b-59b
    Subchapter B Computation of Taxable Income §§61-291
      Part I Definition of Gross Income, Adjusted Gross Income, Taxable
        Income, Etc. §§61-68
      Part II Items Specifically Included in Gross Income §§71-90
      Part III Items Specifically Excluded from Gross Income §§101-140
      Part IV Tax Exemption Requirements for State and Local Bonds
      §§141-150
      Part V Deductions for Personal Exemptions §§151-153
      Part VI Itemized Deductions for Individuals and Corporations §§161-199
      Part VII Additional Itemized Deductions for Individuals §§211-224
      Part VIII Special Deductions for Corporations §§241-249
      Part IX Items Not Deductible §§261-280h
      Part X Terminal Railroad Corporations and Their Shareholders §§281-281
      Part XI Special Rules Relating to Corporate Preference Items §§291-291
    Subchapter C Corporate Distributions and Adjustments §§301-385
    Subchapter D Deferred Compensation, etc. §§401-436
    Subchapter E Accounting Periods and Methods of Accounting §§441-483
    Subchapter F Exempt Organizations §§501-530
    Subchapter G Corporations used to Avoid Income Tax on Shareholders §§531-565
    Subchapter H Banking Institutions §§581-597
    Subchapter I Natural Resources §§611-638
    Subchapter J Estates, Trusts, Beneficiaries, and Decedents §§641-692
    Subchapter K Partners and Partnerships §§701-777
    Subchapter L Insurance Companies §§801-848
    Subchapter M Regulated Investment Companies and Real Estate Investment Trusts
      §§851-860L
    Subchapter N Tax Based on Income from Sources within or without the United States
      §§861-999
    Subchapter O Gain or Loss on Disposition of Property §§1001-1111
    Subchapter P Capital Gains and Losses §§1201-1298
    Subchapter Q Readjustment of Tax between Years and Special Limitations
      §§1301-1351
    Subchapter R Election to Determine Corporate Tax on Certain International
      Shipping … §§1352-1359
    Subchapter S Tax Treatment of S Corporations and Their Shareholders §§1361-1379

Most of the Code's subchapters are divided into parts. The parts provide a natural grouping of provisions that address essentially the same issue. Not all sub-chapters are divided into parts, and occasionally the parts are not numbered consecutively. For instance, the parts of Chapter 1, Subchapter A (i.e., normal income taxes) are as follows:

Part I	Tax on Individuals
Part II	Tax on Corporations
Part III	Changes in Rates during a Taxable Year
Part IV	Credits against Tax
Part V	Not Used
Part VI	Alternative Minimum Tax
Part VII	Environmental Tax

Exhibit 3-9 shows the Table of Contents to Subtitle A (Income Taxes) of the Code with the "Parts" level shown for Subchapters A, B, and C. To save space, the "Parts" level is not shown for the other subchapters.

The most important division of the Internal Revenue Code for the tax researcher is the section, because the Code is arranged so that its primary unit is the section number. The sections currently are numbered 1 through 9833, although not all of the numbers are used. Each section number is used only once in the Code. The researcher can refer to a specific provision of the Internal Revenue Code by its section number and not be concerned about duplication in another part of the law. Indeed, the most common element of the jargon of the tax practitioner community is the Code section number, and tax researchers must learn to identify important tax provisions merely by the corresponding section number.

Code sections can be divided into various smaller elements for the convenience of the drafter or user of the section. A section can contain subsections, paragraphs, subparagraphs, and clauses. Sections are denoted by numbers (1, 2, etc.), subsections by lowercase letters (a, b, etc.), paragraphs by numbers, subparagraphs by capital letters (A, B, etc.), and clauses by lowercase roman numerals (i, ii, etc.). In citing a Code section, one uses parentheses for each division that occurs after the section number.

There are some exceptions to the general formatting of Code section citations. For example, Congress has inserted Code sections in between other consecutive sections and has had to use a capital letter [e.g., Section 25A(b)(1) or Section 280F (a)(1)] to accomplish this. The Code skips the subsections in certain cases, such as Section 212(2). Exhibit 3-10 provides a specific interpretation of a Code section citation.

Although there are nearly a thousand Code sections, certain ones contain basic principles that affect most tax situations (Exhibit 3-11). The tax researcher should be familiar with this group of Code sections for efficient analysis of his or her clients' tax problems.

Where to Find the Internal Revenue Code

The amended Internal Revenue Code can be found in several places. National publishers such as RIA, WestlawNext, and CCH publish paperback versions of the Code for use by tax practitioners. In addition, the text of the Code may be found in most commercial tax services and as Title 26 of the United States Code.

EXHIBIT 3-10: Interpreting a Code Section Citation

Section 121(b)(2)(A)(ii)

→	*Section number 121*
→	*Subsection b*
→	*Paragraph 2*
→	*Subparagraph A*
→	*Clause ii*

Section 121	SEC. 121. EXCLUSION OF GAIN FROM SALE OF PRINCIPAL RESIDENCE
Subsection(a)	(a) Exclusion
	Gross income shall not include gain from the sale or exchange of property if, during the 5-year period ending on the date of the sale or exchange, such property has been owned and used by the taxpayer as the taxpayer's principal residence for periods aggregating 2 years or more.
Subsection(b)	(b) Limitations
Paragraph(1)	(1) In general
	The amount of gain excluded from gross income under subsection (a) with respect to any sale or exchange shall not exceed $250,000.
Paragraph(2)	(2) Special rules for joint returns
	In the case of a husband and wife who make a joint return for the taxable year of the sale or exchange of the—property—
Subparagraph(A)	(A) $500,000 Limitation for certain joint returns
	Paragraph (1) shall be applied by substituting "$500,000" for "$250,000" if—
Clause(i)	(i) either spouse meets the ownership requirements of subsection (a) with respect to such property;
Clause(ii)	(ii) both spouses meet the use requirements of subsection (a) with respect to such property; and
Clause(iii)	(iii) neither spouse is ineligible for the benefits of subsection (a) with respect to such property by reason of paragraph (3)

The type of tax service will indicate the probable location of the original language of the Code in the service. Typically, an annotated tax service (refer to Chapter 2 to review this definition) will include the text of the Code with the related section's discussion. On the other hand, a topical tax service typically reproduces the text of the Code in an appendix to pertinent chapters or volumes of the service.

The U.S. Code and the Internal Revenue Code (which is Title 26 of the U.S. Code) can also be found at various Internet sites. An example of such a site would be **http://uscode.house.gov.**

Occasionally, a tax researcher needs to refer to a source that originated from the Internal Revenue Code of 1939. Many of the provisions of the 1986 (and 1954) Code can be found in the 1939 Code. Exhibit 3-12 gives examples of 1986 Code sections and their 1939 Code equivalents.

EXHIBIT 3-11:   Some Important Code Sections

Section Number	Contents
1	Individual Tax Rates
11	Corporate Tax Rates
61	Definition of Gross Income
62	Deductions for Adjusted Gross Income
162	Trade or Business Deductions
163	Interest Deduction
164	Deduction for Taxes
165	Losses
167, 168, 179	Depreciation, Cost Recovery
212	Production-of-Income Expenses
312	Corporate Dividends
351	Forming a Corporation
368	Mergers, Acquisitions, Corporate Break-Ups
469	Passive Activities
501	Tax-Exempt Status
721	Forming a Partnership, LLC
861	Sourcing of International Income and Deductions
904	Foreign Tax Credit
1245	Depreciation Recapture
1504	Consolidated Taxable Income
6662	Penalties for Inaccurate Tax Filings

EXHIBIT 3-12:   Examples of 1986 Code Sections Derived from the 1939 Code

1986 Code Section	1939 Code Section
§61, Gross Income Defined	§22(a)
§71, Alimony and Separate Maintenance Payments	§22(k)
§103, Interest on State and Local Bonds	§22(b)(4)
§151, Allowance of Deductions for Personal Exemptions	§25(b)
§162, Trade or Business Expenses	§23(a)(1)
§172, Net Operating Loss Deduction	§122
§212, Expenses for Production of Income	§23(a)(2)
§301, Distributions of Property	§22(e), 115(a), (b), (d), (e)
§316, Dividends Defined	§115(a) and (b)
§701, Partners, not Partnership, Subject to Tax	§181

Other useful indices to the Code itself are provided in commercial tax research services. For example, several useful tables are available from the CCH IntelliConnect Tax Service under its "Current IRC Finding Lists." In Cross-Reference Table I, 1939 Code sections are cross-referenced to their 1954 (and 1986) counterparts. In Table II, current Code sections are cross-referenced to the 1939 Code. Table III cross-references the Code sections within the current Code.

These three tables can be useful to the tax researcher when he or she needs to find a 1939 Code section number, perhaps in interpreting a court case that addresses a pre-1954 Code issue, or in identifying situations where a Code section is referred to elsewhere in the current Code, or perhaps to find out whether other Code sections provide information bearing on the section being reviewed.

One other publication will prove to be valuable if the researcher is addressing issues that predate the 1954 Code. Seidman's Legislative History of Federal Income Tax Laws details the historical evolution of the early tax law. It explains how certain provisions evolved into their current form in the Code.

Most tax services also contain information about the history of each Code section. Typically, at the end of the text of each Code section, or as a related page that can be accessed by linking, the editors include a list of the Public Laws that have altered or amended the section. This listing generally includes a reference to the section as it existed prior to amendment as well as the effective date of the amendment to the law. The tax researcher must be careful to consider the impact of any such amendments. Exhibit 3-13 illustrates the Public Law history with respect to a specific Code section.

EXHIBIT 3-13: Recent History for Code Section 101

In 2006, P.L. 109-280, Sec. 863(a), added subsec. (j) P.L. 109-280, Sec. 863(c)(1), substituted "subsection (f), and subsection (j)" for "and subsection (f)" in para. (a)(1), effective for life insurance contracts issued after 8/17/2006, for a contract issued after 8/17/2006 pursuant to an exchange described in Code Sec. 1035 for a contract issued on or prior 8/17/2006. For purposes of the preceding sentence, any material increase in the death benefit or other material change shall cause the contract to be treated as a new contract except that, in the case of a master contract (within the meaning of Code Sec. 264(f)(4)(E)), the addition of covered lives shall be treated as a new contract only with respect to such additional covered lives.

In 2003, P.L. 108-121, Sec. 110(b)(1), added para. (i)(4) P.L. 108-121, Sec. 110(b)(2), added "or astronauts" after "victims" in the heading of subsec. (i), effective for amounts paid after 12/31/2002, with respect to deaths occurring after 12/31/2002.

In 2002, P.L. 107-134, Sec. 102(a), added subsec. (i), effective for tax. yrs. end. before, on, or after 9/11/2001. Sec. 102(b)(2) of this Act, provides:

"(2) Waiver of limitations. If refund or credit of any overpayment of tax resulting from the amendments made by this section is prevented at any time before the close of the 1-year period beginning on the date of the enactment of this Act by the operation of any law or rule of law (including res judicata), such refund or credit may nevertheless be made or allowed if claim therefore is filed before the close of such period."

Interpreting the Internal Revenue Code

One of the greatest problems for a tax researcher is the interpretation of the Internal Revenue Code. Often, Code provisions are long, interrelated, and confusing. For example, several sentences in the Code exceed 300 words; one of them exceeds 400 words. In researching a client's tax problem, one must read each Code section that might apply. Many times, a single phrase or clause in the section may prevent the client from being subject to the provision or may contain other unexpected implications for the client's situation.

A researcher, in his or her initial review, may find the topical index, which is included by most publishers of the Code, a useful tool in locating a starting point or the relevant Code section. In reading, interpreting, and evaluating a selected Code section, the tax researcher must be especially critical of the language used throughout the section. Many, if not most, Code sections contain a general rule, followed by specific conditions that must be satisfied in order to apply the provision and situations under which the taxpayer is not subject to general rule. In some cases, the exceptions to the general rule are further modified to provide for exceptions to the general exceptions. Moreover, some exceptions to a Code section are addressed not within the same section, but in another section of the Code. Therefore, all relevant provisions must be read carefully.

In addition to being aware of the required conditions for application of a section, as well as the exceptions thereto, the researcher must be aware of the definitions of terms used in the section; pertinent definitions may be given within the section or in some other provision of the Code. These definitions may be significantly different from the common use of the term.

In §7701, the text defines many of the terms used throughout the Code, but these definitions may be superseded by material contained within the applicable Code section. In addition, the researcher may need to look beyond the Code, such as to the Regulations or other authority, to determine the conditions that a specific term may encompass. In all cases, the researcher should avoid jumping to premature conclusions until a thorough analysis of all relevant Code sections has been completed.

The tax researcher must be careful not to overlook words that connect phrases, such as "and" and "or." These words have very different logical meanings, and even when the words are "hidden" at the end of the previous clause or subparagraph, they may significantly change the outcome of a research project. The word "and" is conjunctive; the word "or" is disjunctive. If the word "and" lies between two phrases, both of them must be true for the provision to apply to the client's problem. However, if the word "or" lies between two phrases, then only one of them must be true for the provision to apply.

The researcher also must be careful with words that modify percentage or dollar amounts. The phrases "less than 50 percent," "more than 50 percent," and "not less than 50 percent" have very different meanings in determining whether the provisions of a section apply. The researcher also must distinguish between such terms as "30 days" and "one month," because they usually identify different time periods.

Conflicting code sections can also be problematic as illustrated below.

EXAMPLE 3-2

Paul is a roofing contractor and has a truck he uses 100 percent of the time in his business. The truck cost $35,000 three years ago, and Paul has claimed cost recovery deductions of $24,920 on the truck, which leaves him an adjusted basis of $10,080. Paul sells the truck for $22,080, resulting in a gain of $12,000 on the truck. How is he to treat this gain for tax purposes?

In the Internal Revenue Code, Paul finds that when depreciable property used in a trade or business [§1231(b)] is sold, the gain is treated as a long-term capital gain [§1231(a)]. Thus, he might report the gain on his tax return as a long-term capital gain. In §1245(a), however, Paul discovers that gain on depreciable personal property (in this case, the truck) is ordinary income to the extent of depreciation claimed since 1961. Thus, §1245 would indicate the gain is ordinary, not long-term capital.

How is the problem resolved? In §1245(d), Paul finds a directive that the recapture provision "shall apply notwithstanding any other provision of this subtitle [of the Code]." As a result, he must report the gain as ordinary income on his tax return, not long-term capital gain.

If Paul had read only §1231 of the Code and not §1245, he would have arrived at a different conclusion about the gain. In many situations, when Code sections conflict, the resolution of the conflict may not be as easy as in this example.

When analyzing a provision that recently has been changed by Congress, a researcher must be very careful to cross-reference all of the uses of terms whose definitions have been affected by the new law. Often, Congress does not use the care necessary to ascertain that all of the "loose ends" of the new provisions have been tied up. In recent years, almost every major change in the tax law has been followed by a "technical corrections act" to remove errors in implementing and interpreting the new provisions of the law as well as to clarify problems that arise in integrating the new provisions with the existing provisions of the Code. Most of these corrections are identified by practitioners whose clients' situations are adversely affected by a given reading of the amended law. Thus, the typical technical corrections act testifies as much to the thoroughness of the practitioners' research as to shoddy drafting of the law by Congress.

Because the provisions of the Internal Revenue Code change frequently, the researcher must be aware of the effective dates of the various changes to the law. A provision may not go into effect immediately upon its adoption by Congress. The date of the act with which the change in law is passed is not always indicative of the effective date of the provision. Often, various provisions under the same tax law will become effective on different dates and, in fact, may have effective dates that precede the date of the tax act. Similarly, when a provision of the tax law is deleted from the Code, the provision may be left in effect for a designated period of time before it actually expires. Transitional rules may also apply. The effective date for a change in the tax law usually may be found in the explanation of the Public Laws, which follows the pertinent Code section (see Exhibit 3-13). In some cases, the researcher may need to look to the explanation under another Code section for the effective date of a provision. The researcher must be careful to align the client's facts with the effective law at the pertinent dates or a serious mistake could be made in the research conclusion.

Finally, the tax researcher must be aware that not all of the answers to a tax question will be found in the Code. The Code may be silent concerning the problem at hand, the application of Code language to the fact situation at hand may not be clear, or Code sections may appear to be in conflict. Thus, the researcher must look for an answer from other sources, such as tax treaties, administrative rulings (see Chapter 4), judicial decisions (see Chapter 5), or secondary sources of the law. Alternatively, the controlling law may be found in other parts of the Code, such as tariff or bankruptcy laws. Exhibit 3-14 lists examples of Federal laws other than the Code that affect specific tax matters.

EXHIBIT 3-14: Examples of Federal Laws Other Than the Internal Revenue Code That May Affect a Tax Transaction

- Administrative Procedure Act
- Alaska Native Claims Settlement Act
- Atomic Energy Act Tax Provision
- Bank Holding Company Act of 1956
- Civil Rights Attorneys' Fees Awards Act of 1976
- Financial Institutions Reform, Recovery, and Enforcement Act of 1989
- Metric Conversion Act of 1975
- Merchant Marine Act: Capital Construction Fund
- New York City Pension Act
- Organic Act of Guam

SUMMARY

The three major sources of statutory tax law are the Constitution, tax treaties, and the Internal Revenue Code. The tax researcher must thoroughly understand each of these sources and the interrelationships among them. The Constitution is the basis for all Federal laws. The tax treaties are agreements between countries, negotiated by the President and approved by the Senate, that cover taxpayers subject to the tax laws of both countries. The authority of a tax treaty may equal or exceed that of a Code section. The greatest volume of tax statutes is found in the Internal Revenue Code, which is Title 26 of the United States Code. The Code contains the tax laws that Congress has passed, and it is the basic document for most U.S. tax provisions.

QUIZ YOURSELF

Reinforce the tax research information covered in this chapter by completing the online quizzes located at the Federal Tax Research Web site at **www.cengagebrain.com.** At the CengageBrain.com home page, search for the *Federal Tax Research*, 9e ISBN (1111221642) using the search box at the top of the page. This will take you to the product page where you can access the quizzes.

KEY WORDS

By the time you complete this chapter, you should be comfortable discussing each of the following terms. If you need additional review of any of these items, return to the appropriate material in the chapter or consult the glossary to this text.

Committee Report, p. 94	Joint Conference Committee, p. 93	statutory sources, p. 86
Finance Committee, p. 93	primary authorities, p. 86	tax treaties, p. 90
Internal Revenue Code, p. 97	secondary authorities, p. 86	Ways and Means Committee, p. 93

DISCUSSION QUESTIONS

1. What are the three primary statutory sources of U.S. Federal tax law?

2. Discuss the effect of *Pollock v. Farmers' Loan and Trust Co.* on the development of U.S. income tax laws.

3. The Sixteenth Amendment to the Constitution had a significant effect on the U.S. income tax. What was it?

4. Discuss briefly the events leading to the passage of the Sixteenth Amendment to the U.S. Constitution.

5. What did the U.S. Supreme Court hold in *Flint v. Stone Tracy Co.* in 1911?

6. Tax protesters who file "frivolous" tax returns or bring "frivolous" proceedings before the U.S. Tax Court are subject to certain fines or other penalties. What are the grounds for imposing each penalty? What is the maximum amount of each penalty?

7. Discuss the powers of taxation that are granted to Congress by the U.S. Constitution. Are any limits placed on the powers of Congress to so tax?

8. Have the Federal courts ever held Federal estate and gift taxes to be unconstitutional?

9. What is a tax treaty? Explain the purpose of a tax treaty. What matters generally are covered in a tax treaty?

10. How is a tax treaty terminated?

11. When an Internal Revenue Code section and a tax treaty provision appear to conflict, which usually prevails?

12. Describe the ratification process for a tax treaty between the United States and another country.

13. The tax researcher must be able to find descriptions of tax treaties to solve certain tax problems. List different locations where a tax researcher might find a tax treaty.

14. Briefly summarize the usual steps of the legislative process for the development of Federal tax legislation.

15. As a bill proceeds through Congress, various Committee Reports are generated. List the three Committee Reports that typically are prepared for a new tax law.

16. When are Committee Reports useful to a tax researcher?

17. What is a Public Law number? In P.L. 100-203, what do the "100" and the "203" indicate?

18. Where would a tax researcher find pertinent Committee Reports? List at least four publications and their publishers that include tax-related Committee Reports. Is there an index that would help a tax researcher locate a specific Committee Report? If so, where might such an index be found?

19. In addition to the Committee Reports, which are byproducts to the development of tax legislation, what other report may be of value to the tax researcher analyzing a new provision of the tax law? Why?

20. Discuss the evolution of today's Internal Revenue Code.

21. The Internal Revenue Code is Title 26 of the United States Code. How is the Internal Revenue Code subdivided?

22. How are the subtitles of the Internal Revenue Code identified? What generally is contained in a subtitle?

23. In the citation §101(a)(2)(B), what does the "a" stand for? What do the "2" and the "B" indicate to a tax researcher?

24. In the citation §1031(a)(3)(B), what does the "a" stand for? What do the "3" and the "B" indicate to a tax researcher?

25. Are there any exceptions to the general formatting rules for a Code section? Give examples.

26. In what subchapter of Chapter 1, Subtitle A are located the Code sections relating to:
    a. Corporations?
    b. Mutual funds?
    c. Tax-exempt organizations?

27. What Code section contains the statute for the definition of:

    a. Gross income?

    b. The interest deduction?

    c. Depreciation and cost recovery?

28. What Code section contains the statute for the definition of:

    a. A dependent?

    b. Bad debts?

    c. Alimony payments?

29. The tax researcher must be careful not to overlook connecting words such as "and," "or," "at least," and "more than." Explain why this is important.

30. Not all statutory tax laws are found in the Internal Revenue Code. Is this statement true or false? Discuss briefly.

EXERCISES

31. Locate Section 163 of the Code and answer the following. Section 163 is part of which:

    a. Title

    b. Subtitle

    c. Chapter

    d. Subchapter

32. Locate Section 1245 of the Code and answer the following. Section 1245 is part of which:

    a. Title

    b. Subtitle

    c. Chapter

    d. Subchapter

33. Locate the Committee Reports associated with each of the following Code sections using a tax service such as RIA Checkpoint. Give the Public Law (P.L.) number of the most recent committee for each Code section.

    a. Section 25A

    b. Section 117

    c. Section 162

34. Locate the Committee Reports associated with each of the following Code sections using a tax service such as RIA Checkpoint. Give the Public Law (P.L.) number of the most recent committee for each Code section.

    a. Section 24

    b. Section 243

    c. Section 222

35. Log on to http://waysandmeans.house.gov, the Ways and Means Committee of the U.S. House of Representatives Web site, and answer the following questions:

    a. Who is the chair of the committee?

    b. What is the total number of members on the committee?

    c. How many of the members are from your home state? If none, say so.

    d. The Ways and Means Committee has several subcommittees. Name three of these subcommittees and indicate who chairs each subcommittee.

36. What is found in each of the following subtitles of the Internal Revenue Code?
    a. Subtitle B
    b. Subtitle F
    c. Subtitle A
    d. Subtitle C

37. What is found in each of the following subtitles of the Internal Revenue Code?
    a. Subtitle D
    b. Subtitle H
    c. Subtitle K
    d. Subtitle P

38. Each subtitle of the Internal Revenue Code contains several chapters. How are chapters identified? What generally is included in a chapter of the Code?

39. Identify the general content of each of the following chapters of the Internal Revenue Code:
    a. Chapter 11
    b. Chapter 61
    c. Chapter 1
    d. Chapter 12

40. Chapters of the Internal Revenue Code are subdivided into subchapters. How are subchapters identified? What generally is contained in a subchapter?

41. Correctly cite the italicized sentence indicated by the dart (▶) in the following passage from the Code:

SECTION 74. PRIZES AND AWARDS
    a. General rule
       Except as otherwise provided in this section or in section 117 (relating to qualified scholarships), gross income includes amounts received as prizes and awards.
    b. Exception for certain prizes and awards transferred to charities
       Gross income does not include amounts received as prizes and awards made primarily in recognition of religious, charitable, scientific, educational, artistic, literary, or civic achievement, but only if—

    1. the recipient was selected without any action on his part to enter the contest or proceeding;

    2. ▶*The recipient is not required to render substantial future services as a condition to receiving the prize or award; and*

    3. the prize or award is transferred by the payor to a governmental unit or organization described in paragraph (1) or (2) of section 170(c) pursuant to a designation made by the recipient.

42. Correctly cite the italicized sentence indicated by the dart (▶) in the following passage from the Code:

SECTION 263A. CAPITALIZATION AND INCLUSION IN INVENTORY COSTS OF CERTAIN EXPENSES
    a. Nondeductibility of certain direct and indirect costs

    1. In general—In the case of any property to which this section applies, any costs described in paragraph (2)—

       A. in the case of property which is inventory in the hands of the taxpayer, shall be included in inventory costs, and
       B. ▶ *in the case of any other property, shall be capitalized.*

    2. Allocable costs

43. What is the general content of each of the following subchapters of Chapter 1, Subtitle A, of the Internal Revenue Code?
    a. Subchapter C
    b. Subchapter K
    c. Subchapter S
    d. Subchapter E

44. What is found in each of the following subchapters of Subtitle A, Chapter 1 of the Internal Revenue Code?
    a. Subchapter B
    b. Subchapter E
    c. Subchapter L
    d. Subchapter F

45. Which subchapter of Subtitle A, Chapter 1 of the Internal Revenue Code contains the provisions related to the following:
    a. Deferred Compensation
    b. Partners and Partnerships
    c. Corporate Distribution and Adjustments
    d. Banks

46. Which Internal Revenue Code sections are found in each of these subchapters of Subtitle A, Chapter 1?
    a. Subchapter J
    b. Subchapter A
    c. Subchapter I
    d. Subchapter P

47. Which Internal Revenue Code sections are found in each of these parts of Subtitle A?
    a. Subchapter A, Part IV
    b. Subchapter C, Part II
    c. Subchapter B, Part VIII
    d. Subchapter A, Part I

48. What is covered in Subtitle A, Chapter 2 of the Internal Revenue Code? What Internal Revenue Code sections are included in Chapter 2?

49. What is found in each of the following subchapters of Chapter 1, Subtitle A, of the Internal Revenue Code?
    a. Subchapter D
    b. Subchapter H
    c. Subchapter P
    d. Subchapter L

50. What is the official name of P.L. 108-27? What year was that law enacted? Where did you find your answer?

51. What is the official name of P.L. 99-514? What year was that law enacted? Where did you find your answer?

52. The most important division of the Internal Revenue Code is the section. Sections usually are subdivided into various smaller elements. Name several of these elements and state how they are denoted.

53. Do section numbers repeat themselves or is each one unique?

54. Identify the general contents of each of the following Internal Revenue Code sections:
    a. §61
    b. §162
    c. §1
    d. §212

55. Identify the general contents of each of the following Internal Revenue Code sections:
    a. §62
    b. §163
    c. 11
    d. §164

56. Locate Section 217 of the Code. It is found in the:
    a. Subtitle of the Code
    b. Chapter
    c. Subchapter
    d. Part

57. Locate Section 2036 of the Code. It is found in the:
    a. Subtitle of the Code
    b. Chapter
    c. Subchapter
    d. Part

58. Use a tax service (e.g., RIA Checkpoint, LexisNexis, CCH IntelliConnect) to answer the following questions:
    a. Which service did you use?
    b. What is the general content of Internal Revenue Code §28?
    c. What is the general content of Internal Revenue Code §141?
    d. What is the general content of Internal Revenue Code §166?
    e. Print a copy (maximum of one page) of any one of the above Code sections and attach it to your answer.

59. Use a tax service (e.g., RIA Checkpoint, LexisNexis, CCH IntelliConnect) to answer the following questions:
    a. Which tax service did you use?
    b. What is the general content of Internal Revenue Code §117?
    c. What is the general content of Internal Revenue Code §165?
    d. What is the general content of Internal Revenue Code §304?
    e. Print a copy (maximum of one page) of any one of the above Code sections and attach it to your answer.

60. Use a tax service (e.g., RIA Checkpoint, LexisNexis, CCH IntelliConnect) to answer the following questions:
    a. Which tax service did you use?
    b. What is the general content of Internal Revenue Code §25A?
    c. What is the general content of Internal Revenue Code §67?
    d. What is the general content of Internal Revenue Code §280G?
    e. Print a copy (maximum of one page) of any one of the above Code sections and attach it to your answer.

61. Name several locations where a tax researcher would find the text of the current Internal Revenue Code.

62. If a tax researcher wants to know if there is an equivalent 1939 Code section for a specific 1986 Code section, how would he or she locate it?

63. One important problem that faces a tax researcher is interpretation of the Internal Revenue Code. Comment on each of the following interpretation problems:
    a. Exceptions to a Code section
    b. Words that connect phrases, such as "and" and "or"
    c. Recent changes in the Code
    d. Effective dates
    e. Words that modify percentages, dollar amounts, or time

64. Comment on the statement, "All tax questions can be answered using the Internal Revenue Code."

65. Does the United States have an income tax treaty with any of the following countries? If it does, in what year was the treaty signed? State where you found this information.
    a. Japan
    b. United Kingdom
    c. Egypt
    d. Germany

66. Does the United States have an estate tax treaty with any of the following countries? If it does, in what year was the treaty signed? State where you found this information.
    a. Canada
    b. Finland
    c. Hungary
    d. Italy

67. Does the United States have an income tax treaty with any of the following countries? If it does, in what year was the treaty signed? State where you found this information.
    a. Australia
    b. Iceland
    c. Jamaica
    d. Sri Lanka

68. Use a tax service (e.g., RIA Checkpoint, LexisNexis, CCH IntelliConnect) to locate §117 of the Internal Revenue Code. Answer the following questions:
    a. Which tax service did you use?
    b. How many subsection(s) does §117 include?
    c. How many paragraph(s) does §117(b) include?
    d. How many subparagraph(s) does §117(d)(2) include?
    e. Print a copy (maximum of one page) of this section and attach it to your answer.

69. Use a tax service (e.g., RIA Checkpoint, LexisNexis CCH IntelliConnect) to locate §385 of the Internal Revenue Code. Answer the following questions:
    a. Which tax service did you use?
    b. How many subsection(s) does §385 include?
    c. How many paragraph(s) does §385(b) include?
    d. Print a copy (maximum of one page) of this section and attach it to your answer.

70. Use a tax service (e.g., RIA Checkpoint, LexisNexis, CCH IntelliConnect) to locate §280C of the Internal Revenue Code. Answer the following questions:
    a. Which tax service did you use?
    b. How many subsection(s) does §280C include?
    c. How many paragraph(s) does §280C(b) include?
    d. How many subparagraph(s) does §280C(b)(2) include?
    e. Print a copy (maximum of one page) of this section and attach it to your answer.

71. When was each of the following sections originally enacted? State how you obtained this information.
    a. §843
    b. §131
    c. §469
    d. §263A

72. In which subtitle, chapter, and subchapter of the 1986 Code are each of the following sections found?
    a. §32
    b. §172
    c. §2039
    d. §6013

73. List the first three section numbers and titles of each of the following subchapters of Chapter 1 of the Internal Revenue Code:
    a. Subchapter B
    b. Subchapter E
    c. Subchapter J
    d. Subchapter S

74. Identify the equivalent section of the current Code for each of the following sections of the 1939 Code. If there is no equivalent section, say so.
    a. §1
    b. §113(a)
    c. §22(a)
    d. §115(a)
    e. §181

75. Use a computer tax service (e.g., RIA Checkpoint, LexisNexis, CCH IntelliConnect) to locate the following Code sections. What other Code sections reference each of the sections you found? State which computer tax service you used to complete this assignment.
    a. §72
    b. §307
    c. §446

76. Name the article and section of the U.S. Constitution that gives Congress the power to levy a tax.

77. Enumerate the Code sections that contain the chief tax law provisions on the following topics:
    a. S corporations
    b. Personal holding company tax
    c. Gift tax
    d. Tax accounting methods

78. Use an Internet site to determine how many Senators are on the Senate Finance Committee. Who is the Chair of the Finance Committee? State where you found this information.

79. Use an Internet site to determine how many Representatives are on the House Ways and Means Committee. Who is the Chair of the Ways and Means Committee? State where you found this information.

80. Use an Internet site to determine what is contained in each of the following. State where you found this information.
    a. U.S. Const. art. I, §9 cl. 3
    b. U.S. Const. art. I, §8 cl. 1
    c. U.S. Const. art. II, §2 cl. 2

81. Locate and print the first page of a House Ways and Means Committee Report using an Internet site. State where you found this information.

RESEARCH CASES

82. Private G. I. Jane was a soldier in the Iraq War. Her salary was $2,600 per month, and she was in the war zone for eight months. How much of her salary is taxable for the eight months? In answering this case, use only the Internal Revenue Code for your research.

83. Carol received a gift of stock from her favorite uncle. The stock had a fair market value of $30,000 and a basis to the uncle of $10,000 at the date of the gift. How much is taxable to Carol from this gift? In answering this case, use only the Internal Revenue Code for your research.

84. Maria is an independent long-haul trucker. She receives a speeding ticket for $500, which she pays. Can Maria deduct the ticket on Schedule C? In answering this case, use only the Internal Revenue Code for your research.

85. Julie loaned her friend Nathan $2,500. Nathan did not repay the debt and skipped town. Can Julie claim any deduction? In answering this case, use only the Internal Revenue Code for your research.

86. In December of 20x1, Ann's 12-year-old cousin, Susan, came to live with her after Susan's parents met an untimely death in a car accident. In 20x2, Ann provided all normal support (e.g., food, clothing, education) for Susan. Ann did not formally adopt Susan. If Susan lived in the household for the entire year, can Ann claim a dependency exemption for her cousin for the tax year? In answering this case, use only the Internal Revenue Code for your research.

87. John and Maria support their 21-year-old son, Bill. The son earned $10,500 last year working in a part-time job. Bill went to college part time in the spring semester of the current year. To complete his degree, Bill started school full time in the fall. The fall semester at Bill's college runs from August 20 to December 20. Can John and Maria claim Bill as a dependent on the current year's tax return, even if Bill earns this level of gross income? Assume any dependency test not mentioned has been met. In answering this case, use a computer tax service with only the Internal Revenue Code database selected. State your keywords and which computer tax service you used to arrive at your answer.

88. George and Linda are divorced and own a house from the marriage. Under the divorce decree, Linda pays George $3,000 per month alimony. Since the real estate market has collapsed in the area where they live, George and Linda cannot sell the house. Since they are still friends, they decide to live in separate wings of the house until the real estate market recovers. If George and Linda live together for the entire current year, can Linda claim a deduction for the alimony paid to George? In answering this case, use a computer tax service with only the Internal Revenue Code database selected. State your keywords and which computer tax service you used to arrive at your answer.

89. Juan sold IBM stock to Richard for a $10,000 loss. Richard is the husband of Juan's sister, Carla. How much of the loss can Juan deduct in the current year if Juan's taxable income is $55,000 and he has no other capital transactions? In answering this case, use a computer tax service with only the Internal Revenue Code database selected. State your keywords and which computer tax service you used to arrive at your answer.

90. Tex is a rancher. This year her herd of cattle was infested with hoof-and-mouth disease and had to be destroyed. Tex's insurance policy reimburses her for an amount in excess of the tax basis in the cattle, thereby creating an "insurance gain." After receiving the insurance proceeds, Tex buys a new herd of cattle. Can Tex defer the recognition of this insurance gain on the destroyed herd? In answering this case, use a computer tax service with only the Internal Revenue Code database selected. State your keywords and which computer tax service you used to arrive at your answer.

91. Betty owed Martha $5,000. In payment of this debt, Betty transferred to Martha a life insurance policy on Betty, with a cash surrender value of $5,000. The face value of the policy is $100,000. Martha names herself as beneficiary of the policy and continues to make the premium payments. After Martha has paid $15,000 in premiums, Betty dies and Martha collects $100,000. Is any of the $100,000 Martha received taxable? In answering this case, use a computer tax service with only the Internal Revenue Code database selected. State your keywords and which computer tax service you used to arrive at your answer.

92. On May 1, Rick formed a new corporation, Red Inc. He spent $3,000 in legal fees and paid the state $600 in incorporation fees. Red Corporation started operating its business on May 10. Can Rick or Red Corporation deduct either of these organizational fees? In answering this case, use a computer tax service with only the Internal Revenue Code database selected. State your keywords and which computer tax service you used to arrive at your answer.

93. This year, there were massive brush fires in the interior of Mexico. Amy gave $10,000 to the Mexican Relief Foundation, which is organized in Mexico City. The funds were used to provide food, clothing, and shelter to the victims of the Mexican fires. Is Amy's charitable contribution deductible for income tax purposes? In answering this case, use a computer tax service with only the Internal Revenue Code database selected. State your keywords and which computer tax service you used to arrive at your answer.

94. Curtis is 50 years old and has an IRA with substantial funds in it. His son, Curtis Jr., was accepted to Yale University upon graduating from high school. Curtis had not planned for this and needs to draw $25,000 per year out of his IRA to help pay the tuition and fees at Yale. What are the tax consequences of the withdrawals from the IRA? In answering this case, use a computer tax service with only the Internal Revenue Code database selected. State your keywords and which computer tax service you used to arrive at your answer.

95. Cathy Coed is a full-time senior student at Big Research University (BRU). Cathy is considered by most as a brilliant student and has been given a $35,000-per-year scholarship. In the current year, Cathy pays the following amounts to attend BRU:

Tuition	$26,000
Required Lab Fees	$300
Required Books and Supplies	$1,000
Dorm Fees	$7,500

What are the tax consequences (i.e., how much is income) of the $35,000 current year's scholarship to Cathy? In answering this case, use a computer tax service with only the Internal Revenue Code database selected. State your keywords and which computer tax service you used to arrive at your answer.

96. Dennis is an executive of Gold Corporation. He receives a one-for-one distribution of stock rights for each share of common stock he owns. On the date of distribution, the stock rights have a fair market value of $2 per right, and the stock has a fair market value of $20 per share. Dennis owns 10,000 shares of the stock

with a basis of $5 per share. If Dennis does not make any special elections with regard to the stock rights, what is his basis in the rights?

a. Locate the Code section(s) that deals with this situation. State the section number(s).

b. Review the Code section(s). Does it raise a need for new information to solve this question?

c. Are you able to reach a conclusion about the research question from this Code section? If so, what is your conclusion(s)?

97. Kurt purchased a new Toyota hybrid automobile that gets 50 miles per gallon of gasoline. Determine if Kurt gets any special Federal tax breaks for purchasing this energy-saving car. If so, how are such tax breaks calculated?

a. Locate the Code section(s) that deals with this situation. State the section number(s).

b. Review the Code section(s). Does it raise a need for new information to solve this question?

c. Are you able to reach a conclusion about the research question from this Code section? If so, what is your conclusion(s)?

98. Monica purchased two acres of land with an old building on it for $1 million. The purchase was made to acquire the land for a new store she wanted to open on the property. Shortly after completing the purchase, Monica pays $80,000 to have the old building demolished. How does Monica treat the $80,000 demolition payment for tax purposes?

a. Locate the Code section(s) that deals with this situation. State the section number(s).

b. Review the Code section(s). Does it raise a need for new information to solve this question?

c. Are you able to reach a conclusion about the research question from this Code section? If so, what is your conclusion(s)?

99. Lihue Inc. sells timeshares in Hawaii. Gene buys a timeshare out of the inventory of timeshares for sale by Lihue Inc. Gene agrees to pay them $10,000 down, and Lihue Inc. will finance a seven-year note for the balance of the purchase price at the current market rate of interest. Can Lihue Inc. use the installment method to report their gain on the sale of the Hawaiian timeshare to Gene?

a. Locate the Code section(s) that deals with this situation. State the section number(s).

b. Review the Code section(s). Does it raise a need for new information to solve this question?

c. Are you able to reach a conclusion about the research question from this Code section? If so, what is your conclusion(s)?

100. Sara Student is a full-time freshman at Small State University (SSU). Her tuition for the year is $42,000, which is paid by Sara's mother, Susan. Sara also has a job as a model, earning substantial money; therefore, Sara does not qualify as Susan's dependent. Can Sara's mother claim the American Opportunity Credit for the tuition she paid? Can Sara claim the American Opportunity Credit on any unused portion of the tuition?

a. Locate the Code section(s) that deals with this situation. State the section number(s).

b. Review the Code section(s). Does it raise a need for new information to solve this question?

c. Are you able to reach a conclusion about the research question from this Code section? If so, what is your conclusion(s)?

101. David Dental, DDS and his unmarried partner Sally Surgeon, MD have lived together for the past five years. Both are at the peak of their careers and decide to buy a new "show case" home in La Jolla, California. After looking at several homes in the area they buy one for $2 million. They put a 20 percent down payment ($400,000) on the house and finance the balance ($1.6 million). Each takes out a separate mortgage for $800,000 for a total $1.6 million. There is no other debt (e.g., a home equity loan) on the residence. Both David and Sally are single taxpayers and are your tax clients. Each pays $48,000 on their respective mortgages in the current year. You are in the process of preparing their 2009 tax returns.

a. Locate the Code section(s) that deals with this situation. State the section number(s).

b. Review the Code section(s). Does it raise a need for new information to solve this question?

c. Are you able to reach a conclusion about the research question from this Code section? If so, what is your conclusion(s)?

102. Dr. Stephen Kolbert is a professor of television and movie production at Hollywood University (and thus an employee of the university). He often meets with his doctoral students, who call him Dr. K, in his home. In his home, Dr. K has a room that he uses solely to conduct business related to the classes he teaches at Hollywood University. In the room, he and his students review the movies and shows the students have made to satisfy requirements in their doctoral program. Dr. K has an office on campus, but he has found that his movie and show reviews are more efficient when he and his students can watch the programs on his 72-inch LED flat-screen television and sit on the comfortable couch in his home office rather than the 19-inch television and chairs in his office.

a. Locate the Code section(s) that deals with this situation. State the section number(s).

b. Review the Code section(s). Does it raise a need for new information to solve this question?

c. Are you able to reach a conclusion about the research question from this Code section? If so, what is your conclusion(s)?

103. Odiferous Chemical Company (OCC) manufactured pesticides that were toxic. Over the course of several years, the toxic waste contaminated the air and water around the company's plant. Several employees and people living near the plant suffered toxic poisoning, and the Environmental Protection Agency cited the company for violations. In District Court, the judge found OCC guilty and imposed a fine of $15 million, which was paid to the EPA by OCC. You have been asked to assess the deductibility of the payment of the fine.

a. Locate the Code section(s) that deals with this situation. State the section number(s).

b. Review the Code section(s). Does it raise a need for new information to solve this question?

c. Are you able to reach a conclusion about the research question from this Code section? If so, what is your conclusion(s)?

CHAPTER 4

Administrative Regulations and Rulings

LEARNING OBJECTIVES

- Identify the most important administrative sources of the Federal tax law.
- Distinguish among the structure, nature, and purpose of Regulations, Revenue Procedures, and IRS Rulings.
- Describe how to locate and how to interpret the precedential value of administrative sources of the tax law.
- Explain the elements of common citations for Regulations and other IRS pronouncements.
- Detail the contents and publication practices of the Internal Revenue Bulletin and the Cumulative Bulletin.

CHAPTER OUTLINE

THE INTERNAL REVENUE SERVICE (IRS), part of the U.S. Treasury Department, is responsible for the administration of the income tax law. The administrative process consists of both interpreting and enforcing the tax laws. The IRS interprets the law by issuing various pronouncements, examples of which include Treasury Regulations, Revenue Rulings, Revenue Procedures, and Private Letter Rulings requested by taxpayers. Enforcement of the tax law by the IRS consists primarily of systematically auditing tax returns and administering an appeals process for taxpayers to arbitrate disagreement with audit results (see Chapters 13 and 14). In addition, the IRS administers a collection process to collect overdue taxes. The Treasury Secretary delegates the ongoing administrative responsibilities for the tax law to the Commissioner of the IRS, who is a presidential appointee.

To facilitate the IRS's administration of the tax laws, the Code authorizes the Treasury Secretary (or his or her delegate) to prescribe the Rules and Regulations necessary to administer the Code. According to §7805(a):

> *Except where such authority is expressly given by this title to any person other than an officer or employee of the Treasury Department, the Secretary shall prescribe all needful rules and regulations for the enforcement of this title, including all rules and regulations as may be necessary by reason of any alteration of law in relation to internal revenue.*

This Code section gives the IRS general authority to issue binding Rules and Regulations concerning Title 26 of the United States Code. In practice, most of the IRS's pronouncements are written by IRS staff or by the Office of the Chief Counsel of the IRS, who is an Assistant General Counsel of the Treasury Department.

The tax researcher must be especially familiar with the four major types of pronouncements that may be forthcoming under this authority: Regulations, Revenue Rulings, Revenue Procedures, and Letter Rulings. Each of these categories of rulings is issued for a different purpose and carries a different degree of authority. The first three of these categories generally are published by the IRS, while the Letter Rulings (and other pronouncements) typically are not published by any government agency. The remainder of this chapter addresses the nature and location of each of these administrative pronouncements.

Regulations

The **Regulations** constitute the IRS's—and, thereby, the Treasury's—official interpretation of the **Internal Revenue Code**. Regulations are issued in the form of **Treasury Decisions (TDs)**, which are published in the Federal Register and, sometime later, in the Internal Revenue Bulletin, discussed later in this chapter. At least 30 days before a TD is published in final form, however, it must be issued in proposed form, allowing interested parties time to comment on it. As a result of the comments received during this process of public hearings, the IRS may make changes in the TD before its final publication.

Before and during the hearings process, the TDs are referred to as **Proposed Regulations** and, unlike Final Regulations, do not have the effect of law. After the hearings are completed, and changes (if any) have been made to the text of the TD, the TD is published in final form. Final Regulations are integrated with previously approved TDs and constitute the full set of IRS Regulations. After this integration has occurred, the TD designation usually is dropped, and the pronouncement simply is referred to as a "Regulation."

Observers have identified two distinct categories of Regulations, general and legislative. **General Regulations** are issued under the general authority granted to the IRS to interpret the language of the Code, usually under a specific Code (or Committee Report) directive of Congress, and with specific congressional authority. An example can be found under §212, Expenses for the Production of Income. This short Code section has many pages of interpretive Regulations, providing taxpayers with operational rules for applying this provision to tax situations.

SPOTLIGHT ON TAXATION

Quotation

"The hardest thing in the world to understand is the income tax."

—Albert Einstein

With respect to **Legislative Regulations**, the IRS is directed by Congress to fulfill effectively a lawmaking function and to specify the substantive requirements of a tax provision. Regulations that are ordered by the Code in this manner essentially carry the authority of the statute itself and are not easily challenged by taxpayers. Such authority is granted because, in certain (especially technical) areas of the tax law, Congress cannot or does not care to address the detailed or complex issues that are associated with an otherwise defined tax issue. Accordingly, Congress directs the IRS to pronounce Regulations on the matter. For example, Congress delegated to the IRS the authority to prescribe Regulations necessary to carry out the provisions of §135, which grants an exclusion for interest on certain U.S. savings bonds used for higher education expenses, including Regulations requiring record keeping and information reporting. Another example of this legislative authority is found in §385, which directs the IRS to prescribe Regulations to distinguish debt from equity in "thinly capitalized" corporations. Legislative Regulations bear the greatest precedential value of any IRS pronouncement.

Temporary Regulations

In addition to Proposed and Final Regulations, the IRS periodically issues **Temporary Regulations** in response to a congressional or judicial change in the tax law or its interpretation. Temporary Regulations are not subject to the public hearings procedure that typifies the development of a Final Regulation, and they are effective immediately upon publication. Although they are effective immediately, the IRS must simultaneously issue the Regulations in proposed form; the Temporary Regulations expire three years after issuance pursuant to the statute.[1] Temporary Regulations arc issued to provide the taxpayer with immediate guidance concerning a new provision of the law, perhaps concerning filing requirements that must be satisfied immediately or the clarification of definitions and terms.

Until a Temporary Regulation is replaced with the Final Regulation under a Code section, the tax researcher should treat the Temporary Regulation as though it were final. Thus, Temporary Regulations are fully in effect and must be followed until they are superseded, whereas Proposed Regulations, having been issued only to solicit comments and to expose the IRS's proposed interpretation of the law, need not be followed as if they were law.

---

[1] IRC §7805.

Effective Date of Regulations

In general, a new Regulation is effective on the date on which such Regulation is filed with the Federal Register.[2] However; there are certain situations in which a Regulation can be effective retroactively, including the following:

- The Regulation is filed or issued within 18 months of the date of the enactment of the statutory provision to which the Regulation relates.

- The Regulation is designed to prevent abuse by taxpayers.

- The Regulation corrects a procedural defect in the issuance of a prior Regulation.

- The Regulation relates to internal Treasury Department policies, practices, or procedures.

- The Regulation may apply retroactively by congressional directive.

- The Commissioner also has the power to allow taxpayers to elect to apply new Regulations retroactively.

In situations where a Regulation applies retroactively, it technically can apply starting with the date of the underlying Code section to which it relates. However, the statute of limitations may limit the application of a retroactive Regulation in many situations.

Citing a Regulation

Tax practitioners use a uniform common system for citing specific Regulations. Each Regulation is assigned a unique number by the Treasury, which is broadly based on the Code section being interpreted in that Regulation. An example of this citation system appears in Exhibit 4-1.

The number to the left of the period in a Regulation citation indicates the type of issue that is addressed in the pronouncement. The most commonly encountered types of Regulations include the following:

Regulation Type	Topic
1	Income Tax
20	Estate Tax
25	Gift Tax
31	Employment Tax
301	Procedural Matter

By being familiar with this arbitrary numbering system used by the Regulations, the tax researcher immediately can identify the general issue that is addressed in a pronouncement. Note that these numbers indicating the type of issue addressed in the Regulation do not necessarily correspond to the chapter numbers of the Code sections that address the same issues.

The number to the immediate right of the period in the citation of a Regulation indicates the Code section to which the Regulation relates. In the Exhibit 4-1, example of a full citation, one can determine that this is an income tax Regulation dealing with §162 of the Internal Revenue Code. The numbers and letters to the right of the section number denote the Regulation number and smaller divisions of the pronouncement. Regulation numbers typically are consecutive, starting with 0 or 1, and follow the general order of the issues that are addressed in the corresponding Code section. However, the Regulation numbers, paragraphs, and so on do not necessarily correspond to the subsection or other division designations of the underlying Code section.

---

[2]IRC §7805(b).

EXHIBIT 4-1: Interpreting a Regulation Citation

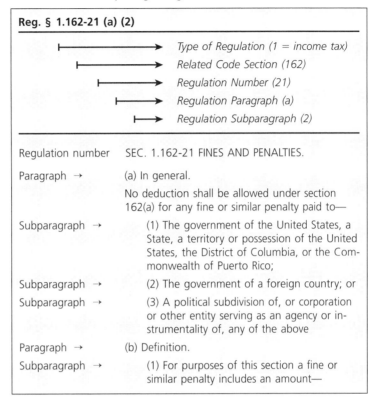

Regulation number	SEC. 1.162-21 FINES AND PENALTIES.
Paragraph →	(a) In general.
	No deduction shall be allowed under section 162(a) for any fine or similar penalty paid to—
Subparagraph →	(1) The government of the United States, a State, a territory or possession of the United States, the District of Columbia, or the Commonwealth of Puerto Rico;
Subparagraph →	(2) The government of a foreign country; or
Subparagraph →	(3) A political subdivision of, or corporation or other entity serving as an agency or instrumentality of, any of the above
Paragraph →	(b) Definition.
Subparagraph →	(1) For purposes of this section a fine or similar penalty includes an amount—

The numbering system for Temporary Regulations is similar to the numbering system for the Final and Proposed Regulations; however, usually the reference to, or citation of, a Temporary Regulation will include a "T" designating the temporary nature of the Regulation. Reg. §1.280H-1T(b)(3) is an example of a citation for a Temporary Regulation under Code §280H.

A Regulation can also be cited in a more formal legal format. For instance, the Regulation in Exhibit 4-1 could be alternatively cited as: 26 CFR § 162-21(a)(2). In this case, the "26" is the number of the Title of the U.S. Code for the Internal Revenue Code, and "CFR" is the abbreviation for Code of Federal Regulations.

Assessing Regulations

In the course of tax practice, the researcher occasionally is faced with a question concerning the validity of a Regulation. If the practitioner disagrees with the scope or language of the Regulation, he or she bears the burden of proof of showing that the Regulation is improper. This can be difficult. Many Regulations simply restate the Code or congressional Committee Reports; they are known as "hard and solid" Regulations. Moreover, because of the authority delegated to the IRS, Legislative Regulations have the full force and effect of law. Finally, the Supreme Court views General Regulations as also having the force and effect of law, unless they conflict with the statute.[3] Thus, a taxpayer's challenge to a Regulation typically must assert an improper exercise of IRS power or an overly broad application of a rule.

---

[3]Maryland Casualty Co. v, U.S., 251 U.S. 342 (1920).

In questioning the provisions of a Regulation, the tax researcher must be aware of several accuracy-related penalties Congress has enacted in the Internal Revenue Code. For example, a penalty is assessed equal to 20 percent of any underpayment of tax where the underpayment is found to be due to "negligence" on the part of the taxpayer.[4] Generally, negligence includes any failure to make a reasonable attempt to comply with the Code or any evidence of disregard of Treasury Rules or Regulations. Thus, if a practitioner chooses to ignore an administrative element of the tax law, he or she must possess substantial authority to do so to avoid this penalty or others of its kind. See Chapter 14 for a more detailed examination of these provisions.

Locating Regulations

When TDs are final, they are published in the **Internal Revenue Bulletin**, a weekly newsletter of the IRS. Most commercial tax services also reproduce the Regulations in their materials; annotated services usually include the text adjacent to the language of the Code and the related court case notes, and topical services usually provide an appendix that includes the edited Regulations for the volume or chapter that discusses the pertinent issue. Paperback or hardbound editions of the tax Regulations also are available from several commercial publishers, including Research Institute of America (RIA) and Commerce Clearing House (CCH), typically as a companion to a similar edition of the Code.

Revenue Rulings

Revenue Rulings are second to Regulations as important administrative sources of the Federal tax law. A Revenue Ruling is an official pronouncement of the National Office of the IRS. It deals with the application of the Code and Regulations to a specific factual situation, usually one that has been submitted by a taxpayer. Thus, many Revenue Rulings indicate how the IRS will treat a given taxpayer transaction. In addition, Revenue Rulings provide taxpayers with needed information, such as applicable Federal interest rates and other items required by taxpayers. These rates are used for complying with required tax law calculations.

Revenue Rulings do not carry the force and effect of Regulations. Nevertheless, they still provide excellent sources of information for tax researchers. In fact, they are published chiefly for the purpose of guiding taxpayers. Therefore, even for a tax researcher whose client did not submit the original request for the Ruling, the result of the Ruling is of value if it concerns a transaction similar in nature, structure, or effect to the client's situation. However, reliance should not be placed on a Revenue Ruling if it has been affected by subsequent legislation, Regulations, Rulings, or court decisions.

Revenue Rulings adhere to a general internal structure, as illustrated in Exhibit 4-2. The typical structure is as follows:

Issue: A statement of the issue in question.

Facts: The facts on which the Revenue Ruling is based.

Law and analysis: The IRS's application of current law to the issue in the Revenue Ruling.

Holding: How the IRS will treat the transaction.

---

[4]IRC §6662.

EXHIBIT 4-2: Revenue Ruling Excerpt

Rev. Rul. 2010-5, 2010-4 I.R.B. 312

Issues
(1) Is a tax return preparer liable for penalties under sections 7216 and 6713 when the preparer discloses to a professional liability insurance carrier tax return information required by the insurance carrier to obtain or maintain professional liability insurance coverage?

(2) Is a tax return preparer liable for penalties under sections 7216 and 6713 when the preparer discloses to the preparer's professional liability insurance carrier tax return information required by the insurance carrier to promptly and accurately report a claim or a potential claim against the tax return preparer, or to aid in the investigation of a claim or potential claim against the tax return preparer?

(3) Is a tax return preparer liable for penalties under sections 7216 and 6713 when the preparer discloses tax return information to the preparer's professional liability insurance carrier in order to secure legal representation under the terms of the insurance policy or to an unrelated attorney for the purpose of evaluating a claim or potential claim against the tax return preparer?

* * *

Facts
Tax Return Preparer A prepared income tax returns during the 2009 filing season and expects to prepare income tax returns in the 2010 filing season. During 2010, A expects to disclose to insurance agents or other insurance company representatives tax return information required to obtain or maintain professional liability insurance coverage, including information necessary to obtain price quotes from the insurance companies. The disclosed information would include a list of client names and descriptions of the services A provided to those clients. A also expects to disclose to its professional liability insurance carrier tax return information required by the terms of the insurance policy to promptly and accurately report, and to aid in the investigation of, a claim or potential claim against A, including client names, descriptions of services A provided to the named clients, a description of the claim or potential claim of professional negligence, misconduct, or fraud, and, when necessary, copies of tax returns relevant to the claim or potential claim. Finally, A expects to disclose to its professional liability insurance carrier tax return information required by the terms of the insurance policy to obtain legal representation provided by the insurance carrier under the terms of the insurance policy related to a claim or potential claim of professional negligence, misconduct, or fraud, or to an unrelated attorney for the purpose of evaluating a claim or potential claim of professional negligence, misconduct, or fraud.

* * *

Law
Section 7216(a) establishes a criminal penalty that is applicable to tax return preparers who knowingly or recklessly disclose or use any information furnished to them for, or in connection with, the preparation of tax returns for any purpose other than to prepare, or assist in preparing, any such returns.

Section 7216(b)(3) establishes an exception to the penalty for disclosures or uses of information which are permitted by regulations prescribed by the Secretary.

Section 6713(a) establishes a civil penalty that is applicable to tax return preparers who disclose or use any information furnished to them for, or in connection with, the preparation of tax returns for any purpose other than to prepare, or assist in preparing, any such returns.

Section 6713(b) provides that the rules of section 7216(b) shall apply for purposes of section 6713.

* * *

Analysis

Issue 1. Obtaining and Maintaining Professional Liability Insurance.
Insurance companies offer professional liability coverage to tax return preparers to insure against potential claims arising from the tax return preparers' negligence, misconduct, or fraud in connection with the preparation or processing of tax returns. A tax return preparer may obtain professional liability insurance coverage in order to protect itself from such claims of negligence, misconduct, or fraud.

Issue 2. Reporting and Investigating Claims.
Services provided by a professional liability insurance carrier include investigation and management of claims or potential claims arising in connection with the preparation of tax returns by the covered tax return preparer. In order to request coverage for a claim or potential claim, a tax return preparer is required to promptly and accurately report claims or potential claims to its professional liability insurance carrier.

* * *

Holdings
(1) Tax Return Preparer A is not liable for penalties under sections 7216 and 6713 when A discloses to a professional liability insurance carrier tax return information required by the insurance carrier to obtain or maintain professional liability insurance coverage, including obtaining price quotes for such insurance coverage.

* * *

Drafting Information
The principal author of this revenue ruling is Molly K. Donnelly of the Office of Associate Chief Counsel (Procedure & Administration). For further information regarding this revenue ruling, contact Ms. Donnelly at (202) 622-4940 (not a toll-free call).

Revenue Ruling Citations

Revenue Rulings are published weekly by the IRS in the Internal Revenue Bulletin, which is discussed in more detail later in this chapter. An example of a citation of a Revenue Ruling is as follows:

Rev. Rul. 2010-5, 2010-4 I.R.B. 312, where

2010-5 is the Revenue Ruling number (the fifth Revenue Ruling of 2010).

2010-4 is the weekly issue of the Internal Revenue Bulletin (the fourth week of 2010).

I.R.B. is the abbreviation for the Internal Revenue Bulletin.

312 is the page number where the Ruling starts in the Internal Revenue Bulletin.

Revenue Rulings in the I.R.B. (referred to as a temporary citation) are published in twice-yearly bound volumes, named the **Cumulative Bulletin** (C.B.) by the Government Printing Office (referred to as a permanent citation). An example of such a C.B. citation would be:

Rev. Rul. 96-58, 1996-2 C.B. 6, where:

96-58 is the Revenue Ruling number (the 58th Revenue Ruling of 1996).

1996-2 is the volume number of Cumulative Bulletin (volume 2 of 1996).

C.B. is the abbreviation for the Cumulative Bulletin.

6 is the page number.

Note the two-digit year (96) in this citation. Tax practitioner should be aware of the historical C.B. citation system because many of the older Revenue Rulings, which are still in effect, may have research value in future years. Since the IRS started (in 1999) numbering the I.R.B.s in consecutive page numbers across issues, the use of the C.B. citation has become less common. As a result, the Cumulative Bulletins are currently a compilation of the I.R.B.s for the appropriate period.

Locating Revenue Rulings

Generally, the tax researcher must examine every applicable Revenue Ruling before a tax research project is complete. Revenue Rulings can be found in the Internal Revenue

Bulletin and by using commercial tax research databases as discussed in Chapter 2. Prior to 1953, Revenue Rulings were known by different names, including Appeals and Review Memorandum (ARM), General Counsel's Memorandum (GCM), and Office Decision (OD). These early rulings still may have some application in client situations if the IRS has not revoked them or modified them in any way. A tax researcher cannot ignore such rulings simply because they are old.

Revenue Procedures

Revenue Procedures deal with the internal practice and procedures of the IRS in the administration of the tax laws. They constitute the IRS's way of releasing information to taxpayers. For example, when the IRS releases specifications for facsimile tax forms generated by a computer service, or informs the public about areas in which it will no longer issue Revenue Rulings, it issues a Revenue Procedure to that effect. Although a Revenue Procedure may not be as useful as a Regulation or a Revenue Ruling in the direct resolution of a tax research problem, the practitioner still should be familiar with all of the pertinent Procedures.

Revenue Procedures are issued in a manner similar to that for Revenue Rulings. They are published in the weekly Internal Revenue Bulletin. The IRS issues approximately 50 Revenue Procedures per year. (For example, there were 56 in 2009.)

SPOTLIGHT ON TAXATION

Factoid

Between 1954 and 2007, the IRS issued approximately 20,000 Revenue Rulings and Revenue Procedures. This is an average of about 400 Revenue Rulings and Revenue Procedures per year. But the average since 2000 has been less than half of that number.

A Revenue Procedure is cited using the same system as that for Revenue Rulings. Thus, a typical current Revenue Procedure would have the following citation: Rev. Proc. 2010-20, 2010-14 I.R.B. 528.

A Revenue Procedure is reproduced in Exhibit 4-3. Revenue Procedures can be found in the same publications in which Revenue Rulings are located.

Letter Rulings

The tax researcher is also interested in the letter rulings that are issued by the IRS in several forms, including Private Letter Rulings, Determination Letters, and Technical Advice Memoranda. The IRS does not publish these items in any official collection, but they are available from several commercial sources, as will be discussed later in this chapter.

Private Letter Rulings

The National Office of the IRS issues **Private Letter Rulings** in response to a taxpayer's request for the IRS's position on a specified tax issue. The IRS has the authority to decline to issue Letter Rulings under certain conditions, such as where the problem is one of an inherently factual nature. The content, format, and procedures that are used for

EXHIBIT 4-3:   Revenue Procedure Excerpt

Rev. Proc. 2010-20, 2010-14 I.R.B. 528

1. PURPOSE

This revenue procedure provides a safe harbor under section 118(a) of the Internal Revenue Code for the treatment of a Smart Grid Investment Grant (SGIG) under 42 U.S.C. 17386 made by the United States Department of Energy (DOE) to a corporation for qualifying investments under the Smart Grid Investment Matching Grant Program as authorized by section 1306 of the Energy Independence and Security Act of 2007 (Pub. L. 110-140), as amended by section 405, Division A of the American Recovery and Reinvestment Act of 2009 (Pub. L. 111-5).

2. BACKGROUND

Section 118(a) of the Code provides that in the case of a corporation, gross income does not include a contribution to the capital of the taxpayer.

Section 1.118-1 of the Income Tax Regulations provides that section 118 applies to contributions to capital made by a person other than a shareholder, for example, property contributed to a corporation by a governmental unit for the purpose of enabling the corporation to expand its operating facilities.

Section 362(c)(2) of the Code requires a basis reduction in a corporation's property when the corporation receives money from a nonshareholder as a contribution to its capital.

42 U.S.C. 17386 provides that DOE shall establish a Smart Grid Investment Matching Grant Program to make grants for qualifying investments. Under 42 U.S.C. 17386, an SGIG may not be used for ongoing or routine operating and maintenance expenditures.

3. SCOPE

This revenue procedure applies to corporate taxpayers that receive an SGIG under 42 U.S.C. 17386 from DOE. This revenue procedure does not apply to noncorporate taxpayers, or to grants under 42 U.S.C. 17384 (Smart Grid technology research, development, and demonstration).

4. PROCEDURE

The Internal Revenue Service will not challenge a corporation's treatment of an SGIG made by DOE to the corporation as a nonshareholder contribution to the capital of the corporation under section 118(a) of the Code if the corporation properly reduces the basis of its property under section 362(c)(2) and the regulations thereunder.

5. EFFECTIVE DATE

This revenue procedure is effective March 10, 2010.

6. DRAFTING INFORMATION

The principal author of this revenue procedure is David McDonnell of the Office of Associate Chief Counsel (Passthroughs & Special Industries). For further information regarding this revenue procedure contact Mr. McDonnell at (202) 622-3040 (not a toll free call).

Revenue Rulings apply with respect to Private Letter Rulings. The IRS does not publish its reply in the Internal Revenue Bulletin. Rather, it sends its response only to the taxpayer who submitted the request. An excerpt of a Private Letter Ruling is shown in Exhibit 4-4.

The process is as follows. The taxpayer asks the letter ruling application IRS to disclose its interpretation of the Code, Regulations, and pertinent court cases for a transaction the taxpayer describes; the description should include a statement of the business purpose for the transaction. For instance, if two corporations plan to merge, one of them might request a Private Letter Ruling to find out whether the IRS believes that the Code's tax-favored reorganization provisions will apply to the anticipated merger. In many cases, if the IRS asserts that the transaction will not receive a treatment favorable to the taxpayer, it will suggest means by which the transaction could be restructured to obtain the favorable treatment.

As mentioned, a Private Letter Ruling is issued only to the taxpayer who requests the ruling. However, Private Letter Rulings are included in the list of authorities

EXHIBIT 4-4: Private Letter Ruling

Private Letter Ruling 201016040 S Corps.—Damages Payments—Creation Of Second Class Of Stock.

Dear [Redacted Text]:

This responds to a letter dated September 4, 2009, and subsequent correspondence, submitted on behalf of X, requesting a ruling under § 1361(b)(1)(D) of the Internal Revenue Code.

Facts

According to the information submitted, X made an election to be treated as an S corporation effective D1. X subsequently discovered that due to some inadequate advice it received, some of the shareholders of X suffered financial damages. These shareholders sought compensation for the damages sustained. X seeks a ruling that such payments to compensate some of its shareholders for these damages will not constitute issuance of a second class of stock, which would jeopardize X's S corporation status under § 1361(b)(1)(D).

Law and Analysis

§ Section 1361(a)(1) provides that the term "S corporation" means, with respect to any taxable year, a small business corporation for which an election under § 1362(a) is in effect.

§ Section 1361(b)(1) defines the term "small business corporation" as a domestic corporation that is not an ineligible corporation and that, among other things, does not have more than one class of stock.

Section § 1.1361-1(l)(1) of the Income Tax Regulations provides that, except as provided in § 1.1361-1(l)(4) (relating to instruments, obligations, or arrangements treated as a second class of stock), a corporation is treated as having only one class of stock if all outstanding shares of stock of the corporation confer identical rights to distribution and liquidation proceeds.

§ Section 1.1361-1(l)(2)(i) provides that the determination of whether all outstanding shares of stock confer identical rights to liquidation and distribution proceeds is made based on the corporate charter, articles of incorporation, bylaws, applicable state law, and binding agreements (collectively, the governing provisions).

Conclusion

Based solely on the facts submitted and representation made, we conclude that the damages payments to some of X's shareholders does not create a second class of stock. Therefore, X will be treated as continuing to be an S corporation, provided that X's S corporation election is not otherwise terminated under § 1362(d).

Except as expressly provided herein, no opinion is expressed or implied as to the federal tax consequences of the facts described above under any other provision of the Code. In particular, no opinion is expressed as to whether X is an S corporation for federal tax purposes.

This ruling is directed only to the taxpayer requesting it. § Section 6110(k)(3) of the Code provides that it may not be used or cited as precedent.

Pursuant to the power of attorney on file with this office, a copy of this letter will be sent to X and X's other authorized representative.

Sincerely,

David R. Haglund
Chief, Branch 1
Office of Associate Chief Counsel
(Passthroughs and Special Industries)

constituting "substantial authority" upon which a taxpayer may rely to avoid certain statutory penalties.[5] Letter Rulings are, in any case, an important source of information because they indicate how the IRS may treat a similar transaction.

Private Letter Rulings also constitute an important IRS stimulus for new Revenue Rulings. When the IRS comes across an unusual transaction that it believes to be of general interest, or when it receives a flurry of Letter Ruling requests concerning

---

[5]Reg. §1.6662-4(d)(3)(iii).

very similar factual situations, a Private Ruling may be converted into Revenue Ruling form and published in official administrative sources. The IRS must notify the taxpayer of its intention to disclose the ruling, and the taxpayer has the right to protest such disclosure. Before publication, all aspects of the new ruling, including the statement of facts, are purged of any reference to the taxpayer's name or other identifying information.

SPOTLIGHT ON TAXATION

Factoid

The IRS has issued almost 100,000 Letter Rulings and Technical Advice Memoranda since 1980. As a result, a tax researcher is faced with an average of over 3,000 new research documents every year just from this one source of authority.

Technical Advice Memoranda

A **Technical Advice Memorandum** is issued by the IRS's National Office, making it similar in this regard to the Private Letter Ruling and different from the Determination Letter. The Technical Advice Memorandum, however, concerns a completed transaction. Whereas a Private Letter Ruling typically is requested by a taxpayer prior to completing a transaction or filing a tax return, a Technical Advice Memorandum usually is requested by an agent when a question arises during an audit that cannot be answered satisfactorily by the local office.

Similar to the Private Letter Ruling, a Technical Advice Memorandum applies strictly to the taxpayer for whose audit it was requested, and it cannot be relied on by other taxpayers. However, once again the information that is contained in the memorandum may be useful to the tax researcher for the insight that it gives concerning the thinking of the IRS relative to a given problem area in taxation.

These memoranda are not included in any official IRS publication, but they are open for public inspection and available from commercial tax research services, as will be discussed in the next section. If the facts or the holding of a Technical Advice Memorandum are felt by the IRS to be of general interest, the memorandum may be converted into Revenue Ruling format and published by the IRS in the Internal Revenue Bulletin.

Determination Letters

A **Determination Letter** is similar in purpose and nature to a Private Letter Ruling, except that it is issued by a local office of the IRS rather than by the national office of the IRS. Because a Determination Letter is issued by a lower-level IRS official, it usually deals with issues and transactions that are not overtly controversial. For instance, the trustee of a pension plan might request a Determination Letter to ascertain whether the plan is qualified for the Code's tax-favored deferred compensation treatment.

Determination Letters usually relate to completed transactions rather than to the proposed transactions that typically lead to the issuance of a Private Letter Ruling. Determination Letters are not included in any official IRS publication, but they are available to the tax researcher from commercial tax research services.

Public Inspection of Written Determinations

The public may request copies of IRS Letter Rulings from the government in lieu of using a subscription commercial tax research service.[6] Included under this provision are Private Letter Rulings, Determination Letters, and Technical Advice Memoranda. Before any public inspection is allowed, however, the IRS is required to remove the taxpayer's name and any other information that might be used by a third party to identify the taxpayer.[7] In addition, the IRS is required to purge the document of any items that could affect national defense or foreign policy, trade secrets, financial information, data relative to the regulation of financial institutions, geographical data, and items that could invade personal privacy. If the taxpayer opposes the disclosure of the written determination, he or she can bring the matter before the IRS and the Tax Court prior to the scheduled disclosure.

Once all of the required data have been removed from the written determination, it must be made open for public inspection online and at such places as the Treasury Secretary designates in the Regulations. Information of this type is available in Washington, D.C., and at selected other locations.

The precedential value of any of these written determinations is strictly limited.[8] Overall, such pronouncements may not be cited as authority in a tax matter by either the taxpayer or the IRS. However, Letter Rulings can be used as "examples" of IRS treatment of similar factual patterns when dealing with the IRS. For example, tax practitioners could suggest that a Letter Ruling be used as guidance in a similar situation during an audit. However, an IRS agent need not follow a Letter Ruling issued to a different taxpayer.

Taxpayers may rely on Private Letter Rulings, Technical Advice Memoranda, Actions on Decisions, General Counsel Memoranda, and other similar documents published by the IRS in the Internal Revenue Bulletin, to avoid certain understatement of tax penalties. Nevertheless, use of such pronouncements for this purpose does not expand the general precedential value of these pronouncements with respect to determining a taxpayer's tax liability.

Written Determination Numbering System

Because the IRS issues thousands of Letter Rulings per year, it assigns a nine-digit document number to each written determination for identification purposes. The first four digits indicate the year in which the ruling was issued, the next two numbers denote the week, and the last three digits indicate the number of the ruling for the week. Thus, a lengthy but unique identifier is created for each pronouncement. For example, the number of a Letter Ruling can be interpreted as follows:

Ltr. Rul. 200917024, where

2009 is the year the Ruling is issued.

17 is the week of the year the Ruling is issued.

024 indicates that this is the twenty-fourth Ruling issued that week.

Before 2000, only a two-digit date was used to signify the year in which the ruling was issued (e.g., 9814026).

Locating Written Determinations

The tax researcher needs access to written determinations to complete many tax research projects. Selected written determinations can be found in summary form in the major tax

---

[6] IRC §6110(f).

[7] IRC §6610(c).

[8] IRC §6110.

services. However, if the tax researcher needs access to the full text of a large number of IRS pronouncements, an electronic database is the best approach.

Other IRS Pronouncements

The IRS issues several other types of information that can be of value to the tax researcher, including acquiescences and nonacquiescences, the Internal Revenue Bulletin, Chief Counsel Memoranda, and other miscellaneous publications.

Acquiescences and Nonacquiescences

When the IRS loses an issue or decision in court, the Commissioner may announce an acquiescence or nonacquiescence to the decision. An **acquiescence** indicates that the court decision, although it was adverse to the IRS, will be followed in similar situations. The Commissioner determines, at his or her own discretion, the degree of similarity required before the IRS will follow the result that is unfavorable to itself.

A **nonacquiescence** indicates that the IRS disagrees with the adverse decision in the case and will follow the decision only for the specific taxpayer whose case resulted in the adverse ruling. If the IRS wishes to express agreement with only part of the decision that is settled in the taxpayer's favor, the Commissioner may nonacquiesce with respect to certain issues. Finally, an acquiescence or nonacquiescence is not issued if the IRS prevails in a court case, because it likely agrees with all pertinent holdings.

Nonacquiescence may indicate to the tax practitioner that the IRS is likely to challenge a similar decision for the taxpayer in a case that has a similar factual situation. However, the issuance of an acquiescence does not necessarily mean that the IRS agrees with the adverse decision, but only that it will not pursue the matter in a (similar and) subsequent case. Each of these items of information can be useful when the practitioner prepares for, or anticipates, a court challenge to the client's position in a tax matter.

As mentioned, if the IRS has acquiesced to a case, then the taxpayer can rely on that decision as a precedent that will be followed by agents for similar fact patterns. If the IRS has nonacquiesced, however, the taxpayer must evaluate whether to pursue a similar fact pattern in court. Such factors as the cost of litigation plus the probability of winning must be appraised before proceeding with a case similar to one with which the IRS has nonacquiesced.

Occasionally, the IRS changes (with an attendant retroactive effect on taxpayers) its acquiescence or nonacquiescence position by withdrawing the original pronouncement. For example, in U.S. *v. City Loan and Savings*, 287 F.2d 612 (CA-6, 1961), the court allowed the IRS to withdraw an acquiescence on an issue-by-issue, but not taxpayer-by-taxpayer, basis. This change may occur after only a short time passes or many years later. Such a change in the IRS's position typically is accompanied by a brief explanation of the reason for the change—for example, because of a contrary holding in a subsequent court case or a change in the agency's policy concerning the issue.

IRS acquiescence decisions are driven by related litigation costs, revenue effects, and administrative and policy directives. The Service issues acquiescences/nonacquiescences as **Actions on Decision (AOD)**, relative to the following court decisions:

- Regular Tax Court
- Memorandum Tax Court
- District Court
- Court of Federal Claims
- Courts of Appeal

IRS Actions on Decision are published in the Internal Revenue Bulletin, and thereafter in the Cumulative Bulletin. They are prepared by the office of the Associate Chief Counsel (Litigation). AODs are public documents, and they generally include the following:

- The issue decided against the government

- The pertinent facts

- A discussion of the reasoning supporting the acquiescence/nonacquiescence decision[9]

Exhibit 4-5 reproduces an acquiescence from the Internal Revenue Bulletin in which the IRS indicates its position on a case. A citator (see Chapter 8) also can be used to locate and interpret acquiescence and nonacquiescence decisions.

EXHIBIT 4-5: Action on Decision Excerpt

Action on Decision 2010-001, 2010-22

June 1, 2010

Subject: *Tidewater Inc. and Subsidiaries and Tidewater Foreign Sales Corporation v. United States*, 565 F. 3d 299 [103 AFTR 2d 2009-1682] (5th Cir. 2009), aff'g No. 06-875, 2007 U.S. Dist. LEXIS 77147 (E.D. La. October 17, 2007)

Issue:
Whether certain time charters entered into between members of Taxpayer's controlled group and unrelated customers are leases under I.R.C. § 7701(e).

Discussion:
Tidewater Inc. and certain of its subsidiaries ("Taxpayer") own ocean-going vessels used in the offshore energy industry in foreign and domestic waters. For tax years 1998–2000, Taxpayer bareboat chartered the vessels to certain of its operating company subsidiaries. Taxpayer and the Service agree that the bareboat charters were leasing transactions. In turn, the operating companies time chartered the vessels to unrelated customers. Each time charter obligated the operating company to provide the customer with a named ocean-going vessel with certain capabilities and a crew to operate that vessel for a specified period of time.

Taxpayer and the Service disagreed about whether the commissions paid to Tidewater FSC (a foreign sales corporation ("FSC") under former § 922) in connection with the charters qualified for the preferential FSC tax treatment under former §§ 921-927. If the time charters with the unrelated customers were subleases of the vessels, the commissions qualified for the preferential FSC tax treatment; otherwise, if the time charters were contracts for services, the commissions did not qualify. See former I.R.C. § 927(a)(2)(A) and Temp. Treas. Reg. § 1.927(a)-1T(f)(2).

Taxpayer claimed that the time charters constituted subleases of the vessels for purposes of the FSC provisions. The Service disagreed and concluded that the time charters were not leases.

The district court rejected the Government's position that the FSC provisions require an "all or nothing" characterization of the time charters as either a lease or a service contract. *Tidewater Inc. v. United States*, No. 06-875, 2007 U.S. Dist. LEXIS 77147, at 13-14 (E.D. La. October 17, 2007). The court determined that the time charters were, in part, subleases and granted the Taxpayer's motion for summary judgment. The court failed to apply (or even discuss) the factors listed under § 7701(e) for determining whether an agreement is a lease. The case was appealed to the United States Court of Appeals for the Fifth Circuit.

* * *

Recommendation:
Nonacquiescence

Reviewers:
Edward C. Schwartz
Attorney
(Income Tax & Accounting)

---

[9]*Taxation with Representation Fund v. IRS*, 485 F. Supp. 263 (DDC, 1990).

Approved:
William J. Wilkins
Chief Counsel
Internal Revenue Service
George J. Blaine
Associate Chief Counsel
(Income Tax & Accounting)

THIS DOCUMENT IS NOT TO BE RELIED UPON OR OTHERWISE CITED AS PRECECENT BY TAXPAYERS

After the IRS issues such a pronouncement, any reference to the citation for the case includes the abbreviation either "Acq" or "Nonacq" (or, occasionally, "NA") to indicate the subsequent development. The AOD itself should not be cited as an IRS precedent, though.

Internal Revenue Bulletin

The IRS's official publication for its pronouncements is the Internal Revenue Bulletin. Most IRS Revenue Rulings and Revenue Procedures, and the agency's acquiescences and nonacquiescences to regular Tax Court decisions, are published in the Internal Revenue Bulletin. This reference bulletin also includes the following information, all of which can be useful to the tax researcher.

- New tax laws, issued by Congress as Public Laws
- Committee Reports underlying tax statutes
- Procedural rules
- New tax treaties
- TDs (which become Regulations)
- Other notices

Interested parties can subscribe to the Internal Revenue Bulletin by contacting the IRS. Alternatively, some of the commercial tax services include subscriptions to, or reproductions of, all of the issues of the Internal Revenue Bulletin. The Internal Revenue Bulletin is available by subscription in hard copy, and online in html and .pdf formats. See Exhibit 4-6 for an example of an Internal Revenue Bulletin.

Chief Counsel Memoranda

The office of the IRS's Chief Counsel periodically generates memoranda that may be of use to the tax researcher. Although the IRS does not publish these memoranda in any official document, they are available from commercial publishers. A **Technical Memorandum (TM)** summarizes and explains published Regulations. **General Counsel Memoranda (GCM)** are generated upon the request of the IRS, typically as a means to assist in the preparation of Revenue Rulings and Private Letter Rulings. In addition, the Chief Counsel's office gives various forms of advice called Chief Counsel Advise (CCA) to IRS offices and personnel. IRS Chief Counsel Pronouncements are summarized in Exhibit 4-7.

These documents are available for public inspection and can be found on most computer-based tax services.

Announcements and Notices

The IRS issues **Announcements and Notices** concerning items of general importance to taxpayers. Announcements are public pronouncements that have immediate or short-term

EXHIBIT 4-6: Internal Revenue Bulletin

Internal Revenue

bulletin

**Bulletin No. 2010-18
May 3, 2010**

HIGHLIGHTS
OF THIS ISSUE
These synopses are intended only as aids to the reader in
identifying the subject matter covered. They may not be
relied upon as authoritative interpretations.

INCOME TAX

Rev. Rul. 2010–12, page 617.
**Federal rates; adjusted federal rates; adjusted federal
long-term rate and the long-term exempt rate.** For purposes of sections 382, 642, 1274, 1288, and other sections
of the Code, tables set forth the rates for May 2010.

Notice 2010–37, page 654.
**Renewable electricity production, refined coal produc-
tion, and Indian coal production; calendar year 2010
inflation adjustment factors and reference prices.** This
notice announces the calendar year 2010 inflation adjustment
factors and reference prices for the renewable electricity production credit, refined coal production credit, and Indian coal
production credit under section 45 of the Code.

EMPLOYEE PLANS

T.D. 9479, page 618.
Final regulations under section 9812 of the Code provide guidance on the requirements imposed on group health plans by
the Paul Wellstone and Pete Domenici Mental Health Parity and
Addiction Equity Act of 2008 (MHPAEA), generally prohibiting
plans from imposing financial requirements or treatment limitations with respect to mental health or substance use disorder
benefits that are more restrictive than those imposed with respect to medical/surgical benefits under the plan.

EXCISE TAX

T.D. 9479, page 618.
Final regulations under section 9812 of the Code provide guidance on the requirements imposed on group health plans by
the Paul Wellstone and Pete Domenici Mental Health Parity and
Addiction Equity Act of 2008 (MHPAEA), generally prohibiting
plans from imposing financial requirements or treatment limitations with respect to mental health or substance use disorder
benefits that are more restrictive than those imposed with respect to medical/surgical benefits under the plan.

TAX CONVENTIONS

Announcement 2010–27, page 657.
The competent authorities of the United States and Belgium entered into the following agreement regarding the types of pension plans established in either Contracting State that will be
deemed to generally correspond to a pension plan recognized
for tax purposes in the other Contracting State as required by
paragraphs 7 and 9 of Article 17 (Pensions, Social Security, An-
nuities, Alimony, and Child Support) of the Convention Between
the Government of the United States of America and the Government of the Kingdom of Belgium for the Avoidance of Double
Taxation and the Prevention of Fiscal Evasion with Respect to
Taxes on Income, signed at Brussels on November 27, 2006.
The Agreement is entered into under paragraph 3 of Article 24
(Mutual Agreement Procedure).

(Continued on the next page)

Finding Lists begin on page ii.

Department of the Treasury
Internal Revenue Service

EXHIBIT 4-7: IRS Chief Counsel Pronouncements

Document	Purpose
Technical Memorandum (TM)	TMs are prepared to summarize and explain published Regulations.
General Counsel Memoranda (GCM)	GCMs assist in the preparation of Revenue Rulings and Private Letter Rulings.
Chief Counsel Advice (CCA)	CCAs are written advice or instruction from the IRS national office issued to field employees.
Action on Decision (AOD)	AODs are prepared when the IRS loses a case in a court. They convey the IRS decision to acquiesce/nonacquiesce.
Field Service Advice (FSAs)	FSAs are nonbinding advice, guidance, and analysis provided by IRS National Office attorneys to IRS field personnel.
Chief Counsel Notices (CCNs)	CCNs are temporary directives the IRS national office uses to disseminate policies, procedures, instructions, and/or delegations of authority to Chief Counsel employees.
Service Center Advice (SCAs)	SCAs are guidance provided by the IRS national office to IRS service centers and related IRS functions concerning their tax.

value, such as an approaching deadline for making an election. Notices contain guidance involving substantive interpretations of the Code or other provisions of the law that usually have long-term application. A tax practitioner may rely on an IRS Announcement or Notice as authority for an action, but should confirm his/her understanding of the released material using appropriate research techniques. Exhibit 4-8 reproduces a typical Notice. Both Notices and Announcements are published in the weekly Internal Revenue Bulletin.

Miscellaneous Publications

The IRS publishes numerous general and specialized documents to help taxpayers. Some of the more common ones include the following:

- Publication 3, Armed Forces' Tax Guide
- Publication 17, Your Federal Income Tax
- Publication 54, Tax Guide for U.S. Citizens and Resident Aliens Abroad
- Publication 225, Farmer's Tax Guide
- Publication 334, Tax Guide for Small Business
- Publication 463, Travel, Entertainment, Gift, and Car Expenses
- Publication 519, U.S. Tax Guide for Aliens
- Publication 520, Scholarships and Fellowships
- Publication 521, Moving Expenses
- Publication 575, Pension and Annuity Income
- Publication 589, Tax Information on S Corporations

Each of these documents is available directly from the IRS, both in print and electronic formats. See Exhibit 4-9 for an excerpt from an IRS publication from the IRS Web site. In addition, several of the commercial tax publishers offer copies of these lay-oriented publications. Furthermore, any library that is designated as a government depository receives all of these documents in hard copy. Finally, many of the above publications can be ordered from the IRS in Spanish language editions.

EXHIBIT 4-8: IRS Notice

Notice 2007-10

This notice announces that the Treasury and the IRS will amend §301.7701-2(b)(8) of the Procedure and Administration Regulations to add the Bulgarian aktsionerno druzhestvo entity to the list of entities that are always treated as corporations under section 7701 of the Internal Revenue Code (Code).

1. BACKGROUND

The IRS and Treasury issued final regulations concerning the classification of business entities under section 7701 of the Code on December 18, 1996 (check-the-box regulations). See generally, TD 8697 (1997-1 C.B. 215; 61 FR 66584) and §§301.7701-1 through 3. Under the check-the-box regulations, a business entity generally can elect its classification for federal tax purposes. However, §301.7701-2(b)(8) provides a list of certain foreign business entities that are always classi-fied as corporations for federal tax purposes (the per se corporation list).

On December 16, 2005, the IRS and Treasury published regulations (TD 9235, 2006-4 I.R.B. 338; 70 FR 74658) under section 7701 of the Code adding certain foreign business entities to the per se list of corporations. These regulations were in response to the adoption by the Council of the European Union of a Council Regulation (2157/2001 2001 O.J. (L 294)) (the EU Regula-tion) that recognized a new business entity, the European public limited liability company (Societas Europaea or SE).

The SE is a public limited liability company. The EU Regulation provides general rules that govern the formation and opera-tion of an SE and supplements those rules for specified issues and issues it does not otherwise address by reference to the laws with respect to public limited liability companies for the country in which the SE has its registered office. An SE must have a registered office in one of the Member States of the European Economic Area (which includes all Member States of the European Union plus Norway, Iceland, and Liechtenstein). For further background see TD 9197 (2005-1 C.B. 985; 70 FR 19697) and Notice 2004-68 (2004-2 C.B. 706).

As of January 1, 2007, Bulgaria will become a member of the European Union. Accordingly, an SE will be eligible to have its registered office in Bulgaria and those SEs with a registered office in Bulgaria will, to a certain extent, be subject to the laws of the public limited liability company in Bulgaria. As a result, and consistent with TD 9235, it is appropriate for the IRS and Treasury to add the public limited liability company for Bulgaria to the per se list.

2. DISCUSSION

The IRS and Treasury will issue temporary and proposed regulations that will modify §301.7701-2 to include the Bulgarian aktsio-nerno druzhestvo on the per se corporation list. This entity has been identified as the public limited liability company in Bulgaria.

3. EFFECTIVE DATE

The temporary and proposed regulations to be issued adding the Bulgarian aktsionerno druzhestvo to §301.7701-2(b)(8) generally will apply to such entities formed on or after January 1, 2007. However, they shall also apply to an entity formed before such date upon a 50 percent or greater change of ownership subsequent to such date.

The principal author of this notice is Ronald M. Gootzeit of the Office of Associate Chief Counsel (International). For further information regarding this notice contact Ronald M. Gootzeit at (202) 622-3860 (not a toll-free call).

EXHIBIT 4-9: IRS Publication 3 (Armed Forces' Tax Guide) Excerpt

---

Armed Forces Reservists

If you are a member of a reserve component of the Armed Forces and you travel more than 100 miles away from home in connection with your performance of services as a member of the reserves, you can deduct your travel expenses as an ad-justment to income on line 33 of Form 1040 rather than as a miscellaneous itemized deduction. The deduction is limited to the amount the federal government pays its employees for travel expenses. For more information about this limit, see Per Diem and Car Allowances in chapter 6 of Publication 463.

Member of a reserve component. You are a member of a reserve component of the Armed Forces if you are in the Army, Navy, Marine Corps, Air Force, or Coast Guard Reserve, the Army National Guard of the United States, the Air National Guard of the United States, or the Reserve Corps of the Public Health Service.

How to report. If you have reserve-related travel that takes you more than 100 miles from home, you should first complete Form 2106, Employee Business Expenses, or Form 2106-EZ, Unreimbursed Employee Business Expenses. Then include in the total on line 33 of Form 1040 your expenses for reserve travel over 100 miles from home, up to the federal rate, from line 10 of Form 2106 or line 6 of Form 2106-EZ. Write "RC" and the amount of these expenses in the space to the left of line 33 of Form 1040. Subtract this amount from the total on line 10 of Form 2106 or line 6 of Form 2106-EZ and deduct the balance as an itemized de-duction on line 20 of Schedule A (Form 1040). See Armed Forces reservists under Miscellaneous Itemized Deductions, later.

These documents are prepared from the government's point of view. For instance, if a lower court has ruled against the IRS on a given matter that is addressed in a Publication, the text of the document probably will not mention the possibility that the IRS's official position will be found to be incorrect on appeal. Although IRS Publications can be the source of some basic information that is useful for laypersons, or in a tax compliance context, the tax researcher should not rely on or cite such a reference in a professional research report.

Although the IRS Publications contain useful information, the tax researcher must be careful when relying on them. IRS Publications typically do not cite the Code, Regulations, or other authority on which the information included therein is based. In fact, the IRS disclaims any responsibility for damages that the taxpayer may suffer in erroneously relying on its Publications, and it may, in fact, take positions that are contrary to those that are included in the Publications in certain court cases or appeals hearings.

SUMMARY

Administrative pronouncements provide the tax researcher with a significant amount of information from and about the IRS. The primary IRS pronouncements that are of interest to the tax researcher include the Regulations, Revenue Rulings, Revenue Procedures, and Letter Rulings. The tax practitioner who performs competent research must be aware of the content and format of each of these items, know how to locate them, appreciate the precedential value of each, and understand how each might affect the client's tax problem. Exhibit 4-10 summarizes the most commonly encountered IRS pronouncements.

EXHIBIT 4-10: Common IRS Pronouncements

Pronouncement	Purpose
Regulation	The official Treasury or IRS interpretation of a portion of the Internal Revenue Code
Revenue Ruling	The IRS's application of the tax law to a specific fact situation and other information for taxpayers (e.g., interest rate adjustments)
Revenue Procedure	A statement of IRS practice or procedure that affects taxpayers or the general public
Announcement Notice	IRS release that has immediate or short-term value
	Guidance involving substantive interpretations that has longer term application
Private Letter Ruling	Statement issued by the National Office of the IRS at a taxpayer's request, applying the tax law to a proposed transaction
Determination Letter	Statement issued by the District Director in response to a taxpayer request, concerning the application of the tax law to a specific completed transaction
Acquiescence	Acceptance by the IRS of a court decision that was held in the taxpayer's favor. Published as an Action on Decision.
Nonacquiescence	Notice that the IRS still disagrees with a court decision that was held in the taxpayer's favor. Published as an Action on Decision.
Treasury Decision	A Regulation is promulgated or amended
Technical Advice Memorandum	A letter ruling issued on a completed transaction, usually during an audit

QUIZ YOURSELF

Reinforce the tax research information covered in this chapter by completing the online quizzes located at the Federal Tax Research Web site at **www.cengagebrain.com.** At the CengageBrain.com home page, search for the *Federal Tax Research*, 9e ISBN (1111221642) using the search box at the top of the page. This will take you to the product page where you can access the quizzes.

KEY WORDS

By the time you complete this chapter, you should be comfortable discussing each of the following terms. If you need additional review of any of these items, return to the appropriate material in the chapter or consult the glossary to this text.

acquiescence, p. 132
Actions on Decision (AOD), p. 132
Announcements and Notices,
  p. 134
Cumulative Bulletin, p. 126
Determination Letter, p. 130
General Counsel Memoranda
  (GCM), p. 134

General Regulations, p. 120
Internal Revenue Bulletin, p. 124
Internal Revenue Code, p. 120
Legislative Regulations, p. 121
nonacquiescence, p. 132
Private Letter Rulings, p. 127
Proposed Regulations, p. 120
Regulations, p. 120

revenue procedures, p. 127
revenue rulings, p. 124
Technical Advice Memorandum,
  p. 130
Technical Memorandum (TM),
  p. 134
Temporary Regulations, p. 121
Treasury Decisions (TDs), p. 120

DISCUSSION QUESTIONS

1. What department and agency of the U.S. government has the responsibility to administer the Federal tax laws?

2. Section 7805(a) of the Internal Revenue Code authorizes the IRS to perform what activities?

3. The IRS issues numerous pronouncements. Name the four that are the most important in conducting Federal tax research.

4. Define the terms Regulation and Treasury Decision. Where are TDs published so that interested parties can comment on them?

5. "A tax researcher should not ignore Proposed Regulations." Comment on this statement.

6. Define and distinguish between General and Legislative Regulations.

7. In the citation, Reg. §1.212-3, what do the "1," the "212," and the "3" indicate?

8. Answer the following questions about this citation: Reg. §20.2039-1(a).
   a. What does the "20" stand for?
   b. What does the "2039" stand for?
   c. What does the "1" stand for?
   d. What does the "(a)" stand for?

9. Answer the following questions about this citation: Reg. §1.274-6T(a)(2).
   a. What does the "1" stand for?
   b. What does the "274" stand for?
   c. What does the "6T" stand for?
   d. What does the "(a)" stand for?
   e. What does the "(2)" stand for?

10. Answer the following questions about this citation: 26 CFR § 163-10(a)(2).
   a. What does the "26" stand for?
   b. What does the "163" stand for?
   c. What does the "6T" stand for?
   d. What does the "(a)" stand for?
   e. What does the "(2)" stand for?

11. Answer the following questions about this citation: 26 CFR § 61-21(a)(3)
    a. What does the "26" stand for?
    b. What does the "61" stand for?
    c. What does the "21" stand for?
    d. What does the "(a)" stand for?
    e. What does the "(3)" stand for?

12. Give the number that is associated with each of the following categories of Regulations:
    a. Estate Tax Regulations
    b. Income Tax Regulations
    c. Gift Tax Regulations
    d. Procedural Regulations
    e. Employment Tax Regulations

13. Give the type of Regulation associated with each of the following Regulation numbers:
    a. 31
    b. 301
    c. 25
    d. 601
    e. 20

14. What are Temporary Regulations? What weight do they carry in the tax researcher's analysis?

15. The burden of proof is on the taxpayer to prove that a provision of the Regulations is improper. How could this affect one's tax research?

16. In general, what is the effective date of a new Regulation?

17. Give at least three locations where a tax researcher can find the complete text of a Regulation.

18. What is a Revenue Ruling?

19. Describe the structure of a typical Revenue Ruling.

20. Where are Revenue Rulings initially published by the IRS? Where are the rulings permanently published in hardbound editions?

21. Explain each of the elements of this citation: Rev. Rul. 2009-32, 2009-12 I.R.B. 621.

22. Explain each of the elements of this citation: Rev. Rul. 96-41, 1996-2 C.B. 8.

23. What is the correct citation for Revenue Ruling 2002-55, which is found on page 529 of the second Cumulative Bulletin volume for 2002?

24. What is the correct citation for Revenue Procedure 94-36, which is found on page 682 of the first Cumulative Bulletin volume for 1994?

25. What resources are available to help the tax researcher who wishes to check the current status of a Revenue Ruling?

26. Of what relevance to the tax practitioner is a Revenue Procedure?

27. Where can a tax researcher find copies of Revenue Procedures?

28. Construct the permanent C.B. citation for the fifth Revenue Procedure of 2001, which was published in the second week of the year. It is published on page 164 of the appropriate document.

29. Identify three types of Letter Rulings that are of interest to the tax researcher. Indicate whether each of these rulings is published by the IRS.

30. Which office of the IRS issues Private Letter Rulings? Who requests such a ruling? What kinds of issues are addressed therein?

31. Sometimes a Private Letter Ruling is generalized and included in an official IRS publication. What form does this recast private ruling take?

32. What is a Determination Letter? Which office of the IRS issues Determination Letters? What kinds of issues are addressed therein?

33. What is a Technical Advice Memorandum? Who requests it? What kinds of issues are addressed therein? Does the IRS include Technical Advice Memoranda in any official publication?

34. Discuss the precedential value of Private Letter Rulings, Determination Letters, and Technical Advice Memoranda. What role do these items play in conducting tax research?

35. Which IRS documents are open to public inspection under §6110?

36. What is the precedential value of an IRS written determination under §6110?

37. Explain each of the elements of this citation: Ltr. Rul. 9615032.

38. Where can a tax researcher find copies of written determinations?

39. One of the most important IRS publications is the Internal Revenue Bulletin. How often is this document published? Name six items that typically are published in the Internal Revenue Bulletin.

40. Explain each of the elements of this citation: Rev. Proc. 2004-16, 2004-10 I.R.B. 559.

41. Explain each of the elements of this citation: Rev. Proc. 2000-41, 2000-2 C.B. 317.

42. Distinguish between a citation with "I.R.B." in it and one with "C.B." in it.

43. Discuss the difference between a Revenue Ruling and a Revenue Procedure.

44. In what publication(s) would a tax researcher find the official listing of the IRS acquiescences and nonacquiescences to a Tax Court decision?

45. Can the IRS change its position on acquiescences or nonacquiescences?

46. Must the IRS acquiesce or nonacquiesce to every issue in a court decision?

47. What is the purpose of each of the following?
    a. Technical Memorandum (TM)
    b. General Counsel's Memorandum (GCM)
    c. Action on Decision (AOD)

48. What is the purpose of each of the following?
    a. Field Service Advice (FSA)
    b. Chief Counsel Notices (CCN)
    c. Service Center Advice (SCA)
    d. Chief Counsel Advice (CCA)

49. Give the title of each of the following:
    a. Publication 17
    b. Publication 225
    c. Publication 334

50. Give the title of each of the following:
    a. Publication 3
    b. Publication 463
    c. Publication 520

51. What is an IRS Announcement? When is it used? In your opinion, could a tax practitioner rely on an IRS Announcement as authority for a tax return position?

52. What is an IRS Notice? When is it used? In your opinion, could a tax practitioner rely on an IRS Notice as authority for a tax return position?

53. Why should the tax researcher exercise caution in relying on an IRS publication, such as published instructions to tax forms, in undertaking a research project?

EXERCISES

54. Locate Revenue Ruling 99-56. Explain the effect of that ruling on previous Treasury Department pronouncements.

55. Briefly describe the subject of each of the following Letter Rulings. State the type [Private Letter Ruling (PLR), Field Service Advice (FSA), Service Center Advice (SCA), etc.] of each Letter Ruling.
    a. 200034026
    b. 200113016
    c. 200113020
    d. 200113023

56. Correctly cite the italicized sentence indicated by the dart (▶) in the following passage from the Regulations:

    SEC. 1.162-21 FINES AND PENALTIES.
    a. In general.
       No deduction shall be allowed under section 162(a) for any fine or similar penalty paid to—
       (1) The government of the United States, a State, a territory or possession of the United States, the District of Columbia, or the Commonwealth of Puerto Rico;
       (2) ▶ *The government of a foreign country; or*
       (3) A political subdivision of, or corporation or other entity serving as an agency or instrumentality of, any of the above

57. Correctly cite the italicized sentence indicated by the dart (▶) in the following passage from the Regulations.

    SEC. 1.1362-1 ELECTION TO BE AN S CORPORATION.
    a. In general.
       Except as provided in section 1.1362-5, a small business corporation as defined in section 1361 may elect to be an S corporation under section 1362(a). An election may be made only with the consent of all of

the shareholders of the corporation at the time of the election. See section 1.1362-6(a) for rules concerning the time and manner of making this election.

b. ▶ *Years for which election is effective.*
An election under section 1362(a) is effective for the entire taxable year of the corporation for which it is made and for all succeeding taxable years of the corporation, until the election is terminated.

58. Briefly describe the subject of each of the following Letter Rulings. State the type [Private Letter Ruling (PLR), Field Service Advice (FSA), Service Center Advice (SCA), etc.] of each Letter Ruling.
    a. 200414014
    b. 200235002
    c. 200411001
    d. 199950003

59. What is the subject of each of the following Revenue Rulings?
    a. Rev. Rul. 2007-4
    b. Rev. Rul. 2006-36
    c. Rev. Rul. 2003-73
    d. Rev. Rul. 95-29

60. What is the subject of each of the following Revenue Procedures?
    a. Rev. Proc. 2007-11
    b. Rev. Proc. 2005-78
    c. Rev. Proc. 2001-45
    d. Rev. Proc. 98-11

61. Read and summarize Announcement 2010-28.

62. Read and summarize Notice 2010-26.

63. Read and summarize Private Letter Ruling 201014040.

64. Read and summarize Technical Advice Memorandum 201014051.

65. What is the subject of each of the following IRS Announcements?
    a. Announcement 2006-52
    b. Announcement 2004-90
    c. Announcement 99-27

66. What is the subject of each of the following IRS Notices?
    a. Notice 2007-2
    b. Notice 2007-91
    c. Notice 95-50

67. What is the subject of each of the following IRS Notices?
    a. Notice 89-114
    b. Notice 99-51
    c. Notice 2000-28

68. What is the subject matter of each of the following Technical Advice Memoranda?
    a. TAM 9015001
    b. TAM 199914034
    c. TAM 200050005

69. What is the subject matter of each of the following Technical Advice Memoranda?
    a. TAM 200703019
    b. TAM 200651033
    c. TAM 9853001

70. Briefly describe the subject matter of each of the following TDs:
    a. T.D. 8346
    b. T.D. 8780
    c. T.D. 8915

71. For each of the following Code sections, how many Treasury Regulations have been issued? Give the total number of such Regulations and the number of the last Regulation.
    a. §102
    b. §143
    c. §301
    d. §385

72. For each of the following Code sections, how many Treasury Regulations have been issued? Give the total number of such Regulations and the number of the last Regulation.
    a. §25A
    b. §119
    c. §180
    d. §305

73. What is the current status of each of the following Revenue Rulings?
    a. Rev. Rul. 95-35
    b. Rev. Rul. 94-17
    c. Rev. Rul. 87-34

74. What is the current status of each of the following Revenue Rulings?
    a. Rev. Rul. 2002-80
    b. Rev. Rul. 2001-31
    c. Rev. Rul. 98-13

75. Locate the pronouncement at 1989-1 C.B. 76.
    a. What is the number assigned to this written determination?
    b. What is the issue(s) addressed in this written determination?
    c. What is the holding in this written determination?

76. Locate the pronouncement at 2000-2 C.B. 333.
    a. What is the number assigned to this written determination?
    b. What is the subject matter discussed in this written determination?

77. Locate the pronouncement at 2004-10 I.R.B. 550.
    a. What is the number assigned to this written determination?
    b. What is the subject matter discussed in this written determination?

78. Locate the pronouncement at 2007-17 I.R.B. 990.
    a. What is the number assigned to this written determination?
    b. What is the subject matter discussed in this written determination?

79. Locate the pronouncement at 2006-40 I.R.B. 528.
    a. What is the number assigned to this written determination?
    b. What is the subject matter discussed in this written determination?

80. What is the current status of each of the following IRS pronouncements?
    a. Notice 2001-26
    b. Revenue Ruling 2000-41
    c. Revenue Procedure 89-31
    d. Announcement 99-110

81. What is the current status of each of the following IRS pronouncements?
    a. Notice 2004-29
    b. Revenue Ruling 2004-28
    c. Revenue Procedure 93-15
    d. Announcement 99-41

82. A member of a tax-exempt business league makes deposits into a strike fund. The contribution reverts to the taxpayer if the fund is terminated. Are these deposits tax deductible?

    Database to search: IRS Letter Rulings

    Keywords: business, league, strike, fund

83. Can proceeds from a life insurance policy be included in a decedent's gross estate if the policy was purchased by an S corporation for an employee-shareholder?

    Databases to search: the Code and IRS Letter Rulings Keywords: Sec. 2042, life, insurance, estate, inclusion

84. Is a veterinary medical corporation a "personal service corporation" for purposes of the required use of the flat 35 percent tax rate?

    Database to search: Revenue Rulings

    Keywords: veterinary, personal, service, corporation

85. Are homeowners who claim an itemized deduction for interest paid on adjustable rate mortgages and then receive refunds in a later year required to show the refunds as taxable income?

    Database to search: Notices

    Keywords: adjustable, rate, mortgage, refund

86. Are points paid by homebuyers on VA and FHA loans deductible in the year the house is purchased?

    Database to search: Revenue Procedures

    Keywords: loan, origination, fees, VA, FHA

RESEARCH CASES

87. Lance asks you to explain why his employer, the Good Food Truck Stop, an establishment that employs more than 30 waiters/waitresses, included $2,400 in tip income on his Form W-2 for the year. Lance always has kept track of the tips he actually received, and he has reported them in full on his tax return.

88. Joe incurred $38,000 of investment interest expense in the current year. He also generated $35,000 in dividend income and had a $65,000 passive loss for the year. What is the amount of Joe's interest deduction?

89. Georgia won the Massachusetts lottery, which means that she will receive $28,000 a year for the next 30 years. Georgia purchased the lucky ticket in March, and she was selected the winner in June. Georgia regularly spent $100 a month on lottery tickets, one-third for Massachusetts tickets and two-thirds for Vermont tickets.

    a. What is Georgia's gross income from this prize?

    b. Is there any corresponding deduction?

90. Dieter won the lottery this year, which means that he will receive $400,000 a year for the next 30 years. The present value of Dieter's prize is about $3,750,000. Conscious of the tax benefits of income shifting, Dieter irrevocably assigned one-fifth of every annuity payment to his daughter Heidi. What are the effects of these events on Dieter's taxable income?

91. Ace High and Lady Luck live together and have pooled their funds for several months to purchase food and other household necessities and to buy an occasional state lottery ticket. Ace used part of these pooled funds to buy a lottery ticket that won $3 million. When they discovered that the lottery proceeds could be paid only to one recipient under state law, Ace and Lady executed a "separate ownership agreement." The agreement created an equal interest in the ticket for both Ace and Lady. Must Ace pay gift tax on the transfer of a one-half interest in the ticket to Lady? What is the value of the gift?

92. Shaky Savings & Loan has a depositor named Olive who opened an account last year. At that time, Olive gave Shaky her Social Security Number (SSN) as a taxpayer identification number (TIN). The IRS notified Shaky that Olive's SSN was invalid. This year, Shaky asked Olive for a corrected number, which she provided. Later this year, the IRS notified Shaky that the new SSN also was invalid. What should Shaky do at this point about backup withholding on Olive's account? Prepare (in good form) a research memorandum to the file.

93. Alpine Corporation is a qualified small business corporation eligible to elect S corporation status. Albert is a shareholder in Alpine. On February 1 of the current year, Albert dies before signing the proper S corporation election form. The stock passes to Albert's estate. Ellen is appointed executor of Albert's estate on May 1 of the current year. On March 10 of the current year, Alpine filed Form 2553, the election form to be an S corporation, properly signed by all March 10 shareholders, and Ellen (the executrix) on behalf of Albert. Is this a valid S corporation election? Prepare (in good form) a research memorandum to the file.

94. Joe Bacillus owns Bacillus's Italian Restaurant. A friend of Joe's who owns a sports bar comes to Joe and wants to form a partnership with Joe to buy an old building, renovate it, and then move both the restaurant and the sports bar into it along with other tenants. Joe would like to make this investment. He needs approximately $200,000 for his share of the buy-in of the partnership that will purchase, renovate, and manage the building. Because of other recent large expenses, however, Joe finds himself short of cash at the present time. His only large liquid asset is his self-directed IRA, which currently owns $225,000 in stock and

bonds. Joe proposes that he direct the IRA to sell the securities and to use the proceeds to invest in the building renovation partnership. Conduct appropriate research (including a computer search) to determine if Joe's plan is workable. Prepare (in good form) a research memorandum to the file.

95. The Pima and Southern Railroad (PSRR) is a small railroad operating in rural Arizona. It exists by carrying freight to remote areas of the southwest. This year the PSRR needs to replace a 30-mile section of its track. The PSRR has bids from a contractor to replace the track for the following amounts:

Cost of new track	$ 5,000,000
Installing new track	3,000,000
Road bed grading and improvements	2,500,000
Removing old track (net of salvage)	1,500,000
Total	$12,000,000

The old track is fully depreciated, and the cost shown is net of $200,000 salvage value received for the scrap metal. The new track is an improved type, and it is expected to last 35 to 40 years. The controller of PSRR, Casey Jones, comes to you and wants to know the tax treatment of the above expenditures. He specifically wants to know if any costs can be deducted or if all must be capitalized and written off over a period of years. He is also concerned about any potential problems with the uniform capitalization rules under §263A. Prepare (in good form) a research memorandum to the file.

96. Your client, Ned Bovine, purchased a $2 million life insurance policy from the Nickel Life Insurance Co. (NLIC) of Dime Box, Texas. Ned's wife is the beneficiary of the policy. The policy was purchased 10 years ago when Nickel Life Insurance was a mutual insurance company. In the current year, Nickel Life Insurance converted from a mutual company to a stock company in a tax-free reorganization. As part of the conversion, Ned received 800 shares of the new publicly traded (NASDAQ) Nickel Life Insurance Company. Three weeks after receiving the shares, Ned sold all his shares at $15 each. The total premiums paid by Ned on the policy before the conversion was $20,000.

a. Locate the IRS pronouncement(s) that deals with this situation. State the pronouncement number(s).

b. Review the IRS pronouncement(s). Does it raise a need for new information to solve this question?

c. Are you able to reach a conclusion about the research question from this IRS pronouncement(s)? If so, what is your conclusion(s)?

97. At age 65, Carlota's financial position was better than her health. She had a large balance in an IRA that she wanted to move to a different IRA. Carlota withdrew $100,000 from the IRA and planned to roll the funds over into another IRA. Unfortunately, she died before completing the rollover. Carlota's son, Andres, discovered what his mother had done a week after her death. Andres was both executor of Carlota's estate and beneficiary of her IRA.

Can Andres, in his role as executor, complete the rollover for his deceased mother by depositing the $100,000 in another IRA within the 60-day rollover period?

a. Locate the IRS pronouncement(s) that deals with this situation. State the pronouncement number(s).

b. Review the IRS pronouncement(s). Does it raise a need for new information to solve this question?

c. Are you able to reach a conclusion about the research question from this IRS pronouncement(s)? If so, what is your conclusion(s)?

98. The Venganza Tribe is a Federally recognized Indian tribal government described in IRC §7701(a)(40)(A). The Venganza Tribe would like to invest some of its cash resulting from its newly opened casino in a real estate development, Vista de Basura Inc., an S corporation. Is the Indian tribal government an eligible shareholder for S corporation purposes?

a. Locate the IRS pronouncement(s) that deals with this situation. State the pronouncement number(s).

b. Review the IRS pronouncement(s). Does it raise a need for new information to solve this question?

c. Are you able to reach a conclusion about the research question from this IRS pronouncement(s)? If so, what is your conclusion(s)?

99. Fred Forgetful parks his personal car on a hill in sunny California and fails to properly set the brake or curb the wheels. As a result of Fred's negligence, the car rolls down the hill, damages Lucky's front porch, injures Lucky (who was sitting on the porch), and damages Fred's car. Due to the accident, Fred is forced to pay the following unreimbursed amounts:

Medical expenses for Lucky's injuries	$5,500
Repairs to Fred's car	7,000
Repairs to Lucky's porch	8,500
Fine for traffic violation	275

Using only the Regulations and Code, determine which of these payments, if any, would qualify for casualty loss treatment (before any percentage limitations) as to Fred.

100. Your client, Mustang Racing Parts Inc. (MRP), is engaged in the production, transmission, distribution, and sale of racing headers for Ford Mustangs (inventory property). The client is also involved in the distribution of other racing parts manufactured by other suppliers (inventory property). During the tax year, MRP produces numerous identical dies and molds using standardized designs and assembly line techniques (noninventory property). The dies and molds are mass-produced. MRP uses the dies and molds to produce particular automobile racing components and does not hold them for sale. The dies and molds have a three-year recovery period for purposes of §168(c). The client wants to know if it can elect to use the "simplified service cost method" to calculate the amount capitalized under §263A on the dies and molds.

a. Locate the IRS Letter Ruling that deals with this situation. State the Letter Ruling number.

b. Review the IRS Letter Ruling. Does it raise a need for new information to solve this question?

c. Are you able to reach a conclusion about the research question from this IRS Letter Ruling? If so, what is your conclusion(s)?

101. Your client, Manny Mendacious, invested $70,000 in the stock of a new start-up company that opened a chain of fried pickle fast-food restaurants call "the Cooked Cucumber." As might be expected, this venture has not been very successful, and Manny's stock has lost its value. Manny knows that worthless securities are normally treated as a short-term capital loss (STCL), which means the $3,000 annual maximum deduction and other limits apply. While talking to one of his co-investors he discovers that her tax adviser (Shamus Sham, the taxman) contends that if a taxpayer "abandons" a security it is not subject to the STCL treatment. Manny is very excited about this and is anxious to assert he "abandoned" the Cooked Cucumber stock and deduct the entire $70,000 loss in the current year.

a. Locate the Proposed Regulation that deals with this situation. Give the Proposed Regulation's citation.

b. Review the Proposed Regulation. Does it raise a need for new information to solve this question?

c. Are you able to reach a conclusion about the research question from this Proposed Regulation? If so, what is your conclusion(s)?

102. David Dental, DDS and his unmarried partner Sally Surgeon, MD have lived together for the past five years. Both are at the peak of their careers and decide to buy a new "show case" home in La Jolla, California. After looking at several homes in the area, they buy one for $2 million. They put a 20 percent down payment ($400,000) on the house and finance the balance ($1.6 million). Each takes out a separate

mortgage for $800,000 for a total $1.6 million. There is no other debt (e.g., a home equity loan) on the residence.

a. Locate the Chief Counsel Advice (CCA) that deals with this situation. Give the Chief Counsel Advice's (CCA) citation.

b. Review the Chief Counsel Advice (CCA). Does it raise a need for new information to solve this question?

c. Are you able to reach a conclusion about the research question from this Chief Counsel Advice (CCA)? If so, what is your conclusion(s)?

Judicial Interpretations

WHEN A DISPUTE BETWEEN the Internal Revenue Service (IRS) and a taxpayer cannot be settled through the administrative appeals process (Chapter 13), the taxpayer can seek relief via the judicial system. The taxpayer may select one of three courts in which to initiate litigation with the IRS. These courts are the Tax Court, U.S. District Courts, and the U.S. Court of Federal Claims. If a taxpayer or the IRS disagrees with a lower court decision, an appeal may be made to the appropriate Court of Appeals and then, finally, to the U.S. Supreme Court. In this chapter we examine the Federal court system, learn to locate various Federal tax judicial decisions, and discuss the use of those decisions in solving tax research problems.

Federal Court System

When a taxpayer and the IRS cannot reach an agreement concerning a specific tax matter using the administrative review process (i.e., audits and appeals, which are discussed in Chapter 13), the dispute may be settled in the Federal court system, where either the taxpayer or the IRS may initiate legal proceedings. A taxpayer may decide to initiate proceedings as a final attempt to recover an overpayment of tax the IRS refuses to refund or to reverse a deficiency assessment determined by the IRS. Alternatively, the IRS may initiate proceedings to assert its claim to a deficiency, to enforce the collection of taxes, or to impose civil or criminal penalties on the taxpayer.

Judicial decisions are the third primary source of the tax law. The Internal Revenue Code is the chief statutory basis for Federal tax laws, and the administrative pronouncements of the IRS interpret provisions of the Code and explain their application. Frequently, however, additional issues and questions arise regarding the proper interpretation or intended application of the law that are not answered either in the law itself or in the administrative pronouncements. The judicial system is left with the task of resolving these questions. In this process, additional tax law is generated that can carry the full force of the statute itself.

Often, recurring litigation in an area of innovative or unexpected judicial decisions regarding tax matters will result in Congress enacting legislation that codifies certain judicial decisions. The practitioner must be familiar with the workings of this judicial system, which has the ability to stimulate tax laws and influence future legislative developments. In addition, in the event an issue is litigated in the court system, the tax practitioner must be familiar with the precedential value of court cases and the process for review of the court's decision.

Most disagreements with the IRS are resolved through the administrative process of appeals. Judicial decisions should be given significant weight in arriving at a conclusion or recommendation to a tax problem; however, caution should be exercised when it is apparent from the IRS's prior actions that a given position is almost certain to result in litigation. The costs of litigation, in terms of both money and time, may be prohibitive for certain taxpayers.

All litigations between a taxpayer and the government begins in a trial court. If the decision of the trial court is not satisfactory to one of the parties, then the trial court decision may be appealed. The appellate court will review the trial court decision, often hear new evidence and arguments, and then either uphold the trial court's decision, modify it in some way, or reverse it.

The Federal court system consists of three trial courts and two levels of appellate courts. The three trial courts are the U.S. Tax Court, the U.S. District Courts, and the

U.S. Court of Federal Claims. The two appellate courts are the U.S. Court of Appeals and the U.S. Supreme Court. Each of the trial courts has different attributes and is designed to serve in a different capacity in the Federal judicial system. Exhibit 5-1 diagrams the existing Federal court system. An appeal from any of the three trial courts is to the appropriate U.S. Court of Appeals. The taxpayers and the IRS have no direct access to the Supreme Court or any Court of Appeals.

EXHIBIT 5-1:   Federal Tax System—Tax Cases

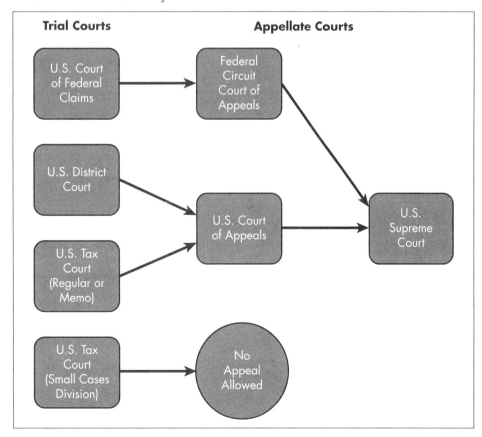

SPOTLIGHT ON TAXATION

Most Litigated Tax Issues

Internal Revenue Code §7803(c)(2)(B)(ii)(X) requires the National Taxpayer Advocate to identify the 10 tax issues most often litigated in the Federal courts, classified by the types of taxpayer affected.

The 2009 Annual Report to Congress lists the following 10 issues:

1. Collection Due Process hearings (§§ 6320, 6330)
2. Summons enforcement (§§ 7602(a), 7604(a), 7609(a))
3. Trade or business expenses (§ 162(a) and related *Code* sections)
4. Gross income (§ 61 and related *Code* sections)
5. Accuracy-related penalty (§ 6662)
6. Frivolous Issues Penalty (§ 6673 and related appellate-level sanctions)
7. Civil Actions to Enforce Federal Tax Liens or to Subject Property to Payment of Tax (§ 7403)
8. Failure to file penalty (§ 6651(a)(1)) and estimated tax penalty (§ 6654)
9. Family status issues (§§ 2, 24, 32, and 151)
10. Relief from joint and several liability for spouses (§ 6015).

Legal Conventions

Burden of Proof   In most litigation, the party initiating the case has the burden of convincing the court that he is correct with respect to the issue. Historically, however, in most civil tax cases the Internal Revenue Code placed the burden of proof on the taxpayer, whether or not he or she initiated the case, except in cases of such items as hobby losses, fraud with intent to evade tax, and the accumulated earnings tax.

However, the burden of proof shifts to the IRS in a few situations.[1] The IRS assumes the burden of proof in any court proceeding on income, gift, estate, or generation-skipping tax liability with respect to factual issues, provided the taxpayer:

• Introduces credible evidence of the factual issue.

• Maintains records and substantiates items as presently required under the Code and Regulations.

• Cooperates with reasonable IRS requests for meetings, interviews, witnesses, information, and documents.

For corporations, trusts, and partnerships with net worth exceeding $7 million, the burden of proof remains on the taxpayer.[2] The burden of proof also automatically shifts to the IRS if the IRS uses statistics to reconstruct an individual's income, or if the court proceeding against an individual taxpayer involves a penalty or addition to tax.

When reading a published opinion, the tax researcher should note whether the decision was based on the IRS's or the taxpayer's failure to meet a needed evidentiary burden, or whether the IRS or the taxpayer established the position with sufficient proof. The first situation should be considered a weaker precedent than the second. Understanding the "strength" of a court decision is an important part of tax research.

[1]IRC §7491.
[2]IRC §7491(a)(2)(C).

Tax Confidentiality Privilege The attorney-client privilege of confidentiality also applies in tax matters to nonattorneys authorized to practice before the IRS, such as certified public accountants (CPAs) and enrolled agents, as identified in Chapter 1. The nonattorney-client privilege may be asserted only in a noncriminal tax proceeding before the IRS or Federal court.[3] The confidentiality privilege usually does not apply to the preparation of tax returns or the giving of accounting or business advice.

The nonattorney-client privilege does not extend to written communications between a tax practitioner and a corporation in connection with the promotion of any tax shelter, nor does it apply to the client's work papers used to determine tax expense for financial statements.

CPAs and enrolled agents need to understand the rules regarding tax confidentiality as they have been applied to attorneys so as to be aware of the privilege limits. Usually, these rules are determined by state law, and the Federal confidentiality privilege cannot extend beyond the protection granted by state law, as it is currently interpreted.

Common Legal Terminology Following are some of the common legal terms likely to be encountered by the tax researcher:

- *Ad hoc.* For one particular or special purpose. For example, an ad hoc committee might be formed to solve a certain problem.

- *Ad valorem.* According to value. This term is used in taxation to designate an assessment of taxes based on property value.

- *Appellant.* The party who appeals a decision, usually to a higher court.

- *Bona fide.* In good faith and without fraud or deceit.

- *Certiorari (writ of).* The process by which the U.S. Supreme Court agrees to hear a case, based on the appeal of a lower court decision by one of the parties involved in that decision.

- *Collateral estoppel.* When an issue of fact has been determined by valid judgment, that issue cannot be litigated again by the same parties in future litigation.

- *Covenant.* An agreement or promise to do or not to do something.

- *De facto.* In fact or reality; by virtue of accomplishment or deed.

- *De jure.* In law or lawful; legitimate.

- *Defendant.* In civil proceedings, the party that is responding to the complaint; usually the one that is being sued in some matter.

- *Deposition.* A written statement of a witness under oath, normally taken in question-and-answer form.

- *Dictum (dicta).* A statement or remark in a court opinion that is not necessary to support the decision.

- *En banc.* A decision by the full court instead of a single judge or a selected set of judges. The larger number sits in judgment when the court feels there is a particularly significant issue at stake.

---

[3]IRC §7525(a)(1).

- *Enjoin.* To command or instruct with authority; a judge can enjoin someone to do or not to do some act.

- *Habeas corpus (writ of).* The procedure for determining if the authorities can hold an individual in custody.

- *Nolo contendere.* A party does not want to fight or continue to maintain a defense; the defendant will not contend a charge made by the government; "no contest."

- *Non obstante veredicto (n.o.v.).* Notwithstanding the verdict; a judgment that reverses the determination of a jury.

- *Nullity.* Something in law that is void; an act having no legal force.

- *Parol evidence.* The doctrine that renders any evidence of a prior understanding of the parties to a contract invalid if it contradicts the terms of a written contract.

- *Per curiam.* An opinion "by the court" that expresses its decision in the case but whose author is not identified.

- *Plaintiff.* The one who initially brings a lawsuit.

- *Prima facie.* At face value; something that is obvious and does not require further support.

- *Res judicata.* The legal concept that bars relitigation on the same set of facts. Because of this concept, taxpayers must make sure that all of the issues they want (or do not want) to be litigated are included in a case. Once the case is decided, it cannot be reopened.

- *Slip opinion.* An individual court decision published separately shortly after the decision is rendered.

- *Vacate.* A reversal or abandonment of a prior decision of a court.

Tax Court

The U.S. **Tax Court** is a specialized trial court that hears only Federal tax cases. Established by the Code and not directly by the U.S. Constitution,[4] its jurisdiction is limited to cases concerning the various Internal Revenue Codes and Revenue Acts that were adopted after February 26, 1926. Before 1943, the Tax Court was known as the **Board of Tax Appeals** (BTA); it was an administrative board of the Treasury Department rather than a true judicial court. In 1943, the BTA became the U.S. Tax Court, an administrative court, and its status was upgraded in 1969 to that of a full judicial court, with enforcement powers.

Nineteen judges hear Tax Court cases. Each judge is appointed to a 15-year term by the President of the United States, with the advice and confirmation of the Senate. This appointment must be based solely on the grounds of the judge's fitness to perform the duties of the office. A Tax Court judge may be removed from his or her position by the President, after notice and opportunity for public hearing, because of inefficiency, neglect of duty, or malfeasance in office, but for no other reason.

To alleviate the heavy caseload of the appointed Tax Court judges, the Chief Judge of the Court periodically designates additional special trial judges to hear pertinent cases

---

[4]IRC §7441.

for a temporary period. Limited primarily by the budget granted by Congress, these temporary appointments are useful in decreasing the waiting period for taxpayers who wish to be heard before the Court. The decisions of these special judges carry the full authority of the U.S. Tax Court. Senior judges are retired judges who still hear cases from time to time by invitation of the Chief Judge.

Tax Court judges are tax law specialists, not generalists. Typically, they have acquired many years of judicial or tax litigation experience before being appointed to the Tax Court. Thus, if a taxpayer wants to argue a technical tax issue with the IRS, the Tax Court usually is the best trial-level forum in which to try the case. Tax Court judges are better able to understand such issues than would be a judge in a more general court.

SPOTLIGHT ON TAXATION

Tax Law Complexity

"We have from time to time complained about the complexity of our revenue laws and the almost impossible challenge they present to taxpayers or their representatives who have not been initiated into the mysteries of the convoluted, complex provisions affecting the particular corner of the law involved. ... Our complaints have obviously fallen upon deaf ears".

—Arnold Raum, U.S. Tax Court Judge

The U.S. Tax Court is a national court, based in Washington, D.C. Its jurisdiction is not limited to a specific geographical region, as is the case with some other Federal courts. Taxpayers need not travel to Washington, D.C. to have a case tried before the Tax Court because some of its judges travel throughout the country and are available to hear taxpayer cases in every major city of the United States several times every year. See Exhibit 5-2 for a map showing cities where the Tax Court occasionally holds trials.

When a case is heard before the Tax Court, it usually is presented before only one of the 19 Tax Court judges. Taxpayers cannot request jury trials before this court. After the judge hears the case, he or she prepares a decision that is reviewed by the Chief Judge of the court. In most instances, the trial judge's opinion stands, but the Chief Judge can designate the opinion for review by the other members of the Tax Court. Upon their agreement with the decision, the opinion is released. If the case involves an unusually important, or novel issue, the entire Tax Court might hear the case. This rare occurrence is identified as an **en banc** sitting of the court.

For a case to be heard, the taxpayer must petition the Court within 90 days of the IRS's mailing of a notice and demand for payment of the disputed amount. The taxpayer need not pay the disputed tax liability before the case is heard.

Tax Court Decisions   The Tax Court issues two kinds of decisions: regular and memorandum. A **Regular decision** (recently 30 to 35 cases per year) generally involves a new or unusual point of law, as determined by the Chief Judge of the court. If the Chief Judge believes that the decision concerns only the application of existing law or an interpretation of facts, then the decision is issued as a **Memorandum decision** (250 to 350 cases per year).

Over the years, however, this classification scheme has not always been strictly followed by the Court. Many of its Memorandum decisions address significant points of law or other issues important to the tax researcher. Accordingly, the researcher should not ignore Memorandum decisions. If issues or points of law pertinent to the problem

EXHIBIT 5-2:   Tax Court Trial Locations (2010)

United States Tax Court Places of Trial

▲ Denotes cities in which only small tax case trials are heard.

at hand are addressed, both Regular and Memorandum decisions of the Tax Court should be considered by the taxpayer.

Because the Tax Court is a national court, it hears cases that may be appealed to Courts of Appeals (discussed later in this chapter) in different geographical regions, or circuits. Because these Courts of Appeals occasionally disagree on tax issues, the Tax Court is faced with a dilemma. For example, one Court of Appeals may have held that a specific item is deductible in computing taxable income, while another has held against such a deduction. Which precedent should the Tax Court follow?

Under *Golsen*,[5] the Tax Court will follow the Court of Appeals that has direct jurisdiction over the taxpayer in question. If the Court of Appeals that has jurisdiction over the taxpayer has not ruled on the matter, then the Tax Court will decide the case on the basis of its own interpretation of the disputed provision.

This **Golsen rule** means the Tax Court may reach opposite decisions, based on identical facts, for taxpayers differentiated solely by the geographical area in which they live. The tax researcher must be aware of the Golsen rule in analyzing cases that may be affected by it.

Small Cases Division   The Tax Court maintains a **Small Cases Division**, which is similar to a small claims court. If the amount of a disputed deficiency, including penalties, or claimed overpayment does not exceed $50,000, then a taxpayer may be heard before the Small Cases Division, upon approval of the Tax Court. The hearing is conducted as

[5]54 T.C 742 (1970).

informally as possible, and the taxpayer may represent him or herself; that is, a (Of course, the taxpayer may be represented by an attorney if he or she so desi elaborate written briefs nor formal oral arguments are required in the Small Cases Division. Issues brought before this forum generally are fact based; for example, does the taxpayer have the necessary documentation to claim the earned income tax credit?

At any time before a decision is final, the Tax Court may interrupt a Small Cases hearing and transfer the case to the regular Tax Court for trial. This might occur, for example, when important facts or issues of law, more suitably heard in the more formal Tax Court context, become apparent only after the Small Cases proceedings have begun.

Small Cases decisions, called Summary Opinions, are not officially published by the government. Nevertheless, they are available for review by tax researchers and taxpayers through commercial publishers. Small Cases Division decisions cannot be used as precedents when dealing with the IRS; however, they do provide insight into how the Tax Court has treated similar tax situations. The decision of the Small Cases judge is final and may not be appealed by the taxpayer or the government. An excerpt from a sample Summary Opinion is presented in Exhibit 5-3.

Locating Tax Court Decisions Tax Court regular decisions are published by the Government Printing Office (GPO) in a set of bound reporters called the Tax Court of the United States Reports. These volumes are cited as "T.C." The Board of Tax Appeals had its own reporter, called the United States Board of Tax Appeals, cited as "BTA."

Memorandum decisions are not published by the GPO. They are included in special-decision reporters that are published by CCH and by RIA. The CCH reporter is titled *Tax Court Memorandum Decisions*, cited as "TCM," and the RIA reporter is known as *RIA Tax Court Memorandum Decisions*, cited as "RIA T.C. Memo." The Tax Court reporter is published twice a year, and both of the memorandum case reporters are published once a year.

Because many months may elapse between the release of a Tax Court decision and its publication in a bound reporter, such decisions receive both a temporary and a permanent citation. The **temporary citation** is structured as follows:

Carl H Jones, III, Carl H. et al. v. Commissioner, 131 T.C. ____ (2008), No. 3, where

131 is the volume number.

T. C. is the abbreviation for the Tax Court Reporter.

___ indicates the page number, which is to be determined later.

No. 3 is the number of the case.

(2008) is the year of the decision.

The temporary citation includes no page number for the case because the opinion has not yet been published. All proper citations either italicize or underline the name of the court case; major elements of the citation are separated by commas. The **permanent citation** for the same case is reported as follows:

Carl H. Jones, III, v. Commissioner, 131 T.C. 25 (2008), where

131 is the volume number.

T. C. is the abbreviation for the Tax Court Reporter.

25 is the page number.

(2008) is the year of the decision.

EXHIBIT 5-3: Tax Court Small Case (Summary Opinion) Excerpt

Indrit Iljazi v. Commissioner, T.C. Summary Opinion 2010-59.

Judge: Opinion by PANUTHOS

Pursuant to Internal Revenue Code section 7463(b), this opinion may not be treated as precedent for any other case.

COUNSEL

Carlton Malben Smith, for petitioner.

Theresa G. McQueeney, for respondent.

Opinion by PANUTHOS

This case was heard pursuant to the provisions of section 7463 of the Internal Revenue Code in effect when the petition was filed. Pursuant to section 7463(b), the decision to be entered is not reviewable by any other court, and this opinion shall not be treated as precedent for any other case. Unless otherwise indicated, all subsequent section references are to the Internal Revenue Code in effect at relevant times.

This proceeding was commenced under section 6015 for review of respondent's determination that petitioner is not entitled to relief from joint and several liabilities with respect to the unpaid tax liability reported on the 2002 joint return petitioner filed with Mary Sue Bacon (Ms. Bacon). The sole issue for decision is whether petitioner is entitled to relief under section 6015(f) for the 2002 tax liability. Respondent concedes petitioner is entitled to the claimed relief, except to the extent that petitioner's claim is time barred.

BACKGROUND

This case was submitted fully stipulated. All stipulated facts are found accordingly, and the attached exhibits are incorporated by reference. Petitioner resided in New York when he filed the petition herein.

Petitioner and Ms. Bacon reported income tax due of $29,360 and submitted a $100 payment with their timely filed 2002 joint income tax return. On November 1, 2003, respondent sent petitioner by certified mail a final notice of intent to levy and notice of his right to a collection due process hearing (CDP notice). The CDP notice was returned to respondent as refused or unclaimed. Ms. Bacon's CDP notice was also returned but listed as undeliverable. On December 2, 2008, respondent received from petitioner a Form 8857, Request for Innocent Spouse Relief, which included the 2002 income tax liability. On February 19, 2009, respondent issued a final determination denying relief under section 6015(f) because the claim was filed more than two years after respondent issued the CDP notice.

On May 11, 2009, petitioner filed a petition in this Court disputing the final determination. After the filing of the petition, respondent sent petitioner's case to the Internal Revenue Service (IRS) Covington Campus Innocent Spouse Operations (CCISO) to determine whether petitioner would be entitled to relief in the absence of the two-year period of limitations imposed by the income tax regulations. As a result of that evaluation, respondent determined that if the request for relief were not time barred, petitioner would be entitled to relief under section 6015(f) as to the portion of the underpayment attributable to the income of Ms. Bacon.

DISCUSSION

Section 6013(d)(3) provides that if a joint return is filed, the tax is computed on the taxpayers' aggregate income and liability for the resulting tax is joint and several. See also sec. 1.6013-4(b), Income Tax Regs. However, the IRS may relieve a taxpayer from joint and several liability under section 6015(f) if, taking into account all the facts and circumstances, it is inequitable to hold the taxpayer liable for any unpaid tax or deficiency and the taxpayer does not qualify for relief under section 6015(b) or (c).

Respondent concedes that petitioner is entitled to the claimed relief but for the two-year period set forth in Rev. Proc. 2003-61, 2003-2 C.B. 296, and the regulations. See sec. 1.6015-5(b), Income Tax Regs.

In *Lantz v. Commissioner*, 132 T.C. 131 (2009), this Court held invalid the Secretary's regulation limiting the period for the right to seek relief under section 6015(f) to two years. The holding of that case did not establish any time within which a request for relief would be considered reasonable and/or timely. Respondent concedes that the only reason for denial was that petitioner's request was made more than two years after the date of the first collection activity. Respondent acknowledges the Lantz Opinion but notes that it is on appeal and that he disagrees with this Court's holding in the case. (1) Respondent does not argue that the amount of time by which petitioner's request exceeded two years is a reason for denial of equitable relief under section 6015(f). Accordingly, there is no reason for this Court to further analyze respondent's claim that the 2-year-period restriction is valid, and we follow the precedent set forth in Lantz. Upon the basis of the foregoing, the Court holds that petitioner is entitled to relief from joint and several liability under section 6015(f).

To reflect the foregoing, Decision will be entered for petitioner.

Most court case citations include the names of both parties involved. Howev
vention is ignored for most Tax Court citations because all such cases involve the tax
payer bringing suit against the government to avoid payment of disputed tax liabilities.
Thus, a traditional citation for the above case would be *Jones, III, Carl H. v. Comm.* (or,
more precisely, *Carl H. Jones, III, v. Commissioner*). Nonetheless, common practice allows the tax researcher to omit the reference to the defendant in the action (i.e., the government or the IRS Commissioner) because such reference could be inferred from the
notation for the court in which the lawsuit is heard.

Once the GPO publishes the decision in the permanent bound edition of the regular
Tax Court cases, the temporary citation becomes obsolete. The same citation procedure
is used with respect to Board of Tax Appeals cases, substituting "BTA" for the "T.C."
identification. Indeed, this procedure for disclosing the citation for a case (i.e., Name–
Volume Number–Reporter–Page Number–Year) is common among all American courts.
Exhibit 5-4 is an example of a regular Tax Court decision.

Using the same citation conventions, the general and permanent citations, respectively, for a Tax Court memorandum decision would appear as follows:

General

Chi Wai, T. C. Memo 2006-179, where

T. C. Memo is a reference to a Tax Court Memorandum decision.

2006 is the year of the decision.

179 is the decision number.

Permanent RIA

Chi Wai, RIA T.C. Memo ¶ 2006-179, where

RIA T.C. Memo is the RIA Tax Court Memorandum reporter.

2006-179 is the paragraph number.

Permanent CCH

Chi Wai, 92 TCM 181 (2006), where

92 is the volume number.

TCM is the CCH Tax Court Memorandum reporter.

181 is the page number.

(2006) is the year of the decision.

One can observe from the general and RIA citations that the opinion was issued in
2006 because all of the Tax Court Memorandum Decisions for that year are cited using
paragraph numbers that begin with "2006." Thus, the reference in parentheses to the
year of the decision is redundant and may be omitted. Again, the citation omits the
reference to the government, typically "v. Comm.," as this is common among all Tax
Court cases.

As we observed with respect to the regular Tax Court decisions, the temporary citation becomes obsolete when the permanent bound edition of the memorandum reporter
is published.

EXHIBIT 5-4: Tax Court Regular Opinion-Excerpt

Jones, III, Carl H. et al. v. Commissioner, 131 TC 25.

Date Issued: 07/28/2008

COUNSEL

James R. Monroe, for petitioners.

Monica J. Miller, Laura A. Price, and Francis C. Mucciolo, for respondent.

VASQUEZ, Judge

Respondent determined a $2,209 deficiency in petitioners' 2003 Federal income tax. After concessions, the issue for decision is whether petitioners are allowed to deduct the cost of a one-on-one course in day trading pursuant to section 212(1).

FINDINGS OF FACT

Some of the facts have been stipulated and are so found. The stipulation of facts and the attached exhibits are incorporated herein by this reference. At the time they filed the petition, petitioners resided in Florida.

Carl H. Jones III (petitioner), an electrical engineer eligible for retirement, was laid off in 2002. Petitioner began day trading in 2002 but had invested in stocks for 35 years. Petitioner spent approximately six in a half hour a day Monday through Friday reviewing, studying, and executing trades. In order to improve his day trading abilities, petitioner signed up for a five-day one-on-one course called DayTradingCourse.com (the course) that he had read about online. (2) The course was held in Cartersville, Georgia, approximately 750 miles from petitioner's home in Florida. Petitioner drove by himself to the course. Petitioner stayed at a modest local hotel just off the interstate highway approximately five miles from the course location.

The course consisted of five days of intensive training and instruction taught by Paul Quillen. Monday through Thursday petitioner received eight hours of instruction daily, and on Friday petitioner received five hours. During the course petitioner learned strategies about day trading, studied Japanese candlestick patterns, and took a psychological exam. During his time in Cartersville petitioner did not participate in recreational activities. In 2003 and as of the date of trial petitioner continued his day trading activity. Petitioners concede that they are not in the trade or business of day trading.

Petitioners claimed $17,563 as miscellaneous itemized deductions on their 2003 joint Federal income tax return. Of that amount $6,053.06 was for the course and related expenses. The total of $6,053.06 consisted of: $5,247 for the course, $ 416.64 for lodging, $224.10 for round trip travel from petitioner's home to and from Cartersville, Georgia, where the course was held, $145.32 for food, and $20 for a course book. On or about March 31, 2006, respondent issued petitioners a notice of deficiency. Petitioners timely petitioned the Court.

OPINION

Petitioners have neither claimed nor shown that they satisfied the requirements of section 7491(a) to shift the burden of proof to respondent with regard to any factual issue. Accordingly, the burden of proof is on petitioners to show that respondent's determination set forth in the notice of deficiency is incorrect. Rule 142(a)(1); *Welch v. Helvering*, 290 [pg. 27] U.S. 111 [12 AFTR 1456], 115 (1933). Deductions are a matter of legislative grace; petitioners have the burden of showing that they are entitled to any deduction claimed. Rule 142(a); New *Colonial Ice Co. v. Helvering*, 292 U.S. 435, 440 [13 AFTR 1180] (1934).

Petitioners claimed the deductions pursuant to section 212(1). Section 212(1) allows as a deduction all the ordinary and necessary expenses paid or incurred during the taxable year for the production or collection of income. Petitioners argue that the course was necessary in order for petitioner to become a better day trader and to maximize profits and minimize losses on his trading activity.

Section 274(h)(7) provides that no deduction shall be allowed under section 212 for expenses allocable to a convention, seminar, or similar meeting. Petitioners argue that the course is not a convention, seminar, or similar meeting as contemplated by section 274(h)(7). We disagree.

* * *

It is important to note that section 274(h)(7) does not preclude deductions pursuant to section 162 (trade or business expenses) for conventions, seminars, or similar meetings. Petitioners concede they were not in the trade or business of day trading and cannot deduct the expenses relating to the course pursuant to section 162.

In reaching our holding herein, we have considered all arguments made by the parties, and to the extent not mentioned above, we find them to be irrelevant or without merit.

To reflect the foregoing, Decision will be entered under Rule 155.

Besides the traditional published sources for Tax Court decisions, these items also are available on computer tax services such as RIA Checkpoint, LexisNexis, and so on. All of the computer services reference the general citation and most give the parallel RIA and CCH reporter citations.

Tax Court Rule 155   When a court reaches a tax decision, it normally will not compute the tax that is due to the government or the refund that is due to a taxpayer. The computation of this amount is left to be determined by the IRS and the taxpayer. The court will compute the tax only if the government and the taxpayer cannot agree. When the Tax Court reaches a decision without calculating the tax, the decision is said to be entered under *Rule 155*. See *Julie A. Toth*, 128 T. C. 1 (2007), for an example of how the Tax Court enters a decision under *Rule 155*. For Tax Court decisions prior to 1974, this practice was referred to as *Rule 50*.

Scope of Tax Court Decisions   The Tax Court may examine an entire tax return for a taxpayer whose case it is hearing. On the other hand, the District Court and Court of Federal Claims can address only the specific issue or issues that are involved in the case. If a taxpayer wants only a specific issue (or issues) litigated in a case, then the District Court or Court of Federal Claims may be a better forum than the Tax Court.

District Courts

The U.S. **District Courts** are another trial-level forum that hears tax cases. Unlike the Tax Court, however, the District Courts hear cases involving legal issues based on the entire U.S. Code, not just the Internal Revenue Code. District Court judges typically are generalists, rather than specialists in Federal tax laws. The same District Court judge might render opinions concerning matters of tax law, civil rights, bank robbery, interstate commerce, kidnapping, and fraud.

The District Courts are further distinguished from the Tax Court in that a taxpayer who disagrees with the IRS may take his or her case to the appropriate District Court only after paying the disputed tax liability; thus, in the typical District Court taxation case, the taxpayer sues the government for a refund of the disputed tax liability.

Numerous District Courts are located throughout the United States, each assigned a geographical area. The designated district can be as small as one city (New York City) or as large as the largest state (Alaska). Typically, the taxpayer will request a hearing before the District Court that has jurisdiction over the location in which he or she lives or conducts business.

District Court cases are heard before one judge, not a panel of judges. In the appropriate District Court, the taxpayer can request a jury trial concerning a tax case (or certain other Federal matters). This opportunity may be useful if the taxpayer wants to argue an "emotional" issue rather than a technical one, or if the taxpayer or his or her associates are particularly credible witnesses (and thus have a good chance of winning a jury trial). Limited to decisions concerning questions of fact, juries apparently occasionally can be persuaded in a tax case to hold for the taxpayer when a judge might not be so inclined.

Because the District Courts are general in nature and do not specialize in tax matters, over time their decisions can vary significantly among the districts. Some of their decisions have important precedential value and can be relied on by the tax researcher; however, many of these decisions are poorly structured or poorly conceived from a technical standpoint and represent candidates for overturn on appeal. The tax researcher must examine these decisions carefully to assess their probable use as a precedent before using them to help solve a client's tax problem.

Locating District Court Decisions   District Court tax decisions are published in three different reporters. West Publishing includes such cases in its *Federal Supplement Series*; citations for these cases include the "F.Supp." or the "F.Supp.2d." abbreviation. The series contains all decisions of the District Courts designated for publication, including those for the numerous nontax cases. Most university and law school libraries subscribe to the *Federal Supplement Series*.

However, it is a waste of money for the tax researcher to subscribe to this series to obtain just the tax decisions that are rendered in the District Courts. Instead, the tax researcher can use special tax case reporters that include only tax decisions selected from all of the decisions of the Federal courts except the Tax Court. (As we discussed earlier, the Tax Court's Regular and Memorandum Decisions are published in specialized reporters, so they do not present a budgeting problem of this sort.)

RIA's specialized tax reporter is titled *American Federal Tax Reports*, abbreviated in citations as **AFTR**. The first series of the reporter includes cases concerning pre-1954 Code litigation, and the second series include cases that address issues relative to the 1954 Code and the third series cases under the 1986 Code, respectively. Includes tax cases issued by federal courts other than the Tax Court. CCH's specialized Federal tax case reporter is known as *United States Tax Cases*, which is abbreviated as **USTC** in traditional citations. Do not confuse this abbreviation with that for the U.S. Tax Court, which we have identified as "T. C." Occasionally, the West citation (F.Supp.) is referred to as the primary citation for a case, and the CCH and RIA reporters are used for secondary citations. The AFTR2d and USTC reporters each publish 1,000 to 1,500 tax cases in a typical year from courts other than the U.S. Tax Court.

Besides the traditional published primary and secondary court reporters, electronic court reporters are also available. The computer-based reporters have their own citations, and they usually cross-reference one or more of the standard printed reporters (West, RIA, and CCH). An illustration of various citations for a District Court case follows.

Court Reporters

West: *Bohall, Patrick L.*, 602 F. Supp. 2d 187 (DCt. D.C., 2009)
RIA: *Bohall, Patrick L.*, 103 AFTR2d 2009-1338 (DCt. D.C.)
CCH: *Bohall, Patrick L.*, 2009-1 USTC ¶ 50,307 (DCt. D.C.)

Each of these citations indicates both the specific District Court that heard the case and the year in which the opinion was issued. Given publication time lags, however, this may not match the year in which the reporter volume was published. Unless necessitated by such a delay, a proper citation need not include in the parentheses the year in which the opinion was issued, in all but a West citation.

Notice that more than one volume of the USTC reporter was published by CCH in 2009, as indicated by the volume number, and that this reporter uses paragraph numbers to organize the opinions. Other elements of the citations are familiar. A complete citation for this case, using traditional form, would appear as follows:

Bohall, Patrick L., 602 F. Supp. 2d 187; 103 AFTR2d 2009-1338; 2009-1 USTC ¶ 50,307 (DCt. D.C.)

Court of Federal Claims

The U.S. **Court of Federal Claims** is the newest of the trial-level courts. Created on October 1, 1982, by the Federal Courts Improvement Act (P.L. 97-164), the U.S. Court of Claims and the U.S. Court of Customs and Patent Appeals were reorganized into two new courts. The trial division of the U.S. Court of Claims became the new U.S. Claims

Court, and the remaining divisions of both courts became the new Court of Appeals for the Federal Circuit, discussed later. The forum was renamed the U.S. Court of Federal Claims in 1992.

Sixteen judges are appointed to the Court of Federal Claims. Its jurisdiction lies in hearing cases concerning all monetary claims against the Federal government, only one type of which is in the form of tax refunds. Thus, the taxpayer must pay the disputed tax and sue the government for a refund in order for the case to be heard in the Court of Federal Claims. Similarly, like the District Court but unlike the Tax Court, the Court of Federal Claims is composed of judges who, with only a few exceptions, are not specialists in technical tax law. The Court of Federal Claims does not allow jury trials on any matter.

The U.S. Court of Federal Claims is a national court located in Washington, D.C. However, because the Court of Federal Claims judges periodically travel to the major cities of the country and hear cases in these various locations, in a manner similar to that of the Tax Court, one need not go to Washington, D.C., to present a case before the Court of Federal Claims.

Moreover, because the Court of Federal Claims is a national court that must follow the decisions only of the Federal District of the Court of Appeals, it is not bound by the geographical Circuit Courts of Appeals that have ruled on similar cases, nor by the Court of Appeals for the circuit in which the taxpayer works or resides. This may be important to a taxpayer whose circuit has held adversely to his or her position on the disputed issue: if the case were presented to the appropriate District Court, or to the Tax Court (recall the Golsen rule), the precedent of the adverse ruling would be adopted by those trial courts, but the Court of Federal Claims is not so bound.

Locating Court of Federal Claims Decisions   Before October 1982, all U.S. Court of Claims decisions concerning both tax and nontax issues were published in *West's Federal Reporter*, second series. (This reporter is now in its third series.) Citations to the reporter use the abbreviations "F.2d" or "F.3d," as the case may be. Current decisions of the U.S. Court of Federal Claims can be found in West's primary reporter, *U.S. Court of Federal Claims*, which can be cited by using the abbreviation "Fed. Cl." In addition, tax decisions of the old U.S. Court of Claims and the new U.S. Court of Federal Claims are available through several secondary published and electronic reporters. U.S. Court of Federal Claims decisions are published in CCH's USTC, RIA's AFTR2d, and other places.

Examine the following proper primary and secondary citations for decisions of the U.S. Court of Federal Claims. All of the elements of these citations are familiar to us. As is most often the situation, when a decision is issued and published in the same year, one need not be redundant in identifying the given year in the body of the citation because the reader can infer the year from other aspects of the listing. A complete citation of the case would include references to all of the publications, in the form indicated previously.

Court Reporters

West: *Esposito v. U.S.*, 70 Fed. Cl. 558 (2006)
CCH: *Esposito v. U.S.*, 2006-2 USTC ¶50,434 (Fed. Cl.)
RIA: *Esposito v. U.S.*, 97 AFTR2d 2006-1733 (Fed. Cl.)

As a general tax court, the U.S. Court of Federal Claims has generated decisions that cannot easily be anticipated. Practitioners usually should pursue a case in the U.S. Court of Federal Claims when the applicable U.S. District and U.S. Tax Court decisions are adverse to the taxpayer or when a nontechnical matter lies at the heart of the taxpayer's case.

Courts of Appeals

The first level of Federal appellate courts is the U.S. **Courts of Appeals**. Like the District Court and Court of Federal Claims, the Courts of Appeals consider issues in both tax and nontax litigation, although the Courts of Appeals generally will hear only cases that involve a question of law. Seldom will a Circuit Court of Appeals challenge the trial court's findings as to the facts.

Congress has created 13 Courts of Appeals: 11 are geographical, in that they are responsible for cases that originate in designated states; one is assigned to Washington, D.C.; and one is known as the Court of Appeals for the Federal Circuit. This last court hears tax and other cases that originate only in the Court of Federal Claims. The other Courts of Appeals consider tax and nontax issues brought from the Tax Court or a District Court for an assigned geographical region.

The 11 geographical Courts of Appeals are organized into geographical circuits, each of which is assigned a number. Practitioners commonly refer to the circuit courts by this number. For example, the Court of Appeals designated to hear cases that originate in Seattle typically is referred to as the Ninth Circuit Court of Appeals. Exhibit 5-5 shows the jurisdiction of each of the 11 geographic Courts of Appeals and District Court jurisdictions. Approximately 20 judges have been appointed to each of the circuit courts. Typically, a three-judge panel hears a Court of Appeals case. Jury trials are not available in these courts. A tax decision from the 11th Circuit Court of Appeals is reproduced in Exhibit 5-6.

A Court of Appeals decision carries precedential weight because each circuit is independent of the others and must follow only the decisions of the U.S. Supreme Court. Because the Supreme Court hears only about a dozen tax cases annually, the Court of Appeals, in most situations, represents the final authority in Federal tax matters. Thus, a researcher generally must follow the holding of a tax decision issued by the Court of Appeals for the circuit in which the client works or resides if the controlling facts or issues of law are sufficiently similar.

Decisions by the circuit court in which the taxpayer works or resides should be given great consideration, even if the researcher has found that another circuit court has held in the taxpayer's favor in a similar case. For example, if a taxpayer lives in San Antonio, and the Fifth Circuit has held that an item similar to the taxpayer's does not qualify as a deduction, then the deduction most likely should not be claimed, even if the Seventh or Eighth Circuit has held that the deduction is available. Under the *Golsen* rule, the unfavorable Fifth Circuit decision will apply to the taxpayer at the trial-court level, even though the U.S. Tax Court will be forced in this example to render opinions that are inconsistent among taxpayers.

If, in the same example however, the Fifth Circuit had not yet ruled on the issue, and the favorable Seventh Circuit ruling is available, then the researcher may be more comfortable in following the decision of the "outside" circuit. Prior decisions of Courts of Appeals are of great importance in the construction of subsequent decisions by another circuit, and the researcher rightly can place precedential value on the holdings of other circuits in anticipating the proper position for a client.

Therefore, in general, the Courts of Appeals decisions most important to a given taxpayer are those issued by the circuit in which he or she works or resides. In addition, however, these observations can be made: Second, Ninth, and D.C. Circuit decisions are especially important because of numerous innovative, unusual, and controversial judicial interpretations of the tax laws, and because their jurisdictions include the two most populous states in the nation and the nation's capital.

EXHIBIT 5-5:   Courts of Appeals and District Court Jurisdictions of the United States.

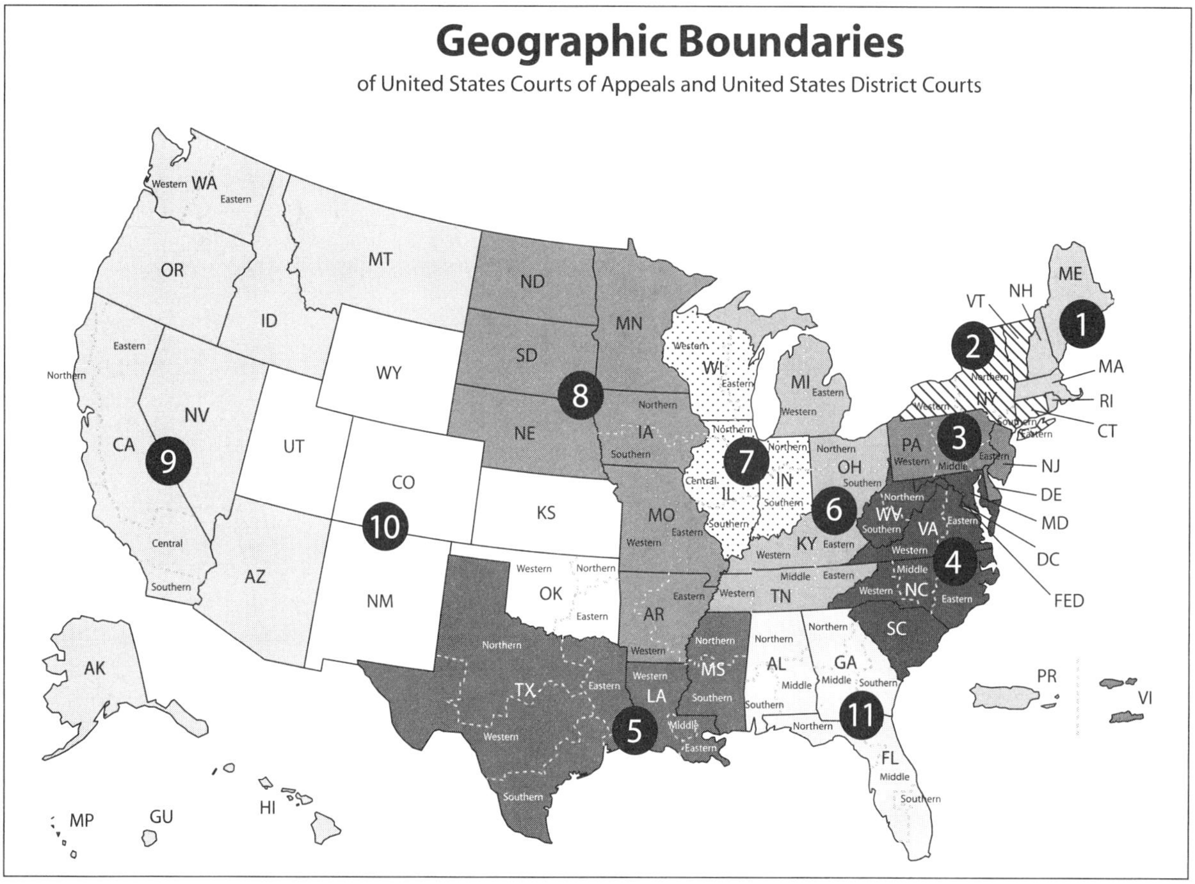

Geographic Boundaries
of United States Courts of Appeals and United States District Courts

Locating Court of Appeals Decisions   Court of Appeals decisions are reported in several general and specialized tax publications. All of the decisions of the various Courts of Appeals designated for publication are included in West's *Federal Reporter* (F.2d or F.3d). Most tax cases from the Courts of Appeals are published in the *United States Tax Cases* (USTC) and in the *American Federal Tax Reports* (AFTR). The familiar

SPOTLIGHT ON TAXATION

Do We Need More Courts?

There is a proposal before Congress to add at least one more circuit to the Courts of Appeals by splitting up the Ninth Circuit. Because of population migration in the past several decades, the Ninth Circuit is seen by some as "too big," constituting about 20 percent of the U.S. population. Another motivation for such a split might be political—the Ninth Circuit is historically the most progressive of the circuits, and this does not always sit well with citizens and their professional advisers in parts of the more conservative Western states.

EXHIBIT 5-6:   Court of Appeals Decision

Daleiden v. Comm., 103 AFTR2d 2009-1330, 2009-1 USTC ¶ 50,279 (CA-11).

Petition for Review of a Decision of the United States Tax Court

Before CARNES, WILSON and KRAVITCH, Circuit Judges.

Roger Daleiden, proceeding pro se, appeals the Tax Court's order of dismissal of his petition for review of the notice of determination. For the reasons that follow, we affirm.

After the IRS determined the Daleidens' tax liabilities for 2001 and sent them a demand for payment, the Daleidens failed to remit payment, and the IRS issued a notice of intent to levy. The Daleidens then requested a Collections Due Process Hearing ("CDP") hearing. Prior to the hearing, the IRS instructed the Daleidens to submit a collection information statement, collection alternatives, and an estimated tax payment. The Daleidens requested a face-to-face CDP hearing and identified the issues they wished to address. Because the IRS determined the arguments were frivolous, it denied a face-to-face hearing and scheduled a telephone hearing. The Daleidens apparently refused to participate in this conference and did not submit any of the requested information. Accordingly, the IRS Appeals Office upheld the assessment of liabilities. The Daleidens then petitioned the Tax Court for review.

The Tax Court set the case for trial for February 11, notified the parties of the date, and warned that the failure to appear could result in dismissal. The court also issued a pre-trial order, instructing the parties to submit stipulations and a pre-trial memorandum and again warned that the failure to comply could result in dismissal.

The Daleidens failed to appear at the trial on February 11 and the IRS moved to dismiss the petition for lack of prosecution. The Tax Court granted the motion to dismiss and sustained the notice of determination issued against Roger. On February 25, the Daleidens filed a motion for a continuance, asserting that Roger's medical condition prevented him from appearing at trial. In support, they submitted a [pg. 2009-1331] letter from Roger's doctor. The Tax Court construed the motion as a motion to vacate the order of dismissal and summarily denied it. This appeal followed.

In his appellate brief, Daleiden argues that the Tax Court improperly conducted a de novo trial and erroneously considered new evidence that was not before the IRS at the CDP hearing. Daleiden, however, raises no claims explaining how the Tax Court erred by dismissing his petition for failure to comply with the court's rules. (2)

When a party fails to make any argument in his appellate brief, we deem the issue abandoned. *Rowe v. Schreiber,* 139 F.3d 1381, 1382 n.1 (11th Cir. 1998). Accordingly, the issue has been abandoned.

Moreover, Daleiden's challenges to the CDP hearing are not properly before us. During a CDP hearing, a taxpayer may raise "any relevant issue relating to the unpaid tax or the proposed levy," possible defenses, and offers of collection alternatives. 26 U.S.C. §6330(c)(2)(A). The taxpayer may challenge the existence or amount of the underlying tax liability, but only if the taxpayer did not receive a Notice of Deficiency. 26 U.S.C. §6330(c)(2)(B).

In this case, Daleiden alleged that the IRS failed to follow procedures, but he did not argue that he never received the notice of deficiency; thus, he would not have been able to challenge the underlying tax liability.

Accordingly, we AFFIRM the Tax Court.

---

citation conventions are used in the following examples of primary and secondary citations for a Court of Appeals decision.

Court Reporters

West: *Hansen v. Comm.,* 471 F.3d 1021 (CA-9, 2006)

RIA: *Hansen v. Comm.,* 98 AFTR2d 2006-8234 (CA-9)

CCH: *Hansen v. Comm.,* 2007-1 USTC ¶ 50, 167 (CA-9, 2006)

In the citations to *Hansen,* the CCH reporter first published this 2006 decision in its first 2007 volume. Thus, the year of issuance must be listed in parentheses. The appeal was from a 2004 Tax Court decision involving a 1991 tax return.

Supreme Court

The U.S. **Supreme Court** is an appellate court and the highest court in the nation. Article III of the Constitution created the Supreme Court and extended to it judicial power "to all cases of law and equity, arising under this Constitution, the laws of the United

States, and treaties. ..." Thus, concerning all areas of Federal law, the Supreme (the final level of appeal and the sovereign legal authority.

The Supreme Court meets and hears cases only in Washington, D.C. If a taxpayer wants to have his or her case heard by the Supreme Court, the taxpayer and counsel must travel to the nation's capital to present the arguments. The Supreme Court is a nine-justice panel; all nine judges hear every case that the Court agrees to consider. The Court does not conduct jury trials.

A U.S. citizen has no automatic right to have his or her case heard by the Supreme Court. Permission to present the case must be requested by a **writ of certiorari**. If the Court decides to hear the case, then "certiorari is granted;" if the Court refuses, then "certiorari is denied." One must treat a Supreme Court decision as having the full force of the law; although Congress might repeal the challenged statute or the Federal administration might refuse to fund or enforce the underlying law and related activities, neither the citizen nor the government can appeal a Supreme Court decision.

As we have discussed, however, certiorari is granted in very few tax cases. Only about a dozen appeals relating to tax issues—state, local, and Federal; income, property, sales, estate, and gift; individual, corporate, and fiduciary—are heard by the Supreme Court in a typical year. In most cases, those petitions granted involve an issue at conflict among the Federal circuits or a tax issue of major importance. For instance, the Court might hear a client's case concerning the inclusion in gross income of life insurance proceeds if many similar cases had been brought before the various Federal courts and tremendous tax liabilities were under dispute, or if two or more of the circuits had issued inconsistent holdings on the matter.

In denying the petition for certiorari, the Supreme Court is not "upholding," or in any way confirming, a lower court decision. Rather, the Court simply does not find the appealed case to be interesting or important enough to consider during its limited sessions. The lower court's decision does stand, but one cannot infer that the decision necessarily is correct or that it should be followed in the future by other taxpayers whose situations are similar. These matters of open-fact tax planning must be analyzed using the tax researcher's professional judgment.

SPOTLIGHT ON TAXATION

The Supreme Court's Love Affair with Tax Law

"If [a United States Supreme Court Justice is] in the doghouse with the Chief [Justice], he gets the crud. He gets the tax cases. ..."
—Harry Blackmun, Supreme Court Justice

Locating Supreme Court Decisions At least four different general and specialized reporters publish all of the tax-related Supreme Court decisions. CCH includes such cases in the *United States Tax Cases* service (USTC), and RIA publishes them in the *American Federal Tax Reports* (AFTR, AFTR2d, or AFTR3d). The GPO publishes the *United States Supreme Court Reports*, which contains all of the tax and nontax decisions of the Court. In common citation convention, references to this service are abbreviated as "U.S." In addition, West Publishing includes all Supreme Court decisions in the *Supreme Court Reporter* (S.Ct.).

In the following examples of proper citations, one can infer from the GPO and West citations that the case was heard by the Supreme Court, and any further reference to that forum (e.g., as United States Supreme Court (USSC) would be redundant). In addition, if a case involves an issue of pre-1954 *Code* tax law, the first series of the AFTR service would be cited. Exhibit 5-7 is an example of a tax decision of the Supreme Court.

Court Reporters

GPO: *U.S. v. Clintwood Elkhorn Mining Co., Et Al.*, 553 U.S. 1 (2008)
West: *U.S. v. Clintwood Elkhorn Mining Co., Et Al.*, 128 S. Ct. 1511 (2008)
RIA: *U.S. v. Clintwood Elkhorn Mining Co., Et Al.*, 101 AFTR2d 2008-1612 (USSC)
CCH: *U.S. v. Clintwood Elkhorn Mining Co., Et Al.*, 2008-1 USTC ¶ 50,281 (USSC)

EXHIBIT 5-7: Supreme Court Decision Syllabus Excerpt

U.S. v. Clintwood Elkhorn Mining Co., Et Al., **101 AFTR2d 2008-1612; 128 S. Ct. 1511; 2008-1 USTC ¶ 50,281 (4/15/2008).**

OPINION

The Internal Revenue Code requires a taxpayer seeking a refund of taxes unlawfully assessed to file an administrative claim with the Internal Revenue Service (IRS) before filing suit against the Government, see 26 U. S. C. §7422(a). Such claim must be filed within three years of the filing of a tax return or two years of the tax's payment, whichever is later, see §6511(a). In contrast, the Tucker Act allows claims to be brought against the Government within six years of the challenged conduct. Respondent coal companies paid taxes on coal exports under a portion of the Code later invalidated under the Export Clause of the Constitution. They filed timely administrative claims and recovered refunds of their 1997–1999 taxes, but sought a refund of their 1994–1996 taxes in the Court of Federal Claims without complying with the Code's refund procedures. Nevertheless, the court allowed them to proceed directly under the Export Clause and the Tucker Act. Affirming in relevant part, the Federal Circuit ruled that the companies could pursue their Export Clause claim despite their failure to file timely administrative refund claims. [1] Held: The plain language of 26 U. S. C. §§7422(a) and 6511 requires a taxpayer seeking a refund for a tax assessed in violation of the Export Clause, just as for any other unlawfully assessed tax, to file a timely administrative refund claim before bringing suit against the Government. PP. 4–12.

((a)) Because the companies did not file a refund claim with the IRS for the 1994–1996 taxes, they may, under §7422(a), bring "[n]o suit" in "any court" to recover "any internal revenue tax" or "any sum" alleged to have been wrongfully collected "in any manner." Moreover, §6511's time limits for filing administrative refund claims—set forth in an "unusually emphatic form," *United States v. Brockamp*, 519 U. S. 347, 350 [79 AFTR2d 97-986]—apply to "any tax imposed by [Title 26]," §6511(a) (emphasis added). Contrary to the companies' claim that these statutes are ambiguous, the provisions clearly state that taxpayers must comply with the Code's refund scheme before bringing suit, including the filing of a timely administrative claim. Indeed, this question was all but decided in *United States v. A. S. Kreider Co.*, 313 U. S. 443 [25 AFTR 1264], where the Court held that the limitations period in the Revenue Act then in effect, not the Tucker Act's longer period, applied to tax refund actions. As was the case there, the current Code's refund scheme would have "no meaning whatever," id., at 448, if taxpayers failing to comply with it were nonetheless allowed to bring suit subject only to the Tucker Act's longer time bar. PP. 4–6.

((b)) The companies nonetheless assert that their claims are exempt from the Code provisions' broad sweep because the claims derive [pg. 2008-1613] from the Export Clause. The principles that a "constitutional claim can become time-barred just as any other claim can," *Block v. North Dakota ex rel. Board of Univ. and School Lands*, 461 U. S. 273, 292, and that Congress has the authority to require administrative exhaustion before allowing a suit against the Government, even for a constitutional violation, see, e.g., *Ruckelshaus v. Monsanto Co.*, 467 U. S. 986, 1018, are fully applicable to unconstitutional taxation claims. The companies' attempt to distinguish Export Clause claims on the ground that the Clause is not simply a limitation on taxing authority but a prohibition carving particular economic activity out of Congress's power is without substance and totally manipulable. There is no basis for treating taxes collected in violation of that Clause differently from taxes challenged on other grounds.

* * *

((c)) The companies' fallback argument—that even if the refund scheme applies to Export Clause cases generally, it does not apply when taxes are unconstitutional on their face—is rejected. *Enochs v. Williams Packing & Nav. Co.*, 370 U. S. 1 [9 AFTR2d 1594], distinguished. PP. 10–12.

473 F. 3d 1373 [99 AFTR2d 2007-613], reversed. Roberts, C. J., delivered the opinion for a unanimous Court.

Case Briefs and Headnotes

Most court reporters contain a brief case summary at the beginning of a case called a **headnote**. Headnotes, which are usually inserted by the court reporter editors, are useful to the researcher by helping to quickly determine if a particular case is of interest. A court case may contain several issues; therefore, there may be several headnotes for any one case. In addition to using headnotes, tax researchers have found that the construction of a concise case brief is of great value to them, both when they return to a client's research problem or planning environment after a period of time passes and in using the given case in constructing a research analysis for another client. However, the reader should be careful to distinguish this concise research tool from the case briefs required as part of the procedure of most court hearings. The latter is a lengthy collection of documents that includes a detailed analysis of all parts of the litigants' arguments.

A proper tax research **case brief** presents in summary fashion, ideally not exceeding one page, the facts, issue(s), holding, and analysis of the chosen court case. From such a brief, the researcher can discover in a very short period whether the full text of the case is of further use in the present analysis. If the briefed case does warrant further examination, the researcher can locate it (or any other cases that are cited in the brief itself) very quickly.

Study carefully the format of the case brief in Exhibit 5-8. Notice that the indicated tax research issues correspond with each of the analyses and holdings of the court, as indicated by the numbers of the brief's outline format. Finally, notice that citations to

EXHIBIT 5-8: Court Case Brief Illustrated

CITATION	*U.S. v. Stephen W. Bentson*, 947 F.2d 1353; 92-1 USTC ¶ 50,048; 68 AFTR2d 5773 (CA-9, 1991).
ISSUE(S)	(1) Does the IRS's failure to comply with the Paperwork Reduction Act (PRA) preclude a taxpayer from being penalized for failing to file a tax return and cause charges against him to be dismissed?
	(2) Could the IRS penalties be avoided because the Form 1040 had not been published in the Federal Register?
	(3) Could the IRS penalties be avoided because of a lack of proof that Bentson had failed to file returns?
FACTS	For the tax year 1982, Bentson filed a "protest tax return." He refused to supply information other than his name, address, social security number, and signature. The rest of his Form 1040 was filled with asterisks, and he attached a statement asserting that to supply other information violated his Fifth Amendment constitutional right. No tax returns could be located for 1983 and 1984. Bentson was charged by the IRS with three counts of willful failure to file tax returns. A District Court bench trial was held. After the close of the government's case, Bentson moved for dismissal, relying on *U.S. v. Kimball*, 896 F.2d 1218, vacated, 925 F.2d 356 (CA-9, 1991).
HOLDING	The District Court granted Bentson's motion as to the first count only. He was found guilty on two counts and sentenced to eight months incarceration followed by three years of probation, and a $2,000 fine. The Ninth Circuit affirmed the lower court's decision.
ANALYSIS	(1) Bentson argued the IRS failed to comply with the Paperwork Reduction Act and relied on the original *U.S. v. Kimball*. This decision was reversed in 1991 (see 925 F.2d 356). The Ninth Circuit held that the public protection provision of the Paperwork Reduction Act is not a defense to prosecution.
	(2) Bentson argued that Form 1040 and the instructions constitute a "rule" for purposes of the Administrative Procedures Act (APA) and therefore must be published in the Federal Register to be valid. The Ninth Circuit ruled this argument had no merit.
	(3) Bentson argued the IRS had not proved he did not file tax returns for 1983 and 1984. This argument was rejected because Bentson had already made a binding judicial admission to the contrary.

other cases, or to administrative proclamations, are complete and somewhat detailed, helping to facilitate further research.

The Internet and Judicial Sources

The Internet provides another way for tax researchers to access judicial sources of tax law. Many law schools, journals, tax publishers, and individuals have set up their own Web sites on the Internet. While not as user friendly as a commercial service, these sites allow anyone with access to the Internet to locate many court decisions. Examples of some of these home pages that have links to other judicial sources are as follows:

- Emory U. School of Law: **www.law.emory.edu**
- Cornell U. School of Law: **www.law.cornell.edu**
- U. of Texas School of Law: **www.utexas.edu/law**
- Practitioners Publishing Co.:   **www.ppc.com**
- Will Yancey's Home Page: **www.willyancey.com**

Computer Tax Service Example

The tax researcher can use a computerized tax service to find court cases of interest. If the researcher knows the case name or citation, he or she can enter it directly and obtain a copy of the case. If the case name or citation is not known, then the researcher can use a computer query to find cases that have addressed the issue at hand.

Your client is involved in a dispute with the IRS over the valuation for estate tax purposes of a closely held business. In the process of getting ready to go to the Tax Court on this matter, you decide to hire an expert witness to justify the client's valuation of the business. During the interviews, one of the experts says that she will use the Capital Asset Pricing Model (CAPM) as the basis for her valuation. You are not sure what the CAPM is and how the courts will react to it. You therefore execute a computer

EXHIBIT 5-9:   RIA Checkpoint CAPM Search Query

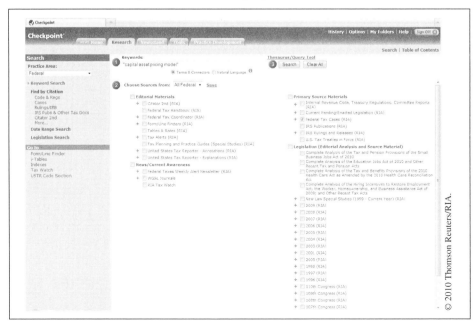

© 2010 Thomson Reuters/RIA.

EXHIBIT 5-10: RIA Checkpoint CAPM Search Result (T. C. Memo Decisions)

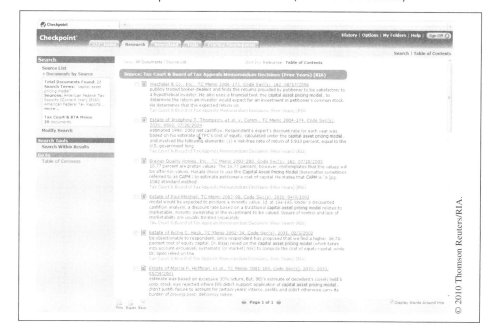

search using RIA Checkpoint to see if there is any information available on the use of the CAPM in tax valuation.

Exhibit 5-9 shows an example of a search query that could be used to find any court cases that have discussed the CAPM. Exhibit 5-10 shows a listing of Tax Court Regular and Memo decisions discussing the use of CAPM in valuing a closely held business. After reviewing these cases, you would conclude that there is a lot of controversy about using the CAPM in nonpublicly traded valuation situations. As a result, you should prepare your client's case using another method of valuation or be prepared to defend your use of the CAPM.

SUMMARY

The tax practitioner must possess a working knowledge of the Federal court system to address tax research problems. The researcher must understand the role of the courts in generating Federal tax law, the relationship of the courts to one another, the Constitution, and the jurisdiction of each court, where to locate an appropriate decision, and how to interpret that decision.

Exhibit 5-11 offers a summary of some of the attributes of the trial-level courts discussed in this chapter. Because of differences among courts, the tax adviser may be inclined to choose one of the trial-level courts

over the others to accommodate the special needs or circumstances of the client.

Exhibit 5-12 summarizes the decisions available in each of the tax case reporter services discussed in this chapter. With the variety of tax publications available, choices must be made so that the practitioner's tax research budget can be used effectively, without sacrifice of his or her ability to solve the client's problems.

Finally, a number of observations concerning citation conventions can be made. Review the citation examples given in this chapter to verify the list shown in Exhibit 5-13 and to add your own observations to it.

EXHIBIT 5-11: Selected Attributes of Trial-Level Courts

Item	Tax Court	District Court	Court of Federal Claims
Jurisdiction	Tax cases only	Legal issues based on entire U.S. Code	Monetary claims against U.S. government
Judges	Tax law specialists	Tax law generalists	Tax law generalists
Domain	National court, but judges travel	Limited geographical Area	National court, but judges travel
Jury trial available?	No	Yes, if question of fact	No
Number of judges	One, reviewed by the chief judge; en banc hearing for certain issues	One	One to five hearing case
Small Cases Division	Yes	Not available	Not available
Payment of tax	Trial, then payment	Payment, then trial	Payment, then trial
Precedents court must follow	Supreme Court; pertinent circuit court; Tax Court	Supreme Court; pertinent circuit court; own District court	Supreme Court; Federal Circuit Court; Court of Federal Claims

EXHIBIT 5-12: Court Decision Reporter Summary

Publisher, Common	I. BY REPORTER		
	Reporter, Common	Decisions Included	
Primary Reporters			
T. C. (B.T.A.)	GPO	Regular Tax Court (BTA) decisions	
TCM	CCH	Tax Court Memorandum decisions	
RIA T. C. Mem. Dec.	RIA	Tax Court Memorandum decisions	
F.Supp	West	District court decisions	
Fed. Cl.	West	Court of Federal Claims decisions	
F.3d (F.2d)	West	Court of Appeals and pre-1982 Court of Claims decisions	
U.S.	GPO	All Supreme Court decisions	
S.Ct.	West	All Supreme Court decisions	
Secondary Reporters			
USTC	CCH	Tax cases from all Federal courts except the Tax Court	
AFTR series	RIA	Tax cases from all Federal courts except the Tax Court	

			II. BY COURT
Court	Publisher	Citation	Reporter
Supreme Court			
All cases	West	S.Ct.	*Supreme Court Reporter*
	GPO	U.S.	*U.S. Supreme Court Reports*
Tax only	CCH	USTC	*U.S. Tax Cases*
	RIA	AFTR series	*American Federal Tax Reports*
Courts of Appeals			
All cases	West	F.3d (F.2d)	*Federal Reporter, 3d (2d) series*
Tax only	CCH	USTC	
	RIA	AFTR series	
Tax Court			
Regular	GPO	T.C.	*Tax Court of the U.S. Reports*
Memo	CCH	TCM	*Tax Court Memorandum Decisions*
	RIA	RIA T.C. Memo	*RIA Tax Court Memorandum Decisions*
District Court			
All cases	West	F.Supp	*Federal Supplement Series*
Tax only	CCH	USTC	
	RIA	AFTR series	
Court of Federal Claims			
All cases post-1982	West	Fed. Cl.	*U.S. Court of Federal Claims*
Tax only	CCH	USTC	
	RIA	AFTR series	

EXHIBIT 5-13: Citation Conventions and Observations

- The common form of a citation is as follows: case name–volume-number–reporter–page number–court–year.
- The AFTR second series began with 1954 IRC cases.
- The B. T. A. became the U.S. Tax Court in 1943.
- The U.S. Court of Claims became the U.S. Claims Court in 1982 and the U.S. Court of Federal Claims in 1992.
- Unless the case was published in a year different from that in which it was heard, the USTC volume number (and many AFTR page numbers) includes a reference to the year, so the year need not be repeated in the citation.
- The S.Ct. and U.S. citations imply that the case was heard in the Supreme Court, so the court abbreviation need not be repeated in the citation.
- The government need not be mentioned in a typical Tax Court citation.
- Although they are not published in a printed court reporter, U.S. Tax Court Small Case Summary Opinions are available after 2000 on computer tax services (e.g., RIA and CCH).

QUIZ YOURSELF

Reinforce the tax research information covered in this chapter by completing the online quizzes located at the Federal Tax Research Web site at **www.cengagebrain.com.** At the CengageBrain.com home page, search for the *Federal Tax Research*, 9e ISBN (1111221642) using the search box at the top of the page. This will take you to the product page where you can access the quizzes.

KEY WORDS

By the time you complete this chapter, you should be comfortable discussing each of the following terms. If you need additional review of any of these items, return to the appropriate material in the chapter or consult the glossary to this text.

AFTR (American Federal Tax Reports), p. 164
Board of Tax Appeals, p. 156
case brief, p. 171
Court of Federal Claims, p. 164
Courts of Appeals, p. 166
District Courts, p. 163

en banc, p. 157
Golsen rule, p. 158
headnote, p. 171
Memorandum decision, p. 157
permanent citation, p. 159
Regular decision, p. 157
Small Cases Division, p. 158

Supreme Court, p. 168
Tax Court, p. 156
temporary citation, p. 159
USTC (United States Tax Cases), p. 164
writ of certiorari, p. 169

DISCUSSION QUESTIONS

1. Who can initiate a court case that deals with a tax matter—the taxpayer or the IRS?

2. Explain the general organization of the Federal court system for cases concerning Federal tax issues.

3. May a taxpayer take his or her tax case directly to the Supreme Court?

4. Who has the burden of proof in most cases involving the tax law? Why?

5. The U.S. Tax Court hears only certain types of cases. Identify those cases.

6. The U.S. Tax Court has undergone an evolution since it was founded. What happened to its structure in 1926, 1943, and 1969, respectively?

7. How many judges sit on the U.S. Tax Court? What is the length of time of the appointment of each judge?

8. The U.S. Tax Court is a national court that meets in Washington, D.C. Does this mean that the taxpayer and his or her attorney must travel to Washington to have a case heard?

9. May a taxpayer have a jury trial in the U.S. Tax Court?

10. What does the term "en banc" mean?

11. Distinguish among a Regular, Memorandum, and Summary decision of the Tax Court.

12. The U.S. Tax Court is a national court that hears cases of taxpayers who may appeal to various geographical Courts of Appeals. How does the Tax Court reconcile the opposite holdings of two or more of these Courts of Appeals for taxpayers who work or reside in different parts of the country?

13. What is the Small Cases Division of the U.S. Tax Court? What is the maximum amount of the deficiency that can be the subject of a Small Cases hearing? Comment on the trial procedures in the Small Cases Division.

14. Where are regular Tax Court decisions published? Illustrate the elements of both a temporary and a permanent regular Tax Court citation. Explain what each part of the citation means.

15. Tax Court Memorandum decisions are not published by the Federal government. However, commercial reporters include these decisions. Illustrate the elements of both a temporary and a permanent citation for a Tax Court Memorandum decision, using both the CCH and RIA reporters. Explain what each part of the citation means.

16. What is the jurisdiction of a U.S. District Court?

17. Can Tax Court Summary Opinions be cited as precedent? Discuss.

18. Must the taxpayer pay the disputed tax deficiency to the government before his or her case will be heard in a District Court? In the U.S. Court of Federal Claims? In the U.S. Tax Court?

19. Which of the trial courts is most appropriate for a taxpayer who wishes to limit the judicial review of the relevant year's tax return to the specific issue(s) involved in the case?

20. Which of the trial courts would best serve a taxpayer litigating an issue of a technical tax nature? Why?

21. Is a Federal District Court a national court? How many judges hear a case brought before a Federal District Court?

22. Name the three court case reporters that publish tax and nontax District Court decisions. Illustrate the elements of a citation that might be found in each reporter. Explain what each part of the citation means.

23. Differentiate between a primary and a secondary case citation.

24. What type of cases are heard by the U.S. Court of Federal Claims?

25. How many judges are appointed to the U.S. Court of Federal Claims?

26. Is the U.S. Court of Federal Claims a national court? Must a taxpayer go to Washington, D.C., to present a case to this U.S. court?

27. Name the three court case reporters that publish U.S. Court of Federal Claims decisions. Illustrate the elements of a citation that might be found in each reporter. Explain what each part of the citation means.

28. Are the U.S. Courts of Appeals national courts? What type of cases do they hear?

29. Identify the circuit court that would hear the case of a taxpayer who lives or works in each of the following areas:
    a. Texas
    b. New York
    c. California
    d. Colorado
    e. A case that is appealed from the U.S. Court of Federal Claims

30. Identify the circuit court that would hear the case of a taxpayer who lives or works in each of the following areas:
    a. Florida
    b. Ohio
    c. North Carolina
    d. Puerto Rico
    e. Guam

31. Identify the circuit court that would hear the case of a taxpayer who lives or works in each of the following areas:
    a. Arizona
    b. Alabama
    c. Vermont
    d. South Carolina
    e. Alaska

32. Identify the circuit court that would hear the case of a taxpayer who lives or works in each of the following areas:
    a. Missouri
    b. Montana
    c. Mississippi
    d. Massachusetts
    e. Michigan

33. Each Court of Appeals has approximately 20 judges. How many of these judges hear a typical case?

34. Name the three court case reporters that publish Court of Appeals decisions. Illustrate the elements of a citation that might be found in each reporter. Explain what each part of the citation means.

35. Can a taxpayer have a jury trial before a Court of Appeals?

36. What is the highest court in the United States? What is its jurisdiction? Where does it hear cases?

37. How does one petition the Supreme Court to hear one's tax case?

38. How many justices are appointed to the Supreme Court? How many hear each case?

39. Why does the Supreme Court hear so few tax cases?

40. Differentiate between the Supreme Court's overturning of a lower court's decision and its denial of a writ of certiorari.

41. Name the four court case reporters that publish Supreme Court decisions. Illustrate the elements of a citation that might be found in each reporter. Explain what each part of the citation means.

42. Is it possible for a taxpayer to have a jury trial before any of the trial courts? Before a Court of Appeals? Before the U.S. Supreme Court?

43. Discuss the precedential value of a Court of Appeals decision. Which Court of Appeals decisions are most important to a specific taxpayer?

44. In the (fictitious) citation *Gomez v. U.S.*, 104 T. C. 123 (2009), what does the "104" stand for? The "T. C."? The "123"?

45. Which court would have issued the (fictitious) *O'Dell v. U.S.*, 98 TCM 86 (2009) decision? What does each element in the citation mean?

46. In the citation *Simons-Eastern v. U.S.*, 354 F.Supp. 1003 (D.Ct., Ga, 1972), the "F.Supp." tells the tax researcher that the decision is from which court?

47. By using only the citation, state which court issued each of the following decisions. If you cannot determine which court by looking at the citation only, say so.
    a. *Davis v. U.S.*, 43 Fed. Cl. 92 (1999)
    b. *D.C. Crummey v. U.S.*, 68-2 USTC ¶ 12,541

    c. *U.S. v. Goode*, 86 AFTR2d 2000-7273

    d. *James v. U.S.*, 81 S.Ct. 1052 (1961)

48. What is a case headnote? How might it be useful to the tax researcher?

49. By using only the citation, state which court issued each of the following decisions. If you cannot determine which court by looking at the citation only, say so.

    a. *Douglas, Christopher*, T.C. Memo 1994-519

    b. *Takaba, Brian G.*, 119 T.C. 285

    c. *Botts, Roy R.*, T.C. Summary Opinion 2001-182

    d. American Airlines, Inc., 40 Fed.Cl. 712

50. What is the common form of a citation shown in Exhibit 5-13?

EXERCISES

51. Locate the court case *Central Labor's Pension Fund v. Heinz*, 541 U.S. 739 (2004). Using only the headnotes answer the following questions:

    a. What was the issue(s) addressed by the court?

    b. What was the ruling of the court?

52. Locate the court case *Fisher v. Comm.*, 105 AFTR2d 2010-2226. Using only the headnotes answer the following questions:

    a. What was the issue(s) addressed by the court?

    b. What was the ruling of the court?

53. Locate the court case *Container Corporation v. Commissioner*, 134 T. C. No. 5 (2010). Using only the headnotes answer the following questions:

    a. What was the issue(s) addressed by the court?

    b. What was the ruling of the court?

54. Locate the court case *Alemasov and Popov*, T. C. Memo. 2007-130. Using only the headnotes answer the following questions:

    a. What was the issue(s) addressed by the court?

    b. What was the ruling of the court?

55. Locate the court case *Angela J. Brown v. Commissioner*, T. C. Summary Opinion 2010-56. Using only the headnotes answer the following questions:

    a. What was the issue(s) addressed by the court?

    b. What was the ruling of the court?

56. Locate the court case *Zimmerman, et al. v. United States*, 2001-1 USTC ¶50,107, 86 AFTR2d 2000-6701. Using only the headnotes answer the following questions:

    a. What was the issue(s) addressed by the court?

    b. What was the ruling of the court?

57. Locate the court case *Anderson Columbia, Inc. V. U.S.*, 54 Fed. Cl. 756 (2002). Using only the headnotes answer the following questions:

    a. What was the issue(s) addressed by the court?

    b. What was the ruling of the court?

58. Find the court decision located at 100 T. C. 32.
    a. What court heard the case?
    b. Who was the judge(s)?
    c. In what year was the case decided?
    d. What was the issue(s) involved?

59. Find the court decision located at 126 T. C. 47.
    a. What court heard the case?
    b. Who was the judge(s)?
    c. In what year was the case decided?
    d. What was the issue(s) involved?

60. Find the court decision located at 133 T. C. No. 8.
    a. What court heard the case?
    b. Who was the judge(s)?
    c. In what year was the case decided?
    d. What was the issue(s) involved?

61. Find the court decision located at T. C. Memo 2010-54.
    a. What court heard the case?
    b. Who was the judge(s)?
    c. In what year was the case decided?
    d. What was the issue(s) involved?

62. Find the court decision located at T. C. Memo. 2001-71.
    a. What court heard the case?
    b. Who was the judge(s)?
    c. In what year was the case decided?
    d. What was the issue(s) involved?

63. Find the court decision located at T. C. Memo. 1992-204.
    a. What court heard the case?
    b. Who was the judge(s)?
    c. What tax year(s) is in question and in what year was the case decided?
    d. What *Code* section(s) was at issue?
    e. What was the issue(s) involved?
    f. Which party prevailed in the decision?

64. Find the court decision located at T. C. Summary Opinion 2003-168.
    a. What court heard the case?
    b. Who was the judge(s)?
    c. What tax year(s) is in question and in what year was the case decided?
    d. What *Code* section(s) was at issue?
    e. What was the issue(s) involved?
    f. Which party prevailed in the decision?

65. Find the court decision located at T. C. Summary Opinion 2006-20.
    a. What court heard the case?
    b. Who was the judge(s)?
    c. What tax year(s) is in question and in what year was the case decided?
    d. What *Code* section(s) was at issue?
    e. What was the issue(s) involved?
    f. Which party prevailed in the decision?

66. Find the court decision located at T. C. Summary Opinion 2010-46.
    a. What court heard the case?
    b. Who was the judge(s)?
    c. What tax year(s) is in question and in what year was the case decided?
    d. What *Code* section(s) was at issue?
    e. What was the issue(s) involved?
    f. Which party prevailed in the decision?

67. Find the court decision located at 2007-1 USTC ¶50,210.
    a. What court heard the case?
    b. Who was the judge(s)?
    c. What tax year(s) is in question and in what year was the case decided?
    d. What *Code* section(s) was at issue?
    e. What was the issue(s) involved?
    f. Which party prevailed in the decision?

68. Find the court decision located at 67 AFTR2d 91-718.
    a. What court heard the case?
    b. Who was the judge(s)?
    c. What tax year(s) is in question and in what year was the case decided?
    d. What *Code* section(s) was at issue?
    e. What was the issue(s) involved?
    f. Which party prevailed in the decision?

69. Find the court decision located at 98 AFTR2d 2006-8309.
    a. What court heard the case?
    b. Who was the judge(s)?
    c. What tax year(s) is in question and in what year was the case decided?
    d. What *Code* section(s) was at issue?
    e. What was the issue(s) involved?
    f. Which party prevailed in the decision?

70. If your last name begins with the letters A–L, read and brief the following cases:
    a. *Sorensen*, T.C. Memo. 1994-175
    b. *Keller*, 84-1 USTC ¶ 9194.

If your last name begins with the letters M–Z, read and brief the following cases:

   c. *Washington*, 77 T. C. 601

   d. *Tellier*, 17 AFTR2d 633

71. If your last name begins with the letters A–L, read and brief the following cases:

   a. *Rownd*, T. C. Memo. 1994-465

   b. *Arnes*, 93-1 USTC ¶ 50,016.

   If your last name begins with the letters M–Z, read and brief the following cases:

   c. *Willie Nelson Music Co.*, 85 T. C. 914

   d. *Independent Contracts, Inc.*, 73 AFTR2d 94-1406

72. Read and brief the following cases:

   a. *Gregory v. Helvering*, 55 S.Ct. 266 (1935)

   b. *Hunt*, T. C. Memo. 1965-172

73. Read and brief the following cases:

   a. *Fulcher, Douglas R.*, T. C. Summary Opinion 2003-157

   b. *The Boeing Company and Consolidated Subs.*, 91 AFTR2d 2003-1088 (123 S.Ct. 1099)

74. Read and brief the following cases:

   a. *Thornton v. Commissioner*, 2003-2 USTC ¶50,695

   b. *Stamoulis v. Commissioner*, T. C. Summary Opinion 2007-38

75. Use a tax service to give two parallel citations for the *U.S. v. D'ambrosia*, a Seventh Circuit Court of Appeals case decided in 2002. Using only the headnote(s), what was the issue(s) in this case?

76. Use a tax service to give three parallel citations for the *Baral v. U.S.*, a Supreme Court case decided in 2000. Using only the headnote(s), what was the issue(s) in this case?

77. Use a tax service to give three parallel citations for the *Falstone, Inc. v. Commissioner,* a Ninth Circuit Court of Appeals case decided in 2003. Using only the headnote(s), what was the issue(s) in this case?

RESEARCH CASES

78. Snidely Limited spent $1 million this year to upgrade its manufacturing plant, which had received several warnings from the state environmental agency about releasing pollution into the local river. Late in the year, Snidely received an assessment of $700,000 for violating the state's Clean Water Act. After he negotiated with the State, which cost $135,000 in legal fees, Snidely promised to spend another $200,000 next year for more pollution control devices, and the fine was reduced to $450,000. How much of these expenditures can Snidely Limited deduct for tax purposes?

79. Last year, only four of 32 professional basketball teams turned a nominal accounting profit. Betty purchased such a team this year. Her taxable loss was determined to be $950,000. Can she deduct this loss?

80. Herbert, a collector of rare coins, bought a 1916 Spanish Bowlero for $2,000 in 1984. He sold the coin for $4,500 in January. Herbert retired from his loading dock job in June and began actively buying and selling rare coins. By December, Herbert's realized gain from such activities was $21,500. What type of taxable income was January's $2,500 gain?

81. Steve is an usher at his local church. Can he deduct commuting expenses for the Sundays that he is assigned to usher for church services?

82. A new member of the San Diego Chargers wants the team to transfer $1 million into an escrow account, in his name, for later withdrawal. The player suggests this payment in lieu of the traditional signing bonus. When is this income taxable to him?

83. Professor Stevens obtained tenure and promotion to full professor status many years ago. Yet, he continues to publish research papers in scholarly journals to satisfy his own curiosity and to maintain his professional prestige and status within the academic community. Publications are also necessary in order for Professor Stevens to receive pay raises at his university. This year, Dr. Stevens spent $750 of his own funds to travel to southern Utah to collect some critical pieces of data for his work. What is the tax treatment of this expenditure?

84. The local electric company requires a $200 refundable deposit from new customers in lieu of a credit check. Landlord Pete pays this amount for all of his new-to-town tenants. Can he deduct the $200 payments on his tax return?

85. High-Top Financing charges its personal loan holders a 2 percent fee if the full loan principal is paid prior to the due date. What is the tax effect of this year's $50,000 of prepayment penalties collected by High-Top?

86. Cecilia died this year, owning mutual funds in her IRA worth $120,000. Under the terms of the IRA, Cecilia's surviving husband, Frank, was the beneficiary of the account, and he took a lump-sum distribution from the fund. Both Cecilia and Frank were age 57 at the beginning of the year.

    a. How does Frank account for the inheritance assuming that he rolls it over into his own IRA in a timely manner?

    b. Would your answer change if Frank were Cecilia's brother?

87. During a properly declared U.S. war with Outer Altoona, Harriet, a single taxpayer, was killed in action. Current year Federal taxable income to the date of Harriet's death totaled $19,000, and Federal income tax withholding came to $2,300.

    a. What is Harriet's tax liability for the year of her death?

    b. What documentation must accompany her final Form 1040?

88. Jerry Baker and his wife Hammi believe in the worship of the "Sea God," which is a very personal religion to Jerry and Hammi. To practice their beliefs, the Bakers want to take a two-week trip to Tahiti this year to worship their deity. The cost (e.g., airfare, hotels) of this religious "pilgrimage" is $5,250. Jerry wants to know if he can deduct the cost of this trip as a charitable deduction on the joint Form 1040, Schedule A.

89. Willie Waylon is a famous country-and-western singer. As an investment, Willie started a chain of barbecue restaurants called Willie's Wonderful Ribs. Willie's friends and associates invested $500,000 in this venture. The restaurant chain failed, and the investors lost all their money. Because of his visibility and status in the entertainment community, Willie felt that he personally had to make good on the losses suffered by the investors, to protect his singing and business reputation. Consequently, he personally paid $500,000 to reimburse the investors for their losses. What are Willie's tax consequences (if any) from the reimbursement?

90. Paul Preppie is an accountant for the Very Big (VB) Corporation of America, located in Los Angeles. When Paul went to work for VB, he did not have a college degree. VB required that Paul earn a B.S. degree in accounting, so he enrolled in a local private university's night school and obtained the degree. VB Corporation does not reimburse employees for attending night school, and because Paul attended a private university the tuition and other costs were relatively expensive. Under California law, once Paul has his degree, he is eligible to sit for the CPA exam and can become a CPA in California. Can Paul deduct any of the $10,500 he paid in tuition and other costs during the current tax year?

    Prepare (in good form) a research memorandum to the file. (See Chapter 2 for an illustration of the structure of a tax memo.)

91. Several years ago, Carol Mutter, a cash-basis taxpayer, obtained a mortgage from Weak National Bank to purchase a personal residence. In December 2009, $8,500 of interest was due on the mortgage, but Carol had only $75 in her checking account. On December 31, 2009, she borrowed $8,500 from Weak Bank, evidenced by a note, and the proceeds were deposited in her checking account. On the same day, Carol issued a check in the identical amount of $8,500 to Weak Bank for the interest due. Is the interest expense deductible for the 2009 tax year?

    Prepare (in good form) a research memorandum to the file. (See Chapter 2 for an illustration of the structure of a tax memo.)

92. Phyllis maintained an IRA account at the brokerage firm ABC. On February 11 of the current year, she requested a check for the balance of her account. She received the check made out in her name and deposited it the same day in a new IRA account at the brokerage firm XYZ. Phyllis then requested a check on May 8 from XYZ, which was deposited in another new IRA account 35 days later. Is the May 8 distribution taxable to Phyllis?

    Prepare in good form a research memorandum to the file. (See Chapter 2 for an illustration of the structure of a tax memo.)

93. Crystal Eros is a devout Pyramidist and a member of the Religious Society of Yanni, a Pyramidist organization. She adheres to the fundamental tenets of Pyramidist theology, including the belief that the Spirit of God is in every person and that it is wrong to kill or otherwise harm another person. Crystal's faith dictates that she not voluntarily participate, directly or indirectly, in military activities. Because Federal income taxes fund military activities, Crystal believes that her faith prohibits her from paying such taxes. Is there any legal substantiation for Crystal's position?

    Prepare (in good form) a research memorandum to the file. (See Chapter 2 for an illustration of the structure of a tax memo.)

94. Last year, your client, Robert Dinero, mailed an automatic extension for his tax return on April 15. He enclosed a check for $10,000 with the extension request. The IRS cashed the check on April 28. Later, the IRS assessed Robert late filing penalties of $2,900 because they claim he did not mail the extension request on time. On the same date, Robert mailed an income tax extension request and check to the state of California. The California check was cashed on April 16. You requested that the IRS send you a copy of the extension request envelope showing the postmark; however, the IRS has lost it. The IRS recently attached Robert's bank account for the $2,900, thereby seizing the funds directly. You have known Robert for years, and he could be described as a good, law-abiding, taxpaying citizen. He always pays his taxes on time, has never been in trouble with the IRS, and is not a tax protester. Robert asks you to recommend whether he should engage a tax attorney and sue for a refund, knowing that the legal fees for such an action will probably exceed $10,000.

    After appropriate research, write a letter to Robert explaining your findings. His address is 432 Lucre Street, Tecate, CA 91980.

95. Your client, Luther Lifo, is an auditing professor who runs a CPA review course. He comes to you with the following tax questions:

    Question One. Luther teaches CPA review courses on either a guaranteed or nonguaranteed basis. Under the guaranteed program, students pay higher tuition and, if they fail the CPA examination, are entitled to a full refund within two weeks of the release of the results. The CPA review course contracts require him to place the tuition in a set-aside escrow account until the students pass the exam; he established the savings account as a trust account for this purpose. The registration fee and tuition must be paid in full before the classes begin. Thus, students enrolled in the class that started in January 20x1 paid their tuition in December 20x0. In 20x0, Luther deposited registration fees and tuition, including $30,000 in guaranteed tuition payments for the winter 20x1 courses, into a checking account. Also during 20x1, he paid refunds to guaranteed students who failed the 20x1 exams from that account. Does Luther report the $30,000 as income in 20x0 or 20x1? How are the refunds paid in 20x1 treated for tax purposes? State the authority for your conclusion.

Question Two. Luther is a majority shareholder in a corporation that owns an office building. He leases space in the building for use in his CPA review course. Luther pays approximately $20 per square foot in annual rent. The corporation leases the remaining space in the building to a LSAT, GMAT, SAT, and GRE review course run by other taxpayers for approximately $10 per square foot. Luther's main intent in negotiating the discounted lease was to secure the additional traffic generated by the other review courses in order to enhance the potential revenue for the CPA review course. What is the amount of rent that Luther can deduct in connection with the CPA review course? State the authority for your conclusion.

After appropriate research, write a letter to Luther explaining your findings. The address is 321 Fifo Street, Temecula, CA 91980.

96. Austin Towers is a convicted former spy for the former Soviet Union. Austin received a communication from a Soviet agent that $2 million had been set aside for him in an account upon which he would be able to draw. Austin was told that the money was being held by the Soviet Union, rather than in an independent or third-party bank or institution, on the petitioner's behalf. Over the next few years, Austin drew approximately $1 million from the account. During that period, Austin filed annual tax returns with his wife showing taxable income of approximately $65,000 per year. Conduct appropriate research to determine Austin's tax liability for the $1 million in spy fees.

After appropriate research, write a letter to Austin explaining your findings. His address is Lompoc Federal Prison, Cell #123, Lompoc, CA 93401.

97. The Reverend Shaman Oracle is an ordained minister in the Church of Prophetic Prophecy in Palm Desert, California. In the current year, Shaman receives payments from the church for his services of $150,000. Of this amount, the church designates $60,000 for compensation and $90,000 as a housing allowance. Shaman and his wife own a home and have actual expenditures during the year for the home of $72,000. The house is located in a well-established rental market, and the fair rental value of the home for the current year is $55,000. Shaman wants to know how he and his wife should report these amounts on their current year's tax return.

After appropriate research, write a letter to Shaman explaining your findings. His address is P.O. Box 1234, Palm Desert, California 92211.

98. Your client, Teddy Chow and his wife Abby, filed a lawsuit to recover damages for personal injuries Teddy sustained in a 2000 auto accident. In 2004, a jury awarded Teddy $1,620,000 in damages. In addition, delay damages in the amount of $1,080,000 were then added to that award, resulting in a total judgment of $2,700,000. The defendants appealed the award, and while the appeal was pending, the parties reached a settlement, which provided for payment to Teddy of $2,550,000. In 2009, after attorney's fees of $850,000 were subtracted, Teddy received $1,700,000. Teddy wants to know how these amounts are treated for tax purposes.

After appropriate research, write a letter to Teddy and Abby explaining your findings. Their address is 654 Hops Street, Golden, CO 78501.

99. Cabrito Ranch Inc. is a family ranch owned and operated by two brothers, Billie and Bubba Cabrito. The corporation made in-kind bonus payments in the form of goats to its two officers (Billie and Bubba) in exchange for their performance of agricultural labor. The two brothers are the only employees to receive goat bonuses. The transfers of the goats to the officers occurred within days of the date Cabrito Ranch would have sold the goats within the ordinary course of its business. The two officers/brothers did not market their bonus goats separately from other Cabrito Ranch goats; rather, the bonus goats were loaded onto the same

trucks and sold to the same goat buyer on the same terms as other Cabrito Ranch goats. The officer/brothers' goats were sold for $70,000 ($35,000 to each brother). Cabrito Ranch wants to know how to treat the cash from the goat bonuses for FICA purposes.

After appropriate research, write a letter to Billie and Bubba explaining your findings. Their address is 247 Angora Road, Mohair, TX 77501.

100. Gwen Gullible was married to Darrell Devious. They were divorced two years ago. Three years ago (the year before their divorce), Darrell received a $250,000 retirement plan distribution, of which $50,000 was rolled over into an IRA. At the time, Gwen was aware of the retirement funds and the rollover. The distribution was used to pay off the couple's mortgage, purchase a car, and for living expenses. Darrell prepared the couple's joint return, and Gwen asked him about the tax ramifications of the retirement distributions. He told her he had consulted a CPA and was advised that the retirement plan proceeds used to pay off a mortgage were not taxable income. Gwen accepted that explanation and signed the return. In fact, Darrell had not consulted a CPA.

One year ago (after the divorce), Gwen received a letter from the IRS saying they had not received the tax return for the last full year of marriage. On advice from a CPA, Gwen immediately filed the return. (She had a copy of the unfiled return.) The IRS notified Gwen that no estimated payments on the retirement distribution had been paid by Darrell, and that she owed $60,000 in tax, plus penalties and interest. The deficiency notice provided that the retirement distribution, less the amount rolled, was income to the couple.

After appropriate research, prepare (in good form) a research memorandum to the file. (See Chapter 2 for an illustration of the structure of a tax memo.) Then write a letter to Gwen explaining your findings. Her address is 678 Surprise Street, Houston, TX 77019.

101. Pealii Loligo owned and operated three "House of Calamari" restaurants from 2002 through 2004. His wife, Cleopatra Decacera, assisted with the management of the restaurants.

In May 2003, Ms. Decacera and Mr. Loligo purchased a $900,000 home. In relation to this home purchase, in 2000 and 2004 they signed mortgage loan applications indicating joint annual incomes of $235,000 and $321,000, respectively. On their 2002 joint Federal income tax return, however, Ms. Decacera and Mr. Loligo reported that they earned no salaries and had net losses of $55,000; and on their 2003 joint tax return, they reported that Mr. Loligo earned a salary of $23,000, and that they had net losses of $77,000.

During 2002–2004, Ms. Decacera and Mr. Loligo paid approximately $70,000 for home furnishings, $30,000 for a swimming pool, and $40,000 for Ms. Decacera's jewelry. In addition, they leased two Mercedes-Benz automobiles and took Ms. Decacera's parents on vacations to Florida and Nevada.

In 2007, Decacera and Loligo were indicted and charged with filing false tax returns in 2002–2004. Loligo pled guilty, while Decacera signed a deferred prosecution agreement and admitted filing false returns. The couple divorced in 2009, and in 2010 the IRS issued a deficiency notice for the 2002–2004 taxes. In September 2010, Ms. Decacera filed a petition in which she requested relief from joint and several liabilities for 2002–2004 income taxes. During January 2011, Mr. Loligo filed his "notice of intervention." In July, an IRS Appeals officer determined that Ms. Decacera did not qualify for Innocent Spouse relief under §6015(f).

After appropriate research, prepare (in good form) a research memorandum to the file. (See Chapter 2 for an illustration of the structure of a tax memo.) Then write a letter to Cleopatra explaining your findings. Her address is 4567 Whome Lane, Escondido, CA 92069.

102. Ned Naive operated several franchised stores, and at the home office's suggestion he consolidated its payroll and accounting functions with Andy the Accountant. Andy is not a CPA. Last year, Andy began embezzling taxpayer's escrowed tax withholdings and failed to remit required amounts for the four quarters. The IRS assessed Ned $10,000 in penalties for failing to make the proper withholding deposits during the year.

After appropriate research, prepare (in good form) a research memorandum to the file. (See Chapter 2 for an illustration of the structure of a tax memo.) Then write a letter to Ned explaining your findings. His address is 4567 Brainless Street, Phoenix, AZ 91234.

103. Phred Phortunate (from Chapter 2) won his state lotto two years ago. His lotto ticket was worth $10 million, which was payable in 20 annual installments of $500,000 each. Phred paid $1 for the winning ticket. The lotto in Phred's state does not allow winners to receive their payout in a lump-sum. Phred wanted all of his money now, so he assigned his future lotto winnings to a Happy Finance Company for a discounted price of $4.5 million. Assignment of lotto winnings is permitted by Phred's state lotto. Phred filed his tax return and reported the assignment of the lotto winnings as a capital gain ($4.5 million–$1) taxable at a 15 percent rate.

After appropriate research to determine if Phred correctly reported his lotto winnings assignment, prepare (in good form) a research memorandum to the file. (See Chapter 2 for an illustration of the structure of a tax memo.) Then write a letter to Phred explaining your findings. His address is 2345 Ecstatic Street, White River Jct., VT 05001.

104. Your client, Gary Gearbox, wholly owned and worked full time for a C corporation in the business of repairing autos. His wife, Tammy, wholly owned and worked full time for another C corporation that provided mobile auto windshields repairs. Both corporations' offices were located in the Gearboxes' home. The corporations paid the Gearboxes rent for the use of this office space. In addition to renting this portion of their home, the Gearboxes also owned five rental properties. On their last three tax returns, the Gearboxes reported net income from leasing office space to their C corporations of $40,000, $24,000, and $22,000, respectively. During these years, the combined losses from the five other rental properties exceeded the income derived from their office leases. On their last three tax returns, the Gearboxes offset the losses from the rental properties against the income from the office leases and, as a result, paid no tax on the rental income paid to them by their corporation.

After appropriate research to determine if Gary and Tammy correctly reported their rental income, prepare (in good form) a research memorandum to the file. Then write a letter to the Gearboxes explaining your findings. Their address is 7895 NASCAR Way, Talladega, AL 35160.

105. Your client Jack Benny and his wife were divorced last year. Jack had been employed by the City of Rancho Cucamonga for 30 years. Jack was a participant in a defined benefit pension plan. He had been eligible to start receiving pension benefits five years ago, but he kept working and did not collect his pension. The divorce decree gave Jack's wife one-half of the community interest in the pension plan. If Jack had retired on the date of the divorce, she would have been entitled to receive $2,200 per month. Because Jack did not retire, however, the divorce court ordered him to pay his former spouse $2,200 per month until he retired. The divorce court also ordered the pension plan to make the same monthly payments to his ex-spouse after his retirement. Jack paid his former spouse $26,400 in the current year as ordered in the divorce decree. Jack is still working and has not yet retired.

After appropriate research to determine if Jack can deduct the payments to his ex-wife as alimony on his current tax return and prepare (in good form) a research memorandum to the file. Write a client letter to Jack with your findings. His address is 543 Camino Disolución, Rancho Cucamonga, CA 91730.

106. Many years ago your client Lucy Hapless (currently single and age 48) started working with Sham Credit Swap (SCS) Inc., where she participated in the company's Section 401(k) plan. Five years ago, she took out a home loan from her 401(k) plan. The loan was repayable with interest through semimonthly payroll deductions over a 10-year term. Lucy made the scheduled payments until she was laid off this early this year. The outstanding balance of the loan became due and payable at the time of Lucy's termination, but she did not have the money to pay off the loan or was she able to refinance it. No payments were made on the loan after her layoff, and the loan went into default. The 401(k) plan sent Lucy a letter, notifying her that she

had a deemed distribution from the plan equal to the then unpaid loan balance of $72,000. The 401(k) plan sent Lucy a check for $98,000, which represented the balance of her plan account less Federal tax withholding of $24,500. Six months ago, when Lucy received the check, deposited the entire $98,000 into her checking account and has been using the money for living expenses, since she has been unable find another job.

After appropriate research to determine if determine Lucy's tax consequences from this Section 401(k) plan loan payoff and prepare (in good form) a research memorandum to the file. Write a client letter to Lucy with your findings. Her address is 789 Hard Luck St., Carefree, AZ 85377.

107. Mary and Manny Muffler were involved in an auto accident several years ago with an uninsured motorist. The uninsured motorist was at fault and caused significant injuries to Mary. Because of her injuries, Mary was unable to work for over a year. At the time of the accident, petitioner and her husband had two vehicles insured under separate automobile liability insurance policies through Farm State Automobile Insurance Co. (Farm State). Both insurance policies were purchased by Mary and her husband and had endorsements for uninsured and underinsured motorist (UM/UIM) coverage with policy limits of $50,000.

Although Mary filed a lawsuit against the motorist who was at fault in her accident, her counsel ascertained that the defendant had neither significant assets nor any insurance. Mary submitted a claim under her UM/UIM coverage to Farm State for compensation for her injuries in the automobile accident. Farm State took the position that petitioner was entitled to recover under the UM/UIM coverage of only one of the two policies held by her and her husband, resulting in an effective policy limit on recovery of $50,000. In taking this position, Farm State relied on anti-stacking provisions in its insurance contracts with petitioner and her husband, under which the insured was precluded from aggregating or "stacking" his or her UM/UIM coverage under multiple Farm State policies. Mary agreed to settle her claim with State Farm for $32,000 plus $18,000 in attorney fees ($50,000 total).

After receiving the $32,000 payment several years ago, Mary became a member of a class action lawsuit against State Farm that alleged that the stacking rules constituted a breach of contract and a breach of a covenant of good faith and fair dealing in their insurance contracts, and that she was entitled to collect on the second policy. State Farm settled the claim. As a result, Mary received an additional $53,000 ($50,000 plus interest) payment pursuant to the settlement agreement as her pro rata portion of the settlement funds. During that year petitioner was issued a Form 1099-MISC, Miscellaneous Income, reflecting the payment.

After appropriate research determine how Mary (who has since divorced Manny) should report the $53,000 payment on her current year's tax return and prepare (in good form) a research memorandum to the file. Write a client letter to Mary with your findings. Her address is 789 Mustang St., Shelby, CA 92111.

PART III

Research Tools

CHAPTER 6

Commercial Tax Services

LEARNING OBJECTIVES

- Apply the research process to actual Federal research problems.
- Become familiar with the major features of tax and legal commercial services.
- Use keyword, citation, and content searches to identify relevant materials in commercial services.
- Identify the comparative strengths and weaknesses of the commercial services.

CHAPTER OUTLINE

WITH EASY AND FREE access to virtually all primary tax sources via the Internet, one might wonder why tax practitioners are willing to bear the substantial costs associated with subscribing to commercial tax and legal services. By organizing the copious assortment of primary and secondary tax law sources, these services facilitate more efficient, effective, and comprehensive searches for solutions to tax questions than a Google or Bing search would produce. Further, tax practitioners are being more closely scrutinized by the IRS and the Securities and Exchange Commission (SEC) as a result of the Sarbanes-Oxley Act and other increases in regulation. This heightened oversight increases the importance of conducting quality tax research that is carefully documented. Commercial services provide a vehicle for conducting this quality research.

One of the most useful products available through commercial services is the editorial explanation and expert analysis of the primary tax sources. As the tax law can be quite complex, the plain English commentary alone can be worth the cost of the services. Thus, the value of a commercial service is to act as an index for and explanations of primary and secondary tax law source materials. Most tax practitioners avail themselves of the benefit of a tax service, as there are services priced to fit the needs (and pocketbooks) of even the smallest tax office.

While one of the main features that practitioners appreciate in a commercial service is the editorial explanation, only reckless (or inadequately trained) tax practitioners confine their analysis to this commentary. The tax services should efficiently direct the researcher to the germane primary sources of the controlling law. It is the ethical and professional duty of tax researchers to evaluate the primary sources themselves and ascertain whether any developments have occurred recently that may change or alter the results of the initial research.

This chapter concretely applies the basic steps for developing effective and efficient tax research based on the process introduced in Chapter 2 and by utilizing the major commercial services to find a solution to an actual tax question. The features of the commercial services, both tax and legal, are explored on this journey.

Tax Services

Traditionally, commercial tax services are classified into two general types: annotated and topical. **Annotated tax services** are organized by Internal Revenue Code section number. They may also be called **Compilations** because they compile an editor's explanation and evaluation with the Code section as well as its recent committee reports and Regulations, and they provide **annotations** (i.e., brief summaries) of related court cases and administrative rulings. **Topical tax services**, on the other hand, divide the tax law into transactions and related subject matter with underlying tax principles as an organizing format. Thus, the material follows logical threads that connect noncontiguous Code sections. Since the electronic services are developed from published services, they are generally organized as topical and annotated databases; however, this structure may not be apparent.

One of the greatest benefits of any Internet service is the currency of the information provided. Most services update in text on a daily or continuous basis. Still, daily updating does not necessarily mean that what happened yesterday will be accessible today; processing time still is required. However, daily updating does mean that as soon as the information is processed it can be entered into the system.

SPOTLIGHT ON TAXATION

The oldest national CPA firm in the United States is Deloitte, which began in 1845 when William Welch Deloitte started his firm in London. In 1880, he opened an office in New York. In 1895, Charles Waldo Haskins and Eiljah Watt Sells joined forces to become the New York firm of Haskins & Sells. In 1952, Deloitte merged with Haskins & Sells to become Deloitte, Haskins & Sells (DHS). It was not until 1989 that DHS merged with Touche Ross to become Deloitte Touche. By 2003, the name of the firm was back to its original name of just Deloitte.

Illustrative Research Example

A research project is utilized to demonstrate the steps in tax research and to explore the essential features of the major tax services. It is important that you attempt the illustrative research project using the tax services available to you. The procedural knowledge necessary to become an effective researcher can only be acquired through hands-on practice. The remainder of this chapter is designed to guide you through the basic commercial services and is not a substitute for you actually performing the research. Using the services as you follow the text presentation of the research steps is a highly effective method of learning this material.

Research Project 6–1. Xandra Zyzzic, a calendar year taxpayer, bought a rental apartment building 20 years ago for $400,000 and has taken $290,000 of cost recovery during the time she has owned the building. In the current year, Lee Sands offers Xandra $440,000 for the building. Not wanting to recognize a large gain on the transaction, Xandra enters into an agreement with qualified like-kind exchange intermediary, Alan Sky. On August 5, year 1, she transfers the apartment to Alan Sky, and Alan transfers the building to Lee in exchange for $440,000. Alan holds the proceeds while Xandra looks for replacement property. On September 4, Xandra identifies a vacant lot as replacement property. On October 1, year 1, Alan notifies Xandra that he has filed for bankruptcy protection and cannot acquire the replacement property. Consequently, Xandra fails to acquire the replacement property. As of December 31, year 1, Alan's bankruptcy proceedings are ongoing and Xandra has received none of the proceeds for her apartment building. It is now April 15, year 2, and time to file the year 1 return. Xandra has no replacement property, no cash, and no apartment building! How does she report this transaction on her tax return?

Approaching the Research Problem

Regardless of the research method used, the starting point in approaching any tax research problem is to formulate the various tax questions to be answered and identify the issues associated with the questions. The tax question for Research Project 6–1 appears to be: What is the appropriate tax treatment of Xandra's failed like-kind exchange? This first formulation of the tax question should not be considered its final version. As the research progresses, other issues are likely to be identified, causing some refinement of the tax research questions and necessitating the development of new ones. Recall the iterative nature of tax research as discussed in Chapter 2 relative to Exhibits 2-1 and 2-2.

Research questions are gradually refined to their final states and all the associated issues are identified. However, this refinement does not guarantee that controlling authority will be found to provide a definite answer to the tax research question. The final conclusion may be that one solution appears more supportable than another. There may be a conflict between the likely interpretation of the facts and circumstances by the IRS and the taxpayer. Considering the probable stance the courts would take may be relevant when weighing the solution to the research question. In most tax research engagements, professional judgment is required because the controlling law is imprecise and can be interpreted differently by the taxpayer, the IRS, and the courts. It is this professional judgment that taxpayers are seeking when they hire CPAs for tax assistance.

Based on the initial question formulated, the main issues in Research Project 6–1 appear to be the taxability of the proceeds from the failed like-kind exchange, the effect of the qualified intermediary's default on completing the exchange due to bankruptcy, and the timing of any gain or loss recognized. Therefore, relevant keywords for this research include like-kind exchange, non-recognition, failed transaction, qualified intermediary, default, bankruptcy, deferred gain, timing gain or loss, and replacement property. It is wise to make an extensive list of possible keywords to lessen the chance of omitting relevant terms. Through a basic knowledge of the Code, we know that like-kind exchanges are governed by IRC §1031, Exchange of Property Held for Productive Use or Investment.

Accessing Tax Information

The key to effective tax research is finding the pertinent material necessary to formulate an informed conclusion about the optimum treatment of the transaction. How the tax services are entered will determine how efficiently the relevant materials are found. A researcher unfamiliar with the topic should start with an editorial explanation and overview of the applicable tax law. This commentary will help the researcher identify the most pertinent elements of the project and introduce the applicable primary tax law. Access to the primary sources from the explanation is easy because the primary sources are generally hyperlinked to their citations. This initial foray into the service is likely to identify other issues to be investigated and more facts that should be collected. Remember that research is an iterative process.

From this initial analysis a researcher may decide that a new, more targeted search is warranted. Once the relevant primary sources are identified, but before they are carefully read, it is necessary to determine which sources are still valid law by checking them through a citator (See Chapter 7 for a full discussion of citators). The fact that the tax service locates a document and places it high on the relevance list does not mean the researcher can assume it is still valid law. The last step is to read carefully the germane primary tax law sources. Only after evaluating the primary sources can the researcher provide educated suggestions as to the optimum treatment for the tax issue in question.

The commercial providers of tax services offer a plethora of tax products (databases) that can be bundled in a variety of ways. This chapter's description of the tax databases within any of the services may not be what is available by subscription to the reader. Each tax professional, firm, or library performs a cost-benefit analysis and purchases only those resources that it finds useful and that it can afford. In addition, the tax services are constantly updating their products to maintain their competitive edges. Therefore, the current appearance of the tax services and products offered may differ from those presented in this text. Nevertheless, the basic methodology described in this text should apply to whatever tax databases and products are available to the reader regardless of their visual presentation.

RIA Checkpoint

Tax services can be entered using three search methods: Keyword, Citation (using citations of primary sources such as a Code section, case name, or ruling number), and

Content (Table of Content and Index). How to use each method will be illustrated using the **Research Institute of America (RIA)** Internet tax service, **RIA Checkpoint**. This is one of the most authoritative and well-known tax services available. The general methodology that applies to RIA Checkpoint also applies to other commercial services.

RIA Checkpoint provides a full gambit of Federal tax information with several different product packages available. The most inclusive package includes all primary tax sources, **Federal Tax Coordinator (FTC)**, **United States Tax Reporter (USTR)**, Citator 2nd Series, **Warren, Gorham & Lamont (WG&L)** journals, WG&L textbooks and treatises, IRS publications, and so on. With so much information available, it is important to limit a search to only those databases that are pertinent to the research project; otherwise, the number of documents retrieved will be overwhelming, and many will be irrelevant.

Exhibit 6-1 shows the opening search screen appearing after the RIA Checkpoint logon screen. The screen is organized to facilitate quick access to the research methods most frequently used by the practitioners. As is visible in Exhibit 6-1, the focus of Checkpoint is on Keyword searches (Arrow A); the Keyword entry box is center screen (Bullet 1). A Table of Contents (TOC) search can be launched by clicking on the button so named at the top of the screen (Arrow B) and Index searches are started either through the TOC or in the left window under Go To (Arrow E). Citation searches are also accessed through the left window (Arrow D).

The discussion of searching in Checkpoint will start with Keyword searching since this is Checkpoint's emphasis, then move to Contents, and finally Citation searches. Before the searching can commence, a practice area needs to be selected in the left window of Exhibit 6-1 (Arrow C). Among the choices are Federal, State & Local, Estate Planning, Pension & Benefits, International, and All Practice Areas. The default area is Federal, and

EXHIBIT 6-1: RIA Checkpoint Opening Search Screen

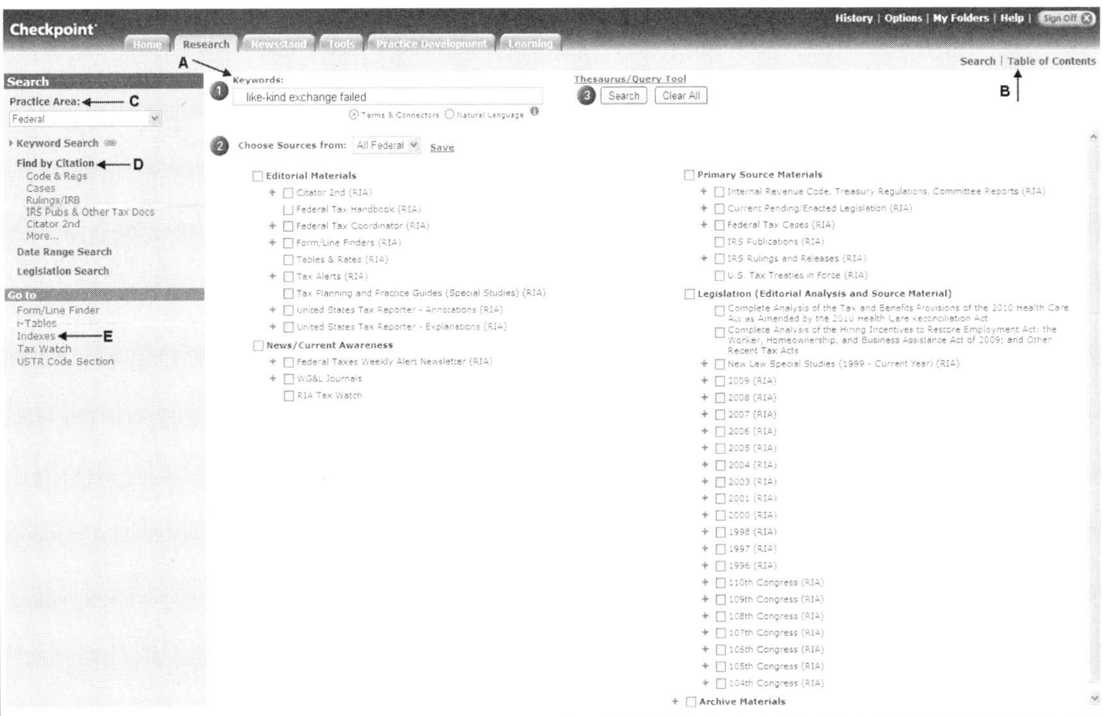

© 2010 Thomson Reuters/RIA.

therefore no changes need to be made for Research Project 6–1 since it involves a Federal income tax problem.

Keyword Search

Checkpoint makes keyword searching appear to be as easy as 1, 2, 3 (Exhibit 6-1). First, enter search terms in the Keywords box at Bullet 1. Second, Choose Sources from the databases listed at Bullet 2. Third, click on the Search button at Bullet 3. If only it was that easy to find the perfect search terms, select just the right database, and have the pertinent search results appear with the click of the mouse! Probably the most difficult part of a keyword search is finding the best words to use that are not so broad that too many irrelevant documents are retrieved and not so narrow that too few relevant documents are found.

RIA offers two types of keyword searches: **Terms & Connectors** and **Natural Language**. With a Natural Language search, the tax question is entered in standard English (natural language) words, phrases (entered within quotation marks), or sentences. The program determines the key terms for searching and relationships among the words (i.e., connectors to apply). This type of search is useful when the researcher is unsure as to which keywords would be the most effective. If keywords can be identified by the researcher, the Terms & Connectors is more appropriate.

For an initial search using Terms & Connectors, the terms *like-kind exchange* and *failed* were entered in the Keywords box of Exhibit 6-1. Editorial Materials, News/Current Awareness, and Primary Source Materials databases were searched. Over 450 documents were retrieved on the Source Documents screen. A **full-text search** looks for each term appearing anywhere in the text of the documents. Thus, every document addressing exchanges with the words *like-kind* and *failed* in it is identified. Court cases, for example, any like-kind exchange controversies where either the taxpayer or the IRS "failed" to prove their position would be identified. Almost 50 percent of the search results are court cases, the majority of which are not applicable to the research project. Common words selected as keywords are likely not to be useful in discriminating relevant documents and therefore should be avoided if possible.

Due to the number of the documents retrieved, our search should be modified in two respects. First, the number of databases searched is reduced. A general understanding of the deductibility of like-kind exchange requirements is first necessary if the researcher is unfamiliar with the topic. Therefore, only editorial materials providing explanations of the tax law such as the FTC and the USTR—Explanations are selected. Additionally, the WG&L Journals are selected because finding an article explaining the topic would be quite helpful in determining the treatment. In addition, the article is likely to have citations to primary sources, thus reducing the searching that the researcher will need to perform. This modification is accomplished by selecting the Modify Search (Arrow 1) on the Source Documents screen in Exhibit 6-2. With this change, approximately 140 documents were retrieved.

Another modification performed to reduce the number of documents retrieved is to place quotation marks around the words *"like-kind exchanges"* indicating that these words should be searched as a phrase. Again, from the Source Document screen in Exhibit 6-2, the Search Within Results (Arrow 2) in the Search Tools option is chosen to make this change. This search option allows the researcher to further search the source documents already identified using additional terms or in our case altered terms. Additional terms can be added, such as *default intermediary*. Running the search with the modified keyword terms and the new databases results in a more reasonable number of documents retrieved in Exhibit 6-2. Through this iterative research process, our first set of search terms became: *failed "like-kind exchange" default intermediary.* The spaces between words are interpreted by Checkpoint as an "and" connection, and quotes require an exact match of the phrase. Accordingly, only documents containing all of these terms are identified. Notice that these terms were entered into the Keywords box in no particular order. If an order is desired, however, **Boolean** connectors may be used. The RIA Boolean connectors are listed in Exhibit 6-3. The list of connectors is available in Checkpoint by clicking on Thesaurus/Query Tool function (Exhibit 6-1, above Bullet 3) or by clicking on the "i" bullet below the keyword entry box (See Exhibit 6-1).

EXHIBIT 6-2: RIA Checkpoint Document Sources

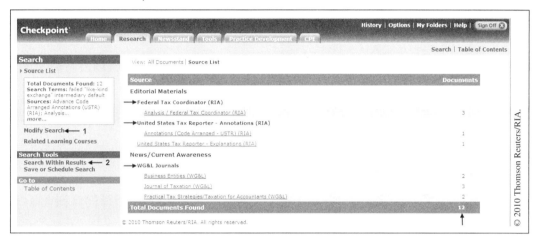

EXHIBIT 6-3: RIA Checkpoint Boolean Connectors

To locate documents:	Use:	Example:
containing any of my keywords	OR, |	funding **OR** deficiency
containing at least one instance of each of my keywords	Space, &, AND	funding deficiency
that contain one keyword but exclude another	^, NOT	funding **NOT** deficiency
containing my exact phrase	" "	"funding deficiency"
containing variations of my keywords	* (asterisk)	deprecia*
disabling automatic retrieval of plurals and equivalencies	# (pound sign)	#damage (retrieves only damage, not damages)
containing single-character variations	? (question mark)	s????holder (retrieves stockholder, shareholder)
containing compound words	- (hyphen)	e-mail (retrieves e-mail e mail, email)

Note: The # character does not turn off the automatic retrieval of possessives (for example, customer's).

Because Checkpoint uses the characters * and / as search connectors, you cannot search for them as you would for other text or characters. If you include these characters in parentheses, they still function as search connectors.

To search for a word or phrase:	Use:	Example:
within **n** words of another (in any order)	/# (where # equals number)	"disclosure exception" **/7** negligence
within **n** words of another (in exact order)	pre/# (where # equals number)	"disclosure exception" **pre/7** negligence
within the same sentence (20 words) as another (in any order)	/s	"disclosure exception" **/s** negligence
within the same sentence (20 words) as another (in exact order)	pre/s	"disclosure exception" **pre/s** negligence
within one paragraph (50 words) as another (in any order)	/p	"disclosure exception" **/p** negligence
within one paragraph (50 words) as another (in exact order)	pre/p	"disclosure exception" **pre/p** negligence

If the researcher is not sure of the best terms to use, synonyms can be added to the keyword search terms by using the built-in Thesaurus (Exhibit 6-1, above Bullet 3). The researcher has the option of including all of the alternatives or customizing the search by choosing which of the synonyms displayed are added to the search. More information on formatting keyword entries can be found in the "Help" feature appearing on every screen.

Using the databases and search terms described, five documents are identified in the FTC and the USTR. Clicking on either of these titles will display the list of retrieved documents in these services. The FTC, RIA's flagship service, is a topical service, whereas the USTR is an annotated service that provides explanations as well as annotations to cases and rulings. As Exhibit 6-4 demonstrates, the FTC document list provides the paragraph number as well as the title of each document and shows the keywords in context with the keywords highlighted. The first document in Exhibit 6-4 (Arrow 2), "Safe harbor method for reporting gain or loss from failed like-kind exchanges due to default by qualified intermediary," appears to be a promising start for our research project. Clicking on the title of the document will retrieve its full-text entry in the Document Display screen (Exhibit 6-5).

Notice that the documents are sorted by relevance (Exhibit 6-4, Arrow 1). The relevance of the documents is determined by an internal formula created by RIA that weighs factors such as density, commonality, and relativity of the search terms in the documents. Rather than being displayed by relevance, the documents may be listed in TOC order by clicking on the Table of Contents sorting option (Exhibit 6-4, Arrow 1).

Since the FTC is a topical service, the main window of the Document Display screen in Exhibit 6-5 presents the Checkpoint explanation for the topic of interest. Checkpoint also offers practical Observations (Arrow 3) that help the practitioner apply the law to client facts. Footnotes are utilized to hyperlink to the primary source substantiations for the editorial views expressed in this service. In our research project the primary source link is to Rev. Proc. 2010-14 (Arrow 2). The discussions presented in such commentaries are not the law, and the paragraph numbers of the FTC should **not** be cited as support by a tax professional. Primary sources are generally the only appropriate documents for supporting a taxpayer's position. Primary sources should be cited only after being examined and analyzed by the researcher.

EXHIBIT 6-4:   RIA Checkpoint Document List

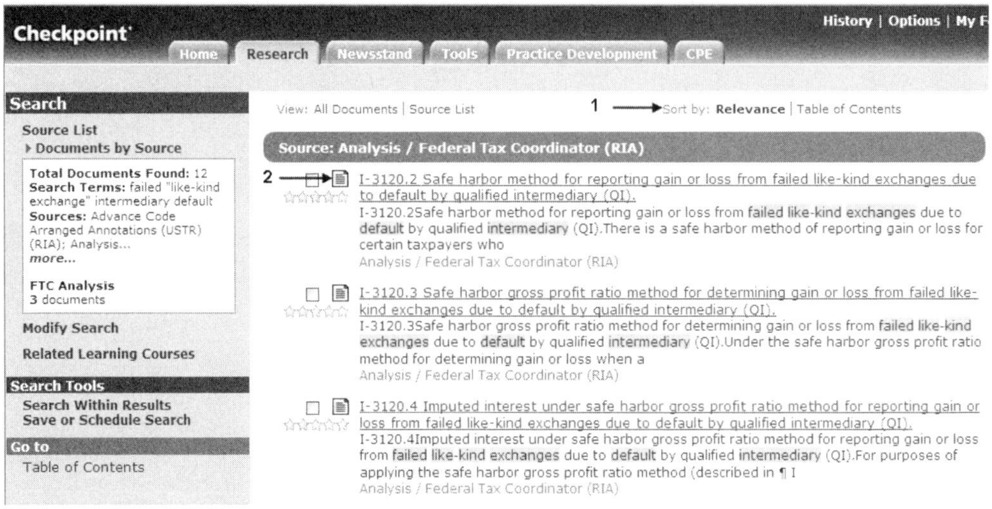

© 2010 Thomson Reuters/RIA.

EXHIBIT 6-5: RIA Checkpoint FTC Explanation

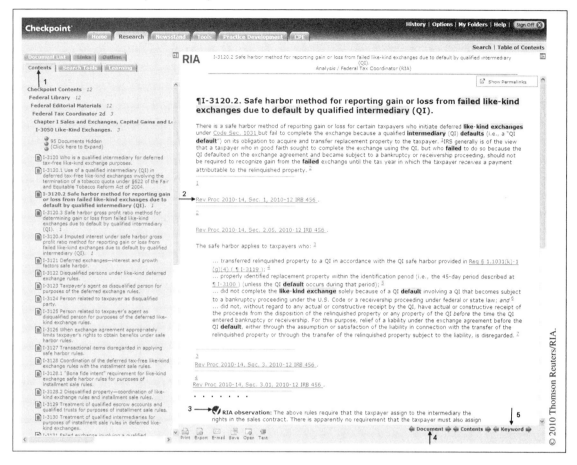

The researcher can decide what to have displayed in the left window of the Document Display screen (Exhibit 6-5, Arrow 1). The Contents displays the documents that would be found before and after the document of interest if the researcher was examining a printed version of the service. This process is handy when the researcher would like to browse other documents closely related to the topic of the research project. Documents found by the search are accessible through the Document arrows (Arrow 4). Clicking on the arrows will scroll though the documents. Finally, the Keyword arrows (Arrow 5) find occurrences of the keywords in the document. The keywords throughout the text are highlighted for easy identification (Exhibit 6-5).

SPOTLIGHT ON TAXATION

Tax Service History

The *United States Tax Reporter*, the annotated tax service offered by RIA, did not start out with this name. Prentice Hall published this tax service from 1924 to 1990 as the *PH Federal Taxes*. In November 1989, Maxwell MacMillan bought the service and merely replaced Prentice Hall's name as the publisher. Then, in September 1991 Thomson acquired Maxwell MacMillan. The *PH Federal Taxes* became part of the RIA offerings in 1992 when its name was changed to the *United States Tax Reporter*.

Contents Search

One very important method of limiting the number of documents retrieved and guaranteeing their pertinence is to employ a contents search either in conjunction with a keyword search or as the only method of searching. This method treats electronic tax services as if they are their counterpart published services. Accordingly, researchers can drill down through either the TOC or Index of a service just like they would thumb through these if they had books in front of them.

TOC Search A TOC search is launched from the opening screen by selecting the Table of Contents option (Exhibit 6-1, Arrow B). For the illustrative Research Project 6–1, we would review the Federal Editorial Materials, and in particular the FTC. Scanning the chapters in the FTC as seen in Exhibit 6-6, Chapter I Sales and Exchanges, Capital Gains and Losses, Cost Recovery Recapture, Depreciation Recapture appears to be relevant. Clicking on the title will display the TOC for the chapter. The researcher can continue to drill down through the contents in Exhibit 6-6 (I-3050 Like-Kind Exchanges) until pertinent individual entries are found (I-3120.2 Safe harbor method for reporting gain or loss from failed like-kind exchanges due to default by qualified intermediary).

This drill-down method can be efficient when the researcher has a good idea of where in the services the relevant documents are likely to be but is having a hard time selecting effective keywords. Our present research problem is a good example. The key terms *failed* and *defaulted* may not have come to mind when reading the description of the problem, but it is obvious that a pertinent document has been located once these terms are seen in the title of an explanation.

EXHIBIT 6-6: RIA Checkpoint Table of Contents

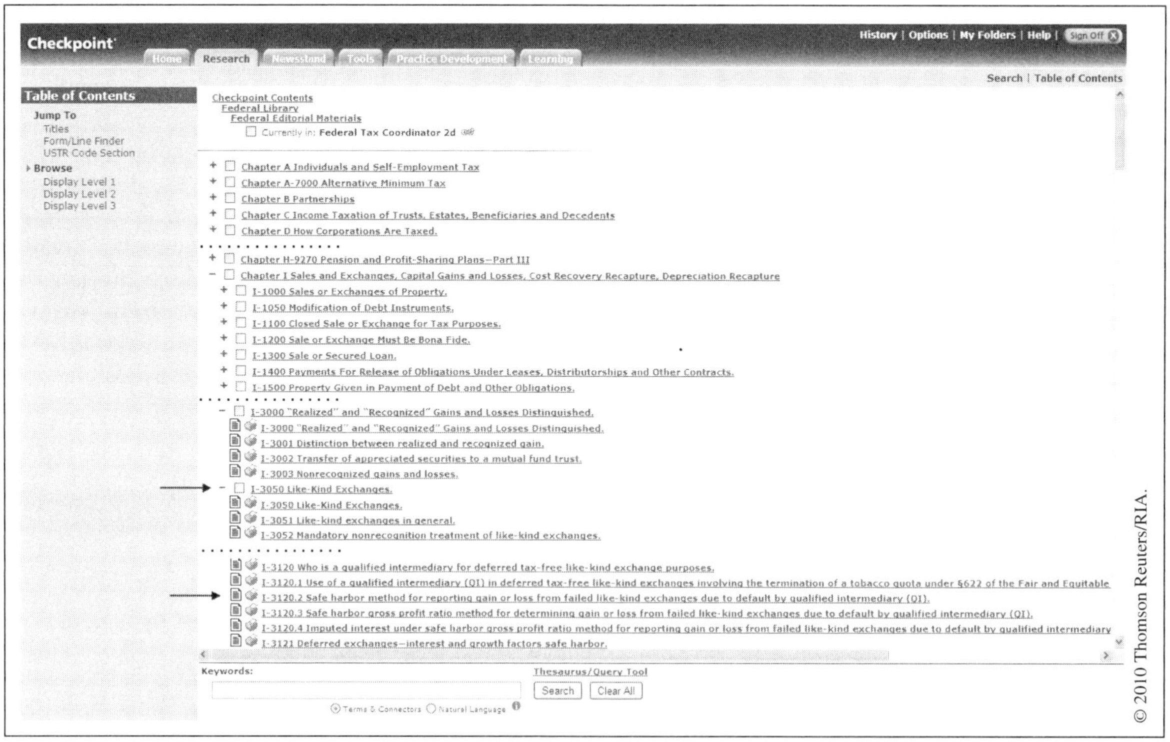

At any point in the drill-down process, a keyword search may be performed on up to 15 topics by checking the box in front of the title (Exhibit 6-6). This search is not limited to the TOC titles as might be presumed; rather, it searches the documents within the titles. Thus, using this method will lead to the same relevant documents as a general keyword. The advantage of this option, however, is that the researcher can limit the chapters of the tax service searched to only those that are pertinent to the issue being researched.

Index Search An Index search was one of the most efficient search methods when tax services were available only in published form. The advantage of an index search is that the *tax meanings of the words* are considered as well as the context in which the words are found because individuals create indexes. The researcher has the ability to use the expertise of the indexer in locating the primary documents of interest. This advantage of indexes holds for the Web services as well. Some researchers find it beneficial to start with an index search to help them identify effective terms for their general keyword searches.

An Index search can be started from two different points in the RIA Checkpoint service. The first method is through the TOC. Federal Indexes is one of the options listed for TOC Searches. The other method is to select Indexes under the Go To heading in the left window of the opening screen (Exhibit 6-1, Arrow E). Only the Federal databases with indexes appear on the displayed screen. These databases include the following:

- Federal Tax Coordinator 2d Topic Index

- Code Arranged Annotations & Explanations (USTR) Topic Index

- RIA's Federal Tax Handbook Topic Index

- Current Code Topic Index

- Final & Temporary Regulations Topic Index

- Proposed Regulations Topic Index

Once a database is selected, the researcher has two options. Clicking on the database will display a listing of the alphabet. From this screen the researcher can select a letter and continue to drill down until the specific topic of interest and the documents are located. This method is similar to using an index for a published service.

As with other TOC searches, a keyword search is possible with any of the indexes. However, these searches differ from other keyword searches in that it is the index entries themselves, and not the underlying documents, that are being searched. For example, selecting the letter "L" within the USTR Topic Index and entering the keywords *like-kind* results in three topics (under the letter "L"), one of which is "like kind exchanges." Clicking on this topic (Exhibit 6-7) leads to the subheading, *intermediaries used for*, and paragraph 10.315.01(27). This explanation also cites Rev. Proc. 2010-14 as providing a safe harbor for failed like-kind exchanges due to the default of a qualified intermediary. Competent researchers always read the primary documents, such as Rev. Proc. 2101-14, and never rely on these brief secondary source explanations when resolving a tax question. The only support recognized by the IRS and courts are primary sources and not the editorial explanations of a tax service.

Tax professionals familiar with search engines such as Google and Bing often are inclined to use a Keyword Search when an Index or TOC search may be more efficient and effective. Experienced tax researchers tend to use TOC, Index, and Citation searches much more frequently as they develop their skills.

EXHIBIT 6-7:   RIA Checkpoint Index Listing

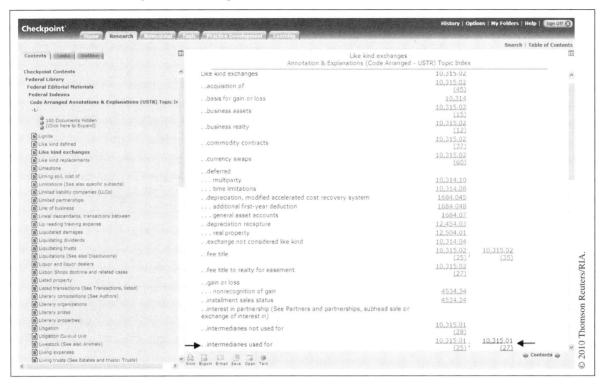

Citation Search

A third approach to searches is the Citation Search. To perform a search by Code section, Regulation, case name, or IRS pronouncements or publications, choose a title under Find a Citation in the left window of the opening screen (Exhibit 6-1, Arrow D). If the type of document you wish to find is not listed in one of these options, the More… heading contains an extensive list of documents that can be searched by citation. After selecting a type of document, Checkpoint provides templates for entering citations and examples for each template. These templates make entering a citation simple because the proper format is provided.

Research Project 6–1 concerns like-kind exchanges, which are governed by §1031. Entering this section number in the Current Code template (Exhibit 6-8) retrieves the full text of §1031, Exchange of Property Held for Productive Use or Investment, as shown in Exhibit 6-9. On careful examination of Exhibit 6-9, the compass symbol can be seen in several locations. Placing the curser over or clicking on this symbol displays a small box in which the exact citation for the particular portion of the document is displayed; [§1031(a)(2)(E) at Arrow 3]. This unique feature is helpful when examining long Code sections or Regulations with complex paragraphing structures. Another feature that will help when examining long documents is the Outline feature in the left window (Arrow 1). If the researcher would like to know where the Code section fits within the Internal Revenue Code, the Contents tab, in the left window, contains this information (Arrow 1). Printing the document, exporting it into a Word file, e-mailing it, or saving it can be accomplished by clicking on the appropriate icon (Exhibit 6-9, Arrow 4). These icons appear at the bottom of each document.

Using the Code section as the beginning point for identifying related documents is simplified by use of the buttons located above the Code section title (Exhibit 6-9, Arrow 2). These buttons will lead the researcher to explanations and annotations in the USTR (Expl and Annot), the FTC topical entries (FTC), relevant primary sources

EXHIBIT 6-8: RIA Checkpoint Code & Regulations Templates

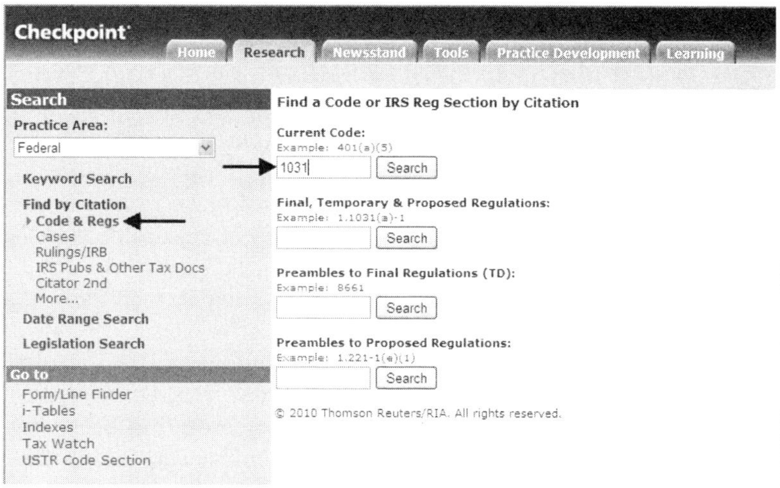

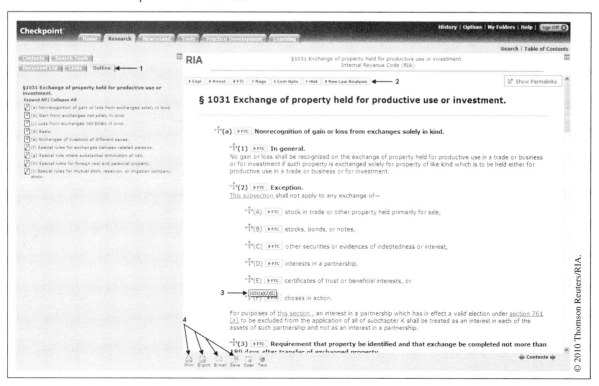

EXHIBIT 6-9: RIA Checkpoint Code Document

(Regs and Com Rpts), history (Hist), and current developments (New Law Analysis). These related features are also available through the Links tab in the left window (Arrow 1). Through these links, the researcher eventually may find the relevant documents desired. However, relying exclusively on Code section searches may be more time consuming than Contents or Keyword searches when there are several Code sections involved in the research issue.

CCH IntelliConnect

After more than four years of reengineering, **Commerce Clearing House (CCH)**, a division of Wolters Kluwer, launched its completely redesigned tax research platform in 2009 called **CCH IntelliConnect**, which has been designed to be intuitive so researchers can start searching effectively with little training. Access to the entire CCH library is available from just one screen. The results can then be narrowed using the filter options provided. A useful new feature allows opening multiple searches (up to six) with the ability to toggle back and forth between them. In addition, for researchers that are performing searches on and off all day, IntelliConnect may be launched in the morning and left open all day. Most other commercial services log off if there are periods of inactivity.

While visually quite different from RIA Checkpoint (compare Exhibit 6-1 with Exhibit 6-10), IntelliConnect supports the same search methods from its opening screen. The differences in the implementation of these methods will be illustrated in this section by again using Research Project 6–1, which will facilitate comparisons of these two tax services.

 SPOTLIGHT ON TAXATION

Tax Service History

The Commerce Clearing House (CCH) service has been in existence since the first U.S. tax law was passed in 1913. Through this long history, CCH has become one of the most recognized publishers of tax products. In 1995, Wolters Kluwer, an international Dutch publishing corporation, acquired CCH from the majority shareholders, including the members of the Thorne family whose great-great grandfather founded the company. This $1.9 billion takeover was the world's largest publishing acquisition at the time.

Keyword Search

The opening screen of CCH IntelliConnect in Exhibit 6-10 is less cluttered than that in RIA Checkpoint. This is due in part to the underlying assumption that initial keyword searches will be of *all* databases available in the researcher's subscription. This assumption is indicated by the Search All Contents as the initial database choice (Exhibit 6-10, Arrow 2). Preferences for the display, searches, and so forth may be personalized as well as the Practice Area databases searched (Arrow 3).

As with RIA Checkpoint, IntelliConnect emphasizes keyword searching; therefore, the Keyword Search box appears in the tools bar and is available from every screen. The Search Options (Arrow 4) enable the researcher to customize word searches by applying a thesaurus to the search terms and by using Boolean Connectors. In addition,

EXHIBIT 6-10: CCH IntelliConnect Opening Search Screen

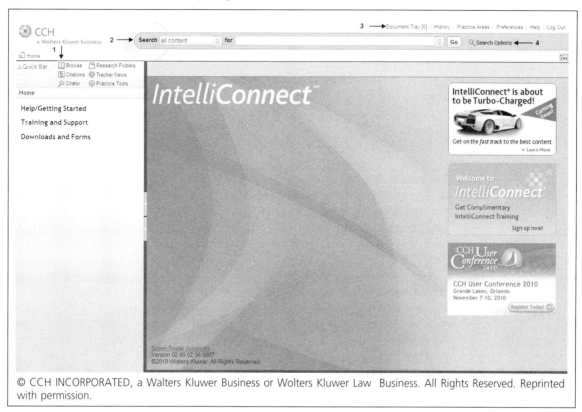

IntelliConnect offers the ability to limit all document searches by dates. When updating previous research that was performed, the "after" date option allows the researcher to locate only new law that has occurred since the initial research, thus saving the time of wading through documents previously reviewed.

To start searching for a solution to Research Project 6-1, the keyword phrase "*like-kind exchanges*" is entered. Since all contents are searched, the document list contains almost 4,100 items. To reduce the list, a Within Results search is selected from the Search pull down menu (Exhibit 6-11, Arrow B), with the terms "*qualified intermediary*" *default* added. As illustrated in Exhibit 6-11, this produces only 38 documents. This list is displayed in the upper center window (Window 2) with hyperlinks to each document. It can be displayed by Relevance or Most Recent Documents (Arrow C). To determine what types of document have been retrieved, the entries under All Results in the left window of Exhibit 6-11 (Window 1) are expanded. Notice that the documents are classified by filters: Document Type, Library, and Jurisdiction. Examining the Document Type reveals that the explanations, journals, and annotations are a reasonable number to examine. Clicking on any one of the headings will change the document list to only those found in the heading selected. For example, by selecting Explanations, the document list only provides explanation documents. The Results by Library also changes to identify only Editorial Content.

Selecting one of the titles displays the full text of the document in the lower center window (Window 3). If the researcher wants to keep this document for later examination, it can be moved to the Document Tray by using the Send to Tray button (Arrow D) and retrieved by clicking on Document Tray (Arrow A). Other documents in the list can be accessed through Window 2 or by using the Prev or Next arrows (Arrow D). This three-pane display allows the researcher to view the results of the search and documents at the same time. The sizes of the windows can be altered to fit the needs of the researcher, and individual windows can be closed if desired.

Content and Citation Searches

Browse   A Table of Content-type search is performed using the Browse function (Exhibit 6-12). The identical drill-down method described for the RIA Checkpoint TOC search is used in a Browse search. CCH offers two main tax databases, **Tax Research Consultant (TRC)** and the **Standard Federal Income Tax Reporter (SFITR)**. TRC's coverage is similar to the RIA Federal tax Coordinator (FTC). The SFITR is organized by Code section like the United States Tax Reporter (USTR). The U.S. Master Tax Guide is also a great source for quick answers to simple research questions.

Drilling down through the Like-kind exchanges entries, as displayed in Exhibit 6-12, illuminates the organization of the SFITR service. First the Code section is provided, then its legislative history, Regulations, and lastly, the Explanations and Annotations. When the document of interest is located (see Triangle) and clicked on, the full text is displayed in the right window.

Index Access to the topical indexes is also found using the Browse function. There is not a separate heading for indexes; rather, the indexes are listed within each source

EXHIBIT 6-11:   CCH IntelliConnect Document Listing & Document

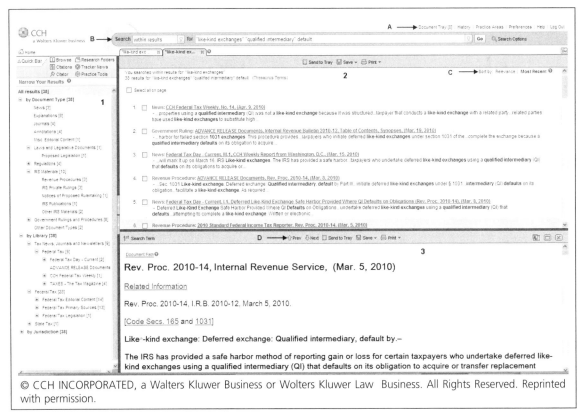

type. For example, access to indexes for the CCH tax databases are provided under the Federal Tax Editorial Content, whereas the index for the Code is located in the Federal Tax Primary Sources. Instead of drilling down through an index, the index entries can be searched using the keyword search method. The statements in the RIA Checkpoint section regarding the usefulness of this searching method apply to CCH IntelliConnect as well. Remember that topics may be indexed in RIA differently than they are in CCH.

Tax Archives   When a client has a prior year's tax return audited, the tax practitioner needs to know what the tax law was in that previous year, not what it is today. IntelliConnect provides practitioners the unique ability to access its tax services as they were in prior years through the Tax Archives (Exhibit 6-13, left screen). The tax services are frozen as of the last day of the year. Thus, the practitioner can determine what the tax laws were (with explanations) from 1986 to today.

Citation   As shown in the left window of Exhibit 6-13, IntelliConnect offers templates for every type of primary and secondary source available in the service though the Citations function (Circled). If the complete citation is known, it can be entered in CCH recognizable format in the general citation box at the top of the page (Arrow 1); otherwise, one of the citation templates is completed (Arrow 2). Either one of these entries is sufficient; both are not necessary. The templates make it easy to retrieve a document without having to know the "official" citation format.

EXHIBIT 6-12:   CCH IntelliConnect Browse & Document

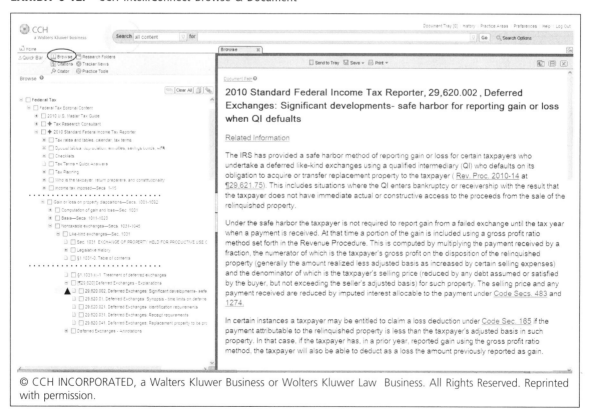

EXHIBIT 6-13: CCH IntelliConnect Citation Template

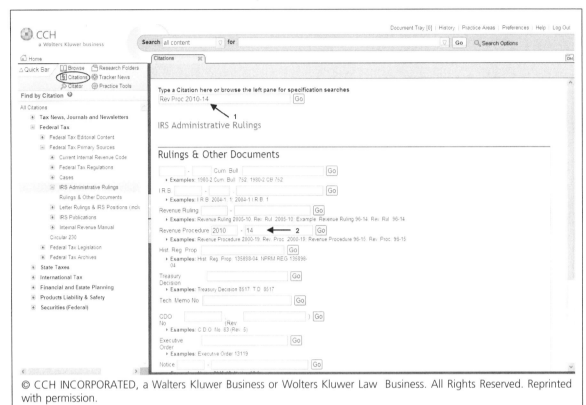

© CCH INCORPORATED, a Walters Kluwer Business or Wolters Kluwer Law Business. All Rights Reserved. Reprinted with permission.

SPOTLIGHT ON TAXATION

Freedom of Information Act

The **Freedom of Information Act (FOIA)**, 5 USC §552, gave the public the right to access IRS records unless they are protected from disclosure. Under this provision, taxpayers have the right to access unpublished documents issued by the IRS, such as Private Letter Rulings and Technical Advice Memorandums. The FOIA applies to records created by Federal agencies, yet records held by Congress and the courts are exempt. State and local government agencies are under each state's own public access laws.

The IRS complies with the FOIA by:

- *Maintaining publicly available materials on the Internet in the IRS Electronic Reading Room of **http://www.irs.gov.***
- *Staffing the IRS Public Reading Room at 1111 Constitution Avenue, NW, Washington, D.C. 20224.*
- *Responding to written requests for agency records not available in the Reading Room.*

Many IRS records are available for sale from the Government Printing Office: **www.gpo.gov.**

BNA Tax & Accounting

BNA Tax & Accounting offers numerous products covering all areas of tax and accounting, some even available on the iPhone, iPad, Blackberry, and Android through the free Quick Tax Reference app. However, it is best known in the tax community as the

SPOTLIGHT ON TAXATION

BNA

In 1926, David Lawrence started the *United States Daily* as the country's "first truly national newspaper." In 1929, Lawrence established **Bureau of National Affairs (BNA)** as a division of the United States New Publishing Company for the purpose of reporting, interpreting, and explaining the workings of the Federal government and its impact on national economics. Since 1947, BNA has been wholly employee-owned, making it the oldest employee-owned company in the United States. After the passage of the 1954 Internal Revenue Code, Leonard L. Silverstein, a former IRS Chief Counsel attorney partnered with BNA to create the Tax Management Portfolios. He realized that there was a need for specialized tax information, written by leading tax practitioners. Today, BNA provides 350 news services and is the largest independent publisher of business and government analysis for professionals.

publisher of the **BNA Tax Management Portfolios (Portfolios)**. The Portfolios are unique because they are written for professionals, by professionals. Practitioners are the preferred authors because they are more sensitive to the information requirements of other practitioners. For this reason, Portfolios are a favorite research tool with those practicing tax. Most commercial tax and legal services (e.g., RIA Checkpoint, CCH IntelliConnect, LexisNexis, and Westlaw) offer the Portfolios on their web platforms. They are also available through the **BNA Tax and Accounting Center (BTAC)**.

Portfolios

The more than-500 BNA Portfolios are classified into five series: Federal Tax; Estates, Gifts, and Trusts; International Tax, State Tax; and Accounting Policy & Practice. The size of the Portfolio library varies as topics are added, deleted, or combined. While the number of Portfolios appears vast, the series is not truly comprehensive. As with any topical service, it would be impossible to cover every issue that a practitioner may encounter in the course of business. However, practitioners that identify a Portfolio on point with an issue generally have completed their search. It is likely that the Portfolio will address the issue in a comprehensive manner.

Each BNA Portfolio begins with a description providing a brief overview of the topic and the order in which the materials are presented. The TOC follows this description. The remainder of the Portfolio contains three sections: (A) Detailed Analysis, (B) Working Papers, and (C) Bibliography and References. The Portfolio sections are updated in response to important tax developments, and when necessary, the complete Portfolio is rewritten.

To find a solution to Research Project 6-1 using BTAC the keywords *"like-kind exchange" intermediary* and *default* were entered into the Quick Search, as seen in Exhibit 6-14 (Arrow 1). Unless specified otherwise, BTAC performs an all-contents search. Similar to CCH IntelliConnect, BTAC employs the three-window format with the search results in the left window and the selected document in the right window. To find the location of the keywords, use the Go to Hit arrows (Arrow 2). Our search resulted in four hits (see numbers preceding the expand boxes) of which the relevant discussion is in the Detailed Analysis of the Portfolio analyzing Exchanges under §1031, Delayed (Forward) Exchanges (Arrow 3).

As with other topical services, the Code, Regulations, Rulings, and court case opinions are integrated into the analysis with citation footnotes, or the relevant portions are included in the text (Arrow 4). In addition to analysis, the authors identify potential pitfalls, probable IRS positions, effective tax planning techniques, and alternative means of structuring transactions in a tax-favorable manner.

EXHIBIT 6-14:   BNA Tax and Accounting Center Detailed Analysis

The Working Papers section of the Portfolios is perhaps the service's most unique and useful feature (Exhibit 6-14, Arrow 5). This material includes practitioner checklists; reproduced IRS forms (interactive for online version and occasionally filled in for an illustrative fact situation); computation worksheets; sample draft agreements and contract clauses; sample board or shareholder resolutions and employment contracts; reproductions of pertinent primary sources; and other practical materials that can assist the professional in implementing tax planning techniques and procedures. For Research Project 6-1, the Worksheet indentified in the search results provides a Sample Qualified Exchange Accommodation Agreement (Arrow 5) with blanks that can be filled in to meet the client's personal needs.

The Bibliography section of a Portfolio has a comprehensive listing of the primary (Official) and secondary (Unofficial) sources of the tax law utilized by the author(s) in preparing the Portfolio. Finally, this section of the Portfolio often includes a listing of journal articles and treatises that are relevant to the Portfolio topic.

Legal Services

Taxation provisions are law and therefore fall under the purview of those in the legal profession. Consequently, research services created for tax attorneys can be used by other tax professionals in performing tax research. This section focuses on the two major legal services, LexisNexis and Westlaw. Since service providers are eager to increase the acceptance of their products by tax professionals in the accounting arena, these publishers are adapting their products to be user friendly to all tax practitioners. Both LexisNexis and

Westlaw offer individual bundling of products, and for their larger accounting firm clients they create special Web interfaces.

While there are numerous legal services that could be examined, this coverage is limited to services to which tax practitioners are most likely to subscribe. Only the tax products offered by these services will be reviewed. Chapter 7 reviews the case law products of these services, and Chapters 8 and 9 provide more detailed information regarding the state and international products available through legal and tax services.

Westlaw

The West Group, an authoritative legal publisher, offers tax research capabilities through its **Westlaw** service. This service is legally oriented because it was designed by attorneys, for attorneys. Due to this orientation toward the legal profession, Westlaw is less represented than RIA and CCH in accounting firms. To capture more of the accounting tax practice market, however, the West Group has developed products specifically for tax research, such as the Tax Platinum Library and Tax Gold Library. Thus, most international, regional, and large local CPA firms subscribe to some portion of the Westlaw service, especially those that hire attorneys into their tax service groups. Virtually all law schools train their students using the Westlaw system.

Data and Access

Westlaw contains more than 2.2 billion documents organized into over 20,000 databases, including BNA Tax Management Portfolios, all of the RIA products, some CCH products, law reviews, legal texts, various tax news services, and the WG&L treatises, manuals, journals, and newsletters. Also included in Westlaw are the popular South-Western Federal Taxation textbook series and a topical tax service, called **Mertens Law of Federal Income Taxation**. Westlaw is accessible via the Internet, wireless mobile devices such as Blackberry, Palm, and Android (Westlaw Wireless), and the iPhone.

Under its continual striving to meet the needs of its users, the West Group has launched a new product called **WestlawNext**, which is powered by a recently developed legal search engine, **WestSearch**, that is designed to perform as if a personal experienced legal researcher is searching WestlawNext for the subscriber. Thus, its aim is to dramatically simplify the research process of Westlaw. For example, rather than having to select a search by citation, terms and connectors, or natural language, the researcher can merely type in a search query and WestlawNext will automatically recognize the format and process the query accordingly. Thus, the terms: *"a failed like-kind exchange due to intermediary default"* entered into the Query box in Exhibit 6-15 will be recognized by WestlawNext as a natural language search format without having to indicate as such. Since WestlawNext is in its infancy, the standard Westlaw will be the focus of this section. The WestlawNext options will be presented as supplemental materials.

Since the West Group creates customized Westlaw Web sites to meet their customer's specific research needs, the appearance of the Westlaw service demonstrated in this chapter may vary from the customized site available to the readers through their schools or employers. The basic searching strategies discussed in this section, however, are similar in all versions of Westlaw.

Searching Westlaw

On the Welcome to Westlaw screen shown in Exhibit 6-16, information about Westlaw's new products (WestlawNext, circled) is provided and interesting legal news is available in the right window. Access to the major features of Westlaw is provided in the left window and the toolbar. The immediate options facilitate searching for a document by citation (Arrow 1), performing a citator search (**KeyCite**) (Arrow 2), or locating a database (Arrow 3). If the researcher is new to Westlaw, the Getting Started Tips function (Arrow 5) is useful. Not only does it offer advice for initiating research, but it also offers access to the Westlaw Help Center.

Using the immediate document searching option, Find this Document by Citation (Exhibit 6-16, Arrow 1), the citation for a document of interest in Research Project 6-1, Rev. Proc. 2010-14, may be entered. While the general format (volume, reporter, page), and the specific details for the citation must be known, spacing and punctuation is optional. Most Federal statutory, administrative or case documents, topical materials, and law review or journal articles may be retrieved by citation. Using WestlawNext, the citation would merely be entered into the Query box (Exhibit 6-15), and WestSearch would recognize format and retrieve the document.

Rather than finding a document, the researcher may want to find a database for a keyword search. The starting point would be Search for a Database (Exhibit 6-16, Arrow 3). Enter either the Westlaw database abbreviation or the actual name of the database. Accessing a database searched frequently is possible through either Recent Databases (databases recently searched) or having the database added to Favorite Databases. Both of these are pull-down menus. If the researcher does not know the specific database to search, the Database Wizard (Exhibit 6-16 Arrow 4) can help. This function

EXHIBIT 6-15: WestlawNext Opening Screen

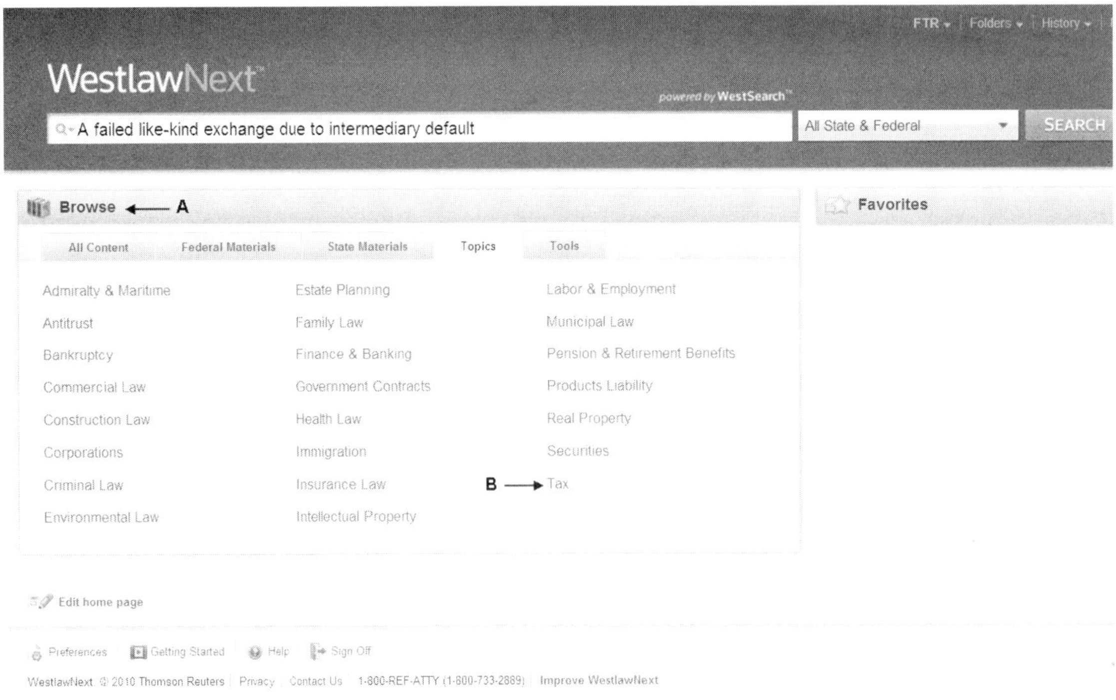

© WestLaw/Thomson Reuters.

EXHIBIT 6-16: Westlaw Welcome Screen

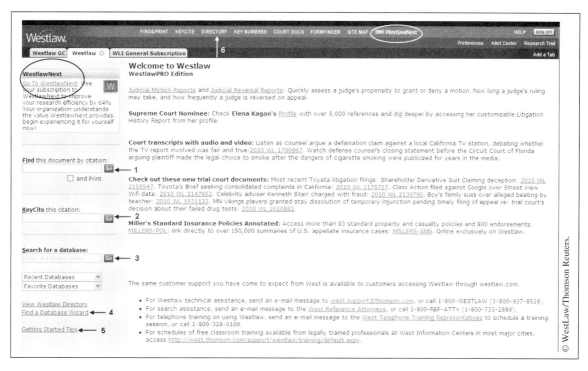

asks a series of questions to determine the category of database being sought. Desiring a taxation database, the Wizard selects the entries listed in Exhibit 6-17.

A final option for locating tax databases is to use the Directory (Exhibit 6-16, Arrow 6). Selecting All Databases, then Taxation in Topical Practice Areas leads to the same Westlaw Directory in Exhibit 6-17 (See Arrow 1 for directory location). The tax databases in WestlawNext are available by clicking on Tax in the Topics Tab in Exhibit 6-15 (Arrow B).

From the Westlaw Search box in Exhibit 6-17 (Arrow 2) on the Taxation Directory screen, the researcher can search the Taxation directory or the entire Westlaw directory of subscribed databases. Since there are no boxes to check in front of the titles, the only method for searching more than one database at a time is to select a combined directory such as Federal Tax Materials Combined (Arrow 3). To discover what is contained in particular databases, click on the "i" ball (circled) and a scope description of the database with a full listing of the sources included will appear.

If the researcher is primarily interested in tax research, the Tax Tab can be added to provide easy access to the tax databases, as Exhibit 6-18 illustrates. The primary and combined databases are listed under the Search window and selected by checking the box (Arrow 1). The researcher can search using a Terms and Connectors (Boolean), Natural Language, or Template keyword query. A thesaurus is available to help in selecting the best words for the search. The thesaurus is not automatically applied; rather, the synonyms are added to the keywords by the researcher. When the Terms and Connectors search option is selected, the list of Westlaw connectors and expanders is provided on screen. These are similar to those of other services, but in Westlaw a space between two words is interpreted as an "or," not as an "and" or phrase connector. An "&" or the word "and" must be included to apply an "and" connection. Westlaw likewise supports an expansive list of field restrictions such as Author, Judge, References, and Year. Finally, the date for the search documents can be limited either by selecting one of the period options provided or by entering specific dates for a period restriction. Expanded lists of Westlaw's connectors, fields, and date options are visible in Exhibit 6-18. Compare Exhibit 6-18 with the search options of WestlawNext in Exhibit 6-15. WestlawNext has made term searching a much simpler task.

The results of the Westlaw search in Exhibit 6-19 are presented with the key words highlighted. If the number of documents retrieved is large, then the researcher can search within this list by selecting the Locate in Result option (Arrow 2). Only the words entered in the Locate in Result search are highlighted in the narrowed list. The flag and letter status symbols (circled) indicate the current standing of the document. For example, a blue H (document 1) indicates the document has some history, yellow flags (documents 2 & 4) warn that the document has been treated negatively, whereas the green C (document 3) has no negative treatment. The meaning of these status symbols is covered fully in Chapter 7 with the discussion of Westlaw's KeyCite.

EXHIBIT 6-17: Westlaw Tax Database Screen

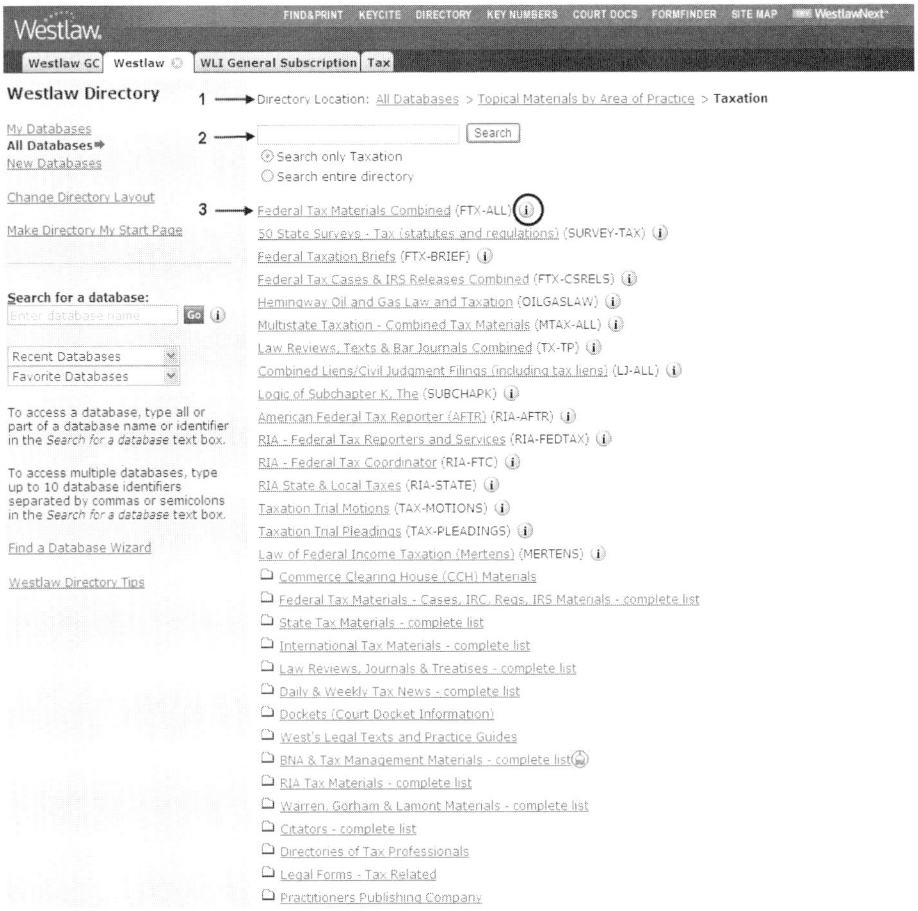

© WestLaw/Thomson Reuters.

In addition, to the documents found in the databases searched by the researcher, Westlaw includes its unique feature, **ResultsPlus** (Exhibit 6-19, Arrow 3). The ResultsPlus is a list of suggested analytical materials relevant to the search topic. The materials appear in law reports, treatises, law reviews, and topical services such as Mertens and BNA Portfolios. As discussed previously, finding an article (or Portfolio) on your research issue can save the researcher substantial time because the research has been completed by the authors and editors in preparing the article.

The Table of Contents (TOC) search option is offered from the Westlaw GC tab on the Search screen (when the database/service has a TOC), and through site map. For the tax databases, TOC searching is available, but it is very limited. Most publications that would have a TOC in print format may be accessed through the TOC option in Westlaw. The TOC search methodology is actively supported by WestlawNext, as is evident by the prominence of Browse on its opening screen (Exhibit 6-15, Arrow A). Each category listed in the Browse section can be expanded as well as most of the databases within the categories. For example, in Exhibit 6-20 each Tax database listed with a TOC can be searched using the drilldown method. A Keyword search can also be performed at any point during a TOC search.

KeySearch

KeySearch uses the **West Key Numbering System**, which organizes key issues found in court cases into approximately 450 numbered topics. These topics are further subdivided with the result that there are more than 100,000 unique Key Numbers! To identify the **Key Number** for the legal topic of interest, select Key Numbers at the top of any page

EXHIBIT 6-18: Westlaw Tax Search Screen

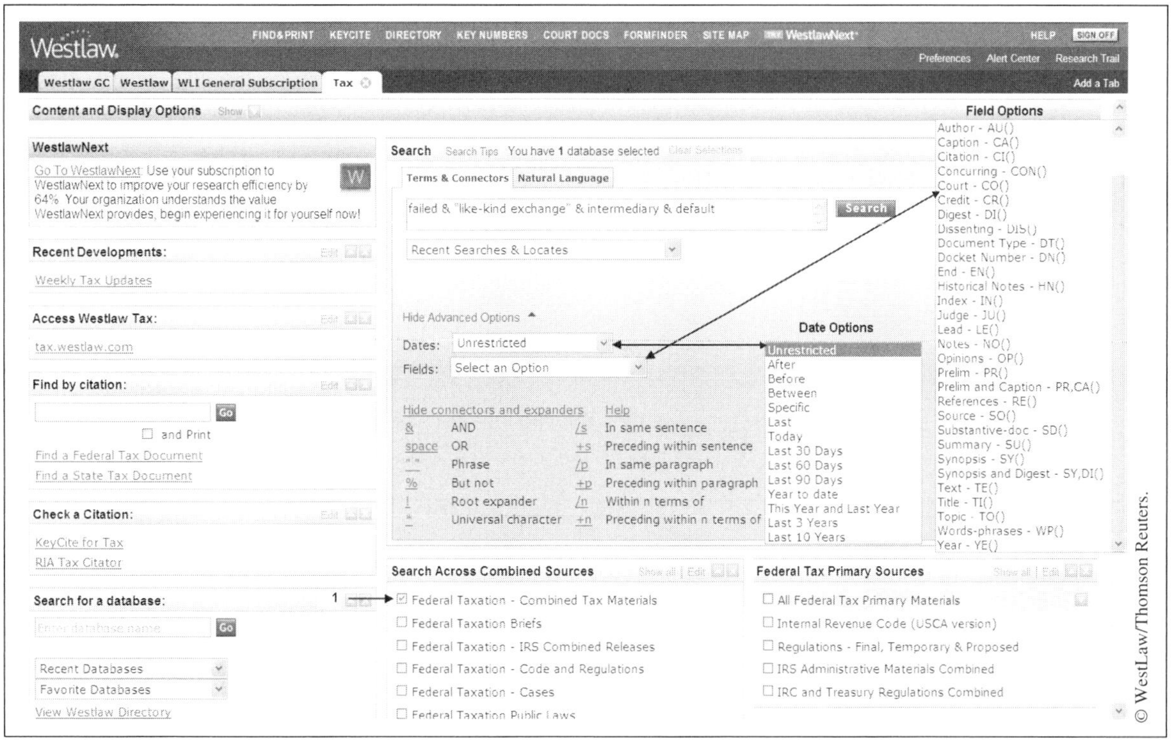

(Exhibit 6-19, Arrow 1) and then perform either a keyword search or drill down through the list of topics. For example, the Key number for Taxation is 371, and the Internal Revenue Code is found in Key Number 220.

The **KeySearch** option, available on the Key Number screen, formulates a query for the researcher based on underlying terms for the topic selected by the researcher and adds the Key Numbers associated with the topic. This type of search is beneficial when the researcher is unfamiliar with the area of tax law and is having difficulty pinpointing keywords to use as search terms. The researcher can determine what type of cases to search or decide to search treatises or journals and law reviews. Only one of these categories, however, may be searched at a time. Other search terms can be added at the researcher's option to ensure the results will be relevant.

LexisNexis

The amount of information available on the **LexisNexis** system is staggering. With more than five billion searchable documents from 34,000 legal, business, and news sources included in LexisNexis, it is possibly the world's largest full-text information resource. About

EXHIBIT 6-19:   Westlaw Search Results

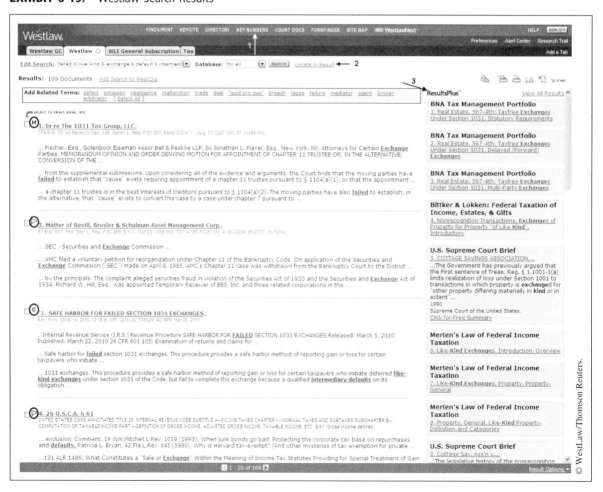

© WestLaw/Thomson Reuters.

the only tax services not available on LexisNexis are its competitors RIA and Westlaw. **Lexis**, for legal (tax) sources, was started in 1973 and **Nexis**, for news, financial, and business information, was started in 1979. In addition to access via personal computers, LexisNexis can be accessed on the practitioner's BlackBerry, Palm, Android, or iPhone.

Tax Center

Realizing how important tax research has become, LexisNexis developed a service exclusively for tax practitioners called **Tax Center**. This service is designed to streamline tax research by having an interface separate from LexisNexis and giving the practitioner the ability to conduct a single search across the full content of this service. Prior to the development of Tax Center, a researcher could not access all the databases within LexisNexis in a single search, as is possible with the RIA and CCH services. Rather, LexisNexis is structured somewhat like a tree. The main libraries are located on the trunk of the tree, and the databases within the libraries are the various branches of the tree. At each level in the database selection process the branch is narrowing until the researcher reaches the end of the branch. For example, in LexisNexis the three areas of Legal, Business & News, and Public Records could not be queried in a single search. Three searches would need to be performed. Thus, allowing a single search across the entire contents of Tax Center does streamline searching in this LexisNexis product.

The tax materials currently available in Tax Center are primary sources (Code, Regulations, cases, IRS pronouncements, and public records) and the analytical materials of

EXHIBIT 6-20: WestlawNext Tax Databases

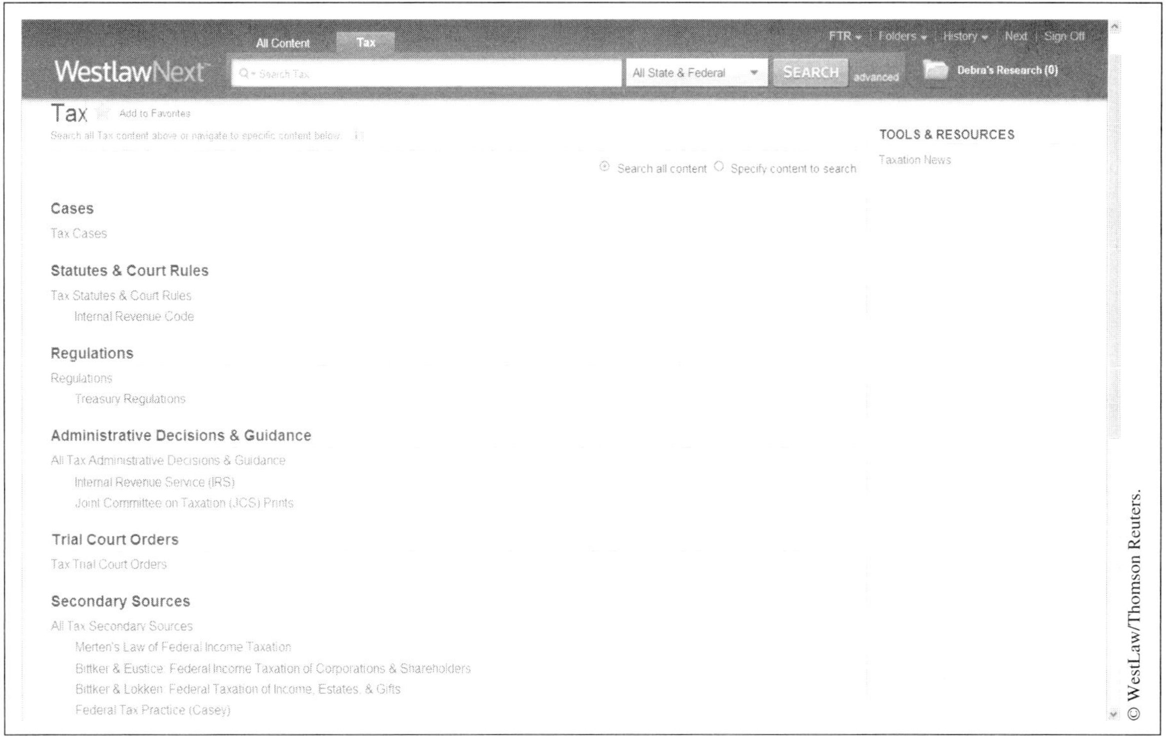

CCH, BNA, **Tax Analysts**, Matthew Bender, and Kleinrock. It has also created its own tax services: LexisNexis **Tax Advisor—Federal Code Reporter** and LexisNexis **Tax Advisor—Federal Topical**. Different packages are available that can be specifically designed for the practice of the tax professional. Consequently, the package utilized in this chapter may vary from the service available to the reader.

Tax Center's opening research option (Exhibit 6-21) presents the practitioner with a wide variety of databases in two sections: Tax Services and Primary Law Sources, and Analytical Sources (Arrows 3 & 4). Each database category offers some choices that are combinations of several sources, while others are only a single source. In the column for Cases, for example, the first choice, Tax Cases, Federal and State, includes all of the other case choices visible in Exhibit 6-21 (Arrow 5). Therefore, it is redundant to select Tax Cases, Federal and State and any of the other Cases options visible. As all of the possible databases for Primary Sources cannot be listed and still have the Analytical Sources visible on the opening screen, an abbreviated list is shown initially. To see all of the options, the researcher would click on the More Sources button (Arrow 6). Since the researcher is limited to a total of 50 sources, checking the boxes by the column headings (IRS, Code & Regulations, and Cases) will select more than the allowed sources and is unnecessary. It is preferable to select combined databases for searching efficiency.

EXHIBIT 6-21: LexisNexis Tax Center Federal Screen

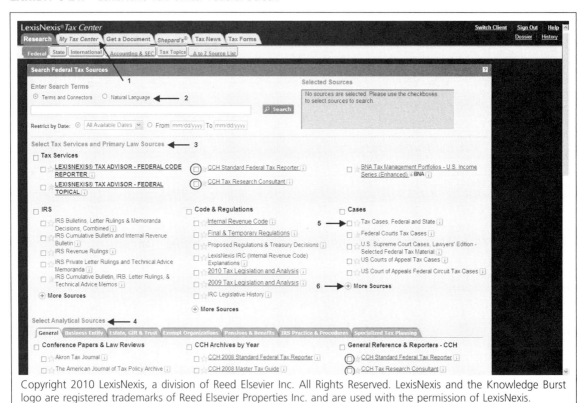

The Analytical Sources (Arrow 4) are divided into several topical areas as well as a general category. The General References & Reporters includes access to CCH materials as well as Tax Analysts publications. All these services with underlined titles (circled) may be expanded with a click to reveal a table of contents for browsing. There are separate categories for CCH Archives and Conference Papers & Law Reviews. As previously mentioned, the CCH archives are useful if the researcher needs to know the tax law in a prior year, for instance, when a client is taking a tax issue to court.

Given the almost overwhelming number of database options, Tax Center includes an option to select databases as Favorites by clicking on the star in front of the title. This provides access to the database through the My Tax Center tab (Arrow 1). Consequently, the researcher can customize Tax Center to support the type of searches most commonly performed. Within the My Tax Center tab, the practitioner may set preferences for the searches and results. For example, the researcher can choose to have the results sorted by relevance or by date. The document view may also be personalized.

Tax Center offers the researcher a choice of Natural Language or Terms and Connectors (Boolean) types of searches (Exhibit 6-21, Arrow 2). Unlike other services, LexisNexis interprets a space between words as signifying a connection of words in a phrase and not as "and" or "or," which are more common. For example, if the researcher enters the words *like-kind exchange intermediate defaults* with no connectors, then LexisNexis identifies only documents with these words appearing next to each other. To search for any occurrence of these words in the document, they must be entered with "and" between them—*like-kind exchange and intermediary and default*. Using a Natural Language search relieves the researcher from remembering to add the "and" connectors.

The results of the natural language keyword search are displayed by Category and Sources in a manner similar to that of RIA Checkpoint. Clicking on a document source provides a list of retrieved documents for that source. Exhibit 6-22 is the Tax Advisor—Federal Topical document germane to Research Project 6-1. When reviewing the document, the researcher can view the document in several modes: TOC, Cite, **key word in context (KWIC)**, full or customized (Exhibit 6-22, Arrow 1). For the KWIC, the researcher may select the number of words providing the context (from 1 to 999). The default is 25. Notice that the document provides the path to its location and its Topical location (§1I:8:14) at least five times on the screen.

The excerpts reproduced in Exhibit 6-22 demonstrate one of the added features of this service; the Practice Tips (Arrow 2). These are similar to the Checkpoint—RIA Observations as both furnish practical suggestions for the practitioner.

Another search option available in LexisNexis is Get a Document. Using this option, documents can be retrieved by Citation (Option 1), Federal Citation (Option 2), and State or Region Citation (Option 3), as illustrated in Exhibit 6-23. The citations must be entered in a format recognized by LexisNexis. If the researcher is not familiar with the LexisNexis format, the Help function (Arrow 1) includes in its index a listing for Citation Format. The formats for administrative document, cases, and tax or legislative documents are provided by example. If one is searching for a case and only the taxpayer's name is known, it is best to use a keyword search in the Research tab and select the level of court from the Cases column. When the researcher is unsure of the judicial level of the case, the combined Federal and state databases or just combined Federal Courts Tax Cases should be selected.

EXHIBIT 6-22: LexisNexis Tax Advisor – Federal Topical

Copyright 2010 LexisNexis, a division of Reed Elsevier Inc. All Rights Reserved. LexisNexis and the Knowledge Burst logo are registered trademarks of Reed Elsevier Properties Inc. and are used with the permission of LexisNexis.

SPOTLIGHT ON TAXATION

The Huge Two

Two companies dominate the realm of providing legal and tax information, Reed Elsevier and Thomson Reuters. These corporations are two of the largest publishing and information providers in the world. Reed Elsevier, an Anglo-Dutch company, is the parent company of LexisNexis; Thomson Reuters owns Westlaw, RIA, and Warren, Gorham & Lamont (WG&L). Since BNA and CCH are each independent companies, they can offer their tax and legal services on both LexisNexis and Westlaw. Thus, through LexisNexis and Westlaw, the tax practitioner can access virtually every major tax publication!

LexisNexis Academic

LexisNexis offers a customized version of its services to academic institutions and public libraries called **LexisNexis Academic**. While the complete LexisNexis flagship service provides full-text documents from more than 6,000 publications, most library

EXHIBIT 6-23:   LexisNexis Get a Document

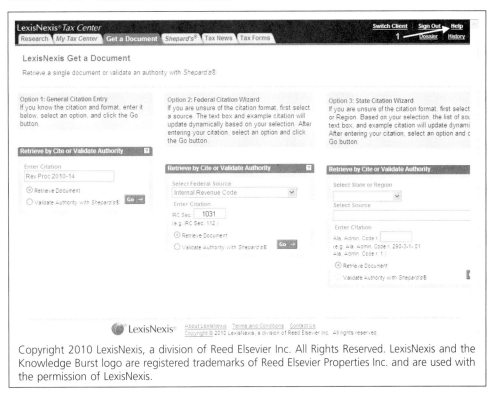

Copyright 2010 LexisNexis, a division of Reed Elsevier Inc. All Rights Reserved. LexisNexis and the Knowledge Burst logo are registered trademarks of Reed Elsevier Properties Inc. and are used with the permission of LexisNexis.

subscriptions do not carry all of the offerings. Thus, the databases available to the reader may differ from that demonstrated in this section.

To perform tax research using Academic, select the US Legal button from the categories in the left window of the opening screen. The legal databases available to the subscriber then appear below the US Legal button as seen in Exhibit 6-24 (Arrows 1 and 2). Choosing Tax Law provides access to primary sources, tax journals, newsletters, and tax law reviews. The tax sources in Exhibit 6-24 may be searched individually or in any combination desired by the researcher, by using either Terms and Connectors or Natural Language keywords if the Power Search is selected (Arrow 7). The entry boxes vary depending on the type of keyword search selected. As is visible in Exhibit 6-24, the connectors available in Academic are furnished in pull-down menus (Arrow 4). To enhance the relevancy of the documents retrieved, date limitations (Specify Date, Arrow 5) can be imposed (options available in the pull-down menu have been moved to the right in Exhibit 6-24 so the menu does not hide the sources).

To access more or specific sources not included in the Tax Law database available in Exhibit 6-24, the Browse Sources (Arrows 3 or 6) may be selected. As Exhibit 6-25 indicates, the Browse Sources option has three numbered steps to follow. Step 1, select Area of Law for how the sources will be browsed. This displays a list of law areas (not shown) and Taxation Law is chosen. Step 2, Filter the sources by country (United States), region (US Federal All, for example), Publication Type (All Publication Types) and source types (multiple, single, or all sources). In Step 3, the researcher selects which categories of legal sources (databases) to view. The sources selected appear in the right frame (Arrow 1) with the ability to remove any or all of them. Clicking the

EXHIBIT 6-24: LexisNexis Academic Legal Screen

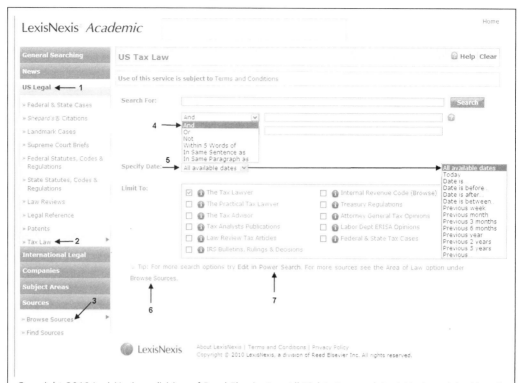

EXHIBIT 6-25: LexisNexis Academic Browse Sources

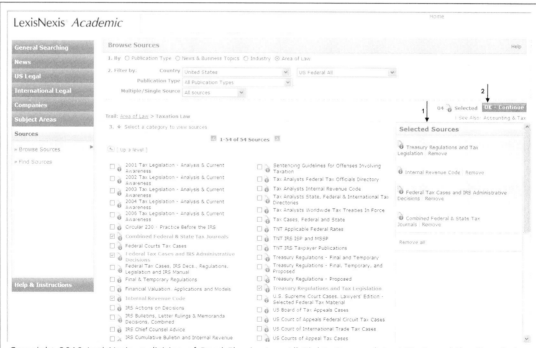

EXHIBIT 6-26: LexisNexis Academic Results Screen

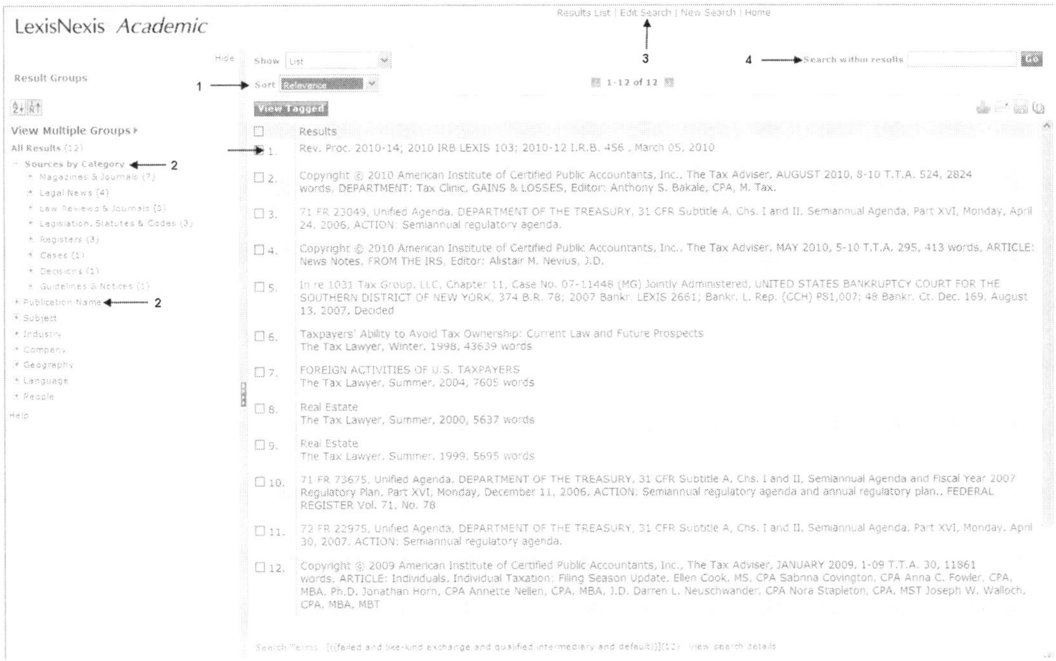

OK Continue button (Arrow 2) accesses the search screen for performing keyword searches.

The results of an Academic search in Exhibit 6-26 may be listed either by relevance, chronological, or publication date (Arrow 1). The results summary in the left window of Exhibit 6-26 also may be personalized to list by category or publication name (Arrows 2). If the documents retrieved are not on point, the researcher may use the Edit Search option (Arrow 3) to return to the original keyword entry box or if too many documents are returned, the Search Within Results option (Arrow 4) allows the researcher to add keywords to narrow the results. Selecting one of the document titles such as # 1, Rev. Proc. 2010-14, displays the document. Academic offers the KWIC (key words in context) view, which highlights the terms entered as keywords. If the Search within results option has been applied, only the words used for narrowing will be KWIC. The documents retrieved are full text and may be downloaded, e-mailed, or printed from the browser.

The improvements made by LexisNexis to Academic have dramatically increased the usefulness of this service for performing tax research. While there are remnants of the prior "tree" organization of the libraries that preempted comprehensive single searches, Academic is a more tax-research-friendly service than in the past.

SUMMARY

There are many commercial services available that can be utilized in performing tax research, and no one service is the best for all practitioners. While the services provide different features, all are most efficient when the organization of the service facilitates research of the issues in a client's tax situation. Thus, each tax service has its place in tax research, and practitioners must determine with which products they are most comfortable and which fit the normal research requirements of their firm.

Changes in technology and the tax services happen on a continuous basis. The same changes occur in the practitioner's business. Consequently, the practitioner's comfort level with products and technology and the research needs will change over time. Practitioners should evaluate their tax resource choices often, at least once a year when it is time to renew their services.

The tax researcher should employ commercial services as gateways to the primary sources and not as a substitute for primary source research. Tax services can make the research process more efficient and productive, but they should not replace a thorough review of primary sources and use of the researcher's professional judgment.

QUIZ YOURSELF

Reinforce the tax research information covered in this chapter by completing the online quizzes located at the Federal Tax Research Web site at **www.cengagebrain.com.** At the CengageBrain.com home page, search for the *Federal Tax Research*, 9e ISBN (1111221642) using the search box at the top of the page. This will take you to the product page where you can access the quizzes.

KEY WORDS

By the time you complete this chapter, you should be comfortable discussing each of the following terms. If you need additional review of any of these items, return to the appropriate material in the chapter or consult the glossary to this text.

annotated tax service, p. 192
annotations, p. 192
BNA Tax and Accounting Center
 (BTAC), p. 209
BNA Tax Management Portfolios
 (Portfolios), p. 209
Boolean, p. 197
Bureau of National Affairs (BNA),
 p. 209
Compilations, p. 192
Commerce Clearning House
 (CCH), p. 204
CCH IntelliConnect, p. 204
Federal Tax Coordinator (FTC),
 p. 195
Freedom of Information Act
 (FOIA), p. 208
full-text search, p. 196
Key Number, p. 215

Key word in context (KWIC), p. 219
KeyCite, p. 212
KeySearch, p. 216
Lexis, p. 217
LexisNexis, p. 216
LexisNexis Academic, p. 220
Mertens Law of Federal Income
 Taxation, p. 211
Natural Language, p. 196
Nexis, p. 217
Research Institute of America
 (RIA), p. 195
ResultsPlus, p. 215
RIA Checkpoint, p. 195
Standard Federal Income Tax
 Reporter (SFITR), p. 206
Tax Advisor—Federal Code
 Reporter, p. 218
Tax Analysts, p. 218

Tax Center, p. 217
Tax Research Consultant (TRC),
 p. 206
Tax Advisor—Federal Topical,
 p. 218
Terms & Connectors (Boolean),
 p. 196
topical tax services, p. 192
United States Tax Reporter
 (USTR), p. 195
Warren, Gorham & Lamont
 (WG&L), p. 195
Westlaw, p. 211
WestlawNext, p. 211
WestSearch, p. 211
West Key Number System, p. 215

DISCUSSION QUESTIONS

1. What is the function of commercial tax services?

2. Compare and contrast the general organization of an annotated tax service with that of a topical tax service.

3. Why would a practitioner need a tax service when most primary tax sources are available for free on the Internet?

4. If commercial services are updated on a daily or continuous basis, explain whether they are current up to the minute.

5. What is the starting point and the process for conducting the research? Will a competent researcher always find a solution to the tax question?

6. What is the key to effective and efficient tax research?

7. With what type of tax service documents should practitioners start, if they are unfamiliar with the topic being researched?

8. Why is it important for you to actually try research projects with the various tax services?

9. What are the three methods for starting a research project in most commercial services? Which does RIA emphasize?

10. Which annotated and topical tax services are included in RIA Checkpoint?

11. What are the two options for entering the Index in RIA Checkpoint? What databases support Index searchers?

12. What is the advantage of using a TOC search? What is the advantage of an Index search?

13. What is the function in RIA Checkpoint of the directional symbol (compass) found in reproduced Code sections or Regulations? Why is it useful?

14. How does CCH IntelliConnect differ from other commercial services in accessing the service after periods of inactivity?

15. Which annotated and topical tax services are included in CCH IntelliConnect?

16. What is the underlying assumption regarding keyword searching in CCH IntelliConnect?

17. Documents retrieved by RIA Checkpoint and CCH IntelliConnect searches can be listed in two orders. What are these orders?

18. CCH IntelliConnect supports date limitations on searches. When is this option useful?

19. When would a practitioner want to search an archived prior year's CCH IntelliConnect tax service?

20. Keyword search in IRA Checkpoint is as easy as 1, 2, 3. Explain what this means. How does the CCH IntelliConnect keyword search compare in ease of use with Checkpoint?

21. How can finding a BNA Portfolio on-point with a practitioner's tax issue be like hiring someone to do the research?

22. How is each BNA Portfolio arranged?

23. Describe the Working Papers section of a BNA Tax Management Portfolio.

24. Who designed Westlaw? What is its target market?

25. The opening screen in Westlaw is oriented to what type of searches?

26. How is a space between keywords interpreted by RIA Checkpoint, CCH IntelliConnect, Westlaw, and LexisNexis?

27. Describe the function of ResultsPlus.

28. What are KeySearch and the West Key Number System?

29. What are the major analytical materials offered through LexisNexis Tax Center?

30. LexisNexis offers a KWIC document view. What is KWIC?

31. What are the three options offered by LexisNexis Get a Document for retrieving documents?

32. What is LexisNexis Academic?

33. How are the tax materials accessed on LexisNexis Academic?

34. Give a summary of the facts for Research Project 6-1.

35. Which national CPA firm is the oldest firm in the United States?

36. Describe the history of the *United State Tax Reporter* currently published by RIA.

37. What family started and was the majority shareholder of CCH until it was purchased by a Dutch publishing corporation?

38. What is the FOIA and how does it apply to IRS documents?

39. What company is the largest independent publisher of business and government analysis?

40. Who are parent companies (owns) of RIA, CCH, Westlaw, and LexisNexis?

EXERCISES

41. Use the RIA Checkpoint Federal Practice Area to answer the following questions:
    a. What are the thesaurus alternatives for "exchange"?
    b. On the search screen, expand the FTC by clicking on the + before the title. What are the subheadings listed?
    c. Expand the IRS Rulings and Releases (RIA). What pronouncement heading has the oldest documents available? From what year are these documents?
    d. There are three access points for current legislation. What are these three points?

42. Use the RIA Checkpoint Federal Practice Area, Go To section to answer the following questions:
    a. What is the title of the lead article for the most recent RIA Tax Watch?
    b. When selecting USTR Code Section, what are the choices given for the first and the second selections that must be made (blue circle 1 and 2)?
    c. What templates are available in the Form/Line Finder?
    d. What tables are available in the "i-Tables" tool?

43. Use the RIA Checkpoint to answer the following questions:
    a. Select the Estate Planning Practice Area. What templates are available for Code & Regs? Now select the Payroll Practice Area. Indicate any differences in the templates available for IRC & Regs.
    b. Select the Federal Practice Area. Under Find by Citation, select More... What is the oldest General Council Memorandum available?
    c. Select the Federal Practice Area. What type of documents may have the Date Range Search applied to them? What are the oldest available dates for these documents?
    d. Select the Federal Practice Area. Under Find by Citation, select More... then Revenue Ruling. List the Revenue Rulings discussing §1245. (Hint: Use Retrieve Rulings By Code Section at Issue.)

44. Use the Home & Tool Tabs in RIA Checkpoint to answer the following questions:
    a. What are the different windows shown on the Home Tab?
    b. With the Savings tool found on the Tool Tab, determine how much you need to start saving now (based on your current age) to have $1 million when you are 65. Use an expected rate of return of 6 percent and expected inflation rate of 2.5 percent. Repeat the process adding 10 years to your current age.
    c. On the Home Tab, under My Quick Links, select Titles. What is the most recent Highlight for New Law Special Study?

    d. With the Tax tool found on the Tool Tab, determine the marginal tax rate for a head of household taxpayer with two dependent children earning $75,000 and having $15,000 in itemized deductions. List the average rate and income tax bracket also.

45. Use the RIA Checkpoint and §681 to answer the following questions:

    a. What is the title of §681 and to what taxpayers does it apply?

    b. What Regulations were issued on this Code Section? What are their titles?

    c. What FTC paragraphs furnish an analysis of the §681(a)? What explanations paragraphs are linked to §681.

    d. List the citations of cases that are linked to §681?

46. Use the RIA Checkpoint Federal Practice Area Indexes to answer the following questions:

    a. What Federal editorial materials have indexes?

    b. In the FTC Topic Index, determine what paragraph defines jigging?

    c. In the Current Code Topic Index, determine what Code section discusses excise taxes on vaccines?

    d. In the Code Arranged Annotations & Explanations (USTR) Topic Index, determine which paragraph discusses the taxation of damages received for false imprisonment.

47. Use the RIA Checkpoint to answer the following questions regarding how bank charge-offs of debts due to orders by Federal or state authorities are treated.

    a. Using *bank, orders, Federal, authorities, charge, debt, worthless,* as keywords, search FTC and determine what paragraph discusses this issue.

    b. Use the same keywords in part a., but search USTR—Explanations. What paragraph discusses this issue?

    c. What primary source is cited by both the FTR and USTR as the source of the solution?

    d. Using a TOC search of the RIA Federal Tax Handbook, what paragraph discusses this issue?

48. Use the RIA Checkpoint to answer the following questions:

    a. Using Form/Line Finder, locate directions for line 15 on Form 1040 for 2008. What is the paragraph number and topic?

    b. What is the mid-term monthly Applicable Federal Rate for the current month?

    c. Select More …, then American Federal Tax Reports (Prior Years). In the Retrieve Case by Name, Tax Years, and so forth, enter 2006 in Year Issued box, S. Ct. in Court example, and Ginsburg in Judge Name. List by citation what case(s) are retrieved.

49. Use the RIA Checkpoint to answer the following questions:

    a. What are the Practice Areas available in Checkpoint?

    b. What materials are offered in the Archive Materials (Search screen bottom right) for 2002?

    c. When would a practitioner want to use the Archive Materials?

    d. Locate repealed §341 using USTR Code Section. What area of the tax law did this section cover and when was the repeal effective?

50. Use the RIA Checkpoint to answer the following questions:

    a. List three Credit Card tools offered on the Tools Tab that would be personally beneficial to your financial planning?

    b. What is the amount of CPE credit available for the On Demand Training: Getting Started with Checkpoint? (Hint: Open Home Tab)

    c. What is the most recent Practice Development listed for California? (Hint: Sort by Jurisdiction.)

51. Use the CCH IntelliConnect Federal Tax database to answer the following questions:

    a. What are the major database categories provided?

    b. Select 1999 in the Federal Tax Achieves. What is the tax bracket (highest marginal rate) for a single individual with taxable income of $65,000? (Hint: Use the Master Tax Guide - 1999.) When would it be useful to know what the IRC was in a prior year?

    c. What is the most recent Action on Decisions listed in Letter Rulings & IRS Positions?

    d. What Federal Tax Legislations does CCH think are worth watching?

52. Use the CCH IntelliConnect Browse to locate Topical Indexes for answering the following questions:

    a. What are the major headings for the letter "Y" in the Internal Revenue Code index?

    b. What countries are listed for the letter "K" in the Tax Research Consultant index?

    c. What is the listing for the letter "Z" in the Gift Tax Detailed Index (found in Financial and Estate Planning)? Include paragraph numbers.

    d. Explain the function of the Topic Navigator that is located in the Practice Tools, Federal Taxes.

53. Use the CCH IntelliConnect Practice Tools to answer the following questions:

    a. Selecting the Federal Taxes heading, determine whether it is more cost effective to buy or lease an auto. The purchase price of the auto is $45,000, the loan term is 36 months, and the interest rate is 8 percent. The lease term is 60 months, and value at the end of the lease term is $10,000. For any other information requested, provide reasonable estimates. Print results.

    b. Selecting the Sales and Property Tax heading, how long can the dormancy period be for a bank account in the state where your college is located?

    c. Selecting Financial and Estate Planning, compare investing in a Traditional versus a Roth IRA based on fictitious information you provide. Print results.

54. Use the CCH IntelliConnect Browse function and select the Federal Tax Editorial Content heading to answer the following questions:

    a. Using Quick Answers Tax Rates and Tables determine what the high-cost localities per diem rate was for the most current period.

    b. In the Interactive Research Aids for Tax Research Consultant, for Individuals, who is the author of the decision tree for qualified moving expenses?

    c. Using the Master Tax Guide, determine whether the Credit for the Elderly is a refundable credit? In what paragraph number is the discussion of this credit located?

    d. What is the most recent Joint Committee on Taxation Blue Book available in the Federal Tax Legislation heading?

55. Use the CCH IntelliConnect Practice Tools database to answer the following questions:

    a. Using the Federal Withholding Calculator, determine what your withholding should be, based on what you would like your income to be upon graduation and your current family situation. Print results.

    b. Using the Depreciation Toolkit, determine the depreciation in year 5 for $45,000 of Dairy Cattle, 150 percent DB method for Farm Property with a half-year convention.

    c. Using the Federal/State Taxes, Tax Calendar, prepare a calendar for the current year for all the taxes for the state within which your college is located. Print one month that shows payment due dates.

    d. Explain whether the Practice Tools offered in the Main Menu (where Browse, Citations, and so forth are located) are the same as in the Practice Tools, listed in the expanding Browse option?

56. Indicate the relevant information requested for CCH IntelliConnect SFITR, paragraph 12,623.025.

    a. What is the title for the paragraph and Code section?

    b. What Regulations apply to this paragraph? Are these Regulations still good law?

    c. What Related Information is available?

57. Use the CCH IntelliConnect, Tax Research Consultant to perform a keyword search on the topic of making an election to defer the determination of whether an activity is a not engaged in for profit (hobby) until after the fourth year.

    a. In what paragraph(s) did you find the discussion of this topic?

    b. What keyword terms did you use for your final search? How many documents did your search retrieve?

    c. What form is filed to make the election?

    d. What Interactive Research Aid is available for determining whether an activity is subject to the hobby loss rules and who wrote it?

58. Use the CCH IntelliConnect, Standard Federal Income Tax Reporter to perform the keyword searches on making an election to defer the determination of whether an activity is a not engaged in for profit (hobby) until after the fourth year.

    a. What Code section and Regulation discusses this election?

    b. In what paragraph(s) did you find editorial discussion of this topic?

    c. What keyword terms did you use for final search? How many documents did your search retrieve?

    d. Compare the keyword search using the Tax Research Consultant with the search using Standard Federal Income Tax Reporter. Which one was more efficient and effective?

59. Use the IntelliConnect Citations to answer the following questions:

    a. What does Notice 2010-50, IRB 2010-27 discuss? What day was it issued?

    b. What document is located at 2010-21 IRB 691? What day was it issued?

    c. What is the title and author of the 2008 *Taxes-The Tax Magazine* article that is retrieved as related information for §381(a)?

    d. What Code section does the Federal Excise Tax Reporter ¶ 34,275.01 involve? In what service and what paragraph is the topic explained?

60. Use the CCH IntelliConnect Federal Tax to answer the following questions:

    a. What is the full name and public law numbers of the 111th Congress legislation that substantively amended the Code?

    b. Is a former IRS employee eligible to become an Enrolled Agent without taking an exam? If yes, what is the procedure? (Hint: Circular 230).

    c. Where can you find guidance on how to defend against IRS levies?

    d. What is the paragraph number in the Standard Federal Income Tax Reporter that discusses nonprofit activities in Oceanography?

61. Use the BNA Tax & Accounting Center to answer the following questions:

    a. When is the next Estate Tax Webinar and who are the speakers?

    b. The American Jobs and Closing Tax Loopholes Act of 2010 originally had a different title. What was this other title?

    c. What are CIP and ISP Papers? Give the full title and paper identifier number of the 2009 paper involving §168(a).

    d. Perform a search of the source documents to locate an IRS publication covering moving expenses.

62. Use the BNA Tax Management Portfolios to answer the following questions:
    a. What is the Portfolio number (and section) that discusses mineral property advance royalties?
    b. In the Portfolio identified in part a, what is demonstrated in Worksheet 4?
    c. What is the Portfolio number (and section) that discusses the deductibility of attorney's fees for bankrupt corporations?
    d. In the Portfolio identified in part c, what is the state Tax Management Portfolio listed in the Unofficial Bibliography?

63. Use the BNA Tax & Accounting Center to answer the following questions:
    a. What options are available in the Advanced Search?
    b. What actions do the following search operators (connectors) perform: spaces between words, question mark (?), and asterisk (*)?
    c. Using a Guided Search, what options are available besides a keyword search?
    d. How does the Go To option function?

64. Use the BNA Tax & Accounting Center to answer the following questions:
    a. Use a Go To search to find Rev. Rul. 90-93. What is the issue in this ruling?
    b. Using a Guided Search, determine what Portfolios cite Rev. Rul. 90-93.
    c. Using an Advance Search, choose the Attorney field and enter the name Dench. Limit the dates to the years from 1995 to 1997. In what case(s) was Dench the lawyer?
    d. Using the Search Indexes & Finding Aids, enter *mortgagor* as the search term. What Portfolios and sections are referenced in the results of this search?

65. Use the BNA Tax Management Portfolios to answer the following questions:
    a. What is the Portfolio number (and section) that discusses the tax consequences to the mortgagor of foreclosure on real estate when the mortgagor is not discharged from the liability?
    b. What is the Rev. Rul. listed in the Official bibliography of the Tax Crimes Portfolio?
    c. What Portfolio contains a Worksheet demonstrating the attribution rules between family members for §267? What is the Worksheet number?

66. Use Westlaw Tax tab to answer the following questions:
    a. Find Rev. Proc. 2010-25. What is the purpose of the procedure?
    b. What publications are available for browsing by table of contents? Where did you find this information?
    c. What is the last numbered chapter for *Mertens Law of Federal Income Taxation*? What chapter numbers are reserved?
    d. What is the quarterly Federal Applicable Rate for long-term for the current period? Where did you find this information?

67. Use the Westlaw Tax tab to answer the following questions:
    a. What are the date and title of the most recent Spotlight Article found in the Weekly Tax Updates?
    b. What daily and weekly news reports are available for Pensions?
    c. What is the specific topic covered in *Mertens Law of Federal Income Taxation*, Chapter 10, §10:10? Who most recently revised this section and on what date?
    d. What is the database identifier for Bittker & Eustice: *Federal Income Taxation of Corporations & Shareholders*? Where did you find this information?

68. Use WestlawNext to answer the following questions:

    a. Using the drill-down TOC method for searching, determine the full titles for §20B:63 in *Mertens Law of Federal Income Taxation*. Who revised this section? What is its Key Number Digest number?

    b. Find the *Armstrong v. Commonwealth of the Northern Mariana Islands* Supreme Court action that occurred in June 2010. Was certiorari granted? What is the WL number for the case?

    c. What journals are available in Taxation News?

    d. What is the topic of Chapter 12, Section 30 (¶12.30) in Bittker & Eustice: *Federal Income Taxation of Corporations* & *Shareholders*?

69. Use the Westlaw GC to answer the following questions:

    a. What is the Chapter section number of the *Sarbanes-Oxley Act in Perspective* for the discussion of sanctions for violations of any provision of Part 205? When was the last update and who is the author?

    b. Select a database to retrieve a search box. What are the thesaurus terms for the intangible asset "patent?"

    c. Give the complete location (from title to section) in the United States Code Annotated (USCA) of the imposition of environmental taxes on petroleum?

    d. In *Mertens Law of Federal Income Taxation*, the chapters designated 25 cover business expenses. There are several lettered Chapter 25s (e.g., Chapter 25A, Chapter 25B). List the lettered chapters for 25. If there is any other numbered chapter designations having more lettered chapters than Chapter 25, provide the number of the chapter.

70. Use the Westlaw GC service to answer the following questions:

    a. Using Find Case by Party Name, locate the 2008 Supreme Court case, *Boulware*. Provide the Federal, Westlaw, RIA and CCH citations for the case.

    b. Under Resources, what is available for Securities?

    c. Select one of the resources in part b. and determine its contents.

    d. Perform a search using Westlaw and WestlawNext to find a document discussing the application of the constructive receipt doctrine to liquidating dividends? What did you find and which platform was easier?

71. Use Westlaw Tax tab to answer the following questions:

    a. The sale of a patent by the original individual inventor generally is treated as a capital gain, even for a professional inventor. Provide the citation for the 1954 House Report that discusses why professionals receive this treatment.

    b. Indicate your search strategy for part a. Include your search terms, databases chosen, and search iterations.

    c. What BNA Portfolios and Mertens documents does ResultsPlus suggest?

    d. What Key Numbers are suggested for this topic?

72. Use WestlawNext to answer the following questions:

    a. What Subchapter of Title 26, Code of Federal Regulations, is reserved?

    b. What is the WL number for Private Letter Ruling 201027033?

    c. What is the key number for medical deductions?

    d. In the *Hargrove* case, why was certiorari granted by the Supreme Court in 2010?

73. Use the Federal area in LexisNexis Tax Center to answer the following questions. (Hint: click on the "i" for information.)

    a. What is the frequency and update schedule for the Federal Courts Tax Cases?

    b. What is the document (Doc) description of the IRC Legislative History?

    c. Who is the publisher of the LexisNexis Tax Advisor—Federal Topical?

d. Select LexisNexis Tax Advisor—Federal Topical database. Perform a natural language search to determine the tax treatment of stock redeemed from a deceased shareholder. Perform the same search using terms and connectors. List your natural search and the number of documents it retrieved. Provide the same information for the terms and connectors search. Explain why one was a more effective search.

74. Use LexisNexis Tax Center to answer the following questions. (Hint: use More Sources.)

   a. What is the update schedule for the IRS Advance Releases?

   b. What law reviews are offered as separate databases?

   c. For the CCH SFTR, what is the earliest year in the Archives?

   d. What is the title of the first article in Tax Analysts *Tax Notes* Today?

75. Use LexisNexis Tax Center to answer the following questions:

   a. Select the Tax Topics tab. There are two search options. The first is a keyword search and what is the second option?

   b. Select the Tax New Tab. What sources are listed under Accounting that can be browsed (underlined titles)?

   c. Select A to Z Source lists. What documents do you find under the letters Q and X?

   d. Select the Accounting & Sec tab. What SEC form databases are available?

76. Use the LexisNexis Tax Center, Select Analytical Sources tabs to answer the following questions:

   a. Select the Specialized Tax Planning tab. What chapter in the Depreciation Handbook discusses amortization of intangible assets?

   b. Select Exempt Organizations tab. What Tax Analysts products are available (More Sources)?

   c. Select the IRS Practice & Procedures tab. In the *Federal Tax Practices and Procedures*, in what section are liens due to bankruptcy and receivership discussed?

   d. Select the Business Entity tab. The *Tax Planning for the Alternative Minimum Tax* discusses the reporting of the Minimum Tax Credit. On what form is this credit computed?

77. Use the LexisNexis Academic Legal Search option to answer the following questions:

   a. Select the Tax Law database and perform a Terms & Connectors search using the following terms: likekind, failed, intermediary with "and" connectors. What 2008 revenue procedure is listed in the results?

   b. Furnish the author's name and publishing law review (with year and volume) for the article "The Like-Kind Exchange Equity Conundrum?"

   c. Using the judge's last name Sotomayor, determine the treatments of the petitions for a writ of certiorari decided on January 11, 2010 for court cases with taxpayers named Lemon. Also provide the full name of each case and from which Court of Appeals is the writ.

   d. When using Terms & Connectors searches what do the following connectors mean: W/10; PRE/ 20; NOT W/seg; and ATLEAST5. (Hint: click on Tips for using search connectors.)

78. Use the LexisNexis Academic Legal Search option, Tax Law to answer the following questions:

   a. What types of sources are provided in the Tax Law library?

   b. Furnish the title of the most recent UCLA law review article by Joshua D. Blank on detecting tax shelters.

   c. One of the sources in the Tax Law is *The Tax Adviser*. What is the coverage period for this journal and how often is this journal published? (Hint: use the "i" button.)

   d. How helpful do you find the two functions "How do I…." and "View additional Tax Law search form topics" in answering search questions?

79. Use LexisNexis Academic Sources by Area of Law, Taxation Law to answer the following questions:

    a. How many United States sources (U.S. Federal All) are available for Treatises & Analytical Materials library?

    b. Locate an article in the Legal News publication database Tax Analysts Tax Publications (Country United States, All Regions) discussing corporate reorganizations and later sale of shares to an ESOP plan qualified for non-recognition treatment that was published in February 2010. Supply the Private Letter Ruling number upon which the article is based and the rulings release date.

    c. Select the Cases for Publication Type for the United States, Northeast region. What states cases are included in the Northeast?

    d. Select the Administrative Materials for Publication Type for the United States, and Region of U.S. Federal All. What sources offer the browse option?

80. Use LexisNexis Academic to answer the following questions:

    a. Select Sources by Publication Type, Filter by Country is United States, Region is U.S. Federal All and Topics is Taxation law. What are the available folders in part 3, Select a category to view sources?

    b. In the Treaties & Analytical Material, who is the publisher of *Policies and Procedures to Prevent Fraud and Embezzlement* and how frequently is this title updated?

    c. In the IRS Practice and Procedure Deskbook, what does Chapter 4, section§ 4:3 discuss?

    d. In the IRS Practice and Procedure Deskbook, what section discusses the dollar limitation for taxes and penalties for filing in the Small Case Division of the Tax Court?

RESEARCH CASES

81. Francis moved in with her mother, Beatrice, when Beatrice's health started to fail. Francis cared for her mother as a devoted child and never expected anything in return. When Beatrice needed to move to a nursing home, she legally transferred the home to Francis for $1,000 and "other valuable consideration." The house had cost Beatrice $50,000 many years ago, and on the date of the transfer it was valued at $150,000. At the time of the transfer, Beatrice was insolvent, as she owed the IRS $250,000 in back taxes and interest for 1990 to 2008. A few months after the transfer of the house, the IRS filed a notice of Federal tax lien for Beatrice's unpaid taxes. The IRS has filed against Francis for $150,000 of her mother's taxes, as Francis is in possession of the only valuable asset Beatrice has owned. Can the IRS collect from Francis?

82. The IRS audited the Loser Corporation's return filed two years ago. This IRS found substantial underreporting of income and is proposing to review Loser's returns for the six prior years. Loser knows it underreported its taxable income on its timely filed tax return five years ago. It reported $80,000 of gross sales, $10,000 product returns, and $60,000 costs of goods sold. Its actual amounts were $100,000 gross sales, $2,000 returns, and $40,000 COGS. Does the IRS have the right to audit this return from five years ago?

83. Magnus has been divorced from his wife, Irina, for three years. In the divorce, Magnus lost custody of the two children he fathered and one adopted child. Irina has moved to Russia to be close to her parents. Magnus misses having children, so he pays for vitro fertilization with his sperm of two anonymous donors' eggs and has the resulting embryos carried by women unrelated to him who give birth to the two children. Can Magnus take the costs for these procedures as a medical expense?

84. Paul and Patty Nelson own a home in Nelsonville, Ohio and maintain apartments in Lexington Kentucky, New York City (part year), and Philadelphia (part year). Their cars are registered, and they have driver's licenses from Kentucky. However, the Nelsons consider Nelsonville their "home" because their house was inherited from Paul's parents and has been in the family for over 150 years. During the year, Paul traveled between Kentucky and Nelsonville numerous times. Patty did not usually accompany Paul, as she works for

a consulting firm on engagements in New York City and Philadelphia. The home office of her employer is in Chicago, but she never works in Illinois. Paul's sales region for his job is Kentucky and Indiana. For purposes of taking expenses while away-from-home, Paul and Patty use their Nelsonville home. Is this correct? Where is the Nelson's tax home?

85. Jason was diagnosed with fibromyalgia three years ago. Since stress increases the symptoms, he left his public accounting job to become an accountant at a manufacturing firm. His symptoms subsided substantially after this move. Then last year, the firm hired a new accounts manager, Sheila, who was very high strung and demanding. Worst yet, Jason uncovers that Shelia is double billing customers that she thinks will not notice. All of this causes Jason terrible stress, and his fibromyalgia flares up such that his doctor insists he take a leave of absence. Shelia fires Jason and Jason sues. When the settlement payment is made for wrongful discharge, Jason receives back wages, attorney fees, and $50,000 identified as nonemployee compensation. Can Jason exclude the $50,000 as a payment for physical pain and suffering?

86. Candidate Feldman ran for Congress in 2010, raising $4.7 million for the campaign, including $800,000 in Federal matching amounts. Five months after his opponent was sworn into office, auditors discovered that Feldman used $500,000 of campaign donations for a personal vacation, taken immediately after the unsuccessful campaign. What are the tax consequences of this use of election funds?

87. Ann is required under a divorce decree to pay alimony of $2,000 per month and child support of $3,000 per month. Ann has only been paying $4,000 per month because she thinks the child support requirement is too high. On Ann's tax return, what portion of the payments does she treat as alimony and what part is considered child support?

88. Which of the following items qualifies for the child care credit claimed by the Rodriguez family?

- Salary for nanny.
- Employer's share of FICA tax for nanny, paid by Rodriguez.
- Employee's share of FICA tax for nanny, paid by Rodriguez.
- Health insurance premiums on nanny, paid by Rodriguez.
- One-half of nanny's hotel bill while on her own during a European vacation, paid by Rodriguez.
- Dry cleaning bills for nanny's clothes soiled by youngsters and paid by Rodriguez.

89. Kenny has been a waiter at the Burger Pitt for four years. The Pitt treats its employees well, allowing them a 60 percent discount for any food that they buy and consume on the premises. This year, the value of this discount for Kenny amounted to $2,500 for days on which he was working, and $1,500 for days when he was not assigned to work but still stopped by during mealtimes. How much gross income must Kenny recognize this year with respect to the discount plan?

90. Ollie died this year in September, after a long illness. His wages prior to death totaled $15,000, and his state taxes thereon came to $600.
   a. Who must file Ollie's last tax return?
   b. How is the return signed?
   c. Who collects Ollie's $440 Federal refund?

91. When Fifi, a sheriff's deputy, was injured on the job, she was allowed under her contract with the state to choose between a $1,000 weekly sick-pay distribution and an $850 weekly workers' compensation payment. Which one should Fifi select?

92. Willie was tired of cleaning up the messes that his wife, Barbara, made in their house. One morning, he found a crumpled facial tissue on the bathroom vanity, so he disgustedly flushed it down the toilet. Unfortunately, the tissue was wrapped around Barbara's engagement ring, which she had removed the previous evening after cutting her finger while shoveling snow. Is the couple allowed a deductible casualty loss for Federal income tax purposes under IRC §165?

93. Louella was born into a low-income family and lives in a poverty-stricken neighborhood. She recently landed a job as wardrobe consultant at High Fashions Ltd., a retailer of expensive women's clothing at an Elm Grove shopping mall. Can Louella claim a §162 business expense deduction on her Federal income tax return for the cost and upkeep of the expensive Yves St. Laurent outfits that she is required to wear on the job?

94. Harriet purchased a variety of birth control devices during the year. To what extent, and under what circumstances, do such items qualify under §213 for a medical expense deduction?

95. Phyllis sued Martin's estate and won a $65,000 settlement. She showed the probate court that she carried out her end of a compensatory arrangement with her companion, where she provided "traditional wifely services" without benefit of matrimony during Martin's life in exchange for all of his estate. Martin left his entire estate to his faithful dog Sparky, via a trust. How much gross income is recognized by Phyllis?

96. How much gross income is recognized by Carol, who received $10,000 damages (two months' salary) for pain and suffering due to the school administration's critical reaction to her negative comments about ineffective recruiting of athletes who graduate with legitimate academic majors?

97. Carol and Jerry, LLP, pays the Good Eats Cafe each month for the lunches the two accountants eat there each work day. While at lunch Carol and Jerry always discuss some business. Often Carol and Jerry invite friends who work at other CPA firms to join them, so they can keep up with what is happening in the accounting community. Are these meals deductible?

98. Lila personally bought three insurance policies on her life. She borrowed $28,500 and prepaid the first five years' worth of annual payments on a whole life policy. In addition, she borrowed $4,200 and paid one of the two required premiums on a group term policy through her professional organization. Finally, she borrowed $3,000 and bought utilities mutual fund shares. The principal and interest of the fund's assets are to be appropriated in a timely fashion by Lila to make payments on a five-premium endowment contract. Interest charges for the three loans were $2,500, $420, and $310, respectively. How much of this interest can Lila deduct?

99. CPA Joe reimburses a client for a $75,000 tax liability that is traceable to Joe's ineffective tax advice. For fear of increasing his already steep malpractice insurance premiums, Joe does not file a claim with the insurer. Can Joe deduct the $75,000 loss?

100. Toni, a gardener, lent Harry, his friend, his new $500 lawn mower. Harry ruined the lawn mower, but replaced it with a $425 model. Later in the same year, Toni lent Harry $5,000 for bail, $3,000 to start a fencing operation, and $15 for a meal. According to Harry's parole officer, none of these items will ever be paid back. Can Toni deduct any of these losses?

101. Three years ago, Geraldine bought a Kandinsky painting for her art collection from a mail-order advertisement for $310,000. This year, Geraldine's art dealer told her that the painting was actually painted by Kansky and is not worth more than $310. What is her deductible loss upon discovery of the forgery?

102. Chickfer Cooperative is a horticultural cooperative located in Arkansas that markets fertilizers created by its members especially for use by commercial greenhouses. It grossed $25 million in sales for the current year. Is Chickfer able to qualify for the domestic production activities deduction?

103. It is 3 a.m. and your access to the university's tax services is down. Find a text version of the Code on the Internet and print §61. Where did you find the Code? Who maintains the site? Does the version of the Code you found use text hyperlinks? What happens when you click on a hyperlink? Download and print a copy of a page with hyperlinks, then click on several hyperlinks and print the pages to which they link.

104. Bob Carburetor is the new owner of Carburetor Cars. Bob's brother Bill has owned an auto dealership for years, Radiator Cars. Bob decides to adopt all of his brother's accounting methods. At Radiator Cars, when a vehicle is sold, the dealership tries to sell an auto service contract. The amounts received for these contracts are placed into an escrow account. The agreements grant the buyers the right to have parts or components covered by the contract repaired or replaced, whenever the covered parts experience a mechanical difficulty. The dealer will provide the services or will reimburse the car buyer for the reasonable cost of repair or replacement. Normally, the buyer returns the vehicle to the dealer for repair, but this is not required. In either case, the repairs or replacements must be authorized in advance by an administrator hired by Radiator Cars. Fees to the administrator of the contracts are paid out of the escrow account. Is this the proper tax treatment for these service contracts?

105. Betty Jo Harris lives in Maine with her son Rick and husband Walter Reed. Rick has Lou Gehrig's disease. Rick's physician encourages Betty Jo to go to a Caregivers of Lou Gehrig's disease conference at the Mayo Clinic in Rochester, Minnesota, so she can learn how to better take care of Rick. Betty takes the advice and flies to Rochester. Besides the cost of the plane ticket, Betty Jo incurs the following types of expenses: meals, lodging, phone calls home, dry cleaning (she dumped her taco salad on her lap at lunch), and conference registration fees. The leading speaker at the conference suggested that caregivers take their patients to destinations in warm climates to improve their state of mind and general condition. When Betty returns home, she arranges a two-month trip (January and February) to the Bahamas for Rick and herself. One week after they have arrived in the Bahamas, Rick's father, Walter, arrives and stays for a couple of weeks. Advise Betty Jo as to whether any of these expenses are deductible as medical expenses.

106. Several years ago, Agnes and Wyman Booth bought a home for $200,000. They lived in the home for 10 years and then moved into an apartment. Unable to immediately sell the home, they rented it for two years earning $24,000 in rents and taking $14,000 in depreciation. After the two rental years, the Booths exchanged the house for $30,000 cash and a duplex worth $300,000. The Booths will hold the duplex as rental property. How much taxable income do the Booths have from the exchange?

107. King & Knight is a personal service corporation that has been in existence for five years. In the current year, it makes a §444 election to have its year-end become October 31. King & Knight incurs an NOL for the current year amounting to $100,000. How should King and Knight treat this NOL for tax purposes?

108. Clarence is a packrat. He has clothes from when he was in high school some 20 years ago that he never wears. He also has household items that have accumulated over the past 15 years. Some of these household items have not been used by Clarence in years and he is not sure if they even work. Clarence is buying a new home and wants to clean out his closets before he moves into his new house. He would like to give all of his old clothes and household items to local charities. What restrictions apply to charitable deductions of old clothes and household items?

109. Ramon, Clarita, and Juan are shareholders in the computer consulting firm, 3Geeks. Since the business has had several years of success, Juan is ready to leave the business and requests to be bought out. After negotiations among the owners, it is agreed that Juan will receive $300,000 for his stock and $500,000 for agreeing not to provide any computer consulting services for one-year starting October 1 of the current year. This $500,000 is the same amount Juan was guaranteed to receive each year as as salary. How should 3Geeks treat the $500,000 payment to Juan?

110. Handy Corporation assists its relocated executives by buying their homes if an acceptable sale cannot be completed before their move. Purchase is made at the appraised value. What is the nature of Handy's gain or loss on the subsequent sale?

111. Walt was convicted of murder and sent to prison for life. Walt continued to profess his innocence. His sister, Wanda, believed him. After spending three years in law school and two years gathering facts, she proved that he was innocent. Walt and Wanda assigned the book, movie, and photo rights concerning their story to Sundance Films for $500,000. How is this payment treated by Walt and Wanda?

112. Hugo was planting a tree when he unearthed 100,000 certificates of ITT bearer bonds, with a current value of $4 million. He speculated that they had been placed there by the former owner of the home (now deceased), at a time when they were worth nearly $400,000. Hugo did not sell the bonds by the end of the year. Must Hugo recognize any gross income with respect to the bonds?

113. Karla is a single parent with two children, ages 7 and 11. She is a full-time student and earns $12,000. Both of her children receive dividends and capital gains from mutual funds acquired for them by their grandparents. Karla has elected to include her children's income on her return for the kiddie tax computation. Since it is on her tax return, does her children's income affect the computation of Karla's earned income credit?

114. At gunpoint, Roger lent $2,000 from the cash register at his hardware store to four large youths who told Roger that they wanted a loan to set up their own business. Not having the phone number of any of the sprightly entrepreneurs, Roger could not recover any of the invested funds. Can Roger claim any deduction with respect to this loan? In what tax year?

115. Phyllis, a Virginia resident, owns some property in Florida. Every year, she travels to Florida (coincidentally, during baseball's spring training season) to inspect the property, initiate repairs, interview new tenants, and search for new properties in which to invest. She also attends about 20 ball games. Determine Phyllis's deductible travel expenses.

116. Bruce wanted to be an Olympic skater. His family paid $12,000 in 2006 and $14,000 in 2007 for travel and training expenses related to skating practices and competitions. Bruce made the 2008 U.S. Olympic team. The U.S. Olympic Committee is an exempt organization. How much of Bruce's expenses are deductible and when?

117. Harold installed a safe and an alarm system and bought a German Shepherd Dog to protect his vintage paperback and comic book collection. What are his deductible items?

118. Donna's and Albert's children attend a parochial grade school. The school charges $1,500 annual tuition and $200 for uniforms for Donna's children, but only $500 tuition and $100 for uniforms for Albert's children because he is a member of the congregation. Albert contributed $800 to the church this year. Can Donna and Albert withdraw amounts out of their children's Coverdell Educational Savings Accounts to pay for this private primary education? What is the amount of Albert's charitable contribution for the year?

119. Julie is a professional singer in the City Symphony Chorus (CSS). CSS requires that all members wear traditional formal wear (i.e., $500 tuxedos for the men and $300 long black gowns for the women) during performances. In addition, because of her annual $15,000 contribution to the CSS patron drive, Julie is a member of the symphony's board of directors. The board chooses the works to be performed, sites for the concerts, and the resident conductor. How much of Julie's $15,300 expenditures on behalf of the exempt orchestra this year can she deduct?

120. The farmers in Whitman County are concerned about the price they are receiving for their crops. They decide to create the Whitman County Farm Commission, whose purpose is to encourage farmers to band together when selling their crops, educate the legislators on farming issues, and instruct farmers on methods to control pests and weeds in the most environmentally safe manner. Does this organization qualify for tax-exempt status?

ADVANCED CASES

121. Helen Hanks, who lives in San Francisco, California, has just been promoted to manager of the divisional office. However, the divisional office is located in Portland, Oregon. Helen's significant other, Tom Hunt, will be moving with her to Portland. Helen's children from a previous marriage will also be joining her in Portland. The children have been living with their father in Spain for the past year.

Helen easily sells the San Francisco house in which she and Tom live. Helen is the sole owner of the house. However, she has a harder time finding the right home in Portland. Helen has to make several trips to Portland before buying a house under construction. It will not be available for occupancy for at least 20 days after she arrives in Portland. Tom accompanied Helen on the house-hunting trips to give his opinion on the houses and to look for a new job.

The actual move takes place as follows. The movers arrive on Wednesday to pack up Helen's and Tom's household items. Thursday, the movers pack up Helen's items from a storage unit located outside of the city along with her sailboat.

The movers then leave for Portland. Helen hires a college student to drive her car to Portland; the driver leaves on Friday. On Saturday, after dropping Helen at the airport for her flight to Portland, Tom leaves to drive his car to Portland via Salt Lake City, Utah, where he also visits his brother. Helen and Tom stayed in a hotel from Wednesday to Friday while still in San Francisco and upon arriving in Portland until the house is ready for occupancy. The moving company stores their household items at its warehouse until Helen and Tom are ready to move into their new house. Helen's children arrive two weeks later.

In November of the current year, Helen pays for all of the costs involved in selling the San Francisco home and moving Tom, the children, and herself to Portland. Helen's employer eventually reimburses her (in March of the next year) for 75 percent of all costs of moving the household items (Helen's and Tom's), Helen's car, and two house-hunting trips. The employer also reimburses Helen for 50 percent of the total hotel and meal costs while she and Tom were in Portland and waiting for the completion of their home. Advise Helen on the tax consequences of the above events.

122. Mark and Leslee Jones were married in 2000. Mark has an MBA from Harvard and worked in the financial markets in New York City. Leslee has a degree in Hotel Administration and worked for the Hilton Hotel until two years ago, when Mark and Leslee moved to California. They moved because Mark lost his job. He had been accused of embezzlement, and formal charges had been filed against him. However, the charges were dropped because the firm for which Mark worked did not want to be involved in a public scandal. Mark admitted the embezzlement to Leslee and promised that if they stayed married and moved, he would never embezzle again. In California, Mark obtained a job as the chief financial officer of a midsize company. His salary, while about 60 percent of his former salary, was still over $200,000.

Mark likes to gamble. He does so by betting on horse races, going to Las Vegas, playing in the stock market, and buying speculative real estate. The reason he had embezzled the money at his former job was to cover his gambling and stock market losses. While in California, he continued to bet on horse races and visit Las Vegas to gamble. Leslee accompanied him to the race tracks and to Las Vegas. Since Mark was known as a big gambler, their rooms were always provided for free, as were any costs associated with their stays in Las Vegas. Leslee would watch Mark gamble for a while, get bored, and then go to see shows or go shopping. Leslee liked to shop and spent thousands of dollars at a time.

As to the investment speculations, Leslee did not help in the decisions to purchase stock or real estate. However, she did sign all purchase-and-sale agreements for real estate, as California is a community property state. Any proceeds from the sales were paid to both Mark and Leslee. She endorsed all checks, which were deposited in their joint checking account. Leslee and Mark both wrote checks out of this account. What Leslee did not know is that Mark had a separate bank account into which he deposited much of his gambling winnings and stock gains.

In the current year, the Jones's prior two tax returns are audited and material omissions are found. The embezzled money never had been reported, gambling gains were substantially understated, and gains on the sale of stock and real estate were omitted from the returns. Shortly after the notice from the IRS as to their findings regarding the audits, Leslee filed for divorce, for obvious reasons.

What tax-related advice do you have for Mark and Leslee? Will Leslee qualify for innocent spouse protection from the tax liabilities? She claims that she had no knowledge of any of the underreporting on their tax returns. Mark and Leslee always used a CPA to prepare their returns.

123. The Griffins were driving in a snow blizzard when a truck hit them as it was sliding off the road. The truck driver received minor injuries, but Wanda and Frank Smith died at the scene of the accident. Amy, their eight-year-old daughter was in the back seat and seriously injured. Amy will eventually recover, but it will take a long time and there will be some lasting physical damage. Frank and Wanda have a will that leaves all their assets to Amy. These assets include their house and its contents, investments, traditional IRAs, 401(k) retirement funds, and a life insurance policy with Amy as the beneficiary. In case of their death, Wanda's only sister, May, is to be guardian of Amy. Frank and Wanda request a trust to be set up for Amy to control the money she will receive.

May filed a lawsuit against the driver of the truck, the company for which he works, and against Frank and Wanda's car insurance company. The accident was determined to be 90 percent the fault of the truck driver and 10 percent the fault of Frank, who was driving. The jury awarded Amy a large sum for the death of her parents and to cover Amy's current and future medical costs. Also received were amounts to cover the medical and funeral costs for Wanda and Frank. Amy received compensation for any mental anguish and for the partial loss of use of her right hand and arm. May was awarded a sum for the loss of her sister, Wanda.

May contacted your supervisor regarding the car accident, the deaths of Frank and Wanda, and the lawsuit. Please advise May on the current tax treatment of the inheritance that Amy is receiving as well as the compensation that Amy and May received from the lawsuit.

CHAPTER 7

Citators and Tax Periodicals

LEARNING OBJECTIVES

- Recognize the importance of citators in the tax research process.
- Comprehend the basic and advanced functionality of citators.
- Use the indexing systems in each of the most popular tax citators.
- Recognize reference conventions and standard abbreviations used in tax citators.
- Update research by using materials in tax citators.
- Identify the comparative strengths and weaknesses of the main tax citators.
- Recognize the usefulness of tax periodicals and their role in the tax research.
- Identify the comparative strengths and weaknesses of the various tax periodicals.
- Use indexes to tax periodicals to facilitate locating pertinent journal articles.

CHAPTER OUTLINE

Besides Confronting The Tremendous volume of tax law, tax practitioners face the added dilemma that the tax law is in a constant state of change. Each year new laws are passed that amend the Internal Revenue Code and new Regulations are issued to provide guidance and revise interpretations of the Code. Every day administrative pronouncements are issued and court cases are decided. This daily change in the tax law makes it very difficult for a tax practitioner to know what law is current and what has been superseded or overruled. This chapter provides the methodology for ensuring that the tax laws, cases, and administrative documents supporting a client's tax position are up-to-date.

Recall from the research process explained in , an evaluation of the relevant primary authority must occur before conclusions can be developed. The evaluation of tax authority includes not only determining whether the authority is still valid but also making judgments regarding the precedential value of the primary sources. How citators help in this evaluation process is the focus of this chapter.

Citators

Law relies heavily on the precedential value of cases, which can be defined as the legal authority established by the case. The legal authority of prior cases is considered when judges are issuing opinions in subsequent cases that contain similar facts or legal issues.

Tax law also relies on the **precedential value** of tax cases and administrative rulings for guidance. The tax law attempts to maintain consistency in the treatment of similar issues so taxpayers can anticipate the acceptable application of the law to their own situations. Each appellate opinion sets a precedent that applies to later cases.

What Is a Citator?

Tax law is in a constant state of flux. The Code is changed frequently by passage of Federal legislation. Regulations are proposed, finalized, and withdrawn. Administrative rulings are issued, modified, superseded, and revoked or made obsolete by changes in the tax law. A case decided at one level may be appealed with the higher court overruling the lower court's decision. A court may see a flaw in the reasoning it or another (equal or lower) court used in deciding an earlier case, or a court may use a different line of reasoning to reach a distinct decision in an area previously reviewed by other courts. When a court takes any action that relies on, rejects, or affects the holding of another case, the acting court refers to the affected case in its opinion. All of this results in a tangle of inter-references among a vast number of cases.

Since practitioners must rely on tax law that is constantly evolving, they must determine if subsequent events have affected the legal standing of the sources upon which they rely. Thus, they need a tool to help them ascertain which legal sources provide strong precedents and which have little or no value. The tax professional could follow the reference threads from case to case or ruling to ruling, but this would be extremely tedious and would only identify earlier cases and rulings and not later sources that may have altered or overruled the case or ruling of interest. This latter information is critical for determining the validity of the document of interest. Fortunately, citators provide this service by following the threads in subsequent sources and summarize, in shorthand form, where the threads lead and what they mean.

A citator is a tool through which a tax researcher can learn the history of a legal source and evaluate the strength of its holdings. Before a researcher relies on the opinion in a case or analysis in a ruling (or even commits the time to read the document), it is important to ascertain its legal standing. Thus, when a case or ruling relevant to a client's tax situation is found, it is imperative that a citator be examined to determine how later legal sources have considered the document of interest. Since the legal profession has long recognized the need for this specialized information, citators were developed in the late 1800s, 100 years before computer searches were possible.

To avoid confusion, it is important to learn the specific terminology that describes references between cases. When one case refers to another case, it **cites** the case. The case making reference to the other case is called the **citing case.** The case that is referenced is the **cited case.** The citing case will contain the name of the cited case and where the cited case can be found. The reference is called its **citation.**

A **citator** is a service that indexes cited cases, gives their full citations, and lists the citing cases and where each citing case can be found. A significant older case, one that establishes an important legal principle, may have been cited by hundreds of other cases. Thus, its entry in a citator would be extremely long and complex. A very recent case, or one examining a narrow aspect of the law, would have few cites, if any.

A citator will not provide all types of information about a case or a ruling. For instance, it does not guide the researcher to documents related to a case or ruling that do not specifically cite it. Also, citators may not always indicate when a case or ruling is no longer valid because of changes in the Code, unless the Code itself specifically identifies the case or a subsequent document makes a specific reference to the Code overriding the case. This is because citators are created by searching primary sources for cites to the case or ruling. A researcher could perform the same search by using the case name or its official cite in a keyword search of databases containing all primary sources. Without access to a tax service, you might try a simple Google or Bing search on the case name. However, sifting through the results would be an arduous task and very inefficient.

Given the tremendous number of court cases and rulings issued annually, the citator is a vital tool in the research process. If the primary sources have not been checked through a citator, the research process is not complete. Thus, only careless or improperly trained practitioners rely on legal sources that have not been checked through a citator.

The various commercial citators organize the lists of citing cases in distinctive schemes. Depending on the researcher's purpose, one citator may be more appropriate than another. For example, one citator may list only citations that have a major impact on the logic or holding of the cited case. Another may list all citations. A researcher, initially checking to make sure a case has not been overruled, would prefer the former. The citations may be annotated to indicate the type of impact the citing case has on the cited case (e.g., modified, overruled, or followed). A trial court case may be appealed, and each appellate court that hears the case creates additional citations. Because each of these decisions may be cited in other documents, a citator can organize cases by jurisdictional level. As each citator is discussed in this chapter, you should consider its suitability for specific research applications. Citators are not a one-size-fits-all type of research tool.

It is important for the researcher to consider a case in context, to trace its judicially derived decision, and to monitor the reaction of subsequent court cases. This is even more important when the opinion is innovative. By using a citator properly, the researcher can review subsequent courts' reactions and determine the strength of the precedent established by the opinion. Before turning to a case, however, the Code and Regulations—the foundation for tax research—should be read and analyzed. Remember, cases and rulings are reviewed to provide guidance in interpreting the statutory and administrative tax law.

Commercial Citators

Of the four citators examined in this chapter, three have editions that exclusively cover tax cases—Commerce Clearing House (CCH), Research Institute of America (RIA), and Shepard's—and one includes tax cases in its law citator—Westlaw. The accuracy of the case citations is very important; consequently, this will be the focus of the citators review in this chapter.

One of the advantages of the CCH and RIA citators is that they allow the researcher to enter case names or citations. Shepard's and Westlaw, on the other hand, accept only citations. All of the citators furnish guidance or have templates for entering citations. The citations reproduced by CCH *are general*, directing the researcher to the first page of the citing case; the other citators give **local citations** (also called pinpoint citations), directing the researcher to the exact page where the cited case is mentioned in the citing case.

For example, *Gregory v. Helvering* (293 US 465) is cited in the Second Circuit Court of Appeals case *Bausch & Lomb Optical Co.*, on page 78 in the Federal Reporter 2d Series case reporter. The CCH citation indicating this citing is *Bausch & Lomb Optical Co.*, 267 F2d 75 (first page of the *Bausch & Lomb Optical Co.* case), whereas the RIA, Shepard's, and Westlaw citators have the cite as *Bausch & Lomb Optical Co.*, 267 F2d 78. Having citations that pinpoint the discussion of the case of interest can be a real time saver when the citing case is long.

Illustrative Citator Example

An actual case, *David A. Gitlitz, Et Ux., et al. v. Commissioner of Internal Revenue* (531 U.S. 206; 121 S. Ct. 701; 87 AFTR2d 2001-417; 2001-1 USTC ¶50147; 2001 U.S. LEXIS 638), will be utilized to demonstrate the various features of the citators. This case involves the proper effect on the shareholders' stock basis when an insolvent S corporation receives a discharge of indebtedness. The insolvent S corporation had two shareholders,

Philip Winn and David Gitlitz, both of whom were assessed deficiencies by the IRS for the tax years 1991 and 1992.

The case has an interesting judicial history. The court of original jurisdiction was the Tax Court, which found for the IRS, in 1998. Winn is listed as the first petitioner in the Tax Court case, and so his name appears as the "case name" in citators. In 1999, the case was appealed to the Tenth Circuit Court of Appeals, which affirmed the Tax Court. Gitlitz is the first petitioner in this case and thus is the "case name" for this decision. The Supreme Court granted certiorari to hear the *Gitlitz* case in 2000 and decided the case in 2001 by reversing the prior decisions. Then the Supreme Court case was overruled in 2002 by Congressional legislation (Job Creation and Worker Assistance Act). The Act added § 108(d)(7)(A) to the Code, ensuring that the original treatment suggested by the Tax Court became law.

It is important that you attempt the illustrative citing project using the citators available to you. The procedural knowledge necessary to become an effective researcher can only be acquired through hands-on practice. The remainder of this section of the chapter is designed to guide you through the basic commercial services and is not a substitute for you actually conducting the precedential value verification. Using the citators as you follow the text presentation is a highly effective method of learning this material.

Shepard's Citators

Shepard's was the first major publisher to truly understand the commercial value of citators. It became the leading publisher of citators and thus its name has become synonymous with the act of citing. In fact, the process of evaluating the validity of a case and locating additional authority is called **Shepardizing** a case. Many attorneys view Shepard's as *the* citator service and all other services as mere imitations. This may have been true at one point in time, but the current competitors have just as much to offer as the "original."

The **Shepard's Citators (Shepard's)** are currently available in print, on CD-ROM, on wireless mobile devices, and exclusively through LexisNexis since the late 1990s. LexisNexis has even created a Shepard's App for iPhones. Just enter the citation and retrieve the Shepard's analysis or the case itself. A current account with LexisNexis is, of course, necessary to use this free App.

Shepard's Citators Shepard's is the only major tax citator whose printed version is organized by case reporter series. Accordingly, the practitioner must know the court reporter citation for the case of interest. Since proper document abbreviation must be entered, Shepard's provides an exhaustive list of examples of proper citation formats with templates for every possible document that can be Shepardized. However, when only the name of a case is known, the lists of proper citation formats are of no help. Using a service such as LexisNexis Academic, which allows the name of the taxpayers be entered in retrieving the case lessens this problem. From the case document, access to Shepard's is available. With the LexisNexis Tax Center service, a keyword search using the name of the taxpayer is performed to retrieve the case. As with Academic, the document offers access to Shepard's at the top of the screen as shown in (Arrow 1).

There are two ways to locate a Shepard's citation format, either via Find Citations or Browse Citations. When using the Find Citations tool, the publication name (reporter for cases) is entered, as shown in Exhibit 7-2. Within the Browse Citations tool, there are so many sample entries that they are indexed themselves. Once the document type of interest is found, clicking on its associated abbreviation displays a template for entering the citation. This is also true for the retrieved abbreviations found in the Find Citations (Exhibit 7-2). The templates are set up in the standard "volume, reporter, page" format.

EXHIBIT 7-1: LexisNexis Tax Center Case Document

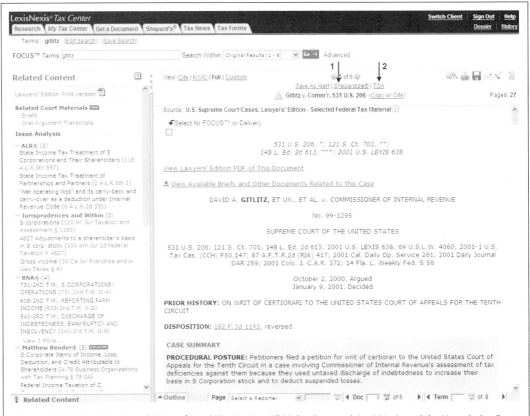

EXHIBIT 7-2: Shepard's Find Citations

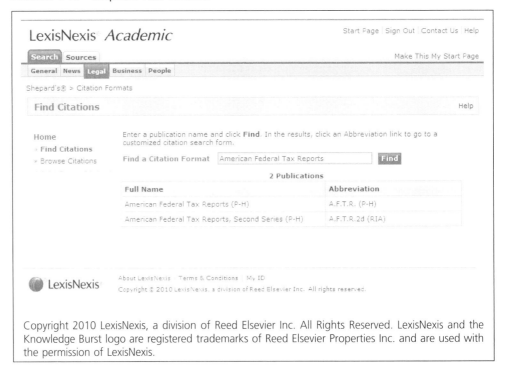

If the researcher knows these three elements of the citation, then the program is forgiving of punctuation and capitalization variations.

Shepard's displays the following information for the case of interest (most of which are visible in Exhibit 7-3):

- Case evaluation symbol (Arrow 1)
- Case citation in proper format and Parallel citations (Arrow 3)
- Shepard's Summary (Arrow 4)
- All prior case history (Arrow 5)
- Treatment by citing cases (not visible)
- Citations to secondary citing sources such as law reviews (not visible)

In examining Exhibit 7-3, the first item listed is the case citation in proper format. Clicking on the citation produces the LexisNexis reporter full-text case document. Each commercial reporter provides information that varies by publisher before the text of the actual case, which is the same in each reporter. For example, LexisNexis includes a case summary (Procedural Posture and Overview) as well as headnotes and core terms. **Headnotes** are the paragraphs in which the editors of the court reporter summarize the court's holdings on each issue of the case.

Since the editors of each reporter analyze the legal points of a case differently, the headnotes for a specific case will not likely correspond across the various reporters. Tax cases may

EXHIBIT 7-3: Shepard's Unrestricted Citator List

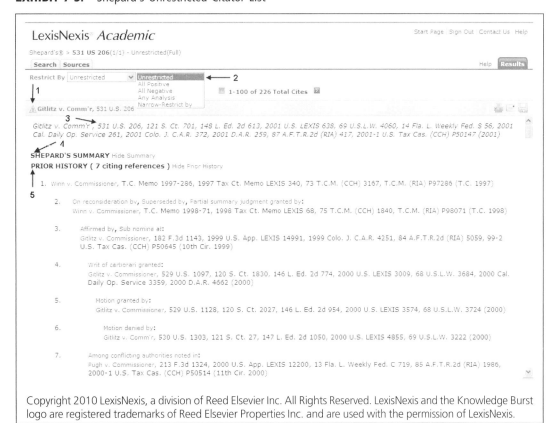

EXHIBIT 7-4:   Shepard's Evaluative Symbols

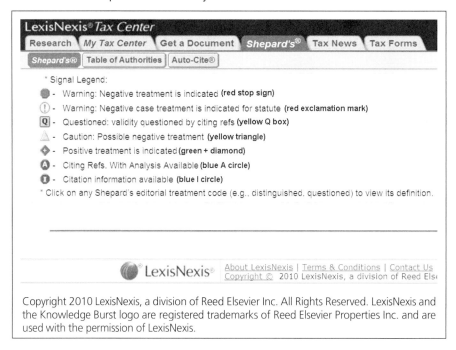

Copyright 2010 LexisNexis, a division of Reed Elsevier Inc. All Rights Reserved. LexisNexis and the Knowledge Burst logo are registered trademarks of Reed Elsevier Properties Inc. and are used with the permission of LexisNexis.

address several issues, and the headnotes help the researcher identify how their particular issue of interest was treated. If the researcher is examining the case document and wants to Shepardize it, links to Shepard's are easily accessible as Exhibit 7-1 (Arrow 1) illustrates.

Preceding the case citation is an easy-to-recognize symbolic evaluation. This enables the researcher to quickly determine the legal standing of a case at-a-glance. Note that the *Gitlitz* case has a yellow triangle symbol (Exhibit 7-3, Arrow 1). The symbols used by Shepard's to indicate the precedential status of the case are given in Exhibit 7-4.

While the warning evaluation is useful, it does not indicate what the negative analysis related to *Gitlitz* is nor does it indicate for which of the 19 headnote issues identified by LexisNexis had the negative analysis. It could be that the negative analysis is for one of the issues in the case that is not of interest to the researcher. Thus, the researcher cannot determine whether the issue in headnote 1 regarding the increase in basis for cancellation of debt was overturned by changes in the tax law.

Shepard's furnishes an extensive list of parallel citations (Exhibit 7-3, Arrow 3). It includes all of the government and major commercial citations along with several unofficial or lesser-known reporter versions. Parallel citations all refer to the same case. Accordingly, the text of the case is the same regardless of which citation is utilized to retrieve the case and, thus, it is not necessary for researchers to list every parallel citation in file memos or client letters; one citation is usually sufficient. LexisNexis citations are not supported with templates by CCH and RIA, and tax professionals are generally not familiar with them.

The prior **direct history** developed by Shepard's gives the complete judicial proceeding for the case of interest (Exhibit 7-3, Arrow 5). For example, the prior direct history of the *Gitlitz* case starts with its original Tax Court Memorandum opinion. On appeal, the Tenth Circuit Court of Appeals affirmed the Tax Court's decision for the government. The taxpayers appealed to the Supreme Court, and the motion for writ of certiorari was granted. The Supreme Court reversed the decision and remanded the case back to the Tenth

Circuit, which vacated its prior decision and remanded the case to the Tax Court with directions for the Tax Court to enter judgment in favor of the taxpayers. Consequently, cases such as this may have prior direct histories with more than two lower court citations when the case has been remanded or other judicial proceedings were required.

The researcher can restrict the citing cases retrieved by Shepard's to all positive, all negative, or any analysis, or the restriction can be customized by type of court or head-note paragraph number (Exhibit 7-3, Arrow 2). This allows the researcher to quickly locate citing cases that address the particular tax issue of interest and in the geographical location of the taxpayer. In addition to the citation of the citing case (and its parallel citations), Shepard's hyperlinks the specific page where the citing case discusses the case of interest and indicates which headnote is linked to the discussion.

Since the numbered headnotes for a specific case do not necessarily correspond among the various reporters, when using headnote numbers to restrict retrieved cases the researcher must be cognizant of which court reporter headnote numbers are pertinent to each citator service. Shepard's also evaluates the discussion of the citing case and categorizes its treatment (e.g., affirmed, cited by, criticized, distinguished, explained, followed) and the operation (e.g., amended, extended, revoked) of the citing cases. These evaluated citing cases are listed beginning with any Supreme Court citing cases and continuing with Federal jurisdiction (Appeals Courts in number order and then District Courts), followed by the U.S. Court of Federal Claims, Tax Court, various state courts, statutes, law reviews and periodicals, treatises, and other secondary sources. Within each of these citing categories, the citations are listed in reverse chronological order (most recent first).

Many researchers prefer to start their analysis of a case with the most recent citing cases and work backward to earlier cases. Using this method, they can quickly identify the current status of the cited case. For example, a steady stream of recent favorable references probably indicates that the precedent of the original case is still valid and strong, whereas either a list of recent negative comments or a scarcity of references may indicate a weak or out-of-date decision. The citator portion of a research project is complete when the researcher is satisfied that the status of the case is sufficiently confirmed.

At this point, some of the citing cases should be examined, especially if the cases found initially support the client's position but the facts are somewhat different. The citing cases may provide support with more similar facts. Hence, those citations designated as "case reconciled," indicating that their facts or opinions are different from those of the cited case and require reconciliation, should be consulted. If the initial cases found have holdings adverse to a client's position, the practitioner should search for cases marked "case distinguished" to identify what factors are relevant to the issuance of an adverse opinion.

The "distinguished" cases usually have facts that are actually different from those of the cited case, thus supporting a different holding. Some of these facts may resemble the facts of the practitioner's client, and therefore they provide the desired support. Similarly, a case denoted as "citing generally" limits the holding of the cited case to a narrow set of facts. This may occur when a higher court has ruled differently on a case with somewhat similar facts or when there has been a change in the tax law. Thus, the holding of the cited case may be inapplicable to the client's factual situation.

Shepard's Table of Authorities Shepard's **Table of Authorities (TOA)** is a type of citator service, but it has a different purpose than regular citators. Rather than furnishing a history of a case and a list of cases citing it, the TOA lists the cases that are cited by the case of interest and to what extent it relied on these cases. This saves the researcher from having to enter each of these cases in the regular citator and consequently it is a tremendous time-saving tool. The TOA is easily accessed from any case document (Exhibit 7-1,

Arrow 2). For our research, the TOA in Exhibit 7-5 lists the cases the Supreme Court cited and relied upon in reaching its opinion in *Gitlitz*.

Examining the cases cited in *Gitlitz* is useful in tracing the logic of the court's decision, whether or not *Gitlitz* supports our client's preferred tax treatment. If *Gitlitz* relies on other cases with negative or weak histories, then some of the reasoning in *Gitlitz* may be flawed. Accordingly, a case that itself has no negative history when checked in the regular citator may appear to be sound law when, in fact, it may be weak as precedent because it relies on cases that have been overruled or have other negative connotations. Thus, less reliance should be placed on the case's findings in this situation.

The TOA lists the cited cases by jurisdiction (e.g., Supreme Court, Circuit Court of Appeals, District Court). For each of these cases, the TOA furnishes the same information that the researcher would obtain if each case was separately checked through the regular Shepard's citator. Thus, for each cited case, the TOA lists the full case name, and its citation (with parallel citations). It also provides an assessment of how the case of interest evaluated the cited cases and the page in the case of interest on which the cited case is discussed. The cited cases themselves are evaluated based on their history and assigned a Shepard's at-a-glance symbol (stop sign, triangle) indicating their current status. As indicated in Exhibit 7-5 (circles), The Supreme Court in *Gitlitz* relied on cases that have been questioned or have negative treatment.

EXHIBIT 7-5:   Shepard's Table of Authorities

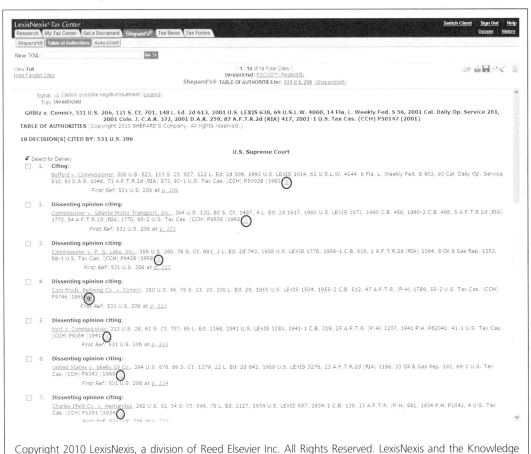

LexisNexis

Besides the Shepard's Citators, LexisNexis contains the Auto-Cite citator and the LEXCITE search system. Each of these is a useful tool for the researcher when verifying a case's value as precedent.

Auto-Cite   LexisNexis created its own citator, **Auto-Cite**, before it acquired Shepard's. Auto-Cite's primary objectives are to provide absolute accurate citations, and to do so within 24 hours of receipt of each case. Not only is Auto-Cite beneficial in determining whether a case opinion is still good law, it also allows researchers to check the standing of Revenue Rulings and Revenue Procedures.

The information retrieved by Auto-Cite includes the correct spelling of the case name, its official citation, the year of the decision, and all official and most unofficial parallel cites. The prior and subsequent case history shows the full litigation history of a case, whereas the subsequent treatment history focuses on opinions that have lessened or negated the case's precedential value. Thus, the service lists citing cases that have overruled, criticized, or in some manner devalued the case of interest. To help quickly analyze whether a case is still good law, Auto-Cite uses at-a-glance symbol designations similar to those of Shepard's. Finally, an interesting feature of Auto-Cite not offered by Shepard's is a listing of documents that have had their precedential value negatively affected by the case of interest.

Auto-Cite is updated at least daily, and it provides accurate information on cases that affect the strength of the cited case. Whereas Shepard's focus is on furnishing a comprehensive direct and **indirect history** of the case, Auto-Cite is a selective list of citing cases that have a significant impact on the validity of the case of interest.

LEXCITE   When researchers want to search the most current legal documents for references to their case of interest, **LEXCITE** is the tool to choose. LexisNexis prides itself on LEXCITE being even more current than Shepard's. As with Shepard's and Auto-Cite, the citation for the case (not the name) must be entered in the standard "volume-reporter-page" convention. LEXCITE ascertains the case's parallel citations, and then it searches for all of the embedded cite references in documents including case law, the Code, Federal Register, IRS pronouncements, and secondary sources such as law reviews and journals. Once the case cite has been located in a document, LEXCITE will identify and highlight subsequent references.

The LEXCITE feature actually searches the full text of the documents available in LexisNexis, which covers more than 1,700 reporters and authorities. The reason for this full text search is because LEXCITE uses the same searching mechanism as a keyword search. Accordingly, the researcher is able to see the references to the case of interest in context and make a personal determination of how the case was evaluated by the document's author. One limitation should be mentioned, however; LEXCITE will not find references to case names only—a court reporter citation must be present for LEXCITE to identify the document as a source.

An advantage of using LEXCITE is that the practitioner can customize the search to retrieve documents addressing only a particular point of law in the cited case by using other search terms in addition to the citation. The jurisdiction, such as only Circuit Court of Appeals, can be specified. Date restrictions are very helpful when updating previous research and one could examine all of the decisions written by a specific judge. This ability to customize the search is particularly useful when assisting a client in litigating a tax issue.

Westlaw Citator System

As discussed in Chapter 6, Westlaw is structured for legal research. It was designed by attorneys for attorneys. Since court cases are essential sources in most areas of law, taxation included, the citation applications are the centerpiece of the Westlaw service. The Westlaw's citators are also very effective for validating statutes, regulations, and administrative rulings. The citators are available in WestlawNext (Westlaw's new platform) as well as Westlaw. While the focus is on Westlaw, differences in the WestlawNext presentation are indicated.

KeyCite   **KeyCite** is available from the opening screen, the always visible toolbar, and most specialized tabs in Westlaw. As with Shepard's Citator, the KeyCite system is designed to be flexible as to citation formats. Also like Shepard's, retrieving cases by taxpayer name is not supported. Most citation formats are accepted as long as the general form of "volume-reporter-page" is used. If the proper document abbreviation is not known, the Publication List in Exhibit 7-6 (Arrow 3) should be reviewed. Since the list contains more than 5,000 documents, it can be scanned by either entering words contained in the document title or entering letters or words with which the document title starts (Arrow 1). As in Exhibit 7-6 (Arrow 2), the researcher must enter the citation in the KeyCite box, using the abbreviation found in the publication. If the researcher is viewing the full text of the case, clicking on the toolbar KeyCite will automatically insert the citation into the search box to facilitate the search.

Westlaw offers more user-friendly methods of finding and citing a case through the Find & Print feature located in the toolbar (Exhibit 7-7, Arrow 1) and the Tax Tab. If the citation is available, it can be entered in the Find by Citation box (Arrow 2). However, when only the taxpayer's name in a court case is known, the case can be retrieved by using Find a Case by Party Name in Exhibit 7-7 (Arrow 3). The taxpayer's name is entered in box 1, and the jurisdiction and/or topic may be used to narrow the search in Selection 2.

EXHIBIT 7-6:   Westlaw KeyCite Publication list

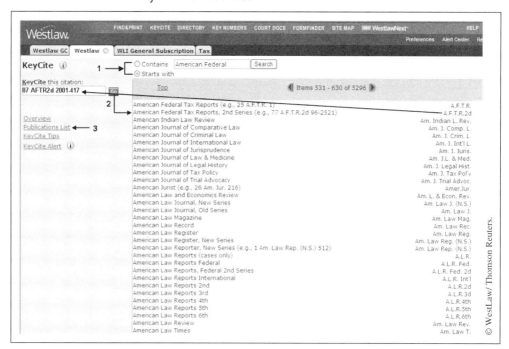

Once the case is found, KeyCite will access the citator information. Find & Print also offers a Publication List (Arrow 4) if the appropriate abbreviations are not known. Clicking on one of these abbreviations displays a template for entering the citation and gives an example of the proper format. The KeyCite available through the Tax tab is the most user-friendly. It automatically displays templates for entering citations, which eliminates the need for determining the abbreviations for any tax documents.

With WestlawNext, the citation or taxpayer name for a case can be entered in the Query box on the opening screen (Exhibit 6-15,). From the retrieved case in Exhibit 7-8, KeyCite is available at the top of the screen (Arrow 1).

History Display   Visible in the left window of Exhibit 7-9, the KeyCite citator offers several display options to the researcher. The current display is Full History, which includes the Direct History, Negative Indirect Citing References, and Court Documents. The *Winn/Gitlitz* case's chronological progression through the courts is listed in the Direct History section of Exhibit 7-9. This progression can also be graphically displayed (Exhibit 7-9 above Arrow 1). This is particularly helpful with a complicated case history such as *Gitlitz*, where after the Supreme Court decision, it is remanded and the lower court decision is vacated. The graph makes sense of the progression. Observe that all of the cases in Direct History have been evaluated as to their precedential value using brief descriptions and KeyCite symbols. Although the symbols of KeyCite are different from Shepard's, their meanings are similar. KeyCite's symbols with their meanings are listed in Exhibit 7-10.

After the Direct History, KeyCite presents the Negative Citing References section, which includes citing cases that adversely affect the precedential value of the case of

EXHIBIT 7-7: Westlaw Find & Print

interest. Phrases indicate whether the cases have criticized, distinguished, limited, questioned, or overruled the cited case's logic or holding. (See triangles in Exhibit 7-9.) Note, in Exhibit 7-9, KeyCite does not indicate that the *Gitlitz* case has been superseded by statute. Rather, it indicates a negative indirect history exists, but it has not been overruled. While being superseded by changes in the tax law is not technically being overruled in the legal sense, the yellow flag does not indicate the true danger of relying on the *Gitlitz* case.

Besides evaluating whether negative citing cases are still good law, KeyCite determines the extent to which citing cases discuss the cited case of interest. This feature is unique to KeyCite and greatly facilitates determining which citing cases should be reviewed. The symbols range from four stars to one star; with four denoting an extended examination of the case and one denoting a brief reference (Exhibit 7-10).

The quotation mark symbol is added if the citing case has quoted the cited case, as is the situation in Exhibit 7-9 with the Nathel case (circled). In WestlawNext the stars have been replaced with the Depth indicator, which also ranges from four to one boxes (see Exhibit 7-11). Four boxes mean the same as four stars. Quotation mark symbols are still added, as seen in Exhibit 7-11. In comparing Exhibits 7-10 and 7-11, the WestlawNext presentation appears more organized and less cluttered. Also, WestlawNext references can be sorted by depth of coverage or by currency of the citing cases (Arrow 1).

Citing References To retrieve a comprehensive list of citing cases, select the **Citing References** option Exhibit 7-9 (Arrow 1). KeyCite retrieved over 700 documents for the *Gitlitz* case, almost all of which are positive cites. The listing starts with the negative cases that are the same as those listed in the Full History. The Positive Cases section is organized by the depth of coverage, starting with the four-star examinations and leading

EXHIBIT 7-8:   WestlawNext Document Screen

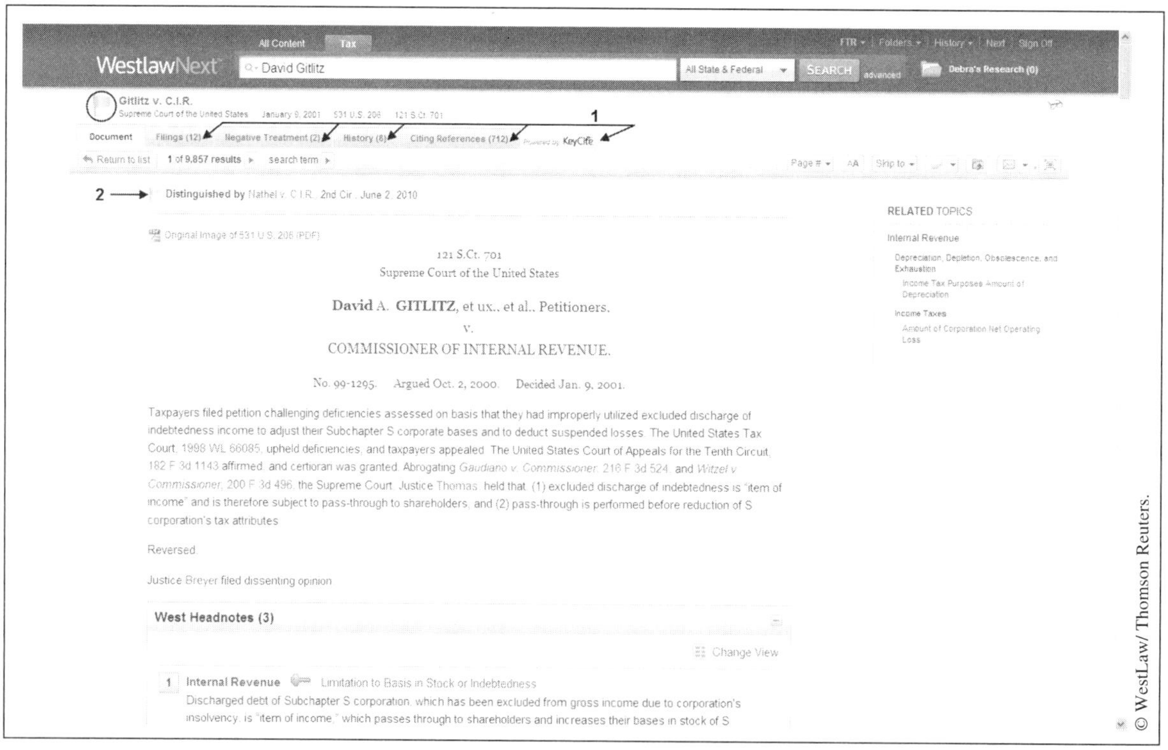

EXHIBIT 7-9: Westlaw KeyCite Full History

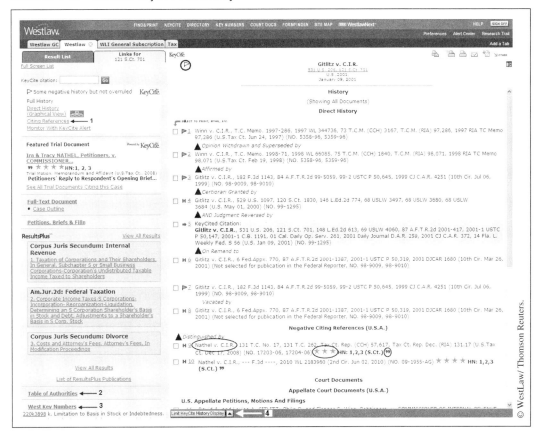

EXHIBIT 7-10: Westlaw KeyCite Evaluative Symbols

to the one-star citing cases. After cases are Administrative Materials, such as IRS Rulings and Congressional provisions. The last section contains secondary source references by journals, law reviews, Bureau of National Affairs (BNA) Portfolios, tax services, and so on. Since the number of documents retrieved can be overwhelming, the Limit KeyCite Display option (Exhibit 7-9, Arrow 4) allows the researcher to limit those retrieved by headnotes (key numbers), location, jurisdiction, date, type of document, and depth of treatment (number of stars).

SPOTLIGHT ON TAXATION

Supreme Court Justices

The U.S. Supreme Court has nine justices who are nominated by the President and approved by the Senate. Approximately 8,000 petitions are filed with the Supreme Court in the course of one year. In addition, some 1,200 applications of various kinds are filed each year that are acted upon by a single justice. As Supreme Court Justices are appointed for life, the ability to nominate a Supreme Court justice accords the President tremendous power to influence future Supreme Court decisions. This is especially true if nominee is relatively young (by Supreme Court standards), such as Chief Justice John Roberts who was only 50 when nominated by President George W. Bush, and Elena Kagan and Sonia Sotomayor, who were 50 and 55 respectively when nominated by President Barack Obama. The following is a list of the Supreme Court justices as of December, 2010:

Name	Date and Place of Birth	Nominating President	Year Installed
John G. Roberts, Jr (Chief Justice).	January 27, 1955 Buffalo, New York	G. W. Bush	2005
Antonin Scalia	March 11, 1936 Trenton, New Jersey	Reagan	1986
Anthony M. Kennedy	July 23, 1936 Sacramento, California	Reagan	1988
Clarence Thomas	June 28, 1948 Pin Point community, Georgia (near Savannah)	G. H. W. Bush	1991
Ruth Bader Ginsburg	March 15, 1933 Brooklyn, New York	W. Clinton	1993
Stephen Breyer	August 15, 1938 San Francisco, California	W. Clinton	1994
Samuel A. Alito	April 1, 1950 Trenton, New Jersey	G. W. Bush	2006
Sonia Sotomayor	June 24, 1954 Bronx, New York	Obama	2009
Elena Kagan	April 28, 1960 New York, New York	Obama	2010

EXHIBIT 7-11:   WestlawNext KeyCite

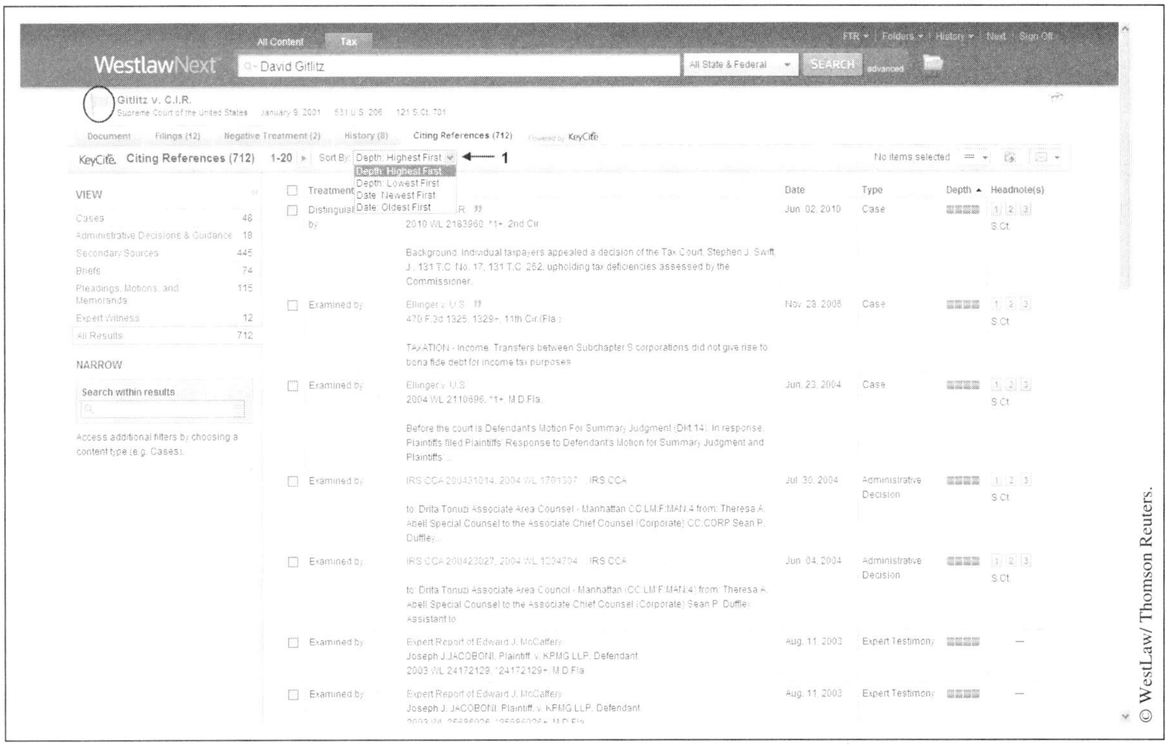

© WestLaw/Thomson Reuters.

The West headnote system has a particularly valuable feature for finding law, the **West Key Number System**. The points of law articulated in a case are classified by the editors into Key Numbers that create an extensive system for organizing case law called the West Key Number Digest. The key number for a topic of interest can be found by drilling down through the Key Numbers alphabetical list. The West Key Number for the *Gitlitz* case is 220K3898, which has been added to Exhibit 7-9 (highlighted below Arrow 3).

ResultsPlus   As discussed in Chapter 6, **ResultsPlus** offers analytical materials relevant to the research. For the *Gitlitz* case, the ResultsPlus in the left window of Exhibit 7-9, suggests discussions of the Code related to the issues in *Gitlitz*. The materials appear in legal encyclopedias (Corpus Juris Secundum and American Jurisprudence), legal reports (American Law Reports), treatises, law reviews, and topical publications such as the BNA Portfolios and Mertens.

Table of Authorities   The Westlaw Table of Authorities (TOA) (Exhibit 7-9, Arrow 2) performs the same function as the Shepard's version (Exhibit 7-5). However, the Westlaw TOA reports more information. As Exhibit 7-12 demonstrates, not only does the TOA list the cases used in supporting the reasoning in *Gitlitz* (with page numbers), Westlaw also denotes how much *Gitlitz* discussed the case by using its four-star depth of treatment symbols. Further, Westlaw identifies which cases *Gitlitz* quotes through its quotation marks symbol. The evaluation symbols are also provided for the cited cases.

EXHIBIT 7-12: Westlaw KeyCite Table of Authorities

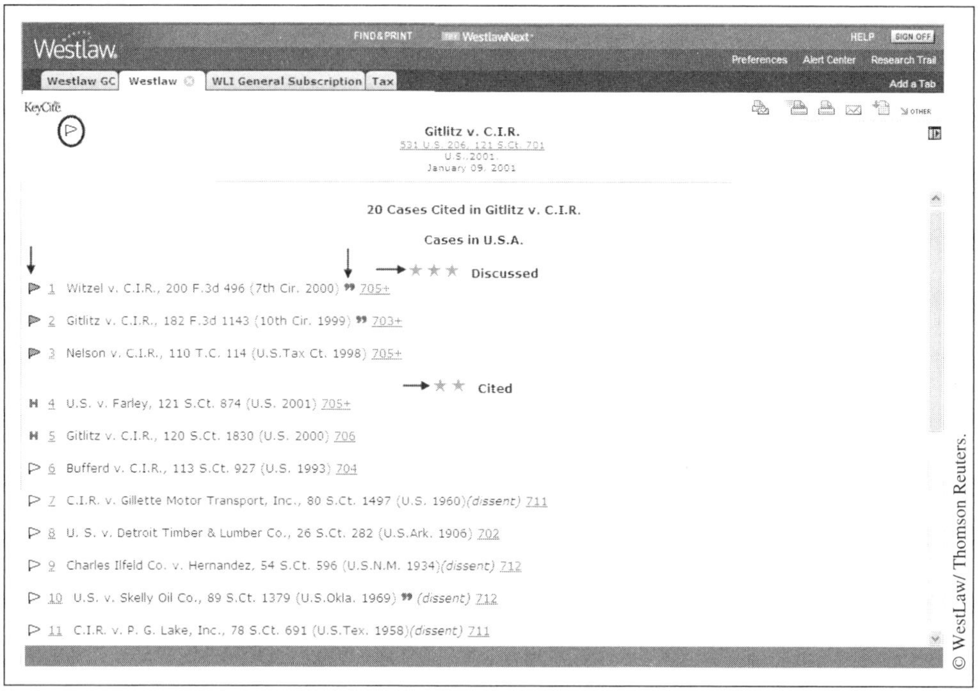

RIA Citator 2nd

While Shepard's and KeyCite citators cover all types of court cases and administrative pronouncements, The Research Institute of America **(RIA) Citator 2nd** focuses strictly on tax documents. This major difference between the Citator 2nd and the legal citators is beneficial to a tax researcher because it narrows the list of citations retrieved to only those that are based on the tax issues in the case. The Citator 2nd's tax coverage is comprehensive including the District Court, Court of Federal Claims, Court of Appeals, and Supreme Court cases reported in RIA's tax court reporter series, American Federal Tax Reporter series (AFTR and AFTR2d), and the Tax Court cases (regular, memorandum, and unpublished), as well as administrative pronouncements (hereafter referred to as rulings) issued by the IRS and Treasury Decisions.

When the plaintiff in a tax case is the U.S. Government, Commissioner of Internal Revenue, Secretary of the Treasury, or an IRS employee; the RIA Citator 2nd does not catalog the case under the plaintiff's name, as is the traditional legal convention. This is because there are thousands of cases in which Eisner, Helvering, Burnet, or other Commissioners or Secretaries of the Treasury initiated the litigation. Rather, the RIA Citator 2nd catalogs all cases by the taxpayer's name. This convention greatly facilitates searching by case name.

Using RIA Citator 2nd The Citator 2nd is accessible from the opening Checkpoint screen. Exhibit 7-13 combines two Checkpoint screens to show the templates for searches by taxpayer (case) name or citation (Arrows 2 and 3). Keyword searches are also supported. For case name searches, the court may be indicated through a supplied list. This is an optional entry; thus, if only the taxpayer name is known, the search can

EXHIBIT 7-13: RIA Citator 2nd Case Name & Citation Templates

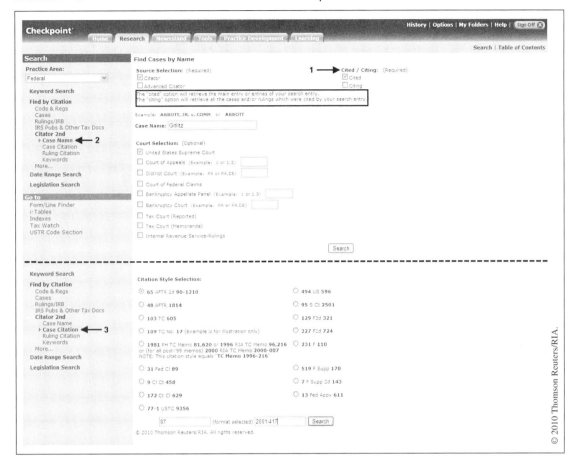

© 2010 Thomson Reuters/RIA.

still be successful. When the citation is known, templates ensure that citations are entered in the proper format.

The researcher must choose (Exhibit 7-13, Arrow 1) whether to retrieve a list of cases and rulings that cite the case of interest (Cited) or a list of cases and rulings cited by the case of interest (Citing). The citing list is similar to Shepard's and Westlaw's TOA. For the Supreme Court *Gitlitz* case, the citing cases are listed in order of relevance and given a star rating. However, the star rating by RIA is not the same as is used in Westlaw. The RIA stars indicate relevance, which may be associated with but is not equal to the coverage afforded of the case by *Gitlitz*.

The result of the Cited search in Exhibit 7-14 is a list of all the *tax* cases citing *Gitlitz*. Observe that the initial entry indicates the *Gitlitz* decision has been overruled by a Congressional action (Arrow 1). Compare Exhibit 7-14 with Shepard's in Exhibit 7-3 and KeyCite in Exhibit 7-9. From the Citator 2nd, the researcher knows immediately that *Gitlitz* has no precedential value whereas both Shepard's and KeyCite only give a warning for the case. Neither indicates that it has been overruled by more recent tax legislation. Thus, while Shepard's and KeyCite list more parallel citations and more extensive judicial (prior) histories than Citator 2nd, the question for the researcher is which service provides the information essential to the project at hand. More information is not necessarily more useful to assessing current law, especially when a vital action by Congress has been omitted from the case history.

Citator 2nd Conventions   Following the judicial history in Exhibit 7-14, the Citator 2nd first lists the citations for cases that are in complete agreement with the cited case. Next, citing cases are listed that discuss the holdings or reasoning of the cited case but do not refer to a specific paragraph or headnote. Finally, cases are listed in order of the headnote issue that they address. The headnote number references allow the researcher to restrict a search to only those citing cases with issues that are relevant to the client's factual situation. The Citator 2nd bases its headnote designations on the AFTR series, as that reporter also is an RIA product. For the *Gitlitz* Supreme Court case, AFTR2d provides only two headnotes. (Shepard's had 19.) The researcher needs to make sure that with the Citator 2nd the AFTR headnote numbers are utilized and not headnote numbers from other reporters, such as those published by West.

Within any of the citing groupings—complete agreement, no specific headnote, Headnote 1, Headnote 2, and so on—citing cases and rulings are listed in the following order:

- U.S. Supreme Court
- U.S. Courts of Appeal

EXHIBIT 7-14:   RIA Citator 2nd Case Results

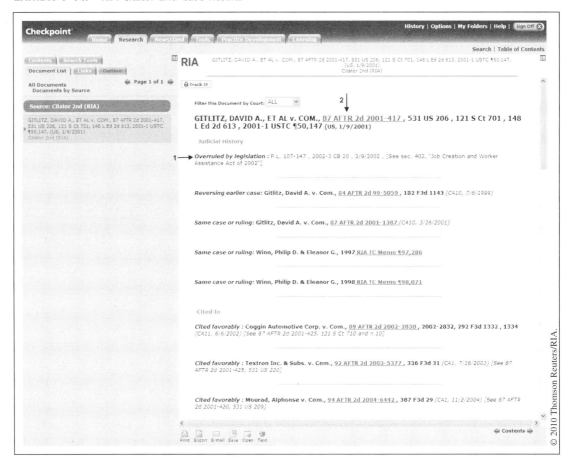

© 2010 Thomson Reuters/RIA.

- U.S. Court of Federal Claims (or predecessor court)

- U.S. District Court

- U.S. Tax Court (or predecessor court—BTA, regular then memorandum decisions)

- State courts

- Treasury Rulings and Decisions

Citing cases within any court or ruling group are arranged in chronological order.

The Citator 2nd includes tax citing cases that discuss or even just cite the case of interest. Therefore, the listings for important cases can be several screens long. Rather than using symbols to indicate how each of these citing cases treated the case of interest, the Citator 2nd uses short, easy-to-understand, descriptive phrases.

AFTR Cases The Citator 2nd AFTR2d case citation is hyperlinked (Exhibit 7-14, Arrow 2) to the full-text RIA reproduction of the *Gitlitz* case in Exhibit 7-15. The main advantages of the AFTR court reporter are that its headnotes address only the tax issues of the case, and it adds the Code sections (Arrow 2) addressed in the case to its Case Information summary, which also includes the level of the court, docket number, date decided, prior history, tax year, disposition of the case, and parallel citations. Knowing the tax year (Arrow 3) for the case can be very beneficial when the tax law is amended after the tax year. This is possible, when, as the *Gitlitz* case illustrates, it can take up to 10 years for the final decision by the courts (tax years 1991 and 1992, and Supreme Court decision 2001). Knowing the disposition of the case (Arrow 4)

EXHIBIT 7-15: RIA Case Document

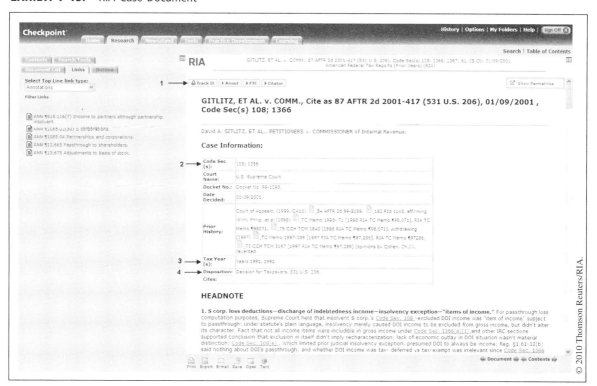

EXHIBIT 7-16:   RIA Citator 2nd Ruling Results

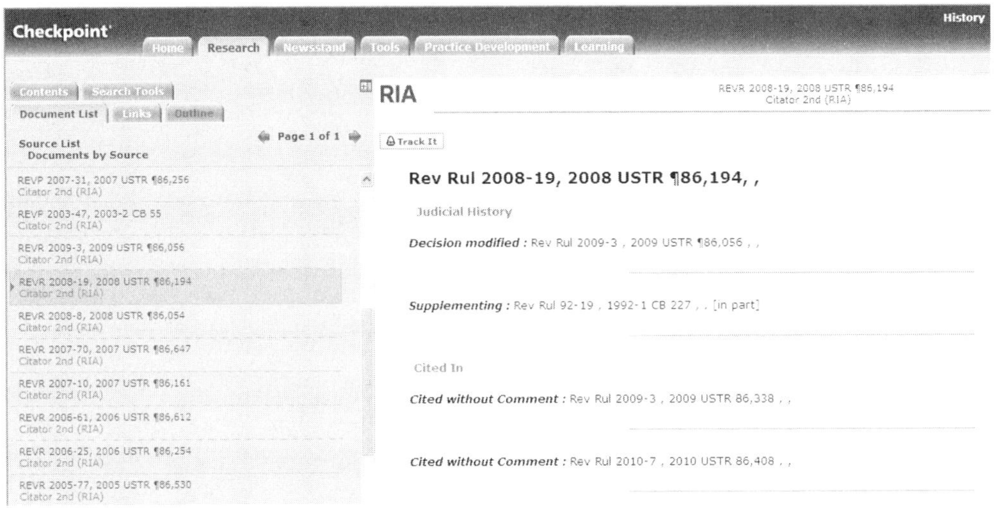

before starting to read the case also may help practitioners to focus their reading of the opinion. It can sometimes be hard to determine the final result of the case merely by reading an opinion from beginning to end!

The Track It in Exhibit 7-15 (Arrow 1) facilitates following developments on the case of interest by sending e-mail notification to the researcher when it is cited in a new case or IRS pronouncement. The four buttons just above the *Gitlitz* case name and citation, in Exhibit 7-15 (Arrow 1), access annotations (Annot) of the case in the United States Tax Reporter (listed in the left window), paragraph references of the case in the Federal Tax Coordinator 2d (FTC), or the case's listing in the Citator 2nd (Citator). References to the annotations also are listed between the headnotes and the opinion (not visible in Exhibit 7-15).

Rulings   Upon identifying administrative rulings (e.g., Revenue Ruling, Revenue Proce-dure, Notice, General Council Memorandums) that appear to support a client's tax posi-tion, it is critical for a researcher to determine if they are still in effect and represent the current view of the IRS. Rulings are continually clarified, modified, superseded, or re-voked, as Exhibit 7-16 illustrates. What is good law at one point (e.g., Rev. Rul. 2008-19 issued March 27, 2008) may not be so a few months later (modified by Rev. Rul. 2009-3 on January 29, 2009).

The steps in checking the validity of rulings are the same as with a court case. The Citator 2nd furnishes templates for most IRS administrative rulings. The search results for rulings provide a hyperlink to the actual ruling and then its judicial history. In this case, the judicial history shows the effect the ruling of interest had on other administra-tive pronouncements, and/or the effect subsequent administrative pronouncements had on the ruling of interest. If there are any citing court cases, these are listed after citing rulings and before lesser pronouncements (such as Notices). As Exhibit 7-16 demon-strates, it is always important to check pertinent pronouncements through a citator.

CCH Citator

The Commerce Clearing House (CCH) IntelliConnect Citator differs dramatically from the other citators examined in this chapter. First, as Exhibit 7-17 (Arrow 1) illustrates, the

EXHIBIT 7-17: CCH Citator Results

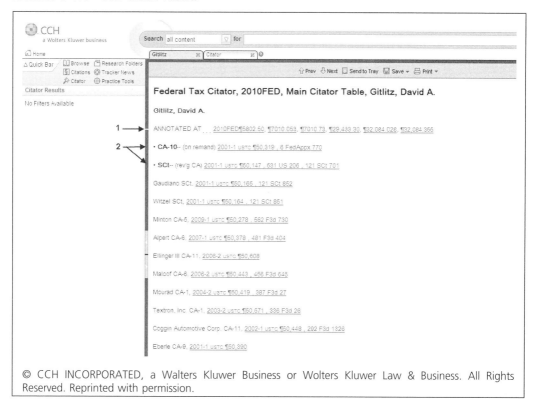

© CCH INCORPORATED, a Walters Kluwer Business or Wolters Kluwer Law & Business. All Rights Reserved. Reprinted with permission.

CCH Citator acts as a Finding Table as well as a citator, by listing paragraph references where the case is examined in the Standard Federal Income Tax Reporter. This feature reduces the searching time required to locate supplemental information regarding a case or ruling of interest. The tax service discussions help the researcher evaluate the case or ruling in the context of relevant Code sections, Regulations, and administrative sources of tax law.

Second, the CCH Citator lists the citing cases for each decision of the case. The court of original jurisdiction, appeals court, and Supreme Court decisions are all in one listing. However, only those citing cases that the CCH editors believe will serve as useful guides in evaluating the cited case's effectiveness as precedent are listed. Thus, the tax researcher is directed to those cases that may be most likely to develop, explain, criticize, or otherwise evaluate a cited case. This is in contrast to the other citators, which provide all of the cases mentioning the cited case and have separate listings for each court-level decision. Although the latter practice provides a level of thoroughness that may be useful, the CCH editorial screening procedure guards against the possibility of being overwhelmed by the sheer volume of citing cases presented. The more selective CCH approach, of course, forces the researcher to rely on an editor's evaluation concerning the usefulness of the citing cases.

Third, the CCH Citator uses a general citation rather than a specific location citation, which means that the citation for the citing case is the first page of the citing case and not the point where the case of interest is discussed by the citing case. If the citing case is long, the researcher can waste valuable time identifying where the citing case discusses the case of interest.

Fourth, the CCH Citator provides the citation to its court reporter, the United State Tax Cases (USTC) and no more than two other parallel citations. It never lists the RIA AFTR series citations (Exhibit 7-17). The other citator services list most if not all parallel citations. CCH also does not have a Table of Authorities or similar type function.

Finally, the CCH Citator does not provide evaluations of the citing cases (Exhibit 7-17), nor references to headnotes. While the CCH USTC provides headnote information and back references to its tax service, it does not number or label this analysis. The omission of these evaluation sources is a significant drawback of the CCH Citator. With cases having numerous issues and lists of citing cases, knowing how each citing case interpreted the different tax issues can substantially reduce the number of cases the researcher reads. The only information that can be gleaned from glancing at the *Gitlitz* Citator entry is that *Gitlitz* is an important case, given the number of cases citing it. One cannot even tell if the Supreme Court decision is still valid, which is critical when relying on the *Gitlitz* case.

Using CCH Citator Similar to the RIA Citator 2nd, the CCH Citator accepts the taxpayer's name and the complete citation, if known. It furnishes templates for entering the citation of the case or ruling of interest. For illustrative purposes, Exhibit 7-18 has entered the case name, complete citation, and cites using the case templates for the *Gitlitz* case. A researcher would actually input data in only one of these search boxes. Not only does the CCH Citator not list AFTR citations, it does not support AFTR citations with a template, nor will it recognize them as complete citations. The RIA Citator, on the other hand, does include templates for USTC (CCH Federal court reporter) citations. Not accepting AFTR citations can cause problems when a journal article, published by WG&L, for

EXHIBIT 7-18: CCH Citator Templates

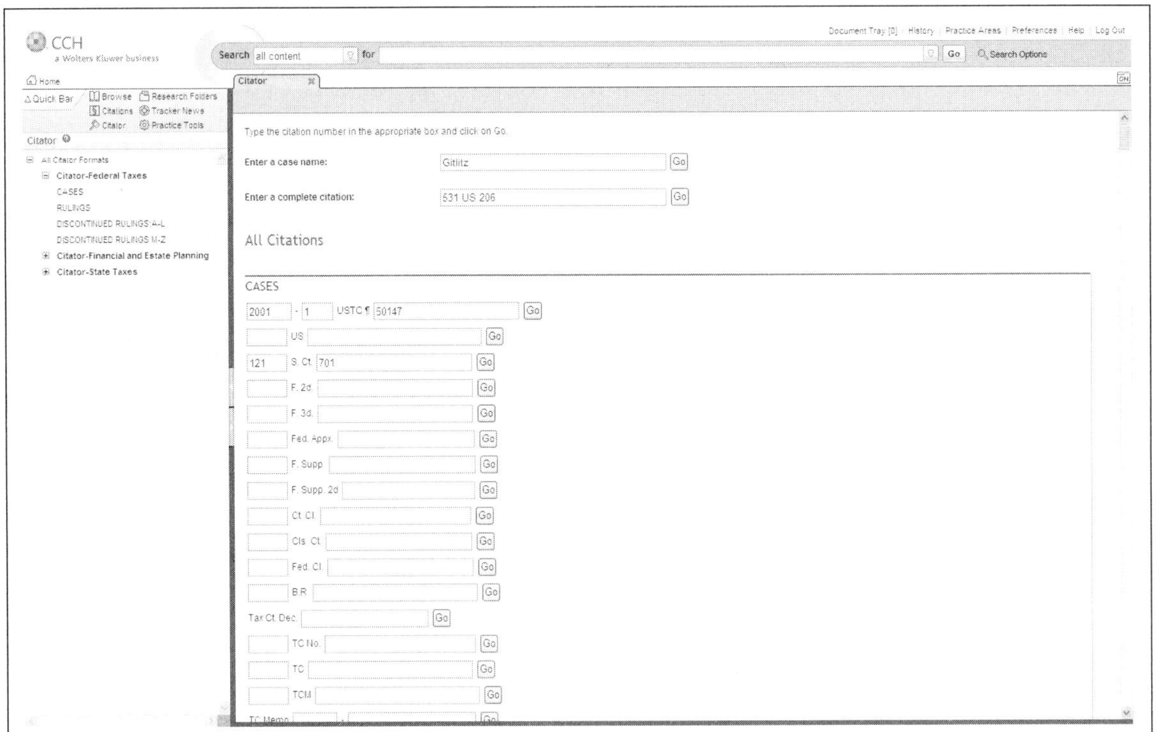

example, contains an AFTR2d cite for a case with a common taxpayer name, but the practitioner has access only to the CCH Citator and CCH court reporters.

Black bullets (Exhibit 7-17, Arrow 2) designate the cases in the direct history of the case of interest. Generally, the highest level court to address the case is listed first, and the trial-level court is listed last. However, due to the reverse chronological order convention, the citation for the *Gitlitz* remand to the Court of Appeals is listed before the Supreme Court case. Next, follows all cases citing the Supreme Court, then the Tenth Circuit regular case followed by its citing cases, and finally the Tax Court Memorandum case. Consequently, the court path chosen by the parties is not as quickly identifiable as with other citators.

Examining the entries in Exhibit 7-17, the citing cases for each court decision are listed by court level and generally in reverse chronology. Unlike Shepard's, the CCH Citator does not list Appeals Court cases in order, or the Circuit or District Court by geographical location. Rather, within Appeals Courts, the cases are listed by date. After listing all court citations, pronouncements are listed by type in a random date order.

The CCH Citator has its drawbacks but it can be the right tool in special circumstances, such as when wanting to find editorial discussion of a case. Each citator has its strengths and weaknesses, which should be considered when selecting an appropriate citator for a particular tax research project.

TAX PERIODICALS

Tax periodicals contain a variety of articles and news briefs that are designed to keep readers up to date in specific or general areas of the tax law. These articles might contain an in-depth review of a recently decided court case, a broad analysis of the factors relevant to a practitioner's decision on whether to make a certain tax accounting election, or a call for reform of a statute by a neutral (or biased) observer. Tax articles can suggest new viewpoints on tax issues, give guidance for solving complex problems, or just explain a new law in a readable form. All of these resources are very useful to tax practitioners.

With the right article that is "on point" with a tax issue, the practitioner is able to, in effect, use the author of the article as a research associate by capitalizing on the author's expert judgments and references, thereby saving hours of research time. Keep in mind, however, that tax periodicals are secondary sources of the tax law and therefore should not be cited as a controlling authority, especially when primary sources supporting the position are available. The article's references can lead to the pertinent primary tax sources. With that caveat aside, researchers who ignore the tax periodicals might be accused, at best, of reinventing the wheel and, at worst, of professional malpractice.

Traditionally, citing articles in professional tax research is limited to two situations: (1) if the researcher is referring to the author's analysis and conclusions as stated in an article and (2) if the researcher cannot find any controlling primary sources of law and a secondary source addresses the issues. Tax articles are now being cited more frequently in case opinions than was true in the past. When lacking both relevant primary law sources and adequate judicial staff, the authors of these case opinions may draw on tax articles to support the views of the court. In any event, it is imperative that researchers understand the practical implications of using secondary law sources.

Citing Articles

The citation for a printed tax journal article should take the following standard form:

> Sanders, Debra, Susan Gill, and Jill Zuber. 2009. Deductibility of bankruptcy costs and the origin of the claim. *The Tax Advisor* 40 (8): at 528.

Notice the proper placement of capital letters, periods, commas, and italics in the citation. The denotation "at 528" indicates that the researcher is referencing or quoting from a specific portion of the article. If the entire article were being referenced, the citation would merely contain the beginning page number of the article. For the citation above, this would be " ... 40 (8): 526."

Unfortunately, the proper citation for articles found on the Internet is not as well established as for printed materials. A problem that complicates matters is deciding how to characterize the Internet material being cited. For example, is the material a journal article, a newsletter, a report, or a blog; who is the author, when was the resource generated? Once all this information is deciphered (and deciphering this may not be easy), a generally safe citation format to follow is that of a printed document with additions or deletions as necessary. The following would be an acceptable format for a journal article found on the Internet:

> Donmoyer, Ryan J. and Margaret Collins. 2009. Grandkids May Benefit as Gift Tax Lapses. *Bloomberg Businessweek* (December 21). Retrieved June 15, 2010 from http://www.businessweek.com/bwdaily/dnflash/content/dec2009/db20091221_242207.htm

Site addresses on the Internet are generally case and punctuation sensitive. Therefore, one should ignore normal grammar rules when providing uniform resource locators (URLs) and place no punctuation (such as a period or a comma) at the end of a URL. It is important to indicate the date on which the document was retrieved because documents and Web site URLs may change or be removed over time.

Types of Periodicals

Tax periodicals can be categorized according to the depth of the coverage of their articles and the audience for which they are written. From the most extensive coverage to the least, they are as follows:

- Annual proceedings
- Scholarly reviews
- Professional journals
- Newsletters

Although each publication has unique attributes, several general characteristics of each category will be identified. This discussion provides an initial introduction to the broad market of secondary source tax commentary.

Annual Proceedings   A number of annual conferences for tax practitioners and academics are conducted every year. Usually sponsored by a professional organization, law school, or educational agency, these conferences generally last from two to five days. The agenda at these conferences may include: lectures, paper presentations with or without discussion, panel discussions, seminars, demonstrations, and luncheon addresses. Often, the conference speakers allow the sponsoring agency to publish their presentations in proceedings from the meeting.

These **annual proceedings** are distributed to the participants at the conference and later to the general public in the form of a collection of articles. Most of these papers exhibit considerable depth of coverage and practical insight by the authors. They can be a valuable resource for the tax researcher. A few of the established academic tax conferences include the following:

- National Tax Association, started in 1907

- New York University Institute on Federal Taxation, first meeting held in 1942

- Penn State Tax Conference, established in 1946

- University of Chicago's Annual Federal Tax Conference, first met in 1947

- University of Southern California's Tax Institute (formerly Major Tax Planning Institute), began in 1948

- Tulane Tax Institute, started in 1952

Scholarly Reviews   All major law schools and a few business schools produce publications referred to as law reviews or academic journals. These publications are edited either by faculty members or by graduate students under the guidance of the school's faculty. Most law reviews also use an outside advisory board comprised of practicing attorneys and law professors at other universities to aid in selecting and reviewing articles. The articles appearing in these scholarly reviews are usually written by tax practitioners, academics, graduate students, or noted commentators.

Some law schools produce journals that are limited to a specific area of law, such as constitutional or labor law. Most of the general **law reviews** feature one to three tax articles per year; however, some law reviews are dedicated exclusively to tax matters. The following are several law reviews that concentrate on taxation issues:

- *Akron Tax Journal* by University of Akron School of Law

- *Ohio Tax Review* by Capital University Law & Graduate Center

- *Florida Tax Review* by University of Florida College of Law

- *Tax Law Review* by New York University School of Law

- *The Tax Lawyer* and *The State and Local Tax Lawyer* by Georgetown University and the ABA

- *Virginia Tax Review* by University of Virginia School of Law

Besides law schools, academic organizations such as the National Tax Association (NTA) and the American Taxation Association (ATA) publish scholarly journals and proceedings from their annual conferences.

Professional Journals   A wide variety of tax journals are published for the purpose of keeping tax practitioners abreast of the current changes and trends in the tax law. This category, commonly referred to as **professional and practitioner journals**, includes publications by professional organizations as well as commercial companies. Examples of the former are the AICPA's *The Tax Adviser* and journals published by state CPA or law societies.

Because the commercial publications are numerous, the tax coverage in these journals can accommodate the needs of the general tax practitioner and those who specialize in a specific area of tax law. For example, journals such as WG&L *Journal of Taxation* and

Practical Tax Strategies or CCH's *Taxes—The Tax Magazine* cover a variety of tax areas, whereas journals such as BNA Tax Management's *The Compensation Planning Journal* or WG&L *Journal of Taxation of Investments* cover specific topics. Further, the articles appearing in these journals also vary greatly in their coverage from very complex with an exceedingly narrow focus to extremely practical "how to" articles designed for immediate implementation. Major changes in the tax law or important tax decisions of the courts spawn numerous articles in the various periodicals on the same or similar topics.

To accommodate the tax practitioner's need for timely information, most of the multi-topic tax journals are published monthly, whereas the more specialized tax journals tend to be issued on a quarterly basis. Practitioners with subscriptions to Internet services may obtain their journals through their online services. For example, a subscriber to RIA Checkpoint may add subscriptions to the WG&L journals. To ensure the quality of their articles, journals seek commentaries prepared by appropriate tax experts. In each case, an editorial review board assesses the timeliness, accuracy, and readability of each article before it is accepted for publication.

Newsletters   The major tax services include a **tax newsletter** as part of their service. The Internet services tend to have daily newsletters, whereas the published services send the newsletters weekly. These newsletters help the subscriber keep abreast of important tax law developments. They are designed to give the practitioner both a capsulated summary of tax law modifications and references to paragraphs within the tax service materials that contain more detailed analysis. Some of these newsletters also publish information concerning tax seminars and professional meetings, short reviews of (or citations for) selected current tax articles, and editorial highlights concerning recent tax developments. Popular newsletters include those published by Tax Analysts, BNA, CCH and RIA.

Tax Analysts   **Tax Analysts** produce a variety of comprehensive state, Federal, and international news, analysis, and commentary publications for tax professionals on a daily, weekly, monthly, and quarterly basis. In addition, Tax Analysts publishes its own tax services, Federal Tax Library and OneDisc. However, what Tax Analysts is best known for in the tax community is its outstanding news publications *Tax Notes* and *Tax Notes Today (TNT)*.

SPOTLIGHT ON TAXATION

Field Service Advice Memorandums

Field Service Advice (FSA) memorandums are available to the tax community thanks to Tax Analysts. In 1993, Tax Analysts filed a request under the Freedom of Information Act to have FSA memorandums become subject to public disclosure. The IRS declined this request, because these documents contained "return information" or were protected by the attorney-client privilege, and therefore were not available for public disclosure. Tax Analysts took the question to court and a 1996 District Court ordered the IRS to release the FSAs to the general public.

The court indicated that FSAs are similar to General Counsel Memoranda (GCMs), also public information. They contain legal analysis and conclusions of the law and are not "return information" under any reasonable interpretation of §6103. Further, just because an IRS attorney declares FSAs to be "return information" does not make them so. FSAs are merely memoranda routinely used by the IRS as guidance in conducting audits and therefore are applied by the IRS in its dealings with the public.

The daily Tax Analysts news services, available only online, offer up-to-the-minute coverage of Federal (*Tax Notes Today*), state (*State Tax Today*), and worldwide (*Worldwide Tax Daily*) tax news. The weekly print series includes *Tax Notes* and *State Tax Notes*, and *Tax Notes International*. The Tax Analysts newsletters also are available through LexisNexis.

Tax Notes Today (TNT) is updated continually throughout the day, not just once a day, so practitioners can be as up-to-date as they desire. The amount of information included in these newsletters is staggering. The TNT, for example, includes the following:

- Commentary and analysis by experts

- Internal Revenue Bulletins, IRS correspondence, and other administrative rulings, Final, Temporary, and Proposed Regulations, as well as public comments on Proposed Regulations

- Congressional actions, legislation, and correspondence including tax committee reports

- Court cases

The content of the weekly *Tax Notes* publication is similar to TNT and the *Weekly Report*, published by BNA (discussed next in this chapter). However, *Tax Notes* includes in-depth analysis of court decisions, regulatory pronouncements, and policy-oriented research submitted by tax professionals and academics, as Exhibit 7-19 illustrates. Special sections provide news and practice tips just for accounting and tax practitioners. To

EXHIBIT 7-19: Tax Analysts Tax Notes

obtain the full text of a document discussed and cited within a *Tax Notes* article, subscribers to an online service such as LexisNexis use *Tax Notes* unique document identification numbers (see underlined numbers in Exhibit 7-19). *Tax Notes* is also available in print subscriptions.

Bureau of National Affairs (BNA)   One of the most important tax newsletters available to practitioners is the **BNA *Daily Tax Report (DTR)*.** The DTR is available online, through wireless devices, including iPhones, and by paper subscription. Subscribers may also receive notification of breaking tax news as soon as it occurs with the DTR Real-Time e-mail alerts. Showing both breadth in coverage and a quality of analysis similar to the Tax Analysts TNT, DTR offers up-to-date information concerning statutory, administrative, and judicial tax law developments that affect state, Federal, and international taxation. In addition, the newsletter provides interviews with government officials, articles reviewing the day's events, and the full text of key documents discussed in the newsletter. In some instances these documents are not available from other tax services. Monthly and quarterly indexes are provided.

DTR offers the equivalent of 30 to 50 pages of single-spaced printed copy every weekday. Because this is clearly too much data to digest every day, the DTR is organized to facilitate accessing only the material of greatest interest to the subscriber. While the content section lists only the title of each note by category, the highlights provide brief paragraphs describing the notes. With hyperlinks, the subscriber can access the actual government document on which the story is based through **TaxCore** (included with subscription to DTR). TaxCore contains a wide variety of full-text primary tax materials that is updated daily. It provides a categorization of sources to facilitate retrieving the document of interest. The source categories include Congressional, Treasury, Court, IRS, State and Local, White House, and International. TaxCore may also be obtained separately from the DTR.

As one would expect, receiving such extensive tax news on a daily basis is an expensive proposition. However, the DTR (as well as many newsletters produced by other publishers) is available online to subscribers of Westlaw, LexisNexis, and various other services. Thus, by subscribing to one of the major tax database systems, the practitioner has access to the DTR at a small or zero incremental cost.

Similar to Tax Analysts, BNA publishes a weekly newsletter as well as a daily one. The **BNA *Weekly Report*** coverage is similar to the DTR, but more in depth. In addition, it contains articles on news and emerging tax topics. The comprehensive index makes it easy to locate items of interest. Besides other weekly, biweekly, and monthly newsletters, BNA publishes journals in the areas of financial planning, real estate, compensation planning, international, and estates, gifts, and trusts. It also has a research service called **Tax Practice Library** that includes a topical service providing analysis, examples, and practice tools such as client letters, line-by-line form guidance, checklists, and interactive tax forms.

CCH AND RIA   CCH and RIA both offer daily and weekly newsletters with their tax services. These news services are current, comprehensive and may be customized by subscribers. This time-saving feature alerts practitioners to tax law changes in their area of specialization, without requiring that they wade through all news articles for the day. E-mail notifications are offered to alert the subscriber when there is breaking news in an area of interest. Access to the full news article and the underlying primary sources is seamlessly provided through hyperlinks.

Locating Relevant Tax Articles

The numerous online indexes facilitate locating tax, business, and law review articles pertinent to the practitioner's research. Depending on the subscription, these search programs can index thousands of periodicals. Most Internet indexes focus on a Keyword Search strategy and allow the researcher to determine the connectors (e.g., and, versus, or) among the words or phrases. Since these indexes are not exclusively for tax research, they will not be reviewed.

Additional resources for locating tax articles are the major tax services. Each service offers access to a variety of journals and law reviews in searchable databases, but no service imparts access to the majority of the tax periodicals. However, the **CCH Federal Tax Articles (FTA)** and the **WG&L Index to Federal Tax Articles (IFTA)** are the two indexes specifically designed for locating tax articles. Unfortunately, both of these indexes are offered only in print and are not available online. This is frustrating for the subscribers to online services, such as IntelliConnect, Checkpoint, and Westlaw, as these indexes would be most useful in an electronic format.

CCH Federal Tax Articles   The FTA index, published by CCH, has many outstanding features that make it one of the best tax indexes available. It is known for the concise abstracts it furnishes for each article cited in the index. Reading these abstracts helps the practitioner reduce false starts that commonly occur when trying to find pertinent articles based solely on their titles. The framework for organizing these abstracts is the Internal Revenue Code.

This organization also expedites finding articles addressing the Code section under investigation by the researcher. CCH updates this index monthly so the citations are timely. Because the FTA current volume (since 2004) is a loose-leaf service, the updates provide new pages that either replace existing pages or are added to the contents of the volume. Besides listing the filing instructions for the new pages, the Report Letter presents the highlights of the most interesting new developments, seminars, and tax conferences.

Approximately 250 journals, law reviews, papers, and proceedings are included in the index. The topics covered in the FTA include Federal income, excise, estate, gift, and employment taxation. The main division of the index, called Articles by Code Section, gives the full citation for each article and its abstract. This cumulative index gives Code section numbers with a brief description of the section as its headings. Articles can also be located by using the topic and author indexes. Each of these indexes refers the researcher to the "Articles by Code Section" division through a system of paragraph numbers.

As previously mentioned, the FTA is only available in print. As the loose-leaf volume accumulates years of monthly updates, it becomes more cumbersome to use. As with any published services, additions to the services processed by editors are printed, shipped, and then filed by the practitioner or an employee. This can result in a substantial time lag, especially if the updates are not filed on a timely basis. Further, there is the likelihood of human filing errors—and a page misfiled is information lost to the researcher. Providing this service online would eliminate these problems with using the FTA.

WG&L Index to Federal Tax Articles   The WG&L IFTA provides citations and occasional summaries for articles covering Federal income, gift, and estate taxation or tax policy that appear in more than 350 periodicals. The index surveys not only traditional tax journals, but also law reviews, major annual tax symposia, and certain economics, accounting, and finance journals. The IFTA is issued in bound quarterly volumes and includes permanent accumulations of references for earlier periods of time. A paperback cumulative supplement augments the main index volumes. Because the supplements are cumulative, the researcher needs to consult only one supplement for recent articles.

The IFTA contains a user's guide that provides the following: explanations of how to use the index; lists of more than 1,500 topical index subject headings; keys to abbreviations of periodical titles; and lists of the periodicals included in older volumes. Further, each cumulative volume and the current supplement also list not only the periodical titles but also the volumes and issue numbers covered by the supplement.

Unlike the CCH index, both the topic and the author indexes contain full article citations. Using the full citations in the author index, the researcher can identify other current articles by the same author pertaining to a specific topic. Authors with several articles on the same topic are more likely to have an expertise in that field, and, thus, their analysis may be more effectual.

Further, the custom of listing citations for each author and topic heading in reverse chronological order (rather than in alphabetical order) expedites finding the most recent publications. Whereas every citation in the CCH index is accompanied by an abstract, only articles judged by the WG&L compilers and Editorial Advisory Board to be of special interest are furnished with a brief summary in the IFTA. Very few articles receive this distinction.

SUMMARY

The tax researcher's job of sorting through the thousands of potentially pertinent Federal tax authorities is simplified by citators. When familiar with these research tools, the current status and precedential value of a specific case or ruling can be determined effectively and quickly. This determination is necessary for the researcher to evaluate the judicial and administrative sources of the tax law that pertain to a client's tax issue.

The Internet services automate virtually all of the tedious mechanical aspects of Sheparding cases and validating citations. Further, they make the retrieval of cited and citing cases seamless. The overview of citators and the act of citing presented in this chapter demonstrate that research is not complete until all primary sources upon which the researcher is relying are found to be currently "good law."

Tax journals and other periodicals not only help researchers locate primary sources of the tax law, but they also enlighten the researcher as to other ways of analyzing a tax issue. Tax articles can synthesize information from the Code, Regulations, and pertinent court cases into a more logical presentation. These articles may help the practitioner identify relevant tax issues or precedents during the research process or in preparing for litigation on a client's behalf. Finally, such publications are an integral part of the means by which the tax professional remains current with respect to the evolution of the Federal tax law.

QUIZ YOURSELF

Reinforce the tax research information covered in this chapter by completing the online quizzes located at the Federal Tax Research Web site at **www.cengagebrain.com.** At the CengageBrain.com home page, search for the *Federal Tax Research*, 9e ISBN (1111221642) using the search box at the top of the page. This will take you to the product page where you can access the quizzes.

KEY WORDS

By the time you complete this chapter, you should be comfortable discussing each of the following terms. If you need additional review of any of these items, return to the appropriate material in the chapter or consult the glossary to this text.

annual proceedings, p. 266
Auto-Cite, p. 251
BNA *Daily Tax Report,* p. 270
BNA *Weekly Report,* p. 270
CCH Citator, p. 263
CCH Federal Tax Articles
   (FTA), p. 271
citation, p. 243
citator, p. 243
cited case, p. 243
cites, p. 243
citing case, p. 243
Citing Reference, p. 254

direct history, p. 248
Headnotes, p. 247
indirect history, p. 251
KeyCite, p. 252
law reviews, p. 267
LEXCITE, p. 251
local citations, p. 244
precedential value, p. 242
professional and practitioner
   journals, p. 267
ResultsPlus, p. 257
RIA Citator 2nd, p. 258
Shepardizing, p. 245

Shepard's Citators (Shepard's),
   p. 245
Table of Authorities (TOA), p. 249
Tax Analysts, p. 268
tax newsletter, p. 268
TaxCore, p. 270
Tax Practice Library, p. 270
Tax Notes, p. 268
Tax Notes Today
   (TNT), p. 268
West Key Number System, p. 257
WG&L Index to Federal Tax
   Articles (IFTA), p. 271

DISCUSSION QUESTIONS

1. Why does the researcher need to determine the precedential value of a case?

2. Why is it difficult to know whether the document retrieved four months ago is still valid law?

3. Describe the function of a citator in the tax research process.

4. Distinguish between the following terms: cited case, citing case, citation, and cites.

5. Citators do not provide all of the information related to a case. What kind of information do citators not provide?

6. Which citators accept only citations and which will accept either case name or citation? Which citators provide templates for entering the citations?

7. Explain the difference between a general directing and a local directing cite. Which services use local directing cites?

8. What does "Shepardizing" mean?

9. Compare the coverage and organization of Shepard's with the RIA and CCH citator services.

10. What is the standard format for a case citation?

11. What are headnotes? Explain whether the headnotes for a given case are set by the court and thus consistent across court reporting services.

12. What is the equivalent of the Shepard's Green + Diamond symbol in Westlaw?

13. What is the function of a TOA? Why is it a useful research tool?

14. Answer the following questions:
   a. What is Auto-Cite, who designed it, and what is its primary objective?
   b. What is LEXCITE, and when would a researcher use this Lexis service?
   c. What is KeyCite, and what event in the late 1990s caused a reorganization of KeyCite?

15. What information regarding citing cases is provided by KeyCite that is not available from the other citation services discussed in this chapter?

16. When is the West Key Number System useful to a researcher?

17. Compare the Shepard's TOA with the Westlaw KeyCite version.

18. What is the major difference in the focus of the citing cases found with a RIA Citator 2nd search and those cases found using Shepard's or KeyCite?

19. Discuss the quality of the RIA Citator 2nd equivalent of the TOA compared to Shepard's and CCH.

20. What symbols are utilized in the RIA Citator 2nd to indicate the treatment given by the cases citing the case of interest?

21. What are the main advantages of the AFTR court reporter?

22. Why must Revenue Rulings identified through a keyword search be checked in a citator?

23. How is the CCH Citator different from the other citators discussed in this chapter?

24. How does the CCH Citator act as a Finding Table?

25. How is the direct history for a case of interest presented in the CCH Citator?

26. How can finding an article on-point with a practitioner's tax issue be like hiring someone to do the research?

27. Why are tax journals and newsletters generally not cited as authority in professional tax research? When would it be appropriate to cite tax journals or newsletters as authority?

28. What does the denotation "at 407" indicate in a tax journal citation?

29. Briefly describe each of the following:
    a. Annual proceedings
    b. Scholarly reviews
    c. Professional journals
    d. Newsletters

30. Who is the publisher of the following newsletters: *Daily Tax Report, Tax Notes,* and the *Weekly Report*?

31. To review a document cited in *Tax Notes*, how does the subscriber obtain access? How is document retrieval achieved for the *Daily Tax Report*?

32. What is the major obstacle to using either the CCH FTA or the WG&L IFTA?

33. What is one of the most outstanding features of the CCH FTA that is not available with most other journal indexes? How does the organizational framework of the CCH FTA differ from that of the WG&L IFTA?

34. What are three methods that can be used to locate articles in the CCH FTA? Can these same three methods of locating an article be used with the WG&L IFTA? Explain your answer.

35. How frequently are the CCH FTA and WG&L IFTA journal indexes updated?

36. Describe approximately how many court cases and rulings are issued each year. Has the number of rulings been increasing or decreasing over the last 30 years?

37. Provide the judicial history of the case that is the basis of Illustrative Citator Example.

38. What publisher was the first to understand the commercial value of citators? What company currently owns this citator service?

39. Why is the responsibility of nominating Supreme Court justices an important presidential power? Which President appointed only one of the current Supreme Court justices? Who is the most recent addition to the Supreme Court?

40. How did Field Service Advice Memorandums become available to the general public?

EXERCISES

41. Use Shepard's citator to answer the following questions:
    a. Provide the full citation for an article starting on page 1 of *Akron Tax Journal* in its 24th volume.
    b. What topic is addressed in the 24th Private Letter Ruling (PLR) issued in the 13th week of 2010? What is the Lexis abbreviated citation?
    c. What is the full citation and parallel citations for Revenue Ruling 1993-48?
    d. What is the Notice citation that is found at 2010-16 IRB 594? What is the Shepard's citation for the Case Note published in the *William Mitchell Law Review* regarding this Notice?

42. Use Shepard's to evaluate *C. G. Services Corp.*, 73 TC 406.
    a. What Shepard's evaluation symbol is associated with the case? What does the symbol mean?
    b. Give either the AFTR or the USTC citation for the 1997 District Court case citing *C. G. Services Corp.*
    c. What is the subsequent appellate history of this case?
    d. There is an article in the 1989 *Tennessee Law Review* on page 661 that cites *C. G. Services Corp.* What is the title of the article and the name of the author(s)?

43. Use Shepard's to evaluate the following case citator: 87 AFTR2d 1706.
    a. What is the name of the case, what was the final court to hear the case and in what year was the case decided?
    b. What Shepard's evaluation symbol is associated with the case? What does the symbol mean?
    c. List the parallel citations (in standard format) for the US, Lexis, and CCH court reporters.
    d. How many Supreme Court cases cite this case? How many cases for the Circuit in which your college is located cite this case?

44. Use Shepard's to evaluate *Stange* (282 US 270).
    a. What are the parallel citations for this case? What precedence symbol is associated with this case?
    b. What is the highest court to have heard this case, and in what year was this case decided?
    c. On what page does the case, *Aiken v. Burnet*, 75 L. Ed 339, cite the *Stange* case? What page would this be if you were using the United States Supreme Court Reports (US)?
    d. The Alaska Supreme Court has cited the *Stange* case. Provide the citation for the case.

45. Use Shepard's to evaluate Revenue Ruling 2005-76l.
    a. What are the full citations listed for this ruling?
    b. What Shepard's evaluation symbol is associated with the case? What does the symbol mean?
    c. Provide the Ruling's subsequent history.
    d. What are the treatise citations for this ruling?

46. Use Shepard's to evaluate the *Fritz W. Hintze* (879 F2d 121) case.
    a. What are the parallel citations for this case? What evaluation symbol is associated with this case?
    b. How many headnotes does *Hintze* have? How many of the headnotes concern civil procedures?
    c. Who were the judges who heard the *Hintze* case? Which judge wrote the opinion?
    d. What was the Supreme Court's view of the *Hintze* case? In what case did the Supreme Court indicate this viewpoint?

47. Use the Shepard's to answer the following questions regarding the *Hinck* (127 S CT 2011) case.
    a. Which Supreme Court justice wrote the *Hinck* opinion? Explain whether the other Supreme Court justices agreed with the written opinion.
    b. What was the court of original jurisdiction for the *Hinck* case, and what court heard the appeal?
    c. What are the parallel citations for the *Hinck* case? What precedence symbol is associated with this case?
    d. What Code section is involved in the *Hinck* case? When was the case argued, and when was it decided?

48. Use the LexisNexis Auto-Cite to locate *Soliman*, 1993 US Lexis 828.
    a. What Lexis evaluation symbol is associated with this case? What event caused the *Soliman* case to receive this symbol?
    b. List the parallel citations (in standard format) for the US, S Ct, AFTR, and CCH court reporters.
    c. What was the court of original jurisdiction? To what circuit was the case appealed?
    d. To what cases did *Soliman* make negative references?

49. Use the LexisNexis Auto-Cite to locate *City of New Britain*, 1954 US Lexis 2751.
    a. What Lexis evaluation symbol is associated with this case? What event caused the *City of New Britain* case to receive this symbol?
    b. What is this case's judicial history?
    c. What U.S. Code Service (USCS) sections cite *City of New Britain*?
    d. What citing cases are listed in the subsequent treatment history section?

50. Use the LexisNexis LEXCITE and enter the following citation: 123 S Ct 1099 and select Federal Courts Tax Cases as the database. [Hint: In the Tax Center Term and Connectors box enter: lexcite (123 S Ct 1099). The citation must be in parentheses]
    a. What is the name of the case with the citation you entered? When was it decided and by what court? (Hint: Open a case and find the cite.)
    b. Provide the Lexis citation for the *Lantz* case that cites the case of interest. When was it decided?
    c. What citing case(s) has (have) a yellow triangle evaluation symbol?

51. Use the LexisNexis LEXCITE and enter the following citation: 5 L Ed 2d 128 and select Federal Courts Tax Cases as the database. [Hint: In the Tax Center Term and Connectors box enter: lexcite (5 L Ed 128). The citation must be in parentheses.]
    a. What is the name of the case with the citation you entered? When was it decided and by what court?
    b. In the "Enter more terms" type "sweepstakes" into the box. There is a 1965 Tax Court case and its Second Court of Appeals case in the citing list. What is the name of this case?
    c. Remove the "sweepstakes" term and select Secondary Sources as the Jurisdiction. What is the full citation for the *University of Colorado Law Review* article citing the case of interest?

52. Use the LexisNexis TOA and evaluate the following citation: 347 US 81.

    a. What are the parallel citations for this case? In what year was this case decided?

    b. How many cases did it cite in developing its decision? Which cited cases have some type of warning associated with them?

    c. What are the jurisdictional levels in which the cases are divided?

    d. On which pages in 347 US 81 are the cases in the TOA cited?

53. Use Westlaw KeyCite to find the following documents.

    a. An article in *New York University Law Review*, volume 84 starting on page 174. Provide its full citation.

    b. The 4th Private Letter Ruling issued in the 15th week of 2010. When was it issued and to what Code section does it apply?

    c. What is the KeyCite recognized abbreviation for the *National Tax Journal*?

    d. What is the title of the 15th IRS News Release issued in 2010?

54. State the proper Westlaw KeyCite citation for the following documents:

    a. An article in *New York University Law Review*, volume 81 starting on page 148.

    b. The 43rd Private Letter Ruling issued in the 29th week of 2007.

    c. The second section of article 16 of the Arkansas State Constitution.

    d. The 34th Field Service Advice issued in the 47th week of 2002.

55. Use Westlaw KeyCite to evaluate *Soliman* 506 US 168.

    a. What are official parallel citations for this case? In what year was this case decided?

    b. Give the names and citation of the cases that state the *Soliman* case has been superseded by statute? Indicate the coverage each case gives *Soliman*.

    c. Using Citing References, determine how much coverage *Duncan* (TC Memo 2000-269) gives to *Soliman*. What evaluation symbol does *Duncan* have and what does it mean?

    d. What ResultsPlus ALR document is offered?

56. Use Westlaw KeyCite to evaluate *Hinck*, 95 AFTR2d 2005-873.

    a. What are official parallel citations for this case? In what year was this case decided?

    b. Using KeyCite History, list each court hearing the case. How did the appeals court treat this case? Did the Supreme Court grant certiorari?

    c. Where is this case discussed in the FTC 2d?

    d. Select Full-Text Document. What are the titles of the headnotes for this case?

57. Use the Westlaw TOA to find the following information about *Shackleford* 262 F3d 1028:

    a. How many cases does *Shackleford* cite in its decision? What is the citation of the earliest case in the cited case list?

    b. What case does *Shackleford* merely mention? On what page is this mention of the case?

    c. How many of the cases cited in *Shackleford* have warning or caution symbols? How does this make you feel about the reasoning in this case?

    d. What is the title of the ResultsPlus Am. Jur. 2d: Federal Taxation offering?

58. Use the Westlaw TOA to find the following information for *Stange*, 282 US 270:

    a. How many cases does *Stange* cite in its decision? What year was the most recent cited case decided?

    b. What case does *Stange* quote? What does the quote discuss?

    c. How many of the cases cited in *Stange* have warning or caution symbols? How does this make you feel about the reasoning in this case?

    d. How many different pages have discussion of cases?

59. Use Westlaw to answer the following questions:

    a. Locate the 2006 *David Bruce Billings* Tax Court case (Hint: use Find & Print). What was the tax issue and what was the decision of the court?

    b. Find the 2007 *David Bruce Billings* Tax Court case. Why are the results of this case different from those of the 2006 case?

    c. What is the KeyCite Key Number for the issue in the 2007 case?

    d. How useful do you think the KeyCite Key Numbering system is in locating cases on income tax issues?

60. Use Westlaw to find the 1988 Prentice Hall Tax Court Memorandum case, *Woodbury*, at paragraph 272.

    a. Select the KeyCite from the toolbar. What is the proper abbreviation for a Prentice Hall Tax Court Memorandum case? Run KeyCite. What is the Westlaw (WL) citation?

    b. Select Find & Print from the toolbar. Find the case by party name. What useful option is available for Specialized Courts? Opening the case, determine what the deficiency was for the taxpayer in 1980.

    c. Open KeyCite from the Tax tab and retrieve the citator data. What evaluation is associated with the case?

    d. Which of the three methods was the easiest to use?

61. Use the RIA Checkpoint Citator to evaluate 39 AFTR2d 77-1008.

    a. What is the name of the case and its parallel citations?

    b. In which District Court was this case heard? How did the court decide?

    c. The issue in this case is liens for taxes. What paragraphs in the USTR provide annotations to this case?

    d. Explain why the FTC paragraphs retrieved by clicking the FTC button above the 1976 case name do not discuss the leins for taxes issue.

62. Use the RIA Checkpoint Citator to evaluate the 1958 *Knetsch* case.

    a. What is its citation? Provide the citations for all the cases generally citing the *Knetsch* case.

    b. What are the citations for the cases that constitute the direct history for the *Knetsch* case?

    c. How many headnotes does the case show? What does each headnote address?

    d. How many Eleventh Circuit Court of Appeals cases cite the *Knetsch* Supreme Court case? List the names of the taxpayers in these cases. What was the easiest method to find this information?

63. Use the RIA Checkpoint Citator 2nd to evaluate the Revenue Procedure 2003-64.

    a. Why are there so many documents retrieved for this citation?

    b. Identify by citation the effect this Procedure had on earlier pronouncements.

    c. Identify by citation the effect later pronouncements had on this Procedure.

    d. What tax issue does this Procedure address?

64. Use the RIA Checkpoint Citator 2nd to evaluate the 2002 *Gwendolyn A. Ewing* Tax Court case.

    a. What is its citation and what tax issues does the case address?

    b. What is the case's direct judicial history?

    c. Where is the case annotated in the United States Tax Reporter?

    d. The *Robert Haag* case cites the 2002 *Ewing* case at 94 AFTR2d 2004-6667. What is the *Haag* case's treatment of the *Ewing* case?

65. Use RIA Checkpoint Citator 2nd to answer the following questions regarding Notice 2010-32:
    a. Besides Notice 2010-32, what other types of pronouncements are retrieved by the search?
    b. What is the history for the Notice?
    c. What is the purpose of the Notice?
    d. Why does Rev Proc 2002-19 appear in the pronouncements retrieved by the Citator 2nd for the citation 2010-32?

66. Use RIA Checkpoint Citator 2nd to evaluate *Deluxe Check Printers, Inc* 15 Cl Ct 175.
    a. What tax years are in question in the case? How was this case treated upon Appeal? What is the citation of the appeals case?
    b. What doctrine is the basis for part B. of the Court of Federal Claims decision? Where is this doctrine discussed in the FTC?
    c. Which cases and rulings distinguish themselves from the *Deluxe Check Printers* Court of Federal Claims case?
    d. What is the number of cases cited by the *Deluxe Check Printers* decision? (Hint: check Citing, NOT cited). Does this number of cases seem logical?

67. Use the RIA Checkpoint Citator 2nd to evaluate the Revenue Ruling 2001-60.
    a. What is the ruling's complete citation?
    b. What was the effect of Rev Rul 2001-60 on Rev Proc 99-49 and Rev Rul 55-290?
    c. Which IRS Revenue Procedures favorably cite Rev Rul 2001-60?
    d. What issue does Rev Rul 2001-60 address?

68. Use the CCH IntelliConnect Citator to answer the following questions regarding Notice 2010-10:
    a. Where is the Notice located in the Internal Revenue Bulletin?
    b. Where is the Notice discussed in the tax services?
    c. To what Code sections does the Notice apply? Who are the principal authors of the Notice?

69. Use the CCH IntelliConnect Citator to evaluate the 1956 *William George* Tax Court case.
    a. What is the citation for the case?
    b. What is the title of the paragraph where *George* is annotated?
    c. What Code section is related to the *George* case?
    d. A Revenue Ruling cites the *George* case. What is the citation and title? How does the Revenue Ruling evaluate the *George* case?

70. Use CCH IntelliConnect Citator to answer the following questions:
    a. Find the discontinued Miscellaneous MS 347; 1950-1 CB 281 ruling (Hint: use CB citation to find it). What is its current standing and why?
    b. Find Court Decision 1787, 1955-2 CB 511. Give the name of the cases and all of its parallel citations.
    c. Find the Treasury Decision 9477. Give the date it was filed with the Federal Register, Code Section to which it applies, and its effect.

71. Use the CCH IntelliConnect Citator to evaluate the 290th Revenue Ruling issued in 1955.
    a. What is its complete Cumulative Bulletin citation? Is this Revenue Ruling still valid?
    b. What tax issue does the Revenue Ruling address?
    c. List the citations of any cases that cite Revenue Ruling 1955-290.
    d. In what paragraph of the CCH service was this ruling initially discussed?

72. Use the CCH and the RIA Citators to locate the *Estate of Edward Kunze* Seventh Circuit case.

    a. What method did you use to find this case?

    b. Do the citators list the same citing cases? Explain your response.

    c. How did the citing cases generally treat the *Kunze* case? Which citator did you use to determine this?

    d. What issues appear to be involved in this case? Which citator did you use to determine this?

73. Use the CCH IntelliConnect Citator to answer the following questions regarding the 19th Revenue Procedure of 2002:

    a. What does this Procedure address? What Code sections are involved?

    b. What is its current status?

    c. What types of pronouncements have cited this Procedure? That is the most current citing of the Procedure?

74. Use the CCH IntelliConnect Citator to evaluate the 2006 *Gwendolyn A. Ewing* case.

    a. What is its citation and what tax issues does the case address?

    b. What is the case's direct judicial history?

    c. Where is the case annotated in the Standard Federal Income Tax Reporter?

    d. The *Robinette* case (2006-1 USTC ¶ 50,213) cites *Ewing*. What is the *Robinette* treatment of the *Ewing* case?

    e. Compare the information retrieved using the CCH Citator and the RIA Checkpoint Citator 2nd (question 64). Which was easier to use, and which provided more relevant information?

75. Find the following law journals and provide the title to the article by the authors indicated:

    a. *Akron Tax Journal:* Volume 25 by Scott Taylor

    b. *Virginia Tax Review*: Volume 29 by Tsilly Dagan

    c. *Florida Tax Review*: Volume 9 by Robert Holo and Jonathan Talansky

    d. *Tax Lawyer:* Volume 63 by David Shores

76. Use the CCH FTA index to answer the following questions:

    a. Provide the proper citation for the most current article discussing §382.

    b. What are the paragraph citation numbers for articles discussing the protection of individual retirement accounts (IRAs) from creditors of bankrupt individuals? What Code section are these articles under?

    c. Provide the proper citation for the most current article by William Skinner.

    d. What is the date on the last update filed in your library's current binder of FTA? (Check behind the tab "Last Report Letter" to find the answer.)

77. Use the WG&L IFTA index to answer the following questions:

    a. Provide the proper citation for the most current article discussing transfer pricing.

    b. Provide the proper citation for the most current article by William Raabe.

    c. What is the most recent supplement in your library?

78. Use the CCH FTA index and the WG&L IFTA for the following tasks:

    a. sing both indexes, find a current article on U.S. citizens living abroad and provide the proper citation for the article. Describe the search strategies you used for each index. Which one proves easier to find the article?

    b. Using both indexes, find a current article on §2511(c), Treatment of Certain Transfers in Trust, and provide the proper citation for the article. Describe the search strategies you used for each index. Which one proves easier to find the article?

c. Using both indexes, find a current article by William M. Funk and provide the proper citation for the article. Describe the search strategies you used for each index. Which one proves easier to find the article?

79. Use the CCH FTA index and the WG&L IFTA for the following tasks:

a. Using both indexes, find a current article on charitable giving and provide the proper citation for the article. Describe the search strategies you used for each index. Which one proves easier to find the article?

b. Using both indexes, find a current article on §213, Medical Expenses, and provide the proper citation for the article. Describe the search strategies you used for each index. Which one proves easier to find the article?

c. Using both indexes, find a current article by Wei-Chih Chiang and provide the proper citation for the article. Describe the search strategies you used for each index. Which one proves easier to find the article?

80. Compare the CCH FTA and the WG&L IFTA regarding ease of locating articles when using the three methods of locating an article (by Code section, by author, and by topic).

RESEARCH CASES

81. Three friends form a film production partnership. Will the operations of this partnership qualify for the domestic production activity deduction in the current year?

82. Can a business traveler to your town use the high-cost-city meal allowance for travel away from home overnight? What would the meal allowance be for a business trip to Washington, D.C.?

83. Nancy and Curtis had not spoken to each other since their mother's funeral in 2001. Nancy broke the family discord this year by selling Curtis a family heirloom, basis to her $14,000, for $1,700. What are the tax consequences of this transaction?

84. Zarco, a very profitable corporation, was owned by Julio, Tilly, and Martinez. Julio and Martinez purchased all of Tilly's Zarco Corporation stock for $50,000 and a $100,000 promissory demand note guaranteed by Zarco. Tilly demanded payment on the note, and Zarco, rather than Julio and Martinez, paid the note. What are the tax consequences of this transaction?

85. Dolores is a limited partner in the Houston Hopes partnership. This year, she was forced under the terms of the agreement to make a $50,000 contribution to capital because the general partners were unable to meet the operating expenses of the entity. Dolores's basis in the partnership prior to the contribution was $40,000, but her at-risk amount was zero because of her limited partner status and her prior-year pass-through losses. What is her at-risk amount after the $50,000 cash call?

86. Steve is a member of a local church. May he deduct as a charitable contribution the commuting expenses for the Sundays that he is assigned to usher?

87. Phil is a used-car manager. To obtain advanced skills in management and marketing, he enrolls in the weekend MBA program at State University, located 20 miles from his home. Does Phil qualify for an educational credit? What items associated with Phil's education are deductible as an employee business expense, assuming that he receives no reimbursements for any of them?

88. Frank and Sharon have been married for five years. Without Frank's knowledge, Sharon has been operating an escort service from the local pub. This year's operations were very profitable. In fact, if Sharon had reported the net escort income, their joint Federal income tax liability would have increased by $50,000. When Sharon finally is nabbed by the police, she is taken to jail. Frank is unable to locate any of Sharon's earnings in their personal bank or brokerage accounts. Can Frank fend off

the IRS's charge that he should pay the $50,000 in tax, plus interest and penalties, from his salary as an engineer?

89. Maria has an unusually strong constitution, which produces the highest quality blood and plasma available for transfusions. She manages to stay healthy while donating blood at the hospital two or three times a week. For each blood donation, the hospital pays Maria $175. Maria drives 40 miles round-trip to the hospital to make her donation. Moreover, she spends about $135 every month for vitamins and other pills prescribed by her physician to ensure that her general health and blood quality do not degenerate in light of her frequent donations. Last year, Maria quit all of her part-time jobs and now survives financially solely by these blood donations. Specify the tax consequences of this regular activity.

90. Chang, a brain surgeon, subscribes to the *Journal of Brain Research*. With a special subscription offer, Chang pays $3,000 this year for the full three-year subscription for this weekly scientific journal. Normally, the journal charges $1,500 for an annual renewal. In what year(s) can Chang deduct this $3,000?

91. Jamie is an elementary school teacher, and her adjusted gross income is $31,000. For this year, she spent $450 of her own funds on special school supplies for those children who could not afford to purchase the necessary supplies. She bought these supplies during a 70-mile round trip to a specialty educational store. Can she deduct any portion of these amounts?

92. Ted's sister, April, was injured while performing her duties as a police officer. She was in the hospital for three weeks before she died from her wounds. The city paid directly to Ted the workers' compensation benefits due to April before she died, as he is April's only surviving relative. How much gross income does Ted recognize upon receiving the benefits?

93. Peggy had been a heavy tobacco user until she joined the Norwood Tobacco Free Program. She had spent a substantial amount of money on nicotine patches and other nonprescription treatments without much success. Her father recently died from lung cancer, and his death made her realize that to kick the habit she would need to get professional help before her smoking created serious medical problems. While she is very pleased at being tobacco free for the first time in 10 years, she is wondering whether any of the vast amounts spent on the cure are deductible.

94. Sally sells her home to Bob and pays $9,000 in points for Bob's mortgage, by receiving $9,000 less in sale proceeds. Determine the tax effects on both parties.

95. Ethel and Rick spent $4,500 in allocable interest and taxes and $1,100 in advertising and maintenance for their "bed and breakfast" inn. This year's rental income from the inn came to $4,900. Determine the tax effects of conducting the B&B using one-third of Ethel and Rick's residence.

96. Carline's son, Leon, 10, is a musical prodigy. Carline, also a musical person, has spent a significant amount of time teaching Leon music and promoting his possible career. When Leon finally receives a recording contract, Carline is designated in the contract to receive one-half of Leon's total earnings. Discuss the proper recognition of gross income and related deductions concerning this arrangement.

97. Barbara owns an incorporated consulting business, for which she has spent years building up its respectable reputation. However, business recently has dropped dramatically due to the unprofessional behavior of Cliff, Barbara's husband. Barbara feels that the only way to protect her business is to divorce Cliff. Cliff demands 50 percent of the stock in Barbara's business. The divorce will be costly because Cliff and Barbara cannot reach an agreement about the business's stock. Are the costs of the divorce deductible to Barbara or to Cliff?

98. Newark Marine Food Service (NMFS) sells hot lunches and snacks to the crews of ships that dock at the Port of Newark. According to custom, the officers of the visiting ships receive a five percent

"commission" from all sales, so that NMFS can retain its "exclusive rights" to the seamen's business. Are the commissions deductible by NMFS?

99. Clara, a community college graduate, works at the Pamper U Hotel in Lake Tahoe. Clara's job is to provide relaxation demonstrations, teach yoga, provide massage therapy, and give lectures on stress management. Since Clara possessed no formal training in any of these subjects, she decided to attend seminars all over the United States on the topics related to her job. She also attended the local university and took physiology classes to learn more about the body and how it functions. Can Clara receive any tax benefits from these educational expenses?

100. John accompanied his wife, Ling, on a business trip to San Diego because Ling is paralyzed from the waist down and confined to a wheelchair. John was not associated with Ling's business directly, but he performed services such as helping Ling overcome architectural barriers, carrying Ling's luggage, facilitating security inspections of Ling at airports, and helped Ling board the airplanes. What is the tax treatment of the incremental expenses for John accompanying Ling on the trip?

101. After his divorce, Brown paid the expenses of maintaining the family home, which continued to be the principal residence of his ex-wife and their three children. Thus, he owns the house, but he no longer lives there. Instead, Brown maintains another home as his principal residence. Can Brown claim head of household status, assuming that the divorce decree grants him the dependency exemptions for his children?

102. Alice, the chair of the School of Accountancy, entertains the faculty at her home each semester and has a holiday party at the end of December for the faculty and their families. When a faculty member is promoted or has a paper published in an exceptionally prestigious journal, Alice hosts a "social hour" at her house. She also sponsors a picnic for the faculty and graduate students at the start of the fall semester to let them get acquainted with each other. To what extent are these expenses deductible?

103. Cambro Construction Company hires union carpenters for home building. Cambro requires, as a condition of employment, that the carpenters provide and maintain various tools of their trade. Cambro pays each carpenter a set amount per hour as a "tool allowance" to cover the costs of the tools. This amount is determined quarterly based on national complied data on the costs of carpenter tools. How should this employee reimbursement be treated for tax purposes?

104. Matt injured Buddy in an automobile accident. The court awarded Buddy $30,000 in damages, but Matt was only able to pay Buddy $12,000. They both then considered the matter closed. Under these terms, compute the amount of gross income to Buddy and Matt from this event.

105. Con man Floyd sold Larry the Library of Congress for $150,000. Since Larry did not have that kind of money, he embezzled the $150,000 from his employer to make the purchase.
    a. How much gross income should Larry and Floyd report as a result of this event?
    b. For tax purposes, how will Larry treat any repayment of the embezzlement to his (former) employer?

106. Reverend Ruth receives a yearly salary of $50,000 and a parsonage allowance of $12,000. She paid $9,000 in rent for the house where she lives, and she spent $1,500 on housing-related purchases. What is her gross income from these items?

107. Jill received a research grant from the University of Minnesota for $10,000 for her time and $3,000 for related supplies and expenses. She purchased a $28,000 Audi the day after depositing the university's check. Jill is a candidate for a master's degree in philosophy and ethics. What is her gross income from the grant?

108. Earl is a golf course superintendent. He recently was hired by the Jack Nicks Corporation to construct an 18-hole course in Wyoming. There will be substantial earthmoving costs in creating the

landscape desired for the course. The fairways will have planted grass, but the greens will be "modern greens" containing sophisticated drainage systems. The greens must be replaced when the underlying drainage systems are replaced. Earl would like to know what costs are expensed and what costs are capitalized either as part of the land or as depreciable assets.

109. Barry's wife, Terra, died in an accident, leaving him with four young children to raise on his own. Shortly after Terra's funeral, Barry and the children move from the house that Barry and Terra owned for eight years, mainly because they needed a change. Barry buys a new house with the help of Lisa, a realtor. Lisa and Barry start dating and, within one year, Barry and Lisa are married. Lisa has four children of her own. Given that neither Lisa's or Barry's homes are large enough for the combined family of eight children, Lisa and Barry both sell their homes and buy a new six-bedroom house. Lisa owned her home for six years, but Barry has owned his most recent house for only one year. All of the houses show realized gains on the sales. How are these sales of personal residences treated for tax purposes?

110. Professor Dodd receives examination copies of text books without charge from book publishers. To what extent should the professor include these books in gross income, if he donates them to a local library and takes a charitable contribution deduction?

111. Tony, a single parent, spent $3,600 on after-school care for his six-year-old son. Tony received $1,200 as aid to families with dependent children from the State Department of Social Services (DSS) for child care as part of the welfare assistance program in which he is enrolled. In determining his child-care credit, how much of the DSS payments are included in gross income, and what is the amount of Tony's child-care costs for computing the child-care credit?

112. Carmella really wants to be an actor but she is having trouble getting that "big break" she so desperately needs. To keep food on the table, Carmella has a small tax preparation business and nets about $30,000 a year. She has received small parts in several movies and on television, earning about $10,000. However, she incurs substantial expenses associated with her acting career that amount to $15,000. Can Carmella deduct her acting expenses and/or can Carmella qualify for the qualified performing artist deduction?

113. Yukio was seriously injured when he fell through an open manhole. Yukio was awarded compensatory damages of $500,000 for his injuries, loss of current wages, reduced future earning ability, and for all of the suffering he incurred and may incur in the future. Is any of the settlement taxable to Yukio? Specifically, is the amount for lost wages taxable?

114. The IRS acquires vast amounts of sensitive information about individual taxpayers. The government is required to keep this information confidential. May a state child-support agency obtain access to an individual's Form 1040 information in determining one's ability to pay child support?

115. John is a shady real estate broker. In 1980, he sells Roy homestead rights to 500 acres in Nevada. In the current year, the land as become moderately valuable and Roy sells his rights to Velma. When Velma tries to exercise the rights, she discovers that Roy never had the rights. She sues Roy for return of money and legal fees. Roy would like to sue John, but he has long since skipped town, never to be found. Roy wants to know if he can claim a theft loss deduction for the damages paid to Velma and all of his court costs due to this breach of title warranty. Roy feels that he was the victim of a swindle when he bought the nonexistent rights from John.

116. Emily's department is required to attend a business meeting in Orlando, Florida. To reduce the costs, the employer charters a 16-passenger plane. Since only 10 employees are attending the meeting, Emily is permitted to bring her husband and daughter along on the flight. How much income will Emily recognize for this fringe benefit?

117. The downturn in the economy created great stress on the housing market and on homeowners. The Federal government developed the Home Affordable Modification Program (HAMP) to help struggling homeowners. Under the plan, homeowners who make timely payments on their modified loans are eligible for Pay-for-Performance Success incentive payments, which are made on their behalf directly to their lenders. Homeowners can receive principal reductions of up to $1,000 per year for up to five years. Are these payments taxable to the homeowner?

118. Ike and Tina were married in 2001 and shortly thereafter purchased a home by taking out a $300,000 mortgage. In 2008, Ike and Tina divorced. The divorce decree gave sole possession and ownership of the house to Ike. However, Tina was to continue making the mortgage payments as part of her pay for spousal maintenance. Are these payments deductible in full or in part by Tina as home interest expense or alimony or are they payments on a debt obligation and not deductible?

119. Todd bought a used speedboat by writing a check for $23,000. When the seller presented the check to Todd's bank, it was rejected, with the bank indicating that Todd no longer had an account at the bank. The seller then requested Todd come back for an item he left behind, but the police were waiting and Todd was arrested for theft. He was handcuffed in front of his family, taken to jail, and put in a holding area with drunks until bail could be arranged. Once it was determined that the bank had made a terrible mistake, Todd sued the bank for false imprisonment and defamation. He received $200,000. While Todd suffered no physical injury from the arrest and detention, he did have nightmares and sought psychological help for several months, and the bank paid the bills. Since Todd was physically held against his will, he thinks the $200,000 is not taxable. Is Todd correct?

120. Rose is a state legislature for a small district located 300 miles from the state capital. Thus, while the legislature is in session (generally 60 days of the year) Rose lives in the capital. If there is a special session, she may have to stay another 30 days. She is rarely gone for more than 100 days. The remainder of the year, Rose is a farmer. Can Rose deduct her costs of attending the legislature as travel expenses because she is away from her home?

ADVANCED CASES

121. Thomas and Nicole Eirgo have been married for 20 years and have three children, Candice, age 18, and twin boys, Trevor and Julian, age 12. Nicole has an undergraduate degree in accounting and worked in public accounting while Thomas was obtaining his law degree. Five years ago they quit their jobs and started TechKnow, a C corporation that develops legal and tax software specifically for accountants and lawyers with high-tech clients. Thomas and Nicole work more than full time at TechKnow and have received only modest salaries. No dividends have been paid. The business has finally started to make substantial profits, but success, unfortunately, has brought problems. Thomas and Nicole have very different opinions regarding TechKnow's future. Thomas would like to continue to reinvest most of the profits for the development of software for other specialties, whereas Nicole would like to focus on the lines they have and enjoy their success by distributing some of the profits. Since they cannot come to an agreement, the earnings are being retained, and no new software is being developed.

These business disagreements are having a disastrous effect on their marriage. The only solution Thomas and Nicole see is to divorce. As might be expected, Thomas and Nicole cannot decide on how to separate their ownership interests in TechKnow. Some options they are considering include redeeming Nicole's stock, having Thomas and/or the children buy the stock, or dividing the business in some manner between the two.

One thing Nicole has decided is to fulfill a lifelong dream of obtaining a doctorate degree in accounting. She will be entering a PhD program in the fall, at which time the divorce should be final. Since Candice also will be attending college, she will live in an apartment with her mother. Thomas will keep the house, and the boys will live with him. Thomas will pay Nicole alimony and child support while she and Candice are in school. The terms and amounts of these payments will be determined at the time the divorce is final.

Advise the Eirgos on the tax consequences of the above events. Support your conclusions with primary citations.

122. Chris and Sue are 50 percent shareholders in the BackBone personal service corporation. BackBone provides chiropractic services in four small towns: Troy, Union, Vista, and Willow. Chris is the main chiropractor in the Troy office, and Sue heads the Vista office. The two other offices have chiropractor employees running the practices, but that is where BackBone's trouble lies. Charlie, the main chiropractor in the Willow office, does not see eye-to-eye with Chris and Sue on management styles. Charlie does not take well to any interference in how he runs the office, the hours he keeps, or the therapy techniques he employs.

Firing Charlie is not an option for two reasons. First, it is difficult to find chiropractors who want to work and live in small towns. Second, and most important, if Charlie were to leave BackBone, he would start his own practice in Willow. He is very good with patients and easily would be able to take at least 80 percent of the clients in Willow. Sue and Chris have noticed that some of the patients in Union drive to Willow because they prefer Charlie to Joe, the chiropractor in their Union office.

Chris and Sue do not want to compete with Charlie and would prefer that the parties would come up with some arrangement that would make everyone happy. They already pay Charlie handsomely, so more salary is not the solution. For Charlie, it seems to be a matter of control. Chris and Sue may be willing to give up control of the Willow office, but they do not want to completely lose the profits this office adds to BackBone.

Chris and Sue have come to you for some suggestions on how to solve this problem with the lowest tax cost. Provide BackBone with several options and the tax consequences of each. Support your conclusions with primary citations.

123. Joe Roberts, 22 years old, is the star of the State University basketball team. He will likely be selected in the first round of the NBA draft. Needless to say, Joe is being wined and dined by several sports agents, and each has been providing Joe with "incentives" to select them as his agent. These incentives range from trips to Las Vegas to Rolex watches. This is all overwhelming for Joe, as he grew up on a farm in Kansas. His parents are also being wined and dined in hopes that Joe's parents can influence him in his choice of agents.

After finally selecting an agent, the time has come to negotiate with the basketball team that selected him. Joe relies completely on the agent in these dealings. Joe is just interested in playing ball, and he does not really care much about the financial details. Joe's agent is in the final negotiating stages with the San Antonio Spurs. The potential offer is $3.5 million for the first year, a signing bonus, and incentive bonuses based on his and the team's performance plus fringe benefits. These benefits will include health and dental insurance, life insurance, a team car, a clothing allowance, a travel allowance for him and his family, free tickets to each game, and all the training and fitness coaching he needs. A retirement plan is a separate benefit to be negotiated.

Joe has come to your firm for tax guidance with regard to the package offered by the Spurs. Provide Joe with a tax analysis of the compensation package. Suggest any tax planning that could help Joe maximize his lifetime wealth.

State Tax Services

- Apply the tax research process to state and local taxes.
- Describe the general constraints of a state taxation system.
- Identify the major features of state tax services.
- Compare and contrast the search methodologies that are available for each of the state tax services.
- Describe which tax services are most appropriate for different research objectives.

CHAPTER OUTLINE

THE STATE AND LOCAL TAX environment is becoming increasingly complex and challenging to navigate due to the states' expansion of their taxing systems. Taxpayers are therefore finding it more difficult to stay abreast of and comply with these evolving state requirements. Thus, state and local tax planning and compliance has become big business for accounting and tax law firms. In today's market, practitioners who service their clients successfully recommend tax solutions that are not only consistent with the client's overall financial goals but also help the client minimize their state and local tax burdens. Consequently, the tax professional must stay current in this area of tax law even though this specialized area can represent an additional burden on the practitioner's time.

There are numerous reasons for emphasizing state and local tax planning. For many businesses this is an untapped planning opportunity in which practitioners can offer an expertise, which is especially important as many of the most productive Federal tax planning opportunities for businesses have been limited by tax law changes. While the amount of any single tax paid to an individual state by a business may be relatively small, in aggregate business taxpayers paid $590 billion in state and local taxes in fiscal year 2009.[1] Coordinated state tax planning can substantially reduce state taxes, especially where the taxpayer operates in a variety of state and local taxing jurisdictions and has some flexibility as to where its property and labor force are located.

All states possess the authority to tax. Generally, local governments must be specifically authorized to impose taxes by state statutory or constitutional provisions. These authorizing provisions, in turn, regulate the rates and operation of local government taxes. Courts in some states, however, have ruled that the power to impose taxes can be implied from broad "home rule" provisions. These rules grant partial autonomy to local government authorities under general state constitutional provisions.

This chapter explores state and local taxation and the resources available for state tax research. Since state and local taxing systems are separate from the Federal tax domain, an overview of state and local taxation is presented before delving into the tax products available to practitioners.

Importance of State and Local Taxes

State and local taxes are playing an ever-increasing role in the tax planning of business and individuals alike. Often, greater revenues are needed to meet the demands of constituents, so states often must raise the tax burdens of citizens. Tax increases for state and local governments can be especially critical when the economy is in a downturn. During these times, the demands for social programs such as welfare and Medicaid build, while the tax bases for states are reduced due to the slow economy. Since most states constitutionally cannot operate at a deficit, the state and local tax obligations become a direct burden for the taxpaying businesses and individuals.

Businesses take the level of state and local taxation into consideration when deciding where to locate a new plant or headquarters. This analysis includes not only business taxes but also the individual taxes of the personnel relocating to the new location. Exhibit 8-1 provides the top and bottom 10 states based on per capita state and local tax burden rank, and also the percentage of personal income represented by that amount. The differences are striking. Note that although Alaska has the largest per capita tax collection, the majority of those are severance taxes for the removal of natural resources and are not a direct burden of Alaska's individual citizens. Vermont, on the other hand, generates the majority of its tax revenue from property taxes. Exhibit 8-2 shows the relative percentages

---

[1]"Total State and Local Business Taxes," Andrew Phillips, Robert Cline, Thomas Neubig and Julia Thayne, March 2010.

EXHIBIT 8-1: Top and Bottom Ten State and Local Tax Collections per Capita 2009

Rank	State	Tax Collection Dollars per Capita	Percent of Personal Income	Largest Source of Tax Revenues
1	Alaska	$7,092	16.4%	Severance*
2	Wyoming	$5,078	10.7%	Severance
3	Vermont	$4,030	10.4%	Property
4	North Dakota	$3,732	9.4%	Severance
5	Connecticut	$3,674	6.6%	Personal Income
6	Hawaii	$3,639	8.7%	Sales
7	New York	$3,328	6.8%	Personal Income
8	Minnesota	$3,259	7.6%	Personal Income
9	Delaware	$3,170	7.9%	Corp. License Fees
10	New Jersey	$3,122	6.1%	Personal Income
41	Colorado	$1,728	4.1%	Personal Income
42	Missouri	$1,728	4.8%	Personal Income
43	Florida	$1,724	4.4%	Sales
44	Arizona	$1,706	5%	Sales
45	Tennessee	$1,659	4.8%	Sales
46	Texas	$1,646	4.4%	Sales
47	South Dakota	$1,642	4.3%	Sales
48	Georgia	$1,636	4.8%	Personal Income
49	New Hampshire	$1,605	3.7%	Sales
50	South Carolina	$1,567	4.9%	Sales

*Severance taxes are imposed on the removal (severance) of natural resources (e.g., oil, gas, coal, other minerals, timber, fish, and so on) from land or water and measured by the value or quantity of products removed or sold.
Source: State Government Tax Collections: 2009, U.S. Bureau of the Census, available at **http://www.census.gov/govs/statetax/**.

of taxes collected by type for all 50 states. Individual income taxes and sales taxes represent the largest categories of taxes at 34 percent and 32 percent, respectively.

Many state constitutions constrain the types of taxes that may be imposed within the state and/or set upper limits on tax rates. Therefore, states may be forced to resort to alternative methods for generating revenues, such as trying to expand the scope of nexus, increase compliance, and impose substantial penalties. As failure to comply with state and local tax laws becomes more costly, businesses and individuals are requesting additional research from their tax professionals to help manage this significant tax burden.

Historical Perspective

Since the time of the early American colonies, payments were made by citizens to their local governing units. Whether these payments were voluntary or required, the purpose of the collections was the same; that is, to support community needs. These early taxing systems were based on the characteristics of the local economy. Accordingly, in the southern states where cotton was the main commodity, taxes were based on imports/exports, whereas taxes in the northern states where many citizens owned land were based on the gross production of farm products and the value of the land. By the end of the eighteenth century, property taxes were becoming popular, and by the mid-nineteenth century, property taxes were the cornerstone of the state and local tax systems.

States relying on property taxes needed to supplement these revenue sources with other kinds of taxes. State income taxes were introduced in Wisconsin in 1911, and gradually they spread to most other states and several municipalities. State sales taxes made an appearance in the early twentieth century, with the first city sales tax imposed by New York in the 1930s. The growth of tax base diversification helped to stabilize state and local governments' revenue yields over time.

In 1970, states were collecting almost $48 billion of taxes per year, and by 2009 this amount had risen to over $715 billion (Exhibit 8-3). Over the last decade, state and local governments' financial burdens have escalated due to cutbacks in Federal aid. These cuts come at

SPOTLIGHT ON TAXATION

State Business Tax Climate 2010

With the myriad differences between states as it relates to sources of income, types of taxes, and tax rates, it can be challenging to determine with any precision exactly what the tax burden will be in a particular state. Tax Foundation, a nonpartisan educational foundation, prepares a tax climate ranking for states, presented below:

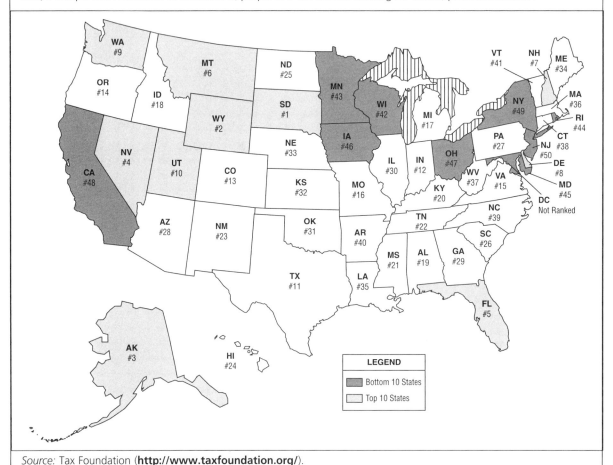

Source: Tax Foundation (**http://www.taxfoundation.org/**).

EXHIBIT 8-2: State and Local Income Tax Collections by Type of Tax 2009

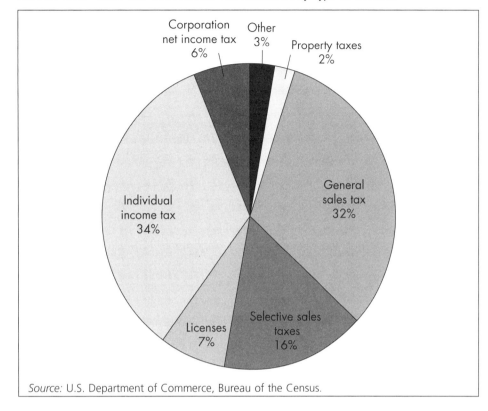

Source: U.S. Department of Commerce, Bureau of the Census.

EXHIBIT 8-3: State Tax Collections

Year	Collections ($B)	Year	Collections ($B)	Year	Collections ($B)
1970	48.0	1985	214.9	2000	551.9
1975	80.1	1990	307.1	2005	650.6
1980	136.9	1995	393.2	2009	715.2

Source: U.S. Bureau of the Census.

a time when citizens are demanding more public services. The combination of these effects has caused the state and local tax burdens to increase substantially over the past 50 years.

Exhibit 8-3 illustrates the increase in the state taxes over time. In 1970, the tax collected by states was $48 billion, whereas by 2009 the amount rose to over $715 billion. Thus, state and local taxes have increased on average by just over 7 percent per year (an increase of almost 1,400 percent over 39 years).

Legal Perspective

Federal and state constitutional provisions play an integral role in state tax planning. The constitutional validity of state tax laws is still challenged in the courts today, whereas the constitutionality of Federal taxes is rarely questioned any more. State and local tax challenges address not only whether the taxes fall within the purview of the state constitution, but also whether the laws are federally constitutional. The Federal clauses most frequently providing the basis for state taxation disputes are the Supremacy Clause related to the hierarchy of tax law, and the Commerce and Due Process Clauses related to the states' power to tax out-of-state individuals and entities.

SPOTLIGHT ON TAXATION

Tax Freedom Day

Every year the Tax Foundation determines "Tax Freedom Day," the hypothetical day when taxpayers have earned enough money to pay all of their taxes and now can "work for themselves." In 2010, the National Tax Freedom Day was April 9. The latest measured tax freedom day was May 1, 2000. Since that time, the date has fluctuated between April 8 and April 27. Depending on the state in which you live, your Tax Freedom Day may be earlier or later than the national average. In 2010, the earliest dates were for Alaska, Louisiana, and Mississippi in late March. The latest dates were for Connecticut (April 27), New Jersey (April 25), and New York (April 23).

TAX FREEDOM DAY AND TAX BURDEN, 1900–2010

Year	Tax Freedom Day	All Taxes as a Percentage of Income
1900	January 22	5.9%
1910	January 19	5.0%
1920	February 13	12.0%
1930	February 12	11.7%
1940	March 7	17.9%
1950	March 31	24.6%
1960	April 11	27.7%
1970	April 19	29.6%
1980	April 21	30.4%
1990	April 21	30.4%
2000	May 1	32.98%
2001	April 27	31.79%
2002	April 17	29.15%
2003	April 14	28.38%
2004	April 15	28.53%
2005	April 21	30.15%
2006	April 24	31.16%
2007	April 24	31.10%
2008	April 16	28.99%
2009	April 8	26.59%
2010	April 9	26.89%

For details, go to **http:// www.taxfoundation.org/taxfreedomday.**

Supremacy

The **Supremacy Clause** in the Federal constitution confers superiority to Federal laws over state laws. That is, Federal laws are "the supreme law of the land" and trump state laws. If a state's constitutional provisions or laws are in conflict with a Federal law, the state provisions are invalid.

Another important application of the Supremacy Clause concerns the taxation by the states of Federal government operations. If states were permitted to tax the Federal government, Federal supremacy would be impinged. Thus, the Supremacy Clause in the Constitution immunizes the Federal government from taxation by the states.

Taxing Out-of-State Taxpayers

Without constitutional limits, states might choose to impose tax on any individual or entity with any connection to that state whatsoever. From a state revenue perspective, such an approach might lead to higher tax revenues, but from the taxpayer's perspective, requirements to file tax returns in every state, even when the taxpayer's connection to that state is minimal, would place an administrative compliance burden that pragmatically, most taxpayers would be unwilling to subject themselves to. As a result, states' power to tax out-of-state individuals and entities has been restricted by the Federal government under two Constitutional clauses and one public law.

Due Process Clause

Section 1 of the 14th Amendment of the Constitution (the **Due Process Clause**) states that " … No state shall make or enforce any law which shall … deprive any person of life, liberty, or property, without due process of law … ." Due process is directed towards the fairness of governmental activities and is concerned with whether the tax in practical terms has a rational relationship to the opportunities, benefits, or protections offered or provided by the state. This "fairness" test is satisfied when an out-of-state entity "purposefully avails itself of the benefits of an economic market in the foreign State."[2] The Supreme Court has applied the Due Process Clause to limit the territorial scope of a state's taxing authority in interstate commerce cases. States have lost cases in two key situations, as follows:

- States seek to tax out-of-state businesses whose connections or nexus with the state are not sufficient to satisfy the Due Process Clause.

- The tax imposed does not fairly reflect the taxpayer's activities in the state.

To be successful in applying a tax, states must prove that the business has more than a de minimis connection to the state and that the taxing base for the interstate enterprise includes only amounts fairly apportioned to its activities within the state. The Due Process Clause does not guarantee that the benefits received by an interstate enterprise will have any direct relationship to the amount of taxes paid to that state. To be fairly related to the services provided by a state, the tax need only be assessed in proportion to the business's activities within the state. As articulated in *Commonwealth Edison Co. v. Montana*, 453 U.S. 609 (1981), "(A) tax … is a means of distributing the burden of the cost of government. The only benefit to which the taxpayer is constitutionally entitled is derived from his enjoyment of the privileges of living in an organized society, established and safeguarded by the devotion of taxes to public purposes."

---

[2]*Quill Corp v. North Dakota*, 504 U.S. 298 (1992).

The Due Process Clause does not require a physical presence by the out-of-state entity for a state to have taxing jurisdiction. Thus, an economic presence rising above a de minimis level is sufficient to tax under the Due Process Clause. However, this same level of contact might not be sufficient to create the substantial nexus within the state as required by the Commerce Clause.

Commerce Clause

Article 1, Section 8, Clause 3 (the **Commerce Clause**) states that "the Congress shall have power … to regulate commerce with foreign nations, and among the several states …". The goal of the Commerce Clause is to create a national economy unencumbered by discriminatory, arbitrary jurisdictional standards of the states. Although phrased as a grant of power to Congress, it has long been interpreted as a constraint on the states' ability to tax interstate trade.

The Commerce Clause has a long history of Supreme Court actions. The interpretation of the clause as it now stands is based on the case *Complete Auto Transit Inc. v. Brady*, 430 US 274 (1977). The case involved a tax being imposed on companies for the privilege of conducting interstate transportation businesses. Corporations involved in intra- and inter-state commerce were all subject to the tax. In unanimously deciding that the tax was valid, the Supreme Court established the four criteria now regarded as controlling as to whether a state may tax interstate commerce without the tax becoming an unreasonable burden.

A tax may be imposed if the activity includes a substantial connection (**nexus**) with the taxing state; the tax burden is fairly apportioned; the tax does not discriminate against interstate commerce; and the tax fairly relates to the services provided by the state. Thus, businesses involved in interstate commerce should be subject to a tax burden related to their fair share of the state's costs of providing benefits to the taxpayer.

In *Quill Corp. v. North Dakota* (1992), the U.S. Supreme Court ruled that the Commerce Clause mandated that a taxpayer must have some *physical presence* in a state to be subject to collection responsibility for the state's use tax. Although Quill deals with use tax not income tax, the Court's discussion of the Due Process and Commerce Clause sheds some light on their application to income taxes. The Quill decision was based on the fact that the burden on an interstate business is so great that it poses a barrier to interstate commerce. It has been suggested that the protection from sales taxation offered by Quill may not last forever. As it gets easier to comply with the use tax obligation, the argument used in Quill becomes less relevant.

Although many of the court cases related to the states' power to define nexus relate to sales tax rather than income taxes, most tax specialists use them interchangeably; however, caution should be used when doing so since sales tax nexus and income tax nexus are likely to be similar but not identical.

Public Law 86-272

The Interstate Income Law (**Public Law 86-272**; 15 USC §§381–384) prevents the income taxation of interstate commerce if a company's only business within the state is the solicitation of orders for sales of tangible personal property. The Supreme Court has clarified that the definition of "solicitation of orders" goes beyond merely making requests for sales—it includes the entire process associated with requesting orders by out-of-state businesses.

Activities that are ancillary to obtaining orders are considered part of the solicitation. Further, activities that are beyond solicitation of orders, but are trivial, are considered de minimis and do not violate the solicitation of orders protection. Having an office located in a state, even if solely for the solicitation of orders, is not de minimis and can subject a business to state taxation.

SPOTLIGHT ON TAXATION

Streamlined Sales Tax Project

Requiring out-of-state and Internet businesses to collect sales taxes on remote sales might impose an overwhelming burden that could severely restrict interstate commerce. There are over 7,500 different taxing jurisdictions in the United States. Texas alone has over a thousand, when considering its local and special taxing districts. In order to find solutions for the complexity in state sales tax systems, the Streamlined Sales Tax Governing Board Inc. was created in 2000.

One of the outcomes of the Board's work is the **Streamlined Sales and Use Tax Agreement**. The purpose of the Agreement is to simplify and modernize sales and use tax administration in order to substantially reduce the burden of tax compliance. The Agreement focuses on improving sales and use tax administration systems for all sellers and for all types of commerce through all of the following:

- *State-level administration of sales and use tax collections.*
- *Uniformity in the state and local tax bases.*
- *Uniformity of major tax base definitions.*
- *Central electronic registration system for all member states.*
- *Simplification of state and local tax rates.*
- *Uniform sourcing rules for all taxable transactions.*
- *Simplified administration of exemptions.*
- *Simplified tax returns.*
- *Simplification of tax remittances.*
- *Protection of consumer privacy.*

Today 23 states have adopted the simplification measures in the Agreement (representing over 31 percent of the population), and more states are moving in that direction. To keep up-to-date on the progress of the Streamlined Sales Tax Project, visit the Governing Board's Web site at **www.streamlinedsalestax.org.**

State Tax Structure

Many states have modeled their income tax structures on the Federal tax system. All of the states have adopted constitutions and typically use three branches of government: legislative, executive, and judicial. Tax statutes are enacted by the state legislatures. These statutes are signed by the state governor, just as Federal tax laws are signed by the President. Regulatory agencies similar to the IRS issue pronouncements on tax matters and administer the tax law. Finally, state courts hear cases regarding tax matters.

Constitution

While each state's taxing system is unique, they are all constrained by the U.S. Constitution and Federal laws. As discussed in the prior section, many clauses of the U.S. Constitution are applied to state taxation, yet only two clauses explicitly restrict state's taxation: the Import/Export Clause and the very specific Duty of Tonnage Clause. Both of these prohibit states from charging taxes on imports or exports without the consent of

Congress. As import/export taxes have become less important at the Federal level, so have these clauses.

Although the Federal laws may appear to dominate state tax issues, it is actually each state's own constitution that is considered the fundamental taxing law because a constitution places the most relevant restrictions on the state's authority to assess taxes. Generally, state constitutions limit the rates and types of taxes that can be imposed, and they require that tax laws show uniformity, equal protection, and have a public purpose. Since elected legislative bodies enact taxes, there is an eminent presumption of validity for a state's taxing laws. It is the ultimate role of the courts to ensure that the legislature acts within the restraints of Federal and state constitutions.

Requiring that tax revenues be generated only for a public purpose is a lofty sounding limitation on a state's ability to tax. However, the definition of "public purpose" is rarely included in constitutions, so the courts have rendered (sometimes vague and broad) interpretations in their decisions for specific taxes. Since the legislature represents a state's citizens, Federal and state courts generally accept the legislative interpretation of the concept.

Legislative

State legislatures are responsible for enacting laws regarding state revenue sources and consequently pass bills amending and augmenting their state's taxing code. While Federal revenue bills constitutionally must start in the House of Representatives, this is not a requirement in all state legislatures. In fact, the jurisdictions of the legislative houses vary from state to state, and there tends to be a significant overlap in their functions. Nebraska avoids this duplication by having only one legislative body. Once the tax bills are passed by the legislatures and signed by the governor, they are incorporated into the state's statutory structure.

State tax codes can provide research challenges for tax practitioners. Each state organizes its tax code based on different criteria and has a different numbering system for its tax law. This means that the practitioner who knows that corporate income tax laws are found in the 300 sections of the Internal Revenue Code (IRC) must conduct a new search for the state corporate income tax laws, if they even exist!

States place varying reliance on the IRC. Some states piggyback most of their individual and business income tax provisions from the IRC, whereas other states have adopted substantial differences. A current trend in state income tax law is to selectively enact changes made by Congress, especially when the Federal changes reduce the state's tax base in a manner the state can ill afford. For instance, some states have refused to adopt the §199 domestic production activities deduction simply because they cannot afford the resulting loss of revenue. Some states adopt Federal income tax law as of a certain time and thus do not adopt the most recent changes that may have been enacted by U.S. legislators. Therefore, the practitioner must be diligent in finding possible differences in state and Federal income tax law when providing tax planning or advice to clients.

Income tax is not the only tax that states utilize, and income taxes may not be the most important revenue generator for the state. In fact, there are several states that do not assess any income taxes. Rather, states rely on a multitude of other taxes, including sales/use, real and personal property, excise on products, severance on natural resources, gaming/gambling, estate/inheritance, and gift taxes. Many states are enacting taxes that are assessed on assets or transactions of service industries, communication and computer operations, and financial enterprises. The mix of taxes varies greatly from state to state. Exhibit 8-4 summarizes the major taxes imposed by each state.

EXHIBIT 8-4:   Selected Taxes Imposed by Each State

State	Income Indiv.	Corp.	Franchise[1]	General Sales	Tangible Personalty[6]	Intangibles	Estate & Inheritance	Gift	Severance[7]
Alabama	Yes	Yes	Yes	Yes	No	Yes	Yes	No	Yes
Alaska	No	Yes	No	Yes[4]	No	No	Yes	No	Yes
Arizona	Yes	Yes	No	Yes	No	No	Yes	No	Yes
Arkansas	Yes	Yes	Yes	Yes	No	No	Yes	No	Yes
California	Yes	Yes	No	Yes	No	No	Yes	No	Yes
Colorado	Yes	Yes	No	Yes	No	No	Yes	No	Yes
Connecticut	Yes	Yes	Yes	Yes	No	No	Yes	Yes	No
Delaware	Yes	Yes	Yes	Yes	No	No	Yes	No	No
District of Columbia	Yes	Yes	No	Yes	No	No	Yes	No	No
Florida	No	Yes	No	Yes	No	Yes	Yes	No	Yes
Georgia	Yes	Yes	Yes	Yes	No	No	Yes	No	No
Hawaii	Yes	Yes	No	Yes	No	No	Yes	No	No
Idaho	Yes	Yes	No	Yes	Yes	No	Yes	No	Yes
Illinois	Yes	Yes	Yes	Yes	No	No	Yes	No	No
Indiana	Yes	Yes	No	Yes	No	No	Yes	No	Yes
Iowa	Yes	Yes	No	Yes	No	Yes	Yes	No	No
Kansas	Yes	Yes	No	Yes	No	Yes	Yes	No	Yes
Kentucky	Yes	Yes	Yes	Yes	No	No	Yes	No	Yes
Louisiana	Yes	Yes	Yes	Yes	No	Yes	Yes	No	Yes
Maine	Yes	Yes	No	Yes	No	No	Yes	No	Yes
Maryland	Yes	Yes	No	Yes	No	No	Yes	No	Yes
Massachusetts	Yes	Yes	No	Yes	No	No	Yes	No	No
Michigan	Yes	Yes	Yes	Yes	No	No	Yes	No	Yes
Minnesota	Yes	Yes	No	Yes	No	No	Yes	No	Yes
Mississippi	Yes	Yes	Yes	Yes	No	Yes	Yes	No	Yes
Missouri	Yes	Yes	Yes	Yes	No	No	Yes	No	No
Montana	Yes	Yes	No	No	No	No	Yes	No	Yes
Nebraska	Yes	Yes	Yes	Yes	No	No	Yes	No	Yes
Nevada	No	No	No	Yes	No	Yes	Yes	No	Yes
New Hampshire	Yes[3]	Yes	No	No[5]	No	No	Yes	No	No
New Jersey	Yes	Yes	No	Yes	No	No	Yes	No	No
New Mexico	Yes	Yes	Yes	Yes	No	No	Yes	No	Yes
New York	Yes	Yes	Yes	Yes	No	No	Yes	No	No
North Carolina	Yes	Yes	Yes	Yes	No	No	Yes	No	No

(Continued)

EXHIBIT 8-4: Selected Taxes Imposed by Each State (*Continued*)

State	Income Ind.	Income Corp.	Franchise[1]	General Sales	Tangible Personalty[6]	Intangibles	Estate & Inheritance	Gift	Severance[7]
North Dakota	Yes	Yes	No	Yes	Yes	Yes	Yes	No	Yes
Ohio	Yes	Yes	Yes	Yes	Yes	No	Yes	No	Yes
Oklahoma	Yes	Yes	Yes	Yes	No	No	Yes	No	Yes
Oregon	Yes	Yes	No	No	No	No	Yes	No	Yes
Pennsylvania	Yes	Yes	Yes	Yes	No	Yes	Yes	No	No
Rhode Island	Yes	Yes	Yes	Yes	No	Yes	Yes	No	No
South Carolina	Yes	Yes	Yes	Yes	No	No	Yes	No	No
South Dakota	No	Yes[2]	No	Yes	Yes	No	Yes	No	Yes
Tennessee	Yes[3]	Yes	Yes	Yes	No	Yes	Yes	Yes	Yes
Texas	No	No	Yes	Yes	No	Yes	Yes	No	Yes
Utah	Yes	Yes	No	Yes	No	No	Yes	No	Yes
Vermont	Yes	Yes	Yes	Yes	No	No	Yes	No	No
Virginia	Yes	Yes	No	Yes	No	No	Yes	No	No
Washington	No	No	No	Yes	No	No	Yes	No	No
West Virginia	Yes	Yes	Yes	Yes	No	No	Yes	No	Yes
Wisconsin	Yes	Yes	No	Yes	No	No	Yes	No	Yes
Wyoming	No	No	Yes	Yes	No	No	Yes	No	Yes

[1]Franchise taxes based on net income are listed here as an income tax and not a franchise tax.
[2]On financial institutions only.
[3]Tax on income from intangibles only.
[4]Local sales tax only.
[5]Sales tax on meals, rooms, rentals, and telecommunications only.
[6]This represents a tax on tangible personalty. Note that all the states, without exception, levy taxes on real property, either on a state or local level.
[7]Severance taxes are taxes on the extraction of natural resources.

Administrative

Once tax statutes are enacted, they must be interpreted and enforced. These duties fall to administrative agencies created by either statute or constitutional provisions. In most states, the Department of Revenue (Department of Taxation, State Tax Commission, etc.) is the main administrative agency for this purpose. Other smaller agencies administer the more specialized taxes such as employment, tobacco, or fuel taxes. California is an exception in that it has two revenue agencies, the Franchise Tax Board (income and franchise taxes) and the State Board of Equalization (most other taxes).

It has been said that whoever has authority to interpret the law is really the lawmaker, and it is the state revenue agencies that play this role for the state tax laws. These agencies publish regulations, rulings, and various other authoritative pronouncements as aids in interpreting and applying the law to a specific situation. As in the Federal system, it is the courts' duty to ensure that the administrative agencies do not overstep their authority.

Most state revenue agencies issue rulings for specific taxpayers, similar in nature to Private Letter Rulings (PLRs) issued by the IRS. As with PLRs, the letters are for the exclusive use of the taxpayer requesting the guidance and usually cannot be relied upon by other taxpayers as authority. These private rulings, however, may provide taxpayers with hints as to the revenue agency's position on a particular issue and, therefore, are useful to the practitioner.

Federal regulations and rulings may be pertinent to state tax issues. For states that piggyback income, estate, or other taxes on Federal statutes, guidance in interpreting the law will come from the Federal pronouncements. As previously stated, the degree to which states follow Federal income tax or other tax law varies greatly.

Judicial

State judicial systems are, for the most part, patterned on the Federal system. Most states use three levels of courts: supreme courts, appeals (appellate) courts, and trial courts. However, some states have only one appeals-level court, whereas others have four levels by adding a county or district trial court with limited jurisdiction. The functions of the levels of state courts are similar to the Federal functions. The trial courts establish the facts and apply the law to these facts. The appeals courts review the trial court's application of the law to the set of facts. They generally rely on the trial court's account of the facts. The state's Supreme Court usually holds powers corresponding to the Federal Supreme Court; it is the final interpretation of an extant law of the state, but its precedents apply only to the state in which it is located. For those states that use only two levels of courts, the functions of the appeals and Supreme courts are conjoined.

While most states do use a three-tier judicial system, it may not be inherently obvious from the court names what their precedential values are. A "superior court" is likely to be a trial court or can be an appellate court, but it probably is not the highest court of the state. Most of the intermediate courts have the words "appeals" or "appellate" in their names. However, the highest court of a state can also be called the "Court of Appeals." In New York, for example, the Supreme Court is its trial court, and its highest court is called the Court of Appeals. The most diversity among states is with the trial courts. There are county, municipal, circuit, district, and superior trial courts, just to name a few. Each state has organized its trial courts to meet the needs of its citizens and judicial system.

Whereas the Federal judicial system includes a court specifically for tax cases, the Tax Court, most states do not have an equivalent. Rather, there may be administrative (quasi-judicial) tribunals authorized to expedite settlements of tax disputes. The decisions of these tribunals generally are available to the public, but they tend to have little precedential value. The findings generally apply only to the taxpayer bringing the dispute. As with other such documents, they can shed light on the state's position on a particular issue.

None of the tax services cull the tax cases from state court reporters and accumulate them into a state tax court service, like the CCH USTC or the RIA AFTR reporters. The tax cases are intermixed in the state reporters with all the other types of cases that state courts hear. Fortunately, the ability to search electronically eliminates any inconvenience that not having dedicated reporters might cause.

Multistate

Companies conducting business in more than one state are subject to multistate taxation. Given the complexity of business organizations, it can be quite difficult to determine what share of business income a state is entitled to tax. In more than 40 of the states that impose a corporate income tax, the starting point in determining state taxable income is Federal taxable income as reflected on the corporate income tax return (Form 1120) or taxable income before the dividends received deduction.

As mentioned earlier, however, each state is free to define taxable income in a manner consistent with that state's system of taxes. As a result, Federal taxable income is often adjusted by whatever differences exist between Federal tax rules and that particular state's tax rules. Common modifications include the following:

- Adding back interest on state and municipal obligations if not exempt for state purposes (net of expenses).

- Subtracting interest on U.S. obligations, which is taxable for Federal purposes but not state purposes (net of expenses).

- Adding back state income taxes deducted in computing Federal taxable income.

- Subtracting refunds of state income taxes.

- Subtracting Federal income tax paid. (A limited deduction is allowed in five states).

- Adding back Federal depreciation, amortization, and depletion in excess of that allowed by the state or subtracting state depreciation, amortization, and depletion in excess of the Federal amount.

- Adjustments of gain or loss on asset dispositions due to depreciation differences.

- Adjustments for differences between Federal and state net operating losses (NOLs).

The income of multistate companies must be divided among the states in which it conducts business. Most states use a system of allocation and apportionment to divide the income. Under this method, certain types of income are traced (allocated) directly to their geographic source or other connection with a state and attributed solely to that state. Other types of income are apportioned among the states in which the corporation is doing business. With apportionment, there is no attempt to trace items of income to the state in which the income was generated. Rather, a formula is used to arrive at an approximation of a business' income that should be attributed to a particular state.

Formula apportionment divides a multistate corporation's tax base among the states in which it does business by applying a fraction representing the ratio of in-state factors to total factors. Historically, the most common apportionment formula has been a three-factor equally weighted formula that considers the ratio of in-state property, payroll and sales to overall property, payroll, and sales. However, today most states use formulas that weight sales more heavily than the other factors.

In most states, nonbusiness income is allocated to a jurisdiction while business income is apportioned. However, it is not always easy to determine if income is business or nonbusiness. In order to create a greater uniformity and consistency in the measurement and determination of business and nonbusiness income, the **Uniform Division of Income for Tax Purposes Act (UDITPA)** was drafted by the National Conference of Commissioners on Uniform State Laws in 1957.

Under UDITPA, business income is defined as income that arises from transactions and activities in the regular course of the taxpayer's business. It includes income from tangible and intangible property if the acquisition, management, and disposition of the property constitute integral parts of the taxpayer's regular trade or business operations. Nonbusiness income is simply defined as all other income.

Interest, dividend, and patent and royalty income can be either business or nonbusiness income. For example, interest derived from notes received from the sale of regular merchandise would be business income. Interest received by banks on loans made to customers is business income, as is interest earned on money held for escrow purchases.

Interest earned from investing excess cash holdings is treated as nonbusiness income. Dividends received from stock held for investment to meet a specific business objective such as bonding or obtaining a source of supply is classified as business income.

In 1967 the **Multistate Tax Commission (MTC)** was created through an organization of state governments called the Multistate Tax Compact. The purposes of MTC are to:

- Facilitate the proper determination of state and local tax liability of multistate taxpayers, including the equitable apportionment of tax bases and settlement of apportionment disputes.

- Promote uniformity or compatibility in significant components of tax systems.

- Facilitate taxpayer convenience and compliance in the filing of tax returns and in other phases of tax administration.

- Avoid duplicative taxation.

The MTC believes that greater uniformity in multistate taxation will ensure that interstate commerce is more fairly taxed, lessen compliance costs for taxpayers and revenue agencies, and reduce the potential for congressional intervention in state fiscal authority. The MTC closely follows state developments in the rules related to allocation and apportionment of taxable income and communicates that information back to member states.

The MTC has strongly encouraged states to adopt the uniform tax laws and abide by its regulations. It has been only moderately successful in this endeavor, however, as only 19 states have become compact members enacting the multistate tax compact into their state laws, while six states are sovereign members who support the general purposes of the MTC. Another 22 states are associate members who participate in commission meetings, programs, and projects. Three states, Delaware, Nevada, and Virginia, are not members.

Participating states may take advantage of the **Joint Audit Program**, which allows the MTC to perform a comprehensive audit of a business's taxes for several states simultaneously. This program replaces individual audit efforts by each state, which can save the states and the taxpayer time and compliance costs.

Another program offered by MTC is the **National Nexus Program**, which is designed to provide education and information to taxpayers to help them understand nexus and business registration requirements. In addition, this program provides litigation support to the states on nexus issues and on identifying potential companies for referral to the joint audit program.

SPOTLIGHT ON TAXATION

Quotation

"The thing generally raised on city land is taxes."

—Charles Dudley Warner

Illustrative Research Example

Sample research projects will be used to demonstrate effective state tax research methods. It is important that you attempt this research project using the various tax services available to you. The procedural knowledge necessary to perform state tax research effectively can be acquired only through hands-on practice. The remainder of this chapter is designed to guide you through the basic tax services—it is not a substitute for your actually performing the research yourself.

Research Project: Vincent Lopez is expanding his Virginia-based accounting practice by entering into some large engagements in Maryland and West Virginia. It is very likely Vincent will need to open a new office to handle the new client business. Vincent would like to know the sales tax implications for this business. Specifically, on which services must Vincent charge sales tax, and are there any tax incentives available to Vincent's firm?

This type of project is very common in state research. Expansion of a business into a new geographic area requires a large number of considerations, including many tax-related issues. It is always important to remember that tax is only one of the many possible consequences of a business decision or transaction, and that tax researchers attention must be given to the relative importance of taxes with regards to all other factors.

RIA State and Local Service

Research Institute of America's RIA Checkpoint State & Local Tax (SALT) service is a comprehensive analysis of state and local taxes for all 50 states and the District of Columbia (D.C.). The service is designed to let the researcher designate the states, type of taxes, and documents to be searched. Any or all of the states' taxes and documents may be searched simultaneously. Essentially all of the taxes imposed by states and most enacted by localities are covered in this service. For a complete list of the taxes and documents included in the RIA SALT service, see Exhibit 8-5.

As with the Federal Checkpoint materials, editorial explanations and annotations are an integral part of this service. The explanations are particularly useful when investigating a state's taxes with which you are unfamiliar, such as the Ohio commercial activity tax (CAT) or the business and occupation (gross revenue) tax of Washington State. The explanations contain links to all the supporting materials, making retrieval a seamless process. The annotations for court and agency decisions also are linked to their primary sources.

Special Features

RIA SALT has many features that were especially developed for this service. These options enhance the effectiveness and efficiency of researching state and local tax issues.

StateNet is a database consisting of all proposed and current enacted regulations and legislation in full text. For proposed legislation, the current status of bills can be tracked through StateNet, which is extremely valuable when a proposed change in the state tax law could have a major impact on the practitioner's clients. Status reports for legislative bills, executive orders, and ballot measures are furnished for each state.

Within the Current Calendars heading is the Effective Date Calendar database, which lists each state's legislative enactment conventions. For example, California's effective date for newly enacted legislation is the following January 1 or as provided in the Act, whereas South Carolina is 20 days after the Governor's approval, or as specified in the Act. Lastly, current legislative calendars are reproduced in StateNet.

The All State Tax Guide is a concise state-by-state analysis of all major taxes, with citations to state materials. The Guide covers interstate law, income allocation and

EXHIBIT 8-5: RIA Search States Tax Type & Document Selection Screen

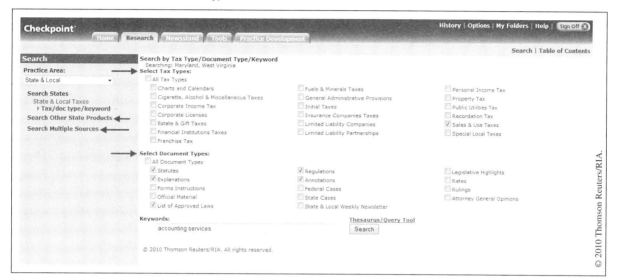

apportionment, uniform acts, and the MTC. It offers numerous tables, charts, and checklists for a variety of tax data as well as calendars for important reporting dates and monthly listings of recently approved state and local tax laws. The list of official state contacts makes it easy to find an address or phone number for taxing authorities.

The latest news on state tax developments is available through the State & Local Taxes Weekly newsletter. This newsletter offers practice-oriented analysis from national experts and breaking news, organized by state, making it easy to identify what is of interest to the practitioner. Also included with the SALT service is the Journal of Multistate Taxation and Incentives. The full-length articles in this journal generally report on multistate tax issues with an emphasis on practical planning opportunities, whereas the short technical comments focus on emerging tax issues for particular states.

The Create-a-Chart feature facilitates the building of multistate charts that can cut across a variety of taxes and/or states. These convenient summary charts can be exported to a word processing or spreadsheet document. The product supports linking information on the charts to controlling authority and/or RIA's explanation paragraphs. These links are maintained when the chart is exported. The practitioner can designate the type of tax (income), a chart type (tax rates, starting point for computing taxable income), and which states to include in the comparison. Over 100 chart types are offered in Create-a-Chart.

The RIA feature, CompareIt, enables the researcher to compare the tax treatment of an item in one state to the treatment in another state or with the Federal treatment. This makes it easy to compare the tax treatment of an item in multiple states, and it eliminates the need to return to the list of documents when performing multiple state searches as would be necessary with Research Project 8–1.

In Exhibit 8-6, for example, first locate the RIA sales tax explanations for Maryland and click on CompareIt, and then you can easily find the West Virginia sales tax explanations by merely clicking on the state name. CompareIt is available only for explanatory materials and not for state statutes or regulations.

As with the Federal databases, the SALT databases can be entered using the three search methods: keyword search, citation, and contents. The multistate search option is different, though. As a variant of a keyword search, it is demonstrated under the Keyword Search heading.

Keyword Search

The opening screen for RIA Checkpoint (Exhibit 6-1, Chapter 6) allows the researcher to choose a practice area. Upon selecting "State & Local," Checkpoint offers a list of the states. All the states or any number of separate states may be designated for the search. At this juncture, one cannot enter keywords. Checkpoint requires that a type of tax and document be specified before a keyword search may occur. Exhibit 8-5 displays the choices for taxes and documents. The offerings appearing on this screen are customized to the state(s) selected in the previous screen. Accordingly, this full list of taxes would not be offered for every state. Again, any or all of the taxes and document databases may be marked for the search.

With respect to Research Project 8–1, Maryland and West Virginia were selected in the list of states, Sales and Use Tax was checked for the Tax Type, and several document types were marked in the document type section (Exhibit 8-5). The search results link to explanations, regulations, and rulings pertaining to the sales taxes on accounting services in Maryland and West Virginia (Exhibit 8-6). By reading these documents, Research Project 8–1 can be analyzed. Rather than designating taxes and documents, the Search Other State Products option is available (Exhibit 8-5). This accesses secondary sources, such as RIA newsletters and journals, in addition to StateNet and Federal cases on state topics. These databases may be searched using keywords or citations depending on the nature of the database.

EXHIBIT 8-6: RIA State & Local Document Screen and CompareIt

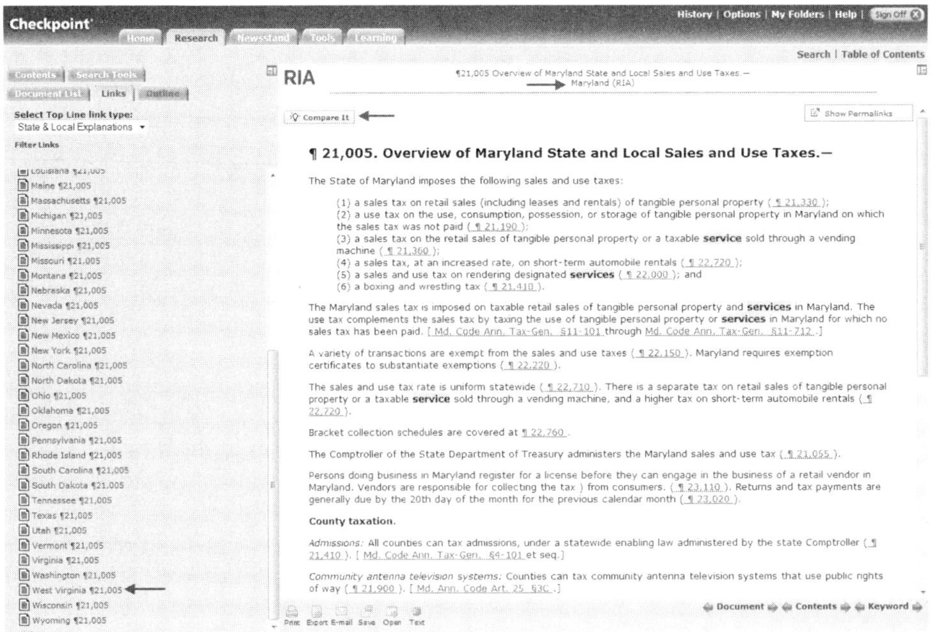

As can be seen in Exhibit 8-7, one of the search choices offered is Search Multiple Sources. A comparison of Exhibits 8-5 and 8-7 reveals that the document categories are not similar for these two keyword search functions. In fact, the Search Multiple Sources is designed for entering keywords, selecting document sources, and searching. This closely resembles the Federal Practice Area keyword search format (Exhibit 6-1, Chapter 6), and the same thesaurus and query tool functions are available.

Along with primary sources, editorial materials, current newsletters, and journals, the Multiple Sources offers the Miscellaneous Multistate Materials database. This database consists of materials from the Multistate Tax Compact, the Multi-state Tax Commission, and the Federation of Tax Administrators. It also contains numerous multistate agreements and acts, formulas for apportionment and allocation of income, and Federal laws on state taxation.

Since the Search Multiple Sources option lacks a tax type indicator, the type of state tax being investigated must be included as a keyword to narrow the results to the particular tax of interest. As seen in Exhibit 8-7, for Research Project 8–1, Maryland (and off-screen West Virginia) was selected from the State and Local Taxes list. The keyword search would need to include "sales taxes" in order to produce results similar to those using Search States in Exhibit 8-5.

Citation Search

Unlike the Federal Practice Area, the SALT materials do not allow state citation searches directly on the opening screen. Rather, only Federal cases on state tax issues may be searched

EXHIBIT 8-7:   RIA Search Multiple Sources Screen

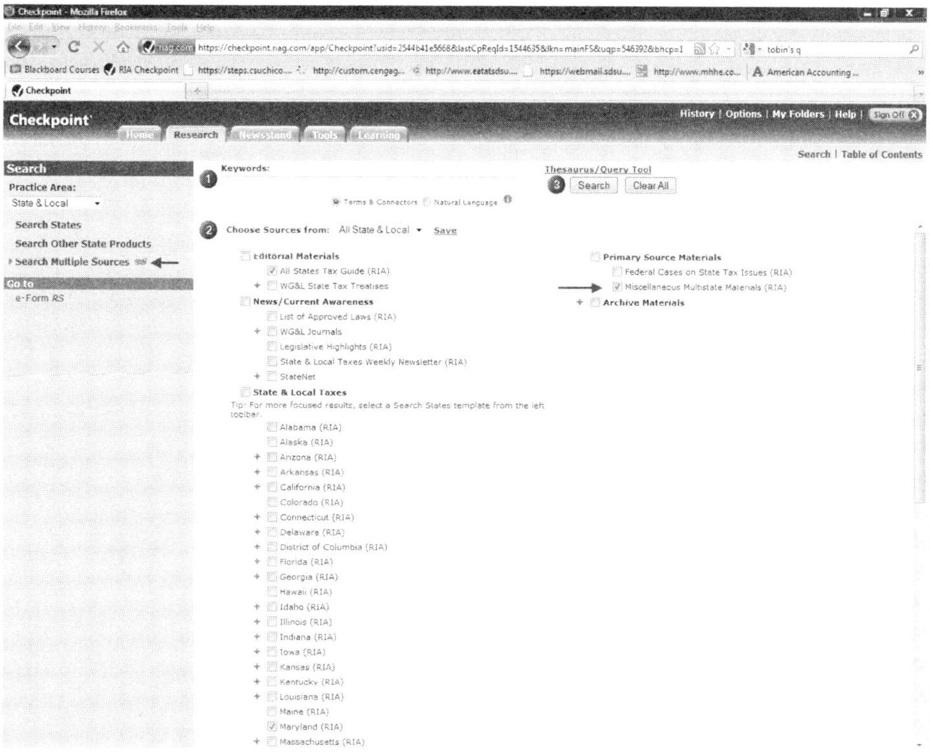

© 2010 Thomson Reuters/RIA.

without selecting a state. The Federal cases may be searched by name of the plaintiff or defendant, citation, or keyword. Since customized templates for the different court reporters are not furnished, the researcher must know the proper format for the citation.

State statutes, regulations, rulings, and cases may be located by citation, but a state must be chosen before these options appear. The citation templates are customized based on the state selected (Exhibit 8-8), and only one state's citations may be searched at a time. If more than one state is chosen in Search States, then the Find by Citation option is not offered.

State Searches also supports a keyword search for courts and rulings using date restrictions. These two searches, Cases by Court/Date and Rulings by Date, also require a state to be selected before the options are accessible because the listing of courts and ruling types are also customized by state. While these are technically keyword search options, the taxpayer's name may be entered as the keyword, thus functioning similar to a citation search. The ability to restrict the search by date is particularly useful when updating a previously searched tax issue.

Contents Search

The RIA SALT service supports Table of Contents (TOC) and Index searches. These methods allow the researcher to treat the tax service as if it were in a printed book. Thus, as in a book, the TOC and Index can be browsed for the topic of interest. In many cases, this methodology for searching is more efficient than the keyword search. By narrowing the search by focusing on the contents of databases, fewer extraneous documents are retrieved when a keyword search is performed. The limitation with this type of search is that only those databases containing tables of contents or indexes are searchable.

The Checkpoint TOC option is available from all screens. Therefore, the researcher does not need to be in the State and Local Practice Area to begin a TOC search. The methodology that is effective in a Federal TOC search also would be appropriate for the SALT search. Besides the editorial materials, StateNet, and newsletters, each state has a listing in the TOC.

One of the most useful subheadings listed for each state is the Index. By drilling down through the Index, the same documents previously identified for Research Project 8–1 can be found. Starting with Maryland and drilling down into Sales—Use and the

EXHIBIT 8-8: RIA Find by Citation Screen

Introduction in the Index, will find the document in Exhibit 8-6. If the listing under the contents is long, using the "Ctrl-F" command to bring up the "Find" box, and entering a relevant term will display the entries desired. These drill-down techniques are efficient in locating pertinent documents; however, the drawback is that each subheading must be examined separately. Access to each state's index is also furnished when it is the only state selected for the Search States option.

CCH Network State Service

Like RIA Checkpoint, Commerce Clearing House's IntelliConnect (CCH) includes a complete state tax service. This research tool allows for keyword searches across as many databases as the researcher would wish to select. For state tax research, CCH has a State Tax library that can be browsed in order to select the specific sources required (Exhibit 8-9).

State Tax Reporters

The backbone of the CCH state tax service is the State Tax Reporters. This service combines detailed explanations, primary source materials, and practical compliance guidance. All of the major taxes imposed by states and localities are covered by the service. Although the CCH explanations are organized by tax type, with links to related primary sources, state material is retrieved by selecting the state(s) of interest. RIA requires the researcher to identify the type of documents to be searched, but CCH assumes all materials are of interest. The list of document types searched can be reduced by selecting the state tax area in the browse sources feature. The State Tax Reporters may also be searched using keywords or the TOC.

Searching the State Tax Reporters for a solution to Research Project 8–1 begins by selecting State Taxes from the choices presented in Exhibit 8-9 and drilling down into the State Tax Reporters, and further refining the selection to Sales and Use taxes and then, if desired, to the specific source of materials on that topic, such as state law (Exhibit 8-10).

EXHIBIT 8-9:   CCH State Tax Library

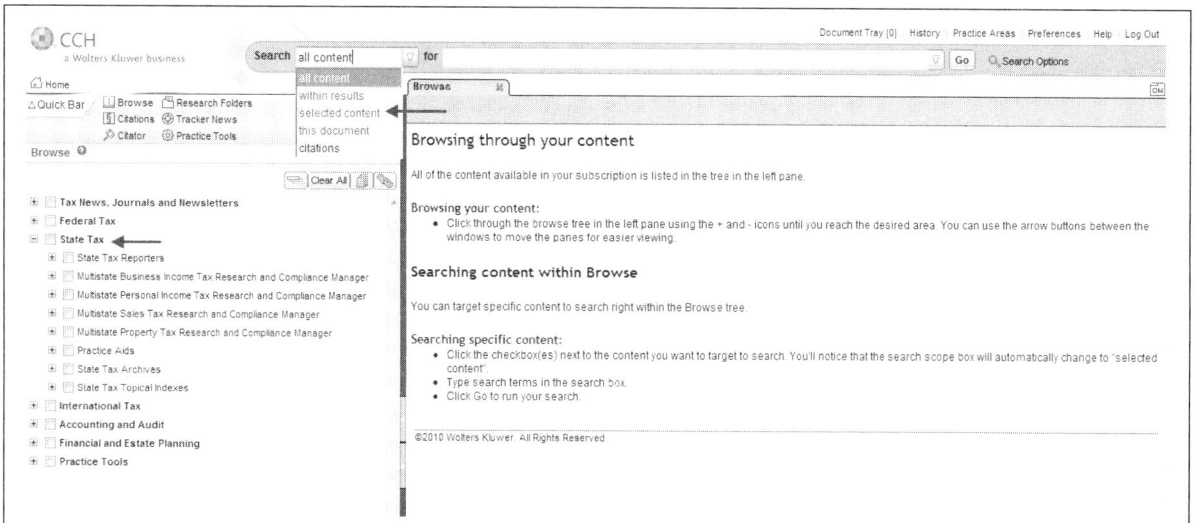

Exhibit 8-10 presents one of the State of Maryland laws related to sales and use tax that contained the keywords searched. The results of the search are displayed in the top box while the selected document is displayed below, providing an opportunity to review the search results in detail.

Multistate Publications

CCH offers several multistate databases, including business, personal, property, and sales tax guides. Each is designed to be an all-in-one guide emphasizing multistate planning yet delivering state-by-state details for every topic. Cost-effective planning ideas are presented, and the "at-a-glance" charts are effective in finding quick answers to each state's treatment of key taxes.

Included with the specialized multistate databases is the *State Tax Guide*. This is similar to the *Master Tax Guide*, as it is intended for finding quick answers to everyday questions on taxes levied in every state. Thus, its treatment of tax issues is very concise—state tax statutes and pronouncements are summarized rather than reproduced. Each state has a page listing its major taxes, tax base and rates, and due dates. There also are charts for most taxes that provide each state's imposition and rates. This publication can be an extremely efficient tool when all that is needed is a short answer to a simple question or a comparison among a few states on a particular tax.

Practice Aids

The latest in state legislative actions is found in the Practice Aids section of the State Tax Tab. This Week's Legislative Activity, Regulatory Activity, Current Year's Final and Pending Legislation, and Prior Year's Enacted Legislation are located in the Practice Aids.

EXHIBIT 8-10: CCH Document Search Results

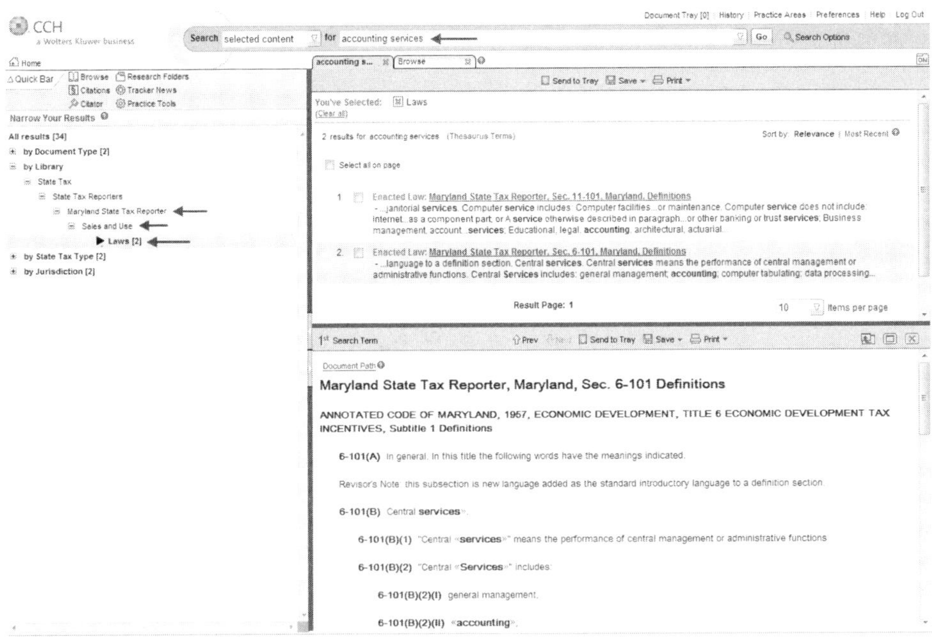

In addition, the Tax Law by State contains primary tax law for each state. The constitution for each state, its revised (consolidated) statutes, city and/or county ordinances, and uncodified (unconsolidated) statutes are obtainable through Tax Law by State.

State Tax Archives

Previous versions of the State Tax Reporters are maintained in the archives to enable research of tax issues for prior years.

Topical Indexes

The last feature in the state tax library is the State Topical Indexes to the Multistate tax guides. Each state also has its own index, but these are accessed through the State Tax Reporter TOC for the state. The major advantage of using an index is that the definition of the term is considered, not just its occurrence in the document.

Citation Search

State citation searches are conducted in the same manner as a Federal citation search. Using Citations from the quick bar and drilling down into the particular state for searching presents templates that are appropriate for state citation searches, as can be seen in Exhibit 8-11.

LexisNexis Academic

The state tax data included in the LexisNexis Academic service are offered through both of the searching engines, Search and Sources. The libraries presented in each are, to some extent, singular. Accordingly, the Search and Sources Tabs each are visited to make a thorough search of the documents available in LexisNexis Academic.

EXHIBIT 8-11: CCH Find by Citation

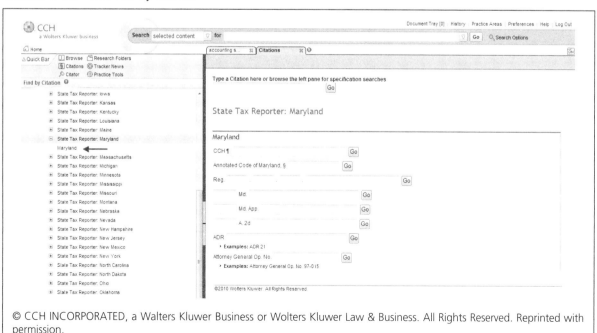

SPOTLIGHT ON TAXATION

State Tax Incentives

All 50 states and the District of Columbia offer some form of tax incentives for business that are considering expanding or relocating to their state. Incentives offered include exemptions or abatements of business, income, property, and sales and use taxes, and they can apply to business activities that create jobs, provide for capital investment, increase research and development expenditures, or are related to certain industries. Businesses evaluating a move or expansion to a new locality should contact the state and local tax commissioner or economic development agency to determine what types of tax incentives are available. The incentives may be quite significant and may help determine the most cost-effective choice of the new location—at least the state and local governments are betting they will. The National Conference of State Legislatures (NCSL) also contains a wealth of economic development and incentive program information (www.ncsl.org).

Search

As with Federal tax research, state tax libraries are located at the Legal button on the Search Tab. Exhibit 8-12 illustrates that the two primary state tax sources are cases

EXHIBIT 8-12: LexisNexis Academic Legal Search

(Federal & State Cases) and statutes (Federal & State Codes). The pull-down menu for the codes is visible for the Select Sources. Notice that a particular state may be selected to search. Cases can be searched by using keywords, plaintiff and/defendant names, citation (examples of proper format are supplied in Citation Help), judge's name, and counsel or firm name. Date restrictions also are possible. Any cases retrieved may be run through the Shepard's Citator to determine their precedential value.

The state code searching is more limited in the number of databases offered. All state constitutions, statutory provisions, court rules, and so on are in a single library. Date restrictions are not permitted.

Sources

When Sources, Taxation Law is selected as the Area of Law in Step 1 and United States is the Country Filter in Step 2, the sources can be filtered further by selecting a region or specific state from the pull-down menu shown in Exhibit 8-13. The categories of sources (Step 3) are customized to the region or state chosen. The sources offered are more expansive than in the Search Tab. Besides the state cases and regulations available through the Search Tab, Sources may contain state revenue decisions, newsletters, journals, IRS pronouncements, and even newspaper articles. The selection of sources varies greatly by state or region. Once the sources are selected, clicking OK-Continue brings the researcher back to the search page with only the selected sources as part of the keyword search.

LexisNexis Tax Center

LexisNexis Tax Center provides state-by-state access to all the state-level tax laws and regulations and a host of analysis and other editorial materials as well. Included are analysis and guidance provided by the LexisNexis Tax Adviser and Bender's State Taxation (Exhibit 8-14). As with the other major tax services, searches are performed by selecting the relevant sources and entering a keyword or search term. Current state tax issues are covered in Tax Analysts *State Tax Notes* available as part of the service.

Westlaw State Services

Westlaw contains an extensive library of databases for state tax research. Exhibit 8-15 shows only part of the list of these databases. Note that the list includes the Bureau of National Affairs (BNA) Tax Management Portfolios devoted exclusively to state taxes and the RIA state series. Besides furnishing access to all state tax statutes, regulations, court cases, and administrative pronouncements, Westlaw enhances the tax practitioner's ability to stay ahead of the curve on new state legislation by providing databases to track current, pending, and proposed state bills. Newsletters such as the BNA Daily Tax Report and the RIA State and Local Taxes Weekly also help keep the practitioner up-to-date.

Find and KeyCite

The opening tab screen, Find a State Tax Document (Exhibit 8-16) allows the researcher to enter the citation for state primary sources. Since the templates for entering citations are based on the state chosen, searching for a specific state document is easy if the general citation is known.

Another method for entering state law citations is to use KeyCite. The citation, however, must be in a format recognized by Westlaw. If the researcher does not know the format, the Publication List can be referenced. Unlike Find by Citation, the KeyCite publication list is not linked to templates for entering the citations.

Directory

There are two ways to access the state databases in the Directory. The first method is through the Topical Materials by Area of Practice and selecting Taxation. The State Tax Materials is one of the files in the list. It contains the complete list of state databases found in Exhibit 8-15.

The second Directory heading leading to state tax materials is the U.S. State Materials. Since a taxation subheading is not displayed as one of the library options, a comprehensive

EXHIBIT 8-13:   LexisNexis Academic Browse Sources

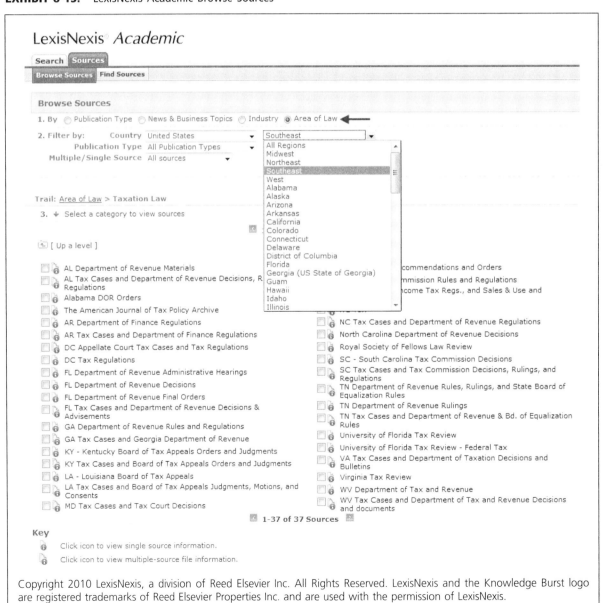

search of *state tax materials* is not possible. By selecting the Other U.S. States subheading, however, access to tax materials is available through each state because Tax Materials is one of the legal topics offered for each state. Thus, each state's tax databases must be

EXHIBIT 8-14: LexisNexis Tax Center State

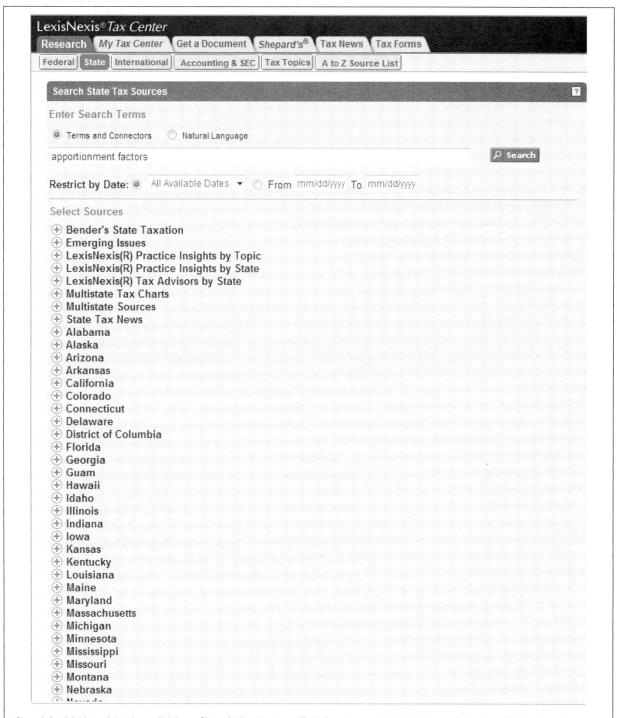

EXHIBIT 8-15: Westlaw State Databases

searched separately. To search across states, the researcher would select from libraries such as Case Law or Statutes & Legislative Services. Drilling down through these libraries, the researcher arrives at databases covering taxation.

Tax Tab

The Tax Tab lists several headings for state taxation (Exhibit 8-16). Show All presents an extended list of the state tax materials and databases (Statutes, Regulations, Cases, and Administrative Decisions) by individual state. Whether selected on the Tax Tab opening screen or after expanding the list, the databases may be searched using either natural language (all terms searched) or terms and connectors. Field filters are available, as is a thesaurus.

One can search some of the state tax databases by TOC. The State Tax Portfolios are listed in the TOC pull-down menu. Further, RIA products and some of the treatises have TOCs that can be browsed.

Practitioners performing state research frequently will want to create state and/or Federal circuit case tab(s) for easy access to these databases. Unfortunately, there are not state tabs dedicated solely to taxation.

BNA State Services

The BNA complements its U.S. Tax Management Portfolios with a State Tax Series. As with the other BNA Portfolios, the state series is topic-driven and features analysis, insights, and guidance from leading state and local tax authorities on a variety of state issues. Some of the Portfolios offer an overview of a tax topic, while others focus on complex income, sales and use, or property tax issues. For topics such as credits and incentives or income taxation, it may take several Portfolios to cover all of the states. The state taxes and a sampling of the types of issues covered by the more than 60 State Portfolios are presented in Exhibit 8-17.

The State Portfolios have the same format as the U.S. series. Each State Portfolio begins with a Portfolio Description, which gives a brief overview of the topic and the order in which the materials are presented. The Portfolios contain the three usual BNA sections: (A) Detailed Analysis, (B) Working Papers, and (C) Bibliography and References. The Portfolio sections are updated in response to state tax changes and, when necessary, the complete Portfolio is rewritten. BNA has been adding new Portfolios to cover emerging issues and to round out the State Portfolios offerings.

When unfamiliar with a state topic, the more general Portfolios furnish a thorough but easy-to-comprehend introduction to the topic. Those Portfolios focusing on a specific technical state topic may assume a certain level of practitioner sophistication and therefore are more difficult for the state research novice. As with the U.S. portfolios, the state statutes, regulations, rulings, and court case opinions are integrated into the analysis with citations footnoted or included in the text. The critical documents cited are reproduced in the working papers section. Other useful aids furnished in the State Portfolios include the following:

- Interactive state forms
- Reproductions of model acts
- Sample sales and use certificates
- Tables, charts, and lists
- State tax administrations' addresses and telephone numbers
- Keyword indexes, state-by-state indexes

EXHIBIT 8-16:   Westlaw State Tax Tab Screen

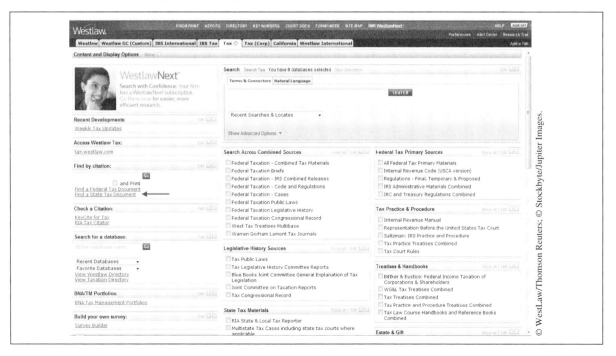

EXHIBIT 8-17:   BNA State Portfolio List

BNA STATE PORTFOLIO TOPICS	
Taxes and Issues Covered	**Issues Covered**
Corporate Income and Franchise Taxes	Procedures and Administration
Gross Receipts Taxes	Managing State Tax Audits
Personal Income Taxes	State Tax Appeal Systems
Property Taxes	State Tax Audit and Collection Procedures
Sales and Use Taxes	Definition of a Unitary Business
Excise Taxes	State Formulary Apportionment
Special Industry Taxes	Choice of Entity
State Environmental Taxes	State Taxation of Pass-Through Entities
State Taxation of Electronic Commerce	Consolidated Returns and Combined Reporting
State Taxation for Specific Industries	Mergers and Acquisitions
State Taxation for Specific States	Business Credits and Incentives
State Environmental Taxes	State Tax Aspects of Bankruptcy
State Taxation of Compensation and Benefits	Doing Business Across State Lines
Limitations on States' Authorities to Tax	Unclaimed Property

Source: www.bna.com

Although BNA does not offer a full state tax service like RIA, CCH, or Westlaw, the State Portfolios and its news reports can compete with any provided by other services. If the practitioner can find a Portfolio that covers the state tax issue of interest, BNA has performed the key research, and all that needs to be done is to apply the results to the facts of the client's situation.

Other Resources

Warren, Gorham & Lamont (WG&L) publishes the *State Taxation* treatise by Jerome R. Hellerstein and Walter Hellerstein. This two-volume treatise, currently in its third edition, is possibly the most comprehensive single work on state and local taxation. The authors have undertaken the ambitious task of assembling a comprehensive review of all state and many local tax laws, plus the court decisions interpreting those laws. Because few published works address state taxation in such a thorough manner, State Taxation has been cited by many state courts and even the U.S. Supreme Court as the authority on state taxation. Westlaw and RIA offer this treatise as part of their SALT services, and it is also available in print.

The *Multistate Corporate Tax Guide* published by CCH is another useful treatise. The Guide focuses on key corporate tax issues in sales and use taxation and income-based taxes for all states and some localities such as New York City and D.C. The treatise provides quick access to each state's position statements on tax issues through numerous charts. Much of the analysis is based on data collected through questionnaires completed by the top state officials who interpret and apply the state laws. To assure timeliness and relevancy of the information, the treatise is updated mid-year with a supplement.

Periodicals and Internet Sites

State tax journals and newsletters contain a variety of articles and news briefs that are designed to keep readers current with regard to developments in general areas of state and local taxation and tax issues specific to a given state. These articles may contain, for example, an in-depth review of a recently decided court case, a broad analysis of state tax factors that should be considered in tax planning, or a call for reform of a statute by a neutral (or biased) observer. The articles can suggest new approaches to tax problems, give guidance for solving complex problems, or just explain a new law in a readable form.

Journals

Two important state taxation journals are the *Journal of Multistate Taxation and Incentives* (WG&L), which releases 10 issues per year, and *Journal of State Taxation* (CCH), published bimonthly. Both of these journals focus on practical solutions to state and local taxation as well as creative planning strategies for multistate business operations and individuals with multistate tax liabilities. These journals keep the subscriber informed on critical areas of state and local taxation nationwide and provide expert assessments of important cases and their potential impacts.

Generally there are reviews of current state legislative issues to keep the reader up-to-date on state proposed, pending, or enacted legislation. Articles may cover legal, accounting, and business aspects of multistate entities. Both journals also focus on incentives offered by states to encourage business growth and expansion.

Newsletters

Tax Analysts publishes two influential state tax periodicals, *State Tax Notes* and *State Tax Today*. Like the Tax Analysts flagship, *Tax Notes*, *State Tax Notes* is an authoritative source for news and commentary on state and local taxation. This weekly publication provides the latest news from all 50 states and D.C., plus in-depth analysis from leading experts in state taxation. Summaries of all judicial, administrative, and legislative developments are also included in *State Tax Notes*.

The purpose of *State Tax Today* is to furnish the most current state tax news on a daily basis. It covers every state, D.C., and U.S. territories. There are links to full-text state documents and U.S. Supreme Court, State Supreme Court, and appellate court decisions. Beside news briefs, *State Tax Today* has in-depth analytical articles, commentaries, and special reports.

Many of the other tax publishers provide state newsletters. For example, the *Tax Management Weekly State Tax Report* is the BNA analog to the Tax Analysts *State Tax Notes*. It gives a state-by-state analysis of state code and regulations, state administrative, judicial court decisions, and state administrative pronouncements, as does *State Tax Notes*. Other state newsletters and reports published by BNA include the following:

- *State Tax Legislation Monitor*
- *State Insights & Commentary*
- *State Tax Regulation Monitor*
- *Weekly State Tax Report*
- *Multistate Tax Report*
- E-mail Highlights notification of the week's state tax highlights

The CCH newsletter is called *State Tax Day*, and RIA's is *State & Local Taxes Weekly*. Both are offered through the publishers' Internet tax services.

Internet Sites

The Tax and Accounting Sites Directory Web site (**www.taxsites.com**) contains links to numerous tax resources on the Internet. The state and local listing has links to each state's taxing agency, legal information, organizations, and government sites. In addition, links to general locators, sales/use tax, news topics, organizations, tax rates and data, state tax guides, and e-commerce tax are included in the state and local screen.

SUMMARY

With so much of a business's tax bill being composed of non-Federal taxes, planning for state and local taxation has become more important to taxpayers and therefore to tax researchers. The research service industry has responded to this escalating need, creating a greater variety of more sophisticated tax research products that are designed to improve the practitioner's efficiency and effectiveness in state and local research. As SALT consulting becomes more of a mainstay for practitioners, tax services will provide more options for research. Consequently, state and local tax research tools likely will be among the fastest-changing components of the major tax services.

QUIZ YOURSELF

Reinforce the tax research information covered in this chapter by completing the online quizzes located at the Federal Tax Research Web site at **www.cengagebrain.com.** At the CengageBrain.com home page, search for the *Federal Tax Research*, 9e ISBN (1111221642) using the search box at the top of the page. This will take you to the product page where you can access the quizzes.

KEY WORDS

By the time you complete this chapter, you should be comfortable discussing each of the following terms. If you need additional review of any of these items, return to the appropriate material in the chapter or consult the glossary to this text.

Commerce Clause, p. 294
Due Process Clause, p. 293
Joint Audit Program, p. 301
Multistate Tax Commission (MTC), p. 301

National Nexus Program, p. 301
nexus, p. 294
Public Law 86-272, p. 294
Streamlined Sales and Use Tax Agreement, p. 295

Supremacy Clause, p. 293
Uniform Division of Income for Tax Purposes Act (UDITPA), p. 300

DISCUSSION QUESTIONS

1. Why are taxpayers emphasizing state and local tax planning?

2. Why have state and local taxes been increasing over recent years?

3. What categories of taxes represent the two largest as a share of total state tax revenues?

4. What tax represents the single largest source of revenue in your state?

5. What state was the first to introduce an income tax? In what year? What was the first city to have a sales tax? In what year?

6. What is Tax Freedom Day? What organization computes Tax Freedom Day? Is Tax Freedom Day coming earlier or later than in the prior years?

7. Describe the different constitutionality challenges with regard to Federal and state taxes.

8. Discuss the supremacy provision in the Federal Constitution.

9. Which clause in the Federal Constitution contains the most significant limitation on state taxing authority?

10. What are the four criteria for imposition of state taxation set forth in Complete Auto Transit Inc.?

11. Explain how the passage of a state tax bill is similar to the passage of a Federal law.

12. When would Federal rulings be pertinent to state tax issues?

13. What is a severance tax?

14. What is UDITPA, and what is its significance with regard to the Multistate Tax Compact?

15. What is the Joint Audit Program that the MTC offers?

16. What are the purposes of the MTC?

17. How is state taxable income typically calculated?

18. What is the most common method of determining a state's share of income of a multistate corporation?

19. What is included in the RIA Checkpoint StateNet?

20. What is the function of the CompareIt feature in RIA?

21. Compare the Multiple Sources search with the State and Local Taxes initial search option in RIA.

22. Discuss the citation search capabilities in the RIA state and local tax practice area.

23. How are specific states' tax laws selected using CCH IntelliConnect?

24. What are some common types of incentives offered by your state?

25. Explain whether one can search the same libraries with the LexisNexis Academic Search engine and its Sources engine.

26. What citator service is used in LexisNexis Academic?

27. What tax service may be offered as one of the state databases in the LexisNexis Academic service?

28. Describe the two methods that work through the Westlaw Directory to search state tax documents.

29. Are the BNA State Portfolios organized by state? If yes, is there a portfolio on each state? If no, what is the organization?

30. What are the different sections in a BNA State Portfolio? How similar are these to the sections provided in the U.S. Income series?

31. Name two state taxation journals and indicate who publishes each.

32. Compare the state tax newsletters published by Tax Analysts and BNA.

33. Why does this chapter not provide a listing of state and local tax Web sites?

EXERCISES

34. Locate the Web site for the MTC.

    a. Define the three levels of membership in the MTC.

    b. Provide a brief summary of one of the latest articles in the Multistate Tax Commission Review. (Hint: Publications are found in Resources.)

    c. What is the Nexus Program? When was it founded?

    d. How does a taxpayer initiate joint audits?

    e. The MTC provides a link to the Federation of Tax Administrators (FTA). What is the title and date of the most recent FTA Meeting?

35. Use the RIA Checkpoint State & Local Practice area to locate the *Bacchus Imports Ltd. v. Herbert H. Dias* case using the Federal Cases in the State Taxes option.

    a. What is the citation for the case, and what court heard this case?

    b. What clauses of the U.S. Constitution is *Bacchus* alleging were violated?

    c. Must the plaintiff and defendant names in the case be entered to find the case? Explain your response.

    d. Read this case. Perform a keyword search to locate the case without using the plaintiff or defendant names. If necessary, use the Search Within Results feature. What keywords did you use for the general search and (if necessary) for your follow-up search?

36. Use the RIA Checkpoint State & Local Practice Area to answer the following questions:

    a. Select the state in which the university you are attending is located and go to the next screen.

    b. What corporate items are provided in the tax type list? Is there a tax on intangibles, mortgages, or stock transfers?

    c. Select Florida (or Washington if your university is in Florida) as the state of interest and go to the next screen. What tax types are different between the two states?

    d. Select the state in which the university you are attending is located. What is the rate of tax per pack of cigarettes? Compare your state's rate to that of Washington State. In what order are the Tax Types listed? In what order are the Document Types listed?

37. Use the RIA Checkpoint State & Local Practice Area to answer the following questions:

    a. For the state of your choice, compare the listing of documents available under the option Select Document Types in the Search States (SALT) with the list for the same state in the TOC.

    b. Using the Index in the TOC for the state of Illinois, what are the listings for the letter "H" under the "stamp" heading?

    c. In the Vermont TOC, what annotation is addressing the constitutionality of land gain taxes found in Recordation?

    d. In the Miscellaneous Multistate Materials TOC, what are the U.S. statute titles listed for Federal Laws on State Taxation?

38. Use the CCH IntelliConnect State Tax to answer the following questions regarding the state in which the university you are attending is located:

    a. What is the title of the most recent article in *State Tax Day* related to this state?

    b. What is the most recent court case for this state?

    c. In the State Tax Reporters, perform a keyword search using the term "escheat." What does this term mean and to what does it apply? In what paragraph did you find the answer?

    d. Using the Topical Index for *Multistate Property Tax Guide*, perform a keyword search for "dining car." Under what headings are there entries for this term?

39. Use the CCH IntelliConnect State Tax to answer the following questions:

    a. Does Hawaii allow estates a personal exemption? If yes, what is the amount and what is the state statute allowing such amount?

    b. Select all states to determine which states provide a personal exemption for estates. Use the keywords "estate" and "personal exemption" in your search. Was this method effective? Explain your response.

    c. Turn on the Thesaurus (use Search Tools). Select a state and perform a keyword search using the term "devise". What synonyms are also searched?

40. Use the CCH IntelliConnect State Tax to answer the following questions:

    a. Did Alaska ever have a personal income tax? If yes, what was the year Alaska repealed the tax?

    b. Use the Multistate Quick Answer Charts to determine the diesel fuel tax for the state in which your university is located. Which state has the highest diesel fuel rate?

    c. What tax legislation was enacted by the state in which your university is located this week (if any)? How about since the beginning of the year?

    d. Determine which states have Jai Alai taxes.

41. Using the LexisNexis Academic Sources option, find the source that contains the Sacramento Bee newspaper and:

    a. Perform a keyword search for "use tax" (as a single term) with the source identified. What is the title of an article published in the *Sacramento Bee* in the last year that addresses a use tax issue?

    b. What sources are available for the state of Florida in the Taxation area of law?

    c. What are the title and author of the most recent article in the *Florida Tax Review* with these three separate keyword terms: property, tax, and abatement? Did you use a natural language or terms and connector search?

42. Use LexisNexis Academic Search option, Legal to answer the following questions:

    a. Locate the following court case: T. C. Memo 1986-512. What is its citation, what court heard it, and when was it decided?

    b. Apply the Shepard's Citator to the above case. How many citing decisions are there for this case? How many headnotes?

    c. Should the finding in this case be relied upon?

43. Use LexisNexis Academic to answer the following questions:

    a. Select Sources, By Area of Taxation—Taxation, Filter by—West. Which states does LexisNexis Academic consider western states?

    b. What treatises and analytical materials are provided for the western states?

    c. Select Search, Legal. In what year was the Missouri constitution adopted?

44. Use the service of your choice (RIA, CCH, LexisNexis, or Westlaw) to answer the following questions:

    a. Locate *Complete Auto Transit Inc. v. Brady*. What is the type of tax that was being examined in the case? Provide two parallel citations for the case and the name of the justice delivering the opinion.

    b. Locate *Quill Corp. v. North Dakota*. What was the disposition of the case by the Supreme Court? Provide two parallel citations for the case and the name of the justice delivering the opinion. Name any judges that filed dissenting opinions.

c. Locate *Wisconsin Department of Revenue v. Wrigley*. What tax years are reviewed by the case? Provide two parallel citations for the case. Who were the attorneys for the respondent and petitioner? Were there any dissenting opinions?

d. Locate *Commonwealth Edition Co. v. Montana*. What is the type of tax that was being questioned in the case? Provide two parallel citations for the case. What two Federal clauses were addressed in the case?

45. Use the Westlaw State Taxes practice area to answer the following questions:
    a. What document types are available under the West State Tax materials for the state of Maine?
    b. What is the latest tax guidance in the state of Maine on the application of sales tax to the rental of bowling shoes?
    c. What section of the Federal Limitations on State and Local Taxation Database results from a search for "*Geoffrey*" in that database?

46. Use the Westlaw State Taxes practice area to answer the following questions:
    a. What is the name of the taxpayer in the CA Franchise Tax Board Decision 88-SBE-022?
    b. According to Hellerstein, does California currently follow a *Joyce* or *Finnigan* rule?

47. Use Westlaw to answer the following questions regarding the *Jensen 178 Cal.App.4th 426* case:
    a. What year was the case decided and by what court?
    b. Examine the headnote. What three holdings did the court determine?
    c. What is the KeyCite "flag" associated with this case?
    d. What two judges concurred with the Judge Boren's ruling?

48. Use the BNA Tax Management Portfolios, Specific States to examine the following questions:
    a. Is there a portfolio for each state? Which state has the most portfolios?
    b. Generally, what are the Portfolio Series numbers for the portfolios that address state business entities and transaction issues?
    c. What are the title and number of the Portfolio that addresses the Federal Constitutional Limitations on State Taxation?
    d. What portfolio discussed the Illinois sales and use tax on professional and personal services?

49. Use the BNA Tax Management Portfolios, State Series for the following questions:
    a. What is the title of State Portfolio 1550? How many worksheets are included in this Portfolio?
    b. Which Portfolio explains the state tax effects of the QSSS election for S corporations?
    c. How many basic forms of drop shipment transactions are there? In which Portfolio did you find your answer?

50. Locate state tax newsletters to answer the following questions:
    a. What is the title of the most recent article in Tax Analyst *State Tax Today* that discusses royalty trusts?
    b. What is the most recent article in BNA *Tax Management Weekly State Tax Reporter* that discusses the streamlining of sales taxes?
    c. What is the title of the most recent article in CCH *State Tax Day* on gasoline taxes?
    d. What is the title of the most recent article in CCH *State Tax Review* that discusses sales tax obligations advertising agencies?
    e. What is the subject of one of the most recent article in RIA *State & Local Taxes Weekly* newsletter?

51. Find an article in the *Journal of Multistate Taxation* and Incentives on the following topics. Provide the authors, title of the article, and date published.
    a. The ad valorem property taxes on a baseball stadium.
    b. Most recent economic incentives provided to the film industry.

   c. Credits and exemptions used by Mississippi to promote the development of broadband technology.

   d. The most recent article on the dividends-received deduction.

52. Use the *Journal of State Taxation* to answer the following questions:

   a. What is the title of the most recent article on Web-related activities and potential nexus problems?

   b. What are the volume and number of the most current issue? What is the lead article?

   c. Who is the current editor of the journal? Is there anyone on the advisory board that is from the university you attend? If yes, list the name(s).

   d. Who is the author of the article titled "Throwback of Foreign Sales?" What are the year, volume, and issue number in which the article appears?

53. Use Internet sites to answer the following questions:

   a. Provide the links to three News & Topics sites provided by Tax Sites for states (www.taxsites.com).

   b. Visit three national associations that are concerned with state tax issues. Provide their URLs.

   c. Visit the Web site of your state's agency responsible for taxation (Department of Revenue for many states). Provide the URL for this agency. For California, provide both agencies' URLs.

   d. Select an adjacent state and give a summary of one of its taxes. (You could use Alaska and Hawaii as a pair.)

RESEARCH CASES

54. Tom and Verna are going to combine their fishing businesses to become more profitable. Tom currently lives in Mississippi and Verna lives in Louisiana. They would prefer to set up the business as an S corporation, but only if it will not be subject to state taxation. Since Verna and Tom live within 20 miles of each other, they do not have a preference as to the state of incorporation. Does it make a tax difference which state they choose?

55. New City, California, charged Rick a real estate transfer tax when his property was relinquished to the Federal Housing Administration (FHA) in its capacity as his loan guarantor. The amount charged was the same as the amount Rick was required to pay the county. Can Rick be required to pay this tax, or should the FHA pay it?

56. TimberCut Corporation transferred all the rights to timber growing on its land located in Spokane County, Washington, to its wholly owned subsidiary, PineCo. The Department of Revenue has imposed a real estate excise tax on TimberCut because PineCo. transferred $1 million cash to TimberCut. Is TimberCut's transfer a sale of timber land subject to the taxes imposed?

57. WaterWorks Corporation has decided to sell off one of its amusement parks located in Texas. Several businesses have been identified as possible buyers. It is unlikely that one of these businesses will purchase all of the assets of the amusement park, but WaterWorks is confident that it can sell all of the assets to various parties within a six-month period. Is this sale subject to Texas sales tax?

58. A tribal nation in Kansas is considering building a gas station to accommodate travelers through their reservation. Before undergoing the considerable expense for construction, the tribal members want to know whether the fuel sold will be subject to state fuel taxes. This will make a difference in the profitability of the project. Is gasoline sold on a federally recognized reservation subject to the fuel tax imposed by Kansas?

59. A town in Vermont wants to charge property tax on a lot and building used by a not-for-profit organization as its administrative office. To be exempt from property taxes, the property must have the following characteristics:

- Be dedicated to public use.
- Have its primary use directly benefit a class of persons who are part of the public.

- Be owned and operated on a not-for-profit basis.
- Does administrative use of the building meet the definition for the exemption?

60. Iowa imposes a tax on the operation of slot machines. The rate is graduated based on slot machine revenues. Can Iowa charge a higher maximum rate to racetrack owners than it does to riverboat owners without violating the equal protection clause of the U.S. Constitution?

61. The Pluto Corporation has been mining ore in Oklahoma for many years. A new mine just developed is producing ore containing uranium. Pluto would like to know the rate of the severance tax on mined uranium, and upon what base the tax is assessed.

62. The Peppermint Partnership operates a successful candy business. It is considering taking the partnership public and becoming a master limited partnership. If it does so, will it be subject to the corporate franchise tax in New York, where its headquarters and operating plant are located?

63. Rodney has been in the South Carolina National Guard for the past 20 years. This is his last year as an active member. Since Rodney turns 65 in August of this year, he will begin collecting Social Security benefits and Guard retirement pay. His employer laid him off in January and Rodney qualified for unemployment compensation. Rodney received severance pay of $50,000 when terminated by his employer. Which of these amounts are taxable to Rodney in South Carolina?

64. Poplar Inc.'s corporate headquarters, plants, and warehouses are located in Vermont. Until this year, all of Poplar's sales have been made in Vermont. Poplar's first out-of-state sale of $1 million (cost of sales, $300,000) is shipped by a common carrier trucking firm from its warehouse to the purchaser's dock in Indiana. The truck stops for gasoline in New York and Ohio, and its driver spends a night in Ohio. To which states must Poplar apportion income from the sale? How much income is taxed in each such state?

65. A religious organization is considering spreading its message into Illinois by opening several churches. As part of its ceremonies, wine is consumed by its members. The church would like to know the consequences for the alcoholic beverage tax if it ferments its own wine. What if, instead of making the wine, the church purchases it from an importing distributor?

66. The Ohio Government Employees Credit Union (Union) was created by merging the Ohio Teachers Bank, the Ohio Transit Credit Association, and the Federal Government Workers Credit Bank. The stock issued by the merged entity is held by those having deposits in Union. Union believes that it is not subject to the Ohio franchise tax (an income tax) because immunity is implied under the Supremacy Clause of the U.S. Constitution. Union believes it is closely connected with the government and thus should be exempt from taxation. Is Union correct in its conclusion that it is not subject to the Ohio franchise tax?

67. Travis Smith and Carmela Jones operate a successful law firm in Portland, Oregon. They are considering opening another office across the Columbia River, in Vancouver, Washington. Travis and Carmela would like to know if they then would be subject to any business or personal taxes in Washington. If they are subject to any taxes, can they use those taxes as a credit or a deduction on their Oregon income tax returns, as taxes paid to another state?

68. Jie Wang wants to open a new funeral parlor in Colorado. She would like to know the sales/use tax implications for this business. Are morticians considered to be rendering services, are they selling tangible personal property, or a combination of both? Specifically, Jie needs to know whether she should contract funeral services as one lump sum, or would it be more beneficial to itemize the charges for caskets, urns, and so on separately from the services offered?

69. Brock and David are equal shareholders of an S corporation that manufactures electric razors. They are interested in opening a plant in the south. They want to know whether Florida or Alabama would be the best state to move to, considering only tax consequences. The main concern is with regard to income taxes

(corporate and personal), franchise taxes, and intangible asset property taxes. Brock and David expect the S corporation to generate $400,000 in annual taxable income.

70. Melkry, an Ohio corporation, provides tugboat services on the Great Lakes to vessels weighing at least 800 tons. Each of Melkry's tugboats weighs approximately 100 tons. Michigan has assessed use tax on repair materials, fuel, and capital assets purchased by Melkry for its operations. Is Melkry subject to the use tax?

71. EmiLu Corporation is a private delivery company that hires independent contractors with their own trucks to deliver car parts to various auto repair shops in Pennsylvania. EmiLu contracts with the manufacturers of the car parts to make the deliveries, and then it hires the drivers in Pennsylvania to deliver the parts. EmiLu has no property, employees, or customers in Pennsylvania. EmiLu is incorporated in Delaware, where all the car part manufacturing customers are located. Is EmiLu subject to the corporate franchise tax in Pennsylvania?

72. Earl and Kathy live on the Big Island of Hawaii in the town of Captain Cook. Because the altitude is high, they have coffee plants growing on their property. Most of their neighbors grow coffee on their property as well. Earl and Kathy collect the coffee from their property and that of their neighbors, and then they dry the coffee in a special building they have constructed on their land. Does this activity affect their qualification for the home exemption for Hawaii property taxes?

73. Chuck Taylor owns a fish processing plant in Alaska. Some of the processing chemicals and fish remains could be considered hazardous wastes. What possible state and local taxes does Chuck need to be concerned about when disposing of these materials?

74. Jefferson W. Clinton is a resident of Arkansas but has not filed an income tax return nor paid any tax liabilities for the years 2004 to 2008. Does Arkansas currently have a tax amnesty program that would relieve Jefferson of some of the penalties and interest on his unpaid liabilities?

75. Chicago Tool and Die Corporation (CTDC) recently purchased an aircraft for the top executives to use for customer visits, transporting employees from one location to another, and for matters relating to acquisitions and lawsuits. Upon purchase, no Illinois sales tax was charged, as the seller did not have Illinois sales tax nexus. The aircraft was hangared in Ohio but made numerous trips (over 200) in and out of Illinois airports. In the year of purchase, was CTDC liable for Illinois use tax?

76. James Bulger works at a sandwich shop in Ames, Iowa. During his coffee break each afternoon, he enjoys a candy bar that his employer sells to him at an employee discount. Candy bars are not exempt from sales tax in Iowa (as food), and his employer charges him sales tax on the purchase. Recently James noticed that his employer was charging him sales tax on the retail sales price ($1), not the employee discount price ($.80) that James actually pays. What is the proper amount to calculate the sales tax on, the actual (reduced) price or the retail price?

77. Sal Bermuda recently invested in a new flavored water that he is bottling and selling at street vendor carts throughout the city of Chicago. Sal's water is flavored with natural ingredients and just a touch of sweetener. Some of Sal's customers have been explaining how happy they are that Sal has not been charging them a $.05 bottled water tax. Sal has never heard of such a tax and is wondering if there are any other taxes aimed specifically at his bottled water product?

78. Apache and Alice Swearingen moved to Minnesota in 2006. Apache retired in early 2009, and the Swearingen's purchased a motor home and started traveling extensively and put their Minnesota home up for sale. Due to lack of interest, however, they took their home off the market late in the year. In 2010 they spent about 15 days in South Dakota. While there they registered a mailbox address with a private company, and using that address obtained South Dakota drivers licenses, opened a bank account, registered to vote, and registered their vehicles in South Dakota. In March 2010, they relisted their Minnesota home for sale. In April 2010 they returned to Minnesota from their road trip to South Dakota (and other states as well), and

in June 2010 they finally sold the home. They spent the rest of 2010 traveling the country in their motor home. Are the Swearingen's required to file a Minnesota resident income tax return for 2010?

79. Evgenia is a resident of California. She recently purchased two computers from an online retailer that did not charge California sales tax. The retailer happened to be offering a steep discount if two computers were purchased in a single transaction. One of the computers she gave to her sister (also a California resident) for her birthday a few days after the computers arrived. Since Evgenia already had a fully functional computer, she stored the other computer for the next 18 months before finally upgrading to a new one. Is Evgenia responsible for California use tax for one, both, or neither computers, and when is the use tax due?

80. Coldbear Inc., a California corporation, recently entered into two new contracts with clients in Georgia and Utah. In order to service those clients, Coldbear will hire a couple of additional employees (based out of California) who will make five or six trips to the client's offices in Utah and Georgia to provide the services required under the contract. Coldbear employees will work at the client's offices in each location and stay in hotels during the trips. (Coldbear does not see any need to open new offices in either state.) Please describe, in detail, how Coldbear will calculate the numerator of the sales apportionment factor for state income tax purposes in all three states (California, Georgia, and Utah).

81. Professional athletes are required by many states to consider "duty days" when determining taxable income. What are duty days? Does the state in which your university is located have duty days? Compare and contrast the definition of duty days between California and Michigan, specifically with reference to different treatment of different sports.

82. Compare and contrast additions to unadjusted Federal income in Utah, Delaware, and New Mexico.

83. Compare and contrast subtractions to unadjusted Federal taxable income for Maine, Montana, and Kansas.

84. Many states use the Internal Revenue Code as the backbone of their tax code. Determine the level of conformity with the Internal Revenue Code for Nebraska, Kansas, Oklahoma, and Missouri. Compare that approach to the one taken by Arkansas.

85. Compare and contrast the rules for allocating nonbusiness gains and losses in Mississippi, Maryland, and Hawaii. Based on the corporate tax rate structure, which state would be most desirable for allocating a nonbusiness gain? How about a nonbusiness loss?

CHAPTER 9

International Tax Services

LEARNING OBJECTIVES

- Describe the basic framework for international taxation.
- Describe and contrast the major features of international tax services.
- Develop search methodologies applicable to each of the international services.
- Identify which tax services are most appropriate for different international research objectives.

THE U.S. DEPARTMENT OF STATE RECOGNIZES 194 countries in the world today, and each can have its own tax rules and regulations. Consequently, global businesses must maneuver through a tangled web of tax laws that are likely to be unfamiliar to most tax professionals. Intricate (sometimes tax-motivated) intercompany transaction flows and transfer pricing further compound the complexity and create an international tax environment that can be an unmanageable labyrinth for many companies.

Fortunately, international tax specialists can help with the perplexing compliance obligations and foster the alignment of company tax strategies with its business needs. The ultimate tax planning goal of most tax directors of large, multinational companies, however, is quite simple—to reduce the company's overall global effective tax rate. Navigating the road that leads to this goal is the challenge. This chapter provides a brief overview of international taxation, especially from a U.S. perspective, and explains some of the more popular international tax research resources available.

Overview of International Taxation

Global business transactions create distinctive tax concerns for both the native country and the temporary resident or transaction country. The native country is where the taxpayer is a citizen or legal resident or where an entity is incorporated or organized. The transaction country is where the income is earned or the transaction completed. International tax provisions generally are concerned with two potential tax situations: the native country's taxation of its citizen's foreign-source income (outbound) and the transaction country's taxation of foreign taxpayers earning income within its borders (inbound).

From an economic perspective, the objective of the international tax rules of each country should be to ensure that the taxing systems interact efficiently and to prevent, to the extent possible, the double taxation of income while encouraging investment within the country's boundaries. At the same time, each country wants to promote global commerce but not erode its domestic tax base for generating revenues. Such tax objectives can be in conflict, and these conflicts are the cause of the complexity and often situation-specific rules found in international tax laws.

International Tax Models

There are two alternative, conceptually "pure" models that countries could base their international tax schemes: worldwide and territorial. Under a **worldwide model,** a country imposes taxes on tax residents based on their worldwide income, regardless of its source. This would include income earned in other countries and even income earned by foreign subsidiaries, whether or not the profits are distributed to the parent. All expenses associated with the earning of foreign income are deductible currently. Since the foreign-earned income also may be taxed by the transaction country, the native country would allow a foreign tax credit for taxes paid to other countries. In practice, no country uses a pure worldwide model of taxation.

Under a **territorial model,** a country taxes only income that is earned within its own borders. A business would not be taxed on income earned outside the native country or income of its foreign subsidiaries, even when the income is repatriated to the parent. Since the foreign income is not taxed within the native country, there is no need for a foreign tax credit. Foreign income is taxed only once, and that is by the foreign country. Accordingly, deductions associated with the foreign income are disallowed. Most territorial models have anti-abuse provisions for certain types of portable income.

The United States uses a blended model that taxes the worldwide income of domestic corporations and the income of foreign entities that is connected with U.S. business. However, U.S. taxes do not apply to the foreign income of U.S.-owned corporations incorporated abroad until that income is brought back to the United States. As a result, a U.S. firm can indefinitely defer U.S. tax on its foreign income until, with some exceptions, such time as the foreign corporation repatriates its earnings back to its U.S. parent.[1] By allowing tax deferral on foreign subsidiary income, the blended model employed in the United States encourages domestic corporations to retain earnings in foreign countries and postpone repatriation as long as possible. Given that most countries enjoy a marginal tax rate lower than the United States, this provides a substantial tax planning opportunity but also causes numerous opportunities for U.S. tax base erosion.

Another important feature of the U.S. tax system is a **foreign tax credit**. Even though the United States taxes worldwide income of domestic entities, it also allows a limited credit for foreign taxes paid. This treatment reduces double taxation that would otherwise apply to income earned overseas and taxed in the foreign jurisdiction. The credit is limited to the amount of U.S. taxes that would be due on the income; thus the United States collects its share of taxes where the U.S. tax rate is greater than that of the foreign country. If foreign taxes exceed the U.S. tax, the excess foreign taxes cannot be credited.

U.S. tax law uses a territorial approach for taxing non-U.S. taxpayers. For instance, the income of a Ugandan citizen is subject to U.S. Federal income tax but only if that income is earned within the United States. The Ugandan's income attributable to sources outside the United States is not taxable within the United States. Thus, the current U.S. international taxing system applies both the worldwide model (for citizens) and the territorial model (for nonresidents) concurrently.

SPOTLIGHT ON TAXATION

Taxation of Residents of U.S. Possessions

In addition to residents of the 50 United States, the reach of Federal taxes may also extend to U.S. possessions. Residents of U.S. possessions may also be subject to U.S. income tax depending on the specific possession and the type of residence. Following are the U.S. possessions: American Samoa, Commonwealth of Puerto Rico, Commonwealth of the Northern Mariana Islands, Guam, and the U.S. Virgin Islands.

Transfer pricing

As businesses expand beyond their country's borders, the legal and supply-chain structures can become extremely complex. For example, a company may develop a technology and secure its rights in one country, manufacture the product in a number of other countries, and distribute the product around the world from several distribution centers. Many firms for both tax and legal purposes will establish separate subsidiaries in each

---

[1]Certain types of portable income and income with little or no economic connection with the foreign country (called Subpart F income) earned by controlled foreign corporations trigger immediate U.S. tax as a constructive dividend.

country. Although for financial statement purposes only the consolidated income will be reported, for each taxing jurisdiction the taxable income earned will depend on the costs that the subsidiaries charge each other at each step of the business process.

Transfer pricing is often used to refer to the price-setting process between related parties. For example, assume a U.S. bicycle manufacturer wishes to sell its products in the Netherlands and establishes a branch in the Netherlands. Under the U.S tax system, all of the income earned (including the branch under the worldwide part of the U.S. system) will be taxable in the United States. However, only the profits earned in the Netherlands will be taxable in that country. If we assume that the product costs $1,000 to produce, $100 to distribute, and is typically sold for $1,200, what should the transfer price to the Netherlands branch be?

One choice might be to set the transfer price at $1,000. Then the Netherlands will tax $200 of profit. On the other hand, perhaps the Netherlands branch does not bear any real risk for the sale of that bicycle and the profits should merely represent the cost to the Netherlands to distribute the bicycle. Thus the transfer price would be $1,100. Extending that idea just a bit further, perhaps the Netherlands branch is merely another cost center of the entire business and does not warrant any profit margin at all. In this case the transfer price equals $1,200.

Each of the alternatives has significant ramifications to the taxing jurisdictions as well as the taxpayers. If tax rates differ between the countries, taxpayers have incentives to manipulate transfer prices in order to report low taxable income in the high-tax country and high taxable income in the low-tax country.

Most countries require a transfer pricing scheme that adheres to an "arm's length" principle, which means that prices should be the same as they would have been had the parties to the transaction not been related to each other. In practice, an arm's-length price may be difficult to establish. As a result, companies with international intercompany transactions may enter into advance pricing agreements (APA) with the IRS. APAs establish a safe-harbor transfer pricing method for the taxpayer.

SPOTLIGHT ON TAXATION

Transfer Pricing

Manipulating transfer prices costs the United States significant tax revenue. A recent study in *Tax Notes International* estimates that the U.S. Treasury lost more than $28 billion in tax revenue in 2007 due to aggressive transfer pricing. In the largest tax dispute in its history, in 2006 the IRS settled a multi-year transfer pricing suit with pharmaceutical company Glaxo SmithKline Holdings for $3.4 billion. In 2008, the company lost a similar suit with the Canada Revenue Agency resulting in additional taxes of $51.5 million. In this suit, the Canadian company purchased ranitidine (the active ingredient in Zantac) from an affiliated company in Switzerland. The price paid by the Canadian company exceeded $1,500 per kilogram at a time when other Canadian drug manufacturers purchased ranitidine at a price of $200 to $300 per kilogram.[2]

---

[2]"Transfer Pricing Costs U.S. at Least $28 Billion," by Martin A. Sullivan, *Tax Notes International,* March 29, 2010 and "GlaxoSmithKline – CRA Wins Landmark Transfer Pricing Case," by Francois Vincent, accessed at **www.kpmg.ca/en/services/tax/GlobalTaxAdviser/issues/200806/article.html** (accessed on May 25, 2010).

Income Sourcing

The geographical source of income has a direct bearing on its tax treatment. U.S. citizens are taxed on their worldwide income, but income earned in other countries may receive tax relief through a number of Code provisions. Foreign taxpayers (also known as non-resident aliens), on the other hand, generally are subject to Federal taxes only on U.S. source income. Consequently, the sourcing rules often are the starting point in researching international tax issues.

Source of Income

The **source determination** of income is dependent on performance location and/or property location. Income from interest and dividends generally is sourced by the residency of the payor. Thus, dividends from a domestic corporation and interest from a state bond are sourced within the United States. To attract foreign investment, however, the United States allows a tax exemption on interest paid from a U.S. bank to a nonresident. For income from property, such as rents, royalties, or gains from property sales, it is the location of the property that is relevant.

Sales of inventory often are sourced by the location of the transaction, not by the origin of the inventory. Thus, inventory purchased in a foreign country but sold within the United States produces domestic sourced income. Income for personal services usually is sourced according to where the services are performed, not the residency of the compensating entity or the citizenship of the personal service provider. Finally, sourcing rules apply to deductions as well as to income.

Source of Deductions

Since the U.S. tax is based on taxable income, deductions and losses must be apportioned between domestic and foreign-source gross income. The U.S. rules for allocation and apportionment are very broad and attempt to match gross income with the deductions incurred to create that income. Deductions for expenses and losses directly related to a transaction or activity are called **"definitely related" deductions** and are relatively simple to allocate. For example, cost of goods sold is allocated to the sales income to which it relates.

SPOTLIGHT ON TAXATION

Organisation for Economic Cooperation and Development

The Organisation for Economic Cooperation and Development (OECD) is an association of countries that believe in democratic governments and market economies. The goals of the OECD are to assist developing countries, support sustainable economic growth, boost employment, raise living standards, maintain financial stability, and generally contribute to world trade. Through its monitoring of world economics, the OECD has become known as one of the most reliable and prolific publishers of economic and social data/statistics. The OECD plays a prominent role in fostering good governance and helps to obtain multilateral economic agreements for individual countries that want to participate in the global economy. It is a forum where peer pressure can act as a powerful incentive. This peer pressure incentive is demonstrated by the OECD's effect on tax havens. In 2000, the OECD issued a list of 41 possible tax havens. By 2009, there were none.

Expenses that are either not attributable to any specific income source or are associated with more than one source are known as **"not definitely related" deductions** and must be apportioned. Typically, these expenses are grouped by class of gross income and then apportioned between foreign and U.S. sourced income. There are also a number of special apportionment rules for items such as interest expense, research and experimentation costs, and losses on sales of real property. All the rules and regulations that govern allocation and apportionment are complex and beyond the scope of this text.

Tax Treaties

Although the calculation of worldwide tax liability is affected by foreign tax laws, international taxation in the United States is governed by the Internal Revenue Code (IRC) and by tax treaties. **Tax treaties**, negotiated by the Treasury Department and signed by the President, are bilateral agreements regarding the treatment of residents (not necessarily citizens) of the foreign country and the United States.

Generally, treaties are negotiated to prevent double taxation by providing reduced tax rates and reduced withholding rates or exempting certain types of income from taxation. The incomes that receive reduced rates and exemptions vary among countries. Most income tax treaties contain what is known as a "saving clause" that prevents U.S. residents from using treaty provisions to avoid taxes on U.S. source income. The United States has tax treaties with more than 60 countries, as enumerated in Exhibit 9-1.

EXHIBIT 9-1:   U.S. Income Tax Treaty Countries

Armenia	Iceland	Poland
Australia	India	Portugal
Austria	Indonesia	Romania
Azerbaijan	Ireland	Russia
Bangladesh	Israel	Slovak Republic
Barbados	Italy	Slovenia
Belarus	Jamaica	South Africa
Belgium	Japan	Spain
Bulgaria	Kazakhstan	Sir Lanka
Canada	Korea	Sweden
China	Kyrgyzstan	Switzerland
Cyprus	Latvia	Tajikistan
Czech Republic	Lithuania	Thailand
Denmark	Luxembourg	Trinidad
Egypt	Mexico	Tunisia
Estonia	Moldova	Turkey
Finland	Morocco	Turkmenistan
France	Netherlands	Ukraine
Georgia	New Zealand	United Kingdom
Germany	Norway	Uzbekistan
Greece	Pakistan	Venezuela
Hungary	Philippines	

Source: **http:// www.ustreas.gov/offices/tax-policy/treaties.shtml**, accessed on July 23, 2010.

The Code and tax treaties may provide conflicting treatment of some types of foreign-sourced income. Unlike most countries, the United States does not consider treaty provisions to take precedence over the Code. Rather, to the extent possible, the Code and treaty should be applied in harmony with each other. If this is not possible, then the most recently issued provision generally prevails. Some U.S. states do not honor the provisions of tax treaties, and U.S.-adopted tax treaties usually do not address state and local tax issues.

If there is no U.S. treaty covering income from a particular country, all taxable income from the country is included in the tax base of the U.S. citizens and residents. This income also is likely to be taxed by the foreign country. To mitigate double taxation of this income, the foreign income exclusion, the foreign tax credit, and other more specific provisions were legislated.

SPOTLIGHT ON TAXATION

The Tax Wedge

Different countries have very different taxes on workers' wages. The OECD tracks something called the "tax wedge," which is the difference between the net earnings that a worker takes home at the end of the year and what it costs to employ that worker. On the employer's side, this cost includes the worker's salary as well as employer contributions for Social Security (e.g., healthcare, pensions). On the worker's side, the negatives are income tax and employee Social Security payments, while the positives include the salary and, possibly, cash benefits.

For example, in the United States the tax wedge for a single worker with no children is calculated by the OECD as follows:

Average cost of labor before taxes	$43,852	
Average wages before taxes	$39,923	
Average social and income taxes	22.4%	
Average wages after taxes	$30,980	$30,980
Tax wedge		$12,871
Tax wedge percentage		29.4%

The tax wedge for a single worker with no children is presented for selected countries:

Country	Tax Wedge Percent
Germany	50.9
France	49.2
Italy	46.5
Czech Republic	41.9
Greece	41.5
Spain	38.2
Netherlands	38.0
Turkey	37.5
OECD Average	36.4
Poland	34.0
United Kingdom	32.5

(continued)

SPOTLIGHT ON TAXATION (CONTINUED)

Country	Tax Wedge Percent
Canada	30.8
United States	29.4
Japan	29.2
Ireland	28.6
Iceland	28.3
Australia	26.7
Korea	19.7
New Zealand	18.4
Mexico	15.3

Source: **www.oecd.org.**

The remainder of this chapter reviews a sample of the commercial international tax service providers. As discussed in Chapter 6, these providers offer a plethora of tax products that can be bundled in a variety of ways. Thus, the tax services described in this chapter may not describe the set of resources available to the reader. Furthermore, the tax services update their products constantly to maintain their competitive edge, and this is especially true in the international arena. Therefore, the current appearance of the tax services may differ from those presented in this text. However, the research concepts still are applicable.

BNA

The Bureau of National Affairs (BNA) has developed myriad products for the tax practitioner who specializes in international taxation. The **BNA Premier International Tax Library** product has three main areas: Portfolios, news and commentary, and references, (see Exhibit 9-2). BNA's signature publication is the Tax Management Portfolios, but BNA also delivers in-depth news coverage, tax planning commentaries, journals, and detailed analysis through special tax services.

BNA Foreign Income Portfolios Library

The **BNA Premier International Tax Library** includes almost 100 BNA Tax Management Portfolios written by leading experts in international taxation and business (see Exhibit 9-3). The topics covered run the gamut from the foreign tax credit, to international aspects of Social Security taxes and foreign estates, to non-tax issues such as the regulation of foreign investments and currency exchange controls. There are more than 10 portfolios dedicated to transfer pricing in the accompanying Transfer Pricing Premier Library; more than 40 portfolios covering the taxation of business operations in specific countries (Country Portfolios); and more than 40 Portfolios covering taxation of U.S. persons' foreign income, taxation of foreign persons' U.S. income, and provisions applicable to U.S. and foreign income. The Country Portfolios address not only income taxation but also indirect taxes, such as the value-added tax (VAT) and other special taxes unique to the various countries.

EXHIBIT 9-2:   BNA ITC Homepage

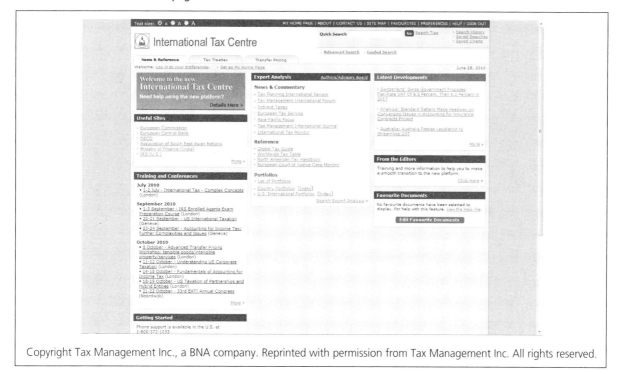

EXHIBIT 9-3:   BNA ITC Portfolios

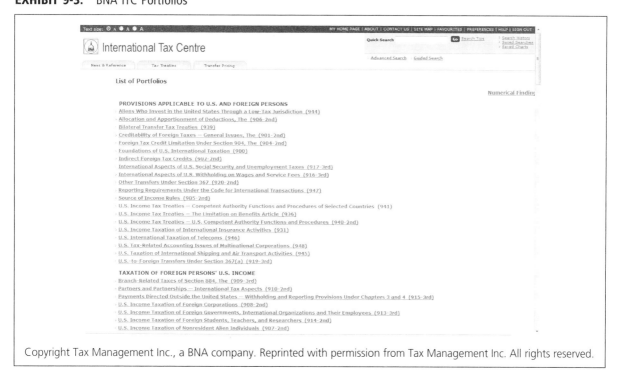

EXHIBIT 9-4:   BNA ITC Global Tax Guides

As with the BNA U.S. Income Library, each BNA Tax Management Portfolio contains excerpts from primary sources, such as the Code, Regulations, and IRS pronouncements. For tax treaties, the Portfolios furnish not only the text but all relevant materials for interpreting the agreements, including technical explanations, legislative histories, and judicial interpretations. Practical advice for complying with the local business and tax laws is offered by notable practitioners in the Detailed Analysis Section. The Working Papers Section contains interactive and IRS forms, sample elections, official documents, and legal forms (some filled-in as examples). These Portfolios are updated regularly.

BNA News and Commentary

The BNA Premier International Tax Library was developed to communicate accurate and detailed analysis of worldwide taxation as well as regular international news updates. Thus, in addition to the Country Portfolios, the Premier International Tax Library offers a variety of news and analysis libraries to the international tax practitioner, shown in Exhibit 9-2. Included are the International Journal and *International Tax Monitor* that follow major tax developments in key jurisdictions; *Tax Planning International Review* and *International Journal*, both providing monthly analysis on international tax developments and treaty changes; and *Tax Planning International* for both Europe and Asia-Pacific Transfer pricing updates are in the accompanying Transfer Pricing Premier Library, featuring the Transfer Pricing Report and *Transfer Pricing International Journal*.

BNA Reference

Including the Portfolios, these sources represent the core of BNA's international reference data. The *Global Tax Guide* provides country-specific information on tax rates for corporate, personal, withholding, and other taxes (see Exhibit 9-4). These rates are summarized in the Worldwide Tax Table, which presents key rate information for many countries in a single source.

EXHIBIT 9-5: BNA ITC Browse Screen

Table of Contents Search Given the organization of the libraries, a search by browsing the libraries can be quite efficient and effective. Simply expand the table of contents (TOC) of any source by clicking on the + boxes preceding the headings (see Exhibit 9-5). However, a simple search of the entire service may be easily performed by entering keywords in the Quick Search box at the top of each screen (Exhibit 9-2). This search retrieves documents containing any of the keywords.

Advanced Search The Advanced Search option furnishes functions much like the RIA or CCH search functions but requiring a selection of source and a keyword. The first step in the search process is to identify the sources to include as part of the search (see Exhibit 9-6). The sources are added to the Current Selections. By clicking next, the keyword search screen appears and keywords and connectors can be used to specify the topics of interest (see Exhibit 9-7). Date restrictions can also be used to narrow the search.

Guided Search The BNA Premier International Tax Library also offers a Guided Search (see Exhibit 9-8). For researchers trying to identify the resources that might best suit a search, the guided search option provides the available databases for each primary area (e.g., news and commentary) in a convenient, listed format and allows for only specific sources to be selected. Keywords can then be used to search for relevant materials.

LexisNexis

LexisNexis has built impressive international tax libraries by amassing documents and services developed by other publishers. The Tax Center and Academic services contain the international publications by BNA, CCH, Wiley, and Tax Analysts as well as publications written by recognized experts in the international field.

Tax Center

The International tab in the LexisNexis Tax Center displays document sources in numerous categories, some of which are displayed in Exhibit 9-9. Primary Law includes various sources of international tax cases as well as cases from specific countries, such as Australia. It also includes country-specific statutes and laws, various legal journals, and news sources that cover the latest in international law revisions.

The researcher may select one, some, or all of these sources and then perform keyword searches by using either the natural language or terms and connectors options. Date restrictions also are available. These restrictions are especially effective when the

EXHIBIT 9-6: BNA ITC Advanced Search Step 1 Screen

EXHIBIT 9-7: BNA ITC Advanced Search Step 2 Screen

EXHIBIT 9-8: BNA ITC Guided Search

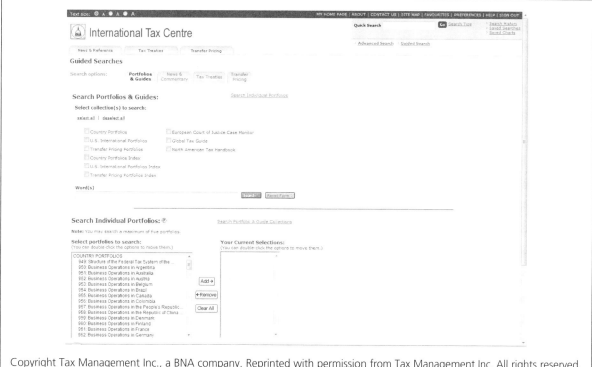

EXHIBIT 9-9: LexisNexis Tax Center International Tab Opening Screen

EXHIBIT 9-10:   LexisNexis Tax Center Doing Business in Guide Screen

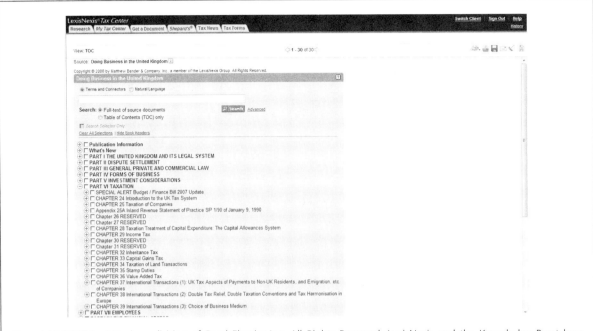

practitioner desires to merely update prior research or needs to know how the law stood in a prior year for such situations as tax audits or court proceedings.

The International Tax Planning heading offers the business primers, "Doing Business in … " for a variety of countries (see Exhibit 9-9). These portfolios provide an overview of the country's business environment, including its taxing structure. Clicking on the icon after the title will either access the document or display the document's TOC, as Exhibit 9-10 shows for the Doing Business in United Kingdom portfolio.

The majority of the Tax Treaties & Analysis resources are products of the Tax Analysts organization. The **Tax Analysts** *Worldwide Tax Treaties* recently added several features to enhance the ability to compare, side by side, income tax treaties. Easy-to-read tables compare the tax rates on various types of income and withholding rates among more than 170 worldwide taxing jurisdictions. The original, in-force, pending, terminated, and unperfected treaties can be viewed separately.

The **CCH** *Tax Treaties Reporter* includes many of the same documents as the Worldwide Tax Treaties. Both have the income and estate tax treaties into which the United States has entered with foreign countries. In addition, the CCH Tax Treaties Reporter contains the exchange of information agreements between the United States and foreign countries, U.S. Regulations relating to treaty articles, reports from the Department of State and the Senate Foreign Relations Committee, as well as administrative rulings and court cases pertinent to the treaties.

The final categories of offerings in the LexisNexis Tax Center are Emerging Issues and News (offscreen in Exhibit 9-9). LexisNexis uses competent country-specific analysts to provide in-depth analysis of emerging tax issues. Additionally, LexisNexis selected one of the most respected sources to supply its daily international news, the **Tax Analysts** *Worldwide Tax Daily*. A sample of the *Worldwide Tax Daily* e-newsletter is presented in Exhibit 9-11. *Worldwide Tax Daily* offers international news on a daily basis, with

EXHIBIT 9-11: Tax Analysts Worldwide Tax Daily

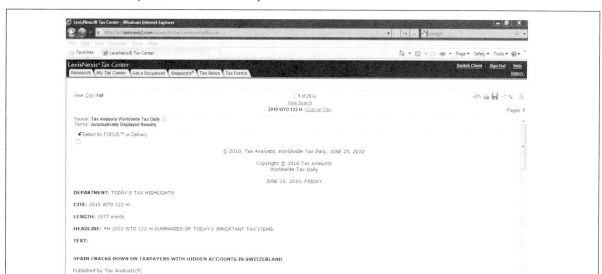

news updates from around the world. The information is organized by countries and international organization.

Tax Analysts also publishes *Tax Notes International,* a weekly publication that provides tax news, commentary, and in-depth analysis of legislative, judicial, and administrative tax developments from more than 180 countries. Full-text tax documents also are available with *Tax Notes International.*

Academic

The international content of LexisNexis Academic is similar to that found in the Tax Center. Academic also relies heavily on Tax Analysts for most of its sources, as Exhibit 9-12 demonstrates. Access to the international documents is easiest through the Sources Tab, as opposed to the Search Tab.

On the Sources Tab, the Browse Sources option requires three choices—numbered 1 through 3 in Exhibit 9-12—to be made before a search can be performed. First, the researcher selects Browsing by one of the following: Publication Type, News & Business Topics, Industry, or Area of Law. Second, Filters are applied by Country, Publication Type, and Multiple/ Single Source. Each of the filters has a pull-down menu, and only one item may be selected. The Country menu is illustrated in Exhibit 9-12. Finally, the researcher selects a Category to View Sources. The researcher may search any or all of the listed sources.

The next step is to click the OK Continue button, which produces the Power Search keyword entry box for natural language or terms and connectors keyword searches.

RIA

Similar to LexisNexis, RIA also offers a variety of international products that may be bundled with RIA Checkpoint (see Chapter 6 for discussion) to meet the particular needs of each practitioner's international research. In the International Practice Area, primary international law and treaties are supplied along with editorial materials by various authors and sources (see Exhibit 9-13). Some of RIA's international products are examined in this section.

EXHIBIT 9-12: LexisNexis Academic International Libraries

EXHIBIT 9-13: RIA International Practice Area Opening Screen

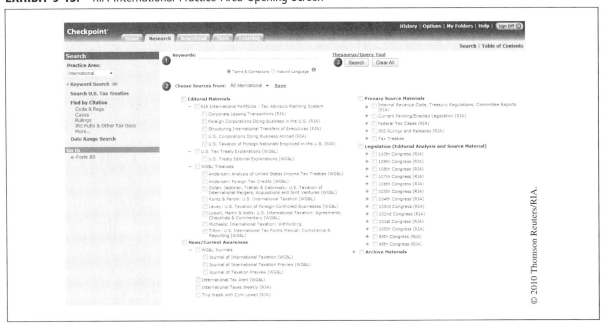

SPOTLIGHT ON TAXATION

International Bureau of Fiscal Documentation (IBFD)

The International Bureau of Fiscal Documentation (IBFD) is a not-for-profit organization organized in 1938 to provide authoritative expertise to tax practitioners around the globe with regard to cross-border taxation. The IBFD relies on independent tax research as well as its research specialists to contribute international tax information and education materials to its customers. Originally the IBFD was simply a tax document repository, but now it focuses on research products, which it distributes to both the private and public sectors.

Because it is an independent agency, the IBFD strives to produce objective and unbiased products, including software, tax courses, personalized client research (for private and government use), daily newsletters, journals, and numerous books on international tax issues. Besides its publications, the IBFD has a library that is regarded as the world's leading resource for international and comparative taxation. Free online access to this library is available at **www.ibfd.org.**

International Tax Products

The **RIA Worldwide Tax Law (WTL)** service is one of the more comprehensive services in the International Practice Area. It offers English translations of tax and commercial laws for approximately 90 countries. Similar to the search methodology used for the State & Local Checkpoint service (see Chapter 8), WTL requires the researcher to select one of eight broad geographical areas and at least one specific country, and then the type of documents desired before a keyword search is performed. From this point, the Checkpoint search and document retrieval proceeds in the same fashion as searching any other Practice Area, as illustrated in earlier chapters of this book.

Another useful service accessible through Checkpoint is the **RIA International Tax Library (ITL)**. Unlike other RIA tax products, ITL is a comprehensive set of analytical treatises and texts. A U.S. bilateral tax treaty database is included for accessing primary sources. Thus, the ITL lacks a central RIA editorial service such as the Federal Tax Coordinator. Newsletters and journals are included to keep the practitioner up-to-date on global taxation.

RIA offers International Portfolios, called the **RIA Tax Advisors Planning System**, that are written by expert practitioners currently in practice. These portfolios, updated monthly, focus on specific issues relevant to taxpayers with international business. Each portfolio includes commentary, advice supported by detailed explanations, integrated planning ideas, and the current rules with citations to the controlling authorities. In addition, practice aids similar in nature to those offered by the Tax Management Portfolios are furnished. The list of RIA portfolios is shorter than BNA's offerings, but the quality is outstanding.

All international subscriptions receive the *RIA International Taxes Weekly*, which is a weekly e-newsletter that covers current developments and emerging issues related to international taxation and is similar to the newsletter delivered with subscriptions to regular RIA Checkpoint.

Checkpoint offers the unique **RIA International Create-a-Chart** function that facilitates the creation of tax comparisons charts with links to controlling authority, detailed explanations, and analysis by WG&L treatises. These links are maintained when the chart

EXHIBIT 9-14:   Westlaw International Directory

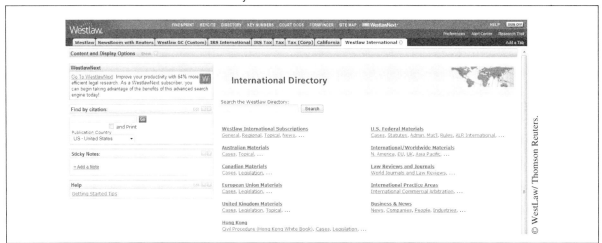

is exported to a word processing file. The Create-a-Chart feature develops personalized charts of pertinent information for countries selected by the practitioner. There are currently more than 75 chart types offered in Create-a-Chart on topics such as alimony, air and ship transport, capital gains, dividends, charitable contributions, and pensions.

Westlaw

Westlaw offers two portals to international taxation materials: through a separate service, Westlaw International, and through the standard Westlaw subscription. Only the standard subscription is examined in this section.

Westlaw can be personalized, allowing the researcher to select up to six tabs to be displayed for those libraries most often searched. The Westlaw International Tab, shown in Exhibit 9-14, provides access to documents on a variety of international topics, one of which is Tax Law (located in Topical under the Westlaw International Subscriptions heading). The databases generally cover U.S. taxation and its treaties, with analysis supplied by the Law of Federal Income Taxation (Mertens) tax service.

Specific country headings, such as Australian and Canadian in Exhibit 9-14, have Tax as one of the Practice Areas and thus provide access to the country's tax laws. However, the countries available may be limited by the user's subscription. Finally, while International Practice Areas might appear a logical avenue for finding tax databases, taxation is not listed under this heading.

Westlaw also offers the IRS International tab. This tab contains many of the same databases available under the International tab but is focused on international tax and has a number of primary and editorial materials, both for the United States and for other countries (see Exhibit 9-15). BNA, WGL, and other popular treatises and analyses are available.

A more fruitful means of entry into Westlaw's international taxation resources is through the Tax library (Tax Tab). This portal furnishes access to the RIA and BNA international materials (primary and editorial) that were discussed previously in this chapter as well as international journals, WG&L treatises, and texts. Exhibit 9-16 provides a partial list of these offerings. Most of the treatises, journals, and texts are not part of a basic subscription, so a premium charge applies to their access.

EXHIBIT 9-15:   Westlaw IRS International Tab

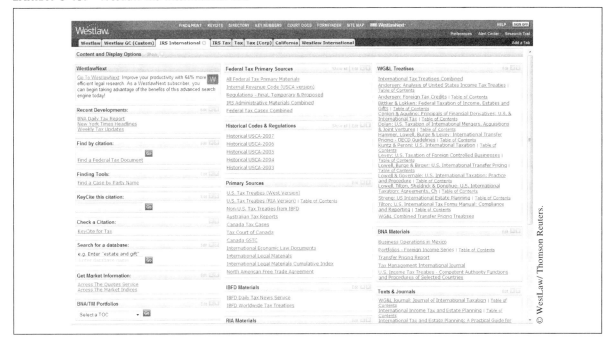

EXHIBIT 9-16:   Westlaw International Tax Journal, Texts, and Treatise Offerings

This list is a sample and is not intended to be comprehensive.

Journals

International Income Tax and Estate Planning

International Tax and Estate Planning: A Practical Guide for Multinational Investors

International Tax Journal

International Tax Review

Journal of International Taxation

United Kingdom Current Awareness Taxation

Treatises

Conlon & Aquilino: Principals of Financial Derivatives: U.S. & International Tax

Dolan: U.S. Taxation of International Mergers, Acquisitions & Joint Ventures

Kuntz & Peroni: U.S. International Taxation

Levey: U.S. Taxation of Foreign Controlled Businesses

Lowell & Governale: U.S. International Taxation: Practice and Procedure

Lowell, Tilton, Sheldrick & Donohue: U.S. International Taxation: Agreements, Checklist & Commentary

Streng: US International Estate Planning

Tilton: U.S. International Tax Forms Manual: Compliance and Reporting

Source: © Westlaw/Thomson Reuters.

CCH

CCH offers numerous international tax products that provides timely and authoritative materials with practical analysis and understandable explanations written by experts in this field. To provide these products, CCH has teamed up with other publishers and authors. For example, CCH offers the BNA international publications and the CCH Global Daily Tax News.

All of the CCH international tax services may be accessed through the IntelliConnect platform, thus simplifying the search process for those practitioners already familiar with this service. Browsing the International Tax area furnishes access to the Tax Treaties, U.S. International Tax Compliance and Planning, and vast array of Worldwide Business Tax Guides. The tax treaties library (see Exhibit 9-17) provides the most complete and up-to-date coverage of more than 7,100 international tax agreements and protocols for more than 200 countries.

Also available are a series of Worldwide Business Tax Guides (see Exhibit 9-18). The Worldwide Business Tax Guides provide a practical, integrated look at the key tax issues in almost 50 countries that arise when planning the development and growth of a corporation's foreign business in a practical, easy-to-read format. Issues such as minimizing risk, reducing costs, and increasing productivity are covered by the in-depth commentary on all forms of doing business in a country.

Service Offerings

Following is a list of some of the most useful resources offered within the CCH International Tax Service. Availability depends upon the level of the researcher's subscription.

- *Worldwide Tax Rates and Answers*. It provides corporate tax rates by country, including national and local tax rates, as well as current forms and instructions for countries around the world.

EXHIBIT 9-17: CCH International Tax Treaties

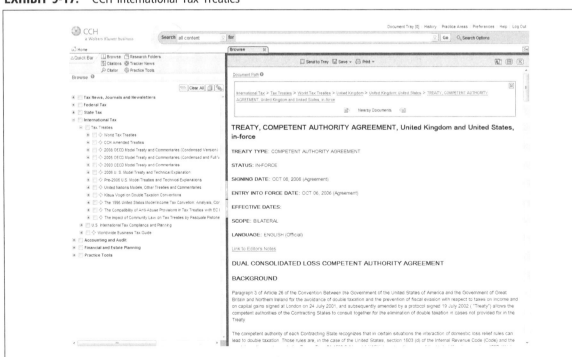

EXHIBIT 9-18: CCH International Worldwide Business Tax Guide

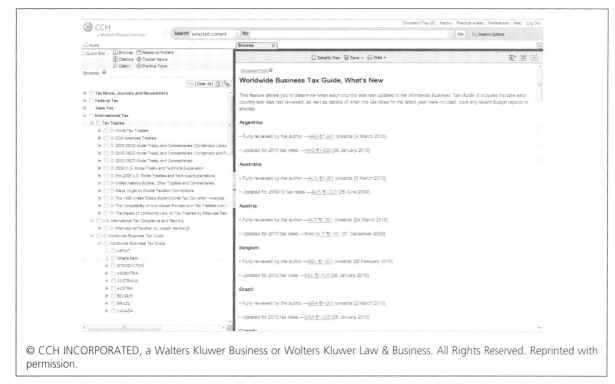

- *Global Transaction Library.* This series of publications is designed to provide guidance on tax planning and compliance for cross-border and international transactions by taking a transactional approach. This service includes *Tax Notes International, International Taxation: Corporate and Individual* by Philip Postlewaite, the *Transfer Pricing Library* that provides four authoritative works on transfer pricing focusing on U.S. transfer pricing laws and international transfer pricing laws, and *International Transfer Pricing Laws: Text and Commentary* that provides coverage of transfer pricing for more than 30 countries.

- *International Tax Planning Library.* This library consists of three comprehensive publications and a practical newsletter exploring tax planning issues from around the world. The three publications cover international tax planning for corporations, expatriates, and migrants, plus offshore financial centers for more than 40 countries.

- *International Tax Treaty Expert Library.* Thousands of treaties (with amended language in context) and related documents, such as diplomatic notes and protocols, are available, and all are in English. The treaties cover income, estate and gift taxes, sea and air transport, and information exchange agreements. Some of the treaties and analytical works included in the service are *Klaus Vogel on Double Taxation Conventions; International Taxation, U.S. Taxation of Foreign Persons & Foreign Income; The Compatibility of Anti-Abuse Provisions in Tax Treaties with EC Law; The Impact of Community Law on Tax Treaties—Issues and Solutions;* and *The 1996 United States Model Income Tax Convention, Analysis, Commentary and Comparison.*

Internet Sites

The Tax and Accounting Sites Directory Web site (**www.taxsites.com**) contains links to numerous tax Web pages, one of which is designated for international tax topics. This is an excellent starting point for Internet international tax searches. Links to tax sites for more than 80 countries are given as well as references to international tax associations and IRS resources. A long list of other sources also is provided. Additionally, the international and regional businesses offer international tax information on their Web sites.

SUMMARY

The world is shrinking as more companies enter the global economy. In 2009, Standard & Poors (S&P) reported that almost 48 percent of revenues of the S&P 500 were earned overseas and that these same companies paid $11.5 billion in foreign taxes. No longer do only large, multinational companies maintain international offices. Now, many middle-market and owner-managed firms are expanding into the international markets of Europe and the Pacific Rim. Thus, it is no longer a luxury to employ staff who are knowledgeable about international taxation.

The demand for international tax services is rapidly growing, and the major players in the research service industry (CCH, LexisNexis, RIA, and Westlaw) continue to expand their international offerings. As the importance of international taxation continues to explode, the tax services will develop more targeted products to serve the needs of the tax practitioners. Consequently, international research tools will likely be among the fastest changing component of the major tax services.

QUIZ YOURSELF

Reinforce the tax research information covered in this chapter by completing the online quizzes located at the Federal Tax Research Web site at **www.cengagebrain.com.** At the CengageBrain.com home page, search for the *Federal Tax Research*, 9e ISBN (1111221642) using the search box at the top of the page. This will take you to the product page where you can access the quizzes.

KEY WORDS

By the time you complete this chapter, you should be comfortable discussing each of the following terms. If you need additional review of any of these items, return to the appropriate material in the chapter or consult the glossary to this text.

BNA Premier International Tax Library, p. 334
CCH *Tax Treaties Reporter*, p. 340
definitely related deductions, p. 331
foreign tax credit, p. 329
not definitely related deductions, p. 332
RIA International Create-a-Chart, p. 343

RIA International Tax Library (ITL), p. 343
RIA *International Taxes Weekly*, p. 343
RIA Tax Advisors Planning System, p. 343
RIA Worldwide Tax Law (WTL), p. 343
source determination, p. 331

Tax Analysts *Worldwide Tax Daily*, p. 340
Tax Analysts *Worldwide Tax Treaties*, p. 340
Tax Notes International, p. 341
tax treaties, p. 332
territorial model, p. 328
transfer pricing, p. 330
worldwide model, p. 328

DISCUSSION QUESTIONS

1. What is an inbound transaction? What is an outbound transaction?

2. What are the major models for developing international taxing systems?

3. What is the worldwide model of international taxation? Explain whether a corporation with only domestic income or a company with foreign income would pay more taxes under this model.

4. What is the territorial model of international taxation? Under this model, what rate of tax does a native corporation pay on its foreign income?

5. Describe whether the United States uses a worldwide or territorial model.

6. What are the general rules for sourcing income?

7. What are the general rules for assigning expenses to certain sources of income?

8. Describe the functions of the OECD.

9. If a provision of the Internal Revenue Code and a tax treaty are in conflict, which rule prevails?

10. What is the tax wedge?

11. Describe the three search alternatives in the BNA International Tax Centre.

12. What kinds of information are provided in the Working Papers Section of the International BNA Tax Management Portfolios?

13. What are the three main areas in the BNA International Tax Centre?

14. What type of information would you expect to find in the document Doing Business in United Kingdom?

15. What organization provides the international news for LexisNexis Tax Center? What is the name of the news publication?

16. What is the easiest method to access the international documents on LexisNexis Academic?

17. What is the International Bureau of Fiscal Documentation?

18. How is the RIA International Tax Library different from other RIA services?

19. Describe the International Create-a-Chart function in RIA Checkpoint.

20. What are the two methods for accessing international tax resources in Westlaw? Which method is most effective?

21. Describe the differences between the International tab and the IRS International tab in Westlaw.

22. What types of information can be found in CCH's Worldwide Tax Guides?

23. CCH offers a number of international tax services available in IntelliConnect. Name at least three.

24. CCH offers a newsletter with its international services. What is the name of the newsletter, and with whom is the letter created?

25. For international taxation, what categories of links does the Tax and Accounting Sites Directory Web site (taxsites.com) employ?

26. Besides the Fortune 500 companies, what companies are expanding into the international markets of Europe and the Pacific Rim?

EXERCISES

27. Use the BNA International Tax Centre to answer the following questions:
    a. What countries are included in Tax Planning International Asia-Pacific?
    b. Using the Tax Treaties tab, prepare a comparison chart of the U.S.-Austria Treaty and the U.S.-Canada Treaty. How do the definitions of permanent establishment differ?
    c. Does Switzerland have a tax treaty with China? Does Switzerland have a treaty with Mexico?

28. Use the BNA International Tax Centre to answer the following questions:

    a. What is the proper citation for the most recent article in the European Tax Service on the United Kingdom's VAT?

    b. Who are the authors of the Tax Management International Forum for the Netherlands?

    c. Use the Quick Search option to determine how many articles Bert Mesdom has written.

29. Use the BNA International Tax Centre to answer the following questions:

    a. What collections are available under the transfer pricing tab when using a Guided Search?

    b. What is the lead report in the most recent International Tax Monitor?

    c. What is the title of the September 2009 article by Ricardo González Orta, Mauricio Martínez, Hernaldo Vega, and Yuri Barrueco in BNA's *International Journal*?

30. Use the BNA International Tax Centre to answer the following questions.

    a. What is the Web site of the Columbian tax authority?

    b. What section of the French tax code provides the general rules for transfer pricing?

    c. Use the Advanced Search option to locate a 2005 article discussing German investment incentives for U.S. film production companies. Provide the title of the article and its author.

31. Use the International Tab of LexisNexis Tax Center to answer the following questions:

    a. Who is the publisher of *International Tax and Estate Planning*?

    b. What is Chapter 5 of the *Foreign Tax & Trade Briefs for India*?

    c. What is the maximum number of sources that can be searched at one time?

32. Use International Tab of LexisNexis Tax Center to answer the following questions:

    a. How many sources are found for a search of William H. Byrnes?

    b. What countries does Djibouti have tax treaties with?

    c. What is Chapter 3, Article 6 of the 2003 OECD Model Income and Capital Tax Convention?

33. Use the International Tax Law Sources of LexisNexis Academic to answer the following questions:

    a. What tax treatment do the Greece-Moldova treaties indicate for earnings of nonresident students? What is the effective date of the agreement?

    b. What is the title and date of the most recent article regarding Iceland in the Tax Analysts' *Worldwide Tax Daily*?

    c. What is the title and date of the most recent article on the European VAT found in the Tax Analysts' *Tax Notes International*?

34. Use RIA materials to answer the following questions:

    a. What international sources are included in the International News/Current Awareness source heading?

    b. What paragraph of the *RIA Tax Treaty Editorial Explanations* discusses rental, royalty, and realty income for the U.S.-Brazil treaty?

    c. What are the title and date of the most recent article in *International Taxes Weekly* that discusses Paul Volcker's comments about additional U.S. taxes?

35. Use RIA materials to answer the following questions:

    a. What are the title and date of the most recent article on Belgium tax incentives appearing in the *Journal of International Taxation*?

    b. What International Create-a-Charts are available for the taxation of students and trainees?

    c. Who are the authors of the treatise titled *U.S. Taxation of International Mergers, Acquisitions & Joint Ventures*?

36. Use the Westlaw International Tab to answer the following questions:
    a. What are the international practice areas listed in the International Directory?
    b. What South American countries are listed in the International/Worldwide Materials?
    c. What are the title and date of the most recent law review article on VAT tax evasion in the European Union found by searching World Journals and Law Reviews in the News and Periodicals of the Westlaw International Subscriptions?

37. Use the Westlaw Tax Tab International Practice Area to answer the following questions:
    a. In which section of BNA Foreign Income Portfolio is there a definition of "foreign capital investment" under Argentine foreign investment law?
    b. On what date did the United States and Ireland enter a totalization agreement that covers social security taxes?
    c. What is the title of Chapter 3, paragraph 3.02 of Anderson's *Foreign Tax Credits* treatise?

38. Use the Westlaw International Tab to answer the following questions:
    a. What BNA Tax Management Portfolio is related to operating a business in Ireland?
    b. According *to Langer on Practical International Tax Planning*, how many totalization agreements with regards to social security does the United States have with foreign countries?
    c. What is the date of the last article in International Tax review to mention the IRS's case against DHL for the transfer pricing of its intangibles?

39. Use CCH IntelliConnect to answer the following questions:
    a. What is the most recent article on UK VAT exemptions in the *Global Daily Tax News*? What does it discuss?
    b. What article of the Tunisia treaty discusses the U.S. taxation of students, apprentices, and trainees from Tunisia?
    c. Who are the authors of the *Worldwide Tax Guide for Italy*?

40. Use CCH IntelliConnect to answer the following questions:
    a. How is a resident of Cyprus defined in its treaty with the United States?
    b. What countries originally entered the tax treaty between Canada and Turkmenistan?
    c. What is the title of Article 26 in the *United Nations Model Double Taxation Convention between Developed and Developing Countries*?

RESEARCH CASES

41. VanDelay, a citizen of the United States but a resident of Dulcinea, is an important sculptor. This year, he came to the United States to appear at an exhibition of his work in San Francisco. The United States has no tax treaty with Dulcinea. Does the $250,000 that VanDelay netted from the show qualify for the §911 earned income exclusion?

42. State University invites Dr. Byko, a Russian citizen, to become a member of the faculty for a three-year period to work on a large grant the university obtained from the National Aeronautics and Space Administration (NASA). Dr. Byko accepts the invitation and enters the United States on a J-1 visa. His university pay is entirely funded by the NASA grant. Based on the Russian treaty, Dr. Byko thinks his income is exempt because it is from a grant. Determine whether Dr. Byko is correct.

43. Haruo, a resident alien, obtained a U.S. divorce from his wife, Wakana, two years ago. Last July Wakana returned to Japan, but Haruo remained in the United States. For all of the current year, Haruo paid alimony

to Wakana in the amount of $10,000 per month. Does Wakana have income subject to U.S. taxation or withholding?

44. Rainbow Corporation has a contract with the National Science Foundation to conduct research in Antarctica. Harriet, a U.S. employee of Rainbow, spent all of last year and part of this year working at McMurdo Station on Ross Island, Antarctica. When filing her return for last year, Harriet excluded her income from the contract, based on the fact that she worked outside of the United States. Her income was not in excess of the excludible ceiling. Is Harriet correct in her treatment of last year's income?

45. Moonsoo, a Republic of Korea citizen, went to San Diego, California on a vacation. Since he liked San Diego, Moonsoo purchased five acres of land on which he wants to build luxury condominiums. He also bought the majority interest in a construction corporation that specializes in condominium construction. Moonsoo could not get the zoning clearance to build the condominiums, so he sold both the land and his stock in the construction corporation. Is Moonsoo taxed in the United States on his gains from these sales?

46. Ireland imposes a tax on the net market value (less certain deduction) of the taxable assets of those individuals residing in Ireland. Although she is a U.S. citizen, Katherine has been residing in Ireland for the past five years. She owns property located in Ireland and in the United States. Much of her property consists of stocks and bonds, but she also has large holdings of land in both countries. Does this Irish tax qualify for the foreign tax credit and/or as a deduction for U.S. tax purposes?

47. Paul Thomas and Karen Jackson are both in the Armed Forces and each receive combat zone pay. Karen is a commissioned officer, whereas Paul is enlisted personnel. How is each taxed on the combat zone pay? How does Paul treat his combat zone pay when computing his Earned Income Tax Credit?

48. Three international students are paid $1,000 a month to be teaching assistants in their university's Department of Accounting. The students from India and China have been in the United States for six years, and the student from Spain arrived one year ago. How is each of the students taxed in the United States for the current year?

49. A group of Russian tourists spent a week in Las Vegas. Kolzak, one of the tourists, was very lucky at the roulette table and won $50,000. Is Kolzak subject to U.S. income tax, and is the casino required to withhold taxes on her winnings?

50. Which of the following payments by International Partners Inc., a Montana corporation, qualifies for the foreign tax credit?
    a. Income tax paid to Germany, covered by an existing treaty.
    b. Income tax paid to Adagio, with which the United States has no income tax treaty.
    c. Value-added tax paid to Largetto, with which the United States has no income tax treaty.
    d. Oil extraction tax paid to Tedesco, with which the United States has no income tax treaty.
    e. Transportation tax paid to Santa Lucia, with which the United States has no income tax treaty. The tax is reduced dollar-for-dollar when International provides consulting services in designing Santa Lucia's new bullet train system. This year, International incurred $1 million in taxes, but it earned a $600,000 reduction for its services.

51. Chris Renaldo, a U.S. tax resident who resides in the United States, heard that the Bank of Spain is paying above market returns for savings accounts. Determine whether interest payments from the bank to Chris will be subject to withholding at the source.

52. Hardy Kicker plays on the U.S. men's soccer team. He recently played in a soccer tournament in South Africa. The South African tournament organizers will pay Hardy $20,000 to play. Determine whether payments to Hardy by the organizers will be subject to tax withholding under South African statute, and separately will they be subject to withholding considering the U.S.-South Africa tax treaty.

53. Sally James is the CFO of a domestic corporation with a small subsidiary in Mexico. The subsidiary earned taxable profits of $1 million for the year just ended. What amount should be accrued for profit sharing for the Mexican employees?

54. Boxian Wu is a real estate developer in China. She recently sold an office building for 4 million yuan. She paid 2 million yuan for the land use rights and 1 million yuan for the cost of developing the building. What is Boxian's Chinese land appreciation tax on the transfer of this real estate?

55. Taylor Joseph has held stock in Foreign Corporation classified as a passive foreign investment corporation for the last three years. Starting with the current year, Foreign will no longer meet the definition of a PFIC. Determine whether Taylor must continue to treat his investment in Foreign as a PFIC.

56. Jamaica Corp. (established under the laws of Jamaica) seeks to borrow funds from a Jamaican financial institution. In order to process the loan, the local Jamaican bank requires that U.S. Corp., the sole shareholder of Jamaica Corp., provide a guarantee on the loan. Jamaica Corp. pays its loan off in accordance with the terms of the loan and no call is made on U.S. Corp.'s guarantee. Does the mere presence of a guarantee require U.S. Corp. and Jamaica Corp. to reflect transfer pricing costs under §482?

CHAPTER 10

Financial Accounting Research

LEARNING OBJECTIVES

- Describe the basics of deferred taxes and accounting for income taxes.
- Explain the source and structure of international accounting standards.
- Identify and use the features of the FASB Accounting Standards Codification Research System.
- Identify which tax services offer accounting research and what information is available.

CHAPTER OUTLINE

FOR BUSINESSES REQUIRED to prepare financial statements in accordance with U.S. **Generally Accepted Accounting Principles (GAAP)** or International Accounting Standards (IAS), the computation of income tax expense requires expertise in accounting for income taxes. Increasingly, tax professionals are finding that an understanding of financial accounting for income taxes is a required competency.

The likelihood of a tax professional being ask to prepare, review, or audit the income tax "provision" reflected in the balance sheet, income statement, and footnotes of financial statements has grown substantially since the passage of the Sarbanes Oxley Act. Simply put, it is no longer enough to understand tax planning and compliance without also gaining a much deeper understanding of accounting for income taxes under the guidance framework applicable to businesses both in the United States and abroad.

In order to effectively work with income tax provisions, a tax professional must be able to understand not only the accounting guidance for income taxes themselves, but also the financial accounting guidance related to other complex business transactions. It is important that the differences between financial statement and tax return be identified and reflected properly in the income tax provision.

Consequently, tax professionals need an understanding of how to research not only the tax law but also financial accounting rules related to businesses. This chapter provides an overview of the topical area most likely to be important to tax researchers, accounting for income taxes, as well as a detailed description of the content, structure, and use of the FASB Accounting Standards Codification Research System (CRS).

Accounting for Income Taxes

Deferred Taxes

Intuitively you might assume that a company would account for income taxes on an "as paid" basis, reflecting the amount of income tax liability actually owed to all jurisdictions for the particular period of time. However, many items of income and expense are not treated the same for financial statement or "book" purposes as they are for tax purposes, and such an income tax number would not meaningfully reflect the income taxes associated with the pre-tax income presented on the financial statements.

A corporation's financial statements are prepared in accordance with GAAP and follow the matching principle in which the expenses related to earning income are reported in the same period as the income, without regard to when the expenses are actually paid. The purpose and objective of the financial statements are very different from the objective of the corporation's income tax return.

Under both U.S. GAAP and IAS, the amount of tax expense reflected in the financial statements is made up of both current and deferred components. While the current tax expense theoretically represents the taxes actually payable to (refund receivable from) the government, the deferred tax expense (or benefit) represents the future tax cost (or savings) connected with income reported in the current-period financial statements.

Differences between the book and the tax basis of items affecting income tax are recorded as deferred tax assets (representing future deductions) or deferred tax liabilities (representing future includable income). Consequently, tax professionals need to be capable of identifying not only the tax treatment of transactions but also the financial statement treatment for the item.

SPOTLIGHT ON TAXATION

Taxes Subject to the Deferred Tax Model

The deferred tax model of taxes applies to all Federal, state, foreign, and local taxes based on income. However, other taxes such as payroll, property, sales, value-added, net capital, or taxes based on capital expenditures are not included. Generally non-income taxes are recognized in the period those costs are incurred for financial statement purposes.

United States Generally Accepted Accounting Principles (GAAP)

In the United States, GAAP comes under the purview of the **Financial Accounting Standards Board (FASB)**. As stated by the FASB:

> *Since 1973, the FASB has been the designated organization in the private sector for establishing standards of financial accounting. Those standards govern the preparation of financial statements. They are officially recognized as authoritative by the SEC (Financial Reporting Release No. 1, Section 101, and reaffirmed in its April 2003 Policy Statement) and the AICPA (Rule 203, Rules of Professional Conduct, as amended May 1973 and May 1979).*

Prior to the 1970s, accounting standards were promulgated by groups formed under the umbrella of the American Institute of Certified Public Accountants (AICPA). Seeking additional independence, primary responsibility was shifted to the FASB in 1973; however, accounting guidance continued to be issued by various groups within the AICPA.

For example, the AICPA continued to issue Statements of Position (SOPs) and Industry Accounting and Auditing Guides. Although subordinate to statements issued by FASB, the guidance continued to have effect until 2009, when the bevy of different sources and statements were brought together into the **FASB Accounting Standards Codification (ASC)**. The ASC now stands as the primary accounting guidance for most businesses.

The U.S. **Securities and Exchange Commission (SEC)** was granted authority for the oversight of the U.S. capital markets in 1934. It is the responsibility of the Commission to:

- Interpret Federal securities laws.

- Issue new rules and amend existing rules.

- Oversee the inspection of securities firms, brokers, investment advisers, and ratings agencies.

- Oversee private regulatory organizations in the securities, accounting, and auditing fields.

- Coordinate U.S. securities regulation with Federal, state, and foreign authorities (**www.sec.gov/about/whatwedo.shtml#create**).

Thus, for public companies, the SEC retains standard-setting authority. In most instances, the SEC continues to rely on the private standard setters. However, the SEC has issued a number of forms of guidance, such as Regulation S-X, Staff Accounting Bulletins, and others that have also been codified by the SEC. Some portion of the SEC guidance is generally available in the ASC as supplemental material.

International Standards

In order to deal with the proliferation of country- or jurisdiction-specific accounting principles, the **International Accounting Standards Board (IASB)** was formed. The principal objectives of this organization are as follows:

- To develop a single set of high-quality, understandable, enforceable, and globally accepted **International Financial Reporting Standards (IFRS)**.

- To promote the use and rigorous application of those standards.

- To take account of the financial reporting needs of emerging economies and small and medium-sized entities (SMEs).

- To bring about convergence of national accounting standards and IFRS to high-quality solutions (**www.ifrs.org/The+organisation/IASCF+and+IASB.htm**).

More than 100 countries now require or permit the use of IFRS or are converging with IASB standards. Exhibit 10-1 shows the level of IFRS adoption as of April 2010. Analysis prepared

EXHIBIT 10-1:   IFRS Adoption

Country	Status for listed companies as of April 2010
Argentina	Required for fiscal years beginning on or after 1 January 2011
Australia	Required for all private sector reporting entities and as the basis for public sector reporting since 2005
Brazil	Required for consolidated financial statements of banks and listed companies from 31 December 2010 and for individual company accounts progressively since January 2008
Canada	Required from 1 January 2011 for all listed entities and permitted for private sector entities including not-for-profit organizations
China	Substantially converged national standards
European Union	All member states of the EU are required to use IFRSs as adopted by the EU for listed companies since 2005
France	Required via EU adoption and implementation process since 2005
Germany	Required via EU adoption and implementation process since 2005
India	India is converging with IFRSs over a period beginning 1 April 2011
Indonesia	Convergence process ongoing; a decision about a target date for full compliance with IFRSs is expected to be made in 2012
Italy	Required via EU adoption and implementation process since 2005
Japan	Permitted from 2010 for a number of international companies; decision about mandatory adoption by 2016 expected around 2012
Mexico	Required from 2012
Republic of Korea	Required from 2011
Russia	Required for banking institutions and some other securities issuers; permitted for other companies
Saudi Arabia	Not permitted for listed companies
South Africa	Required for listed entities since 2005
Turkey	Required for listed entities since 2008
United Kingdom	Required via EU adoption and implementation process since 2005
United States	Allowed for foreign issuers in the US since 2007; target date for substantial convergence with IFRSs is 2011 and decision about possible adoption for US companies expected in 2011.

Source: **http://www.ifrs.org/Use+around+the+world/Use+around+the+world.htm**. © 2010 IFRS Foundation. Used by permission.

by Deloitte shows that of the 173 countries examined, over 90 require the use of IFRS and over 120 require or permit the use of IFRS for companies listed on their stock exchanges.

The FASB continues to pursue convergence with the IASB, and the SEC has expressed an interest in developing a work plan for dealing with a global set of accounting standards. Current international guidance for accounting for income taxes (IAS 12) is similar in many ways to guidance provided in the ASC (ASC 740). Both use a deferred tax framework for reporting income tax expense. Given the existing importance of international accounting standards and the potential for more widespread adoption, tax professionals should continue to monitor changes in international standards related to accounting for income taxes and other relevant transactions.

The FASB Codification

The Codification is the single source of authoritative U.S. GAAP for private companies for interim and annual periods ending after September 15, 2009. All previous U.S. GAAP standards issued by the standard setters described have been superseded. Thus, all other accounting literature not included in the Codification is considered non-authoritative.

For companies registered with the SEC (public companies), the SEC's laws and regulations as well as Federal securities laws continue to apply. Certain guidance is not within the scope of the Codification, such as international accounting standards issued by the IASB, guidance for non-GAAP financial statements such as cash basis, or other comprehensive basis of accounting, governmental accounting standards, and audit guidance.

SPOTLIGHT ON TAXATION

The House of Generally Accepted Accounting Principles (GAAP)

Prior to the Codification, the list of standards and guidance was extensive. Thankfully, the Codification has reduced this to a single source. Pre-codification literature issued by various standard setters include:

1. Financial Accounting Standards Board (FASB)
   a. Statements (FAS)
   b. Interpretations (FIN)
   c. Technical Bulletins (FTB)
   d. Staff Positions (FSP)
   e. Staff Implementation Guides (Q&A)
   f. Statement No. 138 Examples
2. Emerging Issues Task Force (EITF)
   a. Abstracts
   b. Topic D
3. Derivative Implementation Group (DIG) Issues
4. Accounting Principles Board (APB) Opinions
5. Accounting Research Bulletins (ARB)
6. Accounting Interpretations (AIN)
7. American Institute of Certified Public Accountants (AICPA)
   a. Statements of Position (SOP)
   b. Audit and Accounting Guides (AAG)—only incremental accounting guidance
   c. Practice Bulletins (PB), including the Notices to Practitioners elevated to Practice Bulletin status by Practice Bulletin 1
   d. Technical Inquiry Service (TIS)—only for Software Revenue Recognition

The Codification project was a five-year project with the following three primary goals:

1. Simplify user access by codifying all authoritative U.S. GAAP in one spot.

2. Ensure that the codified content accurately represents authoritative U.S. GAAP.

3. Create a codification research system that is up-to-date for the released results of standard-setting activity.

The main advantage of the Codification was a move away from a standards-based model of organization to one based on topical area. For example, guidance for accounting for income taxes, although found primarily in SFAS109, could also be found in a number of other statements, interpretations, and Emerging Issue Task Force findings. Under the Codification, guidance for income taxes is found in ASC 740.

As part of the Codification, the FASB also developed the **FASB Accounting Standards Codification Research System (CRS)**. The goal was to create a research system that should reduce the amount of time and effort required to solve an accounting research issue and ensure that researchers are examining the most current guidance available. Codification users are able to identify all related content in one location much more easily than researching the previous standards. The FASB suggests the following steps when conducting research:

1. Browse the topical structure and related tables of contents. Because all related content is organized topically, users should be able to identify most content by topical browsing.

2. Use the text search feature only for very specific items (for example, guidance about inducements). Text search is based on specific language. Deviations from a selected search expression will lead to certain relevant content being excluded from search results. The CRS incorporates certain tools to help overcome the issue, but searching will always be constrained.

Online access to the Codification is provided by the FASB. Two levels of service are available: a no-cost basic version that allows the user to browse the Codification, print documents, and cross reference to legacy standards; and a fee-based professional version that provides the same functionality as the basic version, as well as search capabilities and some other functionality to assist researchers with their efforts. The FASB has made the professional version available to colleges and universities at a reduced rate.

Structure

As described previously, the Codification is organized by topical area. Each area is broken down into topics, and each topic is further expanded by subtopic, then into sections, and finally into subsections (see example in Exhibit 10-2).

Each area represents a broad category of related guidance such as "Assets." Topics represent a collection of related guidance for a specific area. Subtopics are subsets of the topics and represent a distinct type or scope of the topic. Sections represent a reflection of the nature of the subtopic, such as measurement, disclosure, and recognition. Subsections are the lowest level of the structure and provide even more granular segregation of material when necessary. For example, under the Expenses area is the Income Taxes

EXHIBIT 10-2: Codification Structure

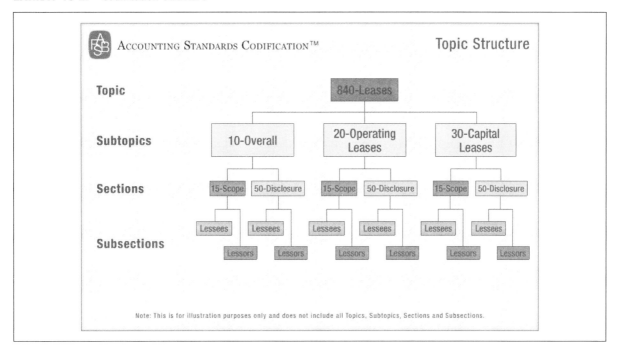

topic and within Income Taxes are a number of subtopics, such as Overall, Intraperiod Tax Allocation, and so forth.

There are also other Topics that intersect with the selected topic. These intersection topics tend to relate to a broad transaction category or an industry (e.g., Interim Reporting or Entertainment-Casinos in Exhibit 10-3). Within the subtopics are sections (Status, Overview and Background, Objectives; see Exhibit 10-4) that are expandable into subsections when available.

To assist with citation of Codification topics, the FASB created a numerical system to identify specific parts of the Codification. Topics are given a three-digit number between 105 and 999 (see Exhibit 10-5).

Intersection topics cut across topics and have a three-digit index as well. For example, topic 270 is Interim Reporting and may be present across any topic within the Codification when such material exists. Most subtopics receive a two-digit number between 0 and 99. Sections are also assigned a two digit number. With the exception of subtopic 10 (Overall) that varies from topic to topic, section numbers assigned are consistent throughout the Codification. For example, Status will be Section 00 across all subtopics in the Codification. A complete listing of the Section framework is presented in Exhibit 10-6. The lowest level of indexing is at the subsection level. Within each subsection is the actual guidance available as a paragraph.

When hierarchy exists within the paragraph structure, the Codification uses the ">" symbol to present the structure. As shown in Exhibit 10-7, the paragraph grouping on >>Instruments Classified as Equity is subordinate to the paragraph grouping >Determination of Temporary Differences. Paragraph numbers are expected to be held constant over time. Therefore, should a paragraph be amended, the content will change but the paragraph number will remain the same. Referencing the ASC should ordinarily take the form of the numerical system inherent in the Codification. To cite the general recognition approach to the interim reporting of income taxes, for example, the proper citation would be ASC 740-270-25-1.

EXHIBIT 10-3:   Codification Topics and Subtopics

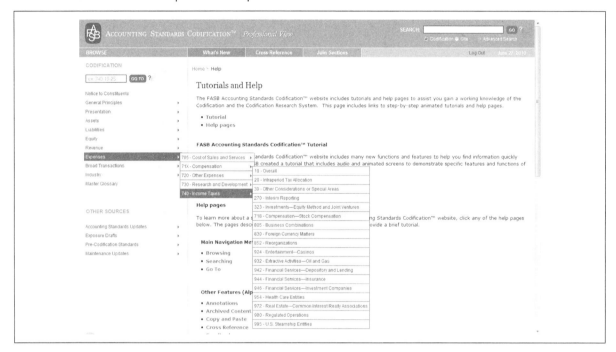

EXHIBIT 10-4:   Codification Section Table of Contents (TOC)

EXHIBIT 10-5: Section Numbering System

Topic Number	Description
105–199	General Principles—Broad conceptual matters
205–299	Presentation—Presentation matters only
305–799	Financial Statement Accounts—Organized in financial statement order—Asset, Liabilities Equity, etc.
805–899	Broad transactions—Cut across multiple financial statement accounts and are transaction-oriented
905–999	Industry—Accounting issues unique to an industry such as Airlines, Software, etc.

EXHIBIT 10-6: Table of Section Numbers

Section	Description	Section	Description
00	Status	40	Derecognition
05	Overview & Background	45	Other Presentation Matters
10	Objectives	50	Disclosure
15	Scope and Scope Exceptions	55	Implementation Guidance and Illustrations
20	Glossary	60	Relationships
25	Recognition	65	Transition and Open Effective Date Information
30	Initial Measurement	70	Grandfathered Guidance
35	Subsequent Measurement	75	XBRL Elements

In addition to providing the complete and current guidance for U.S. GAAP, the Codification also includes a substantial amount of material issued by the SEC applicable to public companies. The structure of SEC information is very similar to that of the rest of the Codification except:

(1) It does not contain the entire population of SEC rules, regulations, interpretive releases, and staff guidance.
(2) Each section is preceded with an "S" to indicate that the material originates from SEC guidance.
(3) Because the SEC releases do not always lend themselves to the Codification framework, the related SEC documentation is provided as issued in section 99. SEC material does not appear as a Section in the browse menus of the Areas and Topics (see Exhibit 10-4); however, the SEC topic materials are presented on the landing page (see Exhibit 10-8).

Browsing

Most research using the Codification is expected to be performed using the browse function. The Codification can be browsed by selecting the specific topic and subtopic desired (see Exhibit 10-8). The page displayed in Exhibit 10-8 is known as a "landing page." All the two-digit subtopics and three-digit intersection topics are displayed on the general topic landing page in an expandable TOC format. By clicking "expand" under the TOC, all of the paragraphs in that topic will be displayed as part of the TOC. Alternatively, any particular subtopic can be expanded by clicking the "+" in front of the title. Note that clicking a broad area or industry topic presented in the TOC on the landing page will

EXHIBIT 10-7: Codification Paragraph Hierarchy

EXHIBIT 10-8: Codification Section Landing Page

bring you to the intersection subtopic within that intersection topic. For example, from the Topic 740 TOC, clicking Topic 718 Compensation–Stock Compensation brings you to the landing page for Topic 718, with a TOC showing the intersection between Topic 718 and Topic 740 (See Exhibit 10-9). In this way the Codification prevents having the same guidance in two places: once under Topic 740 and then again under Topic 718. Instead, the intersection can be found from either topic.

Browsing the *industry* topics works in a slightly different fashion. By selecting an industry topic from the main menu, the landing page offers a listing of the broad areas and topics that intersect that topic (Exhibit 10-10). Clicking one of the section titles brings you to the landing page for that topic. Alternatively, the sections can be "joined" using the Join All Sections button, which then creates a TOC for an industry topic. This allows for continued browsing of that industry topic similar to the other categories of topics and allows the researcher to see all the intersecting guidance for a client's particular industry.

Using the main menu to browse directly to a subtopic is also available (as shown in Exhibit 10-3). By browsing to that level, the subtopic landing page displays the same type of TOC as the topic landing page, but the detail of each section is also displayed (see Exhibit 10-8). Note that a "breadcrumb" describes the location the Codification is displayed at all times at the top of the TOC. By joining all sections, a single document containing all the sections displayed in the TOC is created to allow for a comprehensive review of all the guidance on that subtopic. Note that a complete document that includes all of the content included in the TOC is not created.

Selecting a section from the subtopic menu creates the section page (see Exhibit 10-11). The section page is the primary source of research in most instances. The section page comes with a similar TOC and three tabs: (1) Document, (2) Archive, and (3) What Links Here. Document is the default tab and displays the actual content (subsections and paragraphs selected). The Archive tab will provide a history of the guidance related to that section, and the What Links Here provides a listing of all the other sections within the Codification that contain a link back to the current section.

EXHIBIT 10-9: Codification Intersection

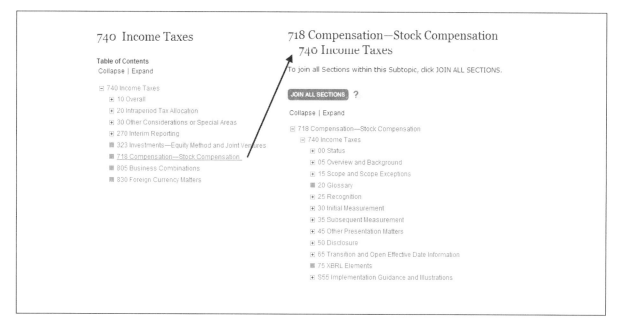

EXHIBIT 10-10:   Codification Industry Section

EXHIBIT 10-11:   Codification Section Page

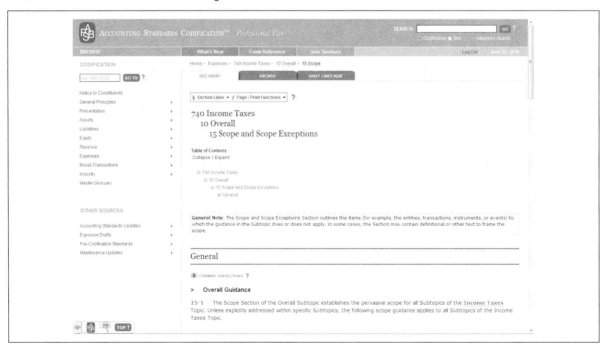

Also available are Section Links that allow for easy links to the other sections within that subtopic (see Exhibit 10-12 on the following page). The section listing contains all of the U.S. GAAP guidance and SEC materials by section number and provides the title to each section. The bolded section provides the name of the current section. This is also available in the breadcrumb at the top of the page.

The Page Functions provide a printer-friendly version of the document, with or without legacy sources. The suggested method to copy and paste materials from the Codification is to use the printer-friendly form of the document prior to the copy-and-paste. An e-mail of the document can also be sent from this menu. From the section page, all of the sections can be combined using the Combine Subsections at the top of the first paragraph, which will create a document that contains all of the subsections within the current subtopic. For example, if the current document is 740-10-15 or Income Taxes (740) Overall (10) Scope and Scope Exceptions (15), using combine subsections will create a document with all subsections of Subtopic 740-10. Any pending guidance that may have been adopted but is not yet effective is also displayed as part of the subsection information. In the event that the exact location of a paragraph is desired, rolling over the paragraph number provides a detailed trail of location within the Codification (see Exhibit 10-13).

Each subtopic includes a glossary section (20) that contains definitions of key words used in that subtopic. The first occurrence of a glossary term in a subsection is also highlighted and linked to that term. If the link is connected to the glossary, then all the locations where that term is used can be displayed by clicking the glossary term itself. The master glossary for all terms can also be found on the main menu.

EXHIBIT 10-13: Codification Rollover Breadcrumb

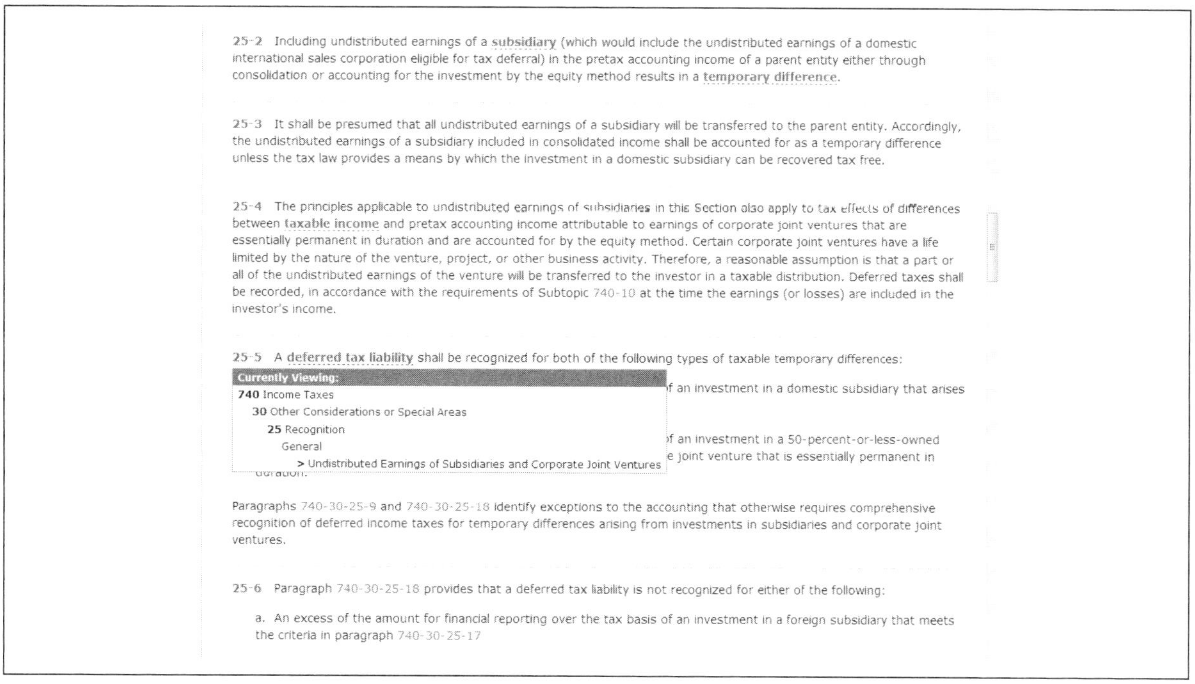

EXHIBIT 10-12:   Codification Sections Links

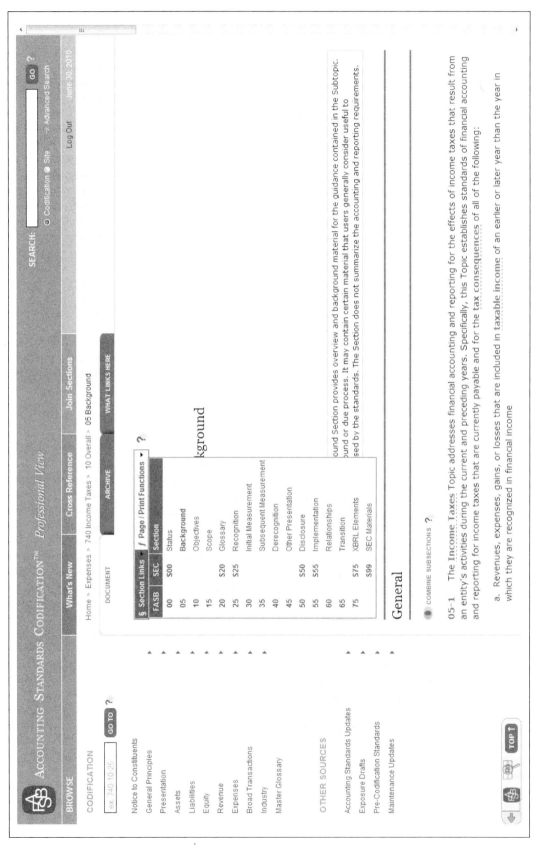

Search

The Codification also possesses a search function similar to those found in the tax services discussed in the prior chapters. Search results include an excerpt from the paragraph and the numerical location within the Codification for each result (see Exhibit 10-14). Narrowing the search results to provide a more precise result can be achieved in several ways. The Related Terms feature presents an opportunity to restrict the search to instances where the original search term and the related words both appear (similar to using the "and" function in the original search).

The search engine identifies commonly used terms and offers them in the related terms list. The number of results in each area is also presented and allows the original search to be restricted to only the areas desired. Unlike related words, the Go button must be clicked after selecting the area to which the search has been restricted. Once a search has been narrowed by area, the search engine then allows additional narrowing, first by topic (see Exhibit 10-15) and then by subtopic. For a more specific search, the advanced search feature allows for the narrowing of search results from the original search point (see Exhibit 10-16).

Go To

The Go To function works in a similar fashion to a "search by citation" in a typical tax service. For instances when the exact location is known, the Codification reference can be typed directly into the Go To box, and the document will be presented immediately. Conveniently, as you type the Codification citation into the box, the system will provide a listing of all available content within that topic, subtopic, or section (see Exhibit 10-17).

EXHIBIT 10-14: Codification Search

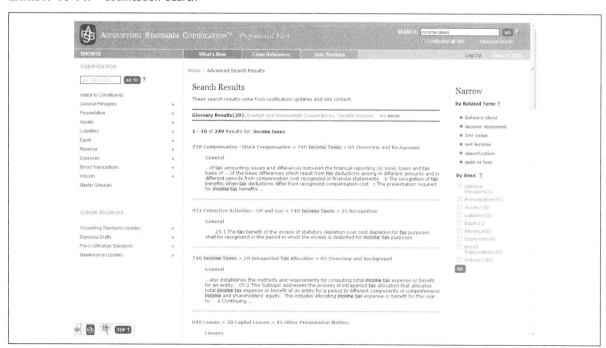

Join Sections

Join Sections allows for all of the related sections of a topic to be joined into a single document so that the guidance across all sections within a topic can be reviewed at one time. For example, if a review of all the disclosure requirements for Topic 740 Income Taxes was desired, the Join Sections feature allows for the selection of Topic 740 and Section 50 (Disclosure) and prepares first a list of all the sections of disclosure available

EXHIBIT 10-15:   Codification Narrow Search

EXHIBIT 10-16:   Codification Advanced Search

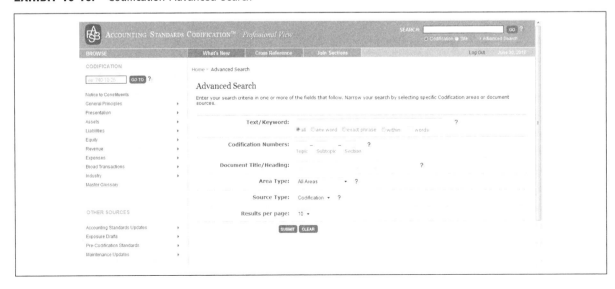

with that topic (see Exhibit 10-18). The desired sections can be selected and then joined into a single document. Drop-down menus are available when selecting topic and section. The joined results will include a TOC similar to those presented when browsing.

Cross Reference

For researchers who either are new to the Codification or are more comfortable with the legacy standards, the Codification system provides a cross-referencing system to allow researchers to locate guidance in the Codification using the old guidance or find the old guidance using the new Codification reference (see Exhibit 10-19). Any of the original standards are available for the cross-reference report (e.g., FAS, FIN, EITF).

EXHIBIT 10-17: Codification Go To

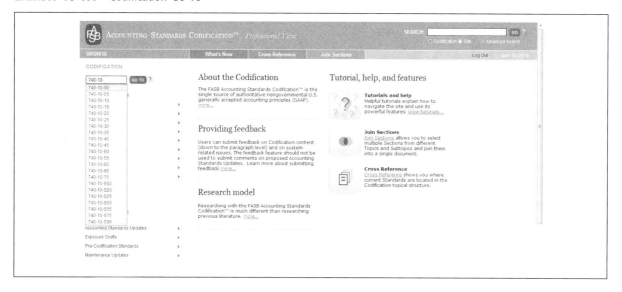

EXHIBIT 10-18: Codification Join Sections

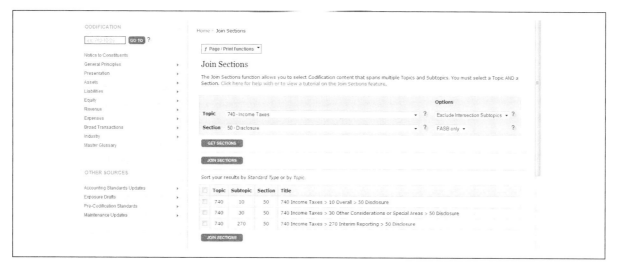

EXHIBIT 10-19:   Codification Cross Reference

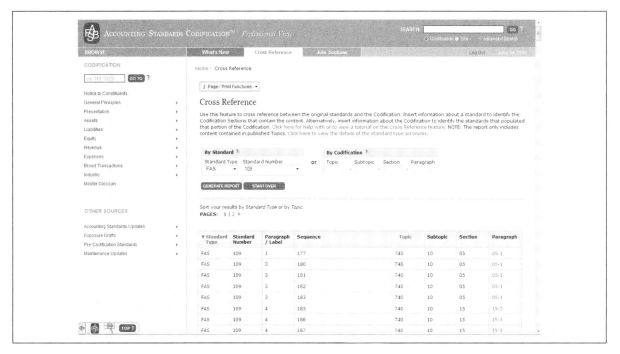

Drop-down menus are available to assist in identifying the proper coding of the old standards. Legacy standard and paragraph numbers are mapped into the Codification at the paragraph level and vice-versa. The Codification paragraph listed in the report is a link to the document itself. Searches for legacy standards using current Codification will provide a report to the original statement and paragraph, but they do not link back to the original document itself. As previously mentioned, cross references to original guidance can also be found by using the print with references function in the Page Functions.

Certain pre-codification legacy standards can be located within the Codification from the homepage (Exhibit 10-3) in the bottom left corner under Other Sources. The legacy guidance is available as indicated in Exhibit 10-20.

EXHIBIT 10-20:   Pre-Codification Standards Available

FASB Pronouncements	AICPA Copyrighted Standards
Statements of Financial Accounting Standards	Accounting Research Bulletins
FASB Interpretations	Accounting Principles Board Opinions
FASB Staff Positions	AICPA Practice Bulletins
FASB Technical Bulletins	AICPA Accounting Interpretations
EITF Abstracts	AICPA Accounting Statements of Position
Derivatives (Statement 133) Implementation Issues	

SPOTLIGHT ON TAXATION

ASC 740

As an example of the importance of financial accounting research for tax professionals and the importance of tax research for audit professionals, ASC 740 requires taxpayers to examine each and every "tax position" taken and for every uncertain tax position, allows tax benefits to be recognized in financial statements only when it is determined that it is "more likely than not" that the tax position can be sustained or when the position is ultimately settled via an audit, negotiation, or a court decision.

A tax position is defined as a position taken in a previously filed return or expected to be taken in a future return. Transactions that create deferred tax assets and liabilities are "tax positions," but transactions that create permanent book/tax differences (or no differences at all) are also tax positions. ASC 740 also requires that the taxpayer distinguish between "highly certain" and "uncertain" positions.

The application of ASC 740 to an uncertain tax position requires that a tax benefit be recognized when it is "more likely than not" (MLTN) to be sustained based on the technical merits of the position. In determining whether the MLTN threshold is met, taxpayers must assume that the tax position will be examined (audited) by the taxing authorities. Ultimately, the conclusion regarding the financial statement recognition takes into account the tax technical merits, facts, and circumstances of the position.

Other Sources

Prior to the codification, guidance was updated through the issuance of a new standard or statement of positions or some other form of standard. Subsequent to codification, changes to guidance are made through **Accounting Standards Updates**. These updates first take the form of an exposure draft during the public comment period. Exposure drafts are proposed updates to the Codification and are indexed numerically to show where the update will ultimately be housed, should it be approved by the Board.

Once approved, the guidance will become "pending content" and will be displayed within the paragraphs of the Codification in the proper positions until such time as the new guidance becomes effective (see Exhibit 10-21). Once effective, the old guidance is removed and placed in the archived data and replaced with the new guidance.

Other Services

The Codification is expected to be the primary source of accounting research. However, many of the companies that provide tax services also offer accounting and audit information within the same platform. Since they operate on the same platform, the research process works in a very similar fashion to that of the tax services, and thus the details of the operations are omitted here. Many offer additional information, however, and a review of the materials available is warranted.

CCH Accounting Research Manager (ARM)

The **CCH Accounting Research Manager (ARM)** provides an online database (with the same IntelliConnect platform) that provides access to accounting, auditing, governmental, and SEC authoritative literature, plus interpretive guidance and the FASB Codification.

EXHIBIT 10-21: Codification Pending Content

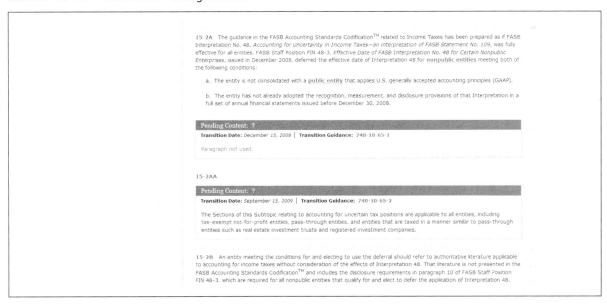

The ARM also provides access to search Form 10-Ks filed with the SEC. In addition, ARM offers a series of knowledge-based audit materials to help professionals conduct audits of certain industries, such as financial institutions or employee benefit plans.

Primary resource information is available for Public Company Oversight Board (PCAOB) rules, releases, and staff materials; IASB accounting standards and IFRIC interpretations; Governmental Accounting Standards Board (GASB) statements and related guidance; Governmental Accounting Office (GAO) auditing standards; and others.

RIA Financial Reporting Manager

RIA offers an accounting base suite as part of its Checkpoint series that has many available components, including GAAP Compliance, SEC Compliance, FASB and IASB materials. Similar to CCH, a bevy of analysis and practice aids are also available such as the Audit and Accounting Disclosure Manual, GAAP Practice Manual, and analysis of international reporting standards.

LexisNexis Tax Center

Part of the LexisNexis Tax Center is an accounting tab that provides a wide variety of materials and analysis on accounting topics. Audit and international accounting materials are provided, such as Wiley GAAP, but the actual U.S. and international standards are not part of the information available.

International Standards

As discussed earlier, international standards are currently promulgated by the IASB. The standards are currently offered free of charge by the IFRS Foundation (**www.iasb.org**). However, the free subscription does not include implementation guidance or the basis for conclusions. A paid subscription is available and includes electronic versions of all

IFRS, older IAS, IFRS Interpretation Committee (IFRIC), and Standing Interpretations Committee (SIC) interpretations and IASB-issued supporting documents, including application guidance, illustrative examples, implementation guidance, bases for conclusions, and all appendices. The paid subscription also includes a search function and the capability to have the standards translated into a variety of languages.

Because one of the intentions of the IASB is to adhere to principle-based standards and because the IASB (and its predecessors) has not issued standards for very long, the body of guidance to comb through for information related to income taxes remains reasonably limited. IAS 12 represents the vast majority of guidance on accounting for income taxes (Section 29 for SMEs). As a result, this book will not cover the research process for IFRS. However, as the popularity of IFRS continues to expand and further progress is made towards convergence with U.S. GAAP, the complexity of IFRS may increase. Meanwhile, many of the tax service providers mentioned above include the international standards as part of their offerings, and thus those tools can be used in the same manner as for tax research.

SPOTLIGHT ON TAXATION

IFRS v. U.S. GAAP

The list of differences between IFRS and U.S. GAAP has been, and continues to be, analyzed over and over as the two systems of accounting guidance evolve and perhaps converge. Most large accounting firms and numerous other sources have analyzed differences on a standard-by-standard or topic-by-topic basis. One difference that even a financial accounting novice would notice is the sheer size difference between the two sets of guidance. U.S. GAAP is currently estimated (even after codification) at about 25,000 pages. Estimates of the international standards are at about 2,500 pages, or 10 percent of the length of U.S. GAAP. Amazingly, the IFRS for SMEs are contained solely within one document of about 250 pages in length. Simplified indeed!

SUMMARY

Tax professionals and CPAs must be able to provide more than just tax advice and compliance services. As the complexity of accounting for income taxes increased dramatically first with the issuance of SFAS No. 109 and then FIN48 on uncertain tax positions, the demands on tax professionals increased dramatically. Tax provision work requires tax professionals to be capable of not only understanding the tax treatment of a transaction, but also the book accounting so that any permanent and temporary differences can be identified and accounted for properly.

Understanding how to navigate the accounting guidance found in the ASC and other sources will enable tax researchers to perform services that are in high demand from accounting firms and businesses of all sizes.

QUIZ YOURSELF

Reinforce the tax research information covered in this chapter by completing the online quizzes located at the Federal Tax Research Web site at **www.cengagebrain.com.** At the CengageBrain.com home page, search for the *Federal Tax Research*, 9e ISBN (1111221642) using the search box at the top of the page. This will take you to the product page where you can access the quizzes.

KEY WORDS

By the time you complete this chapter, you should be comfortable discussing each of the following terms. If you need additional review of any of these items, return to the appropriate material in the chapter or consult the glossary to this text.

Accounting Standards Updates, p. 373

CCH Accounting Research Manager (ARM), p. 373

FASB Accounting Standards Codification (ASC), p. 357

FASB Accounting Standards Codification Research System (CRS), p. 360

Financial Accounting Standards Board (FASB), p. 357

Generally Accepted Accounting Principles (GAAP), p. 356

International Accounting Standards Board (IASB), p. 358

International Financial Reporting Standards (IFRS), p. 358

Securities and Exchange Commission (SEC), p. 357

DISCUSSION QUESTIONS

1. Why should tax professionals know how to conduct financial accounting research?

2. Why are taxes not reflected on financial statements on an "as paid" basis?

3. What two bodies have authority to set accounting standards in the United States?

4. What are the responsibilities of the SEC?

5. Who establishes international accounting standards, and what are their principle objectives?

6. Explain whether U.S. and international accounting standards for income taxes are similar.

7. Why did the FASB undertake the codification project?

8. Describe the hierarchy of elements within the Codification.

9. How do industry sections differ from other sections?

10. What is an intersection section?

11. How can SEC guidance be distinguished from other guidance?

12. What two methods are available to narrow a search in the Codification?

13. Describe how a researcher can find the old standards that became guidance in the Codification.

14. What other services provide accounting information as part of their tax services?

EXERCISES

15. Use the Codification to answer the following:
    a. Under what general area will you find the Income Taxes topic?
    b. What topics are available under the area Equity?
    c. What non-industry subtopics are available in Topic 405 Liabilities?

16. Use the Codification to answer the following:
    a. Use the Master Glossary and search for the term "deferred tax." How many terms result?
    b. Which Broad Transaction areas intersect with Topic 740 Income Taxes?
    c. Which Industry areas intersect with Topic 740 Income Taxes?

17. Use the Codification to answer the following:

  a. What is the citation for the paragraph that provides a description of two basic principles related to accounting for income taxes?

  b. What subtopics of Topic 740 Income Taxes contain sections on implementation guidance?

  c. What is the definition of the term "valuation allowance?"

18. Use the Codification to answer the following:

  a. Perform a Join Sections on Topic 740 and Section 25. What subtopics are on the list?

  b. Using the Search function, search for "push down accounting" and then narrow your search by the Presentation topic. What is the breadcrumb for the resulting paragraph?

  c. Browse to Topic 305, Subtopic 10, Section 05, and then combine all subsections. How many paragraphs are included in the resulting document?

RESEARCH CASES

19. What paragraphs in the ARC discuss the effects of tax holidays on accounting for income taxes?

20. What is the basic recognition threshold for the financial statement effects of a tax position? (Include your citation.)

21. Bradley Corp. took a very aggressive tax position on its tax return in a prior year that the predominance of the evidence indicated that it would be unable to benefit from if detected under review by the taxing jurisdiction. In the current year, the taxing authorities discovered the tax position and reversed the deduction that Bradley had taken. Bradley was required to pay the tax liability associated with the reversal of the tax item. Rather than pursue a settlement with the revenue agent, Bradley has elected to appeal the issue to tax court. Is the issue "effectively settled" under Topic 740?

22. For $1 million, Dempsey Inc. purchased stock in a corporation that held only one asset, an FCC license, and thus is unable to treat the purchase as a business combination. The tax basis in the asset was $0. What method should Dempsey use to assign the value to the asset and the deferred tax liability?

23. Donovan Corp., a calendar year-end company, operates a profitable division in Jurisdiction A. In January 2010, Jurisdiction A enacted a tax law that changed the tax rate structure from 30 percent to 35 percent. Donovan wants to know whether it needs to adjust its 12/31/2009 tax provision to reflect the rate change, and if not in 2009, when does it need to recognize the effect of that change?

24. Altidore Inc. operates a calendar-year-end business that suffers from dramatic seasonal variation in taxable income. For example, it often operates at a net loss for the first two quarters of the year and then operates profitably for the last two quarters and, for as long as anyone can remember, finishes the year with taxable income. The new tax director has been asked to help calculate the deferred tax assets at the end of the first quarter. After looking at the quarterly loss, he claims that since there is no net income, there are no deferred tax assets because the effective tax rate is zero. (Carrybacks and carryforwards are not allowed in this jurisdiction.) Is the tax director correct in his assessment of the effective tax rate for calculating the deferred tax assets?

25. ASC 740 provides a two-step process in accounting for uncertain tax positions. What are these two steps?

26. How are interest and penalties treated on uncertain tax positions? What is the classification of the unrecognized tax benefits?

27. What are the necessary disclosures for uncertain tax liabilities for public companies, and do they differ for non-public companies?

28. According to ASC 740, in what order should tax effects be allocated? (Hint: This has to do with intraperiod allocation.)

29. What are the six exceptions to the basic requirements of ASC 740? Please briefly describe each of the exceptions.

30. Yankee Corporation has suffered a large net operating loss. What are the sources of income to be considered when estimating the future realization of a tax benefit from this loss? Briefly describe each. Provide examples when possible.

31. How and what type of evidence is analyzed to determine the need for a valuation allowance? Describe the process for this analysis.

32. What is the tax basis of an asset under ASC 740? What is the book basis?

PART IV

Implementing the Research Tools

CHAPTER 11

Communicating Research Results

LEARNING OBJECTIVES

- Produce a standard format for the construction of a file memorandum to contain the results of one's research efforts and professional judgment.

- Develop skills in using other methods to communicate research results, including oral presentations and client letters.

CHAPTER OUTLINE

ONCE THE PRACTITIONER HAS begun to develop effective tax research skills, he or she must hone them with practice—whether by working through tax research cases presented as a class exercise in a university course or immediately beginning work for professional clients. Accordingly, the overriding purpose of this chapter is to provide the reader with guidance and opportunities to apply the research skills and examine the tax research resources that have been discussed in previous chapters.

In addition, this chapter discusses the means by which the tax professional conveys the results of a tax research project—in other words, applying some of the judgment and communications skills required. Direction as to the proper format and content of memorandums to the file, of client letters, and of oral presentations is addressed, with development of professional skills the overriding goal.

Communications and the Tax Professional

As we suggested in our initial discussions of the tax research process, illustrated in Exhibit 2-1, a tax research assignment often concludes with some form of communication by the tax professional. The audience for this communication often is the practitioner's supervisor or client, but tax-related communications can take many forms, including the following.

- A telephone call or text message.

- An informal discussion in person or via e-mail.

- A letter prepared for reading by someone at least as familiar with the tax law as the writer.

- A letter prepared for reading by someone less familiar with the tax law than is the writer.

- A letter prepared for reading by someone who is essentially untrained in the tax law.

- An article for publication in a newspaper or magazine directed at the general public.

- An article for publication in a professional journal read by tax generalists.

- An article for publication in a professional journal read by tax specialists.

- A directed discussion among tax peers, such as in a tax department meeting.

- A speech to a general audience.

- A speech at a conference of tax professionals.

- A memorandum to be read in the future by the writer or by a peer with similar training.

- An appearance on a news broadcast or program with a serious tone.

- An appearance on a broadcast with a less serious tone.

- A posting on a general, business, or tax-oriented blog.

For the most part, the tax professional's preparation for these communications is similar. For the purposes of this chapter, we assume that all of the pertinent tax research techniques developed in earlier parts of this text have been planned and conscientiously applied so that the practitioner is qualified and current enough with respect to prevailing tax law to address the audience in terms of the content of the communication. The challenge then becomes how to deliver this information in a manner that will be accepted and understood by the audience.

Communication truly occurs only when the message desired to be sent by the speaker or writer is received by the intended audience. Distractions of all sorts can make this process difficult to accomplish. Thorough research into the nature and expectations of the audience, factors that may interfere with the delivery of the message, and feedback and corrective measures must make up a critical part of the communicator's preparation.

Examples of "noise" that can disrupt the communications process include a mismatching of expectations as to the message, the chosen delivery method, the identity and nature of the sender and receiver of the message, other events competing for the attention of those involved, logistical difficulties, and technological problems. Feedback and corrective devices that can aid in accomplishing the delivery of the desired message include formal and informal evaluation processes, "real-time" opportunities such as question-and-answer periods and written comments received during the drafting of the document, and the sending and receiving of intended and unintended body language or other communicative signals.

Tax professionals generally are virtually untrained as to the application of communication methods in conveying tax messages, but this shortcoming can be remedied. The chief ingredients necessary to become an effective tax-content communicator are the desire to learn and improve as a communicator in general, and the use of every opportunity possible to obtain and develop skills in the delivery of tax information. Given the nature of today's competitive tax profession, plenty of such opportunities for practice exist, and pressures from others who are competing for clients and promotions provide most professionals with more than enough motivation to make improvements in their communication skills.

SPOTLIGHT ON TAXATION

A Career in Taxation

"When I was young, I was taught the story of Jesus and the tax man. The point was that Jesus was good to everyone; so much so that he would even eat with the taxman. The story tells a lot about being good, but it also tells a lot about historical perceptions of the tax collector."

—Christopher Bergin

We begin a more detailed review of the communication process with an examination of the most commonly encountered written communications demanded in the tax practice. The chapter concludes with a discussion of skills needed in delivering spoken communications. In either case, the structure of the communication follows the basic format delineated in Exhibit 11-1.

The Heart of Tax Research Communication: The File Memo

The tax researcher spends most of his or her time reviewing primary and secondary sources of the Federal tax law, redefining pertinent issues, and attempting to discover additional facts concerning the client's situation. On completion of this review, the

EXHIBIT 11-1: The Structure of Technical Tax Communications

Element of the Message	Purposes	Comments
Introduction	Provide a road map for what is to come.	**10 percent of allotted time/space.**
	Place the message in context.	Could include a story/anecdote, current news development, or "object lesson."
	Generate audience interest, if necessary.	
	Set the tone for the message.	
Body	Generally, the technical tax material is presented here.	**80 percent of allotted time/space.**
	Usually follows an order suggested by the hierarchy of the sources of the tax law.	Must be brief, to the point, hard-hitting; not trite or condescending.
	Alternative ordering methods: historical, strengths/weaknesses, cost/benefit.	Identify three to six key points that all readers/listeners must take away from the message.
Conclusion	Tie back to the introduction.	**10 percent of allotted time/space.**
	Reinforce key elements of the message.	Tip off the reader/listener that the conclusion is starting, with: "In closing," "To sum up," or "I'll conclude with …"
	Bring the presentation to a climax. Indicate next steps and follow-up action.	

researcher must integrate the disparate results of the research process into a more usable form.

Thorough practitioners generate a memorandum to the client's file for this purpose. This **file memorandum** is designed to:

- Organize the facts, issues, and conclusions of the project.

- Facilitate a review of the research activities by the practitioner's supervisors or colleagues.

- Allow for a subsequent examination of the research issue by the original researcher or by his or her successor, with respect to the same or another client's identical or related fact situation.

Accordingly, the file memo should be constructed in a general, usable format that lends itself to a quick perusal of the pertinent tax facts and issues. Many accounting and law firms impose a standardized file memo format. If the reader's employer has enacted no such requirement, he or she should consider adopting the format illustrated in Exhibits 2-5 and 11-2. A template for this memo format is available at the Web site for this text located at **www.cengagebrain.com**.

A file memo should include a brief introductory summary of the facts and issues that face the client. In all but the most complex instances, this statement should require no more than two paragraphs. Similarly, the rare footnote at this point of the memo should be restricted to current developments, for example, with respect to an appeal relative to one of the critical cases that is cited in the memo or a statutory amendment.

The file memo then includes a listing of the tax issues that are in dispute and a matching conclusion for each identified issue. This format allows the subsequent reader to determine quickly whether each issue is "pro" or "con" for the taxpayer and limits the time required to sort through a number of such memos. In the support section, a detailed review and evaluation of controlling laws is derived, with full citations presented in the standard forms. The "meat" of the memo is presented here, and the strengths and weaknesses of both sides of the tax argument are developed and discussed. Finally, recommendations for subsequent actions with the client may be enumerated, and other strategies as to tax return or audit positions are identified.

Often, the gathering of the pertinent facts is the most challenging of the tax professional's tasks. Tax engagements typically begin with client contact in the form of a phone call or meeting, followed by an exchange of copies of pertinent documents such as letters, spreadsheets, trusts or wills, contracts, life insurance or annuity agreements, employer handbooks, and diaries or logbooks belonging to the client. In reality, though, the initial determination of the facts is likely to be incomplete for reasons that include the following:

- Taxpayers tend to see the dispute only from their side so that facts and circumstances may be hidden or "forgotten" if they would cast doubt on the ability to determine or document the pro-taxpayer position.

- Taxpayers are not trained in the details of the technical tax law, so they may be unable to determine which documents or other evidence of the facts are important in determining the controlling tax law.

- For tax research that requires the full professional judgment and experience of the practitioner, there may be no clearly controlling tax statute or precedent, facts may be truly incomplete, or they may unfold as the evaluation of tax law occurs. The researcher may discover that issues of taxpayer motive, knowledge, or other circumstances turn on facts that were not immediately known to be critical.

Moreover, fact gathering often turns on such intangible factors as the reliability of the memories of the taxpayers and key witnesses, the ability of witnesses to withstand scrutiny in the deposition and testimony phases of the case, the unanticipated death or disappearance of key parties, the destruction of records due to casualty or computer mismanagement, and the tendency of some taxpayers to "fix the truth" after the fact.

Recalling our language in Chapters 2 and 3, more research engagements entail closed-fact settings than open-fact situations by far, but those facts may be fairly difficult to determine and support in a manner that will satisfy the Internal Revenue Service (IRS) or the courts. Such fact-gathering travails make for interesting anecdotes at conferences of tax practitioners, and they seldom are apparent from the clean, black-and-white statements of facts that accompany file memos and case briefs.

The tone and nature of the file memo should recognize that its readers will be restricted to fellow tax practitioners who are well versed in the Federal tax law. Thus, references to primary and secondary sources of the tax law should be frequent and complete, but usually limited to the tax case reporters that are available in the office of the researcher's firm. One must presume that the ultimate reader of the memo's comments will need no introduction to the hierarchy of the Federal tax system nor to statutory citation practices. In addition, it often is helpful to include pertinent references to one or more of the commercial tax services to which the researcher's firm subscribes, perhaps on a "sticky note" or other attachment to the memo, providing a clear paper trail to facilitate subsequent review and commentary concerning the tax issue.

Seldom will the researcher's efforts result in merely the preparation of a research memorandum to the file. In general, the memo will be accompanied in the file by links to and briefs of one or more pertinent court cases or administrative pronouncements. (Review Exhibit 5-8 and your related class exercises concerning the format and content of a well-constructed court case brief.) In addition, many practitioners append to the file memo photocopies of or network links to prior-year documents, in-house memos, various IRS rulings, and journal articles, much of which features "highlighting;" that is, markup with a literal or virtual pastel marker. These practices are illustrated in Exhibit 11-2.

EXHIBIT 11-2: File Memorandum for Tax Research

Raabe, Whittenburg, Sanders, and Sawyers, CPAs
San Francisco, CA
September 30, 20XX

Relevant Facts

The Browns live in South Dakota. They own their home and hold investments in the debt of several domestic corporations. The interest that they received on this debt was gross income to them. To diversify their portfolio, the Browns took out a sizable second mortgage on their home and applied a portion of the proceeds to some City of Chandler School Bonds. The remainder of the proceeds was used to expand the facilities of Mrs. Brown's dental clinic.

Specific Issues

How much of the mortgage interest paid can be claimed as an itemized deduction by the Browns?

Conclusions

That portion of the mortgage proceeds applied to the dental clinic generates an interest deduction to be claimed against clinic income on Schedule C. No other deduction is allowed.

Support

The Code disallows the deduction of interest on indebtedness that is incurred or continued to purchase or carry obligations, the interest on which is exempt from the Federal income tax. IRC § 265(a)(2). This provision denies the double benefit that would be enjoyed by the taxpayer who would receive tax-exempt income while simultaneously claiming an investment interest deduction for the interest expense paid, for example, by incurring a bank loan and using the proceeds to purchase municipal bonds.

The IRS examines evidence to infer the intent of the taxpayer who is incurring the indebtedness. Under Rev. Proc. 72-18, 1972-1 C.B. 740, a taxpayer who purchases exempt bonds can claim an interest deduction if the debt in question has been incurred for personal reasons (e.g., via a mortgage to finance the purchase of residential property) or for valid business reasons, as long as the borrowing does not exceed legitimate business needs.

Several court decisions have emphasized that the existence of such business motives must be documented clearly, as to both presence and amount. *Wisconsin Cheeseman* v. U.S., 388 F.2d 420 (CA-7, 1968); *Bradford*, 60 T.C. 253 (1973); *Israelson v. U.S.*, 367 F.Supp. 1104 (D.Md., 1973).

Mortgage indebtedness is a classic illustration of an investment that will generate deductible interest expenses for the taxpayer who holds exempt bonds. However, the timing of such a mortgage transaction must be monitored to exhibit the proper motives for the benefit of the IRS. In one case, the taxpayer paid for his home with cash. Only later was an investment program (that included municipal bonds) initiated and a residential mortgage secured. The IRS inferred that the mortgage proceeds were in indirect support of the exempt indebtedness, and the deduction for the mortgage interest was disallowed. *Mariorenzi v. Comm.*, 490 F.2d 92 (CA-8, 1974), 32 TCM 681 (1973). Had the taxpayer secured a mortgage before the home was completed, purchasing the exempt bonds out of savings, it appears that the deduction could have been preserved. The IRS has applied this doctrine outside of the Eighth Circuit, in PLR 8631006.

Because the Browns live in the Eighth Circuit, the *Mariorenzi* doctrine prevails, and no itemized deduction is allowed at all; that is, for that portion of the loan that is applied to the school bonds. Rev. Proc. 72-18 is insensitive to portfolio diversification motives, and no personal motive appears to exist that supports any other possible deduction. According to the logic of these precedents, the Browns should have sold the exempt bonds and then used the proceeds to finance their portfolio acquisitions.

Actions to Be Taken
Prepare letter, review results with client.
Suggest changes in portfolio holdings to regain the deduction.
Preparer: Mary H. Polzin
Reviewer: Char E. Mano

The authors recommend that practitioners restrict such appended material to only those resources that are of utmost importance to reduce both the associated client costs and the volume of the typical memo. In this regard, we believe that an effective statement of facts and issues, followed by a concise synthesis of the controlling law, is far more valuable than a mass of duplicated, small-print tax reference materials.

Evaluating the Sources of Law

The tax researcher will have made a number of judgments and creative applications concerning the client's fact situation before preparing the file memo. For instance, the researcher may select and eliminate competing issues and direct the research process onto one or more pathways to the exclusion of others. Nonetheless, in deriving an analysis of the various elements of the controlling sources of the tax law, the practitioner must choose from among a number of varied interpretations of the statute and of its (interpretive) regulations and court case opinions.

Often the researcher will be guided in this regard by the opinions of the most recent of the court cases discovered. Well-written case opinions typically provide a summary of the evolution of the pertinent tax law and a discussion of the competing interpretations thereof by the parties to the lawsuit. In this manner, the researcher regularly can obtain an indication of both the critical facts and issues that the court has identified in the present case and its interpretation as to the distinguishing features of seemingly relevant precedents. (In reality, most of these sections of the opinion are written by law clerks or law school students who obtain and retain their positions by preparing thorough and insightful file memos of their own!) Moreover, court case opinions often include lengthy dissenting or concurring opinions, from which the researcher can identify additional facts and issues relative to the opinion. Logical and legal leads also might be found in a dissenting opinion that could be pertinent in building an appeal to overturn the majority opinion.

Lacking (or in lieu of) such judicial direction, the researcher's evaluation of the efficacy of a precedent or pronouncement often is guided by no more than a review of the hierarchy of the sources of the Federal tax law. (For a review of these sources, see Chapters 3 through 5.)

In addition, we offer the following points to be considered in the evaluation of a series of apparently conflicting tax laws:

- Regulations seldom are held to be invalid by a court. In the typical year, fewer than a dozen such holdings are issued. Thus, challenges to the provisions of a Regulation should be based on more than a simple challenge to the Treasury's authority or a self-serving competing interpretation of the statute offered by the taxpayer.

- Revenue Rulings and Revenue Procedures, however, are frequently modified or otherwise held to be invalid by a court. Accordingly, the taxpayer's attempted restructuring of the pertinent law in his or her favor with respect to such an administrative pronouncement is more likely to be heard openly by the court and, therefore, to be based on the weight of the competing arguments rather than simply on the Treasury's preemptive interpretive rights.

- The decisions of courts that are higher in the judicial hierarchy should receive additional precedential weight. Given an adequate degree of similarity in fact situations, district and circuit court opinions have direct bearing on the taxpayer only if they were issued in the corresponding jurisdiction. On the other hand, opinions of the national courts like Court of Federal Claims and Tax Court are binding on the taxpayer, even though they were issued with respect to a taxpayer who works or resides in another jurisdiction, unless they are overturned in a pertinent appeal.

- Thus, a taxpayer who works in Wyoming is not bound by decisions of, say, the Seventh Circuit or Alaska District courts. The practitioner should not feel restricted in a trial or appeal hearing by the doctrine of stare decisis. Conversely, an Alaska taxpayer's Court of Federal Claims decision is binding on the Wyoming citizen's Court of Federal Claims case. If this Court of Federal Claims decision was held in a manner that is detrimental to the Wyoming taxpayer, another trial court should be pursued.

- Other factors being equal, decisions of the Second, Ninth, and Federal Circuits should be assigned additional precedential value. Among other reasons, this additional weight can be attributed to the inclusion of the cities of New York and Washington and the state of California in these circuits. Typically, the Ninth Circuit is the first to introduce an innovative or otherwise unusual interpretation of the law, and the Second and Federal Circuits are authoritative in a more traditional vein.

- Older court decisions should be assigned a geometrically declining degree of importance unless they are Supreme Court cases; they are Second, Ninth, or Federal Circuit cases; or they are the only precedents available. The roster and philosophical makeup of a court change over time and often reflect the changing societal culture and philosophies. Thus, recent case opinions are more likely to identify issues that are held to be critical by the sitting judges that the taxpayer will face, and they are likely to be better predictors of the outcome relative to the current taxpayer's issues.

- Tax treatises and journal articles are a useful source by which to identify current, critical tax issues. They also can be utilized in the formation of the practitioner's research schedule because they often include both a comprehensive summary of the evolution of the controlling law and a thorough list of citations concerning prior interpretive court decisions.

- IRS agents are bound only by the Code, administrative pronouncements, and Supreme Court decisions. Some of the most difficult decisions a tax practitioner must face include those in which one must determine whether the time, effort, and expense of litigation will generate a reward that is sufficient to justify, in essence, the construction of new (judicial) tax law; that is, to overcome this narrow scope of the agent's concern.

- Court decisions are never completely predictable. Thus, even if absolutely all of the judicial precedent that is available supports the taxpayer's position, the court still may hold against him or her. Negative decisions may be the result of a poor performance by the attorney, other tax adviser, or witnesses that are heard by the court; changes in the makeup or philosophy of the members of the court; changes in societal mores, as reflected by the court; or an incorrect interpretation of the law by the court that hears the present case. The practitioner, however, can do little more than conduct a thorough tax research analysis concerning the case, identify convincing witnesses, and trust that justice will prevail.

Client Letters

Our discussion to this point in the chapter has concentrated on the communication of tax research by the practitioner to himself or herself or to other tax professionals in a fairly sophisticated document—a memorandum to the file. We now shift the focus for the communication to a different audience, namely, the client, and to a different setting, the written or oral presentation.

By far the most common form of substantive communication between the tax professional and his or her client is the telephone call or e-mail. We must stress the danger inherent in placing too great a dependence on these forms of communication to convey the results of tax research given the intricacies of both the fact situation and the tax adviser's interpretation of controlling law, in most situations. If the telephone or e-mail must be used to convey tax research results (perhaps because of time pressures or convenience), the practitioner should always send a fairly detailed follow-up **client letter**, in hard copy, confirming his or her understanding as to the information that was conveyed and the actions that are to be taken as a result of the call.

SPOTLIGHT ON TAXATION

E-mail Disclaimer

Because of Circular 230 covered opinions rules, most CPAs and other tax advisers include some form of blanket disclaimer in the tag line of all their e-mail and other written correspondence sent to clients. An example of such a disclaimer would be:

Any tax advice included in this written communication was not intended or written to be used, and it cannot be used by the taxpayer, for the purpose of avoiding any penalties that may be imposed by any governmental taxing authority or agency.

Foremost among the attributes of the client letter is its brevity. Except in the most unusual circumstances, it should not exceed two pages. This rule should be violated only when the subject of the research is especially complex or grave, perhaps in anticipation of extended litigation or with respect to a more sophisticated client, where, for instance, one might be tempted to attach a copy (or a "client version") of the research file memo.

The brevity of the client letter is, most often, in response to the desire of the client for "the answer" that has been found concerning the extant tax issues. Clients do tend to see tax issues as black-and-white ones, and they want to know whether they will win or lose with the IRS. Of course, tax practitioners are aware of the colorful world that tax practice presents, and the various shades of emphasis and interpretation sometimes make the view quite murky. Thus, to accommodate the desire of the client, one typically must convey no more than the absolute highlights of the research process.

Another factor that leads to brief client letters is the tax practitioner's professional responsibilities. Responding to client questions is generally easier in a face-to-face meeting. Thus, most practitioners use the client letter to deliver the general conclusions of the research project and to request a follow-up meeting in which questions, comments, and the need for more detail can be addressed.

Exhibits 11-4 and 11-5 illustrate the format and content of typical client letters. The sole difference between these two letters is the degree of sophistication that is possessed by the receiving party.

EXHIBIT 11-3: Sample Client Letter—Sophisticated Client

Raabe, Whittenburg, Sanders, and Sawyers, CPAs
San Francisco, CA
November 19, 20XX
M/M Dale Brown
2472 North Mayfair Road
Fillingham, SD 59990

Dear Dale and Rae,

Thanks again for requesting my advice concerning the tax treatment of your interest expenses. I am sorry to report that only a portion of your expenses can be deducted this year.

I have uncovered a series of court cases in which the IRS has prevailed over the taxpayer's requests for a deduction that is similar to yours. Unfortunately, the Tax Court's position is that interest such as yours is nondeductible, and additional litigation would be necessary to bring about a more favorable result for you.

My efforts have concentrated on the treatment of interest expenses that are incurred by taxpayers who hold exempt bonds while maintaining a bank loan that requires interest payments.

Over the past 30 years or so, a number of Circuit Court decisions have held that a taxpayer effectively must divest himself or herself of investments in such municipal bonds, regardless of portfolio diversification objectives, before a deduction for the interest payments to the bank is allowed. Fortunately, however, an exception exists relative to business-related loans so that interest that is related to Rae's clinic will be allowed as a deduction. Conversely, that portion of the loan that relates to your school bond investment is nondeductible, even though it is secured by your residence.

You may wish to reconsider your use of the mortgage for this purpose, as your tax advantages there from are somewhat limited. This appears to be more palatable for you than would be the alternative of expensive further (and, probably, fruitless) litigation of the issue.

My conclusion is based upon the facts that you have provided me, and upon the efficacy of these somewhat dated court decisions. As you've requested, I've attached a copy of my research memo for you to read and from which you might develop subsequent inquiries. I'm sorry that the news from me wasn't more favorable. If you have any questions or would like further explanation, please don't hesitate to call.

Sincerely,
Mary H. Polzin
for Raabe, Whittenburg, Sanders, and Sawyers, CPAs

In general, the client letter should be structured as follows, perhaps allowing one paragraph for each of the noted topics:

- Salutation/social graces/general conclusion
- Summary of the research project results
- Objective of the report
- Statement of facts and disclaimer as to the scope of the tax professional's knowledge base
- Summary of critical sources of law that lead to result
- Implications of the results
- Assumptions/limitations
- Closing/reference to follow-up meeting/social graces
- Attachments, if any (e.g., engagement letter, file memo, illustrative charts, bibliography), on a separate page

EXHIBIT 11-4: Sample Client Letter—Less Sophisticated Client

Raabe, Whittenburg, Sanders, and Sawyers, CPAs
San Francisco, CA
November 19, 20XX
M/M Dale Brown
2472 North Mayfair Road
Fillingham, SD 59990

Dear Dale and Rae,

Thanks again for requesting my advice concerning the tax treatment of your interest expenses. I am sorry to report that only a portion of your expenses can be deducted this year.

My research has uncovered a series of successes by the IRS in convincing several important courts that interest such as yours should not be allowed as a deduction to reduce your taxes. Unfortunately, the court whose decision initially would prevail upon us would hold against you, and a series of court hearings, over two or three years or so, would be necessary for you to win the case.

This research has been restricted to situations that are similar to yours; that is, in which the taxpayer both owns a municipal bond and owes money to the bank from an interest-bearing loan.

It seems that the IRS would rather have you purchase the municipal bonds with your own money rather than with the bank's. It maintains that you get a double benefit from the non-taxability of the school bond interest income and the deductibility of the interest expense that is paid to the bank. Thus, that portion of the interest that relates to the bond investment is not allowed. A business purpose for the loan salvages the deduction, however, so you can deduct the interest from the loan that relates to Dr. Rae's clinic.

You may just have to live with this situation, as the IRS has been winning cases like these for about 30 years. Yours is not likely to be the one that changes their mind, so you might reconsider your investment in the municipals in the near future.

My conclusion is based upon the facts that you have provided me, and upon the reliability of the court cases that I found. I'm sorry that the news from me wasn't more favorable. If you have any questions or would like further explanation, please don't hesitate to call.

Sincerely,
Mary H. Polzin
for Raabe, Whittenburg, Sanders, and Sawyers, CPAs

Effective written business communication often makes use of the following guidelines. Notice that most of these elements are present in each of the two sample client letters that we have included in this chapter.

- Make your main point(s) in the first paragraph of the communication.

- State a well-defined purpose for the document, and stick to it.

- Avoid "filler" language, such as "at the present time," "the fact that," "as you know," and "enclosed please find."

- Avoid cliches and trendy jargon, such as "interface," "input," "seamless," "hands-on," "state-of-the-art," and any number of sports analogies.

- Follow the 10-80-10 rules of Exhibit 11-1.

- Do not be afraid to revise the letter several times to improve its format or to expand or narrow (as needed) its content. In this regard, allow enough time for the preparation of the document in a professional manner.

- Use the social amenities to your advantage by spelling names correctly, keeping current on the recipient's promotions and current title, and adding handwritten messages at the beginning or end of the document.

- Practice writing until it becomes easier and more enjoyable for you to do. Word processing programs, with the editing and proofreading capabilities that they provide, will aid you in this task. However, do not rely solely on spell-checkers and grammar-checking devices, as they may give you a false sense of security with respect to the accuracy and clarity of your writing.

Comprehensive Illustration of Client File

Exhibit 11-5 provides a comprehensive illustration of the two major elements of a client file: a client letter and a file memo. Notice the degree of correspondence between the two documents in that some portions of the client letter are no more than quotations or paraphrases of the file memo.

EXHIBIT 11-5:   Client File Illustration

CLIENT LETTER
Tax Jockeys Limited
Newport, RI
December 10, 20XX

Harold and Frieda van Briske
2000 Fox Point Heights
Whitefish Bay, RI 02899
Dear Harold and Frieda,

Thank you again for requesting my advice concerning the tax treatment of your prenuptial agreement. I understand that Frieda transferred some appreciated stock to Harold on the morning of the wedding, under the prenuptial agreement. I am happy to report that the transaction will not result in the imposition of any Federal tax for either of you.

My research has uncovered a series of successes by the IRS in convincing several important courts, including the Supreme Court, that an agreement such as yours is not supported by "full and adequate consideration," and, therefore, that it is to be treated as a gift. Although you did not intend for your property transfer to be a gift, the intent of the parties in such agreements does not control for Federal gift tax purposes.

Fortunately, however, the treatment of your transaction as a gift will not result in the imposition of Federal income tax or Federal gift tax. Federal income tax is not imposed upon the transfer because gross income is not recognized by either the donor or donee when a gift is made. Although a gift has occurred, no gift tax is due because the unlimited gift tax marital deduction neutralizes the transfer.

This research has been restricted to fact situations that are similar to yours; that is, in which, pursuant to a prenuptial agreement, a taxpayer surrendered his or her other marital rights in exchange for a sum of money or other property.

My conclusion is based upon the facts that you have given me and upon the reliability of the court cases that I found.

Sincerely,
Karen J. Boucher, CPA, JD, MST for or Tax Jockeys Limited

FILE MEMO
December 10, 20XX
Tax Jockeys Limited
Newport, RI

Relevant Facts
On the morning of their wedding, Frieda gave to Harold $400,000 of appreciated stock, pursuant to a prenuptial agreement. Frieda's basis in the stock was $150,000. In exchange for these securities, Harold surrendered all other marital rights and claims to Frieda's assets, under the terms of the agreement. Harold and Frieda both are residents of Arizona.

Specific Issues
1. What are the gift tax consequences of this exchange?
2. What are the income tax consequences of this exchange?

Conclusions

1. Frieda incurs no gift tax liability as the agreement is executed and implemented.

2. Neither Frieda nor Harold recognizes taxable income as a result of the exchange. Asset basis carries over to Harold, the new owner of the securities.

Support

Issue One

Donative intent on the part of the donor is not an essential element in the application of the gift tax. Reg. § 25.2511-1(g)(1).

The Supreme Court has held that prenuptial transfers in relinquishment of marital rights are not adequate and full consideration in money or money's worth for the transfer of property, within the meaning of IRC §2512 (b). *Merrill v. Fahs*, 324 U.S. 308, 65 S.Ct. 655 (1945); *Comm. v. Wemyss*, 324 U.S. 303, 65 S.Ct. 652 (1945); Reg. § 25.2512-8. Although the van Briske transaction resulted in a gift, no gift tax is imposed due to the application of the annual exclusion and the unlimited gift tax marital deduction. IRC §§ 2503(b) and 2523; Rev. Rul. 69-347, 1969-1 C.B. 227.

IRC § 2501 imposes a tax on the transfer of property by gift; the gift tax is not imposed, though, upon the receipt of property by the donee. Rather, it is the transfer itself that triggers the tax. Since the prenuptial agreement here is enforceable by state law only when consummated by marriage, the transfer has not taken place until after the marriage occurred. Thus, the transfer appears to be eligible for the gift tax marital deduction regardless of the timing of the transfer relative to the marriage ceremony on the wedding day. Even if the securities had been physically transferred to Harold prior to the completion of the ceremonies, the agreement was only enforceable after the couple was married. The IRS likely would not need or attempt to establish the exact moments of both the transfer of the securities and the consummation of the marriage *Archbold*, 42 B.T.A. 453, (1940, Acq. in result only).

Issue Two

Neither Harold nor Frieda recognize any gross income upon Harold's release of his marital rights. Gross income does not include the value of property that is acquired by gift. IRC §102(a); Reg. §1.102-1(a); Rev. Rul. 79-312, 1979-2 C.B. 29; Rev. Rul. 67-221, 1967-2 C.B. 63; *Howard v. C.I. R.*, 447 F.2d 152 (CA-5, 1971).

In the typical gift situation, the donee takes the donor's income tax basis in the transferred property. IRC §§ 1015(a) and 1041(a)(1).

Actions to Be Taken

Prepare letter and review results with client.

Place copy of prenuptial agreement in the client file.

Preparer: Karen J. Boucher

Reviewer: Lynne E. Schoenfeldt

The remainder of the internal file for this hypothetical client would include, among many other possibilities:

- An engagement letter

- A billing and collection history

- Case, regulation, and ruling briefs that are pertinent to the file memo

- Links to important analyses of the client's prevailing tax issues from treatises, journal articles, and other resources

Each consulting firm or tax department has its own formatting requirements with respect to client files. Because document and browser software is so easy to use, the temptation is for the tax researcher to reduce the thickness of the client file, as paper duplications of controlling law and other precedent are deemed unnecessary. This paper reduction movement constitutes a laudable goal.

Yet one must not shortchange the importance of the client file as a road map by which to retrace the researcher's line of thinking that leads to the conclusions and recommendations evidenced in the file memo and client letter. Electronic equivalents of the mind-map of the researcher and of underlining or pastel highlighting of portions of lengthy legal documents must be developed.

Accordingly, every tax researcher must develop or work with a scheme by which to cross reference the steps of the professional critical thinking model undertaken on the client's behalf. This might entail a listing of legal citations and computer files that would bear upon a reconstruction of the researcher's analysis, perhaps in the form of a decision tree or project management summary. Various software applications will be useful in this regard, not the least of which is the "research trail" feature of many electronic tax research products that records the detailed sequencing of commands and decisions made during the online project. Regardless of the form this project diary takes, its importance for professional quality control cannot be overstated.

Oral Presentations of Research Results

Psychologists tell us that most people's greatest fear is speaking before groups of other people. Indeed, the thought of being the only one in the room who is standing, of having your listeners whispering their evaluations of you to each other, of having members of the audience taking notes on (or tape recording) your comments (certainly so that your errors of omission and commission can be parroted back at a later date), and of fielding extemporaneous questions is enough to bring many people to tears.

Yet public speaking is an important part of the tax practitioner's professional life. In many ways, it is the most accurate predictor of success. As politicians have long known, when one is delivering an oral presentation in an effective and professional manner, the audience becomes convinced that all of the other professional qualities that they desire from the speaker are also present. Conversely, an ill-prepared or ill-delivered message can do much to erode the audience's confidence in the speaker, not just with respect to the topic of the presentation but in general.

Thus, it behooves the tax professional to develop skill in public speaking. In contexts that range from presenting an award to a colleague or conducting a staff meeting to presenting a keynote address at the annual tax conference of your peers, such skills can mean the difference between enhancing and damaging your reputation.

SPOTLIGHT ON TAXATION

"Much speech is one thing, well-timed speech is another."
—Sophocles, Oedipus at Colonus

What is advised here is not a series of "tricks" to fool the audience into believing that you are more knowledgeable than you really are. Rather, we now convey some time-tested techniques leading to an effective communication of ideas—from one who has developed a secure base of knowledge in a subject to an audience with a specified background that has a desire to learn more about that subject.

Whether making a presentation of one's results to a supervisor in one's own firm or elaborating on a research project with the client's board of directors, the communication of tax research results poses special problems that make a review of oral communications procedures all the more valuable. Specifically, we can make the following suggestions concerning oral presentations of tax research:

- General preparation for the talk should include a thorough, frank examination of the following set of questions by the presenter. Nearly all of these observations can be characterized as knowledge of the makeup of the audience.

  Why me? Why was I asked to speak? What knowledge or celebrity do I bring to the event?

  What do they want? What does the audience hope to take away from the presentation? Technical knowledge? Relief from stress? Inspiration? Skill development? Amusement or entertainment? Should I present an overview or a detailed technical update or analysis?

  What is their attitude? Is the audience coming to the event curious or anxious to hear from me, or must they be persuaded of the relevance or importance of my topics?

  From what should I stay away? Are there topics that are taboo for this audience, due to their age, experiences, or existing attitudes? One must not alienate the audience, wittingly or unwittingly, in any way if the message is to get across.

  What do they already know? What is the knowledge base of the audience? It would be ideal to speak to a homogeneous audience, especially in the level of knowledge that it brings into the event, but this seldom is the case. One must decide, then, whether to aim at the median knowledge base, above, or below. The stakes are high in exercising this judgment, though, and either repeating what is common knowledge to the group or presenting information at a high level that is accessible to only a few in the audience can make communication impossible.

  Who is the audience? Details as to the audience's demographic characteristics such as age, education, income level, political leanings, and so forth can be vital for tailoring one's style, presentation speed and media, references to literature and popular culture, and use of humor in an effective manner. Remember to play to as many members of the audience as possible, not just the majority of those in attendance or those who were involved directly in hiring or retaining your services.

- Be prepared in the technical aspects of your discussion, particularly the basic research. Spend most of your preparation time on your main points and conclusions rather than on the fine points. If you are caught without a piece of technical information, it is clearly better for you if that information is specific (so that you can refer the questioner to a more detailed reference or to a later, private conversation with you) rather than basic in nature.

- Resist the temptation to tell the audience all that you know about the subject. You almost certainly have neither the time nor the organizational abilities that are necessary to command the attention of the audience for that long a time.

- Direct your remarks to the highlights and general results of the research and allow a questions-and-comments period in which more detailed subjects can be addressed. In this manner, you will provide the greatest amount of information to the greatest number of listeners in the audience.

- Use visual aids effectively. Handouts, slides, or videos can serve to clarify or emphasize your key points (and, not incidentally, to transfer the "spotlight" of the presentation away from you). Most advisers recommend that you not look at the screen repeatedly or read the text of the visual aid word for word along with the audience; rather, use the visual aid as a means of keeping the audience focused on the discussion points by the use of a pointer or other highlighter. Avoid a sequence that allows a "blank screen" for more than a second or two. Inexpensive computer software will assist you in preparing and delivering electronic presentations and in staying on schedule. Use your color laser printer to prepare your visual aids.

- If you are a frequent public speaker, purchase a moderately priced, easy-to-carry projector so that you need not depend on conference center staff to present your slides.

Many speakers are tempted to overuse visual aids, especially because they are so easy to create, even at professional-quality levels, given today's software packages. Visual aids, though, generally should be used only for the following purposes:

- To illustrate ideas that are difficult to convey strictly with words by using a photograph, videotape, map, blueprint, or flowchart.

- To save time by consolidating ideas, committing to a time frame or strategy, or listing conflicting viewpoints or tactics.

- To create interest in a subject, perhaps by presenting the concept in a manner with which the audience is unfamiliar (e.g., an extra-large view, a view from "the other side of the issue," or an evolutionary time or growth line).

- To emphasize a point or concept by highlighting a graphic, picture, mnemonic, or list of key words or concepts.

- To organize the introduction, body, or conclusion of the presentation.

- To introduce humor to the event with a tasteful quotation or cartoon.

- To place ideas in the audience's memories through a visual "take away" item.

A speaker's prepared slides should be designed with care and diligence. When using this technology, as opposed to the hand-drawn flip chart or on-the-fly smart board drawing, one essentially is competing with professional graphic and television artists, and the audience will hold your efforts to these high standards. Most visual and graphic artists offer guidelines for presentation layouts, including the following:

- Use the slide to emphasize pictures, not text or numbers. Except to be able to point to a specific position on the page and keep the members of the audience in the same spot throughout the presentation, do not use your slideshow to duplicate pages of text or spreadsheets with voluminous numbers. Employ graphs, charts, arrows, and other pictorial devices instead.

- When text is involved, use the "six and six" rule: no more than six lines of type, and no more than six words on a line. This directive will help to dictate the font chosen and the corresponding size of print.

- Keep the font style simple. Use sans serif or newspaper-type fonts, not script or modern fonts, unless corporate logos or other protected styles are used. Most designers recommend that no more than two colors of text be used on a slide and that the color scheme of the graphics blend well with that of the text. Be conservative—stick to the primary colors, colors of local sports teams, and multiple shades of gray so as not to frustrate the duplication process for related handout materials.

- Similarly, try to use some background music if your available technology will support it at a professional-quality level. Music can signal the start or end of a presentation or its subunits, a change in direction, or a specific idea.

- On the average, allow at least three minutes of spoken presentation for each slide. Accordingly, limit the number of your slides to the length of your talk in minutes, divided by three. In this way, you will not overproduce your number of slides. If you want to provide your audience with a content outline, use some other medium, not the slides.

- Prepare for the worst: E-mail yourself an extra copy of the slides in case of emergency, and carry your files to the site on a flash drive and on your portable music player. Bring a few sets of hard copy slides as well.

Without exception, determine ahead of the presentation how long your talk is supposed to be and be absolutely certain not to exceed it. You need to be fair to the other speakers, if any, who follow your presentation. Moreover, with very few exceptions the audience also is aware of the schedule for the session, and if the speaker exceeds the allotted time, the audience, at best, will stop paying attention and, at worst, will become restless or angry. Because of their technical nature, most tax presentations should not exceed 45 minutes, and one-half of that time might be ideal for both speaker and audience.

Have an outline for your discussion that includes miniature versions of slides and your business address, phone and fax numbers, and your e-mail and Internet addresses. Use the visual aids to convince the audience that you are following the outline. This will ensure that you will cover the material that you desire; build confidence among the audience as to your speaking abilities; and convince yourself that you are doing a good job in leading the discussion of the assigned topic.

Rehearse your presentation, word for word, at least once. The most effective means of preparing yourself in this manner probably is with a video recorder because your distracting mannerisms (e.g., clearing the throat repeatedly, saying the words "ah" or "you know" too often, or pounding on the lectern) quickly will become apparent. If you do not have a video recorder, use an audio recorder or webcam. Family members or colleagues should not be used for this rehearsal.

Be kind to yourself in evaluating your video performance, but be observant for the following "I didn't know I did that" items:

- In all but the very largest presentation venues, get as physically close to the audience as you can, ideally removing the lectern, stepping down from the stage or platform, and moving to a series of different spots in the room throughout your speaking time. Use a portable mouse device to control your slideshow, but practice using the device an hour before your presentation begins.

- Eliminate nervous and visual distractions, such as jingling coins, playing with pen and marker tops, and adjusting clothing. Minimize the use of crossing your arms, pounding the table, and finger pointing, reserving them as means of emphasizing key points or declaring victory over competing viewpoints.

- Vary the pitch of your voice, avoiding both a dry monotone and a "classic actor" dramatic approach. Many speakers talk too fast or too loud; check yourself throughout the talk on these matters. Test the microphone system before the audience arrives so that you do not need to ask, "Can you hear me in the back?"

- Do not be afraid of silence. Pauses invariably seem longer to the speaker than they do to the audience, so do not let natural breaks in the talk add to your anxiety. In fact, well-paced pauses can relieve tension (both yours and the audience's), signal changes of pace, and allow you to emphasize the importance of certain ideas.

- Do not read directly from your outline, except for a selected quote of three lines or so from the material once or twice in the presentation. Try not to have a separate set of note cards because the tendency again is to break your contact with the audience and hide behind the scripting device. Disguise your notes in the form of comments on hard copies of your slides and flip charts and notes in the margin of your copy of the outline. Keep your eyes up and on the audience.

Avoid references to administrative or "housekeeping" aspects of the event—leave these to be conveyed by the host of the event. Be enthusiastic and positive about your comments— do not apologize for a lack of discussion on a tangential point, a logistical snafu, or a misstatement of fact or law. The audience generally wants you to succeed, so do not undermine this trust with self-destructive comments.

Do not refer to the schedule for the event or other timing issues because they can distract the audience or otherwise detract from conveying your message (e.g., "Only 10 minutes to go," "We may be out of here early," "The previous speakers ran over into my time slot," or "I'll try to get through this quickly, so we can finish on time").

Rehearse the logistical aspects of the presentation, such as the lighting, projectors, or computer presentation software and terminals, before you begin to speak, ideally both the night before and one hour before your presentation. Have adequate numbers and varieties of markers, pointers, flip chart pads, and remote control devices. You do not want to encounter any surprises after it is too late to do anything about them! On your script, notecards, or slide masters, make notes to yourself as to when, for instance, to pass out the handout material, turn on or turn off the projector, or refer to a flip chart.

Avoid clichés, such as opening with a joke, or saying, "It's a pleasure to be here." Do not take the risk of boring or offending the audience with a joke that they may have heard already or that you may not tell effectively under pressure. This is not to suggest that you avoid humor altogether, however. Audiences, and speakers' reputations, thrive on it. If you are sure of your skill in this area, you might venture a joke, but it would probably be wiser to open with a "punch line" summary of some of the most interesting of your results or fact situations.

Have a "Plan B" ready to go—flexibility is the watchword of the effective speaker. If the time actually allowed for your talk is shorter than you had thought due to a misunderstanding or unanticipated events, have a list of topics, videos, or slides that can be eliminated without changing the nature of the talk. Practice your question-and-answer-session skills, especially for occasions where there is more time available than you had anticipated. Do not mention any of these on-the-fly adjustments to the audience—make the changes, do not talk about them.

Observe audience body language and use signals conveying interest, enthusiasm, boredom, or restlessness to your advantage. Make consistent eye contact with the audience, smile when appropriate, and take a few seconds at the completion of the presentation to accept the audience's show of thanks and savor your job well done.

SUMMARY

The tax professional must become proficient in communicating his or her research results. Recipients of these communications might include oneself or one's peers, via the file memorandum; the client, via a brief letter; or a number of other listeners, via an oral presentation. In each case, the practitioner must be sensitive to the needs, backgrounds, and interests of the recipients of the messages without sacrificing professional demeanor or responsibilities.

QUIZ YOURSELF

Reinforce the tax research information covered in this chapter by completing the online quizzes located at the Federal Tax Research Web site at **www.cengagebrain.com.** At the CengageBrain.com home page, search for the *Federal Tax Research*, 9e ISBN (1111221642) using the search box at the top of the page. This will take you to the product page where you can access the quizzes.

KEY WORDS

By the time you complete this chapter, you should be comfortable discussing each of the following terms. If you need additional review of any of these items, return to the appropriate material in the chapter or consult the glossary to this text.

client letter, p. 389

file memorandum, p. 384

TAX RESEARCH ASSIGNMENTS

As we have discussed them in this chapter, develop solutions and appropriate documentation for one or more of the problems that you have worked on in previous chapters or for the following fact situations. In this context, proper format and professional content are of equal importance so that the development of the reader's tax research communication skills will be facilitated.

Specifically, as assigned by your instructor, prepare one or more of the following means of communicating your research results for your chosen problem or case. Be sure to apply the "10-80-10" rule of Exhibit 11-1.

- File memorandum
- Letter to tax-sophisticated client
- Letter to unsophisticated client
- Outline for a tax department meeting
- Article for local business newsweekly
- Speech to local chamber of commerce
- Article for *Practical Tax Strategies*
- Speech to State Bar Association conference
- Presentation to client's board of directors
- Presentation to client's senior counsel
- Posting to the Internet Tax Blog for Practitioners
- Posting to the Internet Tax Help group for taxpayers

RESEARCH CASES

1. Sarah came home one day to find significant water damage in her home. Apparently one of the hoses to her washing machine had worn out and split, spilling water all over the place. Over the next month, mildew appeared as well. Is there any casualty loss deduction for Sarah? Ignore any computational floors and assume that she did not have any homeowners' insurance.

2. Richie is a wealthy rancher in Texas. He operates his ranch through a grantor trust set up by his grandparents. Richie does not like to get his hands dirty, so he hires a professional management company to run the ranch. The property generated a $500,000 loss this year. Can Richie deduct this loss on his Schedule E given the material participation rules of §469?

3. Maggie could not conceive a child using natural means, so she sought out a woman who would donate an egg to be surgically implanted in Maggie so that Maggie could become a mother. Which of the following items are deductible by Maggie in her process to find an egg donor?
    a. Payment to a search firm to find donor candidates.
    b. Payment to Maggie's attorney.
    c. Payment of a fee to the egg donor.
    d. Payment to medical staff to run physiological and psychological tests on the prospective donor.

4. Larry and Mary are in the process of being divorced, and the decree as negotiated allowed alimony payments to Mary of $3,000 on the fifteenth of each month. The divorce was final on July 5, but Mary was short of cash, so Larry made the payments to her starting in March. What is Larry's alimony deduction for the year?

5. Sally incurred a 90-mile round-trip commute every day, mainly because she could not get along with her supervisor at the sales office located four miles from her home. Sally works under a one-year contract, and her assignment to the nearer office is affirmed in the current year's contract, but management has allowed her to travel to the further location. How many deductible commuting miles does Sally accumulate on a work day?

6. Professor White operates a popular bar review course as a sole proprietor. He charges $2,000 tuition to each student, and he guarantees a full refund of the tuition if the student passes an in-course exam but does not pass the actual bar exam on the first try. White is bold enough to do this because the first-time-pass rate is more than 80 percent for the bar exam (as opposed to less than 15 percent for the certified public accountants [CPA] exam). He collected $150,000 tuition for his Fall 2010 review section, but he reported the gross receipts on his 2011 Form 1040 because the grades for those taking the fall review are not released until February 2011. Thus, White asserted that he had no constructive receipt of the tuition until February 2011. Is this treatment correct?

7. Lisa, usually a stay-at-home mother, went to the hospital one day for some outpatient surgery. She hired a babysitter for $35 to watch her four-year-old son while she was gone. What tax benefits are available to Lisa for this cash payment?

8. Same as 7, except that Lisa paid the sitter while she worked as a scout leader for the Girl Scouts.

9. Tex's credit union has provided him with financing to acquire his $200,000 home. The loan is set up as a three-year note with a balloon payment, but the credit union always renews the loan for another three years at the current interest rate. This year, the credit union renewed Tex's loan for the third time, charging $3,000 in points. In what year(s) can Tex deduct this $3,000?

10. Barb and Bob were one-fourth shareholders of a C corporation. When the entity had negative E&P, Barb and Bob secretly withdrew $200,000 in cash, hiding this fact from the other owners. How much gross income do Barb and Bob report?

11. Detail the tax effects to the Prasads of making the §1(g)(7)(a)(iv) election to include their seven-year-old daughter's $10,000 unearned income on their current-year joint return.

12. Eighty percent of the Willigs' AGI comes from their submarine sandwich proprietorship. In 2010, the Willigs lost an IRS audit and owed $12,000 in 2008 Federal income taxes, all attributable to inventory computations in their business. Interest on this amount totaled $3,200. All amounts due were paid by the end of 2010. How much of the interest can the Willigs deduct on their 2010 Schedule C?

13. Al and Amy are divorced. In which of the following cases can legal fees be deducted?
    a. Al pays $5,000 to get the court to reduce his alimony obligation.
    b. Amy pays $5,000 to get the court to increase her alimony receipts.
    c. Al pays Amy's attorney fees in part b, as required by the original divorce decree.

14. Katie is a one-third owner of an S corporation. After a falling-out with the other shareholders, Katie signed an agreement early in January 2010. Under the terms of the agreement, Katie took $200,000 of her capital from the corporation and had eight months to negotiate a purchase of the stock of the other shareholders. She did not complete this task by the end of August 2010. Thus, contrary negotiations began, and on March 1, 2011, Katie sold all of her shares to the remaining shareholders for a $2.5 million gain. For how many of these months does Katie report flow-through income from the S corporation?

15. Can an individual make a contribution to an IRA based on unemployment compensation proceeds received?

16. After an audit was completed, an IRS agent informed Harris of the latter's $10,000 Federal income tax deficiency by leaving a summary memo on Harris's e-mail account. Harris shared this account with his mother, who read the mail first and in a panic confronted Harris with a two-hour "What's this all about?" interrogation. Did the IRS agent violate Harris's right to privacy by using e-mail in this manner?

17. SlimeCo spent $250,000 to build storage tanks for its waste byproducts. This is a recurring expenditure for SlimeCo because once the tanks are filled, new ones must be built. When can SlimeCo deduct the $250,000?

18. Prudence was named a shareholder in her law firm, which operates as an S corporation. Her payments into the capital of the firm were to start in about nine months, when an audit would determine the full value of the firm and a new corporate year would commence. Paperwork with the pertinent state offices was completed, naming Prudence as a shareholder and director, and adding her name to that of the firm. However, Prudence left the firm eight months after the announcement; that is, before she paid any money for shares. Is Prudence liable for tax on her share of the entity's earnings for the eight months?

19. Cal's son has been labeled a "can't miss" NBA prospect since junior high school. This year, while the son is a college freshman and classified as an amateur under NCAA rules, Cal spent $14,000 for special clothing, equipment, camps, and personal trainers to keep improving his son's skills. Can Cal deduct these items?

20. CPA Myrna forgot to tell her client Freddie to accelerate the payment of state income and property taxes in a year when Freddie was in an unusually high tax bracket. Upon discovering the error, the parties negotiated a $15,000 payment from Myrna (and her insurance company) to Freddie to compensate Freddie for Myrna's inadequate professional advice. Is this payment gross income to Freddie?

21. How much of the $100,000 interest that is paid on a loan from Everett National Bank can Ben deduct if he invests the loan proceeds in the following? Consider each item independently.

    a. South Chicago School District bonds

    b. AT&T bonds, paying $125,000 interest income this year

    c. Computer Futures Inc., shares, a growth stock that pays no dividend this year

    d. A life insurance policy on Betty, Ben's wife

22. Lilly leases a car that she uses solely for business purposes. The car would be worth $40,050 on the market, and Lilly paid $7,400 in lease payments this year. How are these items treated on her tax return?

23. You served as an expert witness in taxation in a recent Tax Court case, charging $400 per hour for your services. The LLC client who employed you prevailed in the decision against the government, so now the client is filing to recover your fees from the Treasury under §7430(c)(1)(B)(iii). How much can the client collect?

24. Pete is an engineering professor at State University. Under his contract, Pete's inventions while employed at the university are the property of the Board of Regents, but Pete receives an addition to his salary equal to one-third of the royalties received by the university on his patents. This year, Pete received $75,000 on top of his salary, as royalties allocated to him. Does Pete recognize this amount as ordinary income or capital gain?

25. Dean and Robin owned a family business, each holding the shares as community property. When they were divorced in 2008, the court did not force them to split the shares, citing damage to the business that could occur if the public learned that ownership of the enterprise was changing. Now it is 2012 and Robin wants to remarry. She and her new husband want to have the business retitle one-half of the shares in Robin's name only. The original divorce court agrees in 2012. Is this transfer subject to income tax? Is it subject to gift tax?

26. Dave made a $100,000 cash withdrawal from his IRA. He bought $100,000 of Microcraft stock, and within the rollover period he transferred the stock to another IRA. Does Dave report any gross income?

27. Gold Partners wanted to complete a like-kind exchange just before it liquidated. Accordingly, it sold the real estate it meant to transfer to the other party, and a qualified intermediary held the resulting cash. When the intermediary found acceptable replacement realty, the intermediary transferred cash and the like-kind property directly to the partners, thereby liquidating Gold. Does §1031 apply?

28. HelpCo pays Hank two $100,000 salaries per year, one through its WestCo subsidiary and one through its EastCo subsidiary. How do Hank and HelpCo treat his Social Security tax obligations?

29. Zhang lived in Atlanta from 2007 through 2009 to carry out her duties as an employee of YourTV.com, receiving an annual salary of about $150,000. She was transferred to the San Jose office for 2010 through 2012, and then in 2013 she took an executive position with the Web2.2 LLC in Austin. Zhang owned a home in Atlanta, but she rented an apartment in San Jose. When she withdraws money from her IRA to submit a down payment on her Austin condo, is a 10 percent penalty due?

30. Give three examples of situations where the IRS would waive the two-year rule for applying the §121 exclusion of gain from the sale of a principal residence due to "unforeseen circumstances."

31. LaFollette lives in a condo with Tourneau. The two are not married, but they each hold a one-half interest in the deed for their unit. In the current year, the condo association installed a solar water heater. The

association paid for the water heating system, but it assessed LaFollette and Tourneau $7,500 for this expenditure, as it did for other unit owners. Tourneau was short of funds, so LaFollette paid the entire assessment before the end of the year. Compute LaFollette's §25D credit against her Form 1040 liability for the year.

32. On December 6, Ed Grimely appeared on the game show, "The Wheel of Fate." As a result of his appearance, Grimely won the following prizes:

    a. Assuming that Grimely received all of these prizes by the end of the year, compute his gross income from these prizes.

    b. Will this amount change if Grimely refuses to accept the calliope lessons immediately after the program's taping session is completed?

	Manufacturer's Suggested List Price	Fair Market Value	Actual Cost to the Show
All-expenses-paid trip to Hawaii	$8,432	$6,000	$5,200
One case of Twinkies	16	12	0
Seven music lessons for the calliope	105	35	0
One year of free haircuts	120	60	15

33. Sing-Yi receives a $100 debit card every month from her employer, the Porter Group. The debit card is limited so that it can be used only to purchase fare cards and passes on the Metro Transit line that operates trains and subways in town. Sing-Yi throws away the card when it expires at the end of the month, and she is not required to provide any records to Porter about how the card was used. The card logo says "American Airlines Visa," and Sing-Yi picks her own password for the card. Does the card represent $100 monthly gross income to Sing-Yi? Explain.

34. HardCo spent $4 million this year on a new graphic design for its product, a yo-yo. Under the prior design, HardCo's name and logo only appeared on the box and wrapping paper, which were discarded by most customers once they started using the product. The new design displayed HardCo's name and newer, flashier logo on both sides of the yo-yo, with a paint that also made it glow in the dark. When can HardCo deduct the $4 million?

35. Fred was the owner of three-bedroom cabin in California. During 2010, he contracted with a property management company to rent the cabin to third parties. In exchange for its services, Fred paid the company a 35 percent commission on all rental income received. The property management company was responsible for maintaining the property, cleaning the cabin, paying all utilities, providing linens, etc. The cabin was rented three times during the year for a total of 12 days and nine nights with the average rental period being three days. Fred visited the cabin eight times during the year and stayed 19 nights and 27 days. Fred claimed $15,000 of Schedule E expenses relating to the rental of the cabin on his return under the active rental real estate exception. Was Fred entitled to the deduction?

36. Gina was falsely imprisoned as the result of an auto dealer's criminal complaint against her. Although the charges were later dropped, she was arrested and detained for about eight hours. She was not hurt or abused during the arrest and detention but she did see a psychologist for several sessions. She sued the auto dealership for malicious prosecution and received a $25,000 settlement payment from the company. Can the settlement payment be excluded from income?

37. Four individuals formed Triangle Properties as a C corporation in 2005. The corporation is domiciled in North Carolina. The corporation invested in commercial rental properties that generated passive activity losses. The shareholders made a Subchapter S election for Triangle Properties effective on January 1, 2011. On the date of conversion, Triangle Properties had $118,000 of suspended passive activity losses from its commercial rental properties. In 2011, the properties generated $44,000 of net rental income. Can Triangle Properties carry forward and deduct the suspended passive losses incurred when it was a C corporation against the passive rental income earned while it was an S corporation?

38. Sal was born male but diagnosed with gender identity disorder. As a result, he suffered persistent psychological discomfort with his gender and decided to have a sex change operation. As part of the treatment regimen, Sal had to undergo various hormonal treatments for several years, followed by a period in which he changed his name to Sally and lived for two years as a female before finally having gender reassignment surgery in 2010. Is Sally entitled to a medical deduction for the costs of the hormone treatment, surgeries and related expenses?

39. Jim Jones owns 50 percent of the stock of an S-corporation. In 2010, Jim obtains a health insurance plan providing coverage for Jim, his wife, and their two children. Jim makes all of the premium payments to the plan during 2010 and furnishes proof of the payments to the S-corporation which then reimburses him for the payments and reports the premium payments as wages on Jim's W-2 for the year. Jim reports the amounts as gross income on his 2010 personal tax return. Jim's income from the S-corporation exceeds the amount of premiums for the health coverage and he does not participate in any subsidized health plans maintained by another employer or an employer of his spouse. Is Jim allowed to take a deduction on his personal tax return for the health insurance premiums paid during the year?

ADVANCED CASES

These items require that you have access to research materials other than the Federal tax law and related services. For instance, you might need to refer to an international tax or multistate service or to access Internet sources to prepare your solution for these cases. Consult with your instructor before beginning your work so that you are certain to have available to you all of the necessary research resources for the case(s) that you choose.

40. Tony received some nonqualified and incentive stock options when he worked for his employer in Oregon. When he took a two-year assignment in another country, however, the corporation employing Tony there granted him some options, too. Does Tony have gross income in the other country upon receiving or exercising the non-U.S. options? Assume that Tony was assigned to a corporation based in:
    a. Belgium
    b. Germany
    c. Hong Kong
    d. Canada
    e. The Netherlands

41. Chico is a corporation operating in several states on the accrual basis. Chico received a state income tax refund this year (Year 4) based on the following sequence of events. In which tax year does Chico recognize the refund as gross income?
    Year 1: Generated the operating loss.
    Year 2: Filed the loss carryback form with the state.
    Year 3: Received notice that the refund was approved.
    Year 4: Received the refund check.

42. After her employer transferred her to another town, Rosemary put her house up for sale. After two years of Internet listings, open houses, repairs, and price cuts, a buyer finally came along. By this time, the house

had sat empty for 25 months before the closing occurred, and Rosemary rented it out just to help with the mortgage payments. Rosemary claimed a $40,000 Schedule C loss with respect to the house. Do you agree with this filing position?

43. Edna is a well-paid executive with ADley, a firm that uses stock options and deferred compensation as well as high salaries to compensate its most successful employees. When Edna and Ron were divorced, Ron received the rights to a bundle of these deferred compensation rights. Complete the following table, indicating the required tax results:

Tax Year	Market Price for Edna's Option Transferred to Ron	Event	Tax Consequences to Edna	Tax Consequences to Ron
2005	$9	Divorce is settled.		
2008	$14	Ron exercises stock options with $10 cash payment, then holds stock received.		
2011	$20	Edna terminates employment with ADley; $100 lump sum of deferred compensation is distributed to Ron.		
2013	$22	Ron sells shares received via option contracts.		

44. Wes and Donna were the only members of an LLC, and they fended off unwanted takeover suitors with a clause in the charter that shares could change hands only with unanimous approval from all of the other owners. Wes is now 70 years old, so he wants to start phasing out of the business. He makes a gift of 10 percent of the LLC shares to his son Jeffrey, as agreed to by Donna. The shares are worth $20,000. What is Wes's taxable gift in the year of the transfer to Jeffrey?

45. According to the Tax Foundation, what was the country's Tax Freedom Day in 2010? How has Tax Freedom Day changed since 2000?

46. Chan's only transaction in the United States this year was to sell the biggest office building in Denver at a $100 million gain. Chan has no assets, offices, or employees in the United States. Can he be taxed on the gain? Why or why not?

47. As the result of a Federal audit, your current year Federal taxable income increased by $27,000. By when must you report this adjustment to your state's revenue department? What form is used for this purpose, where do you obtain it, and where is it to be filed?

48. Does your state provide a form with which to file for a manufacturer's exemption from sales/use tax? Which form is used for this purpose, where do you obtain it, and where is it to be filed?

49. For the current period, what is the short-term, quarterly compounded Federal AFR? What is the mid-term rate? What is the long-term exempt interest rate for computing loss carryforwards under §382?

50. SalesCo sold Tom a prepaid phone card for $100 in Year 1. Tom used the phone card for communications services in Year 2. When can your state collect sales/use tax from SalesCo for the sale to Tom?

51. GoodCo donated $40,000 of goods from its inventory to the Red Cross. Does your state require GoodCo to collect or pay sales/use tax on these donated goods?

52. The Downtown Wellness Clinic, a tax-exempt organization, sells memberships to corporations so that their employees can work out before and after office hours. Three blocks away, the Power Up Fitness Center has similar facilities and also wants to sell memberships to corporate neighbors. Is the Clinic subject to Federal income tax on its membership sales?

53. Are Amazon.com and other online sellers required to collect and remit sales tax to your state?

CHAPTER 12

Tax Planning

- Identify several fundamental tenets of tax planning for optimizing tax liabilities.
- Gain perspective on the role of tax planning in tax practice.
- Define and apply several key terms with respect to tax rate schedules.
- Illustrate effective tax planning as found in today's tax profession.

IN THIS CHAPTER WE return to that element of the tax practice consisting of tax planning as it was introduced in Chapter 1. A working knowledge of tax planning concepts is imperative for the researcher because tax avoidance constitutes both an important part of tax practice and a prime motivation in the "open-fact" research context.

For most practitioners, tax research and planning represent the "glamour" end of the business. Properly accomplished tax planning:

- Forces the client to identify financial goals and general means by which to achieve them.

- Allows the tax professional to exercise a higher degree of creativity than in any other part of the practice.

- Affords the practitioner the greatest possible degree of control over the prescribed transactions and the tax consequences.

The tax planning process finds the tax professional in the roles of technical expert, friend, seer, and confessor priest for the client. It offers an opportunity for the most psychologically and financially rewarding work possible in the context of a tax practice.

Economics of Tax Planning, Avoidance, and Evasion

From both the Treasury and the taxpayer viewpoint, taxes can modify individual decisions. Taxes represent an additional cost of doing business or of accumulating wealth. Assuming that economists are correct in speaking about the ways in which a rational citizen makes day-to-day decisions, taxpayers employ tax planning techniques to accomplish the overall goal of wealth maximization.[1] Because taxes deplete the wealth of the taxpayer, planning behavior is designed to reduce the net present value of the tax liability, which is not the same as a simple reduction of taxes in current, nominal dollar terms—an objective that is so often assumed by laypeople, the media, and others, including too many tax advisors.

EXAMPLE 12-1

Sharon can choose between two business plans. One will cost her enterprise $1,000 in taxes today, and the other will cost the business $2,000 in taxes 10 years from now. The plans are identical in all other ways. Prevailing interest rates average 10 percent. Because the present value of the taxes levied with respect to the second alternative is about $800, Sharon should choose the latter plan; that is, the one with the higher nominal dollar tax cost.

If prevailing interest rates average 5 percent during the 10-year planning period, the present value of the taxes levied under the second alternative would be about $1,225, so the first plan, the one that requires an immediate tax payment, should be adopted.

In one important sense, the Federal income tax is its own worst enemy. Taxpayers are rewarded more for finding ways to save taxes than for earning an equal amount in the marketplace. This incentive for tax planning is the result of two rules of tax law.

---

[1]We use "wealth" in its broadest sense here. That is, an individual may choose increased leisure time or other forms of so-called psychic income over traditional forms of wealth. Wealth, the accumulation of which constitutes the overall goal for the specified time period, thus can include measures of happiness, satisfaction, investment, and control over time and other resources.

The first such rule is that the Federal income tax itself is not allowed as a deduction in determining taxable income. Consequently, reducing the amount of income taxes that are paid does not decrease one's allowable deductions and, hence, does not trigger any further increase in taxable income. Instead, the full amount of any tax that is saved increases after-tax income; that is, the tax savings themselves do not constitute taxable income. Unlike most profit-seeking activities, tax planning produces benefits that are completely exempt from income taxation.

The second such rule allows a deduction for any business-related expenses that are incurred in connection with the determination of a tax. Most tax planning costs are deductible by business owners and sole proprietors, although only a few employees will qualify for such a deduction. The net cost of a tax planning project, then, is its gross cost minus the amount of the reduction in the tax liability that is generated by the attendant deduction. In concise terms, the after-tax cost of tax planning can be expressed as follows:

$$\text{ATC} = \text{BTC} \times (1 - \text{MTR}), \quad \text{where}$$
$$\text{ATC} = \textbf{after-tax cost}$$
$$\text{BTC} = \textbf{before-tax cost}$$
$$\text{MTR} = \textbf{marginal tax rate}$$

In relating both rules to tax planning projects, one can see that such endeavors enjoy an economic advantage over most other profit-seeking activities. In evaluating most other investment projects, the decision maker must compare after-tax benefits with after-tax costs. Yet, for tax planning projects, the payoffs are tax-free, while the costs usually remain tax-deductible. Thus, for tax planning activities, one effectively compares pre-tax benefits with after-tax costs.

EXAMPLE 12-2

Shull Corporation, subject to a marginal state and Federal income tax rate of 40 percent, is considering two mutually exclusive alternatives. Alternative 1 is to hire a university accounting major for the summer at a cost of $2,000; his task would be to undertake research on a tax avoidance plan. If it is successful, the plan would save the corporation $1,600 in Federal income taxes.

The probability of success for the plan is estimated at 80 percent. Alternative 2 is to hire a university marketing major for the summer at a cost of $1,800; her task would be to undertake research on a marketing plan. If it is successful, this plan would generate new revenues of $2,000. The probability of such success is estimated to be 85 percent. Which, if either, alternative should Shull pursue?

	Alternative 1	Alternative 2
Before-tax cost	$2,000	$1,800
Tax reduction (40%)	−800	−720
After-tax cost	$1,200	$1,080
Possible pre-tax payoff	$1,600	$2,000
Probability of success	×.80	×.85
Expected pre-tax payoff	$1,280	$1,700
Tax on expected payoff (40%)	−0	−680
Expected after-tax payoff	$1,280	$1,020
Excess of after-tax payoff over after-tax cost	$ 80	$ (60)

Decision: Even though Alternative 2 offers a higher pre-tax payoff, a lower before-tax cost, and a higher probability of success, Alternative 1 should be accepted.

The facts of this example illustrate the apparent built-in economic bias of current tax law for tax planning projects relative to other, seemingly more productive activities.

The analysis of Example 12-2, like most of the illustrations in this book, is based on a "marginal" viewpoint. Its purpose is to determine the effect of the transactions at issue, assuming that all other characteristics of the situation do not change. When it is viewed from this perspective, the after-tax cost of any deductible expenditure decreases if the marginal tax rate is increased. This fact may explain why lower-income taxpayers, who are subject to lower marginal tax rates, engage in tax planning activities less often than do higher-income taxpayers.

EXAMPLE 12-3

Assume the same situation and opportunities as in Example 12-2, except that Shull's marginal tax rate is 20 percent.

	Alternative 1	Alternative 2
Before-tax cost	$2,000	$1,800
Tax reduction (20%)	−400	−360
After-tax cost	$1,600	$1,440
Possible pre-tax payoff	$1,600	$2,000
Probability of success	×.80	×.85
Expected pre-tax payoff	$1,280	$1,700
Tax on expected payoff (20%)	−0	−340
Expected after-tax payoff	$1,280	$1,360
Excess of after-tax payoff over after-tax cost	$(320)	$ (80)

Decision: Accept Alternative 2 because it generates the lesser after-tax loss, or undertake neither (seemingly profitable) project. The change in the marginal tax rate alone resulted in a different decision by Shull.

Tax Rate Terminology

The basic formula for computing a taxpayer's liability is

$$\textbf{Tax Liability} = \textbf{Tax Base} \times \textbf{Rate}$$

Thus, in many respects, the function of a legislative body is to define adequately the appropriate tax base and construct a schedule of tax rates so that the ensuing liabilities will be in accordance with the prevailing revenue and nonrevenue objectives of the tax system. Once a tax has been included in a society's tax structure, legislative efforts seem to focus on slight modifications of the existing tax base and rates; major overhauls, additions, or deletions to the structure rarely are considered. Tax legislation thus usually takes the form of "fine-tuning" the system rather than "changing channels" altogether.

Tax Base

The income tax is the most modern of the taxes that are commonly found in contemporary industrialized societies. Most policymakers believe that a tax that is based on

SPOTLIGHT ON TAXATION

Tax Reform Act of 1986

The last "major" tax reform legislation was probably the Tax Reform Act of 1986 (TRA 86) enacted during the Reagan administration. Among other changes, the TRA 86 broadened the tax base by eliminating many tax shelters, lowered the top individual income tax rate from 50 to 28 percent (while raising the bottom rate from 11 to 15 percent), increased the maximum capital gains tax rate, increased the reach of the alternative minimum tax, and imposed limitations on passive activity losses. TRA 86 also changed the name of the Internal Revenue Code from the Internal Revenue Code of 1954 to the Internal Revenue Code of 1986.

"ordinary taxable income," allowing deductions for the costs of earning such income and for certain personal expenditures, best reflects the capacity of the taxpayer to support government operations.

Previous efforts to base taxation on ability to pay have included taxes on individual consumption and wealth. Consumption taxes are supported by the rationale that the taxpayer receives personal benefit from society in accordance with the amount of goods and services that he or she exhausts during the period; thus, the government should appropriate its share of tax revenue from what people take out of society's "kitty" for personal reasons, not from what they put into it, as is the case under income taxation.

Wealth or property taxes also have been structured to base levies on one's capacity to pay taxes. Most often, wealth taxes take the form of levies against the net holdings of tangible assets that are controlled by the taxpayer at a given time.

Tax Rates

Most tax scholars identify three distinct tax rate structures: proportional, progressive, and regressive, as illustrated in Exhibit 12-1. The classification of a rate structure depends on the trend of the tax rate as the tax base increases. Under a **proportional tax rate** system, the tax rate is constant. For example, a flat income tax assessed at a rate of 24 percent of income regardless of how much income is earned would be an example of a proportional tax. Most sales and property taxes in the United States employ a proportional rate structure.

Under a **progressive tax rate** system, the applicable tax rate increases as the tax base grows larger. The U.S. individual income tax is a progressive tax rate system in which tax rates increase with income.

SPOTLIGHT ON TAXATION

Are Social Security Taxes Regressive?

In 2010 Social Security taxes were imposed on employees at a flat rate of 6.2 percent on all wages up to $106,800. For wages in excess of that amount, there was no additional tax. Technically, the tax is proportional or flat because all covered wages (the tax base) are subject to the same rate of tax. However, many people regard Social Security taxes to be regressive, presumably basing their analysis on the full amount of a taxpayer's income, not just the statutory tax base. Under this view, because the marginal tax rate is zero on wages in excess of $106,800 for the year, the tax is considered regressive.

EXHIBIT 12-1:   Alternative Tax Rate Structures: Graphic Illustrations and Applicable Schedules

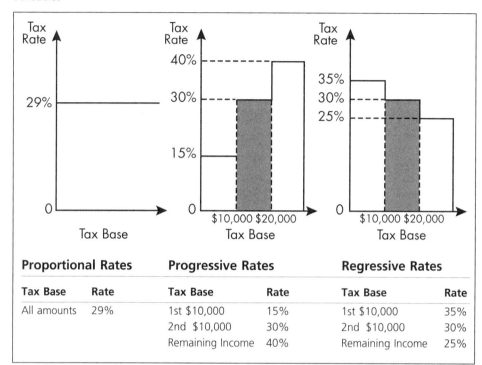

Proportional Rates		**Progressive Rates**		**Regressive Rates**	
Tax Base	**Rate**	**Tax Base**	**Rate**	**Tax Base**	**Rate**
All amounts	29%	1st $10,000	15%	1st $10,000	35%
		2nd $10,000	30%	2nd $10,000	30%
		Remaining Income	40%	Remaining Income	25%

Finally, the tax rate decreases as the tax base grows larger under a **regressive tax rate** structure. Most taxpayers and tax professionals consider regressive tax rates to be unfair. No significant U.S. tax to date has employed a system of regressive tax rates.

Many taxpayers confuse the appropriate meaning of their **marginal tax rate**. Typically, they assume that if a taxpayer is subject to a 36 percent marginal tax rate (i.e., 36 cents is payable in tax on the next dollar of taxable income), he or she owes 36 percent of the *entire* taxable income. One often hears people fall victim to this fallacy, when they state, "I wish I hadn't gotten that raise, because it threw me into a higher tax bracket!" The truth is that even under a system of progressive tax rates, one is never left worse off by earning more money. The higher marginal rates that apply to additional income affect only those increments; the tax liability on the original income layers does not change.

Such comments reflect confusion on the part of the taxpayer concerning marginal tax rate and average tax rate. The **average tax rate** is a simple division of the total tax liability by the corresponding tax base.

EXAMPLE 12-4

Lydia earned $50,000 this year. After applying various deductions, exclusions, and exemptions, though, Lydia's statutory taxable income is $41,000. Assuming the progressive tax rate structure of Exhibit 12-1, Lydia's tax is computed as follows.

$$
\begin{aligned}
15\% \times \$10,000 &= \$\ 1,500 \\
30\% \times \ 10,000 &= \underline{\ 3,000} \\
40\% \times \ 21,000 &= \underline{\ 8,400} \\
\text{Tax liability} &\quad \$12,900
\end{aligned}
$$

Lydia's marginal tax rate is 40 percent, but her average rate is only 31.5 percent ($12,900 tax due ÷ $41,000 taxable income).

The reader should make sure that he or she understands this distinction between marginal and average tax rates because all tax planning analyses should be based on the marginal tax that the individual will pay or save by adopting a particular course of action. The average tax rate is an interesting statistic, but it is solely the marginal rate that affects the change in tax liability and any corresponding changes in taxpayer behavior.

Of course, this definition of statutory taxable income allows for certain deductions, exemptions, and exclusions from total receipts in determining the tax base for the year. Often, because one has received tax-exempt income during the period and because of the tax base's exemptions and standard deduction, an individual controls more receipts than he or she legally must report as taxable income. In this case, the distinction between the nominal and effective average tax rates becomes important.

The **nominal average tax rate** can be computed in Exhibit 12-2 by dividing total tax liability by taxable income. However, before considering Lydia's exclusions, exemptions, and deductions, effectively she had command over $50,000 of income during the year. Thus, Lydia's **effective average tax rate** can be found by dividing the total tax liability by the economic income of $50,000. Exhibit 12-2 summarizes the various tax rate computations that have been introduced in this section.

EXHIBIT 12-2: Various Tax Rate Computations Illustrated

Lydia files a tax return for $50,000 of economic income and $9,000 of exemptions, exclusions, and deductions. Taxable income is $41,000. Tax liability is $12,900 under the prevailing rate system.

Marginal tax rate	40% (from the progressive tax rate schedule, Exhibit 12-1)
Average tax rates	Nominal average rate: $12,900/$41,000 = 31.5%
	Effective average rate: $12,900/$50,000 = 25.8%

Tax Planning in Perspective

The entrepreneurial tax professional should not see tax planning as an end in itself. Rather, especially when dealing with individual clients, tax planning must be seen as part of two sets of major services provided by the practitioner, as illustrated in Exhibits 12-3 and 12-4. As we discussed in Chapter 1, tax planning is part of the entire menu of tax services that the tax professional makes available.

Although the compliance and litigation aspects of the profession increasingly are shared with paraprofessionals (who prepare the bulk of tax returns for many professional firms) or attorneys (when a seemingly irresolvable conflict arises, usually between the client and the IRS), tax planning rightly is initiated by the well-educated and experienced tax practitioner.

Similarly, tax planning is but one of the various types of planning services that a tax professional offers to clients. As the U.S. population collectively ages, the importance of portfolio, estate, and retirement planning has increased. As higher education costs have skyrocketed over the last few decades, education planning has grown in importance as well. Planning for cash and risk contingencies is mandatory for business clients, but even the most modestly endowed of individual clients can benefit from an introduction to such planning.

Thus, to the extent that the tax professional offers tax planning and counseling services, he or she must be facile with the rudiments of the planning process and with the dynamic nature of the evolution of the tax law as it affects planning engagements.

Fundamentals of Tax Planning

As we noted in Chapter 1, tax planning is a completely legal means for saving taxes. The basic objective of such planning is to arrange one's financial activities in a way that will reduce the present value of tax costs such that maximum wealth accumulation can occur in the time period specified.

EXHIBIT 12-3: Tax Planning in the Typical Tax Practice, by Time and Effort of the Professional Staff

EXHIBIT 12-4: Tax Planning in the Client's Wealth Planning Process

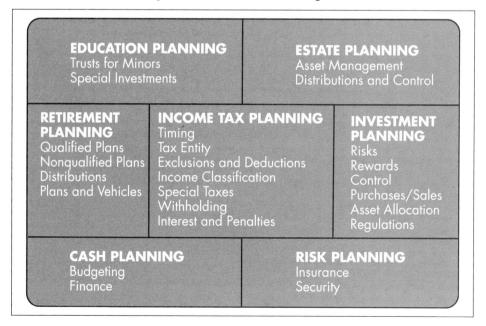

Opportunities for effective tax planning almost always are greater when tax effects are given consideration before transactions are finalized, rather than after they are completed. Decision makers should constantly be alert for tax-optimizing alternatives in the everyday conduct of their affairs. In other words, the first requirement for effective tax planning is tax awareness on the part of decision makers rather than tax expertise by tax professionals.

EXAMPLE 12-5

Russell and Phyllis Cohen, a married couple subject to a 30 percent marginal tax rate, currently are negotiating the purchase of their first home with the Hacienda Heights Construction Company, a land developer. The company has offered to sell the Cohens a house and lot at a price of $250,000 with a 20 percent down payment and 4 percent interest with annual payments for a five-year period. Under these terms, payments would be as follows:

Year	Beginning Balance	Interest	Principal	Total payment
0	$250,000	$ 0	$ 50,000	$ 50,000
1	$200,000	$ 8,000	$ 36,926	$ 44,926
2	$163,074	$ 6,523	$ 38,403	$ 44,926
3	$124,671	$ 4,987	$ 39,939	$ 44,926
4	$ 84,732	$ 3,389	$ 41,537	$ 44,926
5	$ 43,195	$ 1,728	$ 43,195	$ 44,923
Totals		$24,627	$250,000	$274,627

The Cohens are aware that mortgage interest payments are tax-deductible and that the purchase price of a home is not. Thus, they make a counter-offer to purchase the home at a price of $239,246, with $50,000 down and 6 percent interest on annual payments over a five-year period. Under these new terms, Hacienda Heights receives the same cash payments (and gross income) as it did under the original terms. However, the amount of allowable deductions to the Cohens would be increased, with no change in total cash payments.

Year	Beginning Balance	Interest	Principal	Total payment
0	$239,246	$ 0	$ 50,000	$ 50,000
1	$189,246	$11,355	$ 33,571	$ 44,926
2	$155,675	$ 9,340	$ 35,586	$ 44,926
3	$120,089	$ 7,205	$ 37,721	$ 44,926
4	$ 82,368	$ 4,942	$ 39,984	$ 44,926
5	$ 42,384	$ 2,543	$ 42,384	$ 44,927
Totals		$35,385	$239,246	$274,631

Often, decision makers can benefit by recognizing how the rearrangement of a planned transaction can produce tax savings, even if the economic substance of the transaction is left unaltered (or altered very little). In Example 12-5, by reclassifying a portion of their housing expenditures as (deductible) interest rather than (nondeductible) principal, the Cohens were able to increase their allowable deductions and save taxes.

EXHIBIT 12-5:   Goals of Tax Planning Behavior

- Avoiding recognition of taxable income.
- Changing the timing of recognition of income, gains, deductions, losses, and credits.
- Changing tax jurisdictions.
- Changing the character of income.
- Spreading income among related taxpayers.

SPOTLIGHT ON TAXATION

Radical Tax Planning

"A well-timed death is the acme of good tax planning, better even than a well-timed marriage."

—Donald C. Alexander (Former IRS Commissioner)

Tax planning behavior can be characterized as falling into one or more of the general categories enumerated in Exhibit 12-5. Virtually every tax planning technique employed by the tax professional fits one or more of these overriding planning objectives.

Avoiding Recognition of Taxable Income

Taxpayers often can reduce their exposure to taxation by avoiding the accumulation of gross income that must be recognized. This is not to suggest that a taxpayer should avoid accumulating real economic income. As long as marginal tax rates remain less than 100 percent, few people would be willing to go to that extreme. Rather, one usually should strive to obtain economic wealth in some manner that does not create recognized income under the tax law.

EXAMPLE 12-6

Julie earned $3,500 when she sold the crop of fruits and vegetables that she grew, and she was subject to income tax on the full amount. Warren also grew a crop of produce of the same size, but he and his family ate the food. Thus, Warren recognized no gross income and paid no income tax relative to his gardening activities, but his family enjoyed $3,500 worth of fruits and vegetables.

Another method by which one can avoid obtaining recognized income is through the use of debt. Since neither the borrowing of money nor the receipt of funds that previously were lent generates gross income, taxpayers sometimes can use loans to avoid the recognition of taxable income on appreciated investments and enjoy the temporary use of the cash.

EXAMPLE 12-7

Doug owns a tract of land that he acquired many years ago for $10,000. Currently, the land is worth $100,000. Doug needs $50,000 in cash for a business venture. He is considering two alternatives: one is to sell half of the land and the other is to borrow the $50,000 by giving a mortgage on the land. If Doug sells one-half of the land, he will recognize a $45,000 ($50,000 minus one-half of $10,000) taxable gain. However, Doug recognizes no taxable income if he borrows the money, even though the amount that he borrows will be in excess of the basis of the land.

EXAMPLE 12-8

Barbara Ward formed a new corporation by investing $100,000 cash. Following the advice of her tax consultant, Barbara designated $60,000 to be used for the purchase of corporate stock and $40,000 as a loan to the corporation. In this way, if Barbara wants to receive large amounts of cash back from the corporation in the future, the entity simply will repay part or all of the loan principal to her, tax free, rather than making a large (taxable and nondeductible) dividend payment. Barbara also can direct the corporation to pay interest on the loan; such payments are deductible by the corporation. Of course, both interest and dividends are taxable to Barbara when she receives them.

Still another, and perhaps more obvious, way in which one can avoid the recognition of income for tax purposes is to take advantage of the many exclusions that the law permits. For example, an employee might arrange to receive certain non-taxable fringe benefits (such as health insurance) from the employer in lieu of an equivalent value in (taxable) cash salary. This relationship should affect all negotiations as to compensation arrangements: the employer is indifferent between the two choices because both salary and fringe benefit payments are fully deductible against gross income, but the employee's after-tax wealth increases more where tax-free benefits are received.

EXAMPLE 12-9

Lee Schrader, who is subject to a 40 percent overall marginal tax rate, is better off if she receives a tax-free fringe benefit than if she receives an equivalent increase in her salary.

	If Salary Increases	If Fringe Benefit Is Chosen
Value of compensation received	$2,000	$2,000
Tax on employee's compensation	$800	
After-tax increase in employee's wealth	$1,200	$2,000

EXAMPLE 12-10

Albert contributes the maximum amount for the year to a §529 education plan for his daughter. No immediate deduction is allowed, but the earnings in the account never are taxed. Withdrawals similarly are excluded from gross income when they are used for education-related expenses.

EXAMPLE 12-11

Phil designates a portion of his monthly paycheck for medical and child care expenses. No payroll taxes are due on these amounts. Phil's employer reimburses him from these funds when it receives documentation from Phil that he incurred medical and babysitting expenses for the period. By using a "flexible spending plan" such as this one, Phil reduces his total tax liability and has more discretionary income for the year.

Changing the Timing of Recognition of Income, Gains, Deductions, Losses, and Credits

When tax rates are constant, delaying income recognition or accelerating deductions can be beneficial. By delaying the recognition of income, one also delays the payment of the tax and, hence, can continue to enjoy the use of that money. At 4 percent annual interest, the present value of a $1,000 tax that is postponed for 10 years is only $676, a "forgiveness" of almost one-third of the tax "cost." For longer periods and/or higher interest rates, the economic significance of the delay would be even greater. A series of tables computing factors to reflect the time value of money are provided on the end pages in the back of the book.

EXAMPLE 12-12

Janie Heller owns land adjacent to her home that appreciated in value by $5,000 this year. Because she did not sell the land, however, the appreciation in market value was not realized in a market transaction or recognized for income tax purposes. Janie has no recognized income from the land until it is sold.

EXAMPLE 12-13

Mike Jones is a self-employed consultant who uses the cash basis of accounting for tax purposes. Mike finished several consulting jobs late in the year. By postponing billing clients (and receiving cash) to next year, Mike can postpone recognition of taxable income and the resulting tax payment.

EXAMPLE 12-14

George itemizes his deductions and generally gives well over 10 percent of his income to charity each year. He is planning a large charitable gift in January when his church begins a major new capital improvement project. By accelerating the contribution to the current year, George can receive tax savings in the current year rather than next year.

The general principles of delaying income and accelerating deductions are not always optimal. In unusual circumstances, these principles should be violated purposely to produce a desired effect. Again, however, the tax awareness of the parties is utmost in proper planning activities.

EXAMPLE 12-15

Gretchen's cash basis business is unincorporated. It has generated an operating loss of $265,000, which Gretchen can deduct on her tax return. Although there may be other tax uses for this loss, Gretchen may want to accelerate the recognition of other gross income into the current year, for example, by selling appreciated investments or simply sending out bills to customers in a more timely fashion. Realization this year will result in no tax liability for Gretchen because of the loss, so income acceleration should be considered.

EXAMPLE 12-16

Brian's gross income is lower than he expected because of an unanticipated decrease in the sale of his homemade sandals. From a tax standpoint, it may be better to delay deductible expenditures of a discretionary or personal nature (e.g., advertising, medical expenses, and charitable contributions) until business picks up again. In this manner, the value of such deductions will increase, as will the marginal income tax rate to which he is subject.

EXAMPLE 12-17

Matt Young is subject to the AMT for the first time ever this year due to the exercise of incentive stock options received from his employer. State income taxes and property taxes, miscellaneous itemized deductions, among other familiar items, are not allowed as deductions when computing AMT income. Accordingly, Matt should defer the payments of his fourth-quarter state income tax estimates and of the real estate tax on his home until next year, when the usual definitions of taxable income will apply to him again.

EXAMPLE 12-18

Dolores is subject to the AMT this year, so her marginal tax rate is 24 percent, not the usual 36 percent. She might consider accelerating some gross income into the current year to take advantage of this structural decrease in her marginal tax rate. However, the tax adviser must be certain to compare the present values of the resulting taxes, not just the nominal dollar amounts.

EXAMPLE 12-19

Robyn and Chip are concerned about an increase in capital gains tax rates that has been debated in Congress. While the current tax rate on long-term capital gains is 15 percent, it is likely to be 20 percent in the near future. As a result, the couple decides to sell some highly appreciated securities this year rather than waiting until a later year.

Changing Tax Jurisdictions

Tax systems are not universal in breadth, nature, or application. Taxes are adopted by governmental jurisdictions, to be collected from those who live and do business within their boundaries. Often, by moving assets or income out of one tax jurisdiction into another, tax reductions can be effected. Over time, governments tend to modify their tax systems to prevent the "leakage" of tax revenues through such cross-border transactions. Yet, in an effort to attract businesses and resulting jobs into their jurisdictions, governments often retain or create border incentives in the form of tax reductions that are limited in time or scope.

EXAMPLE 12-20

The island country of Ricardo meets its revenue needs with tariffs on the fishing industry. Ricardo never has adopted an income tax system. Harris, a U.S. corporation, could build its new assembly plant through a wholly owned subsidiary incorporated and doing business only in Ricardo, thereby reducing its costs of conducting business because there is no income tax on executive salaries or annual profits. Perhaps by design, Ricardo has attracted new business, profits, jobs, and other benefits through its tax policies.

EXAMPLE 12-21

Judy keeps a log of her travels so that she can document that she is a resident of Florida (a state with no income tax), not New York (a state with a high state tax rate). As a result, Judy's state income tax liability is reduced significantly every year.

EXAMPLE 12-22

RGS Inc. has a manufacturing plant, distribution center, and warehouse in State C and a smaller distribution center in State D. Both States utilize an equally weighted three-factor apportionment formula. State C has a 9 percent corporate tax while State D has a 3 percent tax. Moving the distribution and warehouse now located in State C to State D may reduce the company's overall state income taxes.

Changing the Character of Income

For Federal income tax purposes, several distinct categories of income, deductions, and credits are recognized. The most important of these are as follows:

1. Ordinary income, which is fully taxable, and ordinary deductions, which decrease the tax base dollar for dollar.

2. Investment or "portfolio" income, which usually is fully taxable except for tax-exempt state and local bond interest, and related expenses, which typically can be subtracted only against investment income.

3. Income from passive activities, such as the ownership of rental or "tax shelter" assets, which usually is fully taxable, and related expenses, which can be subtracted only against passive income.

In addition, income from long-term capital gains has often been subject to lower tax rates than ordinary income. This difference in tax rates between ordinary income and capital gain income produces planning opportunities.

EXAMPLE 12-23

Phil Jankowski is the sole shareholder of a management consulting corporation. In addition, he has invested in passive rental activities that generate $40,000 per year in passive losses. According to the Code, such losses from passive activities cannot be applied as deductions to offset fully taxable income, such as from Phil's salary or capital gain transactions. Accordingly, Phil cannot reduce current taxable income by the $40,000 passive loss from his rental activities.

As the dominant shareholder of his corporation, however, Phil may be in a position to salvage the $40,000 deduction. If he reduces his salary from the corporation by $40,000 and takes instead from the corporation a $40,000 properly structured lease payment for the use of specified personal or real property that he owns but the corporation uses, such as office equipment or automobiles, he may be able to create $40,000 in passive income from rental activities, against which the passive loss can be offset.

EXAMPLE 12-24

Amber has $100,000 to invest and is considering a corporate bond that pays 5 percent annual interest or a non-dividend paying stock that is expected to appreciate by 5 percent each year. Assuming that the investments are of similar risk, the tax liability associated with the expected long-term capital gain on the stock will likely be lower than the tax liability associated with the interest income earned on the corporate bonds, which is taxed as ordinary income.

Spreading Income among Related Taxpayers

Because different types of legal entities are taxed separately and at different rates, an individual often can produce an overall tax savings by conducting various business and investment activities within separate taxpaying entities. The progressive nature of the various tax rate schedules further tends to increase the advantage of income splitting. This benefit might result from shifting income, either among different economic entities that are owned by the same individual or among the individual's family members. Accordingly, tax considerations often play an important role both in the selection of organizational forms for a business enterprise and in family financial arrangements.

EXAMPLE 12-25

Bob and Lorraine Whitehead are currently providing for Lorraine's parents' retirement out of after-tax income. Given the Whiteheads' marginal income tax rate of 30 percent, $1,000 of pre-tax income is needed to produce $700 of savings [$1,000 − (0.30 of $1,000) = $700]. Assuming that the parents have a marginal income tax rate of only 18 percent, a transfer to them of $1,000 of pre-tax income, say, by the placement of income-producing assets into an appropriate trust, would raise the after-tax contribution to the parents' retirement to $820 [$1,000 − (0.18 of $1,000)].

EXAMPLE 12-26

Richie Rich makes certain that he makes gifts of highly appreciated securities every year to each of his relatives, using the entire statutory annual gift tax exclusion. This effectively shifts future appreciation and tax on gains to his relatives, who face lower tax rates.

SPOTLIGHT ON TAXATION

Fruits of Tax Planning

"Tax planning is driven by the fact that under a non-neutral tax law, transactions or arrangements whose economic differences are minor can have significantly different tax consequences."

—James W. Wetzler

Exploiting Inconsistencies in the Tax Law

Sometimes, especially when the tax planner can affect the behavior of more than one taxpayer, the tax planning goals can be accomplished by exploiting perceived inconsistencies in the tax system. Multiple taxpayers can exist in the form of family members or related corporations and their shareholders. Several types of systemic inconsistencies can be identified and used by the tax planner.

Inconsistencies between Transactions

Most forms of self-provided in-kind income go unrecognized for tax purposes. Often, however, the same items are not deductible when they are purchased in market transactions. Thus, providing for one's own needs can be an important technique in managing the recognition of taxable income.

EXAMPLE 12-27

Jerry has $50,000 in savings. If the money were invested in securities, the yield on his investment would be taxable, although no deduction would be allowed for his "personal" expense of renting a home. If the $50,000 were invested in a home for his own use, however, the net rental value of the home would escape taxation since such in-kind value is not recognized as gross income under the law.

Inconsistencies between Taxpayers

Inconsistencies often exist between Code sections that control the recognition of income and those that control the allowance of deductions for the same items. When a transaction is between related taxpayers, such inconsistent treatments sometimes can be used to the taxpayers' advantage. The objective in such a situation usually is to structure the terms of the transaction so as to decrease taxable income to the taxpayer group as a whole.

EXAMPLE 12-28

Marilyn is the sole owner-employee of a corporation. To the extent that the corporation pays dividends to Marilyn, she will recognize gross income, but the corporation will receive no deduction. To the extent that Marilyn is paid a reasonable salary, she will recognize gross income and the corporation will receive a deduction. To the extent that she receives certain employee fringe benefits, such as medical insurance, Marilyn is not required to recognize taxable income, and the corporation is allowed an ordinary business expense deduction. In summary, the payment of dividends increases combined taxable income of a shareholder and the corporation, the payment of salary does not change combined taxable income, and providing qualified fringe benefits reduces combined taxable income.

EXAMPLE 12-29

Don and Ann Evans operate a farm, producing a net taxable income of about $30,000 per year. Their nondeductible expenses for housing average $12,000 per year. The Evanses should consider forming a corporation and making a tax-free transfer of all of the farm property to the corporation, including their personal living quarters. As shareholders of the corporation, they could hire themselves as employees, with a requirement that they live on the business premises. The value of the lodging would not be taxable to the Evanses as individuals under §119 of the Code, but it would be deductible as a business expense of the corporation, thus reducing the corporation's taxable income before salaries to $18,000 ($30,000 minus $12,000).

The Evanses then should have the corporation pay them reasonable salaries totaling $18,000. In this manner, taxable income of $18,000 would be taxed directly to them as individuals, and the corporation's taxable income would be reduced to zero, thus avoiding any double taxation. By using this combination of income splitting and an employee fringe benefit, the Evanses could effectively reduce their taxable income (i.e., from $30,000 to $18,000) by the amount of their lodging costs ($12,000), even though such costs are generally nondeductible by both self-employed persons and employees.

This result is based on the assumptions that $18,000 is a reasonable salary for the work that they perform, and that the requirement for living on the farm is for a bona fide business purpose (other than merely for tax avoidance).

Inconsistencies between Years

Another form of inconsistency concerns timing differences in the recognition of income and deductions. Such inconsistencies may relate to the transactions of one taxpayer, or they may concern two taxpayers engaging in a single transaction. In both cases, careful planning to take advantage of tax law inconsistencies can result in a considerable delay in the payment of taxes.

EXAMPLE 12-30

Sarah Carter uses borrowed funds to acquire non-dividend paying corporate stocks. Appreciation on the stocks is not taxed until it is realized on the sale of the shares; yet, Carter might be able to claim investment-interest deductions for the interest that she pays on the borrowed funds.

EXAMPLE 12-31

Harry Fischer is a 40 percent shareholder and junior executive of Able Corporation. Harry's performance incentive bonus is set at 30 percent of the corporation's pre-tax earnings for the year. It is payable on January 31 of the following year. Because the corporation is an accrual-basis taxpayer, the bonus is deductible in the year in which it is earned. As a cash-basis minority shareholder, however, Harry need not recognize the income until the following taxable year (i.e., when he receives it). To the extent of Harry's bonus, the recognition of combined corporate and shareholder income thus is delayed for one year.

EXAMPLE 12-32

Jane Summer is an employee of Orange Corporation and is covered by the company's qualified pension plan. The corporation makes a contribution to the plan for Jane's retirement, which will occur in 30 years. Although Jane will not receive any gross income from the pension benefits until her retirement in 30 years, the corporation is entitled to a current-year business expense deduction.

Avoiding Tax Traps

Ever since the enactment of the first income tax, taxpayers have been trying to find ways to avoid it. Likewise, Congress, the IRS, and the courts have enacted rules and doctrines to prevent, or at least restrict, various avoidance schemes. As a result, current tax law includes a maze of tax traps for the unwary.

Statutory Tax Traps

Many of the statutory provisions encountered in a tax planning context can best be understood when they are viewed as preventive measures; that is, as rules designed by Congress to prevent certain techniques of tax avoidance. However, remember that any transaction that falls within the scope of a given provision, whether or not it is intended as part of a tax avoidance scheme, is subject to that provision. Thus, a basic knowledge of the tax system is necessary for the tax planner if certain disastrous pitfalls are to be avoided.

As we noted earlier in this chapter, income splitting between related taxpayers often can generate significant tax savings. To be effective for tax purposes, though, the income actually must be earned by the separate entities and not merely assigned by means of artificial transactions. Section 482 gives the IRS the power to reallocate both income and deductions among certain related taxpayers so as to reflect "true taxable income."

In applying §482, the regulations indicate that the IRS's right to determine true taxable income is not limited to fraudulent or sham transactions, but also to situations where income inadvertently has been shifted between controlled parties. The courts have held, however, that there truly must be a "shifting" of income before the IRS's power comes into play. Bona fide business transactions that bring tax advantages in their wake should not subject the related parties to reallocation. In concept, at least, §482 can be applied by the IRS only where there has been manipulation of income or deductions by the taxpayers.

Thus, while its boundaries are, in practice, both broad and sometimes hazy, §482 does not prohibit the use of multiple entities for the purpose of earning income. It does, however, give the IRS a potent weapon with which to combat the artificial shifting of income between those entities.

EXAMPLE 12-33

X and Y are two corporations that are fully owned by the same individual. X operates an international airline, and Y owns several hotels that are located in cities served by X. In conjunction with the advertising of its airlines, X often includes pictures of Y's hotels in the airline advertisements. Although the primary benefit of the advertising is to X's airline operations, Y's hotels also obtain patronage by travelers who respond to the ads. X does not charge Y for the advertising. Because an unrelated hotel operator presumably would have been charged for such advertising, the IRS may make an allocation of income from X to Y to reflect the fair market value of the advertising services that were provided.

The "kiddie" tax was created in 1986 to keep parents from sheltering income by putting accounts in the names of their lower-taxed children. Currently it applies to all children under age 19 and full-time students under age 24. In its original form, a portion of investment earnings held by a child was tax-free. Children can still receive a portion of unearned income tax-free. For 2010, the limit is $950, meaning that a child does not have to pay taxes on any interest, dividends, or capital gains up to this amount. The child does have to pay taxes on the next $950, but at his or her lower tax rate. Once unearned income exceeds $1,900, however, the preferential treatment ends. The earnings on those excess earnings are taxed at the parent's top marginal tax rate rather than at the child's usually lower tax rate.

Whereas the objective of this part of the statute may be defensible by some, the broad provision that was enacted to implement it may create undue hardships in some circumstances because it affects all taxpayers, not only those with the now forbidden income-shifting motivation.

EXAMPLE 12-34

Jimmy, age seven, received an inheritance from his grandmother's estate last year. Grandmother wanted Jimmy to attend college someday, so she invested in securities that produce about $10,000 of annual interest income. Jimmy's parents are to see that he accumulates this income for his education. Much of the interest will be taxed at the parents' 40 percent marginal rate, however, and not at Jimmy's lower tax rate, so a smaller after-tax amount of this income will be available for this laudable educational purpose.

Judicial Tax Traps

In the final analysis, the words of the tax law mean only what the courts say that they mean. Often, judicial decisions must be consulted to determine the allowable limits of various Code provisions.

Two pervasive judicial doctrines that often limit the taxpayer's ability to employ effective planning techniques are the concepts of business purpose and substance over form. To be upheld for tax purposes, transactions must possess some non-tax, or "business," purpose in addition to that of tax avoidance. Moreover, there is always the possibility that the court may ignore the form of a transaction if it perceives that such structural false colors cloud the actual substance of the arrangement.

Whenever a series of transactions results in significant tax savings, the IRS may attempt to apply the concept of substance over form by "telescoping" or "collapsing" several transactions into one. If it is upheld by a court, this step-transaction doctrine sometimes can negate what had been a good tax plan (where the steps were viewed as separate transactions). To guard against this possibility, the taxpayer should have a bona fide business purpose for each individual step in the transaction. Of course, documenting non-tax purposes is usually much easier if the various transactions are separated by reasonable time spans since they are then less likely to be viewed as component parts of an overall plan.

EXAMPLE 12-35

Sandra is the sole shareholder of a real estate development corporation. On January 15, she purchased 10 additional shares of stock from her corporation for $100,000. On the same day, she sold a tract of undeveloped land to the corporation for its fair market value of $100,000. To the corporation, the land will be inventory. For Sandra, it had been a capital asset, having been held for investment purposes since its purchase 10 years previously for $20,000.

If these events are viewed as two separate transactions, Sandra will have increased the basis of her investment in the corporation by $100,000 and realized a fully taxable capital gain of $80,000 ($100,000 minus $20,000). The corporation's basis in the land will be $100,000. Thus, if the corporation were to sell the land for $110,000, for example, its income therefrom would be only $10,000 ($110,000 minus $100,000).

Alternatively, if these events are collapsed into a single transaction, Sandra's payment and receipt of cash would be ignored. Instead, she would be viewed as having given a tract of land in exchange for 10 shares of stock of a corporation that she already controls. Under this single-transaction view, Sandra would recognize no taxable capital gain, and the corporation's basis in the stock would be the same as her prior basis, $20,000.

If the corporation were to sell the land for $110,000, its ordinary income would be $90,000 ($110,000 minus $20,000). Taxpayers are restricted to the actual legal forms of the transactions in which they engage, but the IRS has the option of employing the step-transaction doctrine. Thus, the lack of any time lag between the two transactions effectively gives the IRS its choice as to which interpretation it wishes to follow.

SUMMARY

The study of taxes can be viewed as an examination of various ways to optimize one's tax liability. Tax rules that otherwise might seem as dry as a mouthful of sawdust have a way of becoming interesting, stimulating, and challenging when one realizes their economic significance and the resulting implications on human behavior. Tax optimization, therefore, can be viewed both as the heart of professional tax work and as the most important aspect of taxation for non-tax specialists.

QUIZ YOURSELF

Reinforce the tax research information covered in this chapter by completing the online quizzes located at the Federal Tax Research Web site at **www.cengagebrain.com.** At the CengageBrain.com home page, search for the *Federal Tax Research*, 9e ISBN (1111221642) using the search box at the top of the page. This will take you to the product page where you can access the quizzes.

KEY WORDS

By the time you complete this chapter, you should be comfortable discussing each of the following terms. If you need additional review of any of these items, return to the appropriate material in the chapter or consult the glossary to this text.

average tax rate, p. 412
effective average tax rate, p. 413
marginal tax rate, p. 412

nominal average tax rate, p. 413
progressive tax rate, p. 411
proportional tax rate, p. 411

regressive tax rate, p. 412

DISCUSSION QUESTIONS

1. How do taxes fit into the general economic goals of most taxpayers?

2. How might a tax adviser ignoring the present value approach to tax planning arrive at an improper conclusion? Illustrate.

3. Give some examples of U.S. taxes that employ proportional, progressive, and regressive rate structures.

4. Give an example of a transaction between two taxpayers in which an inconsistent treatment is afforded the two taxpayers. Explain how related taxpayers might structure a transaction to take advantage of this inconsistency.

5. Give one or more examples to show how a taxpayer might take advantage of preferential tax rates on long-term capital gains by structuring transactions to produce capital gains rather than ordinary income.

6. Name two types of tax traps and give an example of each.

7. How does the typical tax practitioner divide his or her time among planning, compliance, research, and litigation?

8. What planning engagements can the tax professional offer? Why is he or she in an ideal position to offer these services?

9. Summarize the most important planning services that a tax professional can offer to a client.

10. Why does tax planning analysis focus on the marginal tax rate?

11. When might a taxpayer undertake transactions seemingly opposite to the usual tax planning principles?

12. Higher-income taxpayers tend to engage in tax planning more than do lower-income taxpayers. Why?

13. Is the objective of tax planning always to minimize taxes? Explain.

EXERCISES

14. Using the following codes, identify the basic approach(es) to tax avoidance that are used in each of the following cases:
    AR Avoiding recognition of taxable income
    CT Changing the timing of recognition of income, gains, deductions, losses, and credits
    CJ Changing tax jurisdictions
    CC Changing the character of income
    SI Spreading income among related taxpayers
    None None of the above
    a. Albert invests his savings in tax-exempt state bonds.
    b. Betty invests in non-dividend–paying corporate stocks by using borrowed funds.
    c. Chuck lends $100,000 to his daughter on an interest-free demand note.
    d. Ed invests $100,000 of his savings in a home for his own use.
    e. Frankie invests in a mutual fund that purchases only the indebtedness of the state in which he lives.
    f. At retirement, Tom moves from New York (a state with a high income tax) to Florida (a state with no income tax).

15. Using the codes from Exercise 14, identify the basic approach(es) to tax avoidance that are used in each of the following cases:
    a. Retainer Corp. is a U.S.-owned corporation that was incorporated abroad. The U.S. shareholders do not plan to repatriate earnings back to the United States for many years.
    b. Donna fails to report on her tax return the interest earned on her savings account.
    c. Evelyn has her controlled corporation pay her a salary instead of a dividend during the current year.
    d. Flip operates his business as a regular corporation because of his high marginal tax rate. He plans to sell the corporation in five years.
    e. Georgia grows most of her own food instead of taking a second job.

16. With respect to the system of coding used in Exercises 14 and 15, create one new illustration in each tax planning category.

PROBLEMS

17. Examples 12-2 and 12-3 in this chapter concern a decision between the same two mutually exclusive alternatives under identical conditions, except for the corporation's marginal tax rate. In Example 12-2, where the marginal tax rate was 40 percent, the conclusion was to accept Alternative 1. In Example 12-3, where the marginal tax rate was 20 percent, the conclusion was to accept Alternative 2.

    Determine the marginal tax rate at which the two alternatives would be economic equivalents; that is, they would "break even" and generate the same excess after-tax payoff over after-tax cost. Your answer should be based on all of the conditions and assumptions as stated in Examples 12-2 and 12-3.

18. On creating a new 100 percent-owned corporation, Ben was advised by his tax consultant to treat 50 percent of the total amount that was invested as a loan and 50 percent as a purchase of corporate stock. What tax advantage does this arrangement have over structuring the entire investment as a purchase of stock? Explain.

19. Julia currently is considering the purchase of some land to be held as an investment. She and the seller have agreed on a contract under which Julia would pay $1,000 per month for 60 months, or $60,000 total. The seller, not in the real estate business, acquired the land several years ago by paying $10,000 in cash. Two alternative interpretations of this transaction are (1) a price of $51,726 with 6 percent interest and (2) a price of $39,380 with 18 percent interest. Which interpretation would you expect each party to prefer? Why?

20. George, a high-bracket taxpayer, wishes to shift some of his own taxable income from corporate bonds he owns to his 25-year-old daughter, Debra, so that Debra is taxed on the interest rather than George. One alternative is to make a gift of the interest, and the other is to make a gift of the bonds themselves. Evaluate the pros and cons of each alternative.

21. Assume that a taxpayer can choose when he is to receive $10,000 of fully taxable income. If the taxpayer receives the income at the end of Year 1, he will receive exactly $10,000. If he delays receipt of the income until the end of Year 2, the amount will grow to $11,000. If the taxpayer takes the money at the end of Year 1, he can invest the proceeds and earn a pre-tax return of 10 percent over the next year.

    a. If the taxpayer faces a marginal tax rate of 31 percent in both Year 1 and Year 2, when should he elect to receive the income?

    b. At what pre-tax rate of return, will the taxpayer be indifferent to taking the money in Year 1 and Year 2?

    c. If the taxpayer's marginal tax rate increases to 35 percent in Year 2, when should he elect to receive the income?

    d. What would the tax rate need to be in Year 2 to make the taxpayer indifferent?

22. A taxpayer can invest $10,000 in a taxable 10-year bond that yields an annual pre-tax return of 6 percent or buy land (a capital asset) for $10,000 that is expected to increase at an annual pre-tax rate of 4 percent. The taxpayer expects to hold the bond and the land for 10 years and expects to pay capital gains taxes of 20 percent when the land is sold. The taxpayer's marginal tax rate on ordinary income is expected to be 25 percent throughout the 10-year period.

23. Greg Jones lives in New York City and has the opportunity to rent his condominium during the 2010 Olympic Games. He has two offers—one to rent for 10 days at $500 per day and the other to rent for 16 days at $400 per day. Rental expenses will be negligible. What is your advice to Greg?

24. Should Ferris Corporation elect to forgo the carryback of its $60,000 year 2010 net operating loss? Ferris is subject to a 15 percent cost of capital. Corporate tax rates are as in IRC §11.

a.

Tax Year	Actual or Projected Taxable Income
2009	$700,000
2011	$700,000

b.

Tax Year	Actual or Projected Taxable Income
2009	$70,000
2011	$700,000

c.

Tax Year	Actual or Projected Taxable Income
2009	$70,000
2011	($70,000)
2012	($70,000)
2013	($70,000)
2014	$700,000

25. Should Harris Corporation accelerate $100,000 of gross income into 2011, its first year subject to the AMT? Harris is subject to a 14 percent cost of capital. The corporate AMT rate is a flat 20 percent, and Harris Corporation exceeds the annual AMT exemption phase-out level of income.

a.

Tax Year	Actual or Projected Taxable Income
2012	Regular Tax $700,000
2013	Regular Tax $700,000

b.

Tax Year	Actual or Projected Taxable Income
2012	AMT $700,000
2013	Regular Tax $700,000

c.

Tax Year	Actual or Projected Taxable Income
2012	AMT $700,000
2013	AMT $700,000
2014	AMT $700,000
2015	AMT $700,000
2016	Regular Tax $700,000

26. Paris Corporation holds a $100,000 unrealized net capital gain and a capital loss carryforward that will expire in the current year. Should Paris accelerate the recognition of this gain from next year to this year, assuming a net capital loss carryforward in each of the following amounts? Paris is subject to a 14 percent cost of capital. Its marginal tax rate is 40 percent.

    a. $40,000

    b. $10,000

    c. Repeat parts a and b, but assume that Paris is subject to a 6 percent cost of capital.

27. Maris Corporation put into service $100,000 of equipment that qualifies for its state's 10 percent research credit. To the extent that the credit is claimed, no cost recovery deductions are allowed. Maris is subject to a 14 percent cost of capital. If the credit were not claimed, the property would qualify for cost recovery deductions using a three-year life, straight line with no salvage value, and a half-year convention. The state has a flat income tax rate of 8 percent. What is the net value of the tax credit to Maris Corporation?

CHAPTER 13

Working with the IRS

LEARNING OBJECTIVES

- Describe the organizational structure of the IRS and administrative procedures relative to the audit and appeals process.
- Advise clients as to audit selection factors and probable litigation success.
- Develop decision guidelines as to audit etiquette, working through the appeals system, and constructing taxpayer defenses.

CHAPTER OUTLINE

WE HAVE DISCUSSED VARIOUS aspects of tax practice throughout this text, including both the principles of tax research and the structure of the judicial decision-making process. In this chapter we examine in more detail the workings of the Internal Revenue Service (IRS) and the Treasury Department, with an eye on an overview of the opportunities and challenges that face the practitioner in working with these administrative bodies.

After all, when the researcher has decided that his or her client should prevail with respect to a specified tax issue, a challenge to the IRS must be issued and implemented. In this chapter, we present some of the procedural aspects of this course of action.

Organization of the IRS

The **Department of the Treasury** is responsible for administering and enforcing the internal revenue laws of the United States. However, most revenue functions and authority have been delegated by the Secretary of the Treasury to the **Commissioner of Internal Revenue**. The Commissioner is the chief executive officer of the IRS and is appointed by the President of the United States. The Commissioner is responsible for overall planning and for directing, coordinating, and controlling the policies and programs of the IRS.

The IRS is one of about a dozen bureaus within the Department of the Treasury. It was established by Congress on July 1, 1862, to meet the fiscal needs of the Civil War. At that time, the name of the agency was the Bureau of Internal Revenue. In 1953 the name was changed to the **Internal Revenue Service (IRS).**

The agency has undergone a period of steady growth as the means for financing government operations shifted from the levying of import duties on outsiders to one of internal taxation on U.S. citizens and businesses. This expansion increased substantially after 1913 with the ratification of the Sixteenth Amendment, which authorized the modern income tax on non-corporate entities.

Private sector input is provided through the **IRS Oversight Board**, which functions as part of the Treasury Department. Its major duties include the following:[1]

- Review and approve the IRS's mission, strategic plans, and annual planning documents.

- Review IRS operational functions, including modernization, outsourcing, and training efforts.

- Recommend to the President candidates for Commissioner.

- Review the process of selecting, evaluating, and compensating senior IRS executives.

- Review and approve the IRS annual budget request.

- Ensure the proper treatment of taxpayers.

The Board is designed to function like a corporate board of directors. It is made up of six members of the private sector, appointed to five-year terms by the President, and of the Treasury Secretary, the IRS Commissioner, and a representative of IRS employees. The Board has no authority to affect tax policy, to intervene in IRS personnel or procurement matters, or to affect the processing of individual tax cases.

---

[1]§7802.

IRS National Office

In 2009, the IRS processed more than 236 million returns and collected over $2.3 trillion in tax revenues for the Federal government. It also provided taxpayer assistance through 68 million telephone calls. The IRS consists of a national office in Washington, D.C. and a large, decentralized field organization. Its current mission statement is as follows:

Provide America's taxpayers top quality service by helping them understand and meet their tax responsibilities and by applying the tax law with integrity and fairness to all.

Guiding Principles

- Understand and solve problems from the point of view of the taxpayer.
- Enable IRS managers to be accountable to taxpayers.
- Use balanced measures of performance to measure taxpayer satisfaction, business results, and employee satisfaction.
- Foster open, honest communications.
- Insist on total integrity.

Strategic Plan: Goals and Objectives

- Improve service to make voluntary compliance easier.
  - Objective 1: Incorporate taxpayer perspectives to improve all service interactions.
  - Objective 2: Expedite and improve issue resolution across all interactions with taxpayers, making it easier to navigate the IRS.
  - Objective 3: Provide taxpayers with targeted, timely guidance and outreach.
  - Objective 4: Strengthen partnerships with tax practitioners, tax preparers, and other third parties in order to ensure effective tax administration.
- Enforce the law to make sure everyone meets their obligations to pay taxes.
  - Objective 1: Proactively enforce the law in a timely manner while respecting taxpayer rights and minimizing taxpayer burden.
  - Objective 2: Expand enforcement approaches and tools.
  - Objective 3: Meet the challenges of international tax administration.
  - Objective 4: Allocate compliance resources using a data-driven approach to target existing and emerging high-risk areas.
  - Objective 5: Continue focused oversight of the tax-exempt sector.
  - Objective 6: Ensure that all tax practitioners, tax preparers, and other third parties in the tax system adhere to professional standards and follow the law.

The IRS organizational chart presented in Exhibit 13-1 illustrates that the IRS is organized to facilitate both the processing of tax returns and the carrying out of its broader goals, using a "shared services" model like that used by most large businesses.

The IRS's national office is located in the District of Columbia (D.C.). It is staffed by the office of the Commissioner of Internal Revenue, which includes a Deputy Commissioner and various chief officers and assistants to the Commissioner. The IRS Commissioner is appointed by the President to a renewable five-year term. He or she is the chief

EXHIBIT 13-1: IRS Organizational Chart

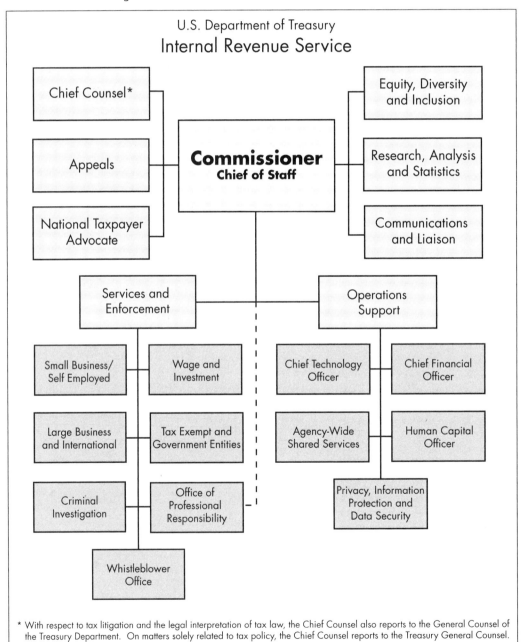

U.S. Department of Treasury
Internal Revenue Service

- Chief Counsel*
- Appeals
- National Taxpayer Advocate

Commissioner
Chief of Staff

- Equity, Diversity and Inclusion
- Research, Analysis and Statistics
- Communications and Liaison

Services and Enforcement
- Small Business/ Self Employed
- Wage and Investment
- Large Business and International
- Tax Exempt and Government Entities
- Criminal Investigation
- Office of Professional Responsibility
- Whistleblower Office

Operations Support
- Chief Technology Officer
- Chief Financial Officer
- Agency-Wide Shared Services
- Human Capital Officer
- Privacy, Information Protection and Data Security

* With respect to tax litigation and the legal interpretation of tax law, the Chief Counsel also reports to the General Counsel of the Treasury Department. On matters solely related to tax policy, the Chief Counsel reports to the Treasury General Counsel.

executive officer of the agency and is charged to administer, manage, conduct, direct, and supervise the execution of the Federal tax laws.[2] The Commissioner's nomination is reviewed by the Senate. He or she advises the President as to the person who should be named Chief Counsel. The Commissioner is the agency's final authority as to the interpretation of tax law.

The **Chief Counsel** is the agency's highest ranking legal adviser. He or she is appointed by the President and reports to the Commissioner, relative to the administration and enforcement of the tax laws. In effect, the Chief Counsel is the IRS's attorney. Rulings and other written determinations are prepared by the Chief Counsel's office.[3] The Chief Counsel represents the agency in Tax Court cases and often assists in preparing proposed legislation, treaties, regulations, and executive orders. Associate Chief Counsels are assigned duties relative to litigation, technical matters, international transactions, and finance and management.

The **National Taxpayer Advocate** administers a taxpayer-intervention system, which is designed to resolve a wide range of tax administration problems that are not remedied through the agency's normal operating procedures or administrative channels.[4] The Advocate reports directly to the Commissioner and works through a system of local Taxpayer Advocates, one of which is located in each state.

The Deputy Commissioner oversees the four primary operating divisions of the IRS and other service and enforcement functions. These operating divisions reflect the major types of tax returns that the agency processes.

The **Wage and Investment (W&I) Division** serves 1040 filers with only wage and investment income (no Schedules C, E, F or Form 2106 for employee business expenses). Most of these filers pay taxes through withholdings, prepare their own returns (rather than using paid preparers), interact with the IRS once a year, and receive refunds.

The **Large Business and International (LB&I) Division** serves approximately 210,000 C-corporations, S-corporations, and partnerships with assets greater than $10 million and certain high-wealth individuals. It is organized along five general industry lines: communications, technology and media; financial services; heavy manufacturing and transportation; natural resources and construction; and retailers, food, pharmaceuticals and healthcare. In addition, the division handles the IRS's international tax compliance efforts including transfer pricing issues and offshore tax evasion and has oversight over the new Foreign Account Tax Compliance Act (FATCA) passed by Congress in 2010.

The **Small Business and Self-Employed (SB/SE) Division** serves about 41 million self-employed taxpayers, nine million small businesses with assets of less than $10 million, and about seven million filers of employment, excise, estate, and gift returns.

The **Tax Exempt and Government Entities (TEGE) Division** comprises three business divisions: employee plans; exempt organizations; and government entities. It serves approximately three million customers that range from small local community nonprofits and municipalities to major universities, huge pension funds, state governments, and participants of complex tax-exempt bond transactions. Although generally paying no

---

[2]§7803(a).

[3]§7803(b).

[4]§7803(c).

income tax, this sector does pay more than $220 billion in employment taxes and income tax withholding.

IRS Service Centers

As electronic filing of returns has increased, the IRS has reduced the number of tax return processing centers. Depending on the state of residence, 1040 paper returns are filed in Atlanta, Austin, Texas, Fresno, California, or Kansas City, Missouri. Tax-exempt and government entities generally file reports and returns in Ogden, Utah. Business returns for partnerships and corporations are generally filed in either Ogden or Cincinnati, Ohio.

The IRS operates major data centers in Memphis and Detroit to support the agency's primary site in Martinsburg, West Virginia. The Detroit site supports administrative computing while most data is processed in Martinsburg and backed up to Memphis. These facilities process seven million transactions per day and run more than 4,500 batch jobs daily as they exchange data with other agencies.

Taxpayer Assistance Orders

The National Taxpayer Advocate can issue a **Taxpayer Assistance Order (TAO)** to suspend, delay, or stop actions where, in the determination of the Advocate, the taxpayer is suffering or about to suffer a significant hardship as a result of the manner in which the IRS is administering the revenue laws.[5] "Hardships" refer to any circumstance that includes an immediate threat of adverse action for the taxpayer, his or her irreparable injury, a delay of more than 30 days in settling the taxpayer's account, or the incurring of significant costs (such as professional advisory fees) to handle the dispute.[6] The IRS action that is the subject of a TAO must be such that it would offend one's sense of fairness, given all the related facts.

Typically, the TAO requires remedial actions, such as a release from the IRS's levy of specific property or the cessation of a collection activity, or it gives the IRS a deadline for action. A TAO is binding on the IRS, short of its rescission by the Advocate, the Commissioner, or a Deputy Commissioner.

A taxpayer applies for a TAO by filing Form 911, Request for Taxpayer Advocate Service Assistance, reproduced as Exhibit 13-2.

Local Taxpayer Advocates

The IRS uses local Taxpayer Advocates in a system designed to help resolve taxpayer problems or complaints that are not being satisfied through regular agency channels. The primary objective of the Advocate system is to provide taxpayers with a representative within the IRS who has access to the pertinent regional, district, or service center official. In addition, the program enables the IRS to identify its own organizational, procedural, and systematic problems and to take corrective action as needed.

The system is not intended to circumvent the existing IRS channels of managerial authority, established administrative procedures, and formal avenues of appeal. Rather, it is designed to ensure that taxpayer problems or complaints that have not been resolved

---

[5] §7811.
[6] §7811(a)(2).

EXHIBIT 13-2: Request for Taxpayer Advocate Service Assistance

OMB No. 1545-1504

Department of the Treasury - Internal Revenue Service

Request for Taxpayer Advocate Service Assistance
(And Application for Taxpayer Assistance Order)

Form **911**
(Rev. 6-2007)

Section I – Taxpayer Information *(See Pages 3 and 4 for Form 911 Filing Requirements and Instructions for Completing this Form.)*

1a. Your name as shown on tax return	2a. Your Social Security Number
1b. Spouse's name as shown on tax return	2b. Spouse's Social Security Number

3a. Your current street address *(Number, Street, & Apt. Number)*

3b. City	3c. State *(or Foreign Country)*	3d. ZIP code

4. Fax number *(if applicable)*	5. E-mail address

6. Employer Identification Number *(EIN) (if applicable)*	7. Tax form(s)	8. Tax period(s)

9. Person to contact	10. Daytime phone number ☐ Check if Cell Phone	11. Best time to call

12. Indicate the special communication needs you require *(if applicable)*

☐ TTY/TDD Line   ☐ Interpreter - Specify language other than English *(including sign language)* _____

☐ Other *(please specify)*

13a. Please describe the tax problem you are experiencing *(If more space is needed, attach additional sheets.)*

13b. Please describe the relief/assistance you are requesting *(If more space is needed, attach additional sheets.)*

I understand that Taxpayer Advocate Service employees may contact third parties in order to respond to this request and I authorize such contacts to be made. Further, by authorizing the Taxpayer Advocate Service to contact third parties, I understand that I will not receive notice, pursuant to section 7602(c) of the Internal Revenue Code, of third parties contacted in connection with this request.

14a. Signature of Taxpayer or Corporate Officer, and title, if applicable	14b. Date signed
15a. Signature of spouse	15b. Date signed

Section II – Representative Information *(Attach Form 2848 if not already on file with the IRS.)*

1. Name of authorized representative	2. Centralized Authorization File (CAF) number
3. Current mailing address	4. Daytime phone number ☐ Check if Cell Phone
	5. Fax number
6. Signature of representative	7. Date signed

Catalog Number 16965S   www.irs.gov   Form **911** (Rev. 6-2007)

EXHIBIT 13-2: Request for Taxpayer Advocate Service Assistance (*continued*)

Section III is to be completed by the IRS only

Section III – Initiating Employee Information

Taxpayer name			Taxpayer Identification Number *(TIN)*	
1. Name of employee	2. Phone number	3a. Function	3b. Operating division	4. Organization code no.

5. How identified and received *(Check the appropriate box)*	6. IRS received date

IRS Function identified issue as meeting Taxpayer Advocate Service (TAS) criteria

☐ (r) Functional referral (Function identified taxpayer issue as meeting TAS criteria).

☐ (x) Congressional correspondence/inquiry not addressed to TAS but referred for TAS handling.
　　　Name of Congressional Representative _____

Taxpayer or Representative requested TAS assistance

☐ (n) Taxpayer or representative called into a National Taxpayer Advocate (NTA) Toll-Free site.

☐ (s) Functional referral (taxpayer or representative specifically requested TAS assistance).

---

7. TAS criteria *(Check the appropriate box.* **NOTE: Checkbox 9 is for TAS Use Only***)*

☐ (1) The taxpayer is experiencing economic harm or is about to suffer economic harm.
☐ (2) The taxpayer is facing an immediate threat of adverse action.
☐ (3) The taxpayer will incur significant costs if relief is not granted (including fees for professional representation).
☐ (4) The taxpayer will suffer irreparable injury or long-term adverse impact if relief is not granted.
☐ (5) The taxpayer has experienced a delay of more than 30 days to resolve a tax account problem.
☐ (6) The taxpayer did not receive a response or resolution to their problem or inquiry by the date promised.
☐ (7) A system or procedure has either failed to operate as intended, or failed to resolve the taxpayer's problem or dispute within the IRS.
☐ (8) The manner in which the tax laws are being administered raise considerations of equity, or have impaired or will impair the taxpayer's rights.
☐ (9) The NTA determines compelling public policy warrants assistance to an individual or group of taxpayers (**TAS Use Only**).

---

8. What action(s) did you take to help resolve the problem *(Must be completed by the initiating employee)*

---

9. State the reason(s) why the problem was not resolved *(Must be completed by the initiating employee)*

---

10. How did the taxpayer learn about the Taxpayer Advocate Service

---

adequately through normal procedures are referred and controlled within the program. When a case is referred to a member of the National Taxpayer Advocate team, he or she will ensure that the problem is not lost or overlooked and that it is resolved as promptly and efficiently as is possible. Typically, the Advocate system is used to resolve billing, procedural, computer-generated, and other problems that taxpayers cannot correct after one or more contacts with the IRS office that is handling the matter.

The National Taxpayer Advocate works through local team members who are responsible for the work that is conducted within his or her jurisdiction. Local Advocates are independent from IRS examination, collection, and appeals functions. They are responsible only to the National Taxpayer Advocate.

Taxpayer Rights

Under three incarnations of the so-called *Taxpayer Bill of Rights*, taxpayers are guaranteed various rights to representation before the IRS, a recording of any proceedings, and an IRS explanation of its position relative to the pertinent disagreement. Specifically, the taxpayer has a right to know why the IRS is requesting information, exactly how the IRS will use the information it receives, and what might happen if the taxpayer does not submit the requested information. Accordingly, prior to an initial audit or collection interview, an IRS employee or officer must explain, orally or in written form, the pertinent aspects of the procedures to come.[7]

A taxpayer may be represented by an attorney, Certified Public Accountant (CPA), or other person who is permitted to represent a taxpayer before the IRS and who has obtained a properly executed power of attorney. Absent an administrative summons, a taxpayer cannot be required to accompany the representative to an interview.[8]

After meeting a 10-day notice requirement, the taxpayer is allowed to make a tape recording of the IRS interview using the taxpayer's own equipment. Similarly, if the IRS intends to record an interview with a taxpayer or his or her representative, it must give a 10-day notice to the taxpayer. In addition, upon receiving a request from the taxpayer and a reimbursement for duplication costs, the IRS must make available to the taxpayer a transcript of the interview or a copy of its tape recording.[9]

To protect the rights of so-called innocent spouses on joint returns, the IRS must inform spouses of their joint and several liability for tax deficiencies, and both spouses must receive separately mailed notices as to audit, appeals, and Tax Court proceedings.[10] This may be especially important where the spouses have divorced or separated subsequent to filing the original joint return.

The Service must inform taxpayers of their rights to representation in carrying out a dispute with the agency. The taxpayer can suspend at any time an interview with IRS personnel so as to include a representative.[11]

With respect to noncriminal tax matters before the IRS or a Federal court, the common law privilege of confidentiality exists between a taxpayer and his or her tax practitioner; that is, one who is authorized to practice before the IRS. The privilege exists with respect to tax advice the practitioner has rendered. These provisions extend existing

---

[7] §7521(b)(1).

[8] §7521(c).

[9] §7521(a); Notice 89-51, 1989-1 CB 691.

[10] §6103(e)(1)(B).

[11] §7521(b)(2).

privilege protection previously only applicable between a taxpayer and his or her attorney. The privilege does not exist with respect to dealings with tax shelters (see Chapter 5).

The Audit Process

The U.S. Federal income tax system is based primarily on an assumption of self-assessment. All persons with taxable incomes that exceed a specific amount are required to prepare an accurate statement of annual income (i.e., an income tax return) and to remit in a timely fashion any amount of tax that is due. In a somewhat paternalistic sense, the IRS uses the examination of returns as an enforcement device to promote such voluntary compliance with the internal revenue laws. In a manner that is somewhat similar to the treatment by a parent of a child who is considering some forbidden behavior, the threat of an IRS audit encourages many taxpayers to report accurately their taxable incomes and to pay any tax liability that remains outstanding.

Because only a small number of tax returns can be audited each year, the IRS attempts to select for examination only those returns that will generate additional revenues for the Treasury. It relies primarily on sophisticated statistical models and computer technology to identify those returns that possess the greatest revenue return for the agency's investment of audit resources. In addition to this scientific selection process, however, a number of returns are manually selected for examination at an examiner's discretion.

Preliminary Review of Returns

All business and individual tax returns are reviewed routinely by IRS personnel and computers for simple and obvious errors, such as the omission of required signatures and Social Security numbers. After this initial review, income tax returns are processed through an automatic data processing system.

One of the most important functions performed by this system is the matching of the information recorded on a return with corresponding data received from third parties, for example, from an employer on Form W-2. This procedure, which is referred to as the Information Document Matching Program (IDMP), has uncovered millions of cases of discrepancies between the amount of income and deductions that recipients have reported on tax returns and corresponding amounts that have been transmitted by third parties. In addition, the IDMP provides the IRS with a means by which to detect taxpayers who fail to file any return at all. In the typical year, about two million taxpayers are sent such failure-to-file inquiries as a result of the matching program.

Mathematical/Clerical Error Program   The Mathematical/Clerical Error Program is one of a number of special programs that are conducted by IRS computers. This program checks every return for mathematical errors, recomputes the tax due after properly applying the numbers that are included in the return, and summarily assesses any additional tax that is due or allows refunds or credits based on (previously) miscomputed deductions or credits. A summary assessment may be made concerning any deficiency that results from a mathematical or clerical error.[12] Consequently, the IRS need not send the taxpayer a formal notice of deficiency (i.e., a 90-day letter, as discussed subsequently in this chapter) before the additional tax is assessed.

---

[12]§6213(b)(1).

SPOTLIGHT ON TAXATION

Math or Clerical Errors Skyrocket

In 2009, the IRS sent out more than 13 million of these notices. While the number of routine math errors has declined sharply due to increases in electronic filing, the program includes 16 types of errors, including the incorrect use of an IRS table, inconsistent entries on a return, omitted information required to substantiate an entry on a return, an entry that claims a deduction or credit in excess of the statutory limit, and failure to provide a taxpayer identification number as well as the catchall "incorrect use or selection of information on a tax return or schedule." In 2009, the most common error concerned the recovery rebate credit.

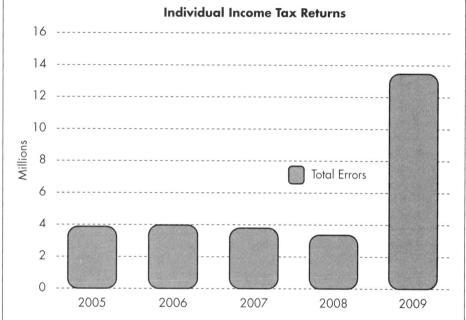

Individual Income Tax Returns

More than 10 million of the 13.5 million math or clerical errors for 2009 concerned the recovery rebate credit. More than 6.2 million of those errors were by taxpayers who were eligible for the credit but failed to claim it, and the IRS computed it for them.

Source: Edward J. Schnee, "Qsub Bank's Tax-Exempt Bond Expense Deductible," *Journal of Accountancy*, June 2010, p. 78. Used by permission.

When a mathematical or clerical error is identified by the service center, the IRS mails the taxpayer a corrected tax computation and requests that he or she pay the additional tax within 10 days of the date of the notice, or 21days if the tax underpayment is less than $100,000. If the deficiency is paid within this period, no interest is charged on the underpayment. If the deficiency is not paid in a timely fashion, however, interest is imposed on the unpaid amount for a period that begins on the date of the notice and demand and ends on the date of payment.

A taxpayer may not petition the U.S. Tax Court with respect to a deficiency that results from a mathematical or clerical error. However, other administrative procedures will allow the taxpayer to contest the summary assessment without first paying the tax.

The IRS must give an explanation of the asserted error to the taxpayer. After receiving this explanation, the taxpayer has 60 days within which to request that the additional tax be abated. If a request for abatement is made, the assessment will be canceled automatically. However, the return is then identified for further examination if the taxpayer cannot justify satisfactorily or substantiate the figures that were included on the original return.

When an error results in a taxpayer overpayment of the tax, the IRS usually sends a corrected computation of the tax, together with a brief explanation of the error and a refund of the excess amount that was paid.

The IRS does not consider such a contact that it makes with the taxpayer to be an examination. Therefore, a taxpayer who is contacted under the Mathematical/Clerical Error Program is not entitled to the administrative remedies that are available to taxpayers who are involved in a formal examination.

Unallowable Items Program   The IRS conducts another program that is similar to the Mathematical/Clerical Error Program called the Unallowable Items Program. Under this program, IRS personnel question items that have been included on individual income tax returns that appear to be unallowable by law. These items include such return elements as an overstatement of the standard deduction, a deduction of Social Security taxes paid, the claiming of an incorrect filing status, the deduction of Federal income taxes, or the deduction of lost (but not stolen) assets as a casualty loss.

If a return is identified as including an unallowable item, the IRS computes the seemingly necessary adjustment in taxes, and the taxpayer is notified by mail. Again, the IRS does not consider the contact that it makes with a taxpayer under the Unallowable Items Program to be an examination.[13] Consequently, it treats an adjustment in this circumstance as a correction of a mathematical or clerical error, and the taxpayer is not sent a formal notice of deficiency.

If the taxpayer is able to explain the questioned item adequately, the assessment is abated. However, the case will be continued as a correspondence or office audit if the taxpayer's response is deemed unsatisfactory.

Selection of Returns for Examination

Each year the IRS determines the approximate number and types of returns that it intends to audit. The national office then prepares an audit plan to allocate its personnel to achieve the desired audit coverage. The primary goal of the IRS in selecting a return for examination is to review only those returns that will result in a satisfactory increase in the tax liability.

Computer and manual methods are used to select returns for examination. Computer programs select certain returns for examination, based on the potential that exists for changes in the tax treatment of certain items on the return. Generally, this is done through the use of mathematical models, including correlations and discriminant functions. IRS personnel also manually select returns that they believe warrant special attention. The Service describes in nontechnical terms its selection procedures in its annual Publication 1. Selection criteria for audits are not disclosed by the Treasury.[14]

Although most of the initial IRS screening of the returns for audit is performed by computers, a more detailed selection procedure then is employed manually in the Examination Division of the local IRS office, where the classification staff ultimately selects those specific cases that will be examined. The number of returns that finally is selected by the staff is based on the examination resource (and other) capabilities of the respective offices.

---

[13]Rev. Proc. 94-68, 1994-2 CB 803.

[14]§6103(b)(2); *Long v. U.S.*, 742 F2d 1173 (CA-9, 1984).

Discriminant Function System   Once a return has been processed through the IRS automated computer program, each return is rated by computer for its audit potential by means of a mathematical model, the **discriminant function formula (DIF).** This formula assigns numeric weights to certain (undisclosed by the IRS) return items, generating a composite score for the return. In this regard, the higher the DIF score, the greater the potential for additional tax payments upon audit. Statistics provided by the Commissioner show a high correlation between DIF scores and such tax modifications, but the specifics of the formula are not disclosed.[15]

When the computer selects a return that has a high probability for an adjustment, as indicated by a high DIF score, an employee at the service center manually inspects the return to confirm its audit potential. If an acceptable explanation for the DIF score cannot be found after this manual examination of the return and its attachments, including explanatory data that the computer did not consider, the return is forwarded to the Examination Division at the appropriate local IRS office.

National Research Program   The **National Research Program (NRP)** is an initiative that is designed to furnish the IRS with statistics concerning the type and number of errors that are made on a representative sample of individual income tax returns. These statistics are used to develop and update the DIF formulas. Under the annual NRP procedures, perhaps 15,000 individual income tax returns are selected randomly for an extremely thorough examination. These returns then are examined comprehensively to determine the degree of their accuracy as filed.

Unlike the treatment that is given returns that are selected for general audit, the NRP examiner may not exercise any judgment in dealing with an item on the return selected for review. All errors are noted and corrected, regardless of their amount. This procedure is necessary to a determination of the actual error patterns that individual income tax returns exhibit so that the statistics that underlie the DIF procedure are free from any major bias.

NRP audits integrate IRS data files with some of those from the Social Security Administration and the Census Bureau. Some of the NRP audits are transparent to the taxpayer. That is, all of the work is done with computer models and IRS personnel, and the taxpayer does not even know that the audit is being conducted. Most of the rest of the procedures require correspondence by mail with the taxpayer, with no in-person contact required. Those whose returns are audited and require such in-person contact likely will need professional assistance to meet the IRS data and documentation demands.

Other Selection Methods   In addition to the previously discussed computerized methods for the identification of returns for IRS examination, returns may be selected manually for a variety of reasons. An examination may be initiated, for instance, because of information that is provided by an informant or because the selected return is linked to another return that is currently under examination, using the Coordinated Industry Case Program. (For example, a partner's return may be selected as a result of a partnership audit.)

Moreover, some returns are reviewed automatically by IRS personnel because the reported taxable income, gross receipts, or total assets exceed a predetermined materiality amount. For instance, individual returns with total positive income of $50,000 or more, or partnership returns with gross receipts or gross income of $500,000 or more, can be selected in this manner. Finally, a return may be selected for examination because the taxpayer has filed a claim for refund or otherwise has indicated that an adjustment in the original amount of tax liability is necessary.

---

[15]*Feltz v. IRS,* 79 AFTR2d 97-747 (DCWWis).

"Economic reality" factors can be considered by the IRS in the selection of returns for audit, but only where the agency has some other evidence that the taxpayer has underreported taxable income for the year. For instance, manual selection of a return and an economic-reality review might occur when an IRS employee, reviewing data in three consecutive filing periods, finds indications that income might be underreported or deductions might be overstated or misclassified. Some of the factors believed to be perused in an economic reality audit include the following:

- Significant increases in interest, dividend, and other investment income.

- Significant decreases in mortgage and other reportable interest paid.

- Significant variance in self-employment or farming income during the period relative to industry norms.

- Business and other expenditures not seemingly justified by income levels.

SPOTLIGHT ON TAXATION

New IRS Enforcement Initiatives

Beginning in 2010 and continuing for the next three years, the IRS will conduct random employment tax audits of approximately 6,000 employers as part of its National Research Program. This initiative will focus on four primary areas: (1) classification of workers as employees or independent contractors; (2) fringe benefits; (3) employee business expense reimbursements; and (4) compensation of owner-employees. As the following graph shows, the IRS expects to earn significant returns on investment on other new IRS enforcement initiatives.

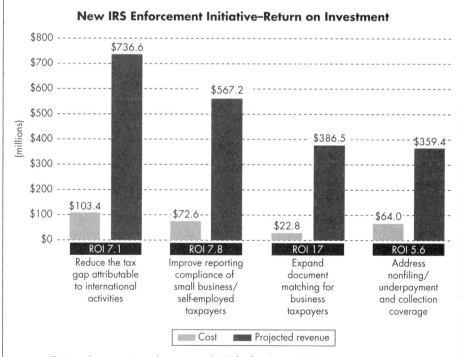

New IRS Enforcement Initiative–Return on Investment

Estimated costs, projected revenue and ROI for fiscal year 2012.

Source: Karen M. Cooley, "Underlying Assets Not Gift Tax Value of Interest in N.Y. LLC," *Journal of Accountancy*, December 2009, p. 72. Used by permission.

EXHIBIT 13-3: Various Audit Statistics

Type of Return	Chances of Audit
Individual Income Tax Returns	**1.0%**
Nonbusiness returns with income under $200,000 (Without earned income tax credit and without schedules C, E, F or Form 2106)	0.4%
Nonbusiness returns with income between $200,000 and $1,000,000	2.3%
Business returns without earned income tax credit and gross receipts less under $25,000	1.1%
Business returns with income between $200,000 and $1,000,000	3.1%
All returns (business and nonbusiness) with income of $1,000,000 or more	6.4%
Corporate Income Tax Returns (except Form 1120-S)	**1.3%**
Small corporations with under $250,000 of total assets	0.7%
Large corporations with over $20,000,000 of total assets	100%
Estate Tax Returns	**9.3%**
Under $5 million gross estate	6.2%
Over $5 million gross estate	1.6%
Partnership Returns	**4%**
S Corporation Returns	**4%**

Chances of Audit   Taxpayers often want to know what their overall probability of selection for an audit might be for a given year. In general, the IRS selects about 1 percent of all returns for examination, outside of the mathematical error program. As can be seen in Exhibit 13-3, the chances of audit vary greatly for different types of tax returns and different size taxpaying entities.

Examinations

After a return is selected for audit, an IRS agent schedules it for a review in either a correspondence, office, or field examination. The type of examination to which the taxpayer is subject generally is determined by the audit potential of the return, the nature of the asserted error, and the type of taxpayer.

Correspondence Examinations

Many times, IRS personnel question only one or two items on a selected return. In these cases, an examination is typically conducted by mail through a **correspondence examination**. The IRS examiner requests that the taxpayer verify the questioned item of income, deduction, or credit by mailing copies of receipts, canceled checks, or other documentation to the district office or service center. If the taxpayer requests an interview, the issues become too complex, or the taxpayer is unable to communicate effectively in writing, the case is referred to the appropriate district office for resolution as an office or field examination.

Issues that typically are addressed in the correspondence audit setting include itemized deductions for interest, taxes, charitable contributions, medical expenses, and simple miscellaneous deductions such as union dues.

A taxpayer who is subject to a correspondence examination is entitled to the same administrative and judicial appeal rights that are allowed to those who are involved in office or field audits.

Office Examinations

When a return that has been selected for examination involves one or more issues that will require some analysis and the exercise of the IRS personnel's judgment, rather than a mere verification of record-keeping requirements, the audit usually is conducted at the pertinent IRS office. An **office examination** also will be scheduled if the examiner believes that an office examination is necessary to guarantee that the taxpayer's legal rights are respected.

If the IRS decides to conduct an office examination, the taxpayer is asked to come to the local IRS office for an interview and to bring any records and documents that support the questioned items. Generally, the auditor is given very little time in which to prepare for the session, and the scope of the examination is limited to the items that are listed in the audit notification letter.

Office audits usually are confined to individuals' income tax returns that include no business income. In recent years, however, the IRS has increased the scope of some office audits to include a limited number of small business returns. Issues that typically are examined in an office audit setting include dependency exemptions; income from tips, rents, and royalties; income from partnerships, estates, and trusts; deductions for travel and entertainment; deductions for bad debts; and casualty and theft losses.

A field examination may be conducted in lieu of an office audit if it is difficult for the taxpayer to bring the requested records to the district office or if the taxpayer for some other valid reason requests that the audit be conducted on his or her premises.

Field Examinations

Examinations that present complex issues that require more advanced knowledge of the internal revenue laws and accounting skills usually are conducted on the taxpayer's premises. A **field examination** is more comprehensive than a correspondence or office audit, and it usually is limited to an examination of corporation and individual business returns. In a field examination, the revenue agent reviews completely the entire financial operations of the taxpayer, including the business history of the taxpayer; the nature, amount, and location of taxpayer assets; the nature of the business operations; the extant accounting methods and system of internal control; and other financial attributes of the entity.

While an office audit ordinarily is limited to the items that are specified in the audit notification letter, a field examination may be open-ended. The agent is free to pursue any unusual items that are recorded in the tax return(s) or the records of the taxpayer (i.e., journals, ledgers, and worksheets) and to investigate other areas of which he or she may be suspicious.

The IRS prefers to conduct the field audit on the taxpayer's premises because the taxpayer's books and records may be more accessible and the agent is better able to observe the taxpayer's business facilities and the scope of its operations. However, it is

SPOTLIGHT ON TAXATION

Average Recommended Additional Tax Per Return After Examination

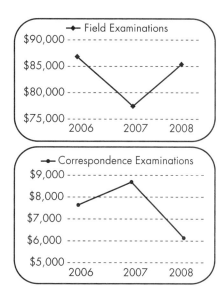

Source: Tina Quinn, "Losses from Interests in LLCs and LLPs Not Presumptively Passive," *Journal of Accountancy*, October 2009, p. 69. Used by permission.

sometimes possible to have the audit conducted at the office of the taxpayer's representative instead. Only one such inspection of taxpayer books and records may be made for a tax year.[16] The Code includes a broad set of restrictions regarding access to the taxpayer's physical office by the IRS.[17] Taxpayers refusing to admit IRS personnel are subject to a $500 fine.[18]

The IRS uses a team approach in its field audits, known as the Coordinated Examination Program, when it examines the returns of large corporate taxpayers. During this type of examination, a large group of IRS agents is used to investigate the operations of the taxpayer. Normally, such an investigation spans more than one IRS district as well.

Dealing with an Auditor

Most practitioners develop over time a list of "dos and don'ts" in negotiating with a government auditor. In the very best case, one will have dealt with the same auditor many times and will have become familiar with the nuances of that particular auditor's mode of operation. Whether this is the case or not, the following guidelines, dictated as much

---

[16]§7605(b).

[17]§7606.

[18]§7342.

by common courtesy and decorum as by ethics and hardcore negotiating techniques, are likely to be useful:[19]

- Do conduct yourself courteously and professionally, showing that you have prepared yourself for the audit.

- Do review the strengths and weaknesses of your position before the agent arrives.

- Do cooperate with the auditor and promptly respond to all requests.

- Do establish internal timetables and responsibilities for completing the audit.

- Do provide the auditor with adequate work accommodations.

- Do not impede the audit process.

- Do not allow the auditor free access to and through the taxpayer's building.

- Do not let the agent browse through taxpayer information.

- Do not volunteer comments or information not requested by the agent.

- Do not attempt to bully or intimidate the auditor.

- Do assign one person to be the primary on-premises contact with the auditor—he or she cannot interview taxpayer employees on a random basis.

- Do verify the auditor's credentials before providing any information.

- Do request that all communications be in writing.

- Do keep track of time spent (by taxpayer, practitioner, and auditor) on the audit.

- Do meet at least daily with the auditor to review issues.

- Do agree to disagree on major irreconcilable issues.

- Do conduct a concluding conference to discuss audit recommendations.

- Do obtain copies of all government work papers affecting the potential assessment.

- Do request clarification on the rest of the appeals process.

Conclusion of Examination

Upon the conclusion of the examination, the IRS auditor or agent must explain to the taxpayer any proposed adjustments to the tax liability. A written **Revenue Agent's Report (RAR)** is prepared by the agent and is given to the taxpayer. The RAR contains a brief explanation of the proposed adjustments and lists the balance due or the overpayment.

The RAR also includes a waiver of the restrictions on assessment, which the taxpayer is asked to sign if he or she agrees with the proposed modifications. This waiver permits the IRS to assess any deficiency in tax immediately without sending the taxpayer a formal notice of deficiency.

Even though the taxpayer may agree with the proposed adjustments to his or her return and sign the form, thereby indicating acceptance of the proposal, the case technically is not closed until the agent's report is reviewed and accepted by the district office

---

[19]Some of the material is adapted from a talk by Robert E. Dallman, Milwaukee WI, "The Audit Process."

review staff. Therefore, it is possible that an agreement that is worked out with the agent may not be accepted by the IRS.

After the taxpayer agrees to any increase in tax, he or she may either make an advance payment of the deficiency and accrued interest, to eliminate additional interest charges, or wait for a formal request for payment from the service center.

If the taxpayer disagrees with the agent's proposals, the IRS makes an immediate attempt to resolve the disagreement. The taxpayer normally is given an opportunity to discuss the proposed adjustments with the agent's group supervisor or with an appeals officer. If an immediate interview is not possible or if the issues remain unresolved after such an interview, the taxpayer receives a preliminary notice of deficiency, which is also referred to as a "30-day letter."

30-Day Letter

When the taxpayer does not agree with the agent's proposed adjustments, a **30-day letter** is issued. This correspondence formally notifies the taxpayer of the examiner's findings, requests that the taxpayer agree to the proposed adjustments, and informs the taxpayer of his or her appeal rights. If the taxpayer does not respond to the notice within 30 days, he or she receives a **statutory notice of deficiency**, also known as a "**90-day letter**," discussed later in this chapter.

The taxpayer has 30 days from the date of the 30-day letter to request a conference with an appeals officer. This request may be made orally with respect to an office examination or if the total proposed additional tax and penalties total $2,500 or less. The taxpayer's appeal must be in written form if the total proposed additional tax and penalties exceed $2,500,[20] and a formal protest, setting forth the specific facts and applicable law or other authority in support of the taxpayer's position, is required if the proposed tax and penalties exceed $10,000.[21]

File a Protest or Go Straight to Court?

In deciding whether to file a protest and request a hearing in the Appeals Office or to allow a 90-day letter to be issued and skip directly to the courts for satisfaction, the taxpayer and his or her adviser must consider a number of factors.[22]

Factors in Favor of the Protest/Appeals Process

- An appeals officer can consider the hazards of litigation. This allows for the possibility of a settlement without the costs of litigation.

- The litigation path remains a possibility even if an appeal is pursued.

- The appeals process allows a further delay in the payment of the disputed tax. This criterion can be important if funds are not available with which to pay the tax or if the taxpayer can earn more on the funds during the administrative period than is assessed in the form of interest.

- During the appeals process, the taxpayer will discover more of the elements of the government's position. In addition, the taxpayer gains additional time in which to formulate or polish his or her own position.

---

[20]Reg. §§601.105(c)(2)(iii) and (d)(2)(iv).

[21]Reg. §§601.105(d)(2) and 601.106(a)(1)(ii)

[22]Saltzman, *IRS Practice and Procedure*, Warren, Gorham & Lamont; ¶ 9.05(1).

- Recovery of some court costs and attorney fees is available if the court finds that the government's case was largely unjustified and all administrative remedies were attempted. Thus, working through the appeals process is required if any costs are to be recovered.

Factors in Favor of Bypassing Appeals

- The likelihood of the government finding and raising new issues during the appeal is eliminated.

- The government receives a psychological message that the taxpayer is firmly convinced of his or her position, and negotiating advantages for the taxpayer may result.

- The conclusion of the dispute, whether for or against the taxpayer, is expedited.

The Appeals Process

To minimize the costs of litigation in both time and money, the IRS encourages the resolution of tax disputes through an administrative appeals process. If a case cannot be resolved at the examination level, the taxpayer is allowed to appeal to a separate division of the IRS, known as the **Appeals Office**.

The Appeals Office has the exclusive and final authority to settle cases that originate in a district that is located within its jurisdiction. This division is under the supervision of the Commissioner of the IRS, with input from the Chief Counsel. The appeals function provides the taxpayer with a final opportunity to resolve tax disputes with the IRS without incurring litigation. Its objective is to resolve tax controversies without litigation on a basis that is fair and impartial to both the government and the taxpayer.

Appeals Conference

The conference with the appeals officer is an informal proceeding. Although the appeals office may require allegations to be submitted in the form of affidavits or declarations under the penalty of perjury, testimony typically is not taken under oath.[23] The taxpayer, or his or her representative, meets with the appeals officer and discusses the dispute informally. According to the IRS's conference and practice rules, the appeals officer is to maintain a standard of strict impartiality toward the taxpayer and the government.

The appeals officer has the authority to settle all factual and legal questions that are raised in the examiner's report. He or she also can settle a tax dispute on the basis of the hazards of litigation. However, no settlement can be made that is based on the nuisance value of the case to the government.

The appeals officer may use a considerable amount of personal judgment in deciding how to handle the disputed issues of a case. He or she can split or trade issues where substantial uncertainties exist as to the law or the facts. On the other hand, the appeals officer may defer action on, or refuse to settle, a case or an issue to achieve greater uniformity concerning the application of the revenue laws and to improve the overall voluntary compliance with the tax laws. An analysis by the U.S. Government Accounting Office (GAO) found that taxpayers who took their case to the IRS appeals division won at least some relief in about 41 percent of cases.

---

[23]Reg. §601.106(c).

90-Day Letter

If the taxpayer and the IRS cannot agree on the proposed adjustments after an appeals conference, the regional director of appeals will issue a statutory notice of deficiency.[24] The statutory notice also is issued if the taxpayer does not request an appeals conference.

A statutory notice of deficiency, commonly referred to as a 90-day letter, must be sent to the taxpayer's last known address by certified or registered mail before the IRS can assess the additional taxes that it believes are due.[25] Once a formal assessment has been made, the IRS is entitled to collect and retain the tax. However, a statutory notice is not required relative to deficiencies that result from mathematical errors or from the overstatement of taxes that were withheld or paid as estimated taxes.

After the statutory notice of deficiency is mailed, the taxpayer has 90 days (150 days if the letter is addressed to a taxpayer who is outside the United States) to file a petition with the U.S. Tax Court for a redetermination of the deficiency. If such a petition is not filed in a timely fashion, the deficiency is assessed and the taxpayer receives a notice and demand for payment of the tax.[26] Once this 90-day period expires, the taxpayer cannot contest the assessment without first paying the tax, filing a claim for refund, and, if the claim is denied by the IRS, instituting a refund suit in a district court or the U.S. Court of Federal Claims. Generally, no assessment or collection effort may be made during the 90-day period, or, if a Tax Court petition is filed, until after the decision becomes final.

A mailing of the statutory notice to the taxpayer's last known address is sufficient to commence the running of the 90-day period, unless the Commissioner has been notified formally of a change of address.[27] The statute does not require that the taxpayer receive actual notice; therefore, a notice that is sent by certified or registered mail to the proper address is effective even though it is never received by the taxpayer himself or herself.[28]

After a case has been scheduled (docketed) for review in the Tax Court, the taxpayer is invited to attend a pretrial settlement conference with an appeals officer and an IRS attorney. However, this conference typically is offered only if the case was not considered previously by the appeals office and if no related criminal prosecution is pending.

If the taxpayer and the IRS agree to settle the dispute at this stage, they will enter into a written agreement stipulating the amount of any deficiency or overpayment. This stipulation is filed with the Tax Court, which will enter a decision in accordance with the agreement. The Tax Court can levy a penalty of up to $25,000 if it determines that the taxpayer did not pursue the available administrative remedies prior to approaching the court.[29]

Possibilities for appeal after completing the trial-level case have been discussed in Chapters 2, 3, and 5. Exhibit 13-4 illustrates the appeals procedures, from the initial

---

[24]§7522.

[25]§§6212(a) and 6212(b)(1).

[26]§6213(c).

[27]§6212(b); *McIntosh v. U.S.,* 85 AFTR2d 98-6501 (SDOh).

[28]§6212(a); *Lifter,* 59 T.C. 818 (1973), and *U.S. v. Ahrens,* 530 F.2d 781 (CA-8, 1976).

[29]§6673(a)(1)(c).

IRS examination to the hearing before the trial-level court. Exhibit 13-5 and Exhibit 13-6 offers sample 30-day and 90-day letters for the reader's perusal.

Entering the Judicial System

If a taxpayer cannot resolve his or her dispute with the IRS administratively, he or she may seek judicial relief. As we have discussed throughout this text, the taxpayer can choose from among the U.S. Tax Court, the pertinent district court, and the U.S. Court of Federal Claims to initiate the lawsuit against the government.

The Tax Court will review the taxpayer's case provided that he or she files a petition with the court within 90 days of the date of his or her statutory notice of deficiency. The district courts and the Court of Federal Claims cannot hear the taxpayer's case unless he or she is suing for a refund. Consequently, the taxpayer first must pay the disputed tax, and then file an (unsuccessful) claim for refund to obtain a judicial review in either of these latter two forums.

EXHIBIT 13-4:   Income Tax Appeal Procedure

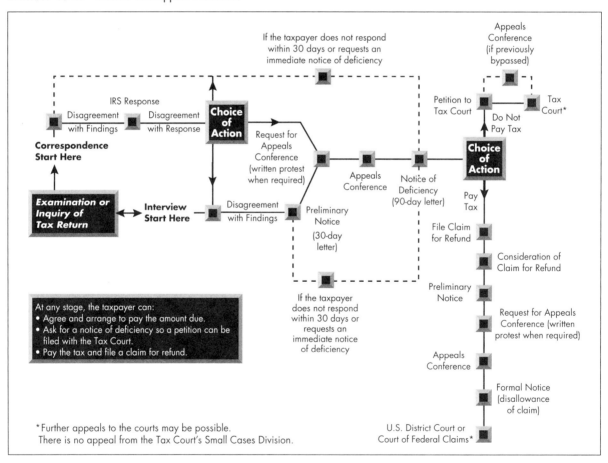

EXHIBIT 13-5: Sample 30-day Letter

Notice of Adjustment—30-Day Letter
IRS   Department of the Treasury
Date:
Social Security or Employee Identification Number:
Tax Year Ended:
Person to Contact:
Contact Telephone Number:
Contact Address:

Dear _____:

Enclosed are two copies of our report explaining why we believe adjustments should be made in the amount of your tax. Please look this report over and let us know whether you agree with our findings.

If you accept our findings, please sign the consent to assessment and collection portion at the bottom of the report and mail one copy to this office within 30 days from the date of this letter. If additional tax is due, you may want to pay it now and limit the interest charge; otherwise, we will bill you. (See the enclosed Publication 5 for payment details.)

If you do not accept our findings, you have 30 days from the date of this letter to do one of the following:

- Mail us any additional evidence or information you would like us to consider.

- Request a discussion of our findings with the examiner who conducted the examination. At that time you may submit any additional evidence or information you would like us to consider. If you plan to come in for a discussion, please phone or write us in advance so that we can arrange a convenient time and place.

- Discuss your position with the group manager or a senior examiner (designated by the group manager), if an examination has been held and you have been unable to reach an agreement with the examiner.

If you do not accept our findings and do not want to take any of the above actions, you may write us at the address shown above or call us at the telephone number shown above within 30 days from the date of this letter to request a conference with an Appeals Officer. You must provide all pertinent documentation and facts concerning disputed issues to the examiner before your case is forwarded to the Appeals Office. If your examination was conducted entirely by mail, we would appreciate your first discussing our findings with one of our examiners.

The Appeals Office is independent of the District Director. The Appeals Officer, who had not examined your return previously, will take a fresh look at your case. Most disputes considered by Appeals are resolved informally and promptly. By going to Appeals, you may avoid court costs (such as the U.S. Tax Court filing fee), clear up this matter sooner, and prevent interest from mounting. An Appeals Officer will promptly telephone you and, if necessary, arrange an appointment. If you decide to bypass Appeals and petition the Tax Court, your case will normally be assigned for settlement to an Appeals Office before the Tax Court hears the case.

Under Internal Revenue Code Section 6673, the Tax Court is authorized to award damages of up to $25,000 to the United States when a taxpayer unreasonably fails to pursue available administrative remedies. Damages could be awarded under this provision, for example, if the court concludes that it was unreasonable for a taxpayer to bypass Appeals and then file a petition in the Tax Court. The Tax Court will make that determination based upon the facts and circumstances of each case. Generally, the Service will not ask the court to award damages under this provision if you make a good faith effort to meet with Appeals and to settle your case before petitioning the Tax Court.

The enclosed Publication 5 explains your appeal rights.

If we do not hear from you within 30 days, we will have to process your case on the basis of the adjustments shown in the examination report. If you write us about your case, please write to the person whose name and address are shown in the heading of this letter and refer to the symbols in the upper right corner of the enclosed report. An envelope is enclosed for your convenience. Please include your telephone number, area code, and the most convenient time for us to call, in case we find it necessary to contact you for further information.

If you prefer, you may call the person at the telephone number shown in the heading of this letter. This person will be able to answer any questions you may have. Thank you for your cooperation.

Sincerely yours,
IRS Examinations
Enclosures:
Examination Report (2)
Publication 5
Envelope

EXHIBIT 13-6:   Sample 90-day Letters

Notice of Deficiency—90-Day Letter
IRS   Department of the Treasury
Date:
Social Security or Employer Identification Number:
Tax Year Ended and Deficiency:
Person to Contact:
Contact Telephone Number:

Dear ___:

We have determined that there is a deficiency (increase) in your income tax as shown above. This letter is a NOTICE OF DEFICIENCY sent to you as required by law. The enclosed statement shows how we figured the deficiency.

If you want to contest this deficiency in court before making any payment, you have 90 days from the above mailing date of this letter (150 days if addressed to you outside of the United States) to file a petition with the U.S. Tax Court for a redetermination of the deficiency. To secure the petition form, write to U.S. Tax Court, 400 Second Street, NW, Washington, D.C. 20217. The completed petition form, together with a copy of this letter must be returned to the same address and received within 90 days from the above mailing date (150 days if addressed to you outside of the United States).

The time in which you must file a petition with the court (90 or 150 days as the case may be) is fixed by law and the court cannot consider your case if your petition is filed late. If this letter is addressed to both a husband and wife, and both want to petition the Tax Court, both must sign the petition or each must file a separate, signed petition.

If you dispute not more than $50,000 for any one tax year, a simplified procedure is provided by the Tax Court for small tax cases. You can get information about this procedure, as well as a petition form you can use, by writing to the Clerk of the Tax Court at 400 Second Street, NW, Washington, D.C. 20217. You should do this promptly if you intend to file a petition with the Tax Court.

You may represent yourself before the Tax Court, or you may be represented by anyone admitted to practice before the court. If you decide not to file a petition with the Tax Court, we would appreciate it if you would sign and return the enclosed waiver form. This will permit us to assess the deficiency quickly and will limit the accumulation of interest. The enclosed envelope is for your convenience. If you decide not to sign and return the statement and you do not timely petition the Tax Court, the law requires us to assess and bill you for the deficiency after 90 days from the above mailing date of this letter (150 days if this letter is addressed to you outside the United States).

If you have questions about this letter, please write to the person whose name and address are shown on this letter. If you write, please attach this letter to help identify your account. Keep the copy for your records. Also, please include your telephone number and the most convenient time for us to call, so we can contact you if we need additional information.
If you prefer, you may call the IRS contact person at the telephone number shown above. If this number is outside your local calling area, there will be a long distance charge to you.

You may call the IRS telephone number listed in your local directory. An IRS employee there may be able to help you, but the contact person at the address shown on this letter is most familiar with your case.

Thank you for your cooperation.

Sincerely yours,
Commissioner
By
Enclosures:
Copy of this letter
Statement
Envelope

SPOTLIGHT ON TAXATION

Deciding to Litigate

One should not consider tax litigation lightly. The additional costs to the taxpayer for attorney and accountant fees, in addition to filing and processing fees and the cost and time involved in gathering supporting documentation for the taxpayer's position, finding and coaching expert and other witnesses, and providing for one's own travel to the site of the hearing, make litigation a costly prospect. Given the right combination of facts and law, though, a suit might be the taxpayer's only chance to achieve an equitable solution.

Remember, nonetheless, that the IRS tends to litigate only cases that it expects to win and that it expects will make good precedent to discourage other taxpayers. Moreover, because many taxpayers represent themselves before the Tax Court, procedural errors occur, usually to the detriment of the taxpayer. Thus, it is not surprising that the deck appears to be stacked against the taxpayer once he or she enters the judicial system.

National Taxpayer Advocate Nina Olson, in her *2009 Annual Report to Congress*, listed the 10 tax issues most litigated in the Federal courts. Of the 923 cases involving those issues, taxpayers prevailed in whole, or in part, in 132, or roughly 14 percent. Taxpayers who were represented by counsel did somewhat better when the numbers were broken down—they won 20 percent, or 54 of 265 cases; pro se taxpayers prevailed in 12 percent, or 78 of 658 cases.

SUMMARY

In counseling clients, the tax professional must be aware of the organization and inner workings of the IRS. Strategic and tactical decisions as to how and when to appeal within the administrative system of the Service, assessing the strengths and weaknesses of the client's case, and determining available remedies can be made only with a thorough understanding of the agency and its operating style. Some of the most valuable advice that a client receives can be in the context of an audit selection letter or the handling of settlement alternatives thereafter.

QUIZ YOURSELF

Reinforce the tax research information covered in this chapter by completing the online quizzes located at the Federal Tax Research Web site at **www.cengagebrain.com**. At the CengageBrain.com home page, search for the *Federal Tax Research*, 9e ISBN (1111221642) using the search box at the top of the page. This will take you to the product page where you can access the quizzes.

KEY WORDS

By the time you complete this chapter, you should be comfortable discussing each of the following terms. If you need additional review of any of these items, return to the appropriate material in the chapter or consult the glossary to this text.

30-day letter, p. 449
90-day letter, p. 449
Appeals Office, p. 450
Chief Counsel, p. 435

Commissioner of Internal Revenue, p. 432
correspondence examination, p. 445
Department of the Treasury, p. 432

discriminant function formula (DIF), p. 443
field examination, p. 446
Internal Revenue Service (IRS), p. 432

DISCUSSION QUESTIONS

1. Why must the tax professional be cognizant of how tax law administration works?

2. What are the major functions of the national office of the IRS?

3. What are the chief responsibilities of:
   a. The IRS Commissioner
   b. The IRS Chief Counsel
   c. The National Taxpayer Advocate
   d. Local Taxpayer Advocates

4. List three of the items included in one of the Taxpayer Bills of Rights.

5. Distinguish between the Math/Clerical Error program and the Unallowable Items program.

6. What are the chances of having a tax return audited this year?

7. What techniques other than the random selection of returns for audit does the IRS use in its enforcement function?

8. Why might it be desirable to settle with an agent rather than continue by appealing to a higher level within the IRS?

9. Relate some of the "audit etiquette" tactics that you have heard taxpayers or tax professionals discuss.

10. Distinguish among the various means by which the IRS selects a tax return for examination. For this purpose, examine the criteria of:
    a. Scope of review
    b. Probability of selection
    c. Preservation of taxpayer constitutional rights

11. Add two items to the "dos and don'ts" list included in the discussion of audit etiquette.

12. Suggest other information documents that the IRS computers could add to the IDMP.

13. Identify several items that you believe are included in the prevailing DIF model.

14. Carol takes some very aggressive positions on her tax return. She maintains, "With the downsizing of the government, my chances of getting caught are virtually zero." Is Carol's approach correct?

15. Should the IRS audit more or fewer returns every year? What issues would you consider in this regard if you were a politician? A wealthy individual?

16. What are the most important activities that the IRS currently is carrying out in its data collection and audit efforts?

EXERCISES

17. Which of the following methods is used to select tax returns for audit? More than one answer may be correct.
    a. DIF procedures
    b. Random samples
    c. Amount of gross income
    d. Type of income, for example, business or wages

18. Which type of audit is used most often to substantiate the reported items of income or deduction for individuals who have only wages?
    a. Field
    b. Office
    c. Correspondence

19. A revenue agent may do which of the following in an attempt to negotiate a settlement after the completion of an audit? More than one answer may be correct.
    a. Attempt to settle an unresolved issue based on the hazards of litigation.
    b. Settle a question of fact.
    c. Reach an agreement that will be accepted unconditionally by the IRS.
    d. Turn the case over to the Appeals Office.

20. When an agreement cannot be reached with a Revenue Agent, a letter is transmitted stating that the taxpayer has 30 days to do which of the following?
    a. File a suit in the U.S. Tax Court
    b. Request an administrative appeal
    c. Pay the tax
    d. Find additional facts to support his or her position

21. A statutory notice of deficiency gives the taxpayer 90 days to do which of the following?
    a. Pay the tax
    b. Request an administrative appeal
    c. File a suit in the U.S. Tax Court
    d. File a protest

22. Make a chart that distinguishes among the various types of examinations that the IRS conducts relative to individual income tax returns; namely, office, correspondence, field, and NRP audits. For this purpose, examine the following criteria:
    a. Scope of review
    b. Type of documentation that typically is required of the taxpayer
    c. Use of IRS personnel time and other resources
    d. Opportunity for agent to use professional judgment in resolving issues

23. Respond to a client's comment: "We have a better than even chance of winning in the Tax Court, according to an article I read. Let's sue the government!"

24. With respect to the Small Cases Division of the U.S. Tax Court, which statement is true?
    a. The taxpayer (but not the IRS) can appeal a contrary judgment.
    b. The IRS (but not the taxpayer) can appeal a contrary judgment.
    c. Either the IRS or the taxpayer can appeal a contrary judgment.
    d. Neither the IRS nor the taxpayer can appeal a contrary judgment.

25. How should the tax professional advise a client whose charitable contributions are double that of the U.S. norm for his or her income level?

26. In early 2011, the IRS selected Amber's 2008 return for audit with respect to Schedule C expenses and employee business expenses claimed on the return. Amber met with an IRS agent who disallowed many of the expenses and claims that Amber owes $2,500 of additional taxes. Discuss Amber's alternatives.

27. Distinguish between the receipt of a 30-day letter and a 90-day letter.

PROBLEMS

28. The President of the United States has hired you to assist in a trim-the-fat program with respect to the Federal government. The President has asked you to recommend specific steps to downsize the bureaucracy of the IRS, from the national office through the district headquarters, by 15 percent. Draft a memo to the President summarizing your recommendations. Augment your memo with diagrams supporting your proposals.

29. The IRS has issued a summons for the tax file held by CPA Ann Whitman for her clients, the Harberts. The file consists of paper and electronic spreadsheets in which Whitman detailed some tax computations using assumptions that the IRS would find to be "too aggressive." In addition, the file includes notes from meetings with the Harberts, income and balance sheet data as to their personal assets, and other technical correspondence, including e-mail messages. In a memo to the tax research file, summarize the current status of the law as to whether the privilege of confidentiality protects these documents from the government.

RESEARCH CASES

30. Your supervisor says that the U.S. Constitution forces the IRS to reveal the make-up of the DIF formula that it uses to select tax returns for audit. Prepare a file memo assessing the supervisor's assertion.

31. Max and Annie are roommates sharing an apartment. Although they know each other well, they have respect for each other's privacy. Thus, when Max's Form 1040 was audited by the IRS, he made no mention of the audit to Annie. When Annie was clearing the answering machine that they shared, she heard the following message: "Max, this is Richard, the IRS auditor. My figures show that you owe the government $10,000 in taxes and another $4,500 in penalties and interest."

    When Annie brought up the message during dinner conversation that night, Max was furious. How could the IRS be so careless as to broadcast this news to a stranger? Did not he have any privacy and confidentiality rights? Max calls you to determine whether he might have a case against the IRS or Richard, the agent. Prepare a file memo assessing Max's position.

32. You have just rendered service for a taxpayer as an expert witness in a case heard by the U.S. Tax Court. The taxpayer is requesting reimbursement for your fees and for those amounts paid to her attorney in presenting the case. Your billing rate for this type of engagement is $500 per hour, the market rate for such services in your city, plus out-of-pocket expenses (e.g., auto mileage, computer charges). How much of your fee will the taxpayer recover?

33. Examine some tax journal articles and treatises to put together a checklist, "How to Prepare for a Tax Audit."

34. Examine some tax journal articles and treatises to put together a checklist, "How to Prepare for an Appeals Conference."

35. Prepare a graph illustrating the trends in IRS audit activity over the past decade. First decide whether you are measuring audited returns, tax dollars recovered by audit, or budget resources dedicated to audit activities. Next decide which types of taxpayers and returns you will be graphing. Then find your data at www.irs.gov.

CHAPTER 14

Tax Practice and Administration: Sanctions, Agreements, and Disclosures

LEARNING OBJECTIVES

- Identify various penalties that may be applied to taxpayers whose returns reflect improper amounts and related computations of interest charges.
- Identify various penalties that may be applied to tax practitioners who fail to perform as directed by the IRS and related computations of interest charges.
- Explain the application of the statutes of limitations and taxpayer-government agreements that may be made with respect thereto.

CHAPTER OUTLINE

THE ADVERSARIAL NATURE OF the Federal tax system has become apparent throughout this text, especially in Chapter 13. The revenue system is based on the notion of self-assessment, but the failure of the taxpayer to comply in detail with the requirements of the structure can lead to painful negotiations with the Internal Revenue Service (IRS) and prolonged litigation.

Yet, the Treasury need not wait for a resolution of the disputed tax issues alone to collect revenues. Penalties and interest play an ever-increasing role in the makeup of the Federal tax system—in many cases, the accumulated penalties and interest assessed by the IRS equal 50 percent of the disputed tax or more.

Interest charges are made by the Treasury so that the taxpayer gains no advantage or disadvantage with respect to the time value of money in deciding how to handle a tax dispute—to the extent that interest rates are developed to parallel those of the rest of the financial market, both parties are indifferent as to cash flow issues, and the negotiations can center on the tax issues alone. Penalties have become more prominent in the Federal tax system for several reasons, as follows:

- In an environment where nominal tax increases are politically unpopular, penalty increases can supplement revenues in a manner that is acceptable to the public.

- Politics aside, penalties increase the tax cost of negotiating with the Treasury and may discourage challenges to tax precedents that are not founded in sound tax law.

- Penalties can bolster the self-assessment process by discouraging taxpayers from behaviors that the Treasury wishes to repress, such as working with tax shelters and ignoring filing deadlines and requirements.

- As professional tax preparers and advisers play a more important role in the development of tax return positions, the behavior of such third parties has increasingly become more and more regulated.

The tax professional must incorporate into the research model the penalty-based "costs" of being too aggressive in taking a tax return or litigation position, and convey the computations of those costs to the client.

We conclude this chapter with a review of alternatives and strategies available to taxpayers in making various compromises and other agreements with the IRS as a result of the examination process. In today's tax practice, the professional must have a full working knowledge of the details of the tax administration process, so as best to serve clients.

Taxpayer Penalties

To promote and enforce taxpayer compliance with our voluntary self-assessment system of taxation, Congress has enacted a comprehensive array of penalties. Tax penalties may involve both criminal and civil offenses. Criminal tax penalties are imposed only after the usual criminal process of law is carried out, in which the taxpayer is entitled to the same constitutional guarantees that are given to non-tax criminal defendants.

Normally, a criminal penalty provides for imprisonment. Civil tax penalties are collected in the same manner as other taxes, and they usually provide only for monetary fines. Criminal and civil penalties are not mutually exclusive; therefore, a taxpayer may be liable under both types of sanctions.

Civil Penalties

The Code imposes two types of **civil penalties**. **Ad valorem penalties** are additions to taxes that are based on a percentage of the delinquent tax. Unlike assessable penalties, ad valorem penalties are subject to the same deficiency procedures that apply to the underlying taxes. **Assessable penalties** typically are expressed as a flat dollar amount. Because of the lack of jurisdiction by the Tax Court or a specific statutory exemption, assessable penalties are not subject to review by the Tax Court. The Code characterizes tax penalties as additions to tax; thus, they cannot subsequently be deducted by the taxpayer.[1]

Civil penalties are imposed when the tax statutes are violated without **reasonable cause**, as the result of **negligence** or unwillful disregard of pertinent rules, or through a willful disobedience or outright **fraud**. The most important civil penalties include the following:

- Failure to file a tax return

- Failure to pay tax

- Accuracy-related penalties

- Failure to pay estimated income taxes

- Failure to make deposits of taxes or overstatement of such deposits

- Giving false information with respect to withholding

- Filing a frivolous return

Failure to File a Tax Return   When a taxpayer fails to file a required tax return, a penalty is imposed unless it is shown that the failure is due to some reasonable cause and not to the taxpayer's willful neglect. The **failure-to-file penalty** is 5 percent of the amount of the tax, less any prior payments and credits, for each month (or fraction thereof) that the return is not filed. The maximum penalty that may be imposed is 25 percent (or five months' cumulative penalty). A fraudulent failure to file is subject to a 15 percent monthly penalty, to a 75 percent maximum.[2]

If the taxpayer's failure to file is due to **willful neglect**, there is a minimum penalty for a failure to file an income tax return within 60 days of the due date, including extensions. This minimum penalty is the lesser of $135, or the full amount of taxes that are

---

[1]§6665(a)(1).

[2]§§6651(a)(1) and (f).

required to be shown on the return. The penalty does not apply if the failure is due to reasonable cause.[3] This penalty is applied in lieu of, rather than in addition to, some other penalty.

No statutory or administrative definition exists for the term "reasonable cause." However, some courts define it to include such action as would prompt an ordinary, intelligent person to act in the same manner as did the taxpayer under similar circumstances. One of the most commonly encountered examples of reasonable cause is the reliance on the advice of competent tax counsel.[4] However, a recent Tax Court decision held that a corporation was liable for employment tax penalties for failure to file its employment taxes on time even though the company had relied on a CPA to file the returns.[5]

Other examples of reasonable cause that the Internal Revenue Manual describes include the following:

- A timely mailed return that is returned for insufficient postage.

- Death or serious illness of the taxpayer or his or her immediate family.

- Destruction of the taxpayer's residence, place of business, or records by fire or other casualty.

- Proper forms that were not furnished by the IRS.

- Erroneous information obtained from IRS personnel.

- A timely mailed return sent to the wrong IRS address.

- An unavoidable absence by the taxpayer.

- An unavoidable inability to obtain records necessary to compute the tax.

- Some other inability to obtain assistance from IRS personnel.

  However, the penalty will not be excused for any of the following reasons:

- The taxpayer lacks the necessary funds with which to pay the tax.[6]

- The taxpayer was hospitalized and suffered from an illness that was not incapacitating.[7]

- The taxpayer was incarcerated.[8]

- The taxpayer allegedly was ignorant of the laws.[9]

To avoid the penalty, the taxpayer must meet the burden of proof that the failure to file (or to pay) was due to reasonable cause. In these situations, the IRS's determination of the penalty is presumed to be correct.

---

[3] §6651(a)(3).

[4] See, for example, *Chamberlin*, TC Memo 2000-50.

[5] *McNair Eye Center*, Inc. TC Memo 2010-81

[6] *Langston*, 36 T.C.M. 1703 (1977).

[7] *Hernandez*, 72 T.C. 1234 (1979).

[8] *Jones*, 55 T.C.M. 1556 (1988).

[9] *Lammerts Estate v. Comm.*, 456 F.2d 681 (CA-2, 1972).

SPOTLIGHT ON TAXATION

When Is a Return Filed?

To avoid the §6651 penalty, a return must be "filed." Some taxpayers think that sending in a blank form, or neglecting to sign the return, is enough to avoid this penalty, but the tax law says otherwise. The taxpayer information must be included in a readable format, almost always on the correct IRS form, mailed by the due date, and signed by the appropriate parties. There must be enough information on the return so as to compute the correct amount of tax; thus, leaving lines or check-boxes empty will void the filing, and the penalty will be assessed.

As electronic filing requirements are imposed on various taxpayers, both to speed up the system and to eliminate the possibility of errors, IRS software will not accept an incomplete or frivolous return. This is also a way to verify tax identification numbers to immediately identify those with other delinquent accounts or with inadequate filing credentials.

Civil penalties also apply for failure to file partnership or S corporation returns. The penalty is a statutory dollar amount of $195 per partner or shareholder for each month (or fraction of a month), up to a maximum of 12 months.[10]

Failure to Pay Tax   If a taxpayer fails to pay either a tax that is shown on his or her return or an assessed deficiency within 10 days of an IRS notice and demand, a **failure-to-pay penalty** is imposed. The 10-day period becomes 21 days when the tax due is less than $100,000.[11] The penalty is 0.5 percent of the required liability, after adjusting for any prior payments and credits, for each month (or fraction thereof) that the tax is not paid—but it increases to 1 percent of the underpaid tax per month after notice and demand is issued by the IRS.[12] The maximum penalty that may be imposed is 25 percent of the outstanding tax. This penalty does not apply if the failure to pay is attributable to a reasonable cause or to the failure to pay an estimated tax for which there is a different penalty.

For this purpose, reasonable cause is defined in a manner that is identical to that discussed in conjunction with the failure-to-file penalty except that, if an individual is granted an automatic filing extension, reasonable cause is presumed to exist provided that the balance due does not exceed 10 percent of the total tax.[13]

The failure-to-file penalty is reduced by the 0.5 percent failure-to-pay penalty for any month in which both apply. Thus, no more than a 5 percent total (non-fraud) penalty typically can be assessed against a taxpayer for any month. Nonetheless, after rendering sufficient notice to the taxpayer, the IRS can assess both the failure-to-pay and the failure-to-file penalties.

A taxpayer can avoid the failure-to-file penalty if an extension of the return's due date is granted by the IRS. With the two exceptions just discussed, however, the failure-to-pay penalty is imposed when the total amount of the tax is not paid by the unextended due date of the return.

---

[10]§6698(b)(1) and 6699(b)(1).

[11]§6651(a)(3).

[12]§§6651(a)(2) and (d)(1). The monthly penalty rate is cut in half for taxpayers paying delinquent taxes under an installment agreement. §6651(h).

[13]§6654(d)(1)(B)(i).

EXAMPLE 14-1

John Gray, a calendar-year taxpayer, filed his 2010 income tax return on October 20, 2011, paying an amount due of $1,000. On April 1, 2011, John had obtained a six-month extension of time in which to file his return. However, he could not assert a reasonable cause for failing to file the return by October 15, 2011 (the extended due date), nor did he show any reasonable cause for failing to pay the tax that was due on April 15, 2011. Gray's failure to file was not fraudulent. As a result, Gray is subject to a $35 failure-to-pay penalty and a $45 failure-to-file penalty, determined as follows:

Failure to pay

Underpayment	$1,000
Penalty percentage	× .005
Penalty per month outstanding	$ 5
Months (or fractions thereof) for which required payment was not made	×7
Failure-to-pay penalty	$ 35

Failure to file

Underpayment	$1,000
Penalty percentage	× .05
Penalty per month outstanding (before reduction)	$ 50
Months (or fractions thereof) for which return was not filed	×1
Unreduced penalty	$ 50
Less: concomitant failure-to-pay penalty (portion of October) [1 month × (.005 × $1,000)]	−5
Failure-to-file penalty	$ 45

Accuracy-Related Penalty   Major penalties relating to the accuracy of the return data, including the existing negligence penalty and the penalty for substantial understatement of income tax liability, are combined in a single Code section. This consolidation of related penalties into a single levy eliminates the possibility of the stacking of multiple penalties when more than one type of penalty applies to a single understatement of tax.

The **accuracy-related penalty** amounts to 20 percent of the portion of the tax underpayment that is attributable to one or more of the following:

- Negligence or disregard of applicable Federal tax rules and Regulations.

- Substantial understatement of income tax.

- Substantial valuation overstatement.

- Substantial overstatement of pension liabilities.

- Substantial understatement of estate and gift tax valuation.

The penalty applies only where the taxpayer fails to show either a reasonable cause for the underpayment or a good-faith effort to comply with the tax law.[14] When the accuracy-related penalty applies, interest on the penalty accrues from the due date of the return rather than merely from the date on which the penalty was imposed.

Occasionally, a valuation overstatement penalty is encountered. This 20 percent penalty applies when an asset value has been overstated on a return, for example, to

---
[14] §6662.

SPOTLIGHT ON TAXATION

Tax Court Rejects TurboTax Defense

In his Senate confirmation hearing, Treasury Secretary Timothy Geithner appeared to blame TurboTax for the errors on his tax returns in which he failed to pay self-employment taxes on the payments he received from the International Monetary Fund. However, in *Parker v. Commissioner*, T.C. Summary Opinion 2010-78 (June 21, 2010), the Tax Court rejected the "TurboTax defense" used by Geithner in refusing to waive the accuracy-related penalty for reasonable cause as provided for by Code Sec. 6664(c).

In so doing, the Court noted that "regardless of the facts and circumstances relating to the case to which petitioner refers involving U.S. Secretary of the Treasury Timothy Geithner, petitioner is required to establish on the basis of the facts and circumstances that are established by the record in his own case that there was reasonable cause for, and that he acted in good faith with respect to the underpayment ...".

substantiate a charitable contribution deduction. It is assessed when the valuation used is 150 percent or more of the actual value, resulting in an underpayment of more than $5,000 ($10,000 for C corporations).

Similarly, a 20 percent transfer tax valuation understatement penalty is assessed where the claimed value is 65 percent or less than the asset's actual value, resulting in an underpayment of over $5,000. The rate of both penalties is 40 percent if a gross valuation misstatement is made; that is, the income tax valuation was at least 200 percent of actual value or the transfer tax value was 40 percent or less of actual value.[15]

The practitioner is likely to encounter two of the elements of this penalty most frequently: negligence or disregard of rules and substantial understatement of tax. In the first penalty, "negligence" includes any failure to make a reasonable attempt to comply with the provisions of the Code.[16] This might occur when the taxpayer fails to report gross income, overstates deductions, or fails to keep adequate records with which to comply with the law. "Disregard" includes any careless, reckless, or intentional disregard of the elements of the tax law.

The negligence component of the penalty is waived when the taxpayer has made a good-faith attempt to comply with the law, as indicated by a full disclosure of the non-frivolous position that may be contrary to that of the IRS. Such disclosure is made by completing Form 8275, the first page of which is reproduced as Exhibit 14-1, and attaching it to the return. If the return position is contrary to the language of a Regulation, Form 8275-R is used.

The second commonly encountered penalty, substantial understatement of income tax, occurs if the determined understatement exceeds the greater of 10 percent of the proper tax liability or $5,000. The understatement must exceed the lesser of the following for a corporation other than an S corporation or a personal holding company:[17]

- 10 percent of the proper tax liability, or

- $10,000, if greater

OR

- $10,000,000

---

[15]§6662(e) through (h).

[16]§6662(c).

[17]§6662(d)(1).

EXHIBIT 14-1:   Disclosure Statement

Form **8275** (Rev. August 2008) Department of the Treasury Internal Revenue Service	**Disclosure Statement** Do not use this form to disclose items or positions that are contrary to Treasury regulations. Instead, use Form 8275-R, Regulation Disclosure Statement. See separate instructions. ▶ **Attach to your tax return.**	OMB No. 1545-0889 Attachment Sequence No. **92**
Name(s) shown on return		**Identifying number shown on return**

Part I   **General Information** (see instructions)

(a) Rev. Rul., Rev. Proc., etc.	(b) Item or Group of Items	(c) Detailed Description of Items	(d) Form or Schedule	(e) Line No.	(f) Amount
1					
2					
3					

Part II   **Detailed Explanation** (see instructions)

1

2

3

Part III   **Information About Pass-Through Entity.** To be completed by partners, shareholders, beneficiaries, or residual interest holders.

Complete this part only if you are making adequate disclosure for a pass-through item.

Note: *A pass-through entity is a partnership, S corporation, estate, trust, regulated investment company (RIC), real estate investment trust (REIT), or real estate mortgage investment conduit (REMIC).*

1 Name, address, and ZIP code of pass-through entity	**2** Identifying number of pass-through entity
	3 Tax year of pass-through entity / / to / /
	4 Internal Revenue Service Center where the pass-through entity filed its return

For Paperwork Reduction Act Notice, see separate instructions.   Cat. No. 61935M   Form **8275** (Rev. 8-2008)

The amount that is subject to this penalty is reduced if the taxpayer either has substantial authority for the position that was taken in the return or makes a full disclosure of a position taken in the return where there is a reasonable basis for the position, on Form 8275 or 8275-R.[18] More specifically, the taxpayer is not subject to this penalty where there is **substantial authority** for his or her position.[19]

For this purpose, "substantial authority" includes the Code, Regulations (proposed and temporary), court decisions, administrative pronouncements, tax treaties, IRS information and press releases, IRS Notices and Announcements, Letter Rulings, Technical Advice Memoranda, General Counsel Memoranda, Committee Reports, and "Blue Book" explanations of tax legislation.[20] Substantial authority does not include conclusions reached in tax treatises, legal periodicals, and opinions rendered by tax professionals.[21]

Clearly, greater weight is placed on the Code and temporary Regulations than will be assigned to Letter Rulings and IRS Notices, but the derivation of a weighted average among all of the competing positions with respect to a given tax question is not likely to be obtained easily.

Civil Fraud If any part of an underpayment of tax is attributable to fraud, a substantial civil penalty is imposed. In addition, the taxpayer may be liable for a criminal penalty, which will be discussed later in this chapter. The civil fraud penalty is 75 percent of the underpayment that is attributable to the fraud.[22]

The burden of proof in a fraud case is on the IRS; it must show a fraudulent intent for the underpayment. This intent usually entails more than mere negligence, but a plan to defraud the government, often including a series of actions over time to evade the tax.

Under an all-or-nothing rule, if the IRS establishes that any portion of an underpayment is attributable to fraud, the entire underpayment is treated as attributable to fraud, and the penalty applies to the entire amount due. If the taxpayer shows that any part of an underpayment is not attributable to fraud, however, then the fraud penalty is not imposed with respect to that amount.[23] Neither the failure-to-file, nor the failure-to-pay penalty, nor the civil accuracy-related penalty, is assessed in these circumstances. However, the penalty for underpayment of estimated tax (discussed later) may still be assessed, and interest is assessed from the (extended) due date of the return.

Fraud is not defined in either the Code or the Regulations. One longstanding judicial definition of fraud describes it as " ... actual, intentional wrongdoing ... the intent required is the specific purpose to evade a tax believed to be owing."[24] This definition has been expanded to include acts that are done without a "bad or evil purpose." In *U.S. v. Pomponio,* the Supreme Court held that "willfulness," which is a crucial element of fraud, is present when the taxpayer's actions constitute " ... a voluntary, intentional violation of a known legal duty."[25] Consequently, the taxpayer's deceptive or misleading conduct distinguishes fraud from mere negligence, or from other actions that are taken to avoid taxation, and not the presence of some (inherent or documented) evil purpose.

---

[18]§6662(d)(2)(B). Tax shelters cannot use this provision.

[19]§6662(d)(2)(B).

[20]Reg. §1.6662-4(d)(iii).

[21]Notice 90-20, 1990-1 CB 328.

[22]§§6663(a) and (b).

[23]§6663(b).

[24]*Mitchell v. Comm.,* 118 F.2d 308, 310 (CA-5, 1941).

[25]429 U.S. 10, 97 S.Ct. 22 (1976).

SPOTLIGHT ON TAXATION

Proving Fraud

The courts factor in the education and experience of the taxpayer in determining whether fraud has occurred. Is the taxpayer "smart" enough in terms of business and accounting training to construct a plan to defraud, and then to carry it out? In cases of a complicated tax law or tax-reduction device, the taxpayer might successfully plead ignorance and avoid the fraud charge.

If a taxpayer is convicted of criminal fraud, he or she cannot contest a civil fraud determination. However, a charge that the taxpayer is guilty of criminal fraud may be contested when a civil fraud determination has been upheld. In a criminal fraud case, the IRS must prove "beyond a shadow of any reasonable doubt" that the taxpayer's actions were fraudulent. In a civil fraud case, there must be "clear and convincing evidence" that the taxpayer committed fraud.

Ordinarily, the evidence that indicates that a taxpayer's conduct was fraudulent is circumstantial. Thus, the court must infer the taxpayer's state of mind from the evidence. Examples of fraud include the following:

- Keeping two sets of books, one in English and one in Japanese.[26]
- Making false accounting entries.[27]
- Destroying books or records.[28]
- Concealing assets or sources of income.[29]
- Consistently understating income or overstating deductions.[30]
- Purposely avoiding the making of business records and receipts.[31]

Failure to Make Estimated Payments   A penalty is imposed on both individuals and corporations who fail to pay quarterly estimated income taxes. This penalty is based on the amount and duration of the underpayment and the rate of interest that currently is established by the Code. This rate, for instance, was 4 percent in mid-2010. Unlike the similar interest computation, however, this penalty is computed without any daily compounding and is not deductible.

The penalty is calculated separately for each quarterly installment. Each penalty period begins on the date on which the installment was required, and it runs through the earlier of either the date that the amount is paid or the due date for filing the return. Any overpayment is first applied to prior underpayments, and the excess is credited to

[26]*Noro v. U.S.,* 148 F.2d 696 (CA-5, 1945).

[27]*U.S. v. Lange,* 161 F.2d 699 (CA-7, 1947).

[28]*U.S. v. Ragen,* 314 U.S. 513, 62 S.Ct. 374 (1942).

[29]*Gendelman v. U.S.,* 191 F.2d 993 (CA-9, 1952).

[30]*Holland v. U.S.,* 348 U.S. 121, 75 S.Ct. 127 (1954) and *Ragen, op.cit.*

[31]*Garispy v. U.S.,* 220 F.2d 252 (CA-6, 1955).

later installments.[32] In this regard, the taxpayer must balance cash flow concerns with the payment requirements of the Code.

EXAMPLE 14-2

The taxpayer is required to have $100 paid in as estimates for the year. Payment schedule A would likely incur an underpayment penalty, while schedule B would not.

Quarter	Schedule A	Schedule B
1	$ 10	$ 40
2	40	10
3	10	40
4	40	10
Total	$100	$100

Individuals   An individual's underpayment of estimated tax is computed as the difference between the amounts that were paid by the quarterly due dates and the least of the following:

- 90 percent of the tax that is shown on the current year's return.

- 100 percent of the prior year's tax, if a return was filed for that tax year of 12 months. The threshold increases to 110 percent if the adjusted gross income reported on that return is more than $150,000.

- 90 percent of the tax that would be figured by annualizing the income that was earned during the year, up to the month in which the quarterly payment is due.[33]

For this purpose, unless the taxpayer can prove otherwise, taxes that are withheld are considered to have been remitted to the IRS in equal quarterly installments.[34]

The underpayment penalty will not apply if less than $1,000 in under-withheld tax is due. Thus, an individual can avoid the estimated tax underpayment penalty if the preceding taxable year included 12 months, the individual did not have any tax liability for the preceding year, and he or she was a citizen or resident of the United States throughout the preceding taxable year.[35]

The IRS can waive the estimated tax underpayment penalty (but not the penalty that is based on the outstanding interest attributable thereto) if the failure to make the payment was due to a casualty, disaster, or other unusual circumstance where it would be inequitable to impose the penalty. The IRS can also waive the penalty if the failure was due to reasonable cause rather than willful neglect during the first two years after the taxpayer retires after reaching age 62, or becomes disabled.[36] The fourth installment penalty is waived if the corresponding tax return is filed with full tax payment by the end of the first month after the tax year-end (January 31 for calendar-year taxpayers).

Corporations   An underpayment on the part of a corporation is defined as the difference between the amount of the installment that would be required to be paid if the

---

[32]§§6654(b) and 6655(b).

[33]§6654(d). The rule is 110 percent of the prior-year tax if that year's AGI > $150,000.

[34]§6654(g).

[35]§§6654(e)(1) and (2).

[36]§6654(e)(3).

estimated tax was equal to 100 percent of the tax that is shown on the return (or, if no return was filed, 100 percent of the actual tax that is due), and the amount that was actually paid on or before the prescribed payment date.[37] The underpayment penalty will not apply if less than $500 in tax is due or if the total payments that are made by the applicable installment date are equal to the least of the following:

1. 100 percent of the non-zero amount of tax that is shown on the corporation's tax return for the preceding year, provided that the preceding year contained 12 months.

2. 100 percent of the current-year tax liability.

3. 100 percent of the tax that is due using a seasonal installment method, or annualizing the current year's income received for (1) the first two or three months, relative to the installment that is due in the fourth month of the tax year, (2) the first three, four, or five months, for the installment that is due in the sixth month, (3) the first six, seven, or eight months, for the installment that is due in the ninth month, or (4) the first nine, ten, or eleven months, for the installment that is due in the twelfth month as elected.[38]

Exception 1 does not apply to a "large corporation;" that is, one that had a taxable income of $1 million or more in any of its three immediately preceding taxable years. To avoid an underpayment penalty, a large corporation can use the prior year safe harbor for the first quarter estimate but must remit quarterly estimated tax payments for the rest of the year that are equal to its current year's tax liability, or it must meet Exception 3, as discussed.[39]

Failure to Make Deposits of Taxes or Overstatements of Deposits   The Code requires employers to collect and withhold income and Social Security taxes from their employees. Amounts that are withheld are considered to be held in a special trust fund for the United States, and they must be deposited in a government depository on or before certain dates prescribed by the statutes and Regulations. An employer who does not have either the inclination or sufficient funds with which to meet its deposit obligations may be tempted to postpone the making of these deposits; that is, to "borrow" from the government the cash provided by employees.

Consequently, the Code imposes heavy civil and criminal penalties on those who are responsible for the failure to make a timely deposit of the withheld funds.[40] A responsible party may be an officer or board member of a corporation rather than the corporation itself, even for charities and other exempt entities.

If an employer fails to deposit on a timely basis taxes that were withheld from employees, a penalty equal to a percentage of the underpayment is imposed. This rate varies from 2 to 15 percent, depending on when the failure is corrected.[41] The penalty may be avoided where the taxpayer can show that his or her actions were due to reasonable cause and not to willful neglect.

---

[37]§6655(b)(1).

[38]§§6655(d), (e), and (f).

[39]§§6654(d)(2) and (g)(2). The prior-year exception can be used in making the first-quarter installment, however. §6654(d)(2)(B).

[40]§6656.

[41]§6656(b)(1).

If any person who is required to collect, truthfully account for, and remit employment taxes willfully fails to do so, a penalty equal to 100 percent of the tax is imposed.[42] Therefore, when a corporate employer willfully does not pay employment taxes to the government that it withheld from an employee, the IRS effectively may collect the tax from those who are responsible for the corporate actions, such as the corporate directors, president, or treasurer.[43]

In addition to the civil penalties that have been discussed, criminal penalties may be imposed in an aggravated case of nonpayment.

Giving False Information with Respect to Withholding All employees are required to give their employer a completed Form W-4, Employee Withholding Allowance Certificate. This form notifies the employer of the number of withholding exemptions that the employee is entitled to claim. The employer then calculates the amount of tax that must be withheld from each employee. A civil penalty of $500 is imposed on any person who gives to his or her employer false information with respect to withholding status or the number of exemptions to which he or she is entitled. This penalty is not imposed where there was a reasonable basis for the taxpayer's statement. Moreover, the IRS may waive all or part of the penalty if the actual income taxes that are imposed are not greater than the sum of the allowable credits and estimated tax payments.[44]

Employers who receive a Form W-4 from an employee, on which he or she claims more than 10 exemptions, must submit a copy of the form to the IRS.[45]

Filing a Frivolous Return A separate $5,000 civil penalty is assessed when the taxpayer is found to have filed a **frivolous return**.[46] Returns of this sort have been used to assert that the taxpayer's Fifth Amendment rights are violated by tax return disclosures,[47] that the taxpayer objects to the use of his or her tax receipts for defense or other uses,[48] that the government can collect taxes only in gold-based coins and certificates (which no longer circulate freely in the United States), or some other argument. Specifically, the penalty applies in the following cases:

- When the return does not contain information by which to judge the completeness of the taxpayer's self-assessment (e.g., if the return is blank).

- When the return contains information or statements that on their face indicate that the self-assessment requirement has not been met (e.g., a "tax protestor" statement is attached).

- The return otherwise takes positions that are frivolous or are meant to impede the administration of the tax law, such as when it takes a return position contrary to a decision of the U.S. Supreme Court, or it is not presented in a readable format.

Other Civil Penalties A variety of other civil penalties may be imposed on taxpayers who fail to comply with the Code. Most of these penalties involve a specialized area of the tax law and ordinarily are not encountered by taxpayers. Consequently, one should be

---

[42]§6672(a).

[43]§§6671(b), 7809(a).

[44]§6682.

[45]Reg. §31.3402(f)(2)-1(g).

[46]§6702.

[47]*Welch v. U.S.*, 750 F.2d 1101 (CA-1, 1985).

[48]*Fuller v. U.S.*, 786 F.2d 1437 (CA-9, 1986).

SPOTLIGHT ON TAXATION

Frivolous Returns

The $5,000 penalty will not be assessed in the course of a typical dispute over the amount of tax due, for example, on an audit where both sides have defensible positions concerning the law. The penalty also is not applied in the case of a mathematical/clerical error. However, the penalty relates to the original return as filed; that is, the penalty is not waived if the taxpayer "fixes" the problem by filing an amended return.

The frivolous-return penalty applies even if the taxpayer legitimately owes a zero tax, and if the taxpayer was not required to file a return (e.g., due to low taxable income) but did so anyway.

aware of the existence of such sanctions and refer to the Code and Regulations when working in such a specialized field to identify the events that might trigger such penalties.

Reliance on Written Advice of the IRS   The Secretary of the Treasury must abate any civil penalty or addition to tax that is attributable to the taxpayer's reliance on erroneous written advice furnished by an IRS officer or employee. This abatement is available only with respect to advice given in response to a specific request by the taxpayer, and it is negated if the IRS error was made due to a lack of information provided by the taxpayer.[49]

Criminal Penalties

In addition to the civil penalties that we have discussed so far, the Code prescribes a number of **criminal penalties** for certain acts of taxpayer noncompliance. The criminal penalties are intended "to prohibit and punish fraud occurring in the assessment and collection of taxes."[50] They are imposed only after the implementation of the constitutional criminal process, under which the taxpayer is entitled to the same rights and privileges as other criminal defendants.

Nature of Criminal Penalties   Criminal and civil penalties are not mutually exclusive. Consequently, a taxpayer may be acquitted of a criminal tax offense but still be liable for a corresponding civil tax penalty. The IRS bears a greater burden of proof with respect to a criminal case. Moreover, the taxpayer holds the right to refuse to answer inquiries that are made by the IRS in a criminal setting if he or she would suffer a loss of some constitutional right by answering.

Ordinarily, criminal prosecutions are limited to flagrant offenses for which the IRS believes it is virtually certain to obtain a conviction. As a result, the IRS usually limits its charges to the civil penalty provisions. In the typical context, according to Section 100 of the *IRS Law Enforcement Manual IX*, criminal prosecutions are limited to cases in which the additional tax that will be generated from a successful prosecution is substantial, the crime appears to have been committed in three consecutive years, or the taxpayer's flagrant or repetitive conduct was so egregious that the IRS believes that it is virtually certain to obtain a conviction. As a result, the IRS usually will not engage in a criminal prosecution when the taxpayer's noncompliance can be corrected by imposing civil penalties.

---

[49]§6404(f).

[50]*U.S. v. White*, 417 F.2d 89, 93 (CA-2).

Criminal Tax Offenses The principal criminal offenses that are addressed by the Code include the following:

- Willful attempt to evade or defeat a tax (i.e., tax evasion)—a felony offense that is punishable by a fine that is not to exceed $100,000 ($500,000 for corporations), reimbursement of the government's cost of prosecution, and/or imprisonment for a period that is not to exceed five years.[51]

SPOTLIGHT ON TAXATION

Tax Criminals

Prosecutions for tax crimes have brought down some highly visible individuals, including political and entertainment figures, but the penalties can be used against any taxpayer as the following IRS information on criminal investigations in the construction industry and medical profession demonstrates:

IRS Criminal Investigation Construction Industry Statistics

	FY 2009	FY 2008	FY 2007
Investigations Initiated	338	268	325
Prosecution Recommendations	149	197	163
Indictments	140	153	140
Convictions	139	150	121
Sentenced	149	140	100
Incarceration Rate*	77.9%	76.4%	70%
Average Months to Serve	29	28	24

*Incarceration may include prison time, home confinement, electronic monitoring, or a combination of all three.
Data Source: **http://www.irs.gov/compliance/enforcement/article/0,,id=163008,00.html.**

IRS Criminal Investigation Medical Professional Statistics*

	FY 2009	FY 2008	FY 2007
Investigations Initiated	104	108	170
Prosecution Recommendations	69	94	103
Indictments	65	83	83
Convictions	57	70	63
Sentenced	69	65	59
Incarceration Rate**	76.8%	72.3%	79.7%
Average Months to Serve	28	19	21

*The data in this table only reflected the occupation of doctor. On October 16, 2009, the data in this table were revised to reflect individuals in all medical professions, including doctors, dentists, nurses, pharmacists, and so forth for all fiscal years.
**Incarceration includes confinement to Federal prison, halfway house, home detention, or some combination thereof.
Data Source: Criminal Investigation Management Information System.

---

[51]§7201.

- Willful failure to collect, account for, and remit any tax, by any person who is required to do so—a felony offense that is punishable by a fine that is not to exceed $10,000, reimbursement of the government's cost of prosecution, and/or imprisonment for a period that is not to exceed five years.[52]

- Willful failure to file a return, supply information, or pay tax or estimated tax—a misdemeanor offense that is punishable by a fine that is not to exceed $25,000 ($100,000 for corporations), reimbursement of the government's cost of prosecution, and/or imprisonment for a period that is not to exceed one year (five years and felony status for returns relative to money laundering rules; that is, large amounts of cash received by a business).[53]

- Willful making, subscribing, or aiding or assisting in the making of a return or other document that is verified by a declaration under the penalties of perjury, and that the person does not believe to be true and correct as to every material matter—a felony offense that is punishable by a fine not to exceed $100,000 ($500,000 for corporations), reimbursement of the government's cost of prosecution, and/or imprisonment for a period that is not to exceed three years.[54]

- Willful filing of any known-to-be-false or fraudulent document—a misdemeanor offense that is punishable by a fine that is not to exceed $10,000 ($50,000 for corporations) and/or imprisonment for a period not to exceed one year.[55]

- Disclosure or use of any information that is furnished to a person who is engaged in the business of preparing tax returns, or providing services in connection with the preparation of tax returns, for purposes other than the preparation of the return—a misdemeanor offense that is punishable by a fine not to exceed $1,000 and/or imprisonment for a period not to exceed one year.[56]

In addition to the penalties just described, the Code prescribes a number of other criminal penalties that ordinarily are not encountered on a regular basis. Most of these penalties involve a specialized area of the tax law. Consequently, one should be aware of the existence of such sanctions and refer to the Code and Regulations when working in such a specialized field to identify them.

Defenses to Criminal Penalties   The standard for conviction in a criminal case is the establishment of guilt beyond a reasonable doubt. With respect to criminal tax cases, taxpayers have had some success in presenting one or more of the following defenses—that is, to establish some doubt in the minds of the court or the jury:

- Unreported income was offset fully by unreported deductions.[57]

- Unreported income was in reality a gift or some other excludible receipt.[58]

---

[52]§7202.

[53]§§7203 and 6050I.

[54]§7206.

[55]§7207.

[56]§7216.

[57]*Koontz v. U.S.*, 277 F.2d 53 (CA-5, 1960).

[58]*DiZenzo v. Comm.*, 348 F.2d 122 (CA-2, 1965).

- The taxpayer was confused or ignorant as to the applicable law; thus, one cannot intend to violate the tax law if he or she does not know what that law is.[59]

- The taxpayer relied on the erroneous advice of a competent tax adviser.[60]

- The taxpayer has a mental disease or defect, so could not have acted willfully to violate the tax law.[61]

- The statute of limitations (discussed later in this chapter) has expired.

- The taxpayer enters a plea bargain and accepts conviction on a lesser offense.

Penalties on Return Preparers

Individuals who prepare income tax returns or refund claims for compensation are subject to a number of disclosure requirements and penalties for improper conduct in the preparation of those documents. These provisions were added to the Code as more and more taxpayers utilized some form of professional assistance in preparing their income tax returns. Moreover, a significant percentage of returns that were prepared by return preparers indicated some fraud potential.

The return preparer penalties apply to all Federal tax returns. Most of them are mild, ranging from $50 for the failure to furnish an identification number to $1,000 for the aiding and abetting of an understatement of a tax liability. As these sanctions may be applied cumulatively, however, their magnitude can become more substantial. In addition, the criminal penalties that may be imposed on the return preparer provide for substantial monetary fines and jail terms.

Some of these rules are discussed in Chapters 1 and 2. For both taxpayer and tax preparer, the penalty system "encourages" a lawful application of the tax rules by all by raising the cost of the tax when specific requirements are violated.

Definition of Return Preparer

A **tax return preparer (TRP)** is any person who prepares for compensation, or employs one or more persons to prepare for compensation, all or a substantial portion of a tax return or claim for income tax refund.[62] A TRP can be an employer, employee, or a self-employed person. This distinction is important because certain penalties are imposed only on a selected type of preparer. For instance, only an employee preparer is subject to a negligence or fraud penalty, unless the employer participated in the wrongdoing. To determine whether the employer or employee return preparer (or both) is liable for a certain penalty, the Regulations that relate to that penalty must be consulted.

A person must prepare a tax return for compensation if he or she is to be subject to the return preparer sanctions. If a return is prepared gratuitously, the preparer is not a TRP. The preparer also must prepare all or a substantial portion of a return if the TRP sanctions are to apply. In determining whether the work that has been performed by the party is substantial, a comparison must be made between the length and complexity of the prepared schedule, entry, or other item and the total liability or refund claim.

---

[59]*U.S. v. Critzer,* 498 F.2d 1160 (CA-4, 1974). This is not a mere disagreement with the law, which is not an acceptable defense. *U.S. v. Schiff,* 801 F.2d 108 (CA-2, 1986), cert. den.

[60]*U.S. v. Phillips,* 217 F.2d 435 (CA-7, 1954).

[61]*U.S. v. Erickson,* 676 F.2d 408 (CA-10, 1982).

[62]§7701(a)(36)(A).

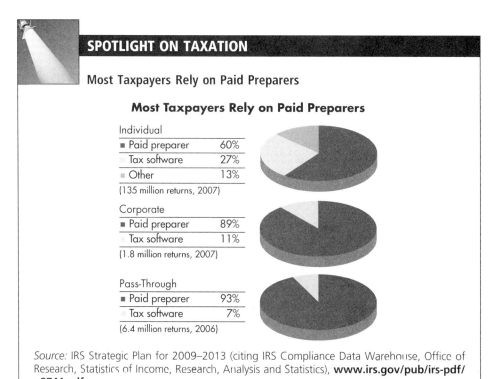

SPOTLIGHT ON TAXATION

Most Taxpayers Rely on Paid Preparers

Most Taxpayers Rely on Paid Preparers

Individual
■ Paid preparer	60%
Tax software	27%
■ Other	13%

(135 million returns, 2007)

Corporate
■ Paid preparer	89%
Tax software	11%

(1.8 million returns, 2007)

Pass-Through
■ Paid preparer	93%
Tax software	7%

(6.4 million returns, 2006)

Source: IRS Strategic Plan for 2009–2013 (citing IRS Compliance Data Warehouse, Office of Research, Statistics of Income, Research, Analysis and Statistics), **www.irs.gov/pub/irs-pdf/ p3744.pdf**.

The Regulations adopt two objective safe harbors in determining what constitutes a substantial portion of a return or claim. If a schedule, entry, or other item involves amounts that are less than $2,000 or less than $100,000 and also less than 20 percent of the gross income (or adjusted gross income, where the taxpayer is an individual) that is shown on the return, then the item is not substantial.[63]

Definition of Return Preparation

In constructing a definition of the TRP, one first must define the domain of return preparation. Return preparation includes activities other than the mere physical completion of a return. The IRS asserts that tax advisers, planners, software designers, and consultants are all tax preparers, even though they may only review the return or give the taxpayer instructions on its completion.

According to the Regulations, one who furnishes a taxpayer or other preparer with "sufficient information and advice so that completion of the return or claim for refund is largely a mechanical matter" is a TRP.[64] However, an adviser is not a TRP when the advice is given with respect to completed transactions or for other than tax return filing purposes.

A person is not a TRP merely because he or she:[65]

- Furnishes typing, reproducing, or other clerical assistance.

- Prepares a return or refund claim of his or her regular employer or of an officer or employee of the employer.

---

[63]Reg. §301.7701-15(b)(2).

[64]Reg. §301.7701-15(a)(1).

[65]§7701(a)(36)(B) and Reg. §§301.7701-5(a)(2) through (7).

- Prepares as a fiduciary a return or claim for refund.

- Prepares a claim for refund during the course of an audit or appeal.

- Provides general tax advice to a taxpayer.

- Is an employee or official of the IRS, while performing job-related duties.

- Prepares the return for no compensation.

- Works for IRS-sponsored programs such as Volunteer Income Tax Assistance, Tax Counseling for the Elderly, or a Low-Income Tax Clinic.

Being classified as a TRP is not directly based on the attainment of a certificate or degree or the completion of continuing education requirements, but on the substantial completion of a tax return for compensation.

Preparer Disclosure Penalties

Five key **preparer penalties** may be imposed on those who do not comply with certain disclosure requirements, as follows:[66]

- A penalty of $50 for each return may be imposed on a TRP if the taxpayer is not given a complete copy of the return when it is presented to him or her for signature.

- A penalty of $50 for each return may be imposed on a TRP if he or she fails to sign the return.

- A penalty of $50 for each return is imposed on a TRP if the preparer's identification number or that of his or her employer, or both, is not listed on each completed return.

- A penalty of $50 for each failure is imposed on a TRP if he or she does not retain a copy of all returns that he or she prepared. Alternatively, he or she may retain a list of all of the taxpayers and their identification numbers for whom returns were prepared for the previous three years.

- A penalty of $50 for each failure to retain, and $50 for each item that is omitted, is imposed on a TRP who does not retain records that indicate the name, identification number, and place of work of each preparer who is employed during the 12-month period that begins on July 1 of each year.

In each instance, the maximum penalty for any calendar year is $25,000.

Preparer Conduct Penalties

The Code contains a number of civil and criminal penalties that may be imposed on return preparers relative to their misconduct. The civil penalties were added to the Code because Congress found that a significant number of return preparers were engaging in improper practices, such as guaranteeing refunds or having taxpayers sign blank returns. Except for the criminal penalty of aiding and assisting in the preparation of a false return, however, there were no lesser sanctions that could be applied to return preparers who were guilty of misconduct.

---

[66]§6695.

Civil penalties that may be imposed on preparers relate to the following:

- Endorsing or negotiating a refund check.

- Negligent understatement or intentional disregard of rules and Regulations.

- Willful understatement of tax liability.

- Failing to be diligent in applying eligibility rules for the earned income tax credit.

- Organizing, or assisting in organizing, or promoting and making or furnishing statements with respect to an abusive tax shelter.

- Aiding and abetting the understatement of a tax liability.

- Disclosure or use of return information for other than return preparation.

Return preparers always have been subject to criminal prosecution for willful misconduct. The two principal criminal preparer penalties involve those who aid or assist in the preparation or presentation of a false return, affidavit, claim, or other document,[67] or disclose or use information for other than return preparation purposes.[68]

Endorsing or Negotiating a Refund Check   A TRP may not endorse or otherwise negotiate an income tax refund check that is issued to another person. A preparer who violates this rule is subject to a $500 penalty.[69]

Understatements Due to Unreasonable Positions   A tax preparer incurs a penalty for each occurrence of an understatement of tax due to the taking of an unreasonable position in the return. A position is "unreasonable" unless there is substantial authority for it.[70]

The substantial authority standard under Code Sec. 6694 should be similar to the substantial authority standard under Code Sec. 6662. In general, substantial authority exists if the weight of authorities supporting the taxpayer's treatment is substantial in relation to the weight of those that take a contrary position. For tax shelters and reportable transactions, the law requires a more stringent "more likely than not" standard [Code Sec. 6694(a)(2)(C)].

Code Sec. 6662(d)(2)(C)(ii) defines a tax shelter as a partnership or other entity, any investment plan or arrangement, or any other plan or arrangement that has as a significant purpose the avoidance or evasion of Federal income tax. A reportable transaction is any transaction for which information must be included with a return or statement because as determined under regulations issued under Code Sec. 6011, the transaction has a potential for tax avoidance or evasion.

The penalty applies to a tax return position that is taken on a Federal tax return or a claim for refund. The amount of the penalty does not relate to the amount of understated tax, which is the manner of computing most tax penalties. Rather, the unreasonable-position penalty is computed as the greater of $1,000 or one-half of the return preparer's fees derived from the engagement.[71]

---

[67] §7206(2).

[68] §7213(a)(3).

[69] §6695(f).

[70] §6694(a)(2)(A).

[71] §6694(a)(1).

The penalty is not applied when the position is properly disclosed under Code Sec. 6662(d)(2)(B)(ii)(I), and the preparer shows both that there is a reasonable basis for the understatement and that the preparer acted in good faith [Code Sec. 6694(a)(3)].

EXAMPLE 14-3

Josie prepares a tax return that includes the claiming of a deduction that is contrary to an extant Revenue Ruling. Because of a new court decision in another circuit that is favorable to the deduction, Josie believes that there is a 70 percent chance that the position would be sustained in a suit relative to the deduction. No unreasonable-position penalty applies to Josie, whether the client wins or loses in court, and she need not disclose in any way her variance from the government position on her return.

EXAMPLE 14-4

Return to the facts of Example 14-3, except that Josie believes that the position has a 30 percent probability of success in a court hearing. To avoid any unreasonable-position penalty, Josie must disclose the position, revealing where and how she has deviated from the government's position relative to the deduction. As long as there is a reasonable basis for the disclosed position and Josie acted in good faith, the penalty can be avoided.

EXAMPLE 14-5

Return to the facts of Example 14-3, except that Josie believes that the deduction has a 5 percent probability of prevailing in court. Josie cannot take this filing position on any tax return. This is a frivolous position and would trigger an unreasonable-position penalty.

Willful Understatement   A preparer is subject to a penalty if any part of an understatement of a taxpayer's liability is attributable to the preparer's willful attempt in any manner to understate the liability, or to the reckless or intentional disregard of IRS rules or Regulations.[72] A preparer is considered to have willfully attempted to understate the tax in this manner if he or she disregards information that has been supplied by the tax payer, or by any other person, in an attempt wrongfully to reduce the taxpayer's levy. The penalty is computed as the greater of $5,000 or one-half of the return preparer's related fees.

Organizing Abusive Tax Shelters   A civil penalty may be imposed on any person who organizes or assists in organizing, or (even indirectly) participates in the sale of any interest in, a tax shelter, and who makes or furnishes a statement regarding an expected tax benefit that the person knows or has reason to know is either false or fraudulent, or contains a gross valuation understatement on a material matter.[73]

For this purpose, a gross valuation understatement is a statement of the value of any property or service that exceeds 200 percent of the amount that is determined to be its correct value, if the value of the property or service is directly related to the amount of

---

[72]§6694(b).

[73]§6700.

any allowable deduction or credit.[74] Accordingly, there does not need to be an understatement of tax before this penalty can be applied. The penalty, equal to one-half of the party's related fees from the engagement, can be triggered without an IRS audit, and it can be based only on the shelter's offering materials.

The amount of a valuation overstatement penalty is the lesser of $1,000 or 100 percent of the gross income that is derived from the activity, or is to be derived, by the taxpayer from the project. The IRS may waive all or a portion of the penalty that is attributable to a gross valuation understatement if there was a reasonable basis for the valuation and it was made in good faith.[75]

Although the penalty is not aimed specifically at tax preparers, but rather at the tax shelter industry itself, professional tax advisers may be subject to the penalty because they often assist in organizing tax shelter projects.

Aiding and Abetting Understatement The Code imposes a civil penalty on any person who aids or assists, or procures or advises, in the preparation or presentation of any portion of a return or other tax-related document, if he or she knows or has reason to believe that the return or other document will be used in connection with any material tax matter, and that this use will result in the understatement of another person's tax liability.[76] This penalty may also be imposed on a person who acts in violation of the statute through a subordinate (e.g., an employee or agent) by either ordering or causing the subordinate to act, or knowing of and not attempting to prevent the subordinate from acting, wrongfully.[77]

The amount of the penalty is $1,000 ($10,000 for corporations) for each understating taxpayer. This penalty may be imposed only once per year for each understating taxpayer who is serviced by the TRP. However, it may be imposed in addition to other penalties. Thus, the preparer may also be prosecuted under the criminal statutes.[78]

Aiding or Assisting in the Preparation of a False Return A criminal penalty may be imposed on any person who willfully aids or assists in the preparation of a return or other document that is false as to any material matter. This penalty is the criminal equivalent to the civil penalty for aiding and abetting the understatement of any tax liability.

A person who is convicted of violating this statute is guilty of a felony and is subject to imprisonment for up to three years and/or may be fined an amount that cannot exceed $100,000 ($500,000 for corporations). This is one of the most severe tax preparer penalties under the Code.[79]

The persons who are prosecuted under this statute usually are accountants or other return preparers. However, a person who supplies false information that is used in the preparation of a return may also be subject to this penalty. The penalty can be assessed when it is merely a false tax-related document (like a Form 1099 or W-4), and not a tax return, that is prepared.

Disclosure or Use of Information by Return Preparers The Code imposes a civil penalty on any return preparer who discloses or uses any tax return information for

[74]§6700(b)(1).

[75]§§6700(a)(2) and (b)(2).

[76]§6701(a).

[77]§6701(c).

[78]§6701(b).

[79]§7206(2).

SPOTLIGHT ON TAXATION

Return Preparer Fraud

Criminal Investigation Statistical Information on Return Preparer Fraud

	FY 2009	FY 2008	FY 2007
Investigations Initiated	224	214	218
Prosecution Recommendations	129	134	196
Indictments	149	142	131
Sentenced	136	124	123
Incarceration Rate[*]	85.3%	81.5%	81.3%
Average Months to Serve	24	18	19

[*]Incarceration may include prison time, home confinement, electronic monitoring, or a combination of all three.

Some return preparers have been convicted of, or have pleaded guilty to, felony charges.

Data Source: **http://www.irs.gov/newsroom/article/0,,id=217788,00.html.**

---

other than the purpose of preparing a tax return. This penalty amounts to $250 per improper use; a preparer's maximum penalty for any calendar year is $10,000. The Code also imposes a criminal penalty on any return preparer who knowingly or recklessly discloses or uses any tax return information for other than the specific purpose of preparing a tax return. One who is convicted of violating this statute is guilty of a misdemeanor and is subject to imprisonment for not more than one year and/or may be fined an amount that cannot exceed $1,000.[80]

The definition of a TRP for purposes of this criminal penalty is broader than that under the civil preparer statutes. For instance, a clerical assistant who types or otherwise works on returns that are completed by the preparer is a TRP for purposes of this provision. However, he or she would not be considered a TRP for purposes of the civil preparer penalty statutes.

The preparer, as here defined, may disclose information that is obtained from the taxpayer without being subject to the civil or criminal penalty if such disclosure is pursuant to any other provisions of the Code, or to a court order.

See Exhibit 14-2 for a summary of the most important of the civil and criminal penalties that may apply to taxpayers, preparers, and shelter distributors.

Injunctions

The IRS is empowered to seek **injunctions** against two classes of persons of interest to our discussion: TRPs and promoters of abusive tax shelters. An injunction is a judicial order that prohibits the named person from engaging in certain specified activities. The courts have broad authority to structure any injunctive relief that is granted to fit the circumstances of the case as appropriate.

---

[80]§§6713 and 7216(a).

EXHIBIT 14-2:   Summary of Tax-Related Penalties

Criminal and civil penalties are not mutually exclusive, so a taxpayer or a preparer may be liable for both. Unlike civil penalties, which are collected in the same manner as would be true for the regular tax, criminal penalties are imposed only after the completion of the normal criminal process, in which the defendant is entitled to a number of constitutional guarantees and other rights, that is, he or she is deemed to be innocent until proven guilty.

IRC Section	Type of Infraction	Penalty
Civil Penalties		
6694(a)	Understatement due to unreasonable position	$1,000 or one-half of income derived, per return
6694(b)	Willful understatement of liability	$5,000 or one-half of income derived, per return
6695(a)	Failure to furnish copy to taxpayer	$50 per failure
6695(b)	Failure to inform taxpayer of certain record-keeping requirements or to sign return	$50 per failure
6695(c)	Failure to furnish identifying number	$50 per failure*
6695(d)	Failure to retain copy or list	$50 per failure
6695(e)	Failure to file correct information return	$50 per failure to file; $50 per omitted item
6695(f)	Negotiation or endorsement of refund checks	$500 per check
6695(g)	Failure to be diligent in applying eligibility rules for earned income tax credit	$100 per failure
6700	Organizing (or assisting in doing so) or promoting and making or furnishing statements with respect to abusive tax shelters	Greater of $1,000 or 100% of gross income derived by preparer from the project
6701	Aiding and abetting an understatement of tax liability	$1,000 per return; $10,000 per return if taxpayer is a corporation
6713	Improper disclosure or use of return data	$250 per improper use; annual maximum $10,000
Criminal Penalties		
7201	Attempt to evade or defeat tax	Felony; fine of not more than $100,000 ($500,000 if a corporation) and/or imprisonment for not more than five years
7202	Willful failure to collect or pay over a tax	Felony; fine of not more than $10,000 and/or imprisonment for not more than five years, plus costs of prosecution
7203	Willful failure to file return, supply information, or pay tax	Misdemeanor; fine of not more than $25,000 ($100,000 if a corporation) and/or imprisonment for not more than one year (five years and felony relative to willful violation of cash receipts rules)
7204	Fraudulent statement or failure to make statement to employees	Fine of not more than $1,000 and/or imprisonment for not more than one year
7205	Fraudulent withholding exemption certificate or failure to supply information	Fine of not more than $1,000 and/or imprisonment for not more than one year
7206	Fraud and false statements; concealing or removing property	Felony; fine of not more than $100,000 ($500,000 if a corporation) and/or imprisonment for not more than three years

(Continued)

EXHIBIT 14-2: Summary of Tax-Related Penalties (*Continued*)

IRC Section	Type of Infraction	Penalty
7207	Fraudulent returns, statements, or other documents	Fine of not more than $10,000 ($50,000 if a corporation) and/or imprisonment for not more than one year
7210	Failure to obey summons in tax matter	Fine of not more than $1,000 and/or imprisonment for not more than one year
7212	Attempts to interfere with administration of internal revenue laws, corruption, threats of force	Fine of not more than $5,000 and/or imprisonment for not more than three years
7216	Disclosure or use of information by preparer of return	Misdemeanor; fine of not more than $1,000 and/or imprisonment for not more than one year

*Annual maximum penalty = $25,000.

Action to Enjoin TRPs

The IRS may seek an injunction against a TRP who is guilty of certain misconduct to prohibit him or her from engaging in such misconduct or from practicing as a return preparer. Before such an injunction can be issued, however, the preparer must have:

- Violated a preparer penalty or a criminal provision of the Code.
- Misrepresented his or her eligibility to practice before the IRS.
- Guaranteed the payment of any tax refund or the allowance of a credit.
- Engaged in other fraudulent or deceptive conduct that substantially interferes with the administration of the tax laws.

In addition, it must be shown that the injunctive relief is appropriate to prevent the conduct from recurring. An injunction to prohibit the person from acting as a TRP may be obtained if the court finds that the preparer continually or repeatedly has engaged in misconduct and that an injunction prohibiting such specific misconduct would be effective.[81]

Action to Enjoin Promoters of Abusive Tax Shelters

The IRS may obtain an injunction against a person who is guilty of promoting abusive tax shelters, or of aiding and abetting an understatement of the tax liability, to prohibit him or her from engaging in such conduct or activities. Before such an injunction is issued, a court must find that injunctive relief is appropriate to prevent this conduct from recurring.[82]

Interest

The Code provides for the payment of interest on underpayments and overpayments of tax, at an adjustable rate, compounded daily. The objective of these provisions is to compensate offended parties for the use of their funds. Moreover, the interest charge

[81] §7407.
[82] §7408.

eliminates the benefits that taxpayers (or the government) could obtain by adopting aggressive positions in the creation or processing of tax returns in order to postpone or avoid the payment of their taxes.

Interest-Computation Conventions

Interest on underpayments is payable at a federally specified rate, from the last date that is prescribed for the payment of the tax to the date on which the tax is actually paid. The last date that is prescribed for payment of the tax is usually the unextended due date of the return that reports the amount of tax that is due.[83]

Interest is compounded on a daily basis.[84] The IRS has published interest-factor tables that automatically calculate the daily compounding for various rates of interest.[85]

The rate of interest that is used for underpayments and overpayments is adjusted quarterly to reflect the Federal short-term interest rate for the first day of the quarter.[86] The new prevailing rate is published in a timely fashion, typically in a Revenue Ruling. Exhibit 14-3 documents the various IRS rates of interest that applied to overpayments and underpayments occurring through September, 2010.

Where the taxpayer is subject to both underpayment and overpayment computations for the same time period, whether the prior disputes involve income, transfer, or employment taxes, the amounts due from and payable to the government are netted, and a zero interest rate applies to those amounts.

EXAMPLE 14-6

Mary Brown, a calendar-year taxpayer, filed her 2009 tax return and showed a balance due of $1,000. The return was filed on June 30, 2010, pursuant to a properly executed extension of time to file, and the tax was paid in full with the return. The prevailing IRS interest rate that applies to Brown's underpayment was 4 percent. She must pay about $8 of interest with her return, determined as follows:

Total tax outstanding	$	1,000
Factor from Rev. Proc. 95-17, for 4 percent		
Interest and 76 days' late payment	×	.008363088
Interest assessed	$	8.36

If Brown does not remit the interest that she owes when she files the return, interest will continue to accrue, on both the tax and the $8.36 of interest itself, until the obligation is paid in full. If this amount is paid within 10 days of the receipt of an IRS notice and demand for payment, however, no further interest accrues.

Interest accrues on the full amount of the tax liability that is appropriate under the Code, regardless of the amount of tax that is entered on the return. Moreover, interest is imposed on an assessable penalty, additional amount, or addition to the tax if these

---

[83]§§6601(a) and (b).

[84]§6622(a).

[85]Rev. Proc. 95-17, 1995-1 CB 556.

[86]§6621.

EXHIBIT 14-3: IRS Overpayment and Underpayment Interest Rates

Period	Rate
Prior to July 1975	6%
July 1, 1975–January 31, 1976	9
February 1, 1976–January 31, 1978	7
February 1, 1978–January 31, 1980	6
February 1, 1980–January 31, 1982	12
February 1, 1982–December 31, 1982	20
January 1, 1983–June 30, 1983	16*
July 1, 1983–December 31, 1984	11*
January 1, 1985–June 30, 1985	13*
July 1, 1985–December 31, 1985	11*
January 1, 1986–June 30, 1986	10*
July 1, 1986–December 31, 1986	9*

*Daily compounding required.

Period	Over-payment Rate*†	Under-payment Rate*†	Large Corporation Under-payment Rate*	Rate for Corporation Over-payments >$10,000*
January 1, 1987–September 30, 1987	8%	9%		
October 1, 1987–December 31, 1987	9	10		
January 1, 1988–March 31, 1988	10	11		
April 1, 1988–September 30, 1988	9	10		
October 1, 1988–March 31, 1989	10	11		
April 1, 1989–September 30, 1989	11	12		
October 1, 1989–March 31, 1991	10	11		
April 1, 1991–December 31, 1991	9	10	12%	
January 1, 1992–March 31, 1992	8	9	11	
April 1, 1992–September 30, 1992	7	8	10	
October 1, 1992–June 30, 1994	6	7	9	
July 1, 1994–September 30, 1994	7	8	10	
October 1, 1994–December 31, 1994	8	9	11	
January 1, 1995–March 31, 1995	8	9	11	6.5
April 1, 1995–June 30, 1995	9	10	12	7.5
July 1, 1995–March 31, 1996	8	9	11	6.5
April 1, 1996–June 30, 1996	7	8	10	5.5
July 1, 1996–April 15, 1998	8	9	11	6.5
April 16, 1998–December 31, 1998	7	8	10	5.5
January 1, 1999–April 15, 1999	6	7	9	4.5
April 16, 1999–April 15, 2000	7	8	10	5.5
April 16, 2000–April 15, 2001	8	9	11	6.5
April 16, 2001–June 30, 2001	7	8	10	5.5
July 1, 2001–December 31, 2001	6	7	9	4.5

(Continued)

EXHIBIT 14-3:   IRS Overpayment and Underpayment Interest Rates (*Continued*)

Period	Over-payment Rate*	Under-payment Rate*†	Large Corporation Under-payment Rate*	Rate for Corporation Over-payments >$10,000*
January 1, 2002–December 31, 2002	5	6	8	3.5
January 1, 2003–September 30, 2003	4	5	7	2.5
October 1, 2003–March 31, 2004	3	4	6	1.5
April 1, 2004–June 30, 2004	4	5	7	2.5
July 1, 2004–September 30, 2004	3	4	6	1.5
October 1, 2004–March 31, 2005	4	5	7	2.5
April 1, 2005–September 30, 2005	5	6	8	3.5
October 1, 2005–June 30, 2006	6	7	9	4.5
July 1, 2006–December 31, 2007	7	8	10	5.5
January 1, 2008–March 31, 2008	6	7	9	4.5
July 1, 2006–December 31, 2007	7	8	10	5.5
January 1, 2008–March 31, 2008	6	7	9	4.5
April 1, 2008–June 30, 2008	5	6	8	3.5
July 1, 2008–September 30, 2008	4	5	7	2.5
October 1, 2008–December 31,2008	5	6	8	3.5
January 1, 2009–March 31, 2009	4	5	7	2.5
April 1, 2009–September 30, 2010	3	4	6	1.5

*Daily computing required.
†After 1998, noncorporate taxpayers use the second column for both underpayments and overpayments. Corporations still receive one percentage point less with respect to their smaller overpayments; that is, the first column applies.

amounts are not paid within 21 calendar days of the date on which the IRS requests its payment. Interest on penalties generally is imposed only from the date of this IRS notice and demand, and not from the due date of the return. However, the fraud, accuracy-related, and failure-to-file penalties run from the (extended) due date of the return.[87]

No interest is charged on criminal penalties or delinquent estimated tax payments. However, recall that a nondeductible penalty is imposed in lieu of interest with respect to delinquent estimated tax payments. This penalty is computed in the same manner as would be the required interest, except that daily compounding of the penalty is not required.

In general, the IRS has no authority to forgive the payment of interest. Consequently, a taxpayer is required to pay the total amount of interest assessed on any underpayment even though the delinquency was attributable to a reasonable cause, including an IRS loss of records and the illness, transfer, or leave of a pertinent IRS employee. However, the IRS can abate such interest where it is attributable to an unreasonable

[87]§6601(e)(2). Interest begins to run after 10 business days for amounts exceeding $100,000.

SPOTLIGHT ON TAXATION

Prepaying Interest

If interest rates are relatively high, some taxpayers consider prepaying the amount of tax in dispute so as to stop the running of interest charges that will be due if the issue is found in favor of the government. A deposit of the tax (and perhaps of related penalty and interest charges) is set up with the Treasury. Such a prepayment might make sense because the prepayment can trigger an immediate interest deduction. In addition, if the taxpayer prevails in the dispute, interest is payable back from the government on the full deposit amount.

error or delay caused by an employee or officer of the IRS in response to the taxpayer's filing a claim on Form 843. Such a delay cannot be traceable to an interpretation of the tax law, but rather must relate to nondiscretionary, administrative, or managerial duties of procedure or return processing, including an IRS loss of records and the illness, transfer, or leave of a pertinent IRS employee.[88]

The government is required to pay interest at the applicable Federal rate to any taxpayer who has made an overpayment of tax. Interest on an overpayment runs from the date of the overpayment to the date on which the overpayment is credited against another tax liability, or, in the case of a refund, to a date that is not more than 30 days before the date of the refund check.

However, the IRS is allowed a specific period in which it may refund an overpayment without incurring interest. This interest-free period runs for 45 days after the unextended due date of the return or, if the return is filed after its due date, for 45 days after it is actually filed. If the refund is not made within this 45-day period, interest begins to accrue from the later of the due date of the return or the date on which the return was actually filed.[89]

EXAMPLE 14-7

Joan Jeffries, a calendar-year taxpayer, filed her 2008 Federal income tax return on October 1, 2011. Her return showed an overpayment of $2,500, for which Jeffries requested a full refund. If the IRS refunds the $2,500 overpayment on or before November 14, 2011, no interest is due from the government. If the refund is paid after November 14, 2011, however, interest accrues from October 1, 2011 through a date that is not more than 30 days before the date of the refund check.

The date that is stated on the government's refund check determines whether the overpayment is refunded within the 45-day interest-free period. The date on which the refund is actually received does not control for this purpose. Thus, an interest-free refund may be paid even though it is not received by the taxpayer until the 45-day period has expired.

---

[88] §6404(e); *Dormer*, TC Memo 2004-167; TD 8789 (1998).

[89] §6611(e).

Applicable Interest Rate

Different rates are used with respect to IRS overpayments and underpayments, as is evident in Exhibit 14-3. The overpayment rate (paid by the IRS) is two percentage points greater than the Federal short-term interest rate, compounded daily, and the underpayment rate (paid to the IRS) is three percentage points greater than the same Federal rate.

Large corporations pay interest at two percentage points higher than the usual underpayment rate. Corporations receive interest on overpayments at one and a half percentage points lower than the usual overpayment rate, where the overpayment exceeds $10,000. Underpayment and overpayment rates are determined for the beginning of each calendar quarter, using the Federal rates in effect for the first month of that quarter.

Statutes of Limitations

The Code establishes a specific period of time, commonly referred to as a **statute of limitations**, within which all taxes must be assessed and collected, and all refund claims must be made. After the pertinent statute of limitations expires, certain actions may not be taken because the expiration establishes an absolute defense for the party against whom legal action is brought. In other words, a taxpayer cannot be required to pay taxes that he or she rightfully owes if these taxes are not assessed and collected within the time periods that the Code has established.

Nature of Statutes of Limitations

Although the statute of limitations appears to be a legal loophole that rewards delinquent taxpayers who avoid detection, Congress believes that, at some point, the right to be free of stale claims must prevail over the government's right to pursue them. If the statutes permitted the lapse of an extended period of time between the initiation of a claim and its pursuit, the defense could be jeopardized because witnesses might have died or disappeared, memories might have faded, and records or other evidence might have been lost.

Moreover, some statutes of limitations are designed solely to protect the government (e.g., the statute of limitations on credits or refunds). A number of such statutes limit the time period within which assessment, collection, and claim for refund or credit activities must be conducted.[90]

Assessment

Assessment of an internal revenue tax generally must be made within three years of the later of the date that the return was actually filed or the unextended due date of the return. A return that is filed prior to its due date, for this purpose, is deemed to be filed on its due date. The assessment period for a return that is filed after the due date starts on the day that follows the actual filing date, regardless of whether the return is delinquent or the due date was extended properly.

The period in which a tax may be assessed is extended to six years if the taxpayer omits from his or her reported gross income an amount that is greater than 25 percent of the reported gross income.[91] For this purpose, §61 gross income is used in the 25 percent computation, with two exceptions. First, the gross income of a business is not

---

[90]§6501.

[91]§6501(e)(1)(A).

reduced by cost of sales. Second, income that is omitted from the return is ignored for purposes of constructing the base for the 25 percent test, if the omission is disclosed in the return or in an attached document.[92]

Although the limitations period is extended for a substantial omission of income, it (surprisingly) is not extended where the taxpayer has overstated the amount of his or her deductions, regardless of the amount of the overstatement.

An exception to the normal three-year assessment period also applies where required information related to certain international transactions and foreign transfers is not disclosed with a return. The statute of limitations is suspended and will not begin until the missing information is supplied to the IRS.[93] All items on the return are subject to adjustment during this time period unless the failure to provide information is due to reasonable cause. If the failure to furnish information is due to reasonable cause, the suspension will apply only to the item or items not furnished, not the entire return.[94]

Irregular Returns A tax may be assessed at any time when a taxpayer files a false or fraudulent return with the intent to evade tax liability.[95] Once the fraudulent return is filed, the limitations period remains open indefinitely. A later filing of a non-fraudulent amended return will not start the running of the three-year (or six-year) limitation period.[96]

When a taxpayer fails to file a return, the tax may be assessed at any time. For this purpose, one's failure to file need not be willful. A taxpayer who innocently or negligently fails to file still is subject to an unlimited period of assessment for the tax.[97]

Acceleration, Extension, and Carryback Effects Generally, the filing of an amended return does not affect the length of the limitations period. However, the limitations period is extended by 60 days if the IRS receives, within 60 days of the expiration of the applicable statute of limitations, an amended return that shows the taxpayer owes an additional tax.[98] This provision was enacted to discourage taxpayers from waiting until the limitations period on an assessment was about to expire before submitting an erroneous amended return.

Prior to the enactment of this provision, it was beneficial for the taxpayer to wait to file an amended return this way because the IRS would not have enough time to assess more tax if an examination of the original return uncovered additional unreported errors or omissions.

The usual three-year assessment period can be reduced to 18 months if a request for a prompt assessment is filed with the IRS.[99] This request usually is made for an income tax return of a decedent or an estate, or for a corporation that is in the midst of a dissolution. Generally, a prompt assessment is requested when all of the involved parties wish to accelerate the final determination of the tax liability.

A deficiency for a carryback year that is attributable to the carryback of a net operating loss, capital loss, or unused research or general business credit can be assessed at any time before the expiration of the limitations period for the year in which the loss

---

[92]§§6501(e)(1)(A)(i) and (ii).
[93]§6501(c)(8)(A).
[94]§6501(c)(8)(B).
[95]§6501(c)(1).
[96]*Badaracco v. Comm.*, 464 U.S. 386, 104 S.Ct. 756 (1984).
[97]§6501(c)(3).
[98]§6501(c)(7).
[99]§6501(d).

occurred or the credit originated. This extension in the period of assessment for the carryback year is necessary to ensure that there is adequate time to process the refund claim and to allow the IRS to examine the return that gave rise to the carryback item.[100] The period for assessment is not extended when a net operating loss, capital loss, or unused credit is carried forward.

IRS-Requested Extensions   An extension of the period of limitations typically is requested by the IRS when an audit or an appellate review cannot be completed until after the statute of limitations expires. The taxpayer is not bound to agree with such a request, but such a refusal may prompt the IRS to stop negotiations prematurely and assess a deficiency against the taxpayer. Although the issuance of a statutory notice of deficiency does not preclude the taxpayer from obtaining a negotiated settlement with the IRS, he or she will be required to undertake a more costly procedure and file a petition with the U.S. Tax Court or pay the assessment and file a claim for refund.

Consequently, a taxpayer normally should not refuse to sign a waiver of the statute of limitations, as requested by the IRS, unless the agent has completed the examination and there exist one or more unagreed-upon issues that the taxpayer is ready to litigate.

Collection

All taxes must be collected within 10 years after a timely assessment has been made.[101] **Collection** can be made either by IRS levy or by the agency's commencement of an action in court. If the tax is not collected administratively by levy within the 10-year period, the IRS must commence an action in court to reduce the assessment to a judgment before the statute of limitation expires.

Once a judgment for the assessed tax is awarded, the tax may be collected at any time after the normal period of collections has expired. Thus, collection is not barred after the 10-year period expires, provided that the IRS has obtained a timely judgment against the taxpayer.

The taxpayer and the IRS may agree to an extension of the normal collection period. The IRS will request such an extension whenever the taxpayer has agreed to extend the period of limitations for assessment of the tax. In addition, the taxpayer may request an extension to allow additional time in which to raise and submit any delinquent taxes. If the taxpayer agrees to extend the period of limitation on collections, the IRS may agree not to seize and sell the taxpayer's property to satisfy the tax liability.

The 10-year period of limitations begins only after an assessment is made. If an assessment can be made at any time, for example, because the taxpayer failed to file a return or filed a fraudulent return, then the tax may be collected within 10 years of the date of assessment, regardless of when it eventually is made.

Claim for Refund or Credit

A taxpayer must file a timely and valid claim at the service center for the district in which the tax was paid to receive a refund or credit of an overpayment of tax. The claim should be made by individuals on Form 1040X, Amended U.S. Individual Income Tax Return, and by corporations on Form 1120X, Amended U.S. Corporation Income Tax Return.

Generally, an overpayment can be refunded or credited only to the person who was subject to the original tax. However, the IRS can apply overpayments to delinquent

---

[100]§§6501(h) through (k).
[101]§6502(a)(1).

support obligations and certain certified non-tax debts that are owed to the Federal government. Refunds in excess of $2 million may not be made until they have been reviewed by the Joint Committee on Taxation.[102]

A taxpayer who reports a net operating loss, capital loss, or credit carryback can accelerate the processing of the refund by filing an Application for Tentative Refund on Form 1045 (for individuals) or Form 1139 (for corporations). The IRS has 90 days from the later of the date on which the application was filed, or the last day of the month in which the return for the loss is due, to examine the application and accept or deny the claim.[103]

If the application is denied, however, the taxpayer cannot bring a suit for recovery of the overpayment because the IRS's determination is only tentative. Instead, the taxpayer must file a refund claim on the appropriate form and wait for six months from the date on which the claim was filed, or until the IRS denies the refund claim, before legal action can be started.

Before a refund or credit can be issued, the IRS must review the taxpayer's claim. Even if the Commissioner agrees that the taxpayer has overpaid a tax, he or she has no authority to refund or credit the overpayment unless the taxpayer files the claim within the allowable period. Any refund of an overpayment that is made after the period for filing a timely claim expires is considered erroneous, and a credit is considered void.

Limitations Period A taxpayer who has filed a return must file a claim for credit or refund within three years of the date on which the return was filed or two years of the date on which the tax was paid, whichever is later. Returns filed early are deemed to be filed on the due date. If the taxpayer did not file a return (e.g., because taxes were withheld from the taxpayer's wages, but the taxpayer did not file a return because his or her taxable income did not exceed the applicable exemptions and standard deduction), the claim for credit or refund must be made within two years of the date on which the tax was paid.[104]

The period within which a claim for credit or refund may be filed is extended when the taxpayer and the IRS agree to extend the statute of limitations on assessments. A claim can be filed within six months after the expiration of the extended assessment period.[105]

Other Extensions The limitations period also can be extended where an overpayment results from a business bad debt or from a discovery of worthless securities.[106] A claim for refund or credit that is attributable to losses sustained from worthless securities or business bad debts may be filed within seven years from the date that the return was due, without regard to any extension for filing the return. This period is extended further if the debt or loss increases a net operating loss carryback since the taxpayer is entitled to three additional years for the filing of a claim that is based on the carryback.[107]

This provision was enacted because the determination of the date on which a debt or share of stock becomes worthless is a question of fact that may not be determined until after the year in which the loss actually occurred. If taxpayers were not allowed

---

[102]§6405(a).

[103]6411(b) and Reg. §1.6411-1(b).

[104]§6511(a).

[105]§6511(c)(2).

[106]§6511(d).

[107]§6511(d)(2)(A).

additional time in which to file refund claims for these items, they could incur substantial losses without the receipt of any tax benefits because the deductions must be taken in the taxable year of the loss, not in a later year.

The period for filing a claim for refund is extended when the claimed overpayment results from the carryback of a net operating loss, capital loss, or certain credits. If a claim for credit or refund is attributable to the carryback of a net operating loss, net capital loss, or business credit, it can be filed within three years of the extended due date of the return for the year in which the losses occurred or the credits originated, rather than within three years of the due date of the return for the carryback year. Again, this provision was enacted because the existence and amount of these items might not be known until after the expiration of the usual three-year period for filing the claim.

Amount of the Credit or Refund If a claim for refund or credit is filed in a timely fashion, the amount of the taxpayer's refund or credit is limited to the portion of the tax that was paid during the three immediately preceding years, plus the period of any extension for filing the return.[108] The amount of tax that is subject to the claim may include amounts that were withheld and estimated payments that were made more than three years before the date on which the claim was filed, because these amounts are all deemed to have been paid on the due date of the return.

If a claim is filed after the three-year period, the amount of any refund or credit is limited to the portion of the tax that was paid during the two years that immediately precede the filing of the claim. This two-year period also is effective if a claim is filed for a year in which a return was not filed. Because this claim relates only to a two-year period, it may not protect payments that were made with the original return.

Suspension of Period of Assessment and Collection

Usually, a tax must be assessed within three years after the filing of a tax return, and it must be collected within six years of the assessment. Under certain circumstances, however, the running of the statutes of limitations on assessment or collection is suspended.

When the IRS mails a statutory notice of deficiency (i.e., a 90-day letter) to the taxpayer, the assessment and collection period is suspended for 150 days (210 days if the letter is addressed to a person who is outside the United States).[109] The statutes of limitations on assessment and collection also are suspended when a case is pending before the U.S. Tax Court. This suspension period begins when the taxpayer files a petition in the Tax Court contesting the deficiency, and it continues until 60 days after the decision of the Tax Court becomes final.

When a taxpayer submits an offer in compromise for consideration by the IRS, the statute of limitations on assessment is suspended. This suspension period begins when the offer is submitted, and it continues until one year after the offer is terminated, withdrawn, or formally rejected.[110]

In addition to the circumstances just discussed, the statute of limitations also can be suspended in the following instances:[111]

- The taxpayer's assets are in the custody of the court.

- The taxpayer is outside the United States for six or more consecutive months.

---

[108]§6511(b)(2)(A).

[109]§6503(a)(1).

[110]Reg. §301.7122-1(f).

[111]§§6503(b) through (f). That section also contains other, less frequently encountered suspension possibilities.

- The taxpayer's assets are wrongfully seized.

- A fiduciary or receiver is appointed in a bankruptcy case.

- The IRS is prohibited under bankruptcy law from any assessment or collection of a tax.

- The collection of excise or termination taxes on certain retirement plans or private foundations is suspended.

Mitigation of Statute of Limitations

Generally, the IRS cannot make an assessment and a taxpayer cannot obtain a refund after the statute of limitations has expired. However, §§1311 through 1314 of the Code include a complex set of rules designed to prevent the taxpayer or the IRS from taking advantage of an oncoming expiration of the period of limitations on assessment, collection, or refunds.

When an error has been made in the inclusion of an item of income, allowance, or disallowance of a deduction or other tax treatment of a transaction that affects the basis of property, the mitigation provisions will allow a submission of the error to be corrected, even though the normal period of limitations has expired for that year.

Statutory Agreements

The Code provides for two types of agreements that may be used to resolve tax disputes; namely, closing agreements and offers in compromise.

Closing Agreements

A **closing agreement** is a formal, written agreement that is made between a taxpayer and the IRS. It is the only agreement that the Code recognizes as being binding. Once it is approved, a closing agreement is final and conclusive on the part of both the government and the taxpayer unless there is a showing of fraud, malfeasance, or a misrepresentation of a material fact, by either party.[112]

The purpose of a closing agreement is either to enable the taxpayer and the IRS to resolve, finally and completely, a tax controversy for any period prior to the date of the agreement and to protect the taxpayer against the reopening of the matter at a later date; or to determine a matter in a tax year that arises after the date of the agreement.

The IRS is authorized to enter into a closing agreement in any case where there appears to be a benefit to the government in closing the case permanently and conclusively, or if the taxpayer demonstrates a need to close the case and the government's interests are not harmed. Typically, a closing agreement is used in cases where the IRS and the taxpayer have made mutual concessions relative to the case, and it is necessary or desirable to bar further actions by either party. Such an agreement also may be used when a corporation is winding up its business affairs or when a taxpayer needs some authentic evidence of his or her tax liability, say, to satisfy creditors.

As a matter of practice, the IRS discourages the use of closing agreements because of their finality. Moreover, the IRS would have a difficult time processing a large number of requests for these agreements. Consequently, it prefers to use a number of informal

---

[112]§7121(b).

agreements that may not resolve conclusively the tax dispute that is under examination or that may not provide for the same degree of finality as would a closing agreement.

Offers in Compromise

The Commissioner can make an **offer in compromise** for any civil or criminal case that does not involve sales of illegal drugs prior to the time that the case is referred to the Justice Department for prosecution or defense. Once the case is referred to the Justice Department, however, the U.S. Attorney General has the final authority to compromise the case.[113] Compromise proposals entailing more than $50,000 in tax also must be supported by an opinion of the Chief Counsel.

In this context, the government will compromise a case only if there is doubt as to the liability or collectibility of the assessed tax. The IRS will not enter into a compromise with the taxpayer if the liability has been established by a valid judgment and if there is no doubt as to the ability of the IRS to collect the amounts that are due.

A compromise agreement may cover the principal amount of tax, plus any corresponding interest or penalties. Ordinarily, the IRS will not compromise a criminal tax case unless it involves a violation of a regulatory provision of the Code or of a related statute that was not deliberately violated with intent to defraud.

A compromise agreement relates to the entire liability of the taxpayer, and it conclusively settles all of the issues for which an agreement is to be made. It is a legally enforceable promise that cannot be rescinded unless there has been a misrepresentation of the assets of the taxpayer by falsification or concealment or a mutual mistake relative to a material fact.

Consequently, a taxpayer cannot decide later to bring a suit for refund with respect to any item that is so compromised. Moreover, if a taxpayer defaults on a compromise agreement, the IRS may collect the original tax liability, less any payments that were actually made, or sue to enforce the agreement.

An offer in compromise typically is made via Form 656, Offer in Compromise, and it must be accompanied by a comprehensive set of the taxpayer's financial statements. The offer may be revoked or withdrawn at any time prior to its acceptance. Page one of Form 656 is reproduced in Exhibit 14-4.

An offer in compromise is perhaps most appropriate in the following circumstances:

- There is doubt as to the taxpayer's liability for the tax (i.e., disputed issues still exist).

- There is doubt as to the collectibility of the tax (i.e., the taxpayer's net worth and earnings capacity are low).

- Payment of the disputed amount would constitute an economic hardship for the taxpayer. For instance, the taxpayer is incapable of earning a living because of a long-term illness or disability, or liquidation of the taxpayer's assets to pay the amount due would leave the taxpayer unable to meet basic living expenses.

The IRS investigates the offer by evaluating the taxpayer's financial ability to pay the tax. In some instances, the compromise settlement includes an agreement for final settlement of the tax through payments of a specified percentage of the taxpayer's future earnings. This settlement procedure usually entails lengthy negotiations with the IRS, but the presumption is that the agency will find terms upon which to enter into a compromise with the taxpayer. The IRS is charged to use a "liberal acceptance policy" in

---

[113]§7122(a).

EXHIBIT 14-4: Offer in Compromise

Form **656** (March 2009)	Department of the Treasury — Internal Revenue Service **Offer in Compromise**	

Attach Application Fee and Payment *(check or money order)* **here.**

Section I　　　　　**Taxpayer Contact Information**	**IRS RECEIVED DATE**

Taxpayer's First Name and Middle Initial　　　Last Name

If a joint offer, spouse's First Name and Middle Initial　　Last Name

Business Name

Taxpayer's Address *(Home and Business) (number, street, and room or suite no., city, state, ZIP code)*

Mailing Address *(if different from above) (number, street, and room or suite no., city, state, ZIP code)*

DATE RETURNED

Social Security Number (SSN) *(Primary)*　　　　*(Secondary)*	Employer Identification Number (EIN) *(EIN included in offer)*　　*(EIN **not** included in offer)*

　 - 　　 - 　　　 - 　　 - 　　　　 - 　　　　 -

Section II　　　　　　　**To: Commissioner of Internal Revenue Service**

I/We *(includes all types of taxpayers)* submit this offer to compromise the tax liabilities plus any interest, penalties, additions to tax, and additional amounts required by law *(tax liability)* for the tax type and period marked below: *(Please mark an "X" in the box for the correct description and fill-in the correct tax period(s), adding additional periods if needed).*

☐ 1040/1120 Income Tax - Year(s) _____

☐ 941 Employer's Quarterly Federal Tax Return - Quarterly period(s) _____

☐ 940 Employer's Annual Federal Unemployment (FUTA) Tax Return — Year(s) _____

☐ Trust Fund Recovery Penalty as a responsible person of *(enter corporation name)* _____,

　 for failure to pay withholding and Federal Insurance Contributions Act taxes (Social Security taxes), for period(s) ending _____

☐ Other Federal Tax(es) [specify type(s) and period(s)] _____

Note: If you need more space, use a separate sheet of paper and title it "Attachment to Form 656 Dated _____." Sign and date the attachment following the listing of the tax periods.

Section III　　　　　　　**Reason for Offer in Compromise**

I/We submit this offer for the reason(s) checked below:

☐ Doubt as to Collectibility — "I have insufficient assets and income to pay the full amount." You must include a complete Collection Information Statement, Form 433-A and/or Form 433-B.

☐ Effective Tax Administration — "I owe this amount and have sufficient assets to pay the full amount, but due to my exceptional circumstances, requiring full payment would cause an economic hardship or would be unfair and inequitable." You must include a complete Collection Information Statement, Form 433-A and/or Form 433-B and complete Section VI.

Section IV　　　　　　　**Offer in Compromise Terms**

I/We offer to pay $_____ *(must be more than zero).* Complete Section VII to explain where you will obtain the funds to make this offer.

Check **only** one of the following:

☐ **Lump sum cash offer** – 20% of the amount of the offer $_____ must be sent with Form 656. Upon written acceptance of the offer, the balance must be paid in 5 or fewer installments.

　　$_____ payable within _____ months after acceptance
　　$_____ payable within _____ months after acceptance
　　$_____ payable within _____ months after acceptance
　　$_____ payable within _____ months after acceptance
　　$_____ payable within _____ months after acceptance

☐ **Short Term Periodic Payment Offer** - Offer amount is paid within 24 months from the date IRS received your offer. The first payment **must** be submitted with your Form 656. You **must** make regular payments during your offer investigation. Complete the following:

　　$_____ will be submitted with the Form 656. Beginning in the month after the offer is submitted *(insert month_____),* on the _____ day of each month, $_____ will be sent in for a total of _____ months. *(Cannot extend more than 24 months from the date the offer was submitted.)*

Catalog Number 16728N　　　　　　　　　www.irs.gov　　　　　　　　　Form **656** (Rev. 3-2009)

compromising with taxpayers and to increase educational efforts so that taxpayer rights and obligations are better known.

The IRS has statutory authority to enter into a written agreement allowing taxes to be paid on an installment basis if that arrangement facilitates the tax collection.[114] The agency encourages its employees to use installment plans, and an individual is guaranteed the right to use an installment agreement when the amount in dispute does not exceed $10,000. The taxpayer uses Form 9465 to initiate the installment plan.

The IRS provides an annual statement accounting for the status of the agreement. The agreement may be modified or terminated later because of inadequate information, a subsequent change in financial condition, or a failure to pay an installment when due or to provide requested information.

SUMMARY

In dealing with tax underpayments, the stakes include more than just the disputed tax. Interest charges accrue, and both the taxpayer and tax adviser can be subjected to significant amounts of civil and criminal penalties. Restrictions on the actions of the taxpayer and practitioner are expressed using such ambiguously defined terms as reasonable cause and substantial authority, such that the lay taxpayer is expected to project accurately the final holding of a judicial forum. Such is the condition of a tax system under which tax rates virtually cannot be raised, yet revenue needs continue to escalate. The tax professional must include these sanctions in the research process, communicating their effects to the client as needed.

QUIZ YOURSELF

Reinforce the tax research information covered in this chapter by completing the online quizzes located at the Federal Tax Research Web site at **www.cengagebrain.com.** At the CengageBrain.com home page, search for the *Federal Tax Research*, 9e ISBN (1111221642) using the search box at the top of the page. This will take you to the product page where you can access the quizzes.

KEY WORDS

By the time you complete this chapter, you should be comfortable discussing each of the following terms. If you need additional review of any of these items, return to the appropriate material in the chapter or consult the glossary to this text.

accuracy-related penalty, p. 464
assessment, p. 488
assessable penalties, p. 461
ad valorem penalties, p. 461
civil penalties, p. 461
closing agreement, p. 493
collection, p. 490

criminal penalties, p. 472
failure-to-file penalty, p. 461
failure-to-pay penalty, p. 463
fraud, p. 461
frivolous return, p. 471
injunctions, p. 481
negligence, p. 461

offer in compromise, p. 494
preparer penalties, p. 477
reasonable cause, p. 461
statute of limitations, p. 488
substantial authority, p. 467
tax return preparer (TRP), p. 475
willful neglect, p. 461

[114]§6159

DISCUSSION QUESTIONS

1. When should prevailing interest rates bear on tax decision making?
   a. The taxpayer is contemplating litigation in either the Tax Court or the Court of Federal Claims.
   b. An understatement of estimated tax payments is discovered late in the tax year.

2. What is the role of the statute of limitations in the Federal income tax system?

3. Describe the civil fraud penalties, the definition of fraud, and the all or nothing rule for civil fraud. What are the differences in individual and corporate penalties for failure to make adequate estimated payments? What is a frivolous return?

4. Explain the imposition of criminal penalties. What is the relationship between criminal and civil penalties? What are the defenses against criminal penalties?

5. Discuss the penalties imposed on TRPs. Who is a preparer, and what is defined as a tax return preparation and what is not preparation?

6. What is an injunction, and when may the IRS seek an injunction?

7. What are the statutes of limitations for the IRS and taxpayers? Why did Congress create them? When can they be shortened, extended, or suspended?

8. How has Congress used tax penalties to discourage the development of certain tax shelters?

9. Define and illustrate the following terms or concepts:
   a. Fraud
   b. Negligence
   c. Reasonable cause
   d. Lack of reasonable cause
   e. Civil penalty conviction
   f. Criminal penalty conviction

EXERCISES

10. Indicate whether the following statements are true or false:
    a. The government never pays a taxpayer interest on an overpayment of tax.
    b. Penalties may be included as an itemized deduction on an individual's tax return.
    c. An extension of time for filing a return results in an automatic extension of the time in which the tax may be paid.
    d. The IRS can compromise on the amount of tax liability if there is doubt as to the taxpayer's ability to pay.
    e. The statute of limitations for assessment of taxes never extends beyond three years from the filing of a return.
    f. There is no statute of limitations relative to a taxpayer's claim for a refund.

11. Indicate whether, after both parties sign a closing agreement, the following result(s) occur. More than one answer may be correct.
    a. The taxpayer still may appeal to a higher level of the IRS.
    b. The interest on the assessment stops accruing immediately.
    c. The agreement is binding on both the taxpayer and the IRS.
    d. The tax must be paid, but a suit for refund can be filed in the District Court or U.S. Court of Federal Claims.

12. Ace filed her 2008 income tax return on January 25, 2009. There was no material understatement of income on her return, and the return was properly signed and filed. The statute of limitations for Ace's 2008 return expires on:

    a. January 25, 2012
    b. April 15, 2012
    c. January 25, 2015
    d. April 15, 2015

13. Blanche filed her 2009 income tax return on April 4, 2010. On December 14, 2010, she learned that 100 shares of stock that she owned had become worthless in 2009. Since she did not deduct this loss on the 2009 return, Blanche intends to file a claim for refund. This claim must be filed by no later than April 15, _____.

    a. 2011
    b. 2014
    c. 2016
    d. 2017
    e. There is no expiration date for the statute of limitations in this context.

14. Carl purposely omitted from his 2008 tax return $40,000 of the gross receipts that he collected as the owner of a restaurant. His 2008 return indicated collective gross receipts of $25,000. The IRS no longer can pursue Carl with the threat of collection of the related tax, interest, and penalties, as of April 15, _____.

    a. 2010
    b. 2013
    c. 2015
    d. 2016
    e. There is no expiration date for the statute of limitations in this context.

15. Diane accidentally omitted from her 2008 tax return $40,000 of the gross receipts that she collected as the owner of a restaurant. Her 2008 return indicated collective gross receipts of $25,000. The IRS no longer can pursue Diane with the threat of collection of the related tax, interest, and penalties, as of April 15, _____.

    a. 2010
    b. 2013
    c. 2015
    d. 2016
    e. There is no expiration date for the statute of limitations in this context.

16. Mike accidentally omitted from his 2008 tax return $4,000 of gross receipts she collected as the owner of a restaurant. His 2008 return indicated collective gross receipts of $35,000. The IRS no longer can pursue Mike with the threat of collection of the related tax, interest and penalties on April 15, _____.

    a. 2010
    b. 2013
    c. 2015
    d. 2016
    e. There is no expiration date for the statute of limitations in this context.

17. Construct a scenario in which the tax adviser should recommend that the client terminate the challenge of the IRS with the following:

    a. Lawsuit

    b. Offer in compromise

    c. Closing agreement

    d. Appeals conference

    e. Office audit

    f. Correspondence audit

18. The client's return is found by the U.S. Tax Court to have included improper business deductions. The court agreed that the taxpayer's position had some statutory and judicial merit, but it held for the government nonetheless. Which of the following could the IRS charge with a preparer penalty?

    a. Taxpayer

    b. Partner of the accounting firm that prepared the return

    c. Employee of the client, who provided the accounting firm with the deduction data

    d. Staff member of the accounting firm, who used the deduction data to prepare the return

    e. Secretary of the accounting firm, who made copies of the return

19. Discuss which penalties, if any, the tax adviser might be charged with in each of the following independent circumstances. In this regard, assume that the tax adviser:

    a. Provided information about the taxpayer's Federal income tax returns to the pertinent state income tax agency.

    b. Provided information about the taxpayer's Federal income tax returns to the pertinent county's property tax agency.

    c. Provided information about the taxpayer's Federal income tax returns to the FBI, which was interested in gathering evidence concerning the client's alleged drug dealing activities.

    d. Suggested to the client various means by which to acquire excludible income.

    e. Suggested to the client various means by which to conceal cash receipts from gross income.

    f. Suggested to the client means by which to improve her cash flow by delaying for six months or more the deposit of the employees' share of Federal employment taxes.

    g. Suggested to the client means by which to improve her cash flow by delaying for six months or more the deposit of the employer's share of Federal employment taxes.

    h. Kept in his safe deposit box the cash receipts referred to in item (e).

20. Discuss which penalties, if any, the tax adviser might be charged with in each of the following independent circumstances. In this regard, assume that the tax adviser:

    a. Suggested that the client invest in a real estate tax shelter.

    b. Provided a statement of assurance as to the accuracy of the financial data that are included in the prospectus of a real estate tax shelter.

    c. Suggested to the promoters of a real estate tax shelter that a specific accounting technique, not recognized by generally accepted accounting principles, should be used to construct the prospectus.

    d. Failed, because of pressing time conflicts, to conduct the usual review of the client's tax return. The IRS discovered that the return included fraudulent data.

    e. Failed, because of pressing time conflicts, to conduct the usual review of the client's tax return. The IRS discovered a mathematical error in the computation of the taxpayer's standard deduction.

21. Julie filed a valid extension for her 2009 tax return giving her until October 15, 2010 to file her return. She filed her return on November 1 and paid $2,000 of tax due. For what period of time will Julie be subject to interest? For what period of time will Julie be subject to the failure-to-file and failure-to-pay penalties?

22. Jim received a six month extension (to October 15, 2011) to file his 2010 tax return. Jim actually filed the return on October 20, 2011, paying the $20,000 amount due at that time. He has no reasonable cause for failing to file the return by October 15 or for failing to pay the tax that was due on April 15, 2011. Compute the failure-to-pay and failure-to-file penalties.

23. Joan filed her unextended 2010 tax return on November 15, 2011, paying the $5,000 amount due at that time. Joan has no reasonable cause for failing to file the return by October 15 or for failing to pay the tax that was due on April 15, 2011. Compute the failure-to-pay and failure-to-file penalties.

PROBLEMS

24. John, a calendar-year taxpayer subject to a 34 percent marginal tax rate, claimed a charitable contribution deduction of $15,000 for a sculpture that the IRS later valued at $10,000. Compute the applicable overvaluation penalty.

25. Samantha, a calendar-year taxpayer subject to a 34 percent marginal tax rate, claimed a charitable contribution deduction of $170,000 for a sculpture that the IRS later valued at $100,000. Compute the applicable overvaluation penalty.

26. Susan, a calendar-year taxpayer subject to a 34 percent marginal tax rate, claimed a charitable contribution deduction of $400,000 for a sculpture that the IRS later valued at $150,000. Compute the applicable overvaluation penalty.

27. Beth, a calendar-year taxpayer subject to a 34 percent marginal tax rate, claimed a charitable contribution deduction of $600,000 for a sculpture that the IRS later valued at $100,000. Compute the applicable overvaluation penalty.

28. Todd, who is subject to a 35 percent marginal gift tax rate, made a gift of a sculpture to Becky, valuing the property at $7,000. The IRS later valued the gift at $15,000. Compute the applicable undervaluation penalty.

29. Greg, who is subject to a 35 percent marginal gift tax rate, made a gift of a sculpture to Karen, valuing the property at $80,000. The IRS later valued the gift at $150,000. Compute the applicable undervaluation penalty.

30. Brian, who is subject to a 40 percent marginal gift tax rate, made a gift of a sculpture to Adam, valuing the property at $100,000. The IRS later valued the gift at $250,000. Compute the applicable undervaluation penalty.

31. Krista, who is subject to a 40 percent marginal gift tax rate, made a gift of a sculpture to Ann, valuing the property at $100,000. The IRS later valued the gift at $500,000. Compute the applicable undervaluation penalty.

32. Compute the overvaluation penalty for each of the following independent cases involving the taxpayer's reporting of the fair market value of charitable contribution property. In each case, assume a marginal income tax rate of 35 percent.

	Taxpayer	Corrected IRS Value	Reported Valuation
a.	Individual	$30,000	$40,000
b.	C Corporation	30,000	50,000
c.	S Corporation	40,000	50,000
d.	Individual	150,000	210,000
e.	Individual	150,000	250,000
f.	C Corporation	150,000	900,000

33. Compute the undervaluation penalty for each of the following independent cases involving the executor's reporting of the value of a closely held business in the decedent's gross estate. In each case, assume a marginal estate tax rate of 50 percent.

	Reported Value	Corrected IRS Valuation
a.	$ 20,000	$ 25,000
b.	100,000	150,000
c.	150,000	250,000
d.	150,000	500,000

34. Kim underpaid her taxes by $15,000. Of this amount, $7,500 was due to negligence on her part because her record-keeping system is highly inadequate. Determine the amount of any negligence penalty.

35. Compute Dana's total penalties. She underpaid her tax by $50,000 due to negligence and by $150,000 due to civil fraud.

36. Trudy's AGI last year was $200,000. Her Federal income tax came to $40,000, which she paid through a combination of withholding and estimated payments. This year, her AGI will be $300,000, with a projected tax liability of $60,000, all to be paid through estimates. Ignore the annualized income method. Compute Trudy's quarterly estimated payment schedule for the year, assuming that she wants to make the minimum necessary payments to avoid any underpayment penalties.

37. When Maggie accepted employment with Martin Corporation, she completed a Form W-4, listing 14 exemptions. Since Maggie was single and had no exemptions, she misrepresented her tax situation in an attempt to increase her cash flow. To what penalties is Maggie exposed?

38. What is the applicable filing period under the statute of limitations in each of the following independent situations?

    a. No return was filed by the taxpayer.

    b. The taxpayer incurred a bad debt loss that she failed to claim.

    c. A taxpayer inadvertently omitted a large amount of gross income.

    d. Same as part c, except that the omission was deliberate.

    e. A taxpayer inadvertently overstated her deductions by a large amount.

39. Kold Corporation estimates that its 2012 taxable income will be $900,000. Thus, it is subject to a flat 34 percent income tax rate and incurs a $306,000 tax liability. For each of the following independent cases, compute the minimum quarterly estimated tax payments that will be required from Kold to avoid an underpayment penalty.

    a. Taxable income for 2011 was ($100,000). Kold carried back all of its loss to prior years and exhausted the entire net operating loss in creating a zero 2011 liability.

    b. For 2011, taxable income was $200,000, and tax liability was $68,000.

    c. For 2010, taxable income was $2 million, and tax liability was $680,000. For 2011, taxable income was $200,000, and tax liability was $68,000.

40. White Corporation estimates that its 2012 taxable income will be $800,000 and its tax liability to be $272,000. For each of the following independent cases, compute the minimum quarterly estimated tax payments that will be required to avoid an underpayment penalty.

    a. White Corporation's 2011 tax return showed taxable income of $700,000 and a tax liability of $238,000.

    b. White Corporation's 2011 tax return showed a net loss and $0 tax liability for the year.

41. Mimi had $40,000 in Federal income taxes withheld in 2010. Due to a sizable amount of itemized deductions, she figured that she had no further tax to pay for the year. For this reason and because of personal problems, and without securing an extension, she did not file her 2010 return until July 1, 2011. Actually, the return showed a refund of $2,400, which Mimi ultimately received. On May 10, 2014, Mimi filed a $16,000 claim for refund of her 2010 taxes.

    a. How much of the $16,000 will Mimi rightfully recover?

    b. How would your analysis differ if Mimi had secured from the IRS an automatic six-month extension of time for filing her 2010 return?

RESEARCH CASES

42. The Bird Estate committed tax fraud when it purposely understated the value of the business created and operated by the decedent, Beverly Bird. Executor Wilma Holmes admitted to the Tax Court that she had withheld several contracts and formulas that, had they been disclosed to the valuation experts used by the government and the estate, would have added $1 million in value to the business and over half that amount in Federal estate tax liabilities. Summary data include the following:

	Reported on Form 706	Other Amounts
Gross estate	$12 million	$1 million understatement
Deductions on original return	$ 2 million	
Interest on estate tax deficiency, professional fees incurred during administration period		$400,000

    Holmes asks you for advice in computing the fraud penalty. Ignore interest amounts. She wonders whether to take the 75 percent civil penalty against the full $1 million understatement or against the $600,000 net amount that the taxable estate would have increased had the administrative expenses been incurred prior to the filing date of the Form 706.

    Write Holmes, an experienced certified public accountant with an extensive tax practice, a letter stating your opinion.

43. Blanche Creek has engaged your firm because she has been charged with failure to file her 2010 Federal Form 1040. Blanche maintains that the "reasonable cause" exception should apply. During the entire tax filing season in 2011, she was under a great deal of stress at work and in her personal life. As a result, Blanche developed a sleep disorder, which was treated through a combination of pills and counseling.

    Your firm ultimately prepared the 2010 tax return for Blanche, but it was filed far beyond the due date. Blanche is willing to pay the delinquent tax and related interest. However, she feels that the failure-to-pay penalty is unfair, as she was ill. Consequently, she could not be expected to keep to the usual deadlines for filing.

    Write a letter to Blanche concerning these matters.

44. The Church of Freedom encourages its members to file "tax protestor" returns with the IRS, objecting to both the government's failure to use a gold standard in payment of tax liabilities, and its sizable expenditures for social welfare programs. These returns routinely are overturned by the tax court as frivolous, with delinquent taxes, penalties, and interest due, and the church has engaged in a longstanding, sometimes ugly battle with the IRS over various constitutional rights. Meanwhile, church members continue to file returns in this manner.

    Ellen overheard church members talking about "roughing up" the IRS agents who were scheduled to conduct an audit of various members' returns. She went to the IRS and informed them of the danger that they might encounter. At the IRS's direction, Ellen then took a key clerical job at church headquarters. In this context, she had access to useful documentation, and over a period of a few months gave to the IRS copies of church mailing lists and computer data. She also helped tape record key conversations among church leaders and search the church's trash for other documents. In other words, Ellen helped the IRS build a case of civil and criminal tax fraud against the church and various members.

All of these materials were given voluntarily to Ellen by church leaders in her context as an employee. Church members never suspected that she was working with the IRS. After delivering the various materials to the IRS, Ellen quit her job with the church and severed all communications with the IRS.

After the parties were charged with fraud, the government's case was found to be insufficiently supported by the evidence, and no penalties were assessed. Afterward, church leaders sued Ellen in her role as IRS informant, charging that she had violated their First Amendment rights of free association and their Fourth Amendment rights against illegal search and seizure. Government employees are immune from such charges, but Ellen was only an informant to the IRS and not its employee. Can the church collect damages from Ellen for informing on them?

45. Butcher attended meetings of tax protestors for many years in which the constitutionality of the Federal income tax and its means of collection were routinely challenged. Members of various protestor groups were provided with materials to assist them in preparing returns such that little or no tax would be due on the basis that, for instance, only gold-backed or silver-backed currency need be submitted to pay the tax or that a tax bill had originated in the Senate rather than the House of Representatives. Some of the groups maintained that no returns need be filed by individuals at all on the grounds that the current law supporting a Federal income tax violates various elements of the U.S. Constitution.

The U.S. Tax Court routinely has overturned such means of avoiding the tax, charging that such protestor returns were frivolously filed and charging the protestors with delinquent taxes, interest, and a variety of negligence and other accuracy-related penalties, especially where taxpayers failed to file altogether. The results of these cases never were discussed in the meetings that Butcher attended, though. Thus, although he never joined any of the groups, Butcher felt comfortable with the arguments of the protestor groups and never filed a Federal income tax return for himself or his profitable sole-proprietorship carpentry business.

When the IRS discovered his failure to file and charged him with tax, interest, and penalties, Butcher went to the tax library and found that judicial precedent and administrative authority were stacked against him. He asked the court for relief from the civil fraud penalties related to his failure to file and failure to pay tax on the basis of his good-faith belief that the tax protestor information he had received was an acceptable interpretation of the law. Under this argument, a taxpayer cannot be found to willfully have failed to file and pay if he or she had a good-faith belief that no such requirement was supported by the Constitution. Should Butcher be required to pay civil fraud penalties?

46. Chang wants to claim a cost recovery deduction for the acquisition of original artwork to be hung in the reception area of her dental office. The paintings were specially chosen because of their tendency to relax the patients who would be viewing them, thereby facilitating the conduct of Chang's business. Chang lives and works in the Fifth Circuit. A recent Eleventh Circuit case seems to support such a deduction, in limited circumstances. Complete the following chart, indicating for each independent assumption the actions that Chang can take without incurring the civil penalty for substantial understatement of taxes, but still maximizing her legitimate deductions for the year.

Probability of Success in Court	Claim the Deduction?	File a Form 8275 Disclosure?
80%		
40%		
20%		
2%		

47. Your client, Lee Ann Harkness, has been accused of criminal tax fraud. A high school dropout, she received hundreds of thousands of dollars over the years from Bentley, an elderly gentleman, in exchange for love and companionship. When Bentley died and Harkness was left out of the will, she sued the estate for compensatory payments earned throughout her years of tending to Bentley. The government now accuses Harkness of fraud in failing to file income and self-employment tax returns for the open tax years. Construct a defense on Harkness's behalf.

48. The Scooter Company, owned equally by Julie (chair of the board of directors) and Jeff (company president), is in very difficult financial straits. Last month, Jeff used the $100,000 withheld from employee paychecks for Federal payroll and income taxes to pay off a creditor who threatened to cut off all supplies. To keep the company afloat, Jeff used these government funds willfully for the operations of the business, but even that effort was not enough. The company missed the next two payrolls, and today other creditors took action to shut down Scooter altogether. From whom and for how much will the IRS assess in taxes and penalties in the matter?

49. For the completion and filing of his 2011 Federal income tax return, Ron retains the services of a tax preparer. Because of a particularly hectic tax preparation season, the preparer does not complete and file the return until June 2012. Is Ron excused from the failure to file and pay penalties under the reasonable cause exception?

50. Joan, a traveling sales representative, kept no formal books and records to summarize her gross receipts for the year, but she retained copies of all customer invoices and reported her gross income for the year from these totals. Is she liable for a negligence penalty under §6662 for failing to keep any books and records?

51. Duane paid his 2005 Federal income taxes in January 2008 in the amount of $10,000, and then paid $4,000 interest and penalties on this amount in May 2009. In April 2011, Duane filed a claim for refund of the $14,000, due to a sizable operating loss from his business in tax year 2010. Can he recover the 2005-related amounts?

52. Tobey was late in filing his Federal income tax refund claim, but he requested an extension of the statute of limitations, citing the financial disability exceptions of §6511(h). Tobey's mother is chronically ill, and he must make four-day-a-week trips to another city to care for her. Will the IRS grant Tobey's request?

The following definitions pertain specifically to the manner in which the identified terms are used in a tax research context. Other uses for such terms are not examined.

30-day letter   A notice from the Internal Revenue Service formally notifying the taxpayer of the results of an examination of the return and requesting that the taxpayer agree to the proposed modifications to the tax liability. A taxpayer's failure to respond to the letter triggers the statutory notice of a tax deficiency, that is, the 90-day letter demanding the payment of the tax or a petition to the tax court.

90-day letter   A statutory notice from the Internal Revenue Service (IRS) that the taxpayer has failed to pay an assessed tax. An issuance of such a letter usually indicates that the taxpayer has exhausted all of his or her appeal rights within the IRS and that the next forum for review will be a trial-level court. Strictly, the taxpayer has 90 days to petition the Tax Court to be relieved of the deficiency assessment. If no such petition is filed, the IRS is empowered to collect the assessed tax.

Accounting Standards Updates   New or revised guidance included in the FASB accounting standards codification when adopted and becoming part of U.S. GAAP.

Accuracy-related penalty   Civil tax penalty assessed where the taxpayer has been negligent in completing the return or is found to have acted with a disregard of Internal Revenue Service rules and regulations, a substantial understatement of the income tax, a substantial valuation or pension liability overstatement, or a substantial transfer tax valuation understatement. A 20 percent penalty usually applies to the pertinent understatement, and related interest accrues from the due date of the return, rather than the date on which the penalty was assessed.

Acquiescence   A pronouncement by the Internal Revenue Service that it will follow the decision of a court case to the extent that it was held for the taxpayer. Announced in the Internal Revenue Bulletin. Modifies the citation for the identified case.

Action on Decision (AOD)   A memorandum prepared when the Internal Revenue Service (IRS) loses a case in a court that recommends the action, if any, that the IRS should take in response to the adverse decision. See also acquiescence, nonacquiescence.

Ad valorem penalties   Additions to tax based on a percentage of the delinquent tax.

Administrative sources   Federal tax law that is created by the appropriate use of power that is granted to the Treasury Department by Congress. These sources of the law have a presumption of the authority of the statute, but they are subject to taxpayer challenge. Such sources include Regulations, rulings, revenue procedures, and other opinions that are used by the Treasury Department or the Internal Revenue Service.

AFTR   The citation abbreviation for the tax case reporter, American Federal Tax Reports. The first series of the reporter includes cases concerning pre-1954 Code litigation, and the second and third series include cases that address issues relative to the 1954 and 1986 Codes, respectively. Includes most tax case opinions issued by Federal courts other than the Tax Court.

American Bar Association (ABA)   The professional organization for practicing attorneys in the United States.

American Institution of Certified Public Accountants (AICPA)   The professional organization of practicing Certified Public Accountants (CPAs) in the United States, namely, the American Institute of CPAs.

Annotated tax service   A commercial tax research reference collection, that is, a secondary source of Federal tax law. Includes Code, Regulation and ruling analysis, judicial case notes, and other indexes and finding lists, organized by Code section number. The two most important annotated services are published by Commerce Clearing House and Research Institute of America.

Annotation   An entry in (especially) an annotated tax service, indicating a summary of a primary source of the Federal tax law that is pertinent to one's research, for example, a court case opinion digest or a reference to a controlling Regulation.

Announcements and Notices   The Internal Revenue Service issues Announcements and Notices concerning items of general importance to taxpayers.

Annual Proceedings   A collection of papers presented at a yearly meeting of tax professionals.

Appeals Office   The internal group of the Internal Revenue Service (IRS) that has the greatest authority to come to a compromise solution with a taxpayer concerning a disputed tax liability. Can consider the "hazards of litigation" in its deliberations. Failure to reach an agreement at this level of the IRS's organization means that the only subsequent appeal by either party to the dispute must be before a court of law.

Assessable penalties   Penalties expressed as a flat dollar amount rather than a percentage of the delinquent tax.

Assessment   The process of the Internal Revenue Service (IRS) fixing the amount of one's tax liability. Although the U.S. tax system exhibits some degree of self-assessment, the IRS has the ultimate authority to assess the liability of every taxpayer.

Auto-Cite   A citator in Lexis; the primary objective of Auto-Cite is to provide accurate citations as soon as possible, within 24 hours of receipt of each case. Auto-Cite can also be used to determine whether cases, Revenue Rulings, and Revenue Procedures are still good law.

Average tax rate   The percentage of a taxpayer's income that is paid in taxes (i.e., computed by dividing the current-year tax liability by the taxpayer's income). The average tax rate is computed as a percentage of total taxable income (this generates the taxpayer's average nominal tax rate) or as a percentage of the taxpayer's total economic income (this generates the taxpayer's average effective tax rate).

BNA Daily Tax Report   A daily collection of the latest Regulations, rulings, case opinions, and other tax law revisions, as well as news reports, press releases, congressional studies and schedules, interviews, and other items of interest to the tax practitioner. Available through the mail and on various electronic tax services. One of the most important tax newsletters published because of its breadth of topics and its quality of analysis. In addition, the newsletter provides interviews with government officials, articles reviewing the day's events, and the full text of key documents discussed in the newsletter.

BNA Premier International Tax Library   A detailed analysis of worldwide taxation, and a source of international news updates, complementing the BNA Foreign Income Library.

BNA Tax Management Portfolios   A topical tax service published by the Bureau of National Affairs in a collection of more than 400 magazine-size portfolios, dedicated to U.S. income, foreign income, and estate and gift taxation. Prepared by an identified expert in the field, each portfolio includes a detailed analysis of the topic, working papers with which to implement planning suggestions, and a bibliography of related literature. Supplemented by a biweekly newsletter, the portfolio series includes a topical index and case name and Code section finding lists.

BNA Weekly Report   The Bureau of National Affairs (BNA) weekly publication that has coverage similar to the BNA Daily Tax Report but provides more depth. In addition, it contains articles on news and emerging tax topics.

Board of Tax Appeals   An earlier name for the U.S. Tax Court, which did not have full judicial status. Opinions are recorded in the Board of Tax Appeals reporter, the citation abbreviation for which is BTA.

Boolean   A deductive logic search that allows for the intersection of terms by using connectors such as "or," "and," or "within # number of words."

Bureau of National Affairs (BNA)   A subsidiary of Tax Management. It offers a wide range of products covering all areas of Federal taxes. It is best known as the publisher of the BNA Tax Management Portfolios (BNA Portfolios). BNA Tax Management also offers electronic tax services, including the Tax Practice Library, and TaxCore.

Case brief   A concise summary of the facts, issues, holdings, and analyses of a court case. Used in a tax research context to allow subsequent review of the case by its author or another party. Includes complete citations of the briefed case, and other items addressed in the brief, to facilitate additional review when necessary.

CCH Citator   A citator published by Commerce Clearing House that is part of the Standard Federal Tax Reporter. The volumes of this loose-leaf service are labeled A to L and M to Z with a Finding List for Rulings in the back of the M to Z volume. This service covers the Federal income tax decisions that have been issued since 1913.

CCH Federal Tax Articles (FTA)   A loose-leaf and bound index to Federal tax articles published by Commerce Clearing House. This index provides concise abstracts for each article cited in the index. The framework for organizing these abstracts is the Code section. More than 250 journals, law reviews, papers, and proceedings are included in the index.

CCH IntelliConnect   The Commerce Clearing House (CCH) Internet platform for its tax research services. It is designed to be intuitive and the entire CCH library can be searched from one screen. It is one of the most well known tax services used by accountants.

CCH Standard Federal Tax Income Reporter   See Standard Federal Tax Income Reporter.

CCH Tax Research Consultant   See Tax Research Consultant.

CCH Tax Treaties Reporter   CCH database that reproduces the full text of U.S. bilateral income, estate and gift tax treaties, exchange of information, totalization (social security), shipping/aircraft tax treaties, protocols, and other related documents on taxation agreements.

CCH's Accounting Research Manager (ARM) A database of financial reporting, auditing, accounting guidance for U.S. government, and international entities offered by CCH.

Chief Counsel The chief legal officer of the Internal Revenue Service. Responsible for making litigation and acquiesce/nonacquiesce decisions, and for developing interpretive material of the agency, including rulings and memoranda.

Circular 230 A tax Regulation detailing the requirements and responsibilities of those who prepare Federal tax returns for compensation. Includes educational, ethical, and procedural guidelines.

Citation A means of conveying the location of a document. Appendix B of this text offers a standard format for citations used by tax researchers.

Citator A research resource that presents the judicial history of a court case and traces the subsequent references to the case. When these references include the citing case's evaluations of the cited case's precedents, the research can obtain some measure of the efficacy and reliability of the original holding.

Cite When one case refers to another case, it cites the latter case.

Cited case With respect to a citator, the original case, whose facts or holding are referred to in the opinion of the citing case.

Citing case With respect to a citator, the subsequent case, which includes a reference to the original (cited) case.

Citing Reference In the Westlaw citator, a listing of all cases that refer to the cited case.

Civil penalty In a tax practice context, a fine or other judgment that is brought against a taxpayer or preparer for a failure to comply with one or more of the elements of the Federal tax law. Examples include penalties for failure to file a return or pay a tax in a timely fashion.

Client letter A primary means by which to communicate one's research results to the client. Includes, among other features, a summary of the controlling fact situation and attendant assumptions, a summary of the critical sources of the tax law that led to the researcher's conclusions, specific implications of the results of the project, and recommendations for client action.

Closed transaction A tax research situation is closed when all of the pertinent transactions have been completed by the taxpayer and other parties, such that the research issues may be limited to the proper nature and amount of disclosure to the

government on the tax return or other document, and to preparation activities relative to subsequent government review.

Closing agreement A form with which the taxpayer and the Internal Revenue Service finalize their computations of a disputed tax liability.

Cohan Rule The doctrine that allows taxpayers to use estimates to claim a tax deduction when they can show that there is some factual foundation on which to base a reasonable approximation of the expense.

Collateral estoppel The legal principle that limits one's judicial exposure relative to a disputed item to one series of court hearings. In a tax environment, the principle can present hardships for the taxpayer who wishes to raise additional issues during the course of a judicial proceeding.

Collection The process by which the Internal Revenue Service extracts an assessed tax liability from a taxpayer. Usually takes the form of the receipt of a check or other draft from the taxpayer, but can include liens or other garnishments of taxpayer assets.

Commerce Clause The clause of the U.S. Constitution indicating that Congress has the power to regulate commerce with foreign nations, among states, and with Native American tribes. It grants powers to Congress and places constraints on the states' ability to tax interstate trade.

Commerce Clearing House (CCH) A major commercial source of text and online information concerning domestic and international tax law.

Commissioner of Internal Revenue The chief operating and chief executive officer of the Internal Revenue Service (IRS). Holds the ultimate responsibility for overall planning and for directing, coordinating, and controlling the policies and programs of the IRS.

Committee Report A summary of the issues that were considered by the House Ways and Means Committee, Senate Finance Committee, or Joint Conference Committee, here relative to proposed or adopted changes in the language of the Internal Revenue Code. Useful in tax research as an aid to understanding unclear statutory language and legislative history or intent. Published in the Internal Revenue Bulletin.

Compilation Broadly, a collection of primary sources, editorial comments, and annotations in a tax service (i.e., its collection of volumes).

Contingent fees The practice under which a professional bases his or her fee for services upon the results thereof. The American Institute of Certified Public Accountants has held that the performance of services for a contingent fee can be unethical; one exception is available, though, where (as in tax practice) the results are subject to third-party actions (here the government, in an audit setting). Several states are relaxing this restriction, allowing certified public accountants to mix the form of their compensation between fixed and contingent fees.

Correspondence examination An audit of one's tax return that is conducted largely by telephone or mail. Usually involves a request for substantiation or explanation of one or more items on a tax return, such as filing status, exemptions, and itemized deductions for medical expenses, interest, taxes paid, charitable contributions, or miscellaneous deductions.

Court of Appeals A Federal appellate court that hears appeals from the Tax Court, Court of Federal Claims, or District Courts within its geographical boundaries. Organized into geographical circuits, although there are additional circuits for Washington, D.C., and for cases appealed from the Court of Federal Claims. Opinions are recorded in the Federal Reporter, various series, and in the American Federal Tax Reports and United States Tax Cases reporter series.

Court of Federal Claims A trial-level court in which the taxpayer typically sues the government for a refund of overpaid tax liability. Hears nontax matters as well in Washington, D.C., or in other major cities. Opinions are reported in the Court of Federal Claims reporter and in the American Federal Tax Reports and United States Tax Cases case reporter series.

Covered Opinions Written advice by practitioners concerning one or more Federals tax issues that are defined in Circular 230, Subpart B, Section 10.35.

Criminal penalty A severe infraction of the elements of the Federal tax law by a taxpayer or preparer. Felony or misdemeanor status for tax crimes can be accompanied by substantial fines or jail terms. Examples of tax crimes include tax evasion and other willful failures to comply with the Internal Revenue Code.

Cumulative Bulletin An official publication of the Internal Revenue Service (IRS), consolidating the material that first was published in the Internal Revenue Bulletin in a (usually semiannual) hardbound volume. Publication alters the proper citation for the contents thereof.

Definitely related deductions Expenses incurred as a result of, or incident to, an activity or in connection with property from which such class of gross income is derived when allocating deductions between foreign and U.S. sources.

Department of the Treasury Responsible for administering and enforcing the internal revenue laws of the United States. The Internal Revenue Service is a bureau of the Treasury Department.

Determination Letter An Internal Revenue Service (IRS) pronouncement issued by the local IRS office, relative to the agency's position concerning a straightforward issue of tax law in the context of a completed transaction.

Direct History In a citator, the listing of the citations to hearings of the cited case by lower level courts.

Discriminant function formula (DIF) A means by which, on the basis of probable return to the Internal Revenue Service in terms of collected delinquent tax liabilities, the Service selects tax returns for examination.

District Court A trial-level court that hears tax and nontax cases. Organized according to geographical regions. Jury trials are available. Opinions are reported in the Federal Supplement Series and in the American Federal Tax Reports and United States Tax Cases reporter series.

Due Diligence The care a reasonable person should take in preparing or assisting in the preparation of, approving, and filing of tax returns, documents, and other papers relating to Internal Revenue service matters. See Circular 230 Subpart B, Section 10.22.

Due Process Clause Found in the Fourteenth Amendment to the U.S. Constitution, the clause (among other things) limits the territorial scope of a state's taxing authority, particularly in regard to interstate commerce.

Effective average tax rate The proportion of a taxpayer's economic income that was paid to the government as a tax liability (i.e., it is computed by dividing the tax liability by the taxpayer's economic income for the year). Economic income includes nontaxable sources of income, such as gifts and inheritances, and tax-exempt interest.

En banc When more than one Tax Court judge hears a case, the court is said to be sitting "en banc".

Enrolled agent (EA) One who is qualified to practice before the Internal Revenue Service by means other than becoming an attorney or certified public accountant. Typically, one must pass a qualifying examination and meet other requirements to become an Enrolled Agent.

Ethical standards Boundaries of social or professional behavior, derived by the culture or its institutions. Tax ethics are described in various documents of governmental agencies or professional organizations.

Fact issue A tax research issue in which the practitioner must determine whether a pertinent question of fact was satisfied by the taxpayer; for example, was an election filed with the government in a timely manner? What was the taxpayer's motivation underlying the redemption of some corporate stock?

Failure-to-file penalty   A penalty imposed on taxpayers who fail to file a required tax return. The penalty can be waived for reasonable cause and is coordinated with the failure to pay penalty.

Failure-to-pay penalty   A penalty imposed on taxpayers who fail to pay a tax that is shown on his or her return. The penalty is generally .5 percent of the required liability for each month that the tax is not paid up to a maximum penalty of 25 percent.

FASB Accounting Standards Codification (ASC)
The source of authoritative generally accepted accounting principles (GAAP) recognized by the FASB to be applied to nongovernmental entities.

FASB Accounting Standards Codification Research System (CRS)   Online system to document and research the FASB Accounting Standards Codification (ASC).

Federal Tax Coordinator   The Research Institute of America (RIA) flagship topical tax service offered through RIA Checkpoint.

Field Examination   An audit of one's tax return that is conducted on the taxpayer's premises. These audits are usually more involved and comprehensive than correspondence or office audits.

File memorandum   A primary means by which to communicate the results of a research project to oneself, one's supervisor, and/or one's successor. Includes, among other features, a statement of the pertinent facts and assumptions, a detailed outline (and citations of) controlling tax law, a summary of the researcher's conclusions, and a listing of action recommendations for the client to consider.

Finance Committee   The committee of the United States Senate that deals with matters of taxation.

Financial Accounting Standards Board (FASB)   The designated organization in the private sector for establishing standards of financial accounting that govern the preparation of financial reports by nongovernmental entities in the United States.

Foreign tax credit   A reduction of U.S. tax liability for taxes paid or accrued to a foreign country on foreign source income and also subject to U.S. tax.

Fraud   In a tax practice context, a taxpayer action to evade the assessment of a tax. Criminal fraud requires a willful intent by the taxpayer. The Internal Revenue Service bears the burden of proof relative to fraud allegations.

Freedom of Information Act (FOIA)   Federal law that requires the Treasury (and other Federal agencies) to release redacted documents to the public. In the tax research context, this allows for the publication of letter rulings and other

Internal Revenue Service written determinations, and their use by the tax professional in the research process.

Frivolous return   A return that does not include enough information to figure the correct tax or that contains information or statements that on their face indicate that the self-assessment requirement has not been met, or takes positions that are meant to impede the administration of the tax law.

Full-text search   A computerized version of a published index. A full-text search locates every occurrence of a word or phrase in every document available for the search.

General Counsel's Memorandum   A memoranda generated upon the request of the Internal Revenue Service, typically as a means to assist in the preparation of Revenue Rulings and Private Letter Rulings.

General Regulation   A Regulation issued under the general authority granted to the Internal Revenue Service to interpret the language of the Code, usually under a specific Code directive of Congress, and with specific congressional authority.

Generally Accepted Accounting Principle (GAAP)   The body of accounting guidance governing the financial reporting by nongovernmental entities contained within the FASB accounting standards codification (ASC).

Golsen rule   Tax Court decisions are appealed to the Court of Appeals for the taxpayer's place of work or residence. The decisions of the Courts of Appeal are not always consistent. Thus, when a taxpayer whose circuit has ruled on a given issue brings a case that includes that issue before the Tax Court, the Tax Court follows the holding of the pertinent circuit, even if the Tax Court disagrees with the holding, or if another circuit has issued a contrary holding. This can lead to contradictory Tax Court rulings, based solely upon the state of the taxpayer's residence.

Headnote   Numbered paragraphs in which the editors of the court reporter summarize the court's holdings on each issue. These paragraphs appear in the court reporters before the text of the actual court case.

Independence   The American Institute of Certified Public Accountants requires the certified public accountant (CPA) who renders an opinion relative to a client's financial statements to be (and to appear to be) independent from the

client. This principle entails restrictions as to the CPA's direct and indirect financial dealings with the client, and its simultaneous role as financial auditor.

Indirect History   In a citator, the listing of cases citing the case of interest. The citator may indicate whether the citing cases positively or negatively affect the precedential value of the cited case.

Injunction   The action by which the Internal Revenue Service or a court prevents (enjoins) a taxpayer, preparer, or tax shelter distributor from undertaking a specified action (e.g., preparing tax returns for compensation or offering a tax shelter for sale).

Internal Revenue Bulletin   An official weekly publication of the Internal Revenue Service that includes Announcements, Treasury Decisions, Revenue Rulings, Revenue Procedures, and other information of interest to the tax researcher.

Internal Revenue Code   The primary statutory source of the Federal tax law, a collection of laws that have been passed by Congress and incorporated in Title 26 of the U.S. Code. The Code was last reorganized in 1954. It is presently known as the Internal Revenue Code of 1986. The chief subdivision of the Code is the section.

Internal Revenue Service (IRS)   A division of the Department of the Treasury, the Federal agency that is charged with the collection of Federal taxes and the implementation of other responsibilities that are conveyed by the Internal Revenue Code.

International Accounting Standards Board (IASB)   The independent standard-setting body responsible for the development and publication of the International Financial Reporting Standards (IFRS).

International Financial Reporting Standards (IFRS)   A single set of high quality financial reporting standards developed by the International Accounting Standards Board (IASB) for use globally.

IRS Oversight Board   A group of at least nine individuals that acts as the board of directors of the Internal Revenue Service. Responsible for overseeing the agency's operational and internal control functions, approving mission plans and strategies, reviewing the agency's budget, and ensuring the proper treatment of taxpayers.

Joint Audit Program   Allows the Multistate Tax Commission to perform a comprehensive audit of a business's taxes simultaneously for several states.

Joint Conference Committee   A committee formed to reconcile differences in versions of a tax bill passed by the United States House and Senate.

Judicial sources   Certain Federal court decisions that have the force of the statute in constructing the Federal tax law. The magnitude of this authority depends upon the level and location of the courts that issued the opinions.

Key number   A means used by the publisher to organize important topics in the tax law. Used as a reference by the tax services and citators published by West.

Key Word in Context (KWIC)   Key word in context, a means by which to display electronic search results.

KeyCite   A Westlaw citator that furnishes a comprehensive direct and indirect history for court cases. The indirect history includes secondary materials that have the cited case in their text. KeyCite allows the researcher to select a full history, negative history, or omit minor cases. This option is not available with the other citators.

KeySearch   A search aid employing the West numbering system of the key issues in court cases. When a researcher identifies the legal topic applicable to the search, this search aid formulates a query based on the underlying terms for the topic based on the key numbers system.

Large Business and International (LB&I) Division   An operating division of the Internal Revenue Service serving large C-corporations, S-corporations and partnerships, certain high-wealth individuals and handling international tax compliance efforts.

Law issue   A tax research question in which one must determine which provision of the Federal tax law applies to the client's fact situation. This entails the evaluation of various statutory, administrative, and judicial provisions with respect to the client's circumstances; for example, is the client's charitable contribution subject to the 30 percent of adjusted gross income limitation?

Law reviews   Scholarly publications of law schools. These publications are edited either by faculty members or by graduate students under the guidance of the school's faculty. Most law reviews also use an outside advisory board comprised of practicing attorneys and law professors at other universities to aid in selecting and reviewing articles. The articles appearing in these publications usually are written by tax practitioners, academics, graduate students, or other noted commentators.

Legislative Regulation   A Regulation by which the Internal Revenue Service is directed by Congress to fulfill a law-making function and to specify the substantive requirements of a tax provision.

LEXCITE   A citator service of Lexis. For the case citation entered, it ascertains parallel citations and then searches for all of the cites in the case law documents. It will find embedded references to a variety of documents such as cases, law reviews, journals, Federal Register, and Revenue Rulings.

Lexis   An Internet service for legal (tax) sources started by LexisNexis in 1973.

LexisNexis   One of the largest legal and news services available on the Internet. An online database resource that allows the researcher to access a database consisting of the text of court cases, administrative rulings, and selected law review articles and to search these files for tax (and other) law sources that may be relevant to the research problem.

LexisNexis Academic   A version of the LEXIS and NEXIS database services designed for use at public libraries, universities, and law schools.

LexisNexis Tax Center   See Tax Center.

Local citation   A citation that directs the researcher to the exact page where the cited case is mentioned in the citing case.

Marginal tax rate   The proportion of the next dollar of gross income (or other increase in the tax base) that the taxpayer must pay to the government as a tax. Thus, the marginal tax rate conveys the proportionate value of an additional deduction, or the cost of an increase to the tax base. Tax-effective decisions must take into account the marginal (and not the average or nominal) tax rate.

Memorandum decision   A decision of the Tax Court that, in the opinion of the chief judge, does not address any new issue of tax law. Accordingly, the government does not publish the opinion. Commerce Clearing House and Research Institute of America each publish annual collections of these Tax Court Memorandum decisions.

Mertens Law of Federal Income Taxation   A topical tax service designed chiefly by and for attorneys.

Multistate Tax Commission (MTC)   Created in 1967 by the Multistate Tax Compact. The MTC adopted the Uniform Division of Income for Tax Purposes Act (UDITPA) as part of its Articles, issued Regulations interpreting the UDITPA, and continues to issue apportionment rules. As of early 2008, there are 47 states participants in MTC.

National Nexus Program   Developed by the Multistate Tax Commission. Its function is to facilitate information sharing among participating states.

National Research Program (NRP)   A means by which the Internal Revenue Service develops its discriminant function formulae. The taxpayer's return is selected randomly for an extensive review, during which every item of income, credit, deduction, and exclusion is challenged by the government. The results of such reviews are used (other than to adjust the examined taxpayer's liability) to delineate criteria by which other axpayers' returns are selected for examination.

National Taxpayer Advocate   Empowered to achieve a temporary delay in the normal enforcement procedures of the Internal Revenue Service, as specified in a Tax-payer Assistance Order.

Natural language   A search where a tax question is entered in standard English (natural language) words, phrases (entered within quotation marks), or sentences. The program determines the key terms for searching and relationships among the words (i.e., connectors to apply). This type of search is useful when the researcher is unsure as to which connectors and keywords would be the most effective.

Negligence   In a Federal tax context, a (nonwillful) failure to exercise one's duty with respect to the Internal Revenue Code or to use a reasonable degree of expected or professional care. Examples include the unacceptable failure to attempt to follow the IRS's rules and Regulations in the preparation of a tax return for compensation.

Nexis   An Internet service for news, financial, and business information, started by LexisNexis in 1979.

Nexus   A sufficient business connection with a locality that gives taxing authority to the locality over the business.

Nominal average tax rate   Determined by an inspection of the applicable rate schedule. The average nominal rate at which the taxpayer's total taxable income is taxed is computed by dividing the taxpayer's total tax liability by his or her taxable income. Tax-exempt income is not included in the denominator of this fraction.

Nonacquiescence   An announcement by the Internal Revenue Service (IRS) that it will not follow the decision of a court in a tax decision that was adverse to the agency. Notation is included in the proper citation of the disputed case. Announced in the Internal Revenue Bulletin.

Not definitely related deductions   Expenses that are not directly related or subject to special apportionment rules when allocating deductions between foreign and U.S. sources.

Offer in compromise   The means by which the government offers to reduce the amount of an assessed tax, usually because of some doubt as to the "litigation-proof" magnitude or collectibility of the tax. A legally enforceable promise that cannot be rescinded, an offer in compromise relates to the entire liability of the taxpayer, and it conclusively settles all of the issues for which an agreement can be made.

Office Examination   An audit of one's tax return that is conduced at a local IRS office. These audits are typically more involved than correspondence audits and often deal with multiple issues that will require some analysis and exercise of judgment by the auditor.

Open transaction   A tax research issue is open when not all of the pertinent transactions have been completed by the taxpayer or other parties, such that the researcher can suggest to the client several alternative courses of action that generate differing tax consequences.

Permanent citation   A Tax Court citation issued to a Tax Court decision containing the case name, volume number, reporter page number, and the year of the decision.

Practice before the IRS   The privilege to sign tax returns as preparer for compensation and to represent others before the Internal Revenue Service (IRS) or in court in an audit or appeal proceeding. This privilege is granted by the IRS and controlled under Circular 230.

Precedential value   A document has precedential value if it can be used as authority, support, or a basis for a subsequent decision in a similar situation.

Preparer penalties   A series of fines and other levies by which the Internal Revenue Service (IRS) encourages tax-payers and preparers to fulfill their responsibilities under the Internal Revenue Code. Examples include penalties for failure to sign returns, keep or furnish copies of returns, and provide required information to Federal agencies.

Primary authority   An element of the Federal tax law that was issued by Congress, the Treasury or Internal Revenue Service, or a Federal court, and thus carries greater precedential weight than elements of the tax law issued by other parties.

Private letter ruling   A written determination published by the Internal Revenue Service relative to its position concerning the tax treatment of a prospective transaction. Strictly, it cannot be applied to any taxpayer other than the one who requested the ruling. Text or summaries thereof are included in various commercial tax services.

Professional and practitioner journal   Journals published by professional organizations and commercial companies. The objective of these journals is to keep tax practitioners abreast of the current changes and trends in the tax law.

Progressive tax rate   If the marginal rates of a tax rate schedule increase as the magnitude of the tax base increases, the schedule includes progressive tax rates.

Proportional tax rate   If the marginal rates of a tax rate schedule remain constant as the magnitude of the tax base increases, the schedule includes proportional tax rates.

Proposed Regulation   An interpretation or clarification of the provisions of a portion of the Internal Revenue Code, issued by the Treasury and available for comment (and possible revision) in a public hearing.

Public Law 87-272   U.S. Federal law that prohibits a state from imposing a net income tax if a company's only state activities are solicitation of orders for sales of tangible personal property which are sent outside the state for approval or rejection and are filled from outside the state.

Realistic possibility   Formerly the standard by which a tax preparer conduct penalty was applied under IRC Section 6694 and the current standard for tax return positions under the AICPA's SSTS No. 1. Under SSTS No. 1, a member should have a good-faith belief that the position has at least a realistic possibility of being sustained administratively or judicially on its merits if challenged.

Reasonable cause   A means by which a taxpayer or preparer can be excused from an applicable penalty or other sanction. For instance, if the taxpayer failed to file a tax return on a timely basis because of illness or if the underlying records were destroyed by natural cause, the taxpayer likely would be excused from the penalty (but not from the tax or any related interest) because of this reasonable cause.

Regressive tax rate   If the marginal rates of a tax rate schedule decrease as the magnitude of the tax base increases, the schedule includes regressive tax rates.

Regular decision   A decision issued by the Tax Court that generally involves a new or unusual point of law, as determined by the Chief Judge of the court.

Regulation   An interpretation or clarification of the provisions of a portion of the Internal Revenue Code, issued by the Treasury under authority granted by Congress. Legislative Regulations directly create the details of a tax law. Both general and legislative Regulations carry the force of the statute, unless they are held to be invalid in a judicial hearing.

Research Institute of America (RIA)   A major commercial source of text and online information concerning domestic and international tax law.

ResultsPlus   A Westlaw feature that provides a list of suggested analytical materials relevant to the topic being searched.

The materials appear in law reports, treatises, law reviews, and topical services such as Mertens and BNA Portfolios.

Revenue Agent's Report   Prepared upon the completion of the examination of a tax return to explain to the taxpayer the sources of any adjustments to the reported tax liability. If the taxpayer agrees to this recomputation, the associated tax, penalty, and interest become due. Lacking such agreement, other aspects of the appeals process are undertaken.

Revenue Procedure   A pronouncement of the Internal Revenue Service concerning the implementation details of a specific Code provision. Published in the Internal Revenue Bulletin.

Revenue Ruling   A pronouncement of the Internal Revenue Service concerning its interpretation of the application of the Code (typically) to a specific taxpayer-submitted fact situation. Published in the Internal Revenue Bulletin. Can be relied upon as precedent by other taxpayers who encounter similar fact patterns.

RIA Checkpoint   The Internet tax service provided by Research Institute of America. This is one of the most authoritative and wellknown Internet tax services available. All services available from Research Institute of America may be accessed by subscription through Checkpoint.

RIA Citator 2nd   Published by Research Institute of America. The Citator 2nd Series is composed of three bound volumes plus paperback supplements, which cover from 1954 to the present. This citator series includes the history of cases that have been decided since 1954 and updates for cited cases appearing in the previous series. Within each volume, the cases are arranged in alphabetical order.

RIA Federal Tax Coordinator   See Federal Tax Coordinator.

RIA International Create-a-Chart   A feature offered by Research Institute of America with its international tax materials. It facilitates the creation of comparison charts for global tax laws. This feature enables the practitioner to summarize pertinent international tax information in a chart that can be exported to a word processing document.

RIA International Tax Library (ITL)   A comprehensive series of tax databases offered by RIA.

RIA International Taxes Weekly   A weekly e-newsletter covering current developments and emerging issues related to international taxation.

RIA Tax Advisors Planning System   A series of portfolios written by expert practitioners currently in practice. These portfolios, updated monthly, focus on specific issues relevant to taxpayers in the international economy, among other topical areas. Each portfolio includes commentary, advice supported by detailed explanations, integrated planning ideas, and current tax rules with citations to the controlling authorities.

RIA United States Tax Reporter   See United States Tax Reporter.

RIA Worldwide Tax Law (WTL)   A tax service offered by RIA that offers English translations of tax and commercial laws for approximately 90 countries.

Secondary authority   An element of the Federal tax law that was issued by a scholarly or professional writer for example, in a textbook, journal article, or treatise, and thus carries less precedential weight than elements of the tax law issued by primary sources.

Securities and Exchange Commission (SEC)   A Federal agency in the United States with responsibilities that include enforcing Federal securities laws and regulating the securities industry. The SEC also has statutory authority to establish financial accounting and reporting standards for publicly held companies in the United States.

Shepardizing   Slang used in the legal profession used to describe the process of using a Shepard's citator.

Shepard's Citator   The only major tax citator that is organized by case reporter series.

Small Business and Self-Employed (SB/SE) Division   An operating division of the Internal Revenue Service serving self-employed taxpayers and small businesses.

Small Cases Division   The Tax Court allows taxpayers whose disputed tax liability does not exceed $50,000 to try the case before the court's Small Cases Division. Procedural rules of the division are somewhat relaxed, and taxpayers often represent themselves. The Small Cases Division decisions are not published, nor can either party appeal the holdings thereof.

Source Determination   In international tax law, different rules apply depending on where the income and deductions are "sourced."

Standard Federal Income Tax Reporter (SFITR)   The Commerce Clearing House (CCH) flagship annotated tax service offered through CCH IntelliConnect.

Statute of limitations   Provides the maximum amount of time within which one or both parties in the taxing process must perform an act, such as file a return, pay a tax, or examine a return. Various time limits apply relative to the Internal Revenue Code, although both parties can, by mutual agreement, extend one or more of these time limitations, if desired.

Statutory notice of deficiency   Synonym for a 90-day letter.

Statutory sources   The Constitution, tax treaties, and the Internal Revenue Code are the statutory sources of the

Federal tax law. They have the presumption of correctness, unless a court modifies or overturns a provision in response to a taxpayer challenge. In this regard, legislative intent and history can be important in supporting the taxpayer's case.

Streamlined Sales and Use Tax Agreement   A set of rules and regulations adopted in whole or in part by certain states intended to simplify and modernize sales and use tax administration in order to substantially reduce the burden of tax compliance.

Substantial authority   A taxpayer penalty may be incurred if a tax return position is taken and not disclosed to the Internal Revenue Service where no substantial authority (generally, statute, Regulation, court decision, or written determination) supports the position.

Supremacy Clause   The clause in the U.S. Constitution that confers superiority to Federal laws over state laws. That is, Federal laws are "the supreme law of the land" and trump state laws. If a state law or constitutional provision is in conflict with a Federal law, the state provision is invalid.

Supreme Court   The highest Federal appellate court. Hears very few tax cases. Approves a writ of certiorari for the cases that it hears. Opinions are reported in the U.S. Supreme Court Reports (citation abbreviation, US); the Supreme Court Reporter (SCt); the United States Reports, Lawyer's Edition (LEd); the American Federal Tax Reports and United States Tax Cases reporter series; and various online services.

Table of Authorities   Is a list of the cases that are a cited reference in the case of interest. The subsequent treatment of these referenced cases is provided. This allows the researcher to evaluate the cases upon which the case of interest relies.

Tax Advisor-Federal Code-Reporter   The LexisNexis annotated service for Code-based research.

Tax Advisor-Federal Topical   The LexisNexis topical tax services that includes validation from Shepard's.

Tax Analysts   A nonprofit entity organized to provide literary forums for the discussion of taxation. It disseminates timely and comprehensive state, Federal, and international tax information through their daily, weekly, and monthly print publications, scholarly books, and electronic database services.

Tax Analysts Worldwide Tax Daily   An international news daily with news updates from around the world, available on LexisNexis and elsewhere. It includes full-text PDF files of international tax documents and treaties discussed in its articles. The information is organized by countries and international organizations.

Tax Analysts Worldwide Tax Treaties   A tax service available on LexisNexis and elsewhere to compare income tax treaties. Side-by-side tables compare the tax rates on various types of income and withholding rates among over 170 worldwide taxing jurisdictions. Original, in-force, pending, terminated, and unperfected treaties can be viewed.

Tax and Accounting Center (TAC)   The Bureau of National Affairs (BNA) Internet tax service platform.

Tax avoidance   The legal structuring of one's financial affairs so as to optimize the related tax liability. Synonym for tax planning.

Tax Center   LexisNexis Internet service exclusively for tax practitioners. This service is designed to streamline tax research by having a separate interface and facilitates a single search across the full tax content.

Tax compliance   An element of modern tax practice in which a practitioner works with a client to file appropriate tax returns in a timely manner and represents the client in administrative proceedings.

Tax Court   A trial-level court that hears only cases involving tax issues. Issues regular and memorandum decisions. Meets in Washington, D.C., and in other major cities. Formerly called the Board of Tax Appeals. Regular opinions are reported in the U.S. Tax Court Reports. Memorandum opinions are published only by commercial tax services.

Tax evasion   The reduction of one's tax liability by illegal means.

Tax Exempt and Government Entities (TEGE) Division   An operating division of the Internal Revenue Service serving employee pension plans, exempt organizations, and government entities.

Tax journal   A periodic publication that addresses legal, factual, and procedural issues encountered in a modern tax practice. As a secondary source of Federal tax law, analyses in tax journals can be used in support of a taxpayer's case before a government agency or, especially, before a court.

Tax litigation   An element of modern tax practice in which a practitioner represents the client against the government in a judicial hearing.

Tax newsletter   A weekly, biweekly, or monthly publication or electronic document, often furnished as part of a subscription to a commercial tax service. Typically provides digest-style summaries of current court case rulings, administrative pronouncements, and pending or approved tax legislation crossreferenced to the organization system of the tax service. Helps the practitioner to keep current relative to the breaking developments in the tax community.

Tax Notes A weekly collection of the latest Regulations, written determinations, case opinions, congressional studies, policy analyses, and other items of interest to the tax practitioner. Available through the mail and on various electronic tax services.

Tax Notes International Weekly publication by Tax Analysts that provides tax news, commentary, and in-depth analysis of legislative, judicial, and administrative tax developments from over 180 countries.

Tax Notes Today Version of the Tax Notes publication that discusses the latest developments in tax rulings, cases, transcripts, studies, and other documents of interest to the tax professional.

Tax planning Synonym for tax avoidance.

Tax Practice Library A basic electronic tax service of Bureau of National Affairs (BNA) furnishing access to primary sources, practice tools, and limited news sources. Rather than relying on the BNA Portfolio Series, Tax Practice Library has developed its own explanatory analysis. Other than offering fewer databases (no BNA Portfolio or journals), this service is almost identical to Portfolio Plus in its searching methods.

Tax Research An examination of pertinent sources of the state, local, and Federal tax law in light of all relevant circumstances relative to a client's tax problem. Entails the use of professional judgment to draw an appropriate conclusion and the communication of such conclusions or alternatives at a proper level to the client.

Tax Research Consultant (TRC) The Commerce Clearing House (CCH) topical tax service offered through CCH IntelliConnect. It is a hybrid between a CCH in-house service and a BNA outside authored topical service.

Tax return preparer (TRP) Any person who prepares for compensation, or employs one or more persons to prepare for compensation, all or a substantial portion of a tax return or claim for income tax refund.

Tax service A commercial tax reference including statutory, administrative, and judicial sources of Federal tax law. Structured to maximize the practitioner's ease of use via a variety of indexes and finding lists. Often includes the text of the pertinent tax authorities and relevant scholarly or professional commentary.

Tax treaty An act of Congress that addresses the application of certain Internal Revenue Code provisions to a taxpayer whose tax base falls under the taxing statutes of more than one country. Published, among other places, in the Internal Revenue Bulletin. Generally, treaties are negotiated to prevent double taxation by providing reduced tax rates, or exempting certain types of income from taxation. The income receiving reduced rates, and tax holidays and exemptions, vary among countries.

TaxCore BNA's web-based source of primary tax resources. Subscribers to several of Bureau of National Affairs' news services receive this service. It provides the hyperlinked primary sources and tax-related documents discussed and cited in the news reports.

Taxpayer Assistance Order The taxpayer uses this request to engage an Internal Revenue Service Taxpayer Advocate to delay the implementation of an IRS action, such as a collection or seizure activity, where it appears that the taxpayer has received less than fair treatment through the administrative procedures of the agency.

Technical Advice Memorandum A pronouncement of the National Office of the Internal Revenue Service stating the agency's position relative to the tax treatment of a taxpayer whose return is under audit. Text or discussion thereof may be included in the body of a commercial tax service.

Technical Memorandum (TM) A document prepared in the production of a Proposed Regulation.

Temporary citation A Tax Court citation issued to a Tax Court decision containing the case name, volume number, reporter, the case number, and the year of the decision. The page number is not included because the opinion has not yet been published.

Temporary Regulation An administrative pronouncement of the Internal Revenue Service, typically concerning the application of a recently enacted or detailed provision of the tax law, especially where there is insufficient time to carry out the publichearings process that usually accompanies the Regulations process. Temporary Regulations carry the force of law, although citations differ from those for permanent Regulations with regard to the prefix.

Terms and Connectors The LexisNexis form of a Boolean search.

Territorial Model A structure of international taxation under which the profits of a business are taxed by the country in which the business is earned.

Topical tax service A professional tax research reference collection, that is, a secondary source of Federal tax law. Includes Code, Regulation, and ruling analysis; judicial case notes; and other indexes and finding lists organized by general topic. The most important topical tax services are published by the Research Institute of America and the Bureau of National Affairs.

Transfer pricing The price-setting process between related parties.

Treasury Decision (TD) A Regulation that has not yet been formally integrated into the published tax Regulation collection. Often issued in the Internal Revenue Bulletin. Typically provides digest-style summaries of current court case rulings, administrative pronouncements, and pending or approved tax legislation crossreferenced to the organization system of the tax service. Helps the practitioner to keep current relative to the breaking developments in the tax community.

Unauthorized practice of law   A prohibited aspect of modern tax practice by nonattorneys, entailing, for example, the issuance of a legal opinion or the drafting of a legal document for the client, for which the practitioner could be subject to legal or professional penalties.

Unconscionable fee   Prohibits charging a fee for tax work that is not in accordance with what is just or reasonable; see Circular 230, Subpart B, Section 10.27(a).

Uniform Division of Income for Tax Purposes Act (UDITPA)   Drafted in 1957 by the National Conference of Commissioners on Uniform State Laws, to create a greater uniformity and consistency in the measurements of business income.

United States Tax Cases (USTC)   The citation abbreviation for the Commerce Clearing House reporter, United States Tax Cases. Includes most of the tax decisions of the Federal courts other than the Tax Court.

United States Tax Reporter (USTR)   The Research Institute of America (RIA) annotated tax service offered through RIA Checkpoint.

Wage and Investment (W&I) Division   An operating division of the Internal Revenue Service serving 1040 filers with only wage and investment income.

Warren, Gorham & Lamont (WG&L)   Publishers of leading tax journals and well respected and influential tax treatises. WG&L is an affiliate of Thomson Reuters.

Ways and Means Committee   The committee of the United States House of Representatives that deals with matters of taxation.

West Key Number System   A means used by the publisher to organize important topics in the tax law. Used as a reference by the tax services and citators published by West.

Westlaw   An online database resource provided by the West Group. Allows the researcher to access a database consisting of the text of court cases, administrative rulings, and selected law review articles and to search these files for tax (and other) law sources that may be relevant to the research problem.

WestlawNext   The Westlaw legal platform with the exclusive search engine WestSearch and other innovative research tools. IT is designed to reduce research time by as much as 50 percent.

WestSearch   The Westlaw search engine that powers WestlawNext. It uses algorithms to identify documents related to the search, even those not containing the search terms, and orders them by relevance. It is designed to perform the same as having a personal experienced legal researcher searching WestlawNext for the subscriber.

WG&L Index to Federal Tax Articles (IFTA)   An index to tax journal articles published by Warren, Gorham & Lamont. It provides citations and occasionally summaries for articles covering Federal income, gift, and estate taxation or tax policy that appear in over 350 periodicals. This index has permanent cumulative indexes provided in paper-bound volumes and is updated quarterly by paperback cumulative supplements. Both the topic and the author indexes contain full article citations.

Willful Neglect   Willful neglect has been interpreted by the courts as a conscious, intentional failure or reckless indifference. Many IRS penalties may be abated due to reasonable cause and not willful neglect.

Worldwide model   A tax system in which a country imposes tax on residents based on their worldwide income, regardless of its source.

Writ of certiorari   Document issued by the Supreme Court indicating the Court will hear the petitioned case. If the case will not be heard, certiorari is said to be denied.

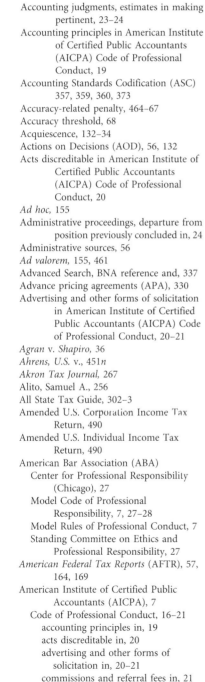